Analytical-Literal Translation of the New Testament of the Holy Bible

Second Edition

Translated by Gary F. Zeolla

authorHOUSE™

1663 LIBERTY DRIVE, SUITE 200
BLOOMINGTON, INDIANA 47403
(800) 839-8640
WWW.AUTHORHOUSE.COM

First published by AuthorHouse 03/02/05

ISBN: 1-4184-7520-3 (e)
ISBN: 1-4184-7519-X (sc)
ISBN: 1-4184-7518-1 (dj)

Printed in the United States of America
Bloomington, Indiana

This book is printed on acid-free paper.

Contents

Appendices

Copyright Information

Preface

The *Analytical-Literal Translation of the New Testament of the Holy Bible* (ALT) is dedicated to the glory of God and the spiritual growth of His people. It is translated by Gary F. Zeolla of Darkness to Light ministry (www.dtl.org).

The purpose of the ALT is to provide a translation of the Greek New Testament that will enable the reader to come as close to the Greek text as possible without actually having to be proficient in Greek. And the name of the ALT reflects this purpose.

"Literal" refers to the fact that the ALT is a word for word translation. All words in the original text are translated—nothing is omitted. The original grammar of the text is retained as much as possible. Any words added for clarity are bracketed, so nothing is added without it being indicated as such.

"Analytical" refers to the detailed "analysis" done on the grammar of the text. The grammar is then translated in way which brings out "nuances" of the original text that are often missed in traditional translations.

In addition, "analytical" refers to the aids that are included within the text which enable the reader to "analyze" and understand the text. Such information is bracketed. It includes the following:

1. Alternative translations for words and phrases.
2. The figurative meanings of words and phrases.
3. Modern-day equivalents for measurement and monetary units and time designations.
4. Explanatory notes.
5. References for Old Testament quotations and other cross-references.

The Greek text used for the ALT is the *Byzantine Majority Text.*[1] The ALT is one of the first translations of the New Testament to utilize this newest and most accurate Greek text. This second edition of the ALT even includes all the updates that were made for the forthcoming second edition of the Byzantine text. So the ALT is based on the most up-to-date and accurate Greek text possible.

This Greek text differs somewhat from the *Textus Receptus* and the Critical Text, the two other Greek texts which are used for translating the Bible. To aid in comparing the ALT with other Bible versions, the most important textual variants between these three Greek texts are listed in an appendix.

So the ALT is the ideal Bible version for studying the Bible. No other Bible version includes all of the above features, and no other Bible version provides the accuracy and attention to detail that the ALT provides.

In preparation for this second edition, the entire text was reviewed numerous times. Changes were made to improve the accuracy and consistency of the translations and to improve the readability. The text was also reformatted so as to reduce the size and cost and to improve the ease of use. So this second edition represents an updated, less expensive, and easier to use version of the ALT.

This second edition of the *Analytical-Literal Translation* is being presented to the Christian public in the belief that the Scriptures are "God-breathed" and that EVERY word of God is important to our salvation and Christian life. As the Scriptures proclaim:

⁴But answering, He said, "It has been written, *'A person will not live on bread alone, but on every word coming out through [the] mouth of God'"* (Matthew 4:4).

²⁸But He said, "But rather, happy [are] the ones hearing the word of God and keeping [fig., obeying] [it]!" (Luke 11:28).

³⁰Now indeed many other signs Jesus also did in the presence of His disciples which have not been written in this scroll. ³¹But these have been written so that you* shall believe [or, be convinced] that Jesus is the Christ, the Son of God, and so that believing you* shall be having life in His name (John 20:30,31).

¹⁶All Scripture [is] God-breathed and [is] beneficial for teaching [or, doctrine], for verification [or, reproof], for correcting faults, for instruction in righteousness [or, the behavior that God requires], ¹⁷so that the person of God shall be fully qualified [or, perfectly fit], having been completely equipped for every good work (1Timothy 3:16,17).

¹²For the word of God [is] living and effective and sharper than every double-edged sword, and [is] penetrating as far as [the] division of both soul and spirit, of both joints and marrow, and [is] able to discern [the] thoughts and intentions of the heart (Hebrews 4:12).

⁵And the One sitting on the throne said, "Look! I am making all things new!" And He says to me, "Write, because these words are true and trustworthy" (Revelation 21:5).

---

¹ Specifically: *The Greek New Testament: Byzantine Textform. Second Edition.* Complied, arranged, and thoroughly updated by Maurice A. Robinson and William G. Pierpont. Publication forthcoming. Dr. Robinson graciously provided a list of all of the updates for the forthcoming text to the translator of the ALT so that this ALT could include these updates. Many thanks to him in this regard.

The ALT follows the main Byzantine text but does not express the footnoted, alternate readings of the text. These indicate places where the Byzantine Greek manuscripts are closely divided. But a list of these alternative readings is posted on the ALT section of Darkness to Light's Web site (www.dtl.org/alt).

Abbreviations and Notations

Following are the meanings of abbreviations and notations seen in the ALT text. More detailed explanations of these notations are given in Appendix #2.

Abbreviations and Notations in Brackets

[the] – Words added for clarity are bracketed. Within bracketed alternative translations, bracketed words indicate words added for clarity, i.e. "[or, the kingdom [of Satan]]" (Matt 8:12) indicates the words "of Satan" are added.

[Isaiah 7:14] – Reference for the preceding OT quote. The quote itself is in italics.

"Yahweh is Salvation" – Meaning of a proper name, placed in quotation marks.

About – Modern-day equivalent for measurements and monetary units.

and elsewhere in – The bracketed information applies to other occurrences of the preceding word or phrase in the given range, but not necessarily to all occurrences.

and throughout/ and in – The bracketed information applies to all occurrences of the preceding word or phrase throughout the given range.

cp. – Cross reference ("compare").

fig., – Possible figurative meaning or paraphrase of preceding literal translation.

Gr. – Transliteration of the Greek word previously translated.

i.e., – Explanatory note ("that is" or "in explanation").

LXX – Septuagint. The OT quote is taken from this third century B.C., Greek translation of the Hebrew OT instead of the Hebrew text.

NT – New Testament

OT – Old Testament

or, – Alternative, traditional, or slightly less literal translation.

see – Cross reference.

Miscellaneous Abbreviations and Notations

ALT – *Analytical-Literal Translation of the New Testament of the Holy Bible*

LORD – Lord – The former indicates the OT verse from which the quote is taken has *Yahweh* (the Hebrew proper name for God). The latter indicates the OT has *adonai* (the general word for "lord").

But – Indicates the use of the Greek strong adversative (*alla*) instead of the weak adversative (*de*, translated as "but" when used in an adversative sense).

you* – Indicates the original is plural (also, your*). With no asterisk the second person pronoun is singular.

you – Indicates the pronoun is emphasized in the Greek text (also, he, she, etc.).

The Gospel According to
Matthew

1 Scroll of [the] genealogy of Jesus Christ, Son of David, Son of Abraham: ²Abraham fathered Isaac, and Isaac fathered Jacob, and Jacob fathered Judah and his brothers, ³and Judah fathered Pharez and Zarah by Tamar, and Pharez fathered Hezron, and Hezron fathered Ram, ⁴and Ram fathered Amminadab, and Amminadab fathered Nahshon, and Nahshon fathered Salmon, ⁵and Salmon fathered Boaz by Rahab, and Boaz fathered Obed by Ruth, and Obed fathered Jesse, ⁶and Jesse fathered David the king.

And David the king fathered Solomon by her [who had been] the [wife] of Uriah, ⁷and Solomon fathered Rehoboam, and Rehoboam fathered Abijah, and Abijah fathered Asa, ⁸and Asa fathered Jehoshaphat, and Jehoshaphat fathered Joram, and Joram fathered Uzziah, ⁹and Uzziah fathered Jotham, and Jotham fathered Ahaz, and Ahaz fathered Hezekiah, ¹⁰and Hezekiah fathered Manasseh, and Manasseh fathered Amon, and Amon fathered Josiah, ¹¹and Josiah fathered Jeconiah and his brothers at the time of the Babylonian captivity.

¹²And after the Babylonian captivity, Jeconiah fathered Shealtiel, and Shealtiel fathered Zerubbabel, ¹³and Zerubbabel fathered Abiud, and Abiud fathered Eliakim, and Eliakim fathered Azor, ¹⁴and Azor fathered Sadok, and Sadok fathered Achim, and Achim fathered Eliud, ¹⁵and Eliud fathered Eleazar, and Eleazar fathered Matthan, and Matthan fathered Jacob, ¹⁶and Jacob fathered Joseph, the husband of Mary, of whom [Gr., *es*, feminine, singular] was born Jesus, the One being called Christ ["the Anointed One"].

¹⁷So all the generations from Abraham to David [were] fourteen generations, and from David to the Babylonian captivity [were] fourteen generations, and from the Babylonian captivity to the Christ [were] fourteen generations.

¹⁸Now the birth of Jesus Christ was in this manner: For His mother Mary, having been promised in marriage to Joseph, before they came together [fig., had sexual relations], was found having in [the] womb [fig., to have become pregnant] by [the] Holy Spirit. ¹⁹But Joseph her husband being righteous and not wanting to publicly disgrace her, intended to privately send her away [fig., divorce her].

²⁰But while he was thinking about these [things], look!, an angel [or, messenger, and throughout NT] of [the] Lord appeared to him in a dream, saying, "Joseph, son of David, you should not be afraid to take Mary [as] your wife, for the [Baby] in her was conceived by [the] Holy Spirit. ²¹And she will give birth to a Son, and you will call His name Jesus ["Yahweh saves"], for <u>He</u> will save His people from their sins."

²²Now this whole [thing] has happened so that the [word] spoken by the Lord through the prophet should be fulfilled, saying, ²³ *"Look! The virgin will have in [the] womb* [fig., *will conceive*]*, and she will give birth to a Son, and they will call His name Emmanuel,"* which is, being translated, *"God with us."* [Isaiah 7:14]

1

²⁴Now Joseph, having been awakened from his sleep, did as the angel of [the] Lord ordered him, and he took his wife, ²⁵and he was not knowing her [fig., was not having sexual relations with her] until she gave birth to her firstborn Son. And he called His name Jesus.

2 Now Jesus having been born in Bethlehem of Judea in [the] days of Herod the king, look!, learned astrologers [or, Magi, and in verses 7,16] from [the] east arrived in Jerusalem, ²saying, "Where is the One having been born King of the Jews? For we saw His star at the rising [of the sun] [fig., in the east], and we came to prostrate ourselves in reverence before Him."

³But Herod the king having heard, was disturbed, and all Jerusalem with him. ⁴And having gathered together all the chief priests and scribes of the people, he began inquiring from them where the Christ [or, the Messiah, and throughout book] would be born.

⁵So they said to him, "In Bethlehem of Judea, for thus it has been written through the prophet, ⁶*'And you, Bethlehem, [in the] land of Judah, you are by no means least among the leaders of Judah, for out of you will come forth a Ruling [One], who will shepherd* [or, *rule*] *My people Israel.'"* [Micah 5:2]

⁷Then Herod, having called the learned astrologers privately, found out from them the exact time of the appearing [of the] star. ⁸And having sent them to Bethlehem, he said, "Go and search carefully for the young Child, but whenever you* find [Him], report back to me, in order that I also, having come, shall prostrate myself in reverence before Him."

⁹So having heard the king, they departed. And look! The star which they saw at the rising [of the sun] [fig., in the east] was going before them, until, having come, it stood over where the young Child was. ¹⁰And having seen the star, they rejoiced exceedingly [with] great joy. ¹¹Then having come to the house, they found the young Child with Mary His mother, and having fallen down, they prostrated themselves in reverence before Him, and having opened their treasure boxes, they presented to Him gifts: gold and frankincense and myrrh [i.e., an expensive incense and ointment, respectively]. ¹²And having been divinely warned in a dream not to return to Herod, they departed to their own region by another way.

¹³Now when they had departed, look!, an angel of [the] Lord appears in a dream to Joseph, saying, "Arise, take the young Child and His mother and be fleeing to Egypt, and be there until I speak to you, for Herod is about to be seeking the young Child to destroy Him." ¹⁴And having risen, he took the young Child and His mother by night and departed to Egypt, ¹⁵and he was there until the death of Herod, so that the [word] spoken by the Lord through the prophet should be fulfilled, saying, *"Out of Egypt I called My Son."* [Hosea 11:1]

¹⁶Then Herod, having seen that he was deceived by the learned astrologers, became extremely enraged; and having sent out [soldiers], he executed all the male children, the [ones] in Bethlehem and in all its borders, from two years old and under, according to the exact time that he found out from the learned astrologers.

[17]Then was fulfilled the [word] spoken by Jeremiah the prophet, saying, [18]*"A voice in Ramah was heard, lamentation and weeping and much mourning, Rachel weeping [for] her children, and she was not wanting to be comforted because they are not."* [Jer 31:15]

[19]Now Herod having come to the end [of his life], look!, an angel of [the] Lord appears in a dream to Joseph in Egypt, [20]saying, "Arise, take the young Child and His mother, and be going to the land of Israel, for the ones seeking the life of the young Child have died." [21]So having arisen, he took the young Child and His mother and came into the land of Israel. [22]But having heard that Archelaus reigns over Judea in place of Herod his father, he was afraid to go there, so having been divinely warned in a dream, he departed to the parts [or, region] of Galilee, [23]and having gone, he settled down in a city being called Nazareth, in order that the [word] having been spoken through the prophets should be fulfilled, "He will be called a Nazarene." [No specific OT passage]

3Now in those days John the Baptist [or, the Immerser, and throughout book] arrives, proclaiming in the wilderness of Judea, [2]and saying, "Be repenting, for the kingdom of the heavens has drawn near!" [3]For this is the [one] having been spoken of by Isaiah the prophet, saying, *"A voice of [one] shouting in the wilderness, 'Prepare the way of [the] LORD; be making His paths straight!'"* [Isaiah 40:3; LXX]

[4]Now John himself was having his clothing [made] from camel's hair and a leather belt around his waist, and his food was locusts and wild honey. [5]Then Jerusalem and all Judea and all the surrounding region of the Jordan [River] were going out to him, [6]and they were being baptized [or, immersed, Gr. *baptizo,* and throughout book] in the Jordan by him, confessing their sins.

[7]But having seen many of the Pharisees and Sadducees coming to his baptism [or, immersion, and throughout book], he said to them, "Brood of vipers! Who warned you* to flee from the coming wrath? [8]Therefore, bear fruit worthy [fig., as evidence] of repentance. [9]And you* should not presume to be saying within yourselves, 'We have Abraham [as our] father,' for I say to you* that God is able to raise children to Abraham out of these stones. [10]But also already the axe is laid to the root of the trees. Therefore, every tree not bearing good fruit is cut down and is thrown into fire.

[11]"I indeed baptize you* in water [or, with water, and throughout book] to [or, because of] repentance. But the One coming after me is mightier [than] I, of whom I am not worthy to carry His sandals, He will baptize you* in [or, with] [the] Holy Spirit, [12]whose winnowing-shovel [is] in His hand, and He will thoroughly clean out His threshing floor and will gather His wheat into the barn, but He will burn the chaff in unquenchable fire!"

[13]Then Jesus arrives from Galilee at the Jordan [River] to John, to be baptized by him. [14]But John tried preventing Him, saying, "I have need to be baptized by You, and You come to me?" [15]But answering, Jesus said to him, "Permit [it] now, for in this way it is fitting for us to fulfill all righteousness." Then he permits Him.

¹⁶And having been baptized, Jesus went up immediately from the water. And look! The heavens were opened to Him, and he [i.e. John] saw the Spirit of God descending like a dove and coming upon Him. ¹⁷And listen! A voice [comes] out of the heavens, saying, "This is My Son—the Beloved—in whom I am well-pleased!"

*4*Then Jesus was led up into the wilderness by the Spirit to be tempted by the Devil ["Slanderer"]. ²And having fasted forty days and forty nights, afterwards He hungered. ³And having approached Him, the Tempter said, "Since You are God's Son, speak, so that these stones shall become loaves of bread." ⁴But answering, He said, "It has been written, *'A person will not live on bread alone, but on every word coming out through [the] mouth of God.'"* [Deut 8:3]

⁵Then the Devil takes Him along to the holy city and sets Him on the pinnacle of the temple, ⁶and says to Him, "Since You are God's Son, throw Yourself down, for it has been written, *'He will give orders to His angels concerning You,'* and *'they will lift You up on [their] hands, lest You strike Your foot against a stone.'"* [Psalm 91:11,12] ⁷Jesus said to him, "Again, it has been written, *'You will not put [the] LORD your God to the test.'"* [Deut 6:16]

⁸Again the Devil takes Him along to a very high mountain and shows to Him all the kingdoms of the world and the glory of them, ⁹and says to Him, "All these I will give to You, if having fallen down, You prostrate Yourself in worship before me." ¹⁰Then Jesus says to him, "Be going away behind Me Satan ["Adversary"]! For it has been written, *'[The] LORD your God you will prostrate yourself in worship before, and Him only will you sacredly serve.'"* [Deut 6:13] ¹¹Then the Devil leaves Him. And look! Angels came and began ministering to Him.

¹²Now Jesus having heard that John was arrested, He departed to Galilee. ¹³And having left Nazareth, having come, He settled down in Capernaum, the [city] by the sea, in the borders of Zebulun and Naphtali, ¹⁴so that the [word] spoken through Isaiah the prophet should be fulfilled, saying, ¹⁵*"Land of Zebulun and land of Naphtali, [the] way of [the] sea, beyond the Jordan, Galilee of the Gentiles, ¹⁶the people, the ones sitting in darkness, saw a great light, and to the ones sitting in [the] region and shadow of death, light rose* [fig., *has dawned*] *on them."* [Isaiah 9:1,2]

¹⁷From that time Jesus began to be proclaiming and to be saying, "Be repenting, for the kingdom of the heavens has drawn near!"

¹⁸Now walking about by the Sea of Galilee, He saw two brothers, Simon, the one being called Peter, and Andrew his brother, casting a net into the sea, for they were fishermen. ¹⁹And He says to them, "Come after Me, and I will make you* fishers of people." ²⁰Then immediately, having left their nets, they followed Him. ²¹And having gone on from there, He saw two other brothers, James the [son] of Zebedee and John his brother, in the boat with Zebedee their father mending their nets, and He called them. ²²Then immediately, having left the boat and their father, they followed Him.

²³And Jesus was traveling around all Galilee, teaching in their synagogues and proclaiming the Gospel [or, Good News, and throughout book] of the kingdom

and healing every disease and every malady among the people. [24]And the fame [or, news] of Him went forth to all Syria. And they brought to Him all the ones having it badly [fig., who were sick], being afflicted with various diseases and pains, and ones being demon-possessed [or, oppressed by demons] and ones being moonstruck [or, lunatics] and paralytics. And He healed them. [25]And large crowds followed Him from Galilee and Decapolis and Jerusalem and Judea and beyond the Jordan [River].

5Now having seen the crowds, He went up into the mountain, and after He had sat down, His disciples came to Him. [2]And having opened His mouth, He began teaching them, saying:

[3]"Happy [or, Blessed, and through verse 11] [are] the poor in spirit, because theirs is the kingdom of the heavens.
[4]Happy [are] the ones mourning, because they will be comforted.
[5]Happy [are] the gentle [or, considerate], because they will inherit the earth.
[6]Happy [are] the ones hungering and thirsting for righteousness, because they will be filled.
[7]Happy [are] the merciful, because they will be shown mercy.
[8]Happy [are] the pure in heart, because they will see God.
[9]Happy [are] the peacemakers, because they will be called sons [and daughters] of God.
[10]Happy [are] the ones having been persecuted for the sake of righteousness, because theirs is the kingdom of the heavens.

[11]"Happy are you* whenever they insult you* and persecute [you*] and by lying say every evil word against you* because of Me. [12]Be rejoicing and be continually glad, because your* reward [is] great in the heavens, for in this manner they persecuted the prophets, the [ones] before you*.

[13]"You* are the salt of the earth, but if the salt becomes tasteless, with what will it be salted? It is good for nothing anymore, except to be thrown out and to be trampled down by people.

[14]"You* are the light of the world; a city standing on a mountain is not able to be hid. [15]Nor do they light a lamp and put it under the measuring basket, but on the lampstand, and it gives light to all the [ones] in the house. [16]In the same manner, let your* light shine before the people, in order that they shall see your* good works and glorify your* Father, the [One] in the heavens.

[17]"Do not suppose that I came to tear down [fig., abolish] the Law or the Prophets; I did not come to tear down but to fulfill. [18]For positively, I say to you*, until the heaven and the earth pass away, by no means shall one iota [i.e., the smallest letter of the Greek alphabet] or one tittle [i.e., a stroke of a letter] pass away from the Law, until all [things] happen. [19]Therefore, whoever breaks one of the least of these commandments, and thus teaches the people, he will be called least in the kingdom of the heavens, but whoever does and teaches [them], he will

be called great in the kingdom of the heavens. [20]For I say to you*, unless your* righteousness greatly exceeds [that] of the scribes and Pharisees, by no means shall you* enter into the kingdom of the heavens.

[21]"You heard that it was said to the ancients: *"You will not murder,"* but whoever murders will be in danger of the judgment. [Exod 20:13; Deut 5:17] [22]But I say to you*, every[one] being enraged at his brother [fig., friend, neighbor, or compatriot, and elsewhere in book] without cause will be in danger of the judgment, and whoever says to his brother, 'Empty-headed fool!' will be in danger of the high council, and whoever says, 'You worthless fool!' will be in danger of the hell [Gr., *gehenna*] of the fire [or, the fiery hell].

[23]"Therefore, if you are bringing your gift to the altar, and there you are reminded that your brother has something against you, [24]leave your gift there before the altar, and be going, first be reconciled to your brother, and then having come, continue bringing your gift. [25]Be coming to terms with your opponent [in a lawsuit] quickly, during which [time] you are with him on the way, lest the opponent hands you over to the judge, and the judge hands you over to the [court] attendant, and you will be cast into prison. [26]Positively, I say to you, by no means shall you get out of there until you pay the last kodrantes [i.e. a small, Roman copper coin worth about 1/500th of an ounce or 0.05 grams of silver].

[27]"You heard that it was said: *'You will not commit adultery.'* [Exod 20:14; Deut 5:18] [28]But I say to you*, every[one] looking on a woman in order to lust after her already committed adultery [with] her in his heart [i.e., the inner self, including the intellect, volition, and emotions, and elsewhere in NT]. [29]But if your right eye causes you to stumble [fig., to sin], pluck it out and cast [it] from you, for it is better for you that one of your body parts perish and not your whole body be cast into hell [Gr., *gehenna*]. [30]And if your right hand causes you to stumble [fig., to sin], cut it off and cast [it] from you, for it is better for you that one of your body parts perish and not your whole body be cast into hell [Gr., *gehenna*].

[31]"Now it was said, *'Whoever divorces his wife must give to her a written notice of divorce.'* [Deut 24:1,3] [32]But I say to you*, whoever divorces his wife, except for a matter of sexual sin [or, fornication, and throughout NT], makes her to be committing adultery; and whoever marries the one having been divorced commits adultery.

[33]"Again, you heard that it was said to the ancients: *'You will not swear falsely, but you will pay to the Lord your oaths.'* [Lev 19:12; Numb 30:2] [34]But I say to you* not to take an oath at all; neither by heaven, because it is the throne of God, [35]nor by the earth, because it is [the] footstool for His feet, nor by Jerusalem, because it is *'[the] city of the great King,'* [cp. Isaiah 66:1; Psalm 48:2] [36]nor shall you take an oath by your head, because you are not able to make one hair white or black. [37]But let your* word be, 'Yes, Yes' [or] 'No, No,' but the [word which is] more [than] these is from the evil [one].

[38]"You* heard that it was said: *'Eye for eye and tooth for tooth,'* [Exod 21:24; Lev 24:20; Deut 19:21] [39]but I say to you* not to resist the evil [one], but whoever will slap you on the right cheek, turn to him also the other. [40]And the one wanting to sue you and to take your tunic, allow to him also the cloak. [41]And whoever will

compel you [to go] one mile, be going with him two. ⁴²Be giving to the one asking of you, and you should not turn away the one wanting to borrow from you.

⁴³"You* heard that it was said, *'You will love your neighbor,'* and you will hate your enemy, [Lev. 19:18] ⁴⁴but I say to you*, be loving your* enemies; be blessing the ones cursing you*; be doing good to the ones hating you*, and be praying on behalf of the ones mistreating you* and persecuting you*, ⁴⁵in order that you* shall become [or, prove to be] sons [and daughters] of your Father, the [One] in the heavens, because He causes His sun to rise on evil [ones] and good [ones], and He sends rain on righteous [ones] and unrighteous [ones]. ⁴⁶For, if you* love the ones loving you*, what reward do you* have? Even the tax collectors do the same, do they not? ⁴⁷And if you* greet [fig., are friendly towards] your* friends only, what more do you* do [than others]? Even the tax collectors do so, do they not? ⁴⁸Therefore, you* will be perfect, just as your* Father, the [One] in the heavens, is perfect.

6"Be taking care not to be doing your* charitable giving before the people, in order to be seen by them; but if not [fig., otherwise], you* do not have a reward from your* Father, the [One] in the heavens. ²So when you are doing charitable giving, you should not sound a trumpet before you like the hypocrites do in the synagogues and in the streets, in order that they shall be praised by the people. Positively, I say to you*, they are receiving their reward in full. ³But when you do charitable giving, do not let your left hand know what the right hand is doing, ⁴in order that your charitable giving shall be in secret, and your Father, the [One] seeing in secret, will Himself reward you in the open.

⁵"And when you are praying, you will not be like the hypocrites, because they affectionately love standing in the synagogues and in the corners of the open streets to be praying, in order that they shall be seen by the people. Positively, I say to you*, they have their reward in full. ⁶But when you are praying, enter into your private room, and having shut your door, pray to your Father, the [One] in secret, and your Father, the [One] seeing in secret, will reward you in the open.

⁷"Now when you* pray, do not use vain repetitions [or, many meaningless words] like the Gentiles, for they suppose that they will be heard by their many words. ⁸Therefore, you* shall not be like them, for your* Father knows what [things] you* have need of before you* ask Him. ⁹Therefore, you*, be praying like this:

Our Father, the [One] in the heavens, let Your name be regarded as holy.
¹⁰Let Your kingdom come.
Let Your will be done, as in heaven, [so] also on the earth.
¹¹Give us today the bread sufficient for the day.
¹²And forgive us our debts [fig., sins], in the same way as we also forgive our debtors [fig., the ones having sinned against us].
¹³And do not lead us into temptation, but deliver us from evil [or, from the evil [one]].

Because Yours is the kingdom and the power and the glory into the ages [fig., forever]! So be it [Gr. *amen*]!

[14]"For, if you* forgive the people their transgressions, your* Father, the [One] in the heavens, will also forgive you,* [15]but if you* do not forgive the people their transgressions, neither will your* Father forgive your* transgressions.

[16]"And when you* are fasting, stop becoming gloomy like the hypocrites, for they disfigure their faces, in order that they shall appear to the people [as] fasting. Positively, I say to you*, they are receiving their reward in full. [17]But when you fast, anoint your head and wash your face, [18]in order that you shall not appear to the people [as] fasting, but [only] to your Father, the [One] in secret, and your Father, the [One] seeing in secret, will reward you.

[19]"Stop storing [or, treasuring] up treasures for yourselves on the earth, where moth and rust destroy, and where thieves break in and steal, [20]but be storing [or, treasuring] up treasures for yourselves in heaven, where neither moth nor rust destroys, and where thieves do not break in nor steal, [21]for where your* treasure is, there will your* heart [fig., inner desire] be also.

[22]"The lamp of the body is the eye. Therefore, if your eye is healthy, all your body will be full of light. [23]But if your eye is bad, all your body will be dark. Therefore, if the light in you is darkness, how great the darkness!

[24]"No one is able to be serving as a slave to two masters, for either he will hate the one and love the other, or he will be devoted to the one and despise the other; you are not able to be serving as a slave to God and to worldly wealth.

[25]"For this reason I say to you*, stop being anxious [about] your* life, what you* shall eat and what you* shall drink, nor [about] your* body, what you* shall wear. Life is more [than] the nourishment, and the body [more than] the clothing, is it not? [26]Look attentively at the birds of the air, for they do not sow nor reap nor gather into barns, and your* heavenly Father provides for them. You* are of much more worth than they, are you* not? [27]But which of you*, by being anxious, is able to add on his height one cubit?

[28]"And why are you* anxious about clothing? Be attentively observing the lilies of the field, how they grow. They do not labor nor do they spin [to make clothing]. [29]But I say to you*, not even Solomon in all his glory was arrayed like one of these. [30]Now if God clothes in such a manner the grass of the field, being [here] today and tomorrow is thrown into the furnace, [He will] much more [clothe] you*, [O you*] of little faith, will He not?

[31]"Therefore, do not be anxious, saying, 'What shall we eat?' or, 'What shall we drink?' or, 'What shall we wear?' [32]For all these [things] the Gentiles seek, for your* heavenly Father knows that you* have need of all these [things]. [33]But be seeking first the kingdom of God and His righteousness, and all these [things] will be added to you.* [34]Therefore, you* should not be anxious for tomorrow, for tomorrow will be anxious for the [things] of itself; sufficient for the day [is] the evil of it.

7 "Stop judging, so that you* shall not be judged, ²for with what judgment you* judge, you* will be judged, and with what measure you* measure, it will be measured to you.* ³But why do you look at the speck, the [one] in your brother's eye, but you do not notice the log, the [one] in your own eye? ⁴Or, how will you say to your brother, 'Allow [me], I shall take the speck from your eye,' and look!, the log [is] in your own eye? ⁵Hypocrite, first take the log out of your own eye, and then you will see clearly to take the speck out of your brother's eye.

⁶"You* shall not give the holy [thing] to the dogs, nor shall you* throw your* pearls before the pigs, lest they trample them among their feet, and having turned around, they tear you* to pieces.

⁷"Be asking, and it will be given to you*; be seeking, and you* will find; be knocking, and it will be opened to you*. ⁸For every[one] asking receives, and the one seeking finds, and to the one knocking it will be opened. ⁹Or what person is [there] from you*, whom, if his son asks [for] a loaf, he will not give to him a stone, will he? ¹⁰And if he asks for a fish, he will not give to him a snake, will he? ¹¹Therefore, if you*, being evil, know [how] to be giving good gifts to your* children, how much more will your* Father, the [One] in the heavens, give good [things] to the ones asking Him! ¹²Therefore, all things, whatever you* shall be wanting that the people shall be doing to you*, in the same manner also you* be doing to them, for this is the Law and the Prophets.

¹³"Enter in through the narrow gate, because wide [is] the gate and spacious [is] the way which leads to the destruction, and many are the ones entering in through it. ¹⁴How narrow [is] the gate and having been constricted [is] the way which leads to the life, and few are the ones finding it!

¹⁵"But be watching out for the false prophets, who come to you* in sheep's clothing, but inwardly are ravenous wolves. ¹⁶By their fruits you* will know them. They do not gather a grape cluster from thorns, or figs from thistles, do they? ¹⁷In the same way, every good tree yields good fruits, but the rotten tree yields evil fruits. ¹⁸A good tree is not able to be yielding evil fruits, nor a rotten tree to be yielding good fruits. ¹⁹Every tree not yielding good fruit is cut down and is thrown into fire. ²⁰Consequently, by their fruits you* will know them.

²¹"Not every one saying to Me, 'Lord, Lord,' will enter into the kingdom of the heavens, but the one doing the will of My Father, the [One] in [the] heavens. ²²Many will say to Me in that day, 'Lord, Lord, we prophesied in Your name, and cast out demons in Your name, and did many miraculous works in Your name, did we not?' ²³And then I will declare to them, 'I never knew you*; be departing from Me, the ones practicing lawlessness!'

²⁴"Therefore, every[one] who hears these words of Mine and does them, I will compare him to a wise man who built his house on the solid rock; ²⁵and the rain came down, and the floods came, and the winds blew, and they beat against that house, and it did not fall, for it had been founded on the solid rock. ²⁶And every[one] hearing these words of Mine and not doing them will be compared to a foolish man who built his house on the sand; ²⁷and the rain came down, and the floods came, and the winds blew, and they beat against that house, and it fell, and its fall was great."

²⁸And it happened, when Jesus finished these words, the crowds were being astonished at His teaching, ²⁹for He was teaching them as [One] having authority and not like the scribes.

8Now when He came down from the mountain, large crowds followed Him. ²And look! A leper [or, one with a skin disease] having come, began prostrating himself in reverence before Him, saying, "Lord, if You are willing, You are able to cleanse me." ³And having stretched out His hand, Jesus took hold of him, saying, "I am willing. Be cleansed!" And immediately his leprosy [or, skin disease] was cleansed! ⁴And Jesus says to him, "See [that] you tell no one. But be going, show yourself to the priest, and offer the gift which Moses commanded, for a testimony to them." [cp. Lev 14:2-57]

⁵Now when He entered into Capernaum, a centurion came to Him, pleading with Him, ⁶and saying, "Lord, my slave boy has been laid in the house a paralytic, being terribly tormented [or, being in great pain]." ⁷And Jesus says to him, "Having come, I will heal him." ⁸And answering, the centurion said, "Lord, I am not worthy that You should enter under my roof, but only say a word, and my slave boy will be healed. ⁹For I also am a person under authority, having under myself soldiers, and I say to this one, 'Go,' and he goes, and to another, 'Be coming,' and he comes, and to my slave, 'Do this,' and he does [it]."

¹⁰So having heard, Jesus marveled and said to the ones following, "Positively, I say to you*, I [have] not found such great faith even in Israel! ¹¹Now I say to you*, many from east and west will come and will be reclined [to eat] with Abraham and Isaac and Jacob in the kingdom of the heavens. ¹²But the sons [and daughters] of the [earthly] kingdom [or, the kingdom [of Satan]] will be cast out into the outer darkness. In that place [there] will be weeping and gnashing of teeth!" ¹³And Jesus said to the centurion, "Be going, and as you believed, let it happen to you." And his slave boy was healed in that hour [or, at that moment]!

¹⁴And Jesus having come into the house of Peter, He saw his mother-in-law having been laid down and sick with a fever. ¹⁵And He took hold of her hand, and the fever left her! And she arose and began serving Him.

¹⁶Now evening having come, they brought to Him many being demon-possessed [or, oppressed by demons], and He cast the spirits out with a word, and He healed all the ones having it badly [fig., who were sick], ¹⁷in order that the [word] having been spoken through Isaiah the prophet should be fulfilled, saying, *"He Himself took our sicknesses, and He bore our diseases."* [Isaiah 53:4]

¹⁸Now having seen large crowds about Him, Jesus gave orders to depart to the other side. ¹⁹And a certain scribe having approached, said to Him, "Teacher, I will follow You wherever You are going." ²⁰And Jesus says to him, "The foxes have dens, and the birds of the air nests, but the Son of Humanity does have [any]where He should lay His head." ²¹Then another of His disciples said to Him, "Lord, permit me first to depart and to bury my father." ²²But Jesus said to him, "Be following Me, and allow the dead to bury their own dead."

²³And when He stepped into the boat, His disciples followed Him. ²⁴And look! A great storm happened in the sea, with the result that the boat was being covered

by the waves, but He was sleeping. ²⁵And having approached, the disciples woke Him up, saying, "Lord, save us! We ourselves are perishing!" ²⁶And He says to them, "Why are you* cowardly, [O you*] of little faith?" Then having arisen, He rebuked [or, gave orders to] the winds and the sea, and [there] became a great calm. ²⁷But the men were amazed, saying, "What sort [of Person] is this, that even the wind and the sea obey [or, are subject to] Him?" [cp. Job 38:25-38; Ps 135:7]

²⁸And when He came to the other side, to the region of the Gergesenes, [there] met Him two [men] being demon-possessed [or, oppressed by demons] coming out from the tombs, very fierce, with the result that no one was able to pass over by that way. ²⁹And listen! They cried out, saying, "What to us and to You [fig., What have we to do with You], Jesus, Son of God? Did You come here before [the] time to torment us?"

³⁰Now [there] was at a distance from them a herd of many pigs being fed. ³¹So the demons began calling on Him, saying, "If You cast us out, permit us to go away into the herd of pigs." ³²And He says to them, "Be going!" So having come out, they went into the herd of pigs. And look! The whole herd of pigs stampeded down the steep bank into the sea and died in the waters. ³³Then the ones feeding [the pigs] fled; and, having gone into the city, they reported all [things] and the [matter] of the ones being demon-possessed [or, oppressed by demons]. ³⁴And look! The whole city came out to meet Jesus; and having seen Him, they implored [Him] that He would depart from their borders.

9And having stepped into the boat, He crossed over and went into His own city. ²And look! They were bringing to Him a paralytic having been laid on a cot. And having seen their faith, Jesus said to the paralytic, "Be having courage, child, your sins have been forgiven you."

³And listen! Some of the scribes said within themselves, "This [Man] blasphemes!" ⁴And Jesus, having known their thoughts, said, "Why are you* thinking evil in your hearts? ⁵For which is easier, to say, 'Your sins have been forgiven,' or to say, 'Get up, and be walking about?' ⁶But so that you* shall know that the Son of Humanity has authority on the earth to be forgiving sins"—then He says to the paralytic, "Having gotten up, take up your cot, and be going to your house." ⁷And having gotten up, he went to his house! ⁸But the crowds having seen were amazed and glorified God, the One having given such authority to people.

⁹And passing by from there, Jesus saw a man sitting at the tax-office, being called Matthew, and He says to him, "Be following Me!" And having stood up, he followed Him.

¹⁰And it happened, as He reclined [to eat] in the house, that look!, many tax collectors and sinners having come, were reclining [to eat] with Jesus and His disciples. ¹¹And the Pharisees having seen, said to His disciples, "Why does your* Teacher eat with the tax collectors and sinners?" ¹²But having heard, Jesus said to them, "The ones being strong [fig., who are healthy] do not have need of a physician, but the ones having [it] badly [fig., who are sick]. ¹³So having gone, learn what it is [fig., what this means], *'I desire mercy and not sacrifice.'* [Hosea 6:6] For I did not come to call righteous [people], but sinners to repentance."

¹⁴Then the disciples of John approach Him, saying, "Why do we and the Pharisees fast much, but Your disciples do not fast?" ¹⁵And Jesus said to them, "The sons of the bridal chamber [fig., the bridegroom's attendants] are not able to be mourning so long as the bridegroom is with them, are they? But days will come when the bridegroom will be taken from them, and then they will fast. ¹⁶But no one puts a patch of a piece of unshrunken cloth on an old garment, for its fullness [fig., the patch] takes from the garment, and [the] tear becomes worse. ¹⁷Nor do they put new wine into old wineskins; but if not [fig., or else] the wineskins are burst, and the wine is poured out, and the wineskins will be ruined. But they put new wine into new wineskins, and both are preserved together."

¹⁸While He is speaking these [things] to them, look!, a certain ruler having come was prostrating himself in reverence before Him, saying, "My daughter just now came to the end [of her life]; but having come, lay your hand on her, and she will live." ¹⁹And Jesus having gotten up followed him, and His disciples.

²⁰And look! A woman suffering from chronic bleeding [for] twelve years, having approached Him from behind, touched the fringe of His cloak. ²¹For she was saying within herself, "If only I shall touch His cloak, I will be cured." ²²Then Jesus having turned around and having seen her, said, "Be having courage, daughter; your faith has cured you." And the woman was cured from that hour!

²³And Jesus having come to the house of the ruler, and having seen the flutists and the crowd being so upset, ²⁴He says to them, "Go away, for the girl did not die, but she is sleeping!" And they began laughing at Him. ²⁵But when the crowd was put out, having gone in, He took hold of her hand, and the girl got up! ²⁶And the report of this went out to that whole land.

²⁷And Jesus passing on from there, two blind men followed Him, crying out and saying, "Be merciful to us, Son of David!" ²⁸Then when He came to the house, the blind men approached Him, and Jesus says to them, "Do you* believe that I am able to do this?" They say to Him, "Yes, Lord." ²⁹Then He touched their eyes, saying, "According to your faith let it happen to you*." ³⁰And their eyes were opened! And Jesus sternly warned them, saying, "Be seeing [that you*] let no one know." ³¹But having gone forth, they spread the news about Him in that whole land.

³²Now as they are going out, look!, they brought to Him a mute man, being demon-possessed [or, oppressed by a demon]. ³³And when the demon had been cast out, the mute [man] spoke! And the crowd was amazed, saying, "Never was [something] like this seen in Israel!" ³⁴But the Pharisees said, "He casts out the demons by the ruler of the demons."

³⁵And Jesus was traveling around all the cities and the villages, teaching in their synagogues and proclaiming the Gospel of the kingdom and healing every disease and every malady among the people. ³⁶Now having seen the crowds, He was moved with compassion concerning them, that they had been distressed and had been dejected, like sheep not having a shepherd. ³⁷Then He says to His disciples, "The harvest indeed [is] plentiful, but the laborers few. ³⁸Therefore, implore the Lord of the harvest, in order that He should send out laborers to His harvest."

10 Then having summoned His twelve disciples, He gave to them power over unclean [or, defiling] spirits so as to be casting them out and to be healing every disease and every malady.

²Now the names of the twelve apostles are these: first Simon, the one being called Peter, and Andrew his brother, James the [son] of Zebedee and John his brother, ³Philip and Bartholomew, Thomas and Matthew the tax collector, James the [son] of Alpheus and Lebbeus, the one having been surnamed Thaddeus, ⁴Simon the Cananean [i.e. Aramaic for "Zealot"] and Judas Iscariot, the one also having betrayed Him.

⁵These twelve Jesus sent out, having given strict orders to them, saying, "You* shall not go into the way of the Gentiles, and you* shall not enter into a city of the Samaritans, ⁶but be going rather to the sheep, the ones having been lost from [the] house of Israel. ⁷Now be going, be proclaiming, saying, 'The kingdom of the heavens has drawn near!' ⁸Be healing [ones] being sick, be cleansing lepers [or, [ones] with a skin disease], be casting out demons; freely you* received, freely give. ⁹You* shall not acquire gold nor silver nor copper coin in your money belt, ¹⁰nor a traveler's bag for [the] journey, nor two tunics nor sandals nor staffs, for the laborer is worthy of his food. [see 1Tim 5:18]

¹¹"But into whatever city or village you* enter, inquire who in it is worthy, and stay there until you* depart. ¹²And as you* enter into the house, greet it. ¹³And if indeed the house is worthy, let your* peace come on it; but if it is not worthy, let your* peace return to you*. ¹⁴And whoever shall not receive you*, nor hear *your words, as you* go out from that house or city, shake off the dust from your* feet. ¹⁵Positively, I say to you*, it will be more tolerable for [the] land of Sodom and Gomorrah in [the] day of judgment than for that city.

¹⁶"Listen! I am sending you* out like sheep in the midst of wolves. Therefore, continue becoming wise as the serpents and innocent as the doves. ¹⁷But be watching out [for] [or, be aware of] the people, for they will hand you* over to local councils [or, courts], and they will scourge you* in their synagogues, ¹⁸and you* will be brought before governors [or, rulers] and kings for My sake, for a testimony to them and to the nations. ¹⁹But whenever they are handing you* over, you* shall not be anxious how or what you* should speak, for it shall be given to you* in that hour what you* will speak; ²⁰for you* are not the ones speaking, but the Spirit of your* Father [is] the One speaking in you*.

²¹"But brother will betray brother to death, and a father [his] child; and children will rebel against parents and will put them to death. ²²And you* will be hated by all because of My name, but the one having endured to [the] end, this [one] will be saved. ²³But whenever they are persecuting you* in this city, be fleeing to the other. For positively, I say to you*, by no means shall you* complete the cities of Israel until the Son of Humanity comes.

²⁴"A disciple is not above the teacher, nor a slave above his lord. ²⁵[It is] enough for the disciple that he become like his teacher, and the slave like his lord. If they called the master of the house Beelzebul [i.e. a Philistine deity, used as a name for the devil], how much more the members of his household? ²⁶Therefore,

do not be frightened [by] them, for nothing has been concealed which will not be revealed, and secret which will not be known.

²⁷"What I am saying to you* in the darkness, be speaking in the light; and what you* are hearing in the ear, be proclaiming on the housetops. ²⁸And stop fearing the ones killing the body, but are not able to kill the soul; but fear rather the One being able to destroy both the soul and the body in hell [Gr., *gehenna*]! ²⁹Two sparrows are sold for an assarion [i.e. a small, Roman copper coin worth about 1/64 of an ounce or 0.22 grams of silver], are they not? And one of them does not fall on the ground without the [will] of your* Father. ³⁰But even the hairs of your* head have all been numbered. ³¹Therefore, do not be frightened; you* are of greater worth than many sparrows.

³²"Therefore, every[one] who will confess Me before the people, I also will confess him before My Father, the [One] in [the] heavens. ³³But whoever denies [or, disowns] Me before the people, I also will deny him before My Father, the [One] in the heavens.

³⁴"You* should not suppose that I came to put peace on the earth; I did not come to put peace, but a sword. ³⁵For I came to *'turn a man against his father, and a daughter against her mother, and a daughter-in-law against her mother-in-law,'* ³⁶and *'the enemies of a person [are] the members of his household.'* [Micah 7:6] ³⁷The one affectionately loving father or mother more than Me is not worthy of Me, and the one affectionately loving son or daughter more than Me is not worthy of Me, ³⁸and whoever does not take his cross and follow after Me is not worthy of Me. ³⁹The one finding his life will lose it, and the one having lost his life for My sake will find it.

⁴⁰"The one receiving you* receives Me, and the one receiving Me receives the One having sent Me. ⁴¹The one receiving a prophet in [the] name of a prophet will take hold of a prophet's reward, and the one receiving a righteous [person] in the name of a righteous [person] will take hold of a righteous [person's] reward. ⁴²And whoever gives one of these little ones a cup of cold water to drink only in the name of a disciple, positively, I say to you*, by no means shall he lose his reward."

11 And it happened, when Jesus finished giving instructions to His twelve disciples, He departed from there to be teaching and to be preaching in their cities.

²But John having heard in the jail [about] the works of Christ, having sent two of his disciples, ³said to Him, "Are You the coming One, or are we looking for a different [one]?" ⁴And answering, Jesus said to them, "Having gone, report to John what you* are hearing and seeing: ⁵blind [ones] receive sight and lame [ones] walk about, leprous [ones] [or, ones with a skin disease] are cleansed and deaf [ones] hear, dead [ones] are raised and the Gospel is proclaimed to poor [ones]. [cp. Isaiah 35:5,6; 61:1] ⁶And happy is [the one] who is not caused to stumble [fig., not offended] because of Me."

⁷Then as these [ones] are going, Jesus began to be saying to the crowds concerning John, "What did you* go out into the wilderness to observe, a reed being shaken by the wind? ⁸But what did you* go out to see? A man having been

clothed in soft garments? Listen! The ones wearing such soft [things] are in the royal houses. ⁹But what did you* go out to see? A prophet? Yes, I say to you*, and more [than] a prophet. ¹⁰For this is [he] concerning whom it has been written, *'Look! I am sending My messenger before Your face* [fig., *ahead of You*], *who will prepare Your way before You.'* [Mal 3:1]

¹¹"Positively, I say to you*, there has not been raised among [those] born of women a greater [one than] John the Baptist, but the [one] least in the kingdom of the heavens is greater [than] he. ¹²But from the days of John the Baptist until now the kingdom of the heavens suffers violence, and violent [ones] take it by force. ¹³For all the prophets and the Law prophesied until John. ¹⁴And if you* are willing to receive [it], he is Elijah, the one about to be coming. [see Mal 4:5] ¹⁵The one having ears to be hearing, let him be hearing [or, be paying attention].

¹⁶"But to what will I compare this generation? It is like young children sitting in marketplaces and calling to their friends, ¹⁷and saying, 'We played a flute for you*, and you* did not dance; we mourned for you*, and you* did not beat your* breasts [fig., lament]. ¹⁸For John came neither eating nor drinking, and they say, 'He has a demon.' ¹⁹The Son of Humanity came eating and drinking, and they say, 'Look! A man, a glutton, and a drunkard, a friend of tax collectors and sinners!' And wisdom was justified [or, vindicated] by her children."

²⁰Then He began to be denouncing the cities in which were done the most of His miraculous works, because they did not repent. ²¹"How horrible it will be to you, Chorazin! How horrible it will be to you, Bethsaida! For if the miraculous works had happened in Tyre and Sidon, the ones having happened in you*, they [would have] repented long ago in sackcloth and ashes. ²²Nevertheless, I say to you*, it will be more tolerable for Tyre and Sidon in [the] day of judgment than for you.* ²³And you, Capernaum, the one having been exalted to heaven, you will be brought down to the realm of the dead [Gr., *hades*], for if the miraculous works had happened in Sodom, the ones having happened in you, it [would have] remained to this day. ²⁴Nevertheless, I say to you*, it will be more tolerable for the land of Sodom in [the] day of judgment than for you."

²⁵At that time answering, Jesus said, "I praise You, Father, Lord of the heavens and of the earth, that You hid these [things] from wise and understanding [ones] and revealed them to young children. ²⁶Yes, Father, for in this way it became good pleasure before You. ²⁷All [things] were handed over to Me by My Father, and no one fully knows the Son, except the Father, nor does anyone fully know the Father, except the Son, and [the one] to whom the Son shall be desiring to reveal [Him]. ²⁸Come to Me, all the ones laboring and having been burdened, and I will give you* rest. ²⁹Take My yoke upon you* and learn from Me, because I am gentle and humble in heart, *'and you* will find rest for your* souls.'* [Jer 6:16] ³⁰For My yoke [is] easy, and My burden is light."

12 At that time Jesus went on [one of] the Sabbaths through the grainfields, and His disciples were hungry, and they began to be picking heads of grain and to be eating. ²But the Pharisees having seen, said to Him, "Look! Your disciples are doing what is not lawful to be doing on a Sabbath!"

³But He said to them, "You* read what David did, when he was hungry, he and the [ones] with him, did you* not? ⁴How he went into the house of God and ate the loaves of bread of the presentation [fig., the consecrated bread], which were not lawful for him to eat nor for the [ones] with him, except for the priests alone? [cp. 1Sam 21:3-6; Exod 29:32-33] ⁵Or you* did read in the Law that on the Sabbaths the priests in the temple desecrate the Sabbath and are blameless, did you* not? ⁶But I say to you*, [something] greater [than] the temple is here. ⁷But if you* had known what is [fig., what this means], '*I desire mercy and not sacrifice,*' [Hosea 6:6] you* [would] not [have] condemned the blameless [ones]. ⁸For the Son of Humanity is Lord of the Sabbath."

⁹And having departed from there, He went into their synagogue. ¹⁰And look! A man was [there] having his hand withered [fig., deformed]; and they questioned Him, saying, "Is it lawful to be healing on the Sabbaths?"—so that they should accuse [or, bring charges against] Him.

¹¹But He said to them, "What person will [there] be of you*, who will have one sheep, and if this [sheep] falls into a ditch on [one of] the Sabbaths, will not take hold of it and raise [it] up? ¹²By how much more then is a person worth than a sheep? Accordingly, it is lawful on the Sabbaths to be doing good." ¹³Then He says to the man, "Stretch out your hand." And he stretched [it] out, and it was restored [as] healthy as the other! ¹⁴But the Pharisees having gone out, plotted against Him in order that they should destroy Him.

¹⁵But Jesus having known, withdrew from there. And large crowds followed Him, and He healed them all. ¹⁶And He warned them that they should not make Him known, ¹⁷in order that the [word] having been spoken through Isaiah the prophet should be fulfilled, saying:

> ¹⁸*Look! My servant whom I chose; My Beloved in whom My soul is well-pleased. I will put My Spirit upon Him, and He will proclaim judgment to the nations.* ¹⁹*He will not quarrel nor cry out, nor will anyone hear His voice in the open streets.* ²⁰*He will not break a bruised reed, and He will not extinguish a smoldering wick, until He sends out justice to victory* [fig., *causes justice to triumph*]. ²¹*And nations will hope* [or, *place their trust*] *in His name.* [Isaiah 42:1-4 (last verse, LXX)]

²²Then was brought to Him [one] being demon-possessed [or, oppressed by a demon], blind and mute; and He healed him, with the result that the blind and mute [person] [was] both speaking and seeing! ²³And all the crowds were amazed and said, "This is not the Son of David, is it?" ²⁴But the Pharisees having heard, said, "This One does not cast out demons, except by Beelzebul."

²⁵So Jesus knowing their thoughts, said to them, "Every kingdom having been divided against itself is laid waste, and every city or house having been divided against itself will not stand. ²⁶And if Satan casts out Satan, he was divided against himself. Therefore, how will his kingdom stand? ²⁷And if I cast out the demons by Beelzebul, by whom do your* sons [fig., followers] cast [them] out? For this reason, they will be your* judges. ²⁸But if by [the] Spirit of God I cast out

the demons, in that case, the kingdom of God already came upon you*. [29]Or how is one able to enter into the house of the strong man and to plunder his property, unless first he binds the strong man? And then he will plunder his house. [30]The [one] not being with Me is against Me, and the [one] not gathering with Me, is scattering.

[31]"For this reason I say to you*, every sin and blasphemy will be forgiven to the people, but the blasphemy against the Spirit will not be forgiven to the people. [32]And whoever speaks a word against the Son of Humanity it will be forgiven to him, but whoever speaks against the Holy Spirit, it will not be forgiven to him, neither in the present age nor in the coming [one].

[33]"Either make the tree good and its fruit good, or make the tree rotten and its fruit rotten, for the tree is known by its fruit. [34]Brood of vipers! How are you* able to be speaking good things, being evil? For out of the abundance of the heart the mouth speaks. [35]The good person out of the good treasure [within him] brings forth good [things], and the evil person out of the evil treasure [within him] brings forth evil [things]. [36]But I say to you*, every idle [or, careless] word which the people shall speak, they will render an account concerning it in [the] day of judgment. [37]For by your words you will be justified [or, declared righteous], and by your words you will be condemned."

[38]Then some of the scribes and Pharisees answered, saying, "Teacher, we want to see a sign from You." [39]But answering, He said to them, "An evil and adulterous [or, unfaithful] generation seeks a sign, and a sign will not be given to it, except the sign of Jonah the prophet. [40]For just as *'Jonah was in the belly of the sea monster three days and three nights,'* so will the Son of Humanity be in the heart [fig., depths] of the earth three days and three nights. [Jonah 1:17] [41]Men, Ninevites, will stand up in the judgment against this generation and will condemn it, for they repented at [or, because of] the proclamation of Jonah. And listen! [One] greater than Jonah [is] here! [see Jonah 3:5] [42][The] Queen of [the] South will be raised up in the judgment against this generation and will condemn it, for she came from the ends of the earth to hear the wisdom of Solomon. And listen! [One] greater than Solomon [is] here! [see 1Kings 10:1-29]

[43]"But when the unclean [or, defiling] spirit goes out from the person, it goes through waterless places seeking rest and does not find [any]. [44]Then it says, 'I will return to my house from where I came out.' And having come, it finds [it] unoccupied, having been swept and having been put in order. [45]Then it goes and takes with itself seven different spirits more evil than itself, and having entered in, they dwell there; and the last [state] of that person becomes worse [than] the first. Thus it will be also for this evil generation."

[46]Now while He is still speaking to the crowds, look!, His mother and brothers had stood outside, seeking to speak to Him. [47]And someone said to Him, "Listen! Your mother and Your brothers have stood outside seeking to speak to You." [48]But answering, He said to the one having spoken to Him, "Who is My mother? And who are My brothers?" [49]And having stretched out His hand toward His disciples, He said, "Look! My mother and My brothers! [50]For whoever does the will of my Father, the [One] in the heavens, he is My brother and sister and mother."

*13*Then on that day Jesus, having gone out from the house, was sitting by the sea. [2]And large crowds were gathered together to Him, with the result that He stepped into the boat to be sitting down. And the entire crowd had stood on the beach.

[3]And He spoke to them many [things] in allegories [or, parables, and throughout book], saying: "Listen! The one sowing went out to be sowing. [4]And in his sowing, some [seed] fell beside the road, and the birds came and devoured them. [5]But others fell on the rocky ground, where it did not have much soil, and immediately it sprouted, because of it not having depth of soil. [6]But [the] sun having risen, it was scorched, and because of it not having root, it withered. [7]But others fell on the thorns, and the thorns came up and choked them. [8]But others fell on the good ground and began yielding fruit, some a hundred[fold] and some sixty[fold] and some thirty[fold]. [9]The one having ears to be hearing—let him be hearing [or, be paying attention]."

[10]And the disciples having come near, said to Him, "Why do You speak to them in allegories?" [11]So answering, He said to them, "To you* it has been given to know the secrets [or, mysteries] of the kingdom of the heavens, but to those [ones] it has not been given. [12]For whoever has, [more] will be given to him, and he will have an abundance; but whoever does not have, even what he has will be taken from him. [13]For this reason I speak in allegories to them, that seeing they do not see, and hearing they do not hear, nor do they understand.

[14]"And in them is fulfilled the prophecy of Isaiah, the one saying:

> *With hearing you* will hear, and by no means will you* understand;*
> *and seeing you* will see, and by no means will you* perceive. [15]For the*
> *heart of this people has become dull* [or, *insensitive*]*, and they heard*
> *heavily with the ears* [fig., *they are hard of hearing*]*, and they closed*
> *their eyes, lest they see with the eyes, and they hear with the ears, and*
> *they understand with the heart, and they turn back, and I will heal them.*
> [Isaiah 6:9,10, LXX]

[16]"But happy are your* eyes because they see, and your* ears because they hear. [17]For positively, I say to you*, many prophets and righteous [ones] desired to see what you* see, and they did not see, and to hear what you* hear, and they did not hear.

[18]"Therefore, you* pay attention to the allegory of the one sowing: [19]Every[one] hearing the word of the kingdom and not understanding [it], the evil [one] comes and snatches away the [word] having been sown in his heart; this is the [seed] having been sown beside the road. [20]But the [seed] having been sown on the rocky ground, this is the [one] hearing the word and immediately receives it with joy. [21]But he does not have root in himself, but is temporary; and affliction or persecution having taken place because of the word, immediately he is caused to stumble [fig., he falls away]. [22]But the [seed] having been sown into the thorns, this is the [one] hearing the word, and the anxiety of this age and the deception of the riches choke the word, and it becomes unfruitful. [23]And the [seed] having been

sown on the good ground: this is the [one] hearing the word and understanding, who indeed bears fruit and produces, some a hundred[fold], but some sixty[fold], but some thirty[fold]."

²⁴Another allegory He set before them, saying: "The kingdom of the heavens was compared to a person sowing good seed in his field. ²⁵But while the people are sleeping, his enemy came and sowed darnel [i.e. a poisonous weed resembling wheat in the early stages of growth] in the midst of the wheat, and he went away. ²⁶So when the stalk sprouted and yielded fruit, then the darnel appeared also. ²⁷So the slaves of the landowner, having approached, said to him, 'Lord, you sowed good seed in your field, did you not? So from where does it have darnel?' ²⁸So he says to them, 'A person, an enemy, did this.' But the slaves said to him, 'So do you want, having gone away, [that] we will gather them up?' ²⁹But he was saying, 'No, lest gathering up the darnel you* uproot the wheat with it. ³⁰Allow both to be growing together until the harvest, and at [the] time of the harvest I will say to the reapers, "Gather up first the darnel and bind them into bundles to burn it, but gather up the wheat into my barn."'"

³¹Another allegory He set before them, saying: "The kingdom of the heavens is like a grain of mustard [or, a mustard seed], which having taken, a person sowed in his field, ³²which indeed is smaller than all the seeds, but when it is grown is largest of the vegetables. And it becomes a tree, with the result that the birds of the air come and nest in its branches."

³³Another allegory He spoke to them: "The kingdom of the heavens is like leaven [or, yeast], which a woman having taken hid in three sata [about 1.5 bushels or 36 liters] of wheat flour, until which [time the] whole was leavened [or, was risen]."

³⁴All these things Jesus spoke in allegories to the crowds, and without an allegory He did not speak to them, ³⁵in order that the [word] having been spoken through the prophet should be fulfilled, saying, *"I will open my mouth in allegories; I will utter things having been hidden from [the] laying of the foundation of [the] world* [or, *from [the] beginning of the creation of [the] universe*, and throughout NT]*."* [Psalm 78:2]

³⁶Then having dismissed the crowds, Jesus came to the house. And His disciples approached Him, saying, "Explain to us the allegory of the darnel of the field." ³⁷So answering, He said to them, "The one sowing the good seed is the Son of Humanity. ³⁸And the field is the world, and the good seed, these are the sons [and daughters] of the kingdom, and the darnel are the sons [and daughters] of the evil one. ³⁹And the enemy, the one sowing them, is the Devil, and the harvest is [the] conclusion of the age, and the reapers are angels. ⁴⁰Therefore, just as the darnel is gathered up and will be burned with fire, so will it be at the conclusion of this age. ⁴¹The Son of Humanity will send out His angels, and they will gather up out of His kingdom all the stumbling blocks [or, everything that offends] and the ones practicing lawlessness. ⁴²And they will throw them into the furnace of fire [or, the fiery furnace]. In that place [there] will be weeping and gnashing of teeth! ⁴³Then will the righteous [ones] shine forth like the sun in the kingdom of their Father. The one having ears to be hearing, let him be hearing [or, be paying attention].

⁴⁴"Again, the kingdom of the heavens is like treasure hid in the field, which a person having found hid, and as a result of his joy, he goes, and all, as much as he has, he sells, and buys that field.

⁴⁵"Again, the kingdom of the heavens is like a person, a merchant, seeking precious pearls, ⁴⁶who having found one very valuable pearl, having gone away, has sold all, as much as he has, and bought it.

⁴⁷"Again, the kingdom of the heavens is like to a dragnet having been cast into the sea, and having gathered together [fish] of every kind, ⁴⁸which, when it was filled, when they dragged [it] up again on the beach, and having sat down, they gathered the good [fish] into containers, but they threw out the rotten [fish]. ⁴⁹In this manner it will be at the conclusion of the age. The angels will go out and will separate the evil [ones] out of [the] midst of the righteous [ones] ⁵⁰and will throw them into the furnace of fire [or, the fiery furnace]. In that place [there] will be weeping and gnashing of teeth!"

⁵¹Jesus says to them, "Did you* understand all these [things]?" They say to Him, "Yes, Lord." ⁵²Then He said to them, "For this reason, every scribe having been made a disciple in the kingdom of the heavens is like a person, a householder, who brings out from his treasury new and old [things]." ⁵³And it happened, when Jesus finished these allegories, He departed from there.

⁵⁴And having come into His hometown, He was teaching them in their synagogue, with the result that they are being astonished and are saying, "From where to this One [or, Where [did] this One [get]] this wisdom and these miraculous powers? ⁵⁵This is the craftsman's Son, is He not? His mother is called Mary, and His brothers [are] James and Joses and Simon and Judas, are they not? ⁵⁶And His sisters are all with us, are they not? So from where to this One all these [things] [or, where then [did] this One [get] all these [things]]?" ⁵⁷And they were caused to stumble because of Him [fig., were having doubts about Him]. But Jesus said to them, "A prophet is not without honor except in his hometown and in his house." ⁵⁸And He did not perform many miraculous works there because of their unbelief.

14 At that time Herod the ruler of the quadrant [or, the tetrarch] heard the report [about] Jesus, ²and said to his servants, "This is John the Baptist! He rose from the dead! And for this reason these miraculous powers supernaturally work in him." ³For Herod having arrested John, bound him and put [him] in prison, because of Herodias, the wife of Philip his brother. ⁴For John kept saying to him, "[It is] not lawful to [or, for] you to be having her!" ⁵And [although] desiring to kill him, he feared the crowd, because they were regarding him as a prophet.

⁶Now as the birthday festivities of Herod were being celebrated, the daughter of Herodias danced in the midst, and she pleased Herod. ⁷And so he promised with an oath to give her whatever she should ask. ⁸So having been instigated by her mother, she says, "Give to me here on a wooden platter the head of John the Baptist!" ⁹And the king was grieved, but because of the oaths and of the ones reclining [to eat] with [him], he commanded [it] to be given. ¹⁰And having sent [guards], he beheaded John in the prison. ¹¹And his head was brought on a wooden platter and was given to the girl, and she brought [it] to her mother. ¹²And his

disciples having come, they took up the body and buried it; and having come, they reported [it] to Jesus.

[13]And having heard, Jesus departed from there in a boat privately to a desolate place. And the crowds having heard followed Him on foot [or, by land] from the cities. [14]And having come out, Jesus saw a large crowd and was moved with compassion for them and healed their infirm [or, sickly] [ones]. [15]But evening having come, His disciples came to Him, saying, "The place is desolate, and the hour already passed by [fig., the time is already late]. Send away the crowds so that, having gone into the villages, they should buy food for themselves."

[16]But Jesus said to them, "They do not have need to go away; you* give [something] to them to eat." [17]But they say to Him, "We do not have [anything] here except five loaves of bread and two fish." [18]Then He said, "Be bringing them here to Me." [19]And having commanded the crowds to be reclined on the grasses [or, areas of grass], having taken the five loaves of bread and the two fish, having looked up to heaven, He bestowed a blessing; and having broken, He gave the loaves of bread to the disciples, and the disciples [gave them] to the crowds. [20]And they all ate and were filled! And they took up the leftover broken pieces of bread—twelve handbaskets full! [21]Now the ones eating were about five thousand men, besides women and young children.

[22]And immediately Jesus compelled the disciples to step into the boat and to be going before Him to the other side, until He sends the crowds away. [23]And having sent away the crowds, He went up into the mountain privately to pray. Now evening having come, He was there alone. [24]But the boat was now in the middle of the sea, being tossed about by the waves, for the wind was against [them].

[25]But in the fourth watch of the night [i.e., between 3:00 - 6:00 a.m.], Jesus went to them, walking about on the sea. [26]And the disciples having seen Him walking about on the sea were terrified, saying, "It is a ghost [or, an apparition]!" And they cried out because of the fear. [27]But immediately, Jesus spoke to them, saying, "Be taking courage! I Am! Stop fearing!" [cp. Exod 3:14]

[28]And answering, Peter said to Him, "Lord, if it is You, command me to come to You on the waters." [29]So He said, "Come!" And having stepped down from the boat, Peter walked about on the waters to come to Jesus. [30]But seeing the strong wind, he was frightened; and having begun to be sinking, he cried out, saying, "Lord, save me!" [31]Then immediately Jesus, having stretched out His hand, took hold of him and says to him, "[O you] of little faith! Why did you waver [or, doubt]?" [32]And when they had stepped into the boat, the wind abated. [33]Then the [ones] in the boat having come, prostrated themselves in worship before Him, saying, "Truly You are God's Son!"

[34]And having crossed over, they came to the land of Gennesaret. [35]And having recognized Him, the men of that place sent out into that whole surrounding region, and they brought to Him all the ones having it badly [fig., who were sick]. [36]And they were pleading with Him that they should only touch the fringe of His garment, and as many as touched [it] were completely cured.

*15*Then scribes and Pharisees from Jerusalem come to Jesus, saying, ²"Why do Your disciples transgress the tradition of the elders? For they do not [ritually] wash their hands whenever they are eating bread." ³But answering, He said to them, "Why do you* also transgress the commandment of God because of your* tradition? ⁴For God commanded, saying, *'Be honoring your father and mother,'* and, *'The one speaking evil of father or mother, let him come to the end [of his life], to [his] death.'* [Exod 20:12; Deut 5:16; Exod 21:17] ⁵But you* say, 'Whoever says to father or mother, "[It is] an offering, whatever you should be benefited from me,"—and by no means shall he [fig., then he has no need at all to] honor his father or his mother.' ⁶And you* nullify [or, disregard] the commandment of God because of your* tradition.

⁷"Hypocrites! Correctly Isaiah prophesied concerning you*, saying ⁸*'This people draws near to Me with their mouth* [fig., *speech*] *and honors Me with the lips* [fig., *words*], *but their heart is far distant from Me. ⁹But in vain* [or, *to no purpose*] *do they worship Me, teaching [as] teachings* [or, *doctrines*], *commandments of people.'"* [Isaiah 29:13, LXX]

¹⁰And having summoned the crowd, He said to them, "Be paying attention, and be understanding. ¹¹The [thing] having entered into the mouth does not defile the person, but the [thing] coming out from the mouth, this defiles the person." ¹²Then His disciples having approached, said to Him, "Do You know that the Pharisees, having heard the word, were caused to stumble [fig., were offended]?" ¹³But answering, He said, "Every plant which My heavenly Father did not plant will be uprooted. ¹⁴Leave them alone. They are blind guides of blind [people], but if a blind [person] guides a blind [person], both will fall into a ditch."

¹⁵But answering, Peter said to Him, "Explain to us this allegory." ¹⁶So Jesus said, "Are you* also still without understanding? ¹⁷Do you* not yet understand that every[thing] entering into the mouth goes into the stomach and is cast out into a latrine? ¹⁸But the [things] coming out from the mouth come out from the heart, and these [things] defile the person. ¹⁹For from the heart come out evil thoughts, murders, adulteries, sexual sins, thefts, false testimonies, blasphemies: ²⁰these are the [things] defiling the person, but to eat with [ritually] unwashed hands does not defile the person."

²¹And Jesus having gone out from there withdrew into the regions of Tyre and Sidon. ²²And look! A woman, a Canaanite, having come out from those borders, called to Him, saying, "Be merciful to me, Lord, Son of David! My daughter is miserably demon-possessed [or, oppressed by a demon]." ²³But He did not answer her a word. And His disciples having approached Him, were asking Him, saying, "Send her away, because she cries out after us."

²⁴But answering, He said, "I was not sent except to the sheep, the ones lost from the house of Israel." ²⁵But having come, she prostrated herself in reverence before Him, saying, "Lord, be helping me!" ²⁶But answering, He said, "It is not good to take the children's bread and to throw [it] to the little dogs." ²⁷But she said, "Yes, Lord, for even the little dogs eat from the crumbs, the ones falling from their lord's table." ²⁸Then answering, Jesus said to her, "O woman, great [is]

your faith! Let it happen to you as you desire." And her daughter was healed from that hour.

²⁹And Jesus having departed from there, went along the Sea of Galilee; and having gone up into the mountain, He was sitting there. ³⁰And large crowds came to Him, having with them [the] lame, blind, mute, crippled, and many others, and they put them down at the feet of Jesus, and He healed them; ³¹with the result that the crowds marveled [or, were amazed], seeing [the] mute speaking, crippled [made] whole, lame walking, and blind seeing; and they glorified the God of Israel.

³²Then Jesus having summoned His disciples, said, "I have compassion on the crowd, because they are already staying with Me three days, and they do not have anything they should eat; and I do not want to send them away hungry, lest they faint on the journey." ³³And His disciples say to Him, "From where to us [fig., Where can we get] in [this] desolate place so many loaves of bread, so as to fill so great a crowd?" ³⁴And Jesus says to them, "How many loaves of bread do you* have?" So they said, "Seven, and a few small fish."

³⁵And He commanded the crowds to recline on the ground. ³⁶And having taken the seven loaves of bread and the fish, having given thanks, He broke [them] and gave [them] to His disciples, and the disciples to the crowd. ³⁷And they all ate and were satisfied! And they took up the leftover broken pieces—seven large baskets full! ³⁸Now the ones eating were four thousand men, besides women and young children. ³⁹Then having sent away the crowds, He stepped into the boat and came into the borders of Magdala.

*16*And the Pharisees and Sadducees having come, testing [Him], asked for Him to show to them a sign from heaven. ²But answering, He said to them, "When evening comes, you* say, '[It will be] fair weather, for the sky is red,' ³and in the morning, 'Today [will be] stormy, for the sky is red [and] overcast.' Hypocrites! The face [fig., appearance] of the sky indeed you* know [how] to be discerning, but the signs of the times you* are not able [to be discerning]! ⁴An evil and adulterous [or, unfaithful] generation seeks a sign, and a sign will not be given to it, except the sign of Jonah the prophet." And having left them, He went away.

⁵And His disciples having come to the other side, forgot to take loaves of bread. ⁶Then Jesus said to them, "Be watching out, and be guarding against the leaven [or, yeast] of the Pharisees and Sadducees." ⁷So they began reasoning within themselves, saying, "Because we took no loaves of bread."

⁸But Jesus having known, said to them, "Why are you* reasoning within yourselves, [you*] of little faith, because you* took no loaves of bread? ⁹Do you* not yet understand, nor remember the five loaves of bread of the five thousand and how many handbaskets you* took up? ¹⁰Nor the seven loaves of bread of the four thousand and how many large baskets you* took up? ¹¹How do you* not understand that [it was] not concerning bread I said to you* to be guarding against the leaven [or, yeast] of the Pharisees and Sadducees?" ¹²Then they understood that He did not say to be guarding against the leaven [or, yeast] of bread, but against the teaching of the Pharisees and Sadducees.

¹³Then Jesus, having come to the regions of Caesarea of Philippi, began asking His disciples, saying, "Who are the people saying Me to be [or, that I am], the Son of Humanity?" ¹⁴And they said, "Some [are saying] John the Baptist; but others, Elijah; but different [ones], Jeremiah, or one of the prophets." ¹⁵He says to them, "But who do you* say Me to be [or, that I am]?" ¹⁶Then answering, Simon Peter said, "You are the Christ, the Son of the living God!"

¹⁷And answering, Jesus said to him, "Happy are you, Simon Bar-Jonah ["son of Jonah"], because flesh and blood did not reveal [it] to you, but My Father, the [One] in the heavens. ¹⁸Now I also say to you, that you are Peter ["a stone"], and on this solid rock I will build my Assembly [or, Church], and [the] gates of the realm of the dead [Gr., *hades*] will not prevail against it. ¹⁹And I will give to you the keys of the kingdom of the heavens, and whatever you bind on the earth will have been bound in the heavens; and whatever you loose on the earth will have been loosed in the heavens." ²⁰Then He gave orders to His disciples that they should tell no one that He is Jesus the Christ ["the Anointed One"].

²¹From that time Jesus began to be showing to His disciples that it is necessary [for] Him to go away to Jerusalem and to suffer many [things] from the elders and chief priests and scribes and to be put to death and on the third day to be raised. ²²And having taken Him aside, Peter began to be rebuking Him, saying, "[May God] be merciful to You, Lord; by no means will this happen to You!" ²³But having turned around, He said to Peter, "Be going away behind Me, Satan! You are a stumbling block to Me, for you do not keep in mind the [things] of God, but the [things] of people."

²⁴Then Jesus said to His disciples, "If anyone desires to come after Me, he must deny [or, disown] himself, and take up his cross, and be following Me. ²⁵For whoever shall be desiring to save his life will lose it, but whoever loses his life for My sake will find it. ²⁶For what is a person benefited if he gains the whole world, but his soul is forfeited? Or what will a person give in an exchange for his soul? ²⁷For the Son of Humanity is about to be coming in the glory of His Father, with His angels, and then He will reward each according to his work. ²⁸"Positively, I say to you*, [there] are some having stood here who will by no means taste of death until they see the Son of Humanity coming in His kingdom."

*17*And after six days Jesus takes along Peter and James and John his brother, and leads them up privately into a high mountain. ²And He was transfigured [or, His appearance was changed] before them; and His face shone like the sun, and His garments became [as] white as the light. ³And look! Moses and Elijah appeared to them, conversing with Him. ⁴Then answering, Peter said to Jesus, "Lord, it is good [for] us to be here. If You desire, You should let us make three tents here: one for You and one for Moses and one for Elijah."

⁵While he is still speaking, look!, a bright cloud overshadowed them. And listen! A voice out of the cloud, saying, "This is My Son—the Beloved—in whom I am well-pleased! Be paying attention to Him!" ⁶And the disciples having heard, they fall on their face[s] and were extremely frightened. ⁷And Jesus having

approached, He took hold of them and said, "Get up, and stop fearing!" ⁸Then having lifted up their eyes, they saw no one, except Jesus only.

⁹And as they come down from the mountain, Jesus commanded them, saying, "You* shall tell no one the vision, until the Son of Humanity rises from [the] dead." ¹⁰And His disciples questioned Him, saying, "Why then do the scribes say that it is necessary [for] Elijah to come first?" [see Mal 4:5] ¹¹Then answering, Jesus said to them, "Elijah is indeed coming first, and he will restore all things. ¹²But I say to you*, Elijah already came, and they did not recognize him, but they did with him whatever they desired; in the same manner the Son of Humanity is also about to be suffering by them." ¹³Then the disciples understood that He spoke to them concerning John the Baptist.

¹⁴And when they came to the crowd, a man approached Him, kneeling before Him, ¹⁵and saying, "Lord, be merciful to my son, for he is moonstruck [or, is a lunatic] and suffers miserably; for frequently he falls into the fire and frequently into the water. ¹⁶And I brought him to Your disciples, and they were not able to heal him."

¹⁷So answering, Jesus said, "O unbelieving [or, faithless] and having been perverted generation, how long will I be with you*? How long will I put up with you*? Be bringing him here to Me." ¹⁸And Jesus rebuked it, and the demon came out from him, and the boy was healed from that hour.

¹⁹Then the disciples having approached Jesus privately said, "Why were we not able to cast it out?" ²⁰So Jesus said to them, "Because of your* unbelief. For positively I say to you*, if you* are having faith like a grain of mustard [or, a mustard seed], you* will say to this mountain, 'Move from here [to] there,' and it will move, and nothing will be impossible to you*. ²¹But this kind does not go out except by prayer and fasting."

²²Now while they are staying in Galilee, Jesus said to them, "The Son of Humanity is about to be betrayed into [the] hands of people, ²³and they will kill Him, and on the third day He will be risen." And they were extremely grieved.

²⁴Now when they came into Capernaum, the ones receiving the didrachmas [i.e. a temple-tax of a silver coin worth about a quarter of an ounce or seven grams of silver] approached Peter, and said, "Your Teacher does not pay the didrachma, does He?" ²⁵He says, "Yes." And when he entered into the house, Jesus anticipated him, saying, "What do you think, Simon? From whom do the kings of the earth receive custom or tribute [or, a tax]? From their sons or from the strangers?" ²⁶Peter says to Him, "From the strangers." Jesus said to him, "In that case, the sons are free. ²⁷But so that we do not cause them to stumble [fig., offend them], going up to the sea, cast [in] a hook, and take up the first fish coming up. And having opened its mouth, you will find a stater [i.e. a silver coin worth two didrachmas]. Having taken that, give [it] to them for Me and you."

18 In that hour [or, At that time] the disciples approached Jesus, saying, "So who is greatest in the kingdom of the heavens?" ²And Jesus having summoned a young child, He set him in the middle of them ³and said, "Positively, I say to you*, unless you* are turned around [fig., changed inwardly] and become like such young children, by no means shall you* enter into the kingdom of the heavens. ⁴Therefore, whoever will humble himself like this young child, he is the greatest in the kingdom of the heavens. ⁵And whoever receives one such child in My name, receives Me.

⁶"And whoever causes one of these little ones who believe in Me to stumble [fig., to sin], it [would be] better for him that a millstone of a donkey [fig., a huge millstone] be hanged on his neck, and he be drowned in the depth of the sea. ⁷How horrible it will be to the world because of the stumbling blocks [fig., the things that cause people to sin]! For it is a necessity [for] the stumbling blocks to come. Nevertheless, how horrible it will be to that person through whom the stumbling block comes!

⁸"But if your hand or your foot causes you to stumble [fig., to sin], cut them off and cast [it] from you! It is better for you to enter into the life lame or crippled, rather than having two hands or two feet, to be cast into the eternal fire. ⁹And if your eye causes you to stumble [fig., to sin], pluck it out and cast [it] from you; it is better for you to enter into the life one-eyed, rather than having two eyes to be cast into the hell [Gr., *gehenna*] of the fire [or, the fiery hell].

¹⁰"Be seeing [that] you* do not despise one of these little ones, for I say to you*, their angels in the heavens through all [fig. always] look at the face of My Father, the [One] in the heavens. ¹¹For the Son of Humanity came to save the ones having been lost.

¹²"What do you think? If a person has a hundred sheep and one of them goes astray, having left behind the ninety-nine, having gone on the mountains, he seeks the one having gone astray, does he not? ¹³And if he happens to find it, positively, I say to you*, he rejoices over it more than over the ninety-nine, the ones not having gone astray. ¹⁴In this manner, it is not [the] will before your* Father, the [One] in the heavens, that one of these little ones perish.

¹⁵"Now if your brother sins against you, be going, and show him his fault between you and him alone; if he hears you, you gained your brother. ¹⁶But if he does not hear [you], take along with you yet one or two, so that *'by [the] mouth of two or three witnesses every word shall be established.'* [Deut 19:15] ¹⁷But if he refuses to listen to them, tell [it] to the assembly [or, church]; but if he also refuses to listen to the assembly, he shall be to you just like the heathen and the tax collector.

¹⁸"Positively, I say to you*, whatever [things] you* bind on the earth will have been bound in heaven, and whatever [things] you* loose on the earth will have been loosed in heaven. ¹⁹Again, positively I say to you*, if two of you* agree together on the earth concerning any matter, whatever they ask, it will be done to [or, for] them from my Father, the [One] in the heavens. ²⁰For where two or three are gathered together in My name, I am there in the midst of them."

²¹Then Peter having approached Him, said, "Lord, how often will my brother sin against me, and I will forgive him, up to seven times?" ²²Jesus says to him, "I do not say to you up to seven times, but up to seventy times seven!

²³"For this reason the kingdom of the heavens was compared to a person, a king, who wanted to settle accounts with his slaves. ²⁴So when he began to be

26

settling the accounts, one debtor was brought near to him [owing] ten thousand talents [i.e. about 950,000 pounds or 420,000 kilograms of gold or silver]. ²⁵But he not having [anything] to repay, his lord commanded him to be sold, and his wife and the children, and all, whatever he was having, and to be repaid. ²⁶So the slave, having fallen down, began prostrating himself in reverence before him, saying, 'Lord, have patience with me, and I will repay you all.' ²⁷Then the lord of that slave, having been moved with compassion, released him and forgave him the debt.

²⁸"But that slave having gone out, found one of his fellow-slaves who was owing to him a hundred denarii [i.e., 100 days' wages], and having seized him, he began choking [him], saying, 'Repay to me if you owe anything!' ²⁹His fellow-slave then, having fallen down at his feet, began pleading with him, saying, 'Have patience with me, and I will repay all to you.' ³⁰But he was not willing, but having gone away, he threw him into prison until he should repay the [amount] being owed.

³¹"But his fellow-slaves, having seen the [things] having been done, were extremely grieved; and having come, they reported to their own lord all the [things] having been done. ³²Then having summoned him, his lord says to him, 'Evil slave! All that debt I forgave you, since you pleaded with Me. ³³It was necessary [for] you also to be merciful to your fellow-slave, just as I also was merciful to you, was it not?' ³⁴And having been enraged, his lord handed Him over to the torturers [or, jailers], until he should repay all being owed to him.

³⁵"In this manner also My heavenly Father will do to you*, unless you* forgive each [one] his brother their transgressions from your* hearts."

19 And it happened, when Jesus finished these words, He departed from Galilee and came into the borders of Judea, beyond the Jordan. ²And large crowds followed Him, and He healed them there.

³And the Pharisees came to Him, testing Him and saying to Him, "Is it lawful for a man to divorce his wife for every cause?" ⁴But answering, He said, "Did you* not read that the One having made [them] from [the] beginning made them male and female; [see Gen 1:27] ⁵and said, *'For this reason, a man will leave behind father and mother and will be joined to [or, be united with] his wife. And they will be—the two—into one flesh [or, the two will become one flesh]?'* [Gen 2:24, LXX] ⁶With the result that they are no longer two, but one flesh. Therefore, what God joined together, stop letting a person separate!"

⁷They say to Him, "Why then did Moses command to *'give a scroll of divorce and to divorce her?'*" [Deut 24:1,3] ⁸He says to them, "Because of your* stubbornness Moses permitted you* to divorce your* wives, but from the beginning it has not been this way. ⁹But I say to you*, whoever divorces his wife [but] not for sexual sin and marries another commits adultery, and the one having married the one having been divorced commits adultery."

¹⁰His disciples say to Him, "If the relationship of the man with the woman is like this, it is better not to marry." ¹¹But He said to them, "All do not accept this word, but [only those] to whom it has been given. ¹²For there are eunuchs [i.e.,

men incapable of having sex] who from [their] mother's womb were so born, and there are eunuchs who were made eunuchs by the people, and there are eunuchs who made themselves eunuchs because of the kingdom of the heavens: the one able to be accepting [it], let him be accepting [it]."

¹³Then young children were brought to Him, so that He should lay His hands on them and pray, but the disciples rebuked them. ¹⁴But Jesus said, "Allow the young children, and stop forbidding them to come to Me, for of such is the kingdom of the heavens." ¹⁵And having laid His hands on them, He departed from there.

¹⁶And look! Someone having approached said to Him, "Good teacher, what good [thing] shall I do that I shall be having eternal life?" ¹⁷But He said to him, "Why do you call Me good? No one [is] good except One—God. But if you desire to enter into that life, keep the commandments." ¹⁸He says to Him, "Which [ones]?" So Jesus said, *"'You will not murder; You will not commit adultery; You will not steal; You will not give false testimony; ¹⁹Honor your father and mother;'* and, *'You will love your neighbor as yourself.'"* [Exod 20:12-16; Deut 5:16-20; Lev 19:18]

²⁰The young man says to Him, "All these I myself obeyed from my youth; what am I still lacking?" ²¹Jesus said to him, "If you desire to be perfect, be going away; sell your possessions and give to [the] poor [ones], and you will have treasure in heaven. And come! Be following Me!" ²²But the young man having heard the word, went away sorrowing [or, distressed], for he was having many possessions.

²³Then Jesus said to His disciples, "Positively, I say to you*, with difficulty will a rich [person] enter into the kingdom of the heavens. ²⁴Now again I say to you*, it is easier [for] a camel to pass through an eye of a needle, than [for] a rich [person] to enter into the kingdom of God."

²⁵So His disciples having heard were extremely amazed, saying, "In that case, who is able to be saved?" ²⁶But Jesus having looked attentively [at them], said to them, "With people this is impossible, but with God all [things are] possible!"

²⁷Then answering, Peter said to Him, "Listen! We left all and followed You! What then will we have?" ²⁸So Jesus said to them, "Positively, I say to you*, that you*, the ones having followed Me, in the Regeneration, when the Son of Humanity sits on [the] throne of His glory, you* also will sit on twelve thrones, judging the twelve tribes of Israel. ²⁹And every[one] who left houses or brothers or sisters or father or mother or wife or children or farms for My name's sake will receive a hundred times as much and will inherit eternal life. ³⁰But many first [ones] will be last, and last [ones] first.

20"For the kingdom of the heavens is like a person, a landowner, who went out early in the morning to hire laborers for his vineyard. ²And having agreed with the laborers for a denarius [for] the day [i.e., a normal day's wage], he sent them into his vineyard. ³And having gone out about [the] third hour [i.e. 9:00 a.m.], he saw others having stood in the marketplace idle. ⁴And he said to those [ones], 'You* also be going into the vineyard, and whatever is just I will give to you.*' 5And they went off. Again, having gone out about [the] sixth and [the] ninth hour [i.e. 12:00 noon and 3:00 p.m., respectively], he did in the same manner. 6Then about the eleventh hour [i.e. 5:00 p.m.], having gone out, he found others having stood idle, and he says to them, 'Why have you* stood here idle the whole day?' 7They say to him, 'Because no one hired us.' He says to them, '<u>You*</u> also be going into the vineyard, and whatever is just you* will receive.'

8"Then evening having come, the lord of the vineyard says to his foreman, 'Call the laborers and pay them their wage, beginning from the last [ones] to the first [ones].' 9And the ones having come about the eleventh hour received each a denarius. 10Then the ones having come first assumed that they will receive more, and <u>they</u> also received each a denarius. 11But having received [it], they began grumbling against the landowner, 12saying, 'These, the last [ones], did one hour, and you made them equal to us, the ones having borne the burden of the day and the scorching heat.'

13"But answering, he said to one of them, 'Friend, I am not doing you wrong. You agreed with me for a denarius, did you not? 14Take [what is] yours, and be going; but I want to give to this [one], the last, as also to you. 15Or is it not lawful for me to do what I want with the [things] of me [fig., my own money]? Is your eye evil [fig., Are you envious] because <u>I</u> am good?' 16In this manner the last will be first, and the first last, for many are called, but few chosen."

17And while Jesus was going up to Jerusalem, He took aside the twelve disciples privately on the road and said to them, 18"Listen! We are going up to Jerusalem, and the Son of Humanity will be betrayed to the chief priests and scribes, and they will condemn Him to death, 19and they will hand Him over to the Gentiles to ridicule and to scourge and to crucify. And on the third day He will rise again."

20Then the mother of the sons of Zebedee, with her sons, approached Him, prostrating herself in reverence [or, in worship] and asking something from Him. 21And He said to her, "What do you want?" She says to Him, "Say [or, Command] that these, my two sons, shall sit one at Your right [hand] and one at Your left in Your kingdom."

22But answering, Jesus said, "You* do not know what you* are asking. Are you* able to drink the cup which <u>I</u> am about to be drinking, or to be baptized [with] the baptism which <u>I</u> am baptized?" They say to him, "We are able." 23And He says to them, "Indeed, My cup you* will drink, and the baptism which <u>I</u> am baptized [with], you* will be baptized. But to sit at My right [hand] and at My left is not Mine to give, <u>but</u> [it is for those] for whom it has been prepared by My Father."

24And the ten having heard, expressed indignation about the two brothers. 25But Jesus having summoned them, said, "You* know that the rulers of the nations domineer over them and their great [ones] tyrannize them, 26but it will not be so among you*; <u>but</u> whoever among you* is desiring to become great, he will be your* servant. 27And whoever among you* is desiring to be first, he must be your* slave. 28Just as the Son of Humanity did not come to be served, <u>but</u> to serve, and to give His life [as] a ransom [or, price of release] for [or, in the place of] many."

²⁹And as they are going out from Jericho, a large crowd followed Him. ³⁰And look! Two blind [ones] sitting beside the road, having heard that Jesus is passing by, cried out, saying, "Be merciful to us, Lord, Son of David!"

³¹But the crowd warned them that they should keep silent. But they began crying out louder, saying, "Be merciful to us, Lord, Son of David!" ³²And having stood still, Jesus summoned them and said, "What do you* desire [that] I should do for you*?" ³³They say to Him, "Lord, that our eyes be opened!" ³⁴So having been moved with compassion, Jesus touched their eyes, and immediately their eyes received [their] sight! And they followed Him.

21 And when they approached Jerusalem and came to Bethsphage, to the Mount of Olives, then Jesus sent two disciples, ²saying to them, "Proceed into the village, the [one] opposite you*, and immediately you* will find a donkey tied up and a colt [or, young donkey] with her; having untied [them], bring [them] to Me. ³And if anyone says anything to you*, you* will say, 'The Lord has need of them.' Then immediately he [will] send them." ⁴Now all this happened that the word spoken through the prophet should be fulfilled, saying, ⁵*"Say to the daughter of Zion, Look! Your King is coming to you, gentle, and having mounted on a donkey, and a colt, [the] son [or, foal] of a beast of burden."* [Isaiah 62:11; Zech 9:9]

⁶So the disciples proceeded, and having done just as Jesus commanded them, ⁷brought the donkey and the colt and laid their coats on them, and sat [Him] on them [i.e. on the coats]. ⁸Then the very large crowd spread their own coats on the road, but others began cutting off branches from the trees and began spreading [them] on the road. ⁹Then the crowds, the ones going in front [of Him] and the ones following, began crying out, saying, "We give praise to You, [Gr., *Hosanna*] to the Son of David! *'Having been blessed [is] the One coming in [the] name of [the] Lord!'* We give praise to You in the highest!" [Psalm 118:26]

¹⁰And when He entered into Jerusalem, the entire city was stirred up, saying, "Who is this?" ¹¹Then the crowds said, "This is Jesus the prophet, the [One] from Nazareth of Galilee."

¹²And Jesus entered into the temple of God and threw out all the ones selling and buying in the temple, and He overturned the tables of the money changers and the seats of the ones selling the doves. ¹³And He says to them, "It has been written, *'My house will be called a house of prayer.'* [Isaiah 56:7] But you* made it a *'hideout for robbers!'*" [Jer 7:11]

¹⁴And lame and blind [people] came to Him in the temple, and He healed them. ¹⁵But when the chief priests and the scribes saw the marvelous [things] which He did, and the children crying out in the temple and saying, "We give praise to You, the Son of David," they expressed indignation. ¹⁶And they said to Him, "Do You hear what these [ones] are saying?" But Jesus says to them, "Yes, did you* never read, *'Out of [the] mouth of young children and nursing infants*

You prepared praise for Yourself?'" [Psalm 8:2, LXX] [17]And having left them, He went forth outside of the city into Bethany, and spent the night there.

[18]But in the early morning returning to the city, He hungered. [19]And having seen a certain fig tree by the road, He came up to it and found nothing on it except leaves only. And He says to it, "Fruit shall no longer come from you into the age [fig., forever]." And immediately the fig tree was withered. [20]And the disciples having seen, were amazed, saying, "How was the fig tree immediately withered?" [21]But answering, Jesus said to them, "Positively, I say to you*, if you* are having faith and do not doubt, not only will you* perform the [sign] of the fig tree, but even if you* say to this mountain, 'Be taken up and be cast into the sea,' it will happen. [22]And all [things], as much as you ask in the prayer, believing, you* will receive."

[23]And when He came to the temple, as He was teaching, the chief priests and the elders of the people came to Him, saying, "By what authority are You doing these [things]? And who gave to You this authority?" [24]But answering, Jesus said to them, "I also will ask you* one word [or, question], which if you* tell me, I also will tell you* by what authority I am doing these [things]. [25]The baptism of John, from where was it? From heaven, or from people?"

So they began reasoning among themselves, saying, "If we say, 'From heaven,' He will say to us, 'Why then did you* not believe him?' [26]But if we say, 'From people,' we fear the crowd, for all hold John as [or, consider John to be] a prophet." [27]And answering Jesus, they said, "We do not know." And He said to them, "Neither do I tell you* by what authority I am doing these [things].

[28]"But what do you* think? A man was having two children, and having approached the first [one], he said, 'Child, be going today; be working in my vineyard.' [29]But answering, he said, 'I will not.' But later, having regretted [it], he went. [30]And having approached the second [one], he spoke in the same manner. Then answering, he said, 'I [am going], lord,' yet he did not go. [31]Which of the two did the will of the father?" They say to Him, "The first [one]."

Jesus says to them, "Positively, I say to you*, the tax collectors and the prostitutes are going before you* into the kingdom of God. [32]For John came to you* in [the] way of righteousness, and you* did not believe him. But the tax collectors and the prostitutes believed him; but you*, having seen, did not regret [it] later [so as] to believe him.

[33]"Be paying attention to another allegory: There was a man, a landowner, who *'planted a vineyard and put a fence around it and dug in it a winepress and built a lookout tower'* and leased it to vineyard keepers and went on a journey. [Isaiah 5:1,2] [34]Then when the season of the fruits drew near, he sent his slaves to the vineyard keepers to receive the fruits of it. [35]And the vineyard keepers having taken hold of his slaves, one they repeatedly beat, and one they killed, and one they stoned. [36]Again he sent other slaves, more than the first [ones], and they did to them in the same manner. [37]So at last he sent to them his son, saying, 'They will respect my son.' [38]But the vineyard keepers having seen the son, said among themselves, 'This is the heir. Come; let us be killing him, and let us take

31

possession of his inheritance!' [39]And having taken him, they threw [him] outside of the vineyard and killed [him].

[40]"Therefore, when the lord of the vineyard comes, what will he do to these vineyard keepers?" [41]They say to Him, "Evil [men]! He will severely destroy them, and he will lease the vineyard to other vineyard keepers, who will render to him the fruits in their seasons." [42]Jesus says to them, "Did you* never read in the Scriptures, *'A stone which the ones building rejected, this [one] has become [the] head of a corner; this happened from [the] Lord, and it is marvelous in our eyes?'* [Psalm 118:22,23] [43]For this reason I say to you*, the kingdom of God will be taken from you* and will be given to a nation [or, people] yielding its fruits. [44]And the one falling on this stone will be broken to pieces, but on whomever it falls, it will crush him."

[45]And the chief priests and the Pharisees having heard His allegories, knew that He [was] speaking about them. [46]And seeking to take Him into custody, they were afraid of the crowds, since they were holding Him as [or, considering Him to be] a prophet.

22And answering, Jesus again spoke to them in allegories, saying, [2]"The kingdom of the heavens was compared to a man, a king, who made marriage festivities for his son. [3]And he sent out his slaves to call the ones having been invited to the marriage festivities, and they were not willing to come. [4]Again he sent out other slaves, saying, 'Say to the ones having been invited, "Listen! I prepared my dinner; my oxen and the fattened calves have been killed, and all things [are] ready; come to the marriage festivities.'" [5]But they, having disregarded [it], went away, one indeed to his own field, but one to his business. [6]But the rest, having taken hold of his slaves, mistreated and killed [them]. [7]And that king having heard, was enraged, and having sent out his soldiers, he destroyed those murderers and set their city on fire.

[8]"Then he says to his slaves, 'The marriage feast indeed is ready, but the ones having been invited were not worthy. [9]So be going on the outlets of the roads [i.e. the roads heading from the city to the countryside], and as many as you* shall find, invite [them] to the marriage festivities.' [10]And those slaves having gone out into the roads, gathered together all, as many as they found, both evil and good [people]. And the marriage-feast [hall] was filled with [ones] reclining [to eat].

[11]"But the king having entered to observe the ones reclining [to eat], saw there a person not having been clothed with [the] clothing of the marriage-feast. [12]And he says to him, 'Friend, how did you come in here, not having [the] clothing of the marriage-feast?' But he was speechless. [13]Then the king said to the servants, 'Tie up his feet and hands; take him away and throw [him] into the outer darkness! In that place [there] will be weeping and gnashing of teeth!' [14]For many are called, but few chosen."

[15]Then the Pharisees having gone, plotted how they shall entrap Him in [some] word. [16]And they send their disciples to Him, with the Herodians, saying, "Teacher, we know that You are truthful, and You teach in truth the way of God, and You are not concerned for anyone, for You do not look to the face of people

[fig., You do not show favoritism to people]. [17]So tell us, what do You think? Is it lawful to give tribute [or, a tax] to Caesar or not?" [18]But Jesus having known their wickedness, said, "Why do you* test Me, [you*] hypocrites? [19]Show to Me the coin [used] for the tribute [or, the tax]." So they brought to Him a denarius [i.e., a Roman, silver coin]. [20]And He says to them, "Whose image [is] this, and the inscription?" [21]They say to Him, "Caesar's." Then He says to them, "So render the [things] of Caesar to Caesar, and the [things] of God to God." [22]And having heard, they were amazed, and having left Him, they went away.

[23]On that day Sadducees approached Him, saying, "[There] is not a resurrection." And they questioned Him, [24]saying, "Teacher, Moses said, *'If anyone dies not having children, his brother will marry his wife, and will raise up seed* [fig., *offspring] to his brother.'* [Deut 25:5] [25]Now seven brothers were with us. And the first [one] having married, came to the end [of his life], and not having seed, he left his wife to his brother. [26]Likewise also the second [one], and the third, to the seventh. [27]Then last of all the woman also died. [28]So in the resurrection, of which of the seven will she be a wife, for all had her?"

[29]But answering, Jesus said to them, "You are led astray [fig., are mistaken], not knowing the Scriptures nor the power of God. [30]For in the resurrection neither do they marry, nor are they given in marriage, <u>but</u> they are like angels of God in heaven. [31]But concerning the resurrection of the dead, you* read the [word] spoken to you* by God, saying, [32]*'I am the God of Abraham and the God of Isaac and the God of Jacob,'* did you* not? [Exod 3:6] God is not a God of dead [ones], <u>but</u> of living [ones]!" [33]And having heard, the crowds were astonished at His teaching.

[34]Now the Pharisees having heard that He silenced the Sadducees, were gathered together. [35]And one of them, a lawyer, questioned, testing Him, and saying, [36]"Teacher, which [is] the great commandment in the Law?" [37]Then Jesus said to him, *" 'You will love [the] Lord your God with your whole heart* [fig., *your entire inner self] and with your whole soul and with your whole understanding.'* [Deut 6:4] [38]This is [the] first and great commandment. [39]But a second [one is] similar to it, *'You will love your neighbor as yourself.'* [Lev 19:18] [40]On these two commandments hang all the Law and the Prophets."

[41]Now the Pharisees having been gathered together, Jesus questioned them, [42]saying, "What do <u>you*</u> think concerning the Christ? Whose Son is He?" They say to Him, "David's." [43]He says to them, "How then does David in [or, by] [the] Spirit call Him 'Lord,' saying, [44]*'The Lord said to my Lord, "Be sitting at My right hand, until I put Your enemies [as] a footstool for Your feet." '* [Psalm 110:1] [45]So if David calls Him 'Lord,' how is He his Son?" [46]And no one was able to answer Him a word, nor dared anyone from that day to question Him any more.

23 Then Jesus spoke to the crowds and to His disciples, [2]saying, "The scribes and the Pharisees [have] sat on the seat of Moses. [3]Therefore, all [things], as many as they tell you* to be observing, be observing and doing, but stop doing according to their works, for they say and do not do. [4]For they bind together heavy and hard to carry burdens and lay [them] on the shoulders of the people, but they are not willing to move them with their finger.

⁵"But all their works they do to be seen by the people, and they enlarge their phylacteries [i.e. small boxes containing Scripture verses], and they extend the fringes of their robes. ⁶They also affectionately love the first couches [fig., places of honor] at the banquets and the first seats [fig., most important places] in the synagogues ⁷and the greetings in the marketplaces, and to be called by the people, 'Rabbi, Rabbi.'

⁸"But you* shall not be called 'Rabbi,' for One is your* Master—the Christ, and you* are all brothers [and sisters]. ⁹And you* shall not call [anyone] your* father on the earth, for one is your* Father, the [One] in the heavens. ¹⁰Neither shall you* be called 'masters,' for one is your* Master—the Christ. ¹¹But the greatest of you* will be your* servant. ¹²And whoever will exalt himself, will be humbled; and whoever will humble himself, will be exalted.

¹³"But how horrible it will be to you*, Scribes and Pharisees, hypocrites! Because you* devour the houses of the widows, [fig., illegally cheat widows' out of their property] and in pretense [or, with a false show] are long [in] praying, because of this you* will receive more severe judgment [or, condemnation]. ¹⁴How horrible it will be to you*, Scribes and Pharisees, hypocrites! Because you* shut off the kingdom of the heavens before the people, for you* do not enter, nor do You* allow the ones entering to enter.

¹⁵"How horrible it will be to you*, Scribes and Pharisees, hypocrites! Because you* travel over the sea and the dry land to make one proselyte [or, convert to Pharisaic Judaism], and whenever it happens, you* make him twice as much a son of hell [Gr., *gehenna*] [as] you* [are]!

¹⁶"How horrible it will be to you*, blind guides, the ones saying, 'Whoever takes an oath by the temple, it is nothing, but whoever takes an oath by the gold of the temple is obligated [to fulfill the oath].' ¹⁷Fools and blind [ones]! For which [is] greater, the gold or the temple, the one sanctifying the gold? ¹⁸And [you* say], 'Whoever takes an oath by the altar, it is nothing, but whoever takes an oath by the gift that is on it is obligated [to fulfill the oath]!' ¹⁹Fools and blind [ones]! For which [is] greater, the gift or the altar which sanctifies the gift? ²⁰Therefore, the one having taken an oath by the altar, takes an oath by it and by all things on it. ²¹And the one having taken an oath by the sanctuary, takes an oath by it and by the One having dwelt in it. ²²And the one having taken an oath by heaven, takes an oath by the throne of God and by the One sitting on it.

²³"How horrible it will be to you*, Scribes and Pharisees, hypocrites! Because you tithe [i.e. give a tenth as an offering] of the mint and the dill and the cumin [i.e., various seasonings] and neglected the weightier [fig., more important] [matters] of the Law: the judgment [or, justice] and the mercy and the faith; these it was necessary to do, and those not to be neglecting. ²⁴Blind guides! The ones straining out the gnat, but swallowing the camel!

²⁵"How horrible it will be to you*, Scribes and Pharisees, hypocrites! Because you* cleanse [or, purify] the outside of the cup and of the dish, but within they are full of violent greed and unrighteousness. ²⁶Blind Pharisee! First cleanse the

inside of the cup and of the dish, so that the outside of them shall also become clean. ²⁷"How horrible it will be to you*, Scribes and Pharisees, hypocrites! Because you* resemble graves having been whitewashed [or, whitewashed graves], which outwardly indeed appear beautiful, but within are full of bones of dead [people] and of all uncleanness [or, impurity]. ²⁸In the same way, you* also indeed outwardly appear to the people [as] righteous, but within you* are full of hypocrisy [or, insincerity] and lawlessness.

²⁹"How horrible it will be to you*, Scribes and Pharisees, hypocrites! Because you* build the graves of the prophets and adorn the tombs of the righteous, ³⁰and you* say, 'If we were [fig., had lived] in the days of our fathers, we would not have been participants with them in the blood of the prophets,' ³¹with the result that you* testify against yourselves that you* are sons of the ones having murdered the prophets. ³²And you* fill up the measure of your* fathers. ³³Serpents! Brood of vipers! How shall you* escape from the judgment of hell [Gr., *gehenna*]?

³⁴"For this reason, look!, I send to you* prophets and wise men and scribes; and [some] of them you* will kill and crucify, and [some] of them you* will scourge in your* synagogues and will pursue from city to city; ³⁵in order that on you* shall come all the righteous blood being poured out on the earth from the blood of Abel the righteous up to the blood of Zacharias, son of Barachias, whom you* murdered between the sanctuary and the altar. [see Gen 4:8-10; 2Chr 24:20-22] ³⁶Positively, I say to you* that all these things will come on this generation.

³⁷"Jerusalem, Jerusalem, the one killing the prophets and stoning the ones having been sent to her! How often I wanted to gather your children together, as a hen gathers her own chickens under the wings, and you* did not want to! ³⁸Look! Your* house is left to you* desolate. ³⁹For I say to you*, by no means shall you* see Me hereafter, until you* say, *'Blessed [is] the One coming in [the] name of [the] LORD!'"* [Psalm 118:26]

24 And having gone out, Jesus was departing from the temple, and His disciples approached Him to point out to Him the buildings of the temple. ²But Jesus said to them, "You* are looking at all these, are you* not? Positively, I say to you*, by no means shall [there] be left here a stone upon a stone which will not be torn down."

³Then as He is sitting on the Mount of Olives, the disciples approached Him privately, saying, "Tell us when these [things] will be? And what [is] the sign of Your Arrival [or, Coming, and throughout book] and of the conclusion of the age?"

⁴And answering, Jesus said to them, "Be watching lest anyone leads you* astray [fig., deceives you*]. ⁵For many will come in My Name, saying, 'I am the Christ'—and they will lead many astray [fig., will deceive many]. ⁶But you* will begin to be hearing of wars and rumors of wars. Take care! Stop being alarmed! For it is necessary [for] all [these things] to take place, but the end is not yet. ⁷For nation will be raised up against nation, and kingdom against kingdom; and [there]

will be famines and plagues and earthquakes in [various] places. ⁸But all these [things are the] beginning of birth pains [fig., of great sufferings].

⁹"Then they will deliver you* up to tribulation [or, affliction] and will kill you*, and you* shall be hated by all the nations on account of My name. ¹⁰And then many will be caused to stumble [fig., will fall away], and they will betray one another and will hate one another. ¹¹And many false prophets will be raised up and will lead many astray [fig., will deceive many]. ¹²And because lawlessness will be increased, the love of the many will be made cold. ¹³But the one having endured to [the] end—this one will be saved. ¹⁴And this Gospel of the kingdom will be proclaimed in the whole inhabited earth for a testimony to all the nations, and then the end will come.

¹⁵"Therefore, when you* see the *'abomination of the desolation'* [or, the *'detestable thing that causes desecration'*], the one having been spoken [of] through Daniel the prophet, having stood in [the] holy place (the one reading, let him be understanding [or, be paying attention]), [Dan 8:13; 9:27; 12:11] ¹⁶then the [ones] in Judea must be fleeing to the mountains. ¹⁷The [one] on the housetop must not be coming down to take the [things] out of his house. ¹⁸And the [one] in the field must not turn back to take up his garments. ¹⁹But how horrible it will be to the ones having in the womb [fig., who are pregnant] and to the ones nursing [babies] in those days! ²⁰But be praying that your* flight shall not be in winter nor on a Sabbath. ²¹For then [there] will be great tribulation [or, affliction], such as has not been from [the] beginning of the world until now, nor never at all shall be. ²²And if those days were not cut short, no flesh would be saved; but because of the chosen ones [or, the elect], those days will be cut short.

²³"Then if anyone says to you*, 'Look! Here [is] the Christ!' or 'Here!' you* shall not believe [him]. ²⁴For false christs and false prophets will be raised up, and they shall give great signs and wonders, so as to lead astray [fig., to deceive], if possible, even the chosen ones [or, the elect]. ²⁵Listen! I have told you* in advance [or, have forewarned you*]!

²⁶"Therefore, if they say to you*, 'Look! He is in the wilderness!' you* shall not go out, [or they say], 'Look! [He is] in the private rooms!' you* shall not believe [them]. ²⁷For just as the lightning comes out from the east and shines as far as [the] west, in this way will also be the Arrival of the Son of Humanity. ²⁸For wherever the carcass shall be, there the vultures will be gathered together.

²⁹"But immediately after the tribulation [or, affliction] of those days, *'the sun will be darkened, and the moon will not give its light, and the stars will fall down'* from heaven [or, the sky], and the powers of the heavens will be shaken. [cp. Isaiah 34:4; Joel 2:10; 2:31] ³⁰And then the sign of the Son of Humanity will appear in heaven [or, the sky]; and then all the tribes of the earth will beat their breasts [fig., will mourn], and they will see the *'Son of Humanity coming on the clouds of heaven* [or, *of the sky*]' with power and great glory! [Dan 7:13] ³¹And He will send out His angels with [the] *'sound of a loud trumpet-blast,'* and *'they will gather together'* His chosen ones [or, elect] from the four winds, from [the] farthest limits of [the] heavens to [the other] farthest limits of them. [Exod 19:16; Deut 30:4]

³²"Now learn the allegory from the fig tree: whenever its branch already becomes tender, and it is putting forth the leaves, you* know that the summer [is] near. ³³In this way also you*, whenever you* see all these [things], you* know that it is near—at [the] doors! ³⁴Positively, I say to you*, this generation [or, race] shall by no means pass away until all these [things] happen. ³⁵The heaven and the earth will pass away, but My words shall by no means pass away.

³⁶"But concerning that day and hour no one knows, not even the angels of the heavens, except My Father only. ³⁷But just as [in] the days of Noah, in this way also will be the Arrival of the Son of Humanity. ³⁸For just as they were in the days before the flood, eating and drinking, marrying and giving in marriage, until which day Noah entered into the ark, ³⁹and they did not know until the flood came and swept all away, in this way also will be the Arrival of the Son of Humanity. [see Gen 6:5-8, 7:1-24] ⁴⁰Then two [people] will be in the field, one is taken, and one is left behind. ⁴¹Two women [will be] grinding in the mill, one is taken, and one is left behind. ⁴²Therefore, keep watching! Because you* do not know in what hour your* Lord is coming. ⁴³But know this, if the homeowner had known in what watch [of the night] the thief is coming, he would have kept watch and would not have allowed his house to be broken into. ⁴⁴For this reason, you* also become ready, because in what hour you* do not think, the Son of Humanity is coming.

⁴⁵"Who then is the faithful and wise slave whom his lord put in charge over his household servants, the [one] to be giving to them food in season [fig., at the proper time]? ⁴⁶Happy [is] that slave, whom his lord having come, will find [him] so doing. ⁴⁷Positively, I say to you*, he will put him in charge over all his property. ⁴⁸But if that evil slave says in his heart, 'My Lord is delaying to come,' ⁴⁹and begins to be beating his fellow-slaves, and to be eating and to be drinking with the [ones] being drunk, ⁵⁰the lord of that slave will come on a day which he does not expect, and in an hour which he does not know, ⁵¹and he will cut him in pieces and will appoint his portion with the hypocrites. In that place [there] will be weeping and gnashing of teeth!

25 ¹"Then will the kingdom of the heavens be compared to ten virgins, who having taken their lamps, went out to the meeting of the bridegroom. ²Now five out of them were wise and the [other] five foolish. ³[Those] who were foolish, having taken their lamps, did not take oil with themselves; ⁴but the wise [ones] took oil in their containers, with their lamps. Now the bridegroom delaying, they all became drowsy and began sleeping.

⁶"But in the middle of the night a cry had been made: 'Look! The bridegroom is coming! You* yourselves be going out to his meeting.' ⁷Then all those virgins were raised, and they trimmed their lamps. ⁸Then the foolish [ones] said to the wise [ones], 'Give to us out of your* oil, because our lamps are being extinguished.' ⁹But the wise [ones] answered, saying, '[No], lest there not be enough for us and for you*. But rather be going to the ones selling, and buy for yourselves.' ¹⁰But while they are going away to buy, the bridegroom came; and the [ones being] ready went in with him into the marriage festivities, and the door was shut.

[11]"But later the rest of the virgins also come, saying, 'Lord, lord, open to us!' [12]But answering, he said, 'Positively, I say to you*, I do not know you*!' [13]Therefore, keep watching! For you* do not know the day nor the hour in which the Son of Humanity is coming.

[14]"For [the kingdom of the heavens is] like a man going on a journey, [who] called his own slaves and entrusted to them his possessions. [15]And to one he gave five talents [i.e. Greek coins, each worth about 95 pounds or 42 kilograms of gold or silver], but to another two, but to another one, to each according to his ability; and he went on a journey immediately. [16]Then the one having received the five talents, having gone, traded with them and made five other talents. [17]In the same manner, also the [one having received] the two, gained also two other [talents]. [18]But the one having received the one, having gone away, dug a hole in the ground and hid his lord's money. [19]Now after a long time the lord of those slaves comes and settles accounts with them.

[20]"And the one having received the five talents, having come, brought five other talents, saying, 'Lord, you entrusted five talents to me, look!, I gained five other talents besides them.' [21]So his lord said to him, 'Well done, good and faithful slave! You were faithful over a few things, I will put you in charge over many things; enter into the joy of your lord.' [22]Then having come also the one having received the two talents, he said, 'Lord, you entrusted two talents to me, look!, I gained two other talents besides them.' [23]His lord said to him, 'Well done good and faithful slave! You were faithful over a few things, I will put you in charge over many things; enter into the joy of your lord.'

[24]"Then having come also the one having received the one talent, he said, 'Lord, I knew you that you are a harsh man, reaping where you did not sow and gathering from where you did not scatter. [25]And having been frightened, having gone away, I hid your talent in the ground. Look! You have [what is] yours!'

[26]"But answering, his lord said to him, 'Evil and lazy slave! You knew that I reap where I did not sow, and I gather from where I did not scatter. [27]Therefore, it was necessary [for] you to give my money to the money changers [or, bankers], and having come, I [would have] received [what is] mine with interest. [28]Therefore, take from him the talent, and give [it] to the one having the ten talents. [29]For to every[one] having, [more] will be given, and he will have an abundance, but from the one not having, even what he has will be taken from him. [30]And throw the worthless slave out into the outer darkness. In that place [there] will be weeping and gnashing of teeth!'

[31]"But when the Son of Humanity comes in His glory, and all the holy angels with Him, then He will sit down on [the] throne of His glory [or, His glorious throne]. [32]And all the nations will be gathered together before Him, and He will separate them from one another, just as the shepherd separates the sheep from the goats. [33]And indeed, He will set the sheep at His right hand and the goats at the left.

[34]"Then the King will say to the [ones] at His right hand, 'Come, the ones having been blessed by My Father, inherit the kingdom having been prepared for you* from [the] laying of the foundation of [the] world. [35]For I was hungry, and

you* gave to Me [something] to eat; I was thirsty, and you* gave Me [something] to drink; I was a stranger, and you* took Me in; ³⁶naked, and you* clothed Me; I was sick, and you* looked after Me; I was in prison, and you* came to Me.'

³⁷"Then the righteous [ones] will answer Him, saying, 'Lord, when did we see You hungering and we fed [You]? Or thirsting and we gave [You something] to drink? ³⁸But when did we see You a stranger and took [You] in? Or naked and we clothed [You]? ³⁹But when did we see You sick or in prison and we came to You?' ⁴⁰And answering, the King will say to them, 'Positively, I say to you*, to the degree that you* did [it] to one of these, the least of My brothers [and sisters], you* did [it] to Me.'

⁴¹"Then He will also say to the [ones] at the left hand, 'Be going away from Me, the ones having been cursed, into the eternal fire, the one having been prepared for the Devil and his angels. ⁴²For I was hungry, and you* did not give to Me [something] to eat; I was thirsty, and you* did not give Me [something] to drink. ⁴³I was a stranger, and you* did not take me in; naked, and you* did not clothe Me; sick and in prison, and you* did not look after Me.'

⁴⁴"Then they also will answer, saying, 'Lord, when did we see You hungering or thirsting or a stranger or naked or sick or in prison, and we did not take care of You?' ⁴⁵Then He will answer them, saying, 'Positively, I say to you*, to the degree that you* did not do [it] to one of these, the least, you* did not do [it] to Me.' ⁴⁶And these will go away into eternal punishment, but the righteous into eternal life."

26 And it happened, when Jesus finished all these words, He said to His disciples, ²"You* know that after two days the Passover is coming, and the Son of Humanity is being handed over to be crucified."

³Then the chief priests and the scribes and the elders of the people were gathered together to the court of the high priest, the one being called Caiaphas. ⁴And they plotted among themselves so that they should seize Jesus by deceit [or, treachery] and kill [Him]. ⁵But they were saying, "Not during the feast, lest there be a riot among the people."

⁶Now Jesus having been in Bethany, in the house of Simon the leper [or, the one with a skin disease], ⁷a woman came to Him having an alabaster jar of very expensive ointment [or, perfume], and she poured [it] on His head as He [was] reclining [to eat]. ⁸But having seen [it], His disciples expressed indignation, saying, "Why this waste? ⁹For this ointment could have been sold for much and been given to [the] poor."

¹⁰But having known, Jesus said to them, "Why do you* cause the woman troubles [fig., bother the woman]? For she worked a good work to Me [or, performed a good deed for Me]. ¹¹For you* always have the poor with yourselves, but you* do not always have Me. ¹²For when this [woman] put this ointment on My body, she did [it] to prepare Me for burial. ¹³Positively, I say to you*, wherever this Gospel is proclaimed in the whole world, what this [woman] did will also be spoken of—in memory of her."

[14]Then one of the twelve, the one being called Judas Iscariot, having gone to the chief priests, [15]said, "What are you* willing to give to me, and I will hand Him over to you*?" So they weighed out for him thirty silver [coins]. [16]And from that time on he began seeking a convenient moment so that he should betray Him.

[17]Now on the first [day] of the [Feast of] Unleavened Bread, the disciples approached Jesus saying to Him, "Where do You desire [that] we will prepare for You to eat the Passover?" [18]So He said, "Be going away into the city, to such a one, and say to him, 'The Teacher says, "My time is near; I am keeping the Passover with you [fig., in your house], with My disciples."'" [19]And the disciples did as Jesus directed them and prepared the Passover.

[20]Now evening having come, He was reclining [to eat] with the twelve. [21]And while they are eating, He said, "Positively, I say to you*, one of you* will betray Me!" [22]And being extremely grieved, they began to be saying to Him, each of them, "Surely Lord, I am not [the one], am I?" [23]But answering, He said, "The one having dipped his hand with Me in the bowl, this [one] will betray Me. [24]Indeed, the Son of Humanity is going away just as it has been written concerning Him. But how horrible it will be to that man through whom the Son of Humanity is betrayed! [It would have been] good for him if that man had not been born!" [25]But Judas, the one betraying Him, answering said, "Surely Rabbi, I am not [the one], am I?" He says to him, "You said [it]."

[26]Now while they were eating, Jesus having taken the bread and having bestowed a blessing upon [it], broke [it] and began giving [it] to the disciples. And He said, "Take, eat; this is My body." [27]And having taken the cup and having given thanks, He gave [it] to them, saying, "Drink from it, all [of you], [28]for this is My blood, the [blood] of the New Covenant, the [blood] poured out on behalf of many for forgiveness of sins. [29]But I say to you*, from now on by no means shall I drink of this fruit of the grapevine until that day when I shall be drinking it with you* new in the kingdom of My Father." [30]And having sung a hymn, they went out to the Mount of Olives.

[31]Then Jesus says to them, "You* will all be caused to stumble [fig, caused to fall away] because of Me on this night, for it has been written, *'I will strike the Shepherd, and the sheep of the flock will be scattered.'* [Zech 13:7] [32]But after I am raised, I will go before you* to Galilee." [33]But answering, Peter said to Him, "Even if all will be caused to stumble [fig., caused to fall away] because of You, yet I will never be caused to stumble." [34]Jesus began saying to him, "Positively, I say to you, on this night, before a rooster crows three times you will deny [or, disown] Me." [35]Peter says to Him, "Even if it is necessary [for] me to die with You, by no means shall I deny [or, disown] You." And likewise said also all the disciples.

[36]Then Jesus comes with them to a place being called Gethsemane. And He says to the disciples, "Sit here until which [time], having gone over there, I pray." [37]And having taken Peter and the two sons of Zebedee, He began to be grieving and to be suffering from distress. [38]Then Jesus says to them, "My soul is deeply grieved to the point of death; stay here and keep watching with Me." [39]And having approached [God] a little [distance away], He fell on His face praying and saying,

"My Father! If it is possible, let this cup pass away from Me. Nevertheless, not as I desire, but as You [desire]."

[40]And He comes to the disciples and finds them sleeping, and He says to Peter, "So! You* were not able to keep watch one hour with Me, were you*? [41]Keep watching and praying so that you* do not enter into temptation; the spirit indeed [is] willing [or, eager], but the flesh [is] weak."

[42]Again a second time having gone away, He prayed, saying, "My Father, if this cup cannot pass away from Me unless I drink it, Your will be done." [43]And having come, He finds them again sleeping, for their eyes had been weighed down. [44]And having left them, having gone away again, He prayed a third time, saying the same thing. [45]Then He comes to His disciples and says to them, "Are you* still sleeping and resting? Look! The hour has drawn near, and the Son of Humanity is being betrayed into the hands of sinners! [46]Be getting up! Let us go. Look! The one betraying Me has come near."

[47]And while He is still speaking, look!, Judas, one of the twelve, came, and with him a large crowd, with swords and clubs, from the chief priests and elders of the people. [48]And the one betraying Him gave to them a sign, saying, "Whomever I kiss; it is He: arrest Him." [49]And immediately, having approached Jesus, he said, "Greetings, Rabbi!" And he affectionately kissed Him. [50]But Jesus said to him, "Friend, for what [or, why] are you here?" Then having approached, they laid hands on Jesus and seized Him.

[51]And look! One of the [ones] with Jesus, having stretched out his hand, drew his sword, and having struck the slave of the high priest, he cut off his ear. [52]Then Jesus says to him, "Put your sword back into its place! For all the ones taking up a sword will die by a sword. [53]Or do you think that I am not able [even] now to call upon My Father, and He will place beside me more than twelve legions [i.e. military units of 6,000 soldiers each] of angels? [54]How then shall the Scriptures be fulfilled, that in this way it is necessary [for it] to happen?"

[55]In that hour [or, At that time] Jesus said to the crowds, "Have you* come out as against a robber [or, an insurrectionist] with swords and clubs to arrest Me? Daily I was sitting with you* teaching in the temple, and you* did not arrest Me. [56]But all this has happened so that the Scriptures of the prophets shall be fulfilled." Then all the disciples having left Him fled.

[57]Then the ones taking Jesus into custody led [Him] away to Caiaphas the high priest, where the scribes and the elders were gathered together. [58]But Peter was following Him from a distance, as far as the courtyard of the high priest; and having entered inside, he was sitting with the [courtyard] attendants to see the end [or, outcome]. [59]Now the chief priests and the elders and the whole High Council [or, Sanhedrin] were seeking false testimony against Jesus, in order that they should put Him to death, [60]but they did not find [any]. And [even with] many false witnesses having come forward, they did not find [any]. [61]But later two false witnesses having come forward, said, "This One said, 'I am able to tear down the temple of God and by three days to build it.'" [cp. John 2:19]

[62]And the high priest having stood up, said to Him, "Do You answer nothing? What are these [men] testifying against You?" [63]But Jesus kept silent. And

answering, the high priest said to Him, "I put You under an oath by the living God, that You tell us if <u>You</u> are the Christ, the Son of God." [64]Jesus says to him, "<u>You</u> said [it]; nevertheless, I say to you*, from now on you* will see *'the Son of Humanity sitting at the right hand of the Power and coming on the clouds of heaven* [or, *of the sky*]!'" [Psalm 110:1; Dan 7:13,14] [65]Then the high priest tore his clothing, saying, "He has blasphemed! What need do we still have of witnesses? Listen! Now you* heard His blasphemy. [66]What do you* think?" And answering, they said, "He is deserving of death." [67]Then they spit into His face and beat Him with their fists, but others slapped [Him] with their hands [or, struck [Him] with a club], [68]saying, "Prophesy to us, O Christ! Who is the one striking You?"

[69]Now Peter was sitting outside in the courtyard. And a certain slave-girl approached him, saying, "<u>You</u> also were with Jesus the Galilean." [70]But he denied [it] before them all, saying, "I do not know what you are saying." [71]Then <u>he</u> having gone out to the porch, another [slave-girl] saw him and says to them there, "This one also was with Jesus of Nazareth." [72]And again he denied [it] with an oath, "I do not know the Man!"

[73]Then after a little while, the ones standing by, having approached, said to Peter, "Surely <u>you</u> also are [one] of them, for even your accent makes you evident [or, gives you away]." [74]Then he began to be calling down curses and to be taking an oath, "I do not know the Man!" And immediately a rooster crowed. [75]And Peter was reminded of the saying of Jesus, He having said to him, "Before a rooster crows three times you will deny [or, disown] Me." And having gone forth outside, he wept bitterly. [cp. Matt 26:34]

27 Now morning having come, all the chief priests and the elders of the people took counsel [or, plotted] against Jesus, so as to put Him to death. [2]And having bound Him, they lead [Him] away and handed Him over to Pontius Pilate the governor.

[3]Then Judas, the one betraying Him, having seen that he was condemned, having felt remorse, brought back the thirty silver [coins] to the chief priests and to the elders, [4]saying, "I sinned, having betrayed innocent blood!" But they said, "What [is that] to us? <u>You</u> will see [to it yourself]!" [5]And having thrown down the silver [coins] in the temple, he departed; and having gone away, he hanged himself.

[6]But the chief priests having taken the silver [coins], said, "It is not lawful to put them into the treasury, since it is [the] price of blood [or, is blood money]." [7]So having taken counsel, they bought with them the field of the potter, for a burial-place for strangers. [8]For this reason, that field was called, "Field of Blood," until this day.

[9]Then was fulfilled the saying having been spoken through Jeremiah the prophet, saying, *"And they took the thirty silver [coins], the price of the One having been priced, whom they priced from the sons of Israel, [10]and gave them for the field of the potter, just as [the] LORD directed me."* [Jer 32:6-9]

[11]Now Jesus stood before the governor. And the governor questioned Him, saying, "Are <u>You</u> the King of the Jews?" But Jesus said to him, "<u>You</u> say [it]." [12]And while He was being accused by the chief priests and the elders, He answered nothing. [13]Then Pilate says to Him, "You hear how many [things] they testify against You, do You not?" [14]And He did not answer him, not even in regards to one charge, with the result that the governor is quite amazed.

[15]Now at the feast the governor was accustomed to [or, was in the habit of] releasing one prisoner to the crowd, [anyone] whom they were desiring. [16]Now they were holding then a well-known [or, notorious] prisoner being called Barabbas. [17]So when <u>they</u> were gathered together, Pilate said to them, "Whom do you* desire [that] I release to you*, Barabbas or Jesus, the One being called Christ?" [18]For he knew that because of envy they handed Him over. [19]But while <u>he</u> is sitting on the judgment seat, his wife sent to him, saying, "Nothing to you and to that Righteous [One] [fig., Have nothing to do with that Righteous One], for many [things] I suffered today in a dream because of Him."

[20]But the chief priests and the elders persuaded the crowds that they should request for themselves Barabbas, but Jesus they should kill. [21]So answering, the governor said to them, "Which of the two do you* desire [that] I release to you*?" Then they said, "Barabbas!" [22]Pilate says to them, "What then should I do with Jesus, the One being called Christ?" They all say to him, "Let Him be crucified!" [23]But the governor said, "For what evil did He do?" But they began shouting all the more, saying, "Let Him be crucified!" [24]So Pilate having seen that he is accomplishing nothing, <u>but</u> rather a commotion is being made, having taken water, he washed his hands in full view of the crowd, saying, "I am innocent of the blood of this Righteous [One]! <u>You*</u> will see [to it yourselves]." [25]And answering, all the people said, "His blood [be] on us and on our children!"

[26]Then he released to them Barabbas. Then after having Jesus beaten with a whip, he handed [Him] over so that He should be crucified. [27]Then the soldiers of the governor, having taken Jesus into the Fortified Palace [or, Praetorium], gathered the entire garrison around Him. [28]And having stripped Him, they put around Him a scarlet cloak. [29]And having woven a victor's wreath [or, crown] out of thorns, they put [it] on His head and a reed in His right hand. And having knelt before Him, they kept ridiculing Him, saying, "Hail! The King of the Jews!" [30]And having spit on Him, they took the reed and began beating [Him] on His head. [31]And when they [had] ridiculed Him, they stripped the cloak off Him, and they put on Him His [own] garments, and they led Him away to crucify [Him].

[32]Then as they are going out they found a man, a Cyrenian, by name Simon: they forced this [man] into service so that he should carry His cross. [33]And having come to a place being called Golgotha, which is being called Place of a Skull, [34]they gave to Him wine vinegar having been mixed with gall to drink. And having tasted [it], He was not wanting to drink [it]. [35]Then having crucified Him, they divided His garments, casting a lot. [36]Then sitting down, they began watching over Him there. [37]And they put up over His head the accusation against Him, having been written, "This is Jesus: the King of the Jews."

[38]At that time being crucified with Him [were] two robbers [or, insurrectionists], one on [His] right hand and one on [the] left. [39]Now the ones passing by were deriding Him, shaking their heads, [40]and saying, "The One tearing down the temple and in three days building [it]—save yourself! Since You are God's Son, come down from the cross!" [41]Then likewise also the chief priests, with the scribes and elders and Pharisees, ridiculing [Him], were saying, [42]"He saved others; He is not able to save Himself! Since He is King of Israel, let Him come down now from the cross, and we will believe in Him! [43]He had confidence in God, let Him now deliver Him, if He wants Him, because He said, 'I am God's Son.'" [44]Now also the robbers [or, insurrectionists], the ones being crucified with Him, were insulting Him with the same [words].

[45]Then from the sixth hour [i.e., 12:00 noon] darkness came over all the land until the ninth hour [i.e., 3:00 p.m.]. [46]But about the ninth hour Jesus cried out with a loud voice, saying [in Aramaic], *"Eli, Eli, lima sabachthani?"* this is, *"My God, My God, why did You abandon Me?"* [Psalm 22:1] [47]Then some of the ones having stood there, having heard, began saying, "This [One] is calling Elijah!" [48]And immediately, one of them having run and having taken a sponge and having filled [it] with wine vinegar and having put [it] around a reed, began giving [it] to Him to drink. [49]But the rest said, "Leave [Him] alone! Let us see if Elijah comes to take Him down."

[50]Then Jesus having again cried out with a loud voice released His spirit. [51]And look! The veil [or, curtain] of the temple was torn in two from top to bottom, and the earth was shaken, and the rocks were split. [52]And the tombs were opened, and many bodies of the holy ones [or, saints] having fallen asleep [fig., having died] were raised. [53]And having come out from their tombs after His resurrection, they went into the holy city [i.e. Jerusalem] and appeared to many. [54]So the centurion and the [ones] with him having watched over Jesus, having seen the earthquake and the [things] having been done, were extremely frightened, saying, "Truly this [One] was God's Son!"

[55]Now many women were there watching from a distance, who followed Jesus from Galilee, ministering to Him, [56]among whom was Mary the Magdalene [or, Mary, a woman from Magdala], and Mary the mother of James and of Joses, and the mother of the sons of Zebedee.

[57]Now evening having come, a rich man from Arimathea came, named Joseph, who also himself was a disciple to Jesus. [58]Having approached Pilate, this one requested for himself the body of Jesus. Then Pilate commanded the body to be given up [to him]. [59]And having taken the body, Joseph wrapped it in clean linen cloth [60]and laid it in his new tomb, which he [had] cut in the rock. And having rolled a large stone against [or, to] the entrance of the tomb, he went away. [61]Now Mary the Magdalene and the other Mary were there, sitting in full view of the grave.

[62]Then the next day, that is after the preparation [day], the chief priests and the Pharisees were gathered together to Pilate, [63]saying, "Lord, we remembered that that deceiver said while yet living, 'After three days I am being raised.' [64]Therefore, command the grave to be secured until the third day, lest His disciples

having come by night should steal Him and say to the people, 'He was raised from the dead,' and the last deception will be worse [than] the first." ⁶⁵Then Pilate said to them, "<u>You</u> have a guard [of soldiers]; be going away; secure [it] as you* know [how]." ⁶So having gone, they secured the grave, having sealed the stone, together with the guard [of soldiers].

28 Now after [the] Sabbaths, at the dawning into [the] first [day] of the week [i.e. early Sunday morning], Mary the Magdalene and the other Mary went [or, came] to see the grave. ²And look! A great earthquake occurred, for an angel of [the] Lord having come down out of heaven, having come to [the tomb], rolled away the stone from the entrance and was sitting on it. ³Now his appearance was like lightning and his clothing white as snow. ⁴But the ones keeping guard shook because of the fear of him, and they became as dead [men].

⁵Then answering, the angel said to the women, "<u>You*</u>, stop being afraid! For I know that you* seek Jesus, the One having been crucified. ⁶He is not here! For He was raised, just as He said! Come, see the place where the Lord was lying. ⁷And go quickly, say to His disciples, 'He was raised from the dead!' And listen! He is going before you* to Galilee; there you* will see Him. Listen! I told you*." ⁸And having gone out quickly from the tomb, with fear and great joy, they ran to report to His disciples.

⁹But as they were going to tell to His disciples, and look!, Jesus met them, saying, "Greetings!" So having approached, they take hold of His feet and prostrated themselves in worship before Him. ¹⁰Then Jesus says to them, "Stop being afraid! Be going, report to My brothers that they should go away to Galilee, and there they will see Me."

¹¹Now while they are going, look!, some of the guard [of soldiers] having come into the city reported to the chief priests all the [things] having happened. ¹²And having been gathered together with the elders, and having taken counsel [or, having plotted], they gave much money to the soldiers, ¹³saying, "Say, 'His disciples having come by night stole Him while we were sleeping.' ¹⁴And if this is heard by the governor, <u>we</u> will persuade him, and we will make you* free from anxiety [fig., will keep you* out of trouble]." ¹⁵So having received the money, they did as they were taught. And this account was spread widely among Jews until this day.

¹⁶But the eleven disciples went to Galilee, to the mountain which Jesus appointed [or, designated] to them. ¹⁷And having seen Him, they prostrated themselves in worship before Him, but some were doubtful. ¹⁸And having approached, Jesus spoke to them, saying, "All authority in heaven and on earth was given to Me. ¹⁹When you* have gone, make disciples of all the nations, baptizing them in the name of the Father and of the Son and of the Holy Spirit, ²⁰teaching them to be observing all [things], as many as I commanded you*. And listen! <u>I</u> am with you* all the days, until the conclusion of the age! So be it!" [Gr. *amen*, and throughout NT].

The Gospel According to

Mark

1 Beginning of the Gospel [or, Good News, and throughout book] of Jesus Christ, God's Son.

²As it has been written in the prophets, *"Look! I am sending My messenger before Your face* [fig., *ahead of You*], *who will prepare Your way before You."* [Mal 3:1] ³ *"A voice of [one] shouting in the wilderness, 'Prepare the way of [the] LORD! Be making His paths straight!'"* [Isaiah 40:3, LXX]

⁴John came baptizing [or, immersing, and throughout book] in the wilderness and proclaiming a baptism [or, immersion, and throughout book] of repentance to [or, for; or, because of] forgiveness of sins. ⁵And all the region of Judea was going out to him, and the inhabitants of Jerusalem, and they were all baptized in the Jordan River by him, they themselves confessing their sins [or, after they themselves confessed their sins]. ⁶Now John had clothed himself with camel's hair and a leather belt around his waist. And he eats locusts and wild honey. ⁷And he began proclaiming, saying, "He is coming after me, the [One] greater than I, of whom I am not worthy, having stooped down, to untie the strap of His sandals! ⁸I indeed baptize you* in water [or, with water, and throughout book], but He will baptize you* in [or, with] [the] Holy Spirit!"

⁹And it happened in those days, Jesus came from Nazareth of Galilee, and He was baptized by John in the Jordan. ¹⁰And immediately coming up from the water, he [i.e. John] saw the heavens being parted and the Spirit like a dove descending upon Him. ¹¹And a voice came out of the heavens, "You are My Son—the Beloved—in whom I am well-pleased!"

¹²Then immediately the Spirit drives Him out into the wilderness. ¹³And He was there in the wilderness forty days, being tempted by Satan. And He was with the wild animals, and the angels were ministering to Him.

¹⁴Now after John was arrested, Jesus came into Galilee proclaiming the Gospel of the kingdom of God, ¹⁵and saying, "The time has been fulfilled and the kingdom of God has come near! Be repenting and believing [or, trusting] in the Gospel!"

¹⁶Now walking about by the Sea of Galilee, He saw Simon and Andrew his brother, [that is] of Simon, casting a net into the sea, for they were fishermen. ¹⁷And Jesus said to them, "Come after Me, and I will make you* to become fishers of people." ¹⁸Then immediately, having left their nets, they followed Him. ¹⁹And having gone on from there a little [further], he saw James, the [son] of Zebedee, and John his brother, and they [were] in the boat mending the nets. ²⁰And immediately He called them. Then having left their father Zebedee in the boat with the hired workers, they went away after Him.

²¹And they are going into Capernaum. And immediately on [one of] the Sabbaths having gone into the synagogue, He was teaching. ²²And they were astonished at His teaching, for He was teaching them as [one] having authority, and not as the scribes.

²³And [there] was in their synagogue a person with an unclean [or, defiling] spirit. And it cried out, ²⁴saying, "Away! What to us and to You [fig., What have we to do with You], Jesus the Nazarene? You came to destroy us! I know You, who You are, the Holy [One] of God!" ²⁵And Jesus rebuked it saying, "Be silenced, and come out from him!" ²⁶Then the unclean [or, defiling] spirit, having torn him back and forth [fig., having thrown him into convulsions] and having cried out with a loud voice, came out from him. ²⁷And they were all shocked, so as to be disputing among themselves, saying, "What is this? What new teaching [or, doctrine] [is] this, that with authority even the unclean [or, defiling] spirits He commands, and they obey Him?" ²⁸So the news of Him went out immediately into the whole surrounding region of Galilee.

²⁹Then immediately, having come out from the synagogue, they went into the house of Simon and Andrew, with James and John. ³⁰Now the mother-in-law of Simon was lying down, being sick with a fever. And immediately they tell Him about her. ³¹And having come near, He raised her up, having taken hold of her hand. And the fever immediately left her! Then she began serving them.

³²Now evening having come, when the sun set, they began bringing to Him all the ones having it badly [fig., who were sick] and the ones being demon-possessed [or, oppressed by demons]. ³³And the whole city had been gathered together near the door. ³⁴And He healed many having it badly [fig., who were sick] with various diseases, and He cast out many demons. But He did not allow the demons to be speaking, because they knew Him.

³⁵Then early in the morning, while it was still quite dark, having risen, He went out and went away into a deserted place, and He was there praying. ³⁶Then Simon and those with him searched eagerly for Him. ³⁷And having found Him, they say to Him, "All are seeking You." ³⁸Then He says to them, "Let us be going into the neighboring market towns, so that there I shall also preach, for this [reason] I have come forth." ³⁹And He was preaching in their synagogues, in all Galilee, and He is casting out the demons.

⁴⁰Then there comes to Him a leper [or, one with a skin disease], calling on Him and kneeling before Him and saying to Him, "If You are willing, You are able to cleanse me." ⁴¹So Jesus having been moved with compassion, having stretched out His hand, took hold of him and says to him, "I am willing. Be cleansed!" ⁴²And He having spoken [this], immediately the leprosy [or, skin disease] went away from him, and he was cleansed!

⁴³Then having sternly warned him, immediately He sent him away, ⁴⁴and He says to him, "See [that] you say nothing to anyone; but be going, show yourself to the priest and bring as an offering for your purification the things Moses directed, as a testimony to them." [Lev 14:2-32] ⁴⁵But that one, having gone out, began to be proclaiming [it] much and to be spreading widely the news, with the result that no longer was He able to openly enter into the city, but He was outside in deserted places, and they kept coming to Him from all directions.

2 And He again entered into Capernaum after [several] days, and it was heard that He is in a house. ²And immediately many were gathered together, with

the result that [there] was no longer [any] room, not even at the door, and He was speaking the word to them. ³Then they come to Him, bringing a paralytic, being carried by four [people]. ⁴And not being able to come near to Him because of the crowd, they unroofed the roof [or, uncovered [a hole in] the roof] where He was, and having dug through, they let down the cot on which the paralytic was lying. ⁵Now Jesus having seen their faith, says to the paralytic, "Child, your sins have been forgiven you."

⁶But some of the scribes were sitting there and reasoning in their hearts, ⁷"Why does this One speak blasphemies like this? Who is able to be forgiving sins except one—God?" ⁸And immediately Jesus, having known in His spirit that they are reasoning in this manner within themselves, said to them, "Why do you* reason these [things] in your* hearts?" ⁹Which is easier, to say to the paralytic, 'Your sins have been forgiven?' or to say, 'Get up yourself, and take up your cot, and be walking about?' ¹⁰But so that you* shall know that the Son of Humanity has authority to be forgiving sins on the earth,"—He says to the paralytic, ¹¹"I say to you, get up yourself! And take up your cot, and be going away to your house." ¹²And he rose up immediately! And having taken up his cot, he went out before all, with the result that all were themselves amazed and [began] to be glorifying God, saying, "We have never seen [anything] like this!"

¹³Then He went out again by the sea. And all the crowd was coming to Him, and He was teaching them. ¹⁴And passing by, He saw Levi, the [son] of Alpheus, sitting at the tax-office. Then He says to him, "Be following Me!" And having stood up, he followed Him. ¹⁵And it happened, while He [was] reclining [to eat] in his [i.e. Levi's] house, [that] also many tax collectors and sinners were reclining [to eat] with Jesus and His disciples, for [there] were many, and they followed Him. ¹⁶And the scribes and the Pharisees, having seen Him eating with the tax collectors and sinners, said to His disciples, "Why is that [One] eating and drinking with those tax collectors and sinners?" ¹⁷Then Jesus, having heard, says to them, "The ones being strong [fig. who are healthy] do not have need of a physician, but the ones having it badly [fig., who are sick]. I did not come to call righteous [ones], but sinners to repentance."

¹⁸Now the disciples of John and those of the Pharisees were fasting, and they come and say to Him, "Why do the disciples of John and those of the Pharisees fast, but Your disciples do not fast?" ¹⁹Then Jesus said to them, "The sons of the bridal chamber [fig., the bridegroom's attendants] in which [time] [fig., while] the bridegroom is with them, are not able to be fasting, are they? As long a time as they have the bridegroom with themselves they are not able to be fasting. ²⁰But days will come when the bridegroom shall be taken from them, and then they will fast in those days.

²¹"And no one sews a patch of a piece of unshrunken cloth on an old garment; but if not [fig., or else] it takes up the new fullness [fig., patch] from the old, and the tear becomes worse. ²²And no one puts new wine into old wineskins; but if not [fig., or else] the new wine bursts the wineskins, and the wine is poured out, and the wineskins will be ruined. But new wine must be put into new wineskins."

²³And it happened, He is going along on [one of] the Sabbaths through the grainfields, and His disciples began to make [their] way, picking the heads of grain. ²⁴And the Pharisees said to Him, "Look! Why are they doing on [one of] the Sabbaths what is not lawful?" ²⁵Then He said to them, "Did you* never read what David did, when he had need and was hungry, he and those with him? ²⁶How he went into the house of God at the time of Abiathar the high priest and ate the loaves of bread of the presentation [fig., the consecrated bread], which it is not lawful to eat, except to the priests, and he gave also to the ones with him?" [cp. 1Sam 21:3-6; Exod 29:32-33] ²⁷And He said to them, "The Sabbath came to be for the sake of humanity, not humanity for the sake of the Sabbath. ²⁸So then, the Son of Humanity is Lord even of the Sabbath."

3 Then He entered again into the synagogue, and a man was there having his hand withered. ²And they were watching Him closely [to see] if He would heal him on [one of] the Sabbaths, so that they should accuse Him. ³And He says to the man, the one having the hand [which] had been withered, "Get up [and come] into the midst [or, [come] forward]!" ⁴Then He says to them, "Is it lawful on the Sabbaths to do good or to do evil? To save life or to kill?" But they were keeping silent. ⁵And having looked around upon them with anger, being deeply grieved at the hardness [fig., stubbornness] of their heart, He says to the man, "Stretch out your hand!" And he stretched [it] out, and his hand was restored healthy like the other! ⁶And the Pharisees having gone out, immediately they began creating a plot with the Herodians against Him in order that they should destroy Him.

⁷Then Jesus withdrew with His disciples to the sea. And a large multitude from Galilee followed Him, and from Judea ⁸and from Jerusalem and from Idumea and beyond the Jordan and the [ones] around Tyre and Sidon—a large multitude having heard what great [things] He was doing, came to Him. ⁹And He told His disciples that a small boat should be kept ready for Him, because of the crowd, so that they would not be pressing upon Him. ¹⁰For He healed many, with the result that they kept pushing their way to Him, so that they could touch Him, as many as were having ailments. ¹¹And the unclean [or, defiling] spirits, when they would see Him, were falling down before Him and were crying out, saying, "You are the Son of God!" ¹²And He would earnestly warn them that they should not make Him known.

¹³And He goes up into the mountain and summons whom He wanted, and they went to Him. ¹⁴Then He appointed twelve, so that they should be with Him, and so that He should send them out to be preaching ¹⁵and to be having power [or, authority] to be healing the diseases and to be casting out the demons.

¹⁶And He gave to Simon [the] name Peter, ¹⁷and James [son] of Zebedee and John the brother of James, and He gave them names—Boanerges, which is [fig., means], "Sons of Thunder," ¹⁸and Andrew and Philip and Bartholomew and Matthew and Thomas and James [son] of Alpheus and Thaddeus and Simon the Cananite [i.e. Aramaic for "Zealot"] ¹⁹and Judas Iscariot, who also betrayed Him.

And they come into a house. ²⁰Then a crowd gathers again, with the result that they are not even able to eat bread. ²¹And the [ones] from His side [fig., His relatives] having heard, they went out to take hold of Him, for they said that He was out of His mind. ²²And the scribes, the [ones] from Jerusalem, having come down, said "He has Beelzebul [i.e. a Philistine deity used as a name for the devil]!" And, "By the ruler of the demons He casts out the demons." ²³Then having summoned them, He began saying to them in allegories [or, parables, and throughout book], "How is Satan able to be casting out Satan? ²⁴And if a kingdom is divided against itself, that kingdom is not able to stand. ²⁵And if a house is divided against itself, that house is not able to stand. ²⁶And if Satan rose up against himself and has been divided, he is not able to stand, but has an end [or, is finished]. ²⁷No one, having entered into his house is able to plunder the property of the strong man, unless he first binds the strong man, and then he shall plunder his house.

²⁸"Positively, I say to you*, that all the sins will be forgiven to the sons [and daughters] of people, also blasphemies, as many as they shall blaspheme. ²⁹But whoever shall blaspheme in regard to [or, against] the Holy Spirit does not have forgiveness into the age [fig., forever], but is in danger of eternal judgment [or, punishment]"— ³⁰because they were saying, "He has an unclean [or, defiling] spirit."

³¹Then His brothers and mother come, and standing outside they sent [word] to Him, calling for Him. ³²And a crowd was sitting around Him. So they said to Him, "Listen! Your mother and Your brothers and Your sisters are outside seeking You." ³³And He answered them saying, "Who is My mother or My brothers?" ³⁴And having looked around in a circle at the ones sitting around Him, He says, "Look! My mother and My brothers! ³⁵For whoever does the will of God, this one is My brother and My sister and mother."

4 And again He began to be teaching by the sea. And a large crowd was gathered to Him, with the result that He, having stepped into the boat, sat [in it] on the sea. And the whole crowd was by the sea on the land.

²And He began teaching them many [things] in allegories. And He was saying to them in His teaching: ³"Be paying attention [to this]! Listen! The one sowing went out to sow. ⁴And it happened, in the sowing, some [seed] fell beside the road, and the birds came and devoured it. ⁵But other [seed] fell on the rocky ground where it was not having much soil, and immediately it sprouted because of it not having depth of soil. ⁶But [the] sun having risen, it was scorched, and because of it not having root, it withered. ⁷And other [seed] fell into the thorns. And the thorns came up and choked it, and it did not give fruit. ⁸And other [seed] fell into the good ground, and it kept yielding fruit, coming up and increasing, and it kept producing: one thirty[fold] and one sixty[fold] and one a hundred[fold]." ⁹And He was saying to them, "The one having ears to be hearing—let him be hearing [or, be paying attention]."

¹⁰But when He came to be alone, those around Him, with the twelve, asked Him [about] the allegory. ¹¹And He was saying to them, "To you* it has been given to know the secret [or, mystery] of the kingdom of God, but to the ones outside,

all the [things] are in allegories, [12]so that, *'Seeing they shall be seeing yet shall not perceive, and hearing they shall be hearing yet shall not be understanding, lest they turn back, and their sins be forgiven to them.'"* [Isaiah 6:9,10, LXX]

[13]Then He says to them, "You* do understand this allegory, do you* not? And how will you* understand all the allegories? [14]The one sowing sows the word. [15]Now these are the [seeds] beside the road where the word is sown: and whenever they hear, immediately Satan comes and snatches away the word, the one having been sown in their hearts. [16]And similarly, these are the [seeds] sown on the rocky ground: which, whenever they hear the word, immediately with joy they receive it. [17]And they do not have root in themselves, but are temporary; afterward, affliction or persecution having come because of the word, immediately they are caused to stumble [fig., fall away]. [18]And these are the [seeds] having been sown into the thorns: the ones hearing the word, [19]and the anxieties [or, cares] of this age [fig, the present life] and the deception of riches and the desires [or, lusts] concerning the remaining [things] entering in, choke the word, and it becomes unfruitful. [20]And these are the [seeds] having been sown on the good ground: who hear the word and receive [it]. And they keep yielding fruit: one thirty[fold] and one sixty[fold] and one a hundred[fold]."

[21]Then He was saying to them, "The lamp does not come so that it should be put under the basket nor under the bed, does it? [It comes] so that it should be placed on the lampstand, does it not? [22]For [there] is not anything hidden which shall not be revealed, nor [which] was kept secret, but that it should come into light. [23]If anyone has ears to be hearing—let him be hearing [or, be paying attention]."

[24]And He was saying to them, "Be watching [or, Beware of] what you* pay attention to. By what measure [or, standard] you* measure, it will be measured to you*, and to the ones hearing [more] will be added to you*. [25]For whoever shall be having, [more] will be given to him, and whoever does not have, even what he has will be taken away from him."

[26]And He was saying, "The kingdom of God is like this: as if a person should cast the seed on the ground [27]and should be sleeping and rising night and day, and the seed should be sprouting and growing. How? He himself does not know. [28]For the earth bears fruit by itself [or, spontaneously]: first a blade, then a head of grain, then full-grown wheat in the head. [29]But whenever the crop yields [its fruit], immediately he sends out the sickle, because the harvest has come."

[30]And He said, "To what shall we compare the kingdom of God, or by what kind of allegory shall we illustrate it? [31][It is] like a grain of mustard [or, a mustard seed], which, whenever it is sown on the earth, is smaller than all of the seeds on the earth. [32]And whenever it is sown, it comes up and becomes larger than all of the vegetables, and it produces large branches, with the result that *'the birds of the air are able to be nesting under its shade.'"* [Ezek 17:23; 31:6]

[33]And with many such allegories He was speaking to them the word, as much as they were able to be hearing. [34]But without an allegory He was not speaking to them, but privately to His disciples He was explaining all.

[35]And on that day, evening having come, He says to them, "Let us cross over to the other side." [36]And having left the crowd, they take Him along, as He was [already] in the boat. And other small boats were also with Him. [37]Then a great storm of wind comes, and the waves were splashing into the boat, with the result that it is already being filled. [38]And <u>He</u> was in the stern, sleeping on the cushion. And they wake Him up and say to Him, "Teacher, You are concerned that we perish, are You not?" [39]And having woken up, He rebuked the wind and said to the sea, "Be silent! Be muzzled [fig., Be still]!" And the wind abated, and [there] was a great calm. [40]And He said to them, "Why are you* so cowardly? How [is it that] you* do not have faith?" [41]Then they feared a great fear. And they were saying to one another, "Who, then, is this, that even the wind and the sea obey [or, are subject to] Him?" [cp. Job 38:25-38; Psalm 135:7]

5 Then they came to the other side of the sea, into the region of the Gadarenes. [2]And <u>He</u> having come out from the boat, immediately a man met him out of the tombs with an unclean [or, defiling] spirit, [3]who was having his dwelling among the tombs. And not even with chains was anyone able to bind him, [4]because <u>he</u> had frequently been bound with shackles and chains. And the chains had been pulled apart by him, and the shackles had been broken in pieces, and none was able to tame him. [5]And through all [fig. continually], night and day, in the mountains and in the tombs, he was crying out and cutting himself with stones.

[6]Now having seen Jesus from a distance, he ran and prostrated himself in reverence before Him. [7]And having cried out with a loud voice, he said, "What to me and to You [fig., What have I to do with You], Jesus, Son of God the Most High? I adjure You [or, place You under an oath] [by] God; You shall not torment me!" [8]For He was saying to him, "Come out from the man, [you] unclean [or, defiling] spirit!"

[9]And He was questioning him, "What [is] your name?" And he answered, saying, "Legion [is] my name, because we are many." [10]And he began calling on Him much, so that He should not send them out of the region.

[11]Now [there] was there, near the mountain, a large herd of pigs being fed. [12]And all the demons pleaded with Him, saying, "Send us into the pigs, so that we shall enter into them." [13]Then immediately Jesus permitted them. And having come out, the unclean [or, defiling] spirits entered into the pigs, and the herd stampeded down the steep bank into the sea (now they were about two thousand), and they were being drowned in the sea.

[14]So the ones feeding the pigs fled, and they reported [it] in the city and in the farms. And they came out to see what it is, the [thing] having happened. [15]And they come to Jesus, and they see the one being demon-possessed [or, oppressed by demons, and through verse 18] sitting and having been clothed and being of sound mind, the one having had the legion. And they were frightened. [16]Now the ones having seen [it] related to them how it had happened to the one being demon-possessed and about the pigs. [17]Then they began to be pleading with Him to go away from their borders.

¹⁸And as <u>He</u> stepped into the boat, the one having been demon-possessed was pleading with Him that he should be with Him. ¹⁹But Jesus did not allow him, <u>but</u> He says to him, "Be going away into your home, to your own [people] and report to them how great [things] the Lord has done to you, and [how] He was merciful to you." ²⁰And he went away and began to be proclaiming in the Decapolis [or, Ten Cities] how great [things] Jesus did to him, and all were marveling.

²¹And Jesus having crossed over in the boat again to the other side, a large crowd was gathered to Him, and He was by the sea. ²²Then look! One of the synagogue leaders, by name Jairus, comes, and having seen Him, he falls at His feet. ²³And he was earnestly pleading with Him, saying, "My little daughter has the last extremity [fig., is at the point of death]. [I ask] that having come, You lay Your hands on her, in order that she shall be cured and will live."

²⁴Then He went away with him. And a large crowd was following Him, and they were pressing upon Him. ²⁵And a certain woman, being with a flow of blood twelve years, ²⁶and having suffered many [things] under many physicians and having spent all the [things] with her [fig., everything that she had] and not having been benefited at all, <u>but</u> rather having come to [be] much worse, ²⁷having heard about Jesus, having come in the crowd behind [Him], she touched His robe. ²⁸For she was saying, "If I just touch His garments, I will be cured." ²⁹And immediately the flow of her blood was dried up, and she knew in her body that she has been healed of that affliction.

³⁰Then immediately Jesus, having known in Himself the power having gone out from Him, having turned around in the crowd, said, "Who touched My garments?" ³¹And His disciples were saying to Him, "You see the crowd pressing upon You, and You say, "Who touched Me!" ³²And He was looking around to see the one having done this. ³³Now the woman, having been afraid and trembling, knowing what had happened to her, came and fell down before Him, and she told to Him all the truth. ³⁴So He said to her, "Daughter, your faith has cured you; be going away in peace and be cured from your affliction."

³⁵As <u>He</u> is still speaking, they come from the synagogue leader, saying, "Your daughter died; why do you still trouble the Teacher?" ³⁶But immediately Jesus, having heard the word being spoken, says to the synagogue leader, "Stop being afraid, only be believing [or, trusting]!" ³⁷And He did not allow anyone to follow with Him, except Peter and James and John, the brother of James.

³⁸Then He comes into the house of the synagogue leader and sees a commotion, weeping, and loud wailing. ³⁹And having gone in, He says to them, "Why are you* so upset and weeping? The young child did not die, <u>but</u> is sleeping!" ⁴⁰And they began laughing at Him. But having sent [them] all out, He takes the father of the young child and the mother and those with Him, and He goes in where the child was lying. ⁴¹And having taken hold of the hand of the young child, He says to her, *"Talitha koumi!"* which is, being translated, "Girl (I say to you), get up!" ⁴²And immediately the girl rose up and was walking about! (for she was twelve years [old]). And they were amazed [with] great amazement. ⁴³And He gave strict orders to them that no one should know [about] this. Then He said [for something] to be given to her to eat.

*6*Then He went out from there and came into His hometown, and His disciples follow Him. ²And [the] Sabbath having come, He began to be teaching in the synagogue. And many hearing were astonished, saying, "Where [did] this One [get] these [things]? And what [is] the wisdom having been given to Him? And [how] are such miraculous works being done through His hands? ³This is the craftsman, the Son of Mary and Brother of James and Joses and Judas and Simon, is it not? And His sisters are here with us, are they not?" And they were caused to stumble because of Him [fig., were having doubts about Him].

⁴But Jesus said to them, "A prophet is not without honor, except in his hometown and among his relatives and in his own house." ⁵And He was not able to do any miraculous work there, except having laid His hands on a few infirm [or, sickly] [people], He healed [them]. ⁶And He marveled because of their unbelief. And He was traveling around the villages in a circuit, teaching.

⁷Then He summons the twelve. And He began to be sending them out two [by] two, and He was giving to them authority [or, power] over the unclean [or, defiling] spirits. ⁸And He gave strict orders to them that they should be taking nothing for the journey, except a staff only—no traveler's bag, no bread, no copper coin [or, money] in their money belt— ⁹but having put on sandals—also, "You* shall not put on two tunics." ¹⁰And He was saying to them, "Whenever you* enter into a house, be staying there until you* depart from there. ¹¹And as many as shall not receive you* nor hear you*, going out from there, shake off the dust that [is] under your* feet for a testimony to [or, against] them. Positively, I say to you*, it will be more tolerable for Sodom or Gomorrah in [the] day of judgment than for that city."

¹²Then having gone out, they began preaching that [people] should repent. ¹³And they were casting out many demons, and they were anointing many infirm [or, sickly] [people] with oil and were healing [them].

¹⁴And Herod the king heard (for His name became well known), and he said, "John, the one baptizing, was raised from [the] dead! And because of this these miraculous powers are supernaturally working in Him." ¹⁵Others were saying, "He is Elijah." But others were saying, "He is a prophet like one of the prophets." ¹⁶But Herod having heard, said, "John whom I beheaded—this is he! He was raised from [the] dead!"

¹⁷For Herod himself, having sent [soldiers], arrested John and bound him in prison on account of Herodias the wife of Philip his brother, because he married her. ¹⁸For John kept saying to Herod, "It is not lawful for you to be having the wife of your brother!" ¹⁹So Herodias was holding a grudge against him and was wanting to kill him, but she was not able, ²⁰for Herod was fearing John, knowing him [to be] a righteous and holy man, and he was protecting him. And having heard him, he was doing many [things], and he would hear him gladly.

²¹And a suitable day having come, when Herod, for his birthday festivities, was making a banquet for his nobles and the commanding officers [or, Chiliarchs] and the most prominent people of Galilee, ²²and the daughter of Herodias herself having come in and having danced and having pleased Herod and the ones

reclining [to eat] with [him], the king said to the girl, "Ask of me whatever you want and I will give [it] to you." ²³And he took an oath with her, "Whatever you ask me, I will give to you—up to half of my kingdom!"

²⁴So having gone out, she said to her mother, "What will I ask for myself?" So she said, "The head of John the Baptist [or, the Immerser]!" ²⁵And having come in, immediately with haste to the king, she asked, saying, "I want that you give to me at once, on a wooden platter, the head of John the Baptist!" ²⁶And the king—[although] having become deeply grieved—because of the oaths and of the ones reclining [to eat] with [him], did not want to regard her [request] as nothing. ²⁷Then immediately the king, having sent an executioner, commanded his head to be brought. ²⁸So having gone, he beheaded him in the prison. And he brought his head on a wooden platter and gave it to the girl, and the girl gave it to her mother. ²⁹Then his disciples having heard, they came and took away his corpse and laid it in a tomb.

³⁰And the apostles are gathered together to Jesus, and they reported all to Him, and how many [things] they did, and how many [things] they taught. ³¹And He said to them, "Come you* by yourselves privately to a desert place, and be resting yourselves a little." For the ones coming and the ones going were many, and they were not even finding time to eat. ³²Then they went away privately into a deserted place in the boat. ³³And they saw them going away, and many recognized Him. And they ran together there on foot [or, by land] from all the cities, and they went before them and came together to Him.

³⁴And having come out [of the boat], Jesus saw a large crowd. And He was moved with compassion on them, because they were like sheep not having a shepherd, and He began to be teaching them many [things]. ³⁵Then the hour already having become late, His disciples having approached Him, say, "The place is desolate, and the hour is already late. ³⁶Send them away so that, having gone away into the surrounding farms and villages, they should buy for themselves loaves of bread, for they do not have something they should eat [or, for they do not have anything to eat]."

³⁷But answering, He said to them, "You* give to them to eat." And they say to Him, "Having gone away, should we buy two hundred denarii [i.e., 200 days' wages] [worth of] loaves of bread and give to them to eat?" ³⁸But He says to them, "How many loaves of bread do you* have? Be going away and see." And when they found out, they say, "Five, and two fish."

³⁹And He commanded for them to make all recline company [by] company on the green grass. ⁴⁰And they reclined group [by] group, by hundreds and by fifties. ⁴¹And having taken the five loaves of bread and the two fish, having looked up to heaven, He bestowed a blessing and broke the loaves of bread in pieces, and He began giving to His disciples so that they should distribute to them, and He divided the two fish to all. ⁴²And they all ate and were satisfied! ⁴³And they took up twelve handbaskets full of broken pieces of bread and of the fish. ⁴⁴And the ones having eaten of the loaves of bread were five thousand men!

⁴⁵And immediately He compelled His disciples to step into the boat and to go on ahead to the other side, to Bethsaida, until <u>He</u> sent the crowd away. ⁴⁶And

having said good-bye to them, He went away into the mountain to pray. [47]And evening having come, the boat was in the middle of the sea, and He [was] alone on the land. [48]And He saw them being tormented [or, straining] in the rowing, for the wind was against them. And about the fourth watch of the night [i.e., between 3:00 - 6:00 a.m.], He comes to them walking about on the sea. And He wanted to pass by them. [49]But having seen Him walking about on the sea, they supposed [Him] to be an apparition, and they cried out. [50]For they all saw Him and were terrified. And immediately He spoke with them and says to them, "Be taking courage! I Am! Stop fearing!" [cp. Exod 3:14] [51]And He went up to them into the boat, and the wind abated. And they were very much utterly amazed within themselves, and they began marveling. [52]For they did not understand concerning the loaves of bread, for their heart had been hardened [fig., they were stubborn in their inner selves].

[53]Then having crossed over, they came to the land [of] Gennesaret and anchored [there]. [54]And they having come out from the boat, immediately [the people] having recognized Him, [55]having run about that whole surrounding region, they began to be carrying on the cots the ones having it badly [fig., who were sick] wherever they would hear that He is there. [56]And wherever He was going, into villages or cities or farms, they were laying the sick in the marketplaces. And they were pleading with Him that they should at least touch the fringe of His garment, and as many as were touching Him were being healed.

7 And the Pharisees and some of the scribes, having come from Jerusalem, are gathered together to Him. [2]And having seen some of His disciples eating bread with defiled [or, ceremonially unclean] hands—that is, not ritually washed—they found fault. [3]For the Pharisees and all the Jews, if they do not wash their hands with [the] fist [fig., in the proper manner], do not eat, keeping the tradition of the elders. [4]And [coming] from the marketplace, unless they baptize [or, ceremonially wash] themselves, they do not eat, and many other [traditions there] are which they received [and] are keeping: [like] baptisms [or, ceremonial washings] of cups and pitchers and brazen vessels and cots.

[5]Afterwards the Pharisees and the scribes ask Him, "Why do Your disciples not walk about [fig., conduct themselves] according to the tradition of the elders? But they eat their bread with ritually unwashed hands." [6]But answering, He said to them, "Correctly did Isaiah prophesy concerning you*, the hypocrites! As it has been written, *'This people honors Me with their lips* [fig., *words*]*, but their heart is far distant from Me.* [7]*But in vain* [or, *to no purpose*] *do they worship Me, teaching [as] teachings* [or, *doctrines*] *[the] commandments of people.'* [Isaiah 29:13, LXX] [8]For having left behind [or, having neglected] the commandment of God, you* keep the tradition of people: baptisms [or, ceremonial washings] of pitchers and cups, and many such other similar things you* do."

[9]And He was saying to them, "[All too] well do you* regard as nothing the commandment of God, so that you* should keep your* tradition. [10]For Moses said, *'Be honoring your father and your mother'*, and, *'The one speaking evil of father or mother, let him be coming to the end [of his life], to [his] death.'* [Exod

20:12; Deut 5:16; Exod 21:17] [11]But you* say, 'If a person says to his father or to his mother, "[It is] Corban (which is, a gift), whatever you should be benefited from me."' [12]And you* no longer allow him to do anything for his father or for his mother, [13][thus] nullifying the word of God for your* tradition which you* handed down. And many such other similar things you* do."

[14]And having summoned all the crowd, He was saying to them, "Be paying attention to Me, all [of you*], and be understanding: [15]There is nothing from outside the person entering into him which is able to defile him, but the [things] coming out from him, those are the [things] defiling the person. [16]If anyone has ears to be hearing, let him be hearing [or, be paying attention]."

[17]And when He entered into a house from the crowd, His disciples began asking Him about the allegory. [18]And He says to them, "So you* also are without understanding! You* do understand that nothing from outside entering into the person is able to defile him, do you* not? [19]Because it does not enter into his heart, but into the stomach, and goes out into the latrine, purifying [or, purging] all the foods." [20]But He was saying, "That [which] comes out from the person, that defiles the person. [21]For from within, out of the heart of people, proceed evil thoughts, adulteries, sexual sins, murders, [22]thefts, covetous desires [or, greed], wicked deeds, deceit [or, treachery], flagrant sexual immorality, an evil eye [fig., envy], blasphemy, arrogance, foolishness. [23]All these evils come out from within and defile the person."

[24]Then having risen from there, He went away into the boundaries of Tyre and Sidon. And having entered into a house, He was wanting no one to know, yet He was not able to escape notice. [25]For a woman having heard about Him, whose little daughter was having an unclean [or, defiling] spirit, having come, she fell at His feet. [26]Now the woman was a Greek, a Syro-Phoenician by race. And she kept asking Him that He would cast out the demon from her daughter.

[27]But Jesus said to her, "Allow the children to be filled first, for it is not proper to take the children's bread and to cast [it] to the little dogs." [28]But she answered and says to Him, "Yes indeed, Lord, but even the little dogs under the table eat from the young children's crumbs." [29]And He said to her, "Because of this word, be going; the demon has gone out from your daughter." [30]And having gone away into her house, she found the demon having gone out and her daughter having been placed on the bed.

[31]And again, having gone out from the borders of Tyre and Sidon, He came to the Sea of Galilee, in the middle of the borders of Decapolis [or, Ten Cities]. [32]And they bring to Him a deaf [person] with a speech impediment, and they plead with Him that He lay His hand on him. [33]And having taken him aside privately, away from the crowd, He put His fingers into his ears, and having spit, He touched his tongue. [34]And having looked up into heaven, He sighed and says to him, "Ephphatha!" which is, "Be opened!" [35]Then immediately his ears were opened, and the bond [fig., impediment] of his tongue was loosed, and he began speaking plainly!

[36]And He gave orders to them that they should tell no one, but as much as He was giving orders to them, all the more abundantly [or, widely] they were proclaiming

[it]. ³⁷And they were utterly astonished, saying, "He has done all [things] well; He makes both the deaf to be hearing and the mute to be speaking!"

8In those days, the crowd being very great and not having anything they should eat, Jesus having summoned His disciples, says to them, ²"I have compassion on the crowd because they are already staying with Me three days and do not have anything they should eat. ³And if I send them away hungry to their home, they will faint on the journey, for some of them come from a distance." ⁴Then His disciples answered to Him, "From where will anyone be able to feed these with bread here in [this] desolate place?" ⁵And He was asking them, "How many loaves of bread do you* have?" So they said, "Seven."

⁶Then He gave strict orders to the crowd to recline on the ground. And having taken the seven loaves of bread, having given thanks, He broke [them] and began giving [them] to His disciples so that they should set [them] before [the people]. And they set [them] before the crowd. ⁷And they were having a few small fish. And having bestowed a blessing upon [them], He said to set them also before [the people]. ⁸So they ate and were satisfied! And they took up leftover broken pieces of bread—seven large baskets. ⁹Now the ones eating were about four thousand! Then He sent them away.

¹⁰And immediately having stepped into the boat with His disciples, He came into the parts [or, district] of Dalmanutha. ¹¹Then the Pharisees came out and began disputing with Him, seeking from Him a sign from heaven, testing Him. ¹²And having sighed deeply in His spirit, He says, "Why does this generation seek after a sign? Positively, I say to you*, no sign will be given to this generation."

¹³Then having left them, having stepped again into a boat, He went away to the other side. ¹⁴And the disciples forgot to take loaves of bread, and they had nothing with them in the boat except one loaf of bread. ¹⁵And He began giving orders to them, saying, "Be watching out! Continually beware of the leaven [or, yeast] of the Pharisees and of the leaven of Herod." ¹⁶Then they began discussing with one another, saying, "[He said this] because we have no loaves of bread."

¹⁷And Jesus having known, says to them, "Why do you* discuss that you* have no loaves of bread? Do you* not yet perceive nor understand? Do you* still have your* heart having been hardened [fig., Are you* still stubborn in your* inner selves]? ¹⁸*'Having eyes, do you* not see? And having ears, do you* not hear?'* [Jer 5:21] And do you* not remember? ¹⁹When I broke the five loaves of bread for the five thousand, how many handbaskets full of broken pieces of bread did you* take up?" They say to Him, "Twelve." ²⁰"But when [I broke] the seven [loaves] for the four thousand, how many large baskets full of broken pieces of bread did you* take up?" And they said, "Seven." ²¹And He was saying to them, "How do you* not understand?"

²²Then He comes into Bethsaida. And they bring to Him a blind [man], and they plead with Him that He should touch him. ²³And having taken hold of the hand of the blind [man], He led him forth outside of the village. And having spit into his eyes, having placed His hands on him, He began asking him if he sees [or, is able to see] anything. ²⁴And he, having looked up, was saying, "I see people

that like trees I see [them] walking about." ²⁵Then He again placed the hands on his eyes and made him look up. And he was restored and saw everyone clearly! ²⁶And He sent him away to his house, saying, "Neither enter into the village, nor tell [it] to anyone in the village."

²⁷Then Jesus went out, and His disciples, into the villages of Caesarea Philippi. And on the way He was questioning His disciples, saying to them, "Who are people saying Me to be [or, [that] I am]?" ²⁸So they answered, "John the Baptist [or, the Immerser], and others Elijah, but others one of the prophets." ²⁹Then He says to them, "But you*, who do you* say Me to be [or, [that] I am]?" So answering, Peter says to Him, "You are the Christ" ["the Anointed One"]. ³⁰And He warned them that they should be telling no one about Him.

³¹Then He began to be teaching them that it is necessary [for] the Son of Humanity to suffer many [things] and to be rejected by the elders and the chief priests and the scribes and to be killed and after three days to rise again. ³²And He was speaking the word plainly. And Peter, having taken Him aside, began rebuking Him. ³³But He, having turned back and having seen His disciples, rebuked Peter, saying, "Be going away behind Me, Satan! For you do not keep in mind the [things] of God, but the [things] of people."

³⁴And having summoned the crowd, with His disciples, He said to them, "Whoever desires to be following after Me, let him deny [or, disown] himself, and take up his cross, and be following Me. ³⁵For whoever is desiring to save his life will lose it, but whoever loses his own life on account of Me and the Gospel, will save it. ³⁶For what will it benefit a person if he gains the whole world and forfeits his soul? ³⁷Or what will a person give in exchange for his soul? ³⁸For whoever is ashamed of Me and of My words in this adulterous [fig., unfaithful] and sinful generation, the Son of Humanity will also be ashamed of him when He comes in the glory of His Father, with the holy angels."

9 And He was saying to them, "Positively, I say to you*, there are some of the ones standing here who by no means shall taste of [fig., experience] death until they see the kingdom of God having come in power."

²Then after six days Jesus takes Peter and James and John and leads them up privately into a high mountain, alone. And He was transfigured [or, His appearance was changed] before them. ³And His garments became radiant, extremely white like snow, such as a bleacher [or, launderer] on the earth is not able to whiten [them]. ⁴Then Elijah with Moses appeared to them, and they were conversing with Jesus. ⁵And answering, Peter says to Jesus, "Rabbi, it is good [for] us to be here. And let us make three tents: one for You and one for Moses and one for Elijah"— ⁶for he had not known what he will [or, should] say, for they were terrified. ⁷And a cloud appeared overshadowing them, and a voice came out of the cloud, saying, "This is My Son—the Beloved! Be paying attention to Him!"

⁸Then suddenly, having looked around, they no longer saw anyone, but Jesus only, with themselves. ⁹Now while they descended from the mountain, He gave orders to them that they should relate to no one what they saw, except when the Son of Humanity rises from [the] dead. ¹⁰And they kept this word to themselves,

questioning together what the rising from [the] dead is. ¹¹Then they began questioning Him, saying, "The scribes say that it is necessary [for] Elijah to come first." [see Mal 4:5] ¹²But answering, He said to them, "Elijah indeed, having come first, restores all [things]. But why has it been written concerning the Son of Humanity that many [things] He shall suffer and be treated with contempt? ¹³But I say to you* that indeed Elijah has come, and they did to him as much as they wanted, just as it has been written concerning him."

¹⁴And having come to the disciples, He saw a large crowd around them, and scribes arguing with them. ¹⁵Then immediately, when the entire crowd saw Him, they were greatly surprised, and running up [to Him], they began greeting Him. ¹⁶And He questioned the scribes, "What are you* arguing about with them?" ¹⁷Then one from the crowd answering, said, "Teacher, I brought my son to You, because he has a mute spirit [i.e., a spirit which makes him mute]. ¹⁸And wherever it seizes him, it tears him [fig., throws him into convulsions]. And he foams at the mouth and gnashes his teeth, and he is withering away. And I spoke to Your disciples that they cast it out, but they were not able."

¹⁹So answering him, He said, "O unbelieving [or, faithless] generation, how long will I be with you*? How long will I put up with you*? Be bringing him to Me." ²⁰And they brought him to Him. And having seen Him, immediately the spirit tore him back and forth [fig., threw him into convulsions], and having fallen on the ground, he began rolling about, foaming at the mouth. ²¹And He questioned his father, "How long a time is it [that] it has happened like this to him?" Then he said, "From childhood. ²²And also, frequently it casts him into the fire and into water, so that it should destroy him. But if You are able to do anything, help us, having compassion on us." ²³So Jesus said to him, "If you are able to believe [or, to have faith]—all [things are] possible to the one believing [or, having faith]!" ²⁴And immediately, having cried out, the father of the young child with tears said, "I do believe [or, I do have faith]! Lord, be helping my unbelief [or, my weak faith]!"

²⁵Now Jesus having seen that a crowd is gathering rapidly, He rebuked the unclean [or, defiling] spirit, saying to it, "Mute and deaf spirit, I command you, come out from him, and you shall no longer enter into him!" ²⁶And having cried out and having greatly torn him back and forth [fig., having thrown him into terrible convulsions], it came out. And he became as dead, with the result that many are saying that he was dead. ²⁷But Jesus, having taken him by the hand, lifted him up, and he stood up.

²⁸And when He came into the house, His disciples began questioning Him privately, "Why were we not able to cast it out?" ²⁹And He said to them, "This kind is able to come out by nothing except by prayer and fasting."

³⁰Then having gone out from there, they were passing through Galilee, and He did not want that any should know. ³¹For He was teaching His disciples, and He was saying to them, "The Son of Humanity is being betrayed into the hands of people, and they will kill Him. And having been killed, the third day He will rise." ³²But they were not understanding the saying, and they were afraid to question Him.

[33]And He came into Capernaum. And being in the house, He began questioning them, "What were you* discussing on the road among yourselves?" [34]But they were keeping silent, for on the road they discussed with one another who [is the] greatest. [35]And having sat down, He called the twelve and says to them, "If anyone desires to be first, he will be last of all and a servant of all." [36]And having taken a young child, He set him in the middle of them. And having taken him in His arms, He said to them, [37]"Whoever receives one like these young children in My name receives Me, and whoever receives Me, does not receive Me, but the One having sent Me."

[38]Then John answered Him, saying, "Teacher, we saw someone casting out demons in Your name, who does not follow us, and we tried to prevent him, because he does not follow us." [39]But Jesus said, "Stop preventing him, for [there] is no one who will perform a miraculous work in [or, on the basis of] My name and will soon [afterwards] be able to speak evil of Me. [40]For [the one] who is not against you* is for you*. [41]For whoever gives you* a cup of water to drink in My name because you* are Christ's, positively I say to you*, he shall by no means lose his reward.

[42]"And whoever causes one of the little [ones] believing [or, trusting] in Me to stumble [fig., to sin], it is better for him if rather a millstone [i.e. a large stone used for grinding grain] is hung around his neck, and he has been cast into the sea.

[43]"And if your hand is causing you to stumble [fig., to sin], cut it off! It is better for you to enter into life crippled, than having your two hands, to go away into hell [Gr., gehenna], into the unquenchable fire, [44]where their worm does not come to the end [of their lives], and the fire is not extinguished.

[45]"And if your foot is causing you to stumble [fig., to sin], cut it off! It is better for you to enter into the life lame, than having your two feet to be cast into hell [Gr., gehenna], into the unquenchable fire, [46]where their worm does not come to the end [of their lives], and the fire is not extinguished.

[47]"And if your eye is causing you to stumble [fig., to sin], cast it out! It is better for you to enter into the kingdom of God one-eyed, than having two eyes, to be cast into the hell [Gr., gehenna] of the fire [or, the fiery hell], [48]where their worm does not come to the end [of their lives], and the fire is not extinguished.

[49]"For every[one] will be salted with fire, and every sacrifice will be salted with salt. [50]The salt [is] good, but if the salt becomes tasteless, by what will you* season [it]? Be having salt in yourselves, and be living in peace with one another."

10 Having risen from there, He comes into the borders of Judea, by the other side of the Jordan. And crowds are again gathering together to Him. And, as He was accustomed, He again began teaching them.

[2]And [some] Pharisees, having come to [Him], questioned Him if it is lawful [for] a husband to divorce a wife, testing Him. [3]But answering, He said to them, "What did Moses command you*?" [4]So they said, "Moses permitted [one] *to write a scroll of divorce and to divorce.'"* [Deut 24:1,3] [5]And answering, Jesus

said to them, "Because of your* stubbornness he wrote you* this command. 6But from [the] beginning of the creation, God *'made them male and female.'* [Gen 1:27] 7*'For this reason, a man will leave behind his father and mother and will be joined to* [or, *united with*] *his wife.* 8*And they will be—the two—into one flesh'* [or, *'the two will become one flesh'*], with the result that they are no longer two, but one flesh. [Gen 2:24, LXX] 9Therefore, what God joined together, stop letting a person separate!"

10And in the house again, His disciples questioned Him concerning the same [matter]. 11And He says to them, "Whoever divorces his wife and marries another commits adultery against her. 12And if a woman divorces her husband and is married to another, she commits adultery."

13And they were bringing to Him young children, so that He should touch them. But the disciples were rebuking the ones bringing [them]. 14But having seen, Jesus expressed indignation. And He said to them, "Allow the young children to be coming to Me; stop forbidding [or, preventing] them, for of such [ones] is the kingdom of God. 15Positively, I say to you*, whoever does not receive the kingdom of God like [or, in the same way as] a young child shall by no means enter into it." 16And having taken them in His arms, having placed His hands on them, He began bestowing a blessing upon them.

17Then as He was going out into [the] road, one having run up and having knelt before Him, began questioning Him, "Good Teacher, what should I do so that I shall inherit eternal life?" 18But Jesus said to him, "Why do you call Me good? No one [is] good except One—God. 19The commandments you know: *'You shall not commit adultery; You shall not murder; You shall not steal; You shall not give false testimony; You shall not defraud; Honor your father and mother.'"* [Exod 20:12-16; Deut 5:16-20] 20But answering, he said to Him, "Teacher, all these I myself obeyed from my youth." 21Then Jesus having looked attentively at him, loved him, and said to him, "One [thing] you lack. Be going away; as many [things] as you have, sell and give to the poor [ones], and you will have treasure in heaven. And come! Be following Me, having taken up the cross." 22But having become appalled at the word, he went away distressed, for he was having many possessions.

23And Jesus having looked around, says to His disciples, "How with difficulty will the ones having possessions [or, riches] enter into the kingdom of God!" 24But the disciples were shocked at His words. So Jesus again answering, says to them, "Children, how difficult it is [for] the ones having confidence in [or, relying on] possessions [or, riches] to enter into the kingdom of God! 25It is easier [for] a camel to enter through the eye of the needle than [for] a rich [person] to enter into the kingdom of God." 26Now they were even more astonished, saying to themselves, "Then who is able to be saved?" 27But having looked attentively at them, Jesus says, "With people it is impossible, but not with God! For all [things] are possible with God!"

28Peter began to say to Him, "Listen! We left all and followed You." 29Answering, Jesus said, "Positively, I say to you*, there is no one who left house or brothers or sisters or father or mother or wife or children or farms for My sake and for the sake of the Gospel, ³⁰who shall not receive a hundred times as much now, in this time, houses and brothers and sisters and mothers and children and farms, with persecutions, and in the coming age, eternal life. ³¹But many first [ones] will be last, and last [ones], first."

³²Now they were on the road going up to Jerusalem, and Jesus was going before them. And they were astonished, and [as they were] following, they were afraid. And having again taken the twelve, He began to be telling them the [things] which were to be happening to Him: ³³"Listen! We are going up to Jerusalem, and the Son of Humanity shall be betrayed to the chief priests and scribes. And they will condemn Him to death, and they will deliver Him to the Gentiles. ³⁴And they will ridicule Him and will scourge Him and will spit on Him and will kill Him, and on the third day He will rise again."

³⁵And James and John, the sons of Zebedee, approached Him, saying, "Teacher, we desire that whatever we ask, You shall do for us." ³⁶So He said to them, "What do you* want Me to do for you*?" ³⁷Then they said to Him, "Grant to us that we shall sit, one at Your right [hand] and one at Your left, in Your glory." ³⁸But Jesus said to them, "You do not know what you* ask. Are you* able to drink the cup which I am drinking and to be baptized [with] the baptism which I am being baptized?" ³⁹So they said to Him, "We are able." Then Jesus said to them, "Indeed, the cup which I am drinking, you* will drink, and the baptism which I am being baptized [with], you* will be baptized [with]. ⁴⁰But to sit at My right and at My left is not mine to give, but [it is for those] for whom it has been prepared."

⁴¹And the ten having heard, began expressing indignation at James and John. ⁴²But Jesus having summoned them, says to them, "You* know that the ones recognized to be ruling the nations domineer over them, and their great [ones] tyrannize them. ⁴³But it will not be so among you*. But whoever shall be desiring to become great among you*, he will be your* servant. ⁴⁴And whoever of you* is desiring to become first, he will be slave of all. ⁴⁵For even the Son of Humanity did not come to be served, but to serve, and to give His life [as] a ransom [or, price of release] for [or, in the place of] many."

⁴⁶And they come to Jericho. And as He is going out from Jericho, with His disciples and a large crowd, a son of Timaeus—Bartimaeus the blind—was sitting beside the road begging. ⁴⁷And having heard that it is Jesus the Nazarene, he began to be crying out and to be saying, "The Son of David—Jesus! Be merciful to me!" ⁴⁸And many began warning him that he should keep silent, but all the more he kept crying out, "Son of David! Be merciful to me!"

⁴⁹And Jesus having stood still, said [for] him to be summoned. And they summoned the blind [man], saying to him, "Cheer up! Get up! He is summoning you." ⁵⁰So he, having thrown off his cloak, having gotten up, came to Jesus. ⁵¹And answering, Jesus says to him, "What do you want [that] I should do for you?" So the blind [man] said to him, "Rabbouni [i.e. Teacher], that I receive [my] sight!" ⁵²Then Jesus said to him, "Be going! Your faith has cured you!" And immediately he received [his] sight! And he began following Jesus on the road.

11 And when they draw near to Jerusalem, to Bethsphage and Bethany, to the Mount of Olives, He sends out two of His disciples ²and says to them, "Be going away into the village, the [one] opposite you*, and immediately entering into it, you* will find a colt [or, young donkey] having been tied, on which no person has sat. Having untied it, bring [it]. ³And if anyone says to you*, 'Why are you* doing this?', you* say, 'The Lord has need of it.' And immediately he [will] send it here."

⁴So they went away and found a colt having been tied by the door outside in the street, and they untied it. ⁵And some of the ones having stood there said to them, "What are you* doing—untying the colt?" ⁶But they said to them just as Jesus commanded, and they gave them permission.

⁷And they brought the colt to Jesus. And they placed their garments on it, and He sat on it. ⁸Then many spread their coats in the road, but others were cutting down leafy branches from the trees and were spreading [them] in the road. ⁹And the ones going before and the ones following began crying out, saying, "We praise You [Gr., *Hosanna*]! *'Having been blessed [is] the One coming in [the] name of [the]* LORD!*'* [Psalm 118:26] ¹⁰Having been blessed [is] the coming kingdom in [the] name of [the] Lord of our father David! We praise You in the highest!"

¹¹And Jesus entered into Jerusalem and into the temple. And having looked around at all [things], the hour already being late, He went out into Bethany with the twelve. ¹²And the next day, after they had come out from Bethany, He was hungry. ¹³And having seen a fig tree from a distance having leaves, He came, if perhaps He will find anything on it. Then having come upon it, He found nothing except leaves, for it was not [the] season for figs. ¹⁴And answering, Jesus said to it, "No longer will anyone eat fruit from you into the age [fig., forever]." And His disciples were listening.

¹⁵And they come into Jerusalem. Then Jesus having gone into the temple, He began to be casting out the ones selling and buying in the temple. And He overturned the tables of the money changers and the seats of the ones selling the doves. ¹⁶And He was not allowing that anyone should carry merchandise through the temple. ¹⁷Then He began teaching [them], saying to them, "Has it not been written, *'My house will be called a house of prayer for all the nations?'* [Isaiah 56:7] But you* made it a *'hideout for robbers!'*" [Jer 7:11]

¹⁸And the scribes and the chief priests heard. And they began seeking how they could destroy Him, for they were fearing Him, because the entire crowd was being astonished by His teaching. ¹⁹And when evening came, He would go forth outside the city.

²⁰Then in the early morning, passing by, they saw the fig tree having been dried up from [the] roots. ²¹And having remembered, Peter says to Him, "Rabbi, look! The fig tree which You cursed has been dried up." ²²And answering, Jesus says to them, "Be having faith in God! ²³For positively, I say to you*, whoever says to this mountain, 'Be taken up and be cast into the sea' and does not doubt in his heart, but believes [or, has faith] that what he says is going to happen, it will be [granted] to him whatever he says. ²⁴For this reason I say to you*, all [things],

as many as while praying you* shall be asking [for], be believing [or, be having faith] that you* are receiving, and it will be [granted] to you*.

²⁵"And whenever you* stand praying, be forgiving, if you* are holding anything against anyone, so that also your* Father, the [One] in the heavens, shall forgive you* of your* transgressions. ²⁶But if you* do not forgive, neither will your* Father, the [One] in the heavens, forgive your* transgressions."

²⁷And they come again into Jerusalem. And in the temple, as He walks about, the chief priests and the scribes and the elders come to Him. ²⁸And they say to Him, "By what authority do You do these [things]? And who gave to You this authority, so that these [things] You are doing?" ²⁹But answering, Jesus said to them, "I will also ask you* one word [or, thing], and [if] you* answer Me, I also will tell you* by what authority I am doing these [things]. ³⁰The baptism of John—was it from heaven or from people? Answer Me." ³¹And they began considering with themselves, saying, "If we say, 'From heaven,' He will say, 'Then why did you* not believe him?' ³²But shall we say, 'From people?'"—they were fearing the people, for all were holding that John was really a prophet. ³³And answering, they say to Jesus, "We do not know." Then answering, Jesus says to them, "Neither do I tell you* by what authority I am doing these [things]."

12 And He began to be speaking to them in allegories: "A man *'planted a vineyard and put a fence around [it] and dug a trough* [i.e. a trench for gathering juice under the wine press] *and built a lookout tower.'* [Isaiah 5:1,2] And he leased it to vineyard keepers and went on a journey. ²Then he sent a slave to the vineyard keepers at the [harvest] time, so that from the vineyard keepers he should receive from the fruit of the vineyard. ³But they, having taken him, repeatedly beat [him] and sent him away empty-handed. ⁴And again he sent to them another slave. And that one, having cast stones at [him], they wounded in the head and sent [him] away, having been treated shamefully. ⁵And again he sent another. And that one they killed. And many others: some repeatedly beating, but others killing.

⁶"Therefore, having still one son—his beloved—he sent even him to them last, saying, 'They will respect my son.' ⁷But those vineyard keepers said to one another, 'This is the heir. Come; let us kill him, and the inheritance will be ours!' ⁸Then having taken him, they killed [him], and threw [him] outside of the vineyard. ⁹Therefore, what will the owner of the vineyard do? He will come, and he will destroy the vineyard keepers, and he will give the vineyard to others. ¹⁰Did you* not even read this Scripture, *'A stone which the builders rejected, this [stone] became [the] cornerstone. ¹¹This came to be from [the] LORD, and it is marvelous in our eyes?'"* [Psalm 118:22,23] ¹²Then they began seeking to take Him into custody—but they feared the crowd—for they knew that He spoke the allegory against them. And having left Him, they went away.

¹³And they send to Him some of the Pharisees and [some] of the Herodians, so that they should trap Him in [some] word. ¹⁴So having come, they say to Him, "Teacher, we know that You are truthful, and You are not concerned for anyone; for You do not look to the face of people [fig., You do not show favoritism to

people], <u>but</u> You teach the way of God in truth. Is it lawful to give tribute [or, a tax] to Caesar or not? ¹⁵Should we give, or should we not give?"

But knowing their insincerity, He said to them, "Why do you* test Me? Be bringing to Me a denarius [i.e., a Roman, silver coin], so that I should see [it]." ¹⁶So they brought [it]. Then He says to them, "Whose image [is] this? And the inscription?" So they said to Him, "Caesar's." ¹⁷And answering, Jesus said to them, "Give back [or, Render] the [things] of Caesar to Caesar and the [things] of God to God." And they were amazed at Him.

¹⁸Then Sadducees come to Him—who say there is not a resurrection—and they questioned Him, saying, ¹⁹"Teacher, Moses wrote to us that *'if someone's brother dies'* (and leaves behind a wife) *'and leaves no children, that his brother shall take his wife and raise up seed* [fig., *offspring*] *to his brother.'* [Deut 25:5] ²⁰[There] were seven brothers. And the first took a wife, and dying, he left no seed. ²¹Then the second took her, and died, and neither did he leave seed. And the third in the same manner. ²²And the seven took her and left no seed. Last of all the woman also died. ²³In the resurrection, whenever they rise, whose wife of them will she be? For the seven had her [as] wife."

²⁴And answering, Jesus said to them, "Is this not the reason you* are led astray [fig., are mistaken]: you* do not know the Scriptures nor the power of God? ²⁵For when they rise from [the] dead, they neither marry nor are they given in marriage, <u>but</u> they are as angels, the [ones] in the heavens. ²⁶But concerning the dead [ones], that they rise: you* have read in the Scroll of Moses (at The Bush), how God spoke to him, saying, *'I [am] the God of Abraham and the God of Isaac and the God of Jacob,'* have you* not? [Exod 3:6] ²⁷He is not the God of dead [ones], <u>but</u> [the] God of living [ones]! Therefore, <u>you*</u> are greatly led astray [fig., mistaken]!"

²⁸Then one of the scribes having approached, having heard them debating, knowing that He answered them well, questioned Him, "Which is [the] first commandment of all?" ²⁹Then Jesus answered him, "[The] first of all the commandments [is], *'Be hearing* [or, *Be paying attention*]*, O Israel! [The] LORD is our God, [the] LORD is one. ³⁰And you will love [the] LORD your God with your whole heart and with your whole soul and with your whole understanding and with your whole strength'* [Deut 6:4,5]—this [is] the first commandment. ³¹And [the] second [is] similar to it, *'You will love your neighbor as yourself'* [Lev 19:18]—no other commandment is greater [than] these."

³²Then the scribe said to Him, "Well [said], Teacher! You have spoken in truth that He is one, and [there] is not another besides Him. [cp. Deut 4:35,39] ³³And to be loving Him with the whole heart and with the whole understanding and with the whole soul and with the whole strength and to be loving one's neighbor as oneself is more [than] all the whole burnt-offerings [or, offerings which are entirely burned] and the sacrifices." [cp. Deut 6:5; Lev 19:18; 1Sam 15:22] ³⁴And Jesus, having seen him, that he answered wisely, said to him, "You are not far from the kingdom of God." And no one dared any longer to question Him.

³⁵Then answering, Jesus was saying, teaching in the temple, "How are the scribes saying that the Christ [or, the Messiah, and throughout book] is [the] Son

of David? ³⁶For David himself said by [the] Holy Spirit, *'The LORD says to my Lord, "Be sitting at My right hand until I put Your enemies [as] Your footstool for Your feet."'* [Psalm 110:1] ³⁷Therefore, David himself calls Him 'Lord.' Then how is He his Son?" And the large crowd was gladly hearing him.

³⁸And He was saying to them in His teaching, "Be watching out for [or, Beware of] the scribes, the ones desiring to be walking about in long robes and [desiring] greetings in the marketplaces, ³⁹and first seats [fig., most important places] in the synagogues and first couches [fig., places of honor] at the banquets; ⁴⁰the ones devouring the houses of the widows [fig., illegally cheating widows out of their property] and in pretense [or, with a false show] are long [in] praying. These will receive more severe judgment [or, condemnation]."

⁴¹And Jesus having sat down opposite the treasury [fig., collection boxes], He began watching how the crowd put copper coin [or, money] into the treasury. And many rich [people] were putting in much. ⁴²Then having come, one poor widow put [in] two lepta [or, two very small copper coins], which are a kodrantes [or, a small copper coin]. ⁴³And having summoned His disciples, He says to them, "Positively, I say to you*, this poor widow has put [in] more [than] all the ones putting into the treasury [fig., the collection boxes]. ⁴⁴For all put in out of their abundance, but she, out of her poverty, all, as much as she was having—she put in her whole livelihood."

13 Then as He goes out from the temple, one of His disciples says to Him, "Teacher, look! What great stones! And what great buildings!" ²And answering, Jesus said to him, "Are you looking at these great buildings? By no means shall a stone be left on a stone which by no means shall not be torn down."

³Then as He sits on the Mount of Olives, opposite the temple, Peter and James and John and Andrew began questioning Him privately. ⁴"Tell us when these [things] will be? And what [is] the sign when all these [things] shall be about to be fulfilled?" ⁵But answering them, Jesus began to say, "Be watching out lest anyone leads you* astray [fig., deceives you*]. ⁶For many will come in My name, saying, 'I Am!'—and they will lead many astray [fig., will deceive many]. ⁷But when you* hear of wars and rumors of wars, stop being alarmed. For it is necessary [for] these [things] to take place, but the end [is] not yet. ⁸For nation will be raised up against nation, and kingdom against kingdom, and there will be earthquakes in [various] places, and there will be famines and disturbances [fig., uprisings]. These [are the] beginnings of birth pains [fig., great sufferings].

⁹"But you*, be watching out [for] yourselves. For they will hand you* over to local councils [or, courts], and you* will be repeatedly beaten in synagogues, and you* will be brought before governors and kings for My sake, for a testimony to them. ¹⁰And to all the nations it is necessary [for] the Gospel first to be proclaimed. ¹¹But when they lead you* away, handing [you*] over, stop worrying beforehand what you* shall speak, neither be thinking about [it]; but whatever shall be given to you* in that hour, this you* are to be speaking, for it is not you* speaking, but the Holy Spirit. ¹²But brother will betray brother to death, and a father [his] child;

and children will rebel against parents and will put them to death. [13]And you* will be hated by all because of My name, but the one having endured to [the] end—this one will be saved.

[14]"Now when you* see the '*abomination of the desolation*' [or, the '*detestable thing that causes desecration*'], the one having been spoken [of] by Daniel the prophet, having stood where it should not be (the one reading, let him be understanding [or, be paying attention]), then the [ones] in Judea must be fleeing into the mountains. [Dan 8:13; 9:27; 12:11] [15]Then the [one] on the housetop must not go down to the house, nor go in to take anything out of his house. [16]And the one being in the field must not return to the [things] behind [him], to take up his garment [or, coat]. [17]But how horrible it will be to the ones having in the womb [fig., who are pregnant] and to the ones nursing [babies] in those days! [18]But be praying that your* flight does not happen in winter. [19]For [in] those days [there] will be tribulation [or, affliction], such as [there] has not been like from [the] beginning of [the] creation which God created, until now, and never at all shall be. [20]And if [the] Lord did not cut the days short, no flesh would be saved; but because of the chosen [or, the elect], whom He Himself chose, He cut the days short.

[21]"Then, if anyone says to you*, 'Look! Here [is] the Christ,' or, 'Look! There!' stop believing [him]. [22]For false christs and false prophets will be raised up, and they will give signs and wonders in order to be leading astray [fig., deceiving], if possible, even the chosen [or, the elect]. [23]But you*, be watching out! Listen! I have told you* all [things] in advance.

[24]"But in those days, after that tribulation, '*the sun will be darkened, and the moon will not give its light. [25]And the stars of heaven* [or, *the sky*] *will be falling,*' and the powers, the [ones] in the heavens, will be shaken. [Isaiah 34:4; Joel 2:10; 2:31] [26]And then they will see '*the Son of Humanity coming in clouds*' with much power and glory! [Dan 7:13] [27]And then He will send out His angels, and He will gather together His chosen [ones] from the four winds, from [the] farthest limits of the earth to [the] farthest limits of heaven.

[28]"Now learn the allegory from the fig tree: whenever its branch already becomes tender and is putting forth the leaves, you* know that the summer is near. [29]So also you*, when you* see these [things] happening, you* know that it is near—at the doors! [30]Positively, I say to you*, this generation [or, race] shall by no means pass away until all these [things] happen. [31]Heaven and earth will pass away, but My words shall by no means pass away.

[32]"But concerning that day or hour no one knows, neither the angels, the [ones] in heaven, nor the Son, except the Father. [33]Be watching! Be staying alert, and be praying! For you do not know when the time is. [34][It is] like a person away from home on a journey, having left his house, and having given the authority to his slaves [or, having put his slaves in charge] and to each [one] his work, commanded also the doorkeeper that he should keep watching. [35]Therefore, keep watching! For you* do not know when the lord of the house is coming—evening, or midnight, or rooster-crowing [fig., before dawn], or early morning—[36]lest, having come suddenly [or, unexpectedly], he finds you* sleeping. [37]So what I say to you*, I say to all—keep watching!"

*14*Now the Passover and the [Feast of] Unleavened Bread were two days away. And the chief priests and the scribes were seeking how, by deceit [or, treachery], having arrested Him, they should be killing Him. ²But they were saying, "Not during the feast, lest perhaps there will be a riot of the people."

³And He being in Bethany, in the house of Simon the leper [or, the one with a skin disease], while He reclines [to eat], a woman came having an alabaster jar of ointment [or, perfume] of very costly, pure nard [i.e., an aromatic oil]. And having broken the alabaster jar, she poured [it] over His head. ⁴But some were expressing indignation to one another and saying, "Why has this waste of the ointment been made? ⁵For this could have been sold for more than three hundred denarii [i.e., 300 days' wages] and given to the poor." And they were harshly criticizing her.

⁶But Jesus said, "Leave her alone! Why do you* cause her troubles [fig., bother her]? She worked a good work to Me [or, performed a good deed for Me]. ⁷For the poor you* always have with yourselves, and whenever you* are desiring you* are able to do them good, but Me you* do not always have. ⁸What she had [or, was able to do], this [woman] did. She undertook beforehand to anoint My body for the burial preparation. ⁹Positively, I say to you*, wherever this Gospel is proclaimed in the whole world, also what this [woman] did will be spoken of—in memory of her."

¹⁰Then Judas Iscariot, one of the twelve, went away to the chief priests so that he could betray Him to them. ¹¹Now having heard, they were glad, and they promised to give to him money [or, silver]. And he began seeking how conveniently [or, how at a convenient time] he should betray Him.

¹²And on the first day of the [Feast of] Unleavened Bread, when they were sacrificing the Passover [or, Paschal Lamb], His disciples say to Him, "Where do You desire [that], having gone away, we should prepare, so that You shall eat the Passover?" ¹³Then He sends out two of His disciples and says to them, "Be going into the city, and a man will meet you* carrying a pitcher of water. Follow him. ¹⁴And wherever he enters, say to the owner of the house, 'The Teacher says, "Where is the guest room, where I shall eat the Passover with My disciples?"' ¹⁵And he will show to you* a large, upstairs room, having been furnished [and] ready. There prepare [it] for us." ¹⁶And His disciples went out and came into the city, and they found [everything] just as He said to them. And they prepared the Passover.

¹⁷Then evening having come, He comes with the twelve. ¹⁸And while they are reclining and eating, Jesus said, "Positively, I say to you*, one of you*, the one eating with Me, will betray Me." ¹⁹So they began to be sorrowful and to say to Him, one by one, "Surely not I, is it?" And another, "Surely not I, is it?" ²⁰But answering, He said to them, "One of the twelve, the one dipping with Me into the bowl. ²¹Indeed, the Son of Humanity is going away, just as it has been written concerning Him. But how horrible it will be to that man through whom the Son of Humanity is betrayed! It was better for him if that man had not been born!"

²²And while they are eating, Jesus having taken bread, having bestowed a blessing upon [it], broke and gave [it] to them, and said, "Take, eat; this is My

body." ²³And having taken the cup, having given thanks, He gave [it] to them, and they all drank of it. ²⁴Then He said to them, "This is My blood of the New Covenant, the [blood] being poured out for many. ²⁵Positively, I say to you*, no longer by any means shall I drink of the fruit of the grapevine until that day when I shall be drinking it new in the kingdom of God."

²⁶And having sung a hymn, they went out to the Mount of Olives. ²⁷Then Jesus says to them, "You* will all be caused to stumble because of Me on this night, because it has been written, *'I will strike the Shepherd, and the sheep will be scattered.'* [Zech 13:7] ²⁸But after I am raised, I will go before you* to Galilee." ²⁹But Peter said to Him, "Even if all will be caused to stumble, but not I." ³⁰And Jesus said to him, "Positively, I say to you that you today, on this night, before a rooster crows twice, three times you will deny [or, disown] Me." ³¹But he kept saying all the more insistently, "Even if it should be necessary [for] me to die with You, by no means shall I deny [or, disown] You." And in the same manner also they all were saying.

³²And they come to a place, the name of which [is] Gethsemane. And He says to His disciples, "Sit here until I pray." ³³Then He takes Peter and James and John with Him, and He began to be greatly disturbed and to be suffering from distress. ³⁴And He says to them, "My soul is deeply grieved, even to death; stay here, and be keeping watch." ³⁵Then having approached [God] a little [distance away], He fell on the ground, and He began praying that if it is possible, the hour should pass away from Him. ³⁶And He was saying, "Dad [Gr. *Abba*], Father! All [things] are possible to You; take this cup away from Me; but not what I desire, but what You [desire]."

³⁷Then He comes and finds them sleeping. And He says to Peter, "Simon, are you sleeping? You were not able to keep watch one hour, were you? ³⁸Keep watching and praying so that you* shall not enter into temptation; the spirit indeed [is] eager [or, willing], but the flesh weak." ³⁹And again having gone away, He prayed, saying the same thing. ⁴⁰Then having returned, He found them again sleeping, for their eyes had been weighed down. And they did not known what they should answer to Him. ⁴¹And He comes the third time and says to them, "Are you* still sleeping and resting? It is enough! The hour came. Look! The Son of Humanity is being betrayed into the hands of the sinners. ⁴²Arise! Let us go. Look! The one betraying Me has come near."

⁴³Then immediately, while He is still speaking, Judas arrives, one of the twelve, and with him a large crowd with swords and clubs, from the chief priests and the scribes and the elders. ⁴⁴Now the one betraying Him had given a prearranged signal to them, saying, "Whomever I kiss, it is He; arrest Him and lead Him away under guard." ⁴⁵And having come, immediately having approached Him, he says to Him, "Rabbi, Rabbi!" And he affectionately kissed Him. ⁴⁶So they laid their hands on Him and arrested Him.

⁴⁷But a certain one of the ones having stood by, having drawn his sword, struck the slave of the high priest and cut off his ear. ⁴⁸And answering, Jesus said to them, "[Why] did you* come out as against a robber [or, insurrectionist] with swords and clubs to arrest Me? ⁴⁹Daily I was with you* teaching in the temple,

and you* did not arrest Me, <u>but</u> [you* are doing so now] so that the Scriptures shall be fulfilled." ⁵⁰And having left Him, they all fled.

⁵¹And one certain young man followed Him, having put a linen cloth on [his] naked [body], and the young men seized him. ⁵²But having left behind the linen cloth, he fled from them naked.

⁵³And they led Jesus away to the high priest. And all the chief priests and the elders and the scribes gather together to him. ⁵⁴And Peter followed Him from a distance, as far as inside the courtyard of the high priest. And he was sitting together with the [courtyard] attendants and warming himself near the fire. ⁵⁵Now the chief priests and the entire High Council [or, Sanhedrin] were seeking testimony against Jesus to put Him to death, and they were not finding [any]. ⁵⁶For many were giving false testimony against Him, but their testimonies were not consistent. ⁵⁷And some having risen up, were giving false testimony against Him, saying, ⁵⁸<u>We</u> heard Him saying, '<u>I</u> will tear down this temple made with human hands, and by three days, I will build another not made with human hands.'" [cp. John 2:19] ⁵⁹But not even in this manner was their testimony consistent.

⁶⁰Then the high priest, having risen up in the middle [of them], questioned Jesus, saying, "You do not answer anything, do You? What do these testify against You?" ⁶¹But He was keeping silent and answered nothing. Again the high priest was questioning Him, and says to Him, "Are <u>You</u> the Christ—the Son of the Blessed [One]?" ⁶²So Jesus said, "<u>I</u> am! And you* will see *'the Son of Humanity sitting at the right hand of the Power'* and *'coming with the clouds of heaven* [or, *the sky*]!'" [Psalm 110:1; Dan 7:13,14]

⁶³Then the high priest, having torn his clothes, says, "What need do we still have of witnesses? ⁶⁴You heard the blasphemy! What does it appear to you*?" Then they all condemned Him to be deserving of death. ⁶⁵And some began to be spitting on Him and to be covering His face [or, blindfolding Him] and to be beating Him with their fists and to be saying to Him, "Prophesy!" And the attendants kept hurling at [fig., kept striking] Him with slaps of their hands [or, with blows from a club].

⁶⁶And Peter being in the courtyard beneath, one of the slave-girls of the high priest comes, ⁶⁷and having seen Peter warming himself, having looked attentively at him, she said, "<u>You</u> also were with Jesus the Nazarene!" ⁶⁸But he denied [it], saying, "I do not know [Him], neither do I understand what you are saying." And he went forth outside into the porch, and a rooster crowed. ⁶⁹And the slave-girl having seen him again, began to be saying to the ones having stood by, "This one is [one] of them." ⁷⁰But he was again denying [it].

And after a little while, again, the ones having stood by said to Peter, "Surely you are [one] of them, for you also are a Galilean, and your accent is like [theirs]." ⁷¹But he began to be invoking a curse upon himself and to take an oath, "I do not know this One of whom you* speak." ⁷²Then a second time a rooster crowed. And Peter remembered the saying which Jesus said to him, "Before a rooster crows twice, you will deny [or, disown] Me three times." And having cast upon [it] [fig., having thought seriously about it], he began weeping. [see Mark 14:30]

15And immediately, in the early morning, the chief priests having created a plot [or, having held a consultation] with the elders and scribes and the whole High Council [or, Sanhedrin], having bound Jesus, they led [Him] away and handed [Him] over to Pilate. ²And Pilate questioned Him, "Are <u>You</u> the King of the Jews?" So answering, He said to him, "<u>You</u> are saying [it]." ³And the chief priests were accusing Him [of] many [things]. ⁴Then Pilate again questioned Him, saying, "You do not answer anything, do You? Look [at] how many [things] they testify against You!" ⁵But Jesus no longer answered anything, with the result that Pilate was amazed.

⁶Now at [the] feast he would release to them one prisoner, whomever they would request. ⁷And [there] was the [one] being called Barabbas, having been bound with the fellow insurrections, who had committed murder in the insurrection. ⁸And the crowd having cried out, began to be asking [him to do] just as he would always do for them. ⁹But Pilate answered to them, saying, "Do you* desire [that] I release to you* the King of the Jews?" ¹⁰For he knew that because of envy the chief priests had handed Him over. ¹¹But the chief priests shook up [fig., incited] the crowd, so that he should rather release Barabbas to them.

¹²So Pilate answering, again said to them, "What then do you* desire [that] I should do to [the One] whom you* call King of the Jews?" ¹³Then they again cried out [or, they shouted back], "Crucify Him!" ¹⁴But Pilate said to them, "But what evil did He do?" But they cried out [or, shouted] all the more, "Crucify Him!"

¹⁵So Pilate, because he was wanting to do [what would] satisfy the crowd, released to them Barabbas. And he handed over Jesus—after having [Him] beat with a whip—so that He should be crucified. ¹⁶Then the soldiers led Him away inside the court, which is [called the] Fortified Palace [or, Praetorium], and they call together the entire garrison. ¹⁷And they clothe Him with a purple robe, and having woven a victor's wreath [or, crown] of thorns, they put [it] on Him. ¹⁸Then they began to be saluting Him, "Hail, the King of the Jews!" ¹⁹And they kept beating His head with a reed and kept spitting on Him, and having placed the knee [fig., having knelt down], they began prostrating themselves in [mock] reverence before Him.

²⁰And when they [had] ridiculed Him, they stripped the purple robe off Him and clothed Him in His own garments. And they led Him out so that they should crucify Him. ²¹And they forced someone passing by into service—Simon, a Cyrenian, coming from [the] countryside (the father of Alexander and Rufus)—so that he should carry His cross. [see Acts 19:33; Rom 16:13] ²²Then they bring Him to the place [called] Golgotha (which is, having been translated, "Place of a Skull)."

²³And they tried giving Him wine having been flavored with myrrh to drink, but He did not take [it]. ²⁴And having crucified Him, they divide His garments, casting a lot on them [to determine] who should take what. ²⁵Now it was the third hour [i.e., 9:00 a.m.] when they crucified Him. ²⁶And the inscription of the accusation against Him had been inscribed—"The King of the Jews."

²⁷And they crucify two robbers [or, insurrectionists] with Him, one on [His] right hand, and one on His left. ²⁸And the Scripture was fulfilled, the one saying, *"And He was numbered with lawless ones."* [Isaiah 53:12]

²⁹And the ones passing by were deriding Him, shaking their heads, and saying, "Ha! The One tearing down the temple and in three days building [it]! ³⁰Save Yourself, and come down from the cross!" ³¹And likewise also the chief priests mocking [Him] to one another, along with the scribes, were saying, "Others He saved; Himself He is not able to save! ³²The Christ! The King of Israel! Let Him come down now from the cross so that we shall see and believe in Him." And the ones being crucified with Him were insulting Him.

³³Now the sixth hour [i.e., 12:00 noon] having come, darkness came over the whole land until the ninth hour [i.e., 3:00 p.m.]. ³⁴And at the ninth hour, Jesus shouted with a loud voice, saying [in Aramaic], *"Eloi, Eloi, lima sabachthani?"*—which is, having been translated, *"My God, My God, why did You abandon Me?"* [Psalm 22:1] ³⁵And some of the ones having stood by, having heard, said, "Listen! He is calling Elijah!" ³⁶So one [of them] having ran and having filled a sponge with wine vinegar and having put [it] around a reed, began giving [it] to Him to drink, saying, "Leave [Him] alone! Let us see if Elijah comes to take Him down."

³⁷But Jesus having released [fig., uttered] a loud cry, breathed His last. ³⁸Then the veil [or, curtain] of the sanctuary was torn in two, from top to bottom. ³⁹And the centurion, the one having stood opposite Him, having seen that, having cried out in such a manner, He breathed His last, said, "Truly this Man was God's Son!"

⁴⁰Now [there] were also women watching from a distance, among whom was both Mary the Magdalene [or, Mary, a woman from Magdala] and Mary the mother of James the less and of Joses, and Salome ⁴¹(who also, when He was in Galilee, would follow Him and would minister to Him), and many other women, the ones having come up together with Him to Jerusalem.

⁴²And now evening having come, since it was the preparation [day] (which is [the day] before the Sabbath), ⁴³Joseph of Arimathea, a prominent member of the High Council, who also himself was waiting for [or, expecting] the kingdom of God, having been brave enough, he went in to Pilate and requested for himself the body of Jesus. ⁴⁴And Pilate was amazed that He was already dead [or, wondered if He was already dead]. And having summoned the centurion, he questioned him if He was already dead. ⁴⁵And having found out from the centurion, he granted the body to Joseph.

⁴⁶And having bought linen cloth and having taken Him down, he wrapped Him in the linen cloth and laid Him in a tomb which had been cut out of rock. And he rolled a stone against [or, upon] the entrance of the tomb. ⁴⁷Now Mary the Magdalene and Mary [the mother] of Joses were watching where He is laid.

16 And the Sabbath having past, Mary the Magdalene and Mary [the mother] of James and Salome bought spices, so that having come they should anoint Him. ²And very early in the morning on the first [day] of [the] week [i.e. early Sunday morning], they come [or, go] to the tomb, the sun having risen. ³And they were saying to one another, "Who will roll away the stone for us from the entrance of the tomb?" [4]Then having looked up, they see that the stone had been rolled away—for it was extremely large. [5]And having entered into the tomb, they saw a young man sitting on the right, having been clothed in a long, white robe, and they were frightened.

[6]And he says to them, "Stop being frightened! You* seek Jesus the Nazarene, the One having been crucified. He was raised! He is not here! Look [at] the place where they laid Him. [7]But be going. Say to His disciples and to Peter that He is going before you* to Galilee; there you* will see Him, just as He said to you*." [8]And having gone out, they fled from the tomb. But trembling and amazement were holding them, and they said nothing to anyone, for they were afraid.

[9]Now having risen in the early morning on the first [day] of the week [i.e. early Sunday morning], He appeared first to Mary the Magdalene, from whom He had cast out seven demons. [10]That one having gone, told the ones having been with Him, while they were mourning and weeping. [11]And those ones, having heard that He is alive and was seen by her, refused to believe.

[12]But after these [things], to two of them, while they are walking about, He was revealed in a different form, while they are going into [the] countryside. [13]And those ones having gone, told to the rest, [but] they did not even believe them.

[14]Later, while they are reclining [to eat], He was revealed to the eleven, and He denounced their unbelief and stubbornness, because they did not believe the ones having seen Him after He had been raised. [15]And He said to them, "Having gone [or, Go] into all the world, proclaim the Gospel to all the creation. [16]The one having believed and having been baptized will be saved, but the one refusing to believe will be condemned. [17]Now these signs will accompany the ones believing: they will cast out demons in My name; they will speak with new tongues [fig., languages]; [18]they will take up serpents, and if they drink anything poisonous, it shall not harm them; they will lay hands on infirm [or, sickly] [people] and they will be well."

[19]So then, after He spoke to them, [the] Lord was taken up into heaven, and He sat at the right hand of God. [20]So having gone out, they preached everywhere, the Lord working with [them] and confirming the word through the accompanying signs. So be it!

The Gospel According to
Luke

1 Since many undertook to arrange in proper order an account about the events having been accomplished among us, ²just as they were handed down to us by the ones having became eye-witnesses and attendants of the Word from the beginning, ³it seemed good also to me, having closely followed [or, having investigated] every[thing] carefully from the beginning, to write [it out] to you in consecutive order [or, in an orderly fashion], most excellent Theophilus, ⁴so that you shall know the certainty [or, exact truth] about which you were instructed.

⁵[There] was in the days of Herod the king of Judea a certain priest by name Zacharias, from [the] division of Abijah, and his wife [was] from the daughters of Aaron, and her name [was] Elizabeth. ⁶Now they were both righteous before God, going in [fig., observing] all the commandments and regulations of the Lord blameless. ⁷And no child was [born] to them, because Elizabeth was barren, and both were advanced in their days.

⁸Now it happened, while he [was] serving as priest in the [appointed] order of his division before God, ⁹according to the custom of the priesthood, he was chosen by lot to offer incense, having entered into the temple of the Lord. ¹⁰And the whole multitude of the people was praying outside at the hour of incense. ¹¹And an angel of [the] Lord appeared to him, having stood on [the] right [side] of the altar of incense. ¹²And having seen [him], Zacharias was disturbed, and fear fell upon him.

¹³But the angel said to him, "Stop being afraid, Zacharias, for your petition was heard, and your wife Elizabeth will bear a son to you, and you will call his name John. ¹⁴And [there] will be joy to you and great happiness, and many will rejoice at his birth. ¹⁵For he will be great before the Lord, and he shall by no means drink wine and strong drink, and he will be filled [with the] Holy Spirit even from his mother's womb. ¹⁶And he will turn many of the sons [and daughters] of Israel to [the] Lord their God. ¹⁷And *he* will go before Him in [the] spirit and power of Elijah, to turn hearts of fathers to children, and disobedient [ones] to the way of thinking of righteous [ones], to make ready a people having been prepared for [the] Lord."

¹⁸And Zacharias said to the angel, "By what [fig., How] will I know this [will happen]? For I am an old man, and my wife is advanced in her days?" ¹⁹And answering, the angel said to him, "I am Gabriel, the one having stood in the presence of God, and I was sent to speak to you and to proclaim the good news to you [of] these [things]. ²⁰And listen! You will be silent and not being able to speak, until which day these [things] occur, because you did not believe my words, which will be fulfilled in their [appointed] time."

²¹And the people were waiting for Zacharias, and they began wondering [why] he [was] delaying in the temple. ²²But having come out, he was not being

able to speak to them, and they realized that he had seen a vision in the temple. And he was making gestures to them and was remaining mute.

²³And it happened, when the days of his sacred service were completed, he departed to his house. ²⁴Now after those days, his wife Elizabeth conceived, and she kept herself in seclusion [for] five months, saying, ²⁵"In this way the Lord has done to me, in [the] days in which He took notice of [me] to take away my disgrace among people."

²⁶Now in the sixth month the angel Gabriel was sent by God to a city of Galilee, to which [is the] name Nazareth, ²⁷to a virgin having been promised in marriage to a man, whose name [was] Joseph, from the house of David. And the name of the virgin [was] Mary. ²⁸And having come in, the angel said to her, "Greetings, [one] having been bestowed grace [or, having been shown kindness]! [cp. Eph 1:6] The Lord [is] with you. You have been blessed among women." ²⁹But having seen [him], she was greatly perplexed at his word and was pondering what sort of greeting this might be.

³⁰And the angel said to her, "Stop being afraid, Mary; for you [have] found favor with God! ³¹And listen! You will conceive in [your] womb, and you will give birth to a Son, and you will call His name Jesus ["Yahweh saves"]. ³²This One will be great, and He will be called [the] Son of the Most High. And [the] Lord God will give to Him the throne of David His father. ³³And He will reign over the house of Jacob into the ages [fig. forever], and of His kingdom there will be no end."

³⁴And Mary said to the angel, "How will this be since I do not know a man [fig., since I am a virgin]?" ³⁵And answering, the angel said to her, "[The] Holy Spirit will come upon you, and [the] power of the Most High will overshadow you, and so the Holy One being born will be called God's Son. ³⁶And listen! Elizabeth your relative, she also has conceived a son in her old age, and this is the sixth month to her, the one being called barren. ³⁷For every word will not be [fig., For nothing is] impossible with God!" ³⁸And Mary said, "Look! The slave of [the] Lord! May it be to me according to your word." And the angel departed from her.

³⁹Now Mary having risen in those days, she went to the mountainous [countryside] with haste, to a city of Judea. ⁴⁰And she entered into the house of Zacharias and greeted Elizabeth. ⁴¹And it happened, when Elizabeth heard the greeting of Mary, the baby leapt for joy in her womb. And Elizabeth was filled with [the] Holy Spirit. ⁴²And she exclaimed with a loud voice, and said, "You have been blessed among women, and the fruit of your womb has been blessed! ⁴³And why [has] this [happened] to me, that the mother of my Lord should come to me? ⁴⁴For listen! When the voice of your greeting came into my ears, the baby in my womb leapt for joy with great happiness! ⁴⁵And happy [or, blessed, and throughout book] [is] the one having believed, for [there] will be a fulfillment to the [things] having been spoken to her from [the] Lord."

⁴⁶And Mary said, "My soul magnifies the Lord, ⁴⁷and my spirit was very glad because of God my Savior. ⁴⁸For He looked with care upon the humble state of His slave. For, look! From now on all generations will consider me to be fortunate.

⁴⁹For the Mighty [One] did marvelous [things] to me, and holy [is] His name. ⁵⁰And His mercy [is] to generations of generations, to the ones fearing Him. ⁵¹He performed mightily with His arm; He scattered proud [ones] in [the] attitude of their heart. ⁵²He brought down rulers from thrones, and He exalted lowly [ones]. ⁵³Hungering [ones] He satisfied with good [things], and [ones] being rich He sent away empty. ⁵⁴He helped Israel His servant, [in order] to remember [His] mercy, ⁵⁵just as He spoke to our fathers, to Abraham and to his seed into the age [fig., to his descendents forever]." ⁵⁶Now Mary remained with her about three months, and she returned to her house.

⁵⁷Then the time was fulfilled to Elizabeth [for] her to give birth, and she bore a son. ⁵⁸And the neighbors and her relatives heard that [the] Lord was magnifying His mercy with her, and they were rejoicing with her. ⁵⁹And it happened on the eighth day [that] they came to circumcise the young child, and they were going to call him by the name of his father Zacharias. ⁶⁰And answering, his mother said, "Not [so], but he will be called John."

⁶¹And they said to her, "[There] is none among your relatives who is called by this name." ⁶²So they began making gestures to his father [as to] what he might want him to be called. ⁶³And having asked for a writing tablet, he wrote, saying, "John is his name." And they were all amazed. ⁶⁴Then his mouth was immediately opened and his tongue, and he began speaking, praising God! ⁶⁵And fear came on all the ones living around them, and all these sayings were being discussed in all the mountainous [countryside] of Judea. ⁶⁶And all the ones having heard [these things], they themselves kept [fig., reflected on] [them] in their hearts, saying, "What then will this young child be?" And [the] hand of [the] Lord was with him.

⁶⁷And Zacharias his father was filled with [the] Holy Spirit and prophesied, saying, ⁶⁸"Blessed [is the] Lord, the God of Israel, because He visited and made redemption for His people. ⁶⁹And He raised up a horn of salvation for us in the house of David His servant, ⁷⁰just as He spoke through [the] mouth of His holy prophets, the [ones] from antiquity, ⁷¹[announcing] salvation from our enemies and from the hand of all the ones hating us, ⁷²[in order] to do mercy with [fig., show mercy to] our fathers and to remember His holy covenant, ⁷³[performing the] oath which He vowed to Abraham our father, ⁷⁴to give to us, [by] having been delivered out of the hand of our enemies, to [be able to] sacredly serve Him without fear, ⁷⁵in holiness and righteousness before Him all the days of our life!

⁷⁶"And you, young child, will be called a prophet of the Most High, for you will go before [the] face [fig., presence] of [the] Lord to prepare His ways, ⁷⁷to give knowledge of salvation to His people by [the] forgiveness of their sins, ⁷⁸because of [the] bowels of mercy [fig., tender mercies] of our God, with which the Rising [Sun] from on high [has] visited us, ⁷⁹to give light to the ones sitting in darkness and [the] shadow of death, to guide our feet into [the] way of peace."

⁸⁰Now the young child was growing and was being strengthened in spirit, and he was in the deserts until [the] day of his public appearance to Israel.

2Now it happened in those days [that] a decree went out from Caesar Augustus [for] all the inhabited earth to be registered. [2]This registration [or, census] was [the] first while Cyrenius was governing Syria. [3]And all began traveling to be registered, each to his own city.

[4]So Joseph also went up from Galilee, from [the] city of Nazareth, to Judea, to the city of David, which is being called Bethlehem, because of his being from [the] house and family of David, [5]to register himself with Mary, the woman having been promised to him in marriage, being pregnant. [6]Then it happened, in their being there [fig., while they were there], the days were completed [for] her to give birth. [7]And she gave birth to her firstborn Son, and she wrapped Him in long strips of cloth and laid Him in the feeding trough [or, manger, and in verses 12,16], because there was no place for them in the guest room [or, inn].

[8]And shepherds were in the same region staying in the fields and watching over their flock [during the] watches of the night. [9]And look! An angel of [the] Lord stood over them, and [the] glory of [the] Lord shone around them, and they feared [with] a great fear. [10]And the angel said to them, "Stop being afraid! For listen! I bring to you* the Gospel [or, Good News, and throughout book] of great joy, which will be to all people. [11]Because a Savior was born to you* today in the city of David, who is Christ [the] Lord! [12]And this [will be] the sign to you*: You* will find a Baby having been wrapped in long strips of cloth, lying in a feeding trough."

[13]And suddenly [there] was with the angel a multitude of the heavenly army [or, host], praising God, and saying, [14]"Glory to God in [the] highest, and peace on earth, good will among people!"

[15]And it happened, when the angels departed from them into heaven, that the men, the shepherds, said to one another, "Let us go then as far as Bethlehem and see this [thing], the one having happened, which the Lord revealed to us." [16]And having hurried, they came and found both Mary and Joseph, and the Baby lying in the feeding trough. [17]So having seen, they spread the news [or, reported accurately] about the word, the one having been spoken to them about this young Child. [18]And all the ones having heard were amazed about the things having been spoken by the shepherds to them. [19]But Mary was keeping [fig., treasuring] all these things, pondering [them] in her heart. [20]And the shepherds returned, glorifying and praising God for all which they heard and saw, just as it was spoken to them.

[21]And when eight days were completed to circumcise Him, then His name was called Jesus, the [name] having been called [fig., given] by the angel before He was conceived in the womb. [22]And when the days of their purification were completed, according to the Law of Moses, they brought Him to Jerusalem to present [Him] to the Lord, [23]just as it has been written in [the] Law of [the] Lord, *"Every male opening a womb will be called holy to the LORD,"* [Exod 13:2,12,15] [24]and to give a sacrifice, according to the [word] having been spoken in [the] Law of [the] Lord, *"A pair of turtle-doves or two young pigeons."* [Lev 12:8]

[25]And look! There was a man in Jerusalem whose name [was] Simeon, and this man was righteous and devout, waiting for [or, expecting] the comforting help of Israel, and [the] Holy Spirit was upon him. [26]And it had been divinely told him by the Holy Spirit [that he would] not see death before he saw the Christ ["the Anointed

One"] of [the] Lord. ²⁷And he came by the Spirit to the temple, and the parents brought in the young Child Jesus, [for] them to do according to the custom of the Law concerning Him.

²⁸Then <u>he</u> took Him into his arms and blessed God and said, ²⁹"Now You are releasing Your slave, Master, according to Your word, in peace. ³⁰Because my eyes saw Your salvation, ³¹which You prepared before [the] face [fig., in the presence] of all the peoples, ³²a light for revelation to Gentiles, and [the] glory of Your people Israel!" ³³And Joseph and His mother [were] marveling at the things being spoken concerning Him.

³⁴And Simeon blessed them, and said to Mary His mother, "Listen! This [One] is set [fig., appointed] for [the] fall and rising up of many in Israel, and for a sign being spoken against ³⁵(but also a sword will pierce your own soul), in order that the thoughts of many hearts shall be revealed."

³⁶And [there] was Anna, a prophetess, a daughter of Phanuel, of the tribe of Asher, this [woman] having advanced in many days, having lived with a husband seven years from her virginity [i.e., her husband died seven years after they were married], ³⁷and she [was] a widow of about eighty-four years [or, then [as] a widow [until] she was about eighty-four years [old]], who was not departing from the temple, sacredly serving night and day with fastings and petitions. ³⁸And <u>she</u>, at that very hour, having come up, began giving thanks to the Lord, and she was speaking about Him to all the ones waiting for [or, expecting] redemption in Jerusalem.

³⁹And when they completed all [things], the ones according to the Law of [the] Lord, they returned to Galilee, to their own city Nazareth. ⁴⁰And the young Child was growing and was being strengthened in spirit, being filled with wisdom, and the grace of God was upon Him.

⁴¹And His parents were traveling yearly to Jerusalem to the feast of the Passover. ⁴²And when He became twelve years old, they having gone up to Jerusalem, according to the custom of the feast, ⁴³and having completed the days, in their returning, the Child Jesus stayed behind in Jerusalem, and Joseph and His mother did not know [it]. ⁴⁴But having supposed Him to be among the group of travelers, they went a day's journey and were looking for Him among their relatives and among their acquaintances. ⁴⁵And not having found Him, they returned to Jerusalem seeking Him.

⁴⁶And it happened, after three days, they found Him in the temple, sitting in [the] middle of the teachers, both listening to them and questioning them. ⁴⁷But all the ones hearing Him were themselves being astonished at His understanding and His answers. ⁴⁸And having seen Him, they were amazed. And His mother said to Him, "Child, why did You [treat] us in this way? Listen! Your father and I, being deeply distressed, were seeking You." ⁴⁹And He said to them, "Why [is it] that you* were seeking Me? Did you* not know that it is necessary [for] Me to be [occupied] in the [things] of My Father?" ⁵⁰And they did not understand the saying which He spoke to them.

⁵¹And He went down with them and came to Nazareth, and He was being subjected to them. And His mother was treasuring all these things in her heart. ⁵²And Jesus kept advancing in wisdom and in stature, and in favor with God and people.

3 Now in [the] fifteenth year of the government of Tiberius Caesar, Pontius Pilate governing Judea, and Herod being ruler of the quadrant [or, the tetrarch] of Galilee, but Philip his brother being ruler of the quadrant of Ituraea and of the region of Trachonitis, and Lysanias being ruler of the quadrant of Abilene, ²in the time of [the] high priest Annas and [the high priest] Caiaphas, [the] word of God came to John, the son of Zacharias, in the wilderness.

³And he went into the whole surrounding region of the Jordan [River], proclaiming a baptism [or, immersion, and throughout book] of repentance to [or, for; or, because of] forgiveness of sins, ⁴as it has been written in a scroll of the words of Isaiah the prophet, saying:

A voice of [one] shouting in the wilderness, "Prepare the way of [the] LORD; be making His paths straight! ⁵*Every valley will be filled and every mountain and hill will be leveled, and the crooked [roads] will be [made] into straight [roads] and the rough [roads made] into smooth roads.* ⁶*And all flesh will see the salvation of God!"* [Isaiah 40:3-5; LXX]

⁷Then he began saying to the crowds coming out to be baptized [or, immersed, and throughout book] by him, "Brood of vipers! Who warned you* to flee from the coming wrath? ⁸Therefore, produce fruits worthy of repentance, and do not begin to be saying within yourselves, 'We have a father, Abraham,' for I say to you*, God is able to raise up children to Abraham out of these stones. ⁹But also the axe is already laid to the root of the trees. Therefore, every tree not producing good fruit is cut down and thrown into fire!"

¹⁰And the crowds began questioning him, saying, "What then will we do?" ¹¹Then answering, he says to them, "The one having two tunics must share with the one not having [any], and the one having food must be doing likewise."

¹²And tax collectors also came to be baptized, and they said to him, "Teacher, what will we do?" ¹³Then he said to them, "Be collecting no more than the [amount] having been instructed to you*." ¹⁴Now [the] ones serving as soldiers also began questioning him, saying, "And what will <u>we</u> do?" And he said to them, "Violently extort money [from] no one nor accuse [anyone] falsely for money, and be content with your* wages."

¹⁵Now the people are anticipating, and all are pondering in their hearts concerning John, whether he might be the Christ [or, the Messiah, and throughout book]. ¹⁶John answered, saying to all, "<u>I</u> indeed baptize you* in water [or, with water, and throughout book], but [One] mightier than I is coming, of whom I am not worthy to loose the strap of His sandals, <u>He</u> will baptize you* in [or, with] [the] Holy Spirit and fire; ¹⁷whose winnowing shovel [is] in His hand, and He will thoroughly clean out His threshing floor and will gather the wheat into His barn, but He will burn the chaff in unquenchable fire!" ¹⁸So then urging many other [things], he was proclaiming the Gospel to the people.

¹⁹But Herod, the ruler of the quadrant [or, the tetrarch], being rebuked by him concerning Herodias the wife of his brother and concerning all the evils which Herod did, ²⁰added also this to all [his other sins] and locked up John in prison.

²¹Now it happened, while all the people [were coming] to be baptized, Jesus also having been baptized, and praying, heaven [or, the sky] was opened, ²²and the Holy Spirit descended in bodily form like a dove upon Him, and a voice came out of heaven saying, "<u>You</u> are My Son—the Beloved—in You I am well-pleased!"

²³And Jesus Himself was about thirty years old when He began [His public ministry], being, as was being supposed, [the] son of Joseph, the [son] of Eli, ²⁴the [son] of Matthat, the [son] of Levi, the [son] of Melchi, the [son] of Janna, the [son] of Joseph, ²⁵the [son] of Mattathias, the [son] of Amos, the [son] of Naum, the [son] of Esli, the [son] of Naggai, ²⁶the [son] of Maath, the [son] of Mattathias, the [son] of Semei, the [son] of Joseph, the [son] of Judah,

²⁷the [son] of Joanan, the [son] of Rhesa, the [son] of Zerubbabel, the [son] of Shealtiel, the [son] of Neri, ²⁸the [son] of Melchi, the [son] of Addi, the [son] of Cosam, the [son] of Elmodam, the [son] of Er, ²⁹the [son] of Jose, the [son] of Eliezer, the [son] of Jorim, the [son] of Matthat, the [son] of Levi, ³⁰the [son] of Simeon, the [son] of Judah, the [son] of Joseph, the [son] of Jonan, the [son] of Eliakim, ³¹the [son] of Melea, the [son] of Mennan, the [son] of Mattatha, the [son] of Nathan, the [son] of David,

³²the [son] of Jesse, the [son] of Obed, the [son] of Boaz, the [son] of Salmon, the [son] of Nahshon, ³³the [son] of Amminadab, the [son] of Aram, the [son] of Hezron, the [son] of Perez, the [son] of Judah, ³⁴the [son] of Jacob, the [son] of Isaac, the [son] of Abraham, the [son] of Terah, the [son] of Nahor, ³⁵the [son] of Serug, the [son] of Reu, the [son] of Peleg, the [son] of Eber, the [son] of Shelah, ³⁶the [son] of Cainan, the [son] of Arphaxad, the [son] of Shem, the [son] of Noah, the [son] of Lamech, ³⁷the [son] of Methuselah, the [son] of Enoch, the [son] of Jared, the [son] of Mahalaleel, the [son] of Cainan, ³⁸the [son] of Enos, the [son] of Seth, the [son] of Adam, the [son] of God.

4 Then Jesus, full of [the] Holy Spirit, returned from the Jordan [River] and was led by the Spirit into the wilderness, ²being tempted forty days by the Devil. And He did not eat anything in those days, and they having been completed, afterward He was hungry. ³And the Devil said to Him, "Since You are God's Son, speak to this stone that it shall become bread." ⁴And Jesus answered to him, saying, "It has been written, *'A person will not live on bread only, <u>but</u> on every word of God.'"* [Deut 8:3]

⁵And the Devil, having brought Him into a high mountain, showed to Him all the kingdoms of the inhabited earth in a moment of time. ⁶And the Devil said to Him, "I will give to You all this authority and their glory, because it has been handed over to me, and I give it to whomever I shall be desiring. ⁷Therefore, if <u>You</u> prostrate Yourself in worship before me all will be Yours." ⁸And answering, Jesus said to him, "Get behind Me, Satan! It has been written, *'You will prostrate yourself in worship before [the] LORD your God, and Him only you will sacredly serve.'"* [Deut 6:13]

⁹And he brought Him to Jerusalem and set Him on the pinnacle of the temple and said to Him, "Since You are God's Son, throw Yourself down from here. ¹⁰For it has been written, *'To His angels He will give orders concerning You, to guard over You'*, ¹¹and, *'They will lift You up on [their] hands, lest You strike Your foot against a stone.'"* [Psalm 91:11,12] ¹²And answering, Jesus said to him, "It has been said, *'You will not put [the] LORD your God to the test.'"* [Deut 6:16] ¹³And having completed every temptation, the Devil departed from Him until an [opportune] time.

¹⁴And Jesus returned in the power of the Spirit to Galilee, and news went out through the whole surrounding region concerning Him. ¹⁵And He began teaching in their synagogues, being glorified by all. ¹⁶And He came to Nazareth, where He had been brought up. And He entered, according to His custom, on the day of the Sabbaths into the synagogue, and He stood up to read aloud [the Scriptures].

¹⁷And a scroll of Isaiah the prophet was handed to Him. And having unrolled the scroll, He found the place where it had been written:

¹⁸*[The] Spirit of [the] LORD [is] upon Me, on account of which He anointed Me to proclaim the Gospel to poor [ones]; He has sent Me to heal the ones having been broken [in] heart* [fig., *who have become despondent within themselves*], *to proclaim deliverance to captives and recovery of sight to blind [ones], to send away [ones] having been oppressed with deliverance,* ¹⁹*to proclaim [the] acceptable year of [the] LORD.* [Isaiah 61:1,2, LXX]

²⁰And having rolled up the scroll, having returned [it] to the attendant, He sat down. And the eyes of all in the synagogue were looking intently on Him. ²¹Then He began to be saying to them, "Today this Scripture has been fulfilled in your* ears." ²²And all were bearing witnesses to Him [or, were speaking well of Him], and they were wondering at the gracious words, the ones having come out from His mouth. And they were saying, "This is the Son of Joseph, is it not?"

²³And He said to them, "Certainly, you* will say this allegory [or, proverb] to Me, 'Physician, heal yourself—as many [things] as we heard having been done in Capernaum, do also here in Your hometown.'" ²⁴Then He said, "Positively, I say to you*, no prophet is accepted in his hometown. ²⁵But I say to you* in truth, many widows were in Israel during the days of Elijah, when the sky was shut for three years and six months, when great famine came upon all the land; ²⁶and to none of them was Elijah sent, except to Zarephath [in] the [region] of Sidon, to a woman, a widow. ²⁷And many lepers [or, ones with a skin disease] were in Israel in the time of Elisha the prophet, and none of them was cleansed, except Naaman the Syrian."

²⁸And all [the people] in the synagogue were filled with rage, hearing these things. ²⁹And having risen, they forced Him outside the city and brought Him as far as [the] brow of the hill on which their city had been built, in order to throw Him down from the cliff. ³⁰But He, having passed through [the] middle of them, went away.

³¹And He went down to Capernaum, a city of Galilee, and was teaching them on [one of] the Sabbaths. ³²And they were being astonished at His teaching, because His word was with authority.

³³And in the synagogue was a man having a spirit of an unclean [or, defiling] demon. And he cried out with a loud voice, ³⁴saying, "Away! What to us and to You [fig., What have we to do with You], Jesus, O Nazarene? Did You come to destroy us? I know You, who You are—the Holy One of God!" ³⁵And Jesus rebuked him, saying, "Be silenced, and come out from him!" And the demon having thrown him down into [the] midst, came out from him, in no way having harmed him. ³⁶And amazement came upon all, and they were conversing with one another, saying, "What [is] this word, that with authority and power He commands the unclean [or, defiling] spirits, and they come out?" ³⁷And a report concerning Him was spreading into every place of the surrounding region.

³⁸Then having risen from the synagogue, He entered into the house of Simon. But Simon's mother-in-law was being afflicted with a high fever, and they asked Him about her. ³⁹And having stood over her, He rebuked the fever, and it left her! Then immediately, having risen, she began serving them.

⁴⁰Then [at] the setting of the sun, all, as many as were having ones being sick [with] various diseases, brought them to Him. Then having put His hands on each one of them, that One healed them. ⁴¹But demons also were coming out from many, crying out and saying, "<u>You</u> are the Christ, the Son of God!" And rebuking [them], He would not allow them to be speaking, because they knew Him to be the Christ.

⁴²Now day having come, having gone out, He went into a deserted place, and the crowds were seeking Him, and they came to Him and were trying to restrain Him [so He would] not be going from them. ⁴³But He said to them, "It is necessary [for] Me to also proclaim the Gospel of the kingdom of God to the other cities, for this [reason] I have been sent." ⁴⁴And He was preaching in the synagogues of Galilee.

5And it happened, while the crowd [was] pressing upon Him to be hearing the word of God, that He had stood beside the lake of Gennesaret. ²And He saw two boats standing beside the lake, but the fishermen, having disembarked from them, were washing their nets. ³Then having stepped into one of the boats, which was Simon's, He asked him to put out a little from the land. And having sat down, He began teaching the crowds from the boat. ⁴Then when He ceased speaking, He said to Simon, "Put out into the deep [water] and let down your* nets for a catch."

⁵And answering, Simon said to Him, "Master, having labored through the whole night we caught nothing, but at Your word I will let down the net." ⁶And having done this, they caught a great number of fish, but their net began breaking. ⁷And they signaled to their partners, the ones having come in the other boat, to help them. And they came and filled both the boats, with the result that they were being sunk.

[8]But Simon Peter having seen, fell down at the knees of Jesus, saying, "Depart from me, because I am a sinful man, O Lord!" [9]For astonishment seized him, and all the [ones] with him, at the catch of the fish which they caught, [10]and likewise also James and John, [the] sons of Zebedee, the ones [who] were partners with Simon. And Jesus said to Simon, "Stop being afraid! From now [on] you will be catching people." [11]And having brought the boats to the land, having left all, they followed Him.

[12]And it happened, in His being [fig., while He was] in one of the cities, that look!, a man full of [or, covered with] leprosy [or, a skin disease], and having seen Jesus, having fallen on [his] face, he implored Him, saying, "Lord, if You are willing, You are able to cleanse me." [13]And having stretched out His hand, He took hold of him, having said, "I am willing. Be cleansed!" And immediately the leprosy [or, skin disease] went away from him! [14]And He gave strict orders to him to tell no one, "<u>But</u> having gone away, show yourself to the priest and bring as an offering for your cleansing [or, purification] just as Moses directed, for a testimony to them."

[15]But all the more the report was going about [fig., spreading] concerning Him, and large crowds were gathering to be hearing [Him] and to be healed by Him of their sicknesses. [16]But He would [often] withdraw into the desert places and [would] be praying.

[17]And it happened, on one of the days, that <u>He</u> was teaching; and Pharisees and teachers of the Law were sitting [there], the ones having come from every village of Galilee and of Judea and of Jerusalem, and [the] power of [the] Lord was [present] for [Him] to be healing them. [18]And look! Men [were] carrying a man on a cot, [who] had been paralyzed, and they were trying to bring [him] in and to lay him before Him. [19]And not having found by what [way] they could bring him in because of the crowd, having gone up on the roof, they lowered him with the stretcher through the tiles into the middle before Jesus. [20]And having seen their faith, He said to him, "Man, your sins have been forgiven you."

[21]And the scribes and the Pharisees began to reason, saying, "Who is this [Man] who speaks blasphemies? Who is able to be forgiving sins, except God alone?" [22]So Jesus having known their thoughts, answering, said to them, "What are you* reasoning in your* hearts? [23]Which is easier to say, 'Your sins have been forgiven you?' or to say, 'Get up, and walk about?' [24]But so that you* shall know that the Son of Humanity has authority on the earth to be forgiving sins"—He said to the one having been paralyzed, "I say to you, get up, and having taken up your stretcher, be going to your house." [25]And immediately having gotten up before them, having taken up [the stretcher] on which he was lying, he went away to his house, glorifying God! [26]And astonishment took hold of [them] all, and they began glorifying God and were filled with fear, saying "We saw remarkable [things] today!"

[27]And after these [things], He went out and saw a tax collector by name Levi sitting at the tax office. And He said to him, "Be following Me!" [28]And having left all behind, having gotten up, he follow Him. [29]And Levi made a great banquet for Him in his house. And [there] was a large crowd of tax collectors and others

who were with them reclining [to eat]. ³⁰And their scribes and the Pharisees began complaining against His disciples, saying, "Why do you* eat and drink with the tax collectors and sinners?" ³¹And answering, Jesus said to them, "The ones being healthy have no need of a physician, but the ones having it badly [fig., those who are sick]. ³²I have not come to call righteous [ones], but sinners to repentance."

³³Then they said to Him, "Why do the disciples of John frequently fast and make petitions, likewise also the [disciples] of the Pharisees, but Yours eat and drink?" ³⁴But He said to them, "You* are not being able to make the sons of the bridal chamber [fig., the bridegroom's attendants] to fast in which [time] [fig., while] the bridegroom is with them, are you*? ³⁵But days will come when also the bridegroom shall be taken away from them, then they will fast in those days."

³⁶Now He also was telling them an allegory [or, parable, and throughout book]: "No one puts a patch of new clothing on old clothing, but if not [fig., or else] the new [cloth] tears, and also [the patch] from the new does not match with the old. ³⁷And no one puts new wine into old wineskins, but if not [fig., or else] the new wine will burst the wineskins, and it will be poured out, and the wineskins will be destroyed. ³⁸Instead, new wine must be put into new wineskins, and both are preserved together. ³⁹And no one having drunk old [wine] immediately desires new, for he says, 'The old is better.'"

*6*Now it happened on the second-first Sabbath [fig., the first Sabbath of the second month] He [was] passing through the grainfields, and His disciples were picking the heads of grain and were eating, rubbing [the husk from the grain] with their hands. ²And some of the Pharisees said to them, "Why are you* doing what is not lawful to be doing on the Sabbaths?" ³And answering, Jesus said to them, "Did you* not even read this, what David did when he was hungry, himself and the ones being with him? ⁴How he went into the house of God and took the loaves of bread of the presentation [fig., the consecrated bread] and ate [them] and gave [them] also to the [ones] with him, which it is not lawful to eat, except only to the priests?" [cp. 1Sam 21:3-6; Exod 29:32-33] ⁵And He was saying to them, "The Son of Humanity is Lord even of the Sabbath."

⁶Now it also happened on another Sabbath, He went into the synagogue and [was] teaching. And a man was there, and his right hand was withered [fig., deformed]. ⁷Now the scribes and the Pharisees were watching closely if He will heal on the Sabbath, so that they should find an accusation against Him. ⁸But He Himself knew their thoughts, and He said to the man, the one having the withered [fig., deformed] hand, "Get up, and stand in the middle!" So having risen, he stood. ⁹Then Jesus said to them, "I will ask you* something: Is it lawful to do good on the Sabbaths, or to do evil? To save life or to kill?" ¹⁰And having looked around at them all, He said to him, "Stretch out your hand!" Then he did so, and his hand was restored whole like the other! ¹¹But they were filled with extreme rage, and they began discussing with one another what they might do to Jesus.

¹²Now it happened in those days, He went out into the mountain to pray and was spending the night in the prayer of God [or, in prayer to God]. ¹³And when it became day, He summoned His disciples, and having chosen from them twelve,

whom also He named apostles: ¹⁴Simon, whom He also named Peter, and Andrew his brother, James and John, Philip and Bartholomew, ¹⁵Matthew and Thomas, James the [son] of Alphaeus, and Simon, the one being called [the] Zealot, ¹⁶Judas [the son; or, the brother] of James, and Judas Iscariot, who also became a traitor.

¹⁷And having come down with them, He stood on a level place with a crowd of His disciples and a large crowd of the people from all Judea and Jerusalem and the costal region of Tyre and Sidon, who came to hear Him and to be healed from their diseases; ¹⁸and the ones being harassed by unclean [or, defiling] spirits, and they were being healed. ¹⁹And the whole crowd was trying to be touching Him, because power was going out from Him, and He was healing [them] all.

²⁰And having lifted up His eyes to His disciples, He said: "Happy [are] the poor, because yours* is the kingdom of God. ²¹Happy [are] the ones hungering now, because you* will be filled. Happy [are] the ones weeping now, because you* will laugh. ²²Happy are you* when people hate you*, and when they exclude you* and insult [or, denounce] [you*] and cast out [fig., scorn] your* name as evil because of the Son of Humanity. ²³Rejoice in that day and leap for joy! For listen! Your* reward [is] great in heaven, for according to these [things] [fig., in like manner] were their fathers doing to the prophets.

²⁴"Nevertheless, how horrible it will be to you*, the rich, because you* are receiving your* comfort in full. ²⁵How horrible it will be to you*, the ones having been satisfied, because you* will be hungry. How horrible it will be to you*, the ones laughing now, because you* will mourn and weep. ²⁶How horrible it will be when people speak well of you*, according to these [things] [fig., in like manner] were their fathers doing to false prophets.

²⁷"But I say to you*, the ones hearing: Be loving your* enemies. Be doing good to the ones hating you*. ²⁸Be blessing the ones cursing you*. Be praying on behalf of the ones mistreating you*. ²⁹To the one striking you on the cheek, be offering also the other; and from the one taking away from you your cloak, do not refuse the tunic also. ³⁰So be giving to every[one] asking of you, and stop demanding back from the one taking away your [belongings]. ³¹And just as you* want that people shall be doing to you*, you* also be doing to them likewise. ³²And if you* love the ones loving you*, what grace [fig., credit] is [it] to you*? For even the sinful love the ones loving them. ³³And if you* are doing good to the ones doing good to you*, what grace [fig., credit] is [it] to you*? For even the sinful do the same. ³⁴And if you* are lending [to the ones] from whom you* hope [or, expect] to receive back, what grace [fig., credit] is [that] to you*? For even sinful [ones] lend to sinners so that they shall receive back the same [amount].

³⁵"Nevertheless, be loving your* enemies, and be doing good, and be lending, hoping for [or, expecting] nothing in return; and your* reward will be great, and you* will be sons [and daughters] of [the] Most High, because He is kind to the ungrateful and evil. ³⁶Therefore, continue becoming merciful, just as your* Father also is merciful. ³⁷And stop judging, and by no means shall you* be judged. Stop condemning, and by no means shall you* be condemned. Be forgiving, and you* will be forgiven. ³⁸Be giving, and it will be given to you*—good measure, having been pressed down and shaken and running over, they will give into your* bosom

[or, lap]. For with the same measure with which you* are measuring, it will be measured to you* in return."

³⁹Then He spoke an allegory to them, "A blind [person] is not able to be leading a blind [person], is he? They will both fall into a ditch, will they not? ⁴⁰A disciple is not above his teacher, but every[one] having been fully trained will be like his teacher. ⁴¹But why do you look at the speck, the [one] in your brother's [fig., friend's, neighbor's, or compatriot's] eye, but you do not notice the log, the [one] in your own eye? ⁴²Or how are you able to be saying to your brother, 'Brother, allow [me], I will take out the speck, the [one] in your eye,' [but] you yourself do not notice the log in your own eye? Hypocrite! First take the log out of your eye, and then you will see clearly to take out the speck, the [one] in your brother's eye.

⁴³"For a good tree does not produce rotten fruit, nor does a rotten tree produce good fruit. ⁴⁴For each tree is known by its own fruit. For they do not gather figs from thorn plants, nor do they pick a grape cluster from a thorn bush. ⁴⁵The good person out of the good treasure of his heart produces the good [thing], and the evil person out of the evil treasure of his heart produces the evil [thing]. For out of the abundance of the heart his mouth speaks.

⁴⁶"And why do you* call Me, 'Lord, Lord,' and do not do what I say? ⁴⁷Every[one] coming to Me and hearing My words and doing them, I will show you* to whom he is like: ⁴⁸he is like a person building a house, who dug and went deep and laid a foundation on the solid rock, but a flood having come, the stream burst upon that house and was not able to shake it, for it had been founded on the solid rock. ⁴⁹But the one having heard and not having done [so], is like a person having built a house on the ground without a foundation, [against] which the stream burst upon, and immediately it fell, and the ruin of that house became great."

7Now when He completed all His sayings in the ears of the people, He entered into Capernaum. ²Then a certain centurion's slave having [it] badly [fig., being ill] was about to be coming to the end [of his life], who was highly valued by him. ³But having heard about Jesus, he sent elders of the Jews to Him, urgently asking Him, in order that having come He would completely cure his slave. ⁴Then having come to Jesus, they began earnestly pleading with Him, saying, "He is worthy to whom You will do this, ⁵for he loves our nation, and he himself built the synagogue [for] us."

⁶Then Jesus began going with them, but [when] He [was] already not far away from the house, the centurion sent friends to Him, saying to Him, "Lord, stop being troubled, for I am not worthy that You should enter under my roof. ⁷For this reason, I did not consider myself worthy to come to You, but say a word, and my slave boy will be healed. ⁸For I also am a man having been appointed under authority, having soldiers under myself. And I say to this [one], 'Go,' and he goes; and to another, 'Be coming,' and he comes; and to my slave, 'Do this,' and he does [it]." ⁹So having heard these things, Jesus marveled at him, and having turned to the crowd following Him, He said, "I say to you*, not even in Israel did I find

so great a faith!" [10]And the ones having been sent, having returned to the house, found the ailing slave being in good health!

[11]And it happened on the next [day], He was traveling to a city being called Nain, and many of His disciples were going along with Him, and a large crowd. [12]Then as He approached the gate of the city, that look!, [a man] having died was being carried out [for burial], an only-begotten [or, one and only] son of his mother, and she [was] a widow, and a large crowd of the city was with her. [13]And the Lord having seen her was moved with compassion towards her, and He said to her, "Stop weeping!" [14]And having approached, He took hold of the open coffin. Then the ones carrying [it] stood still, and He said, "Young man, I say to you, get up!" [15]And the dead [man] sat up and began to speak! And He gave him to his mother. [16]But fear [or, awe] took hold of [them] all, and they began glorifying God, saying, "A great prophet has risen up among us," and, "God [has] visited His people!" [17]And the account of this went out in all Judea about Him, and in all the surrounding region.

[18]And his disciples reported to John about all these [things]. [19]And John having summoned a certain two of his disciples, sent to Jesus, saying, "Are <u>You</u> the Coming [One], or do we look for another?"

[20]So having come to Him, the men said, "John the Baptist [or, the Immerser, and throughout book] sent us to You, saying, 'Are <u>You</u> the Coming [One], or do we look for another?'" [21]Then in that very hour He healed many from diseases and plagues and evil spirits, and to many blind [people] He graciously gave [the ability] to be seeing. [22]And answering, Jesus said to them, "Having gone, report to John what you* saw and heard, that blind [people] receive [their] sight, lame [people] walk, lepers [or, ones with a skin disease] are cleansed, deaf [people] hear, dead [people] are raised, poor [people] have the Gospel proclaimed [to them]. [23]And happy is whoever is not caused to stumble [fig., is not offended] because of Me."

[24]Now the messengers of John having gone away, He began to be saying to the crowds concerning John: "What have you* gone out into the wilderness to see? A reed having been shaken by the wind? [25]<u>But</u> what have you* gone out to see? A man having been dressed in soft [fig., delicate] clothing? Listen! The [ones] in splendid clothes and living in luxury are in the royal [palaces] of kings! [26]<u>But</u> what have you* gone out to see? A prophet? Yes, I say to you*, and much more [than] a prophet. [27]This is [he] concerning whom it has been written, *'Look! I am sending My messenger before Your face [fig., ahead of You], who will prepare Your way before You.'* [Mal 3:1] [28]For I say to you*, no one is a greater prophet among the [ones] born of women than John the Baptist, but the least in the kingdom of God is greater than he."

[29]And all the people having heard, and the tax collectors, they justified God [or, acknowledged God's righteousness], having been baptized with the baptism of John. [30]But the Pharisees and the lawyers rejected the counsel [or, purpose] of God for themselves, not having been baptized by him.

[31]"To what then will I compare the people of this generation? And to what are they similar to? [32]They are similar to young children, the ones sitting in a

marketplace and calling to one another and saying, 'We played a flute for you*, and you* did not dance; we mourned for you*, and you* did not weep!' ³³For John the Baptist came neither eating bread nor drinking wine, and you* say, 'He has a demon!' ³⁴The Son of Humanity came eating and drinking, and you* say, 'Look! A man, a glutton, and a drunkard, a friend of tax collectors and sinners!' ³⁵And wisdom was justified [or, vindicated] by all her children."

³⁶Now a certain one of the Pharisees was asking Him that He would eat with him. And having gone into the house of the Pharisee, He reclined [to eat]. ³⁷And look! A woman in the city, who was a sinner, having known that He is reclining [to eat] in the house of the Pharisee, having brought an alabaster jar of ointment [or, perfume], ³⁸and having stood behind [Him] beside His feet weeping, she began to be wetting His feet with her tears and was wiping [them] dry with the hairs of her head, and she kept affectionately kissing His feet and was anointing [them] with the ointment.

³⁹But the Pharisee, the one having called [or, having invited] Him, having seen, spoke within himself, saying, "This one, if He were a prophet, would have known who and what sort of woman [it is] who is touching Him, that she is a sinner." ⁴⁰And answering, Jesus said to him, "Simon, I have something to say to you." Then he says, "Teacher, say [it]." ⁴¹"[There] were two debtors to a certain creditor. The one was owing five hundred denarii, but the other fifty [i.e., 500 and 50 days' wages, respectively]. ⁴²But when they did not have [anything] to pay back, he freely forgave both. So tell [Me], which of them will love him more?" ⁴³Then answering, Simon said, "I suppose that [it is the one] to whom he freely forgave the greater [amount]." And He said to him, "You judged correctly."

⁴⁴And having turned to the woman, He said to Simon, "See this woman? I entered into your house; you did not give water for My feet, but this [woman] wet My feet with her tears and wiped [them] dry with the hairs of her head. ⁴⁵You did not give a kiss to Me, but this [woman], from what [time] [fig., since] I came in [has] not stopped affectionately kissing my feet. ⁴⁶You did not anoint My head with oil, but this [woman] anointed My feet with ointment. ⁴⁷For this reason, I say to you, her many sins have been forgiven, because she loved much. But [the one] to whom little is forgiven, loves little."

⁴⁸Then He said to her, "Your sins have been forgiven." ⁴⁹And the ones reclining [to eat] with [Him] began to be saying within themselves, "Who is this, who also forgives sins?" ⁵⁰But He said to the woman, "Your faith has saved you; be going in peace."

8And it happened in the next [fig., afterward] that <u>He</u> was traveling through every city and village preaching and proclaiming the Gospel of the kingdom of God, and the twelve [were] with Him, ²and certain women who had been healed of evil spirits and sicknesses: Mary, the one being called Magdalene [i.e. because she was from Magdala], from whom seven demons had gone out, ³and Joanna wife of Chuza, steward of Herod, and Susanna and many others, who were providing for them from their possessions.

⁴Now a large crowd having gathered, and the [people] from every city were coming to Him, He spoke by [way of] an allegory: ⁵"The one sowing went out to sow his seed, and in his sowing, some [seed] indeed fell beside the road, and it was trampled down, and the birds of the sky devoured it. ⁶And other [seed] fell on the rock, and having grown up, it withered away, because of not having moisture. ⁷And other [seed] fell in [the] middle of the thorn plants, and the thorn plants having grown up with [it], choked it. ⁸And other [seed] fell into the good ground, and having grown up, it produced fruit a hundred fold." These [things] saying, He was calling out, "The one having ears to be hearing, let him hear [or, pay attention]!"

⁹But His disciples began questioning Him, saying, "What might this allegory be [fig., What does this allegory mean]?" ¹⁰Then He said, "To you* it has been given to know the secrets [or, mysteries] of the kingdom of God, but to the rest in allegories; so that *'seeing they shall not be seeing, and hearing they shall not be understanding.'* [Isaiah 6:9, LXX]

¹¹"Now this is the [meaning of the] allegory: The seed is the word of God. ¹²Now the [ones] beside the road are the ones hearing, then the Devil comes and snatches away the word from their heart, lest having believed, they are saved. ¹³But the [ones] on the rock [are those] who, whenever they hear, receive the word with joy, and these have no root, who for a time believe, and in time of temptation [or, trial] fall away. ¹⁴But the [seed] having fallen into the thorns, these are the ones having heard, and going, are choked by anxieties and riches and pleasures of [this] life, and do not produce mature fruit. ¹⁵But the [seed] in the good ground, these are such who with an upright and good heart, having heard the word, hold [it] fast and bear fruit with patient endurance.

¹⁶"Now no one having lit a lamp covers it with a container or puts [it] under a bed, but he puts [it] on a lampstand, so that the ones coming in shall be seeing the light. ¹⁷For no[thing] is hidden which will not become evident, nor secret which will not be known and come to light. ¹⁸Therefore, be watching how you* hear, for whoever shall be having, it will be given to him, and whoever shall not be having, even what he seems to be having will be taken away from him."

¹⁹Now His mother and brothers having come to Him, and they were not able to get near to Him because of the crowd. ²⁰And it was reported to Him, saying, "Your mother and Your brothers have stood outside wanting to see You." ²¹But answering, He said to them, "My mother and My brothers are these: the ones hearing the word of God and doing it."

²²And it happened, on one of those days, that He stepped into a boat with His disciples, and He said to them, "Let us cross over to the other side of the lake." And they put out to sea. ²³But as they sailed, He fell asleep. And a storm of wind [fig., a windstorm] came down onto the lake, and they began being swamped and were being in danger. ²⁴Then having approached, they awakened Him, saying, "Master, Master, we are perishing!" And having gotten up, He rebuked the wind and the raging of the water, and they ceased, and it became calm! ²⁵And He said to them, "Where is your* faith?" Then having been afraid, they marveled, saying to

one another, "Who then is this, that He commands even the winds and the water, and they obey Him?"

²⁶And they sailed to the region of the Gadarenes, which is opposite Galilee. ²⁷Then when He got out on the land, [there] met Him a certain man from the city, who was having [fig., was possessed by; or, oppressed by] demons for a long time, and he was not dressing himself with a garment, and he was not living in a house, but in the tombs. ²⁸Now having seen Jesus, and having cried out, he fell down before Him and said with a loud voice, "What to me and to You [fig., What have I to do with You], Jesus, Son of the Most High God? I beg You, do not torment me!" ²⁹For He gave strict orders to the unclean [or, defiling] spirit to come out from the man, for many times it had seized him, and he was being bound with chains and shackles, being guarded; and breaking the bonds, he was being driven by the demons into the uninhabited [areas].

³⁰Then Jesus questioned him, saying, "What is your name?" But he said, "Legion" (because many demons [had] entered into him). ³¹And he kept imploring Him that He would not command them to go away into the bottomless pit [or, the abyss]. ³²Now a herd of many pigs was in that place being fed in the mountain, and they kept imploring Him that He would permit them to enter into these, and He permitted them. ³³Then the demons having gone out from the man, entered into the pigs, and the herd stampeded down the steep bank into the lake and were drowned.

³⁴Now the ones feeding [the pigs], having seen the [thing] having happened, fled and reported [it] in the city and in the fields. ³⁵Then they came out to see the [thing] having happened, and they came to Jesus and found the man from whom the demons had gone out, having been clothed and being of sound mind, sitting at the feet of Jesus, and they were frightened. ³⁶Now the ones having seen [it], reported to them also how the one having been demon-possessed [or, oppressed by demons] was cured. ³⁷And the whole multitude of the surrounding region of the Gadarenes asked Him to go away from them, because they were gripped with great fear. Then having stepped into the boat, He returned.

³⁸Now the man from whom the demons had gone out began begging Him to be with Him, but Jesus sent Him away, saying, ³⁹"Be returning to your house and describe fully what great things God did to you." And he went away proclaiming throughout the whole city what great things Jesus did to him.

⁴⁰Then it happened, when Jesus returned, the crowd received [or, welcomed] Him, for they were all looking for Him. ⁴¹And look! A man came whose name [was] Jairus, and he was an official of the synagogue. And having fallen at the feet of Jesus, he began imploring Him to come to his house, ⁴²because an only-begotten [or, one and only] daughter was to him [fig., he only had one daughter] about twelve years [old], and she was dying. But while He [was] going away, the crowds were pressing against Him.

⁴³And a woman being with a flow of blood for twelve years, who having spent her whole livelihood on physicians was not able to be healed by any, ⁴⁴having approached [Him] from behind, touched the fringe of His cloak. And immediately the flow of her blood stood [fig., stopped]! ⁴⁵And Jesus said, "Who [is] the one

having touched Me?" But all [were] denying [it]. Peter and the [ones] with him said, "Master, the crowds are pressing against You and crowding [You], and You say, 'Who [is] the one having touched Me?'" ⁴⁶But Jesus said, "Someone touched Me, for I knew [that] power has gone out from Me." ⁴⁷So the woman having seen that she did not escape notice, came trembling. And having fallen before Him, declared to Him before all the people for what reason she [had] touched Him, and how she was healed immediately. ⁴⁸Then He said to her, "Take courage, daughter, your faith has cured you. Be going in peace."

⁴⁹While He is still speaking, someone comes from the synagogue leader saying to Him, "Your daughter has died. Stop troubling the Teacher." ⁵⁰But Jesus having heard, answered Him, saying, "Stop being afraid; only be believing, and she will be cured." ⁵¹Then having come to the house, He did not allow anyone to go in, except Peter and John and James and the father of the child and the mother. ⁵²Now they were all weeping and beating their breasts [fig., mourning] for her. But He said, "Stop weeping. She did not die, but is sleeping!"

⁵³And they began laughing at Him, knowing that she [had] died. ⁵⁴But having sent [them] all outside, and having taken hold of her hand, He called out, saying, "Child, be getting up!" ⁵⁵And her spirit returned, and she got up immediately! And He instructed [that something] be given to her to eat. ⁵⁶And her parents were amazed, but He gave strict orders to them to tell no one the [thing] having happened.

*9*Now having called the twelve together, He gave to them power and authority over all the demons and to be healing diseases. ²And He sent them out to be proclaiming the kingdom of God and to be healing the sick. ³And He said to them, "Be taking nothing for the journey, neither staff nor traveler's bag nor bread nor money; neither be having two coats apiece. ⁴And into whatever house you* enter, there be remaining, and from there be departing. ⁵And as many as do not receive you*, going out from that city, shake off even the dust from your* feet as a testimony against them." ⁶Then going out, they began going about through the villages, proclaiming the Gospel and healing everywhere.

⁷Now Herod, the ruler of the quadrant [or, the tetrarch], heard [about] all the [things] being done by Him, and he was thoroughly perplexed, because the [thing] being said by some [was] that John had been raised from [the] dead, ⁸but by some that Elijah [had] appeared, but by others that a prophet, one of the ancient [ones, had] risen. ⁹And Herod said, "I beheaded John, but who is this concerning whom I am hearing such things?" And he was trying to see Him.

¹⁰And the apostles having returned, related to Him what great [things] they did. And having taken them, He withdrew privately to a deserted place [belonging to] a city being called Bethsaida. ¹¹But the crowds having known [or, having found out], followed Him. And having received them, He began speaking to them concerning the kingdom of God and curing the ones having need of healing.

¹²Now the day began to be declining, and the twelve having approached, said to Him, "Send the crowd away, so that having gone away into the surrounding villages and the farms, they shall find lodging and find something to eat, because

here we are in a deserted place." [13]But He said to them, "<u>You*</u> give them [something] to eat." But they said, "We have no more than five loaves of bread and two fish, unless, having gone, <u>we</u> should buy food for all this people." [14]For they were about five thousand men.

But He said to His disciples, "Make them recline in groups [of] fifty each." [15]And they did so, and made all to recline. [16]Then having taken the five loaves of bread and the two fish, having looked up to heaven, He bestowed a blessing upon them and broke [the bread] in pieces and began giving [them] to the disciples to distribute to the crowd. [17]And they all ate and were filled! And twelve handbaskets were taken up of broken pieces of bread having been leftover to them.

[18]And it happened, while He [was] praying alone, the disciples gathered to Him, and He questioned them, saying, "Who do the crowds say Me to be [or, that I am]?" [19]Then answering, they said, "John the Baptist, but others, Elijah, but others, that a prophet, one of the ancient [ones, has] risen." [20]So He said to them, "But you*, who do you* say Me to be [or, that I am]?" Then answering, Peter said, "The Christ of God." [21]But having warned them, He gave strict orders [to them] to say this to no one, [22]saying, "It is necessary [for] the Son of Humanity to suffer many [things] and to be rejected by the elders and chief priests and scribes and to be killed and to rise [on] the third day."

[23]Then He said to [them] all, "If anyone desires to come after Me, he must deny [or, disown] himself and take up his cross and be following Me. [24]For whoever shall be desiring to save his life, will lose it, but whoever loses his life for My sake, this [one] will save it. [25]For what is a person benefited, having gained the whole world, but having lost or forfeited himself? [26]For whoever is ashamed of Me and of My words, this [one] the Son of Humanity will be ashamed of when He comes in His [own] glory and [the glory] of the Father and of the holy angels. [27]But I say to you* truly, [there] are some of the [ones] having stood here who by no means shall taste of death until they see the kingdom of God."

[28]Now it happened, about eight days after these words, that having taken Peter and John and James, He went up into the mountain to pray. [29]And it happened, while He [was] praying, the appearance of His face [became] different, and His clothing [became] dazzling white. [30]And look! Two men began conversing with Him, who were Moses and Elijah, [31]who, having appeared in glory, spoke of His departure [Gr., *exodus*] which He was about to be accomplishing in Jerusalem.

[32]But Peter and the [ones] with him having been overcome with sleep, but having become fully awake, they saw His glory, and the two men having stood with Him. [33]And it happened, as they [were] parting from Him, Peter said to Jesus, "Master, it is good for us to be here; and let us make three tents: one for You and one for Moses and one for Elijah"—not knowing what he [was] saying.

[34]But as he [was] saying these [things], a cloud came and overshadowed them, and they were frightened as they entered into the cloud. [35]And a voice came out of the cloud saying, "This is My Son—the Beloved! Be paying attention to Him!" [36]And after the voice came, Jesus was found alone. And they kept silent, and they reported to no one in those days anything of what they had seen.

[37]Now it happened on the next day, when they had come down from the mountain, a large crowd met Him. [38]And listen! A man from the crowd cried out, saying, "Teacher, I beg You to look with care upon My son, because he is my only-begotten [or, my one and only [son]]. [39]And listen! A spirit seizes him, and suddenly he cries out, and it tears him back and forth [fig., throws him into convulsions], with foaming, and it hardly [ever] departs from him, bruising him. [40]And I begged Your disciples that they would be casting it out, and they were not able."

[41]Then answering, Jesus said, "O unbelieving [or, faithless] and having been perverted generation, how long will I be with you* and put up with you*? Bring your son here." [42]But as he [was] still approaching, the demon dashed him to the ground and threw [him] into convulsions. Then Jesus rebuked the unclean [or, defiling] spirit and healed the child and gave him back to his father. [43]Then they were all amazed at the magnificence of God.

But while all [were] marveling at all [things] which Jesus did, He said to His disciples, [44]"You* put your* ears to these words, for the Son of Humanity is about to be betrayed into the hands of people." [45]But they were failing to understand this saying, and it was concealed from them, so that they did not perceive [the meaning of] it, and they were afraid to ask Him about this saying.

[46]Then a dispute came up among them, [as to] which of them might be the greatest. [47]But Jesus having seen the thought process of their heart [fig., having known what they were thinking within themselves], having taken hold of a young child, set him beside Himself, [48]and said to them, "Whoever receives this young child in My name receives Me, and whoever receives Me receives the One having sent Me. For the one being least among you* all, this one will be great."

[49]Then answering, John said, "Master, we saw someone casting out demons in Your name, and we prevented [or, forbid] him, because he does not follow with us." [50]And Jesus said to him, "Stop preventing [or, forbidding] [him], for who[ever] is not against us is for us."

[51]Now it happened, as the days [were] approaching [for] His ascension, that He fixed His face [fig., made a firm resolve] to go to Jerusalem, [52]and He sent messengers before His face [fig., ahead of Him]. And having gone, they went into a village of Samaritans in order to prepare for Him. [53]And they did not receive Him, because His face was [fig., He had resolved to be] going to Jerusalem. [54]So His disciples James and John having seen [this], said, "Lord, do You want [that] we should tell [fig., command] fire to come down from heaven and to consume them, as also Elijah did?" [55]But having turned, He rebuked them, and said, "You* do not know of what sort of spirit you* are! [56]For the Son of Humanity did not come to destroy people's lives, but to save!" And they went on to another village.

[57]Now it happened, as they [were] going on the road, someone said to Him, "I will follow You wherever You go, Lord." [58]And Jesus said to him, "The foxes have dens, and the birds of the sky nests, but the Son of Humanity does not have [any]where [to] be laying His head." [59]Then He said to another, "Be following Me!" And he said, "Lord, permit me, having gone away, first to bury my father." [60]But Jesus said to him, "Allow the dead to bury their own dead, but you, having

gone away, be proclaiming far and wide the kingdom of God." ⁶¹Then another also said, "I will follow You, Lord, but first permit me to say good-bye to the [ones] in my house." ⁶²But Jesus said to him, "No one having put his hand on a plough, and looking to the [things] behind [fig., looking back], is fit for the kingdom of God."

10 Now after these [things], the Lord appointed also seventy others, and He sent them two each [or, two by two] before His face [fig., ahead of Him] into every city and place where He Himself was about to be going. ²Then He was saying to them, "The harvest truly [is] plentiful, but the laborers [are] few. Therefore, implore the Lord of the harvest in order that He should put forth laborers into His harvest.

³"Be going away. Listen! I am sending you* out as lambs in [the] midst of wolves. ⁴Do not be carrying a money bag nor a traveler's bag nor sandals, and greet no one along the road. ⁵But into whatever house you* shall be entering, first be saying, 'Peace to this house.' ⁶And if a son [fig., person] of peace is there, your* peace will rest on him; but if not, it will return upon you*. ⁷Now be remaining in that very house, eating and drinking the [things] from them, for the laborer is worthy of his pay. Do not keep moving from house to house. [cp. 1 Tim 5:18]

⁸"And into whatever city you* are entering, and they are receiving you*, be eating the [things] being set before you*; ⁹and be healing the sick in it, and be saying to them, 'The kingdom of God has drawn near to you*.' ¹⁰And into whatever city you* are entering, and they are not receiving you*, having gone out into its open streets, say, ¹¹'Even the dust having clung to us from your* city, we ourselves wipe off against you*. Nevertheless, be knowing this, that the kingdom of God has drawn near to you*.' ¹²I say to you*, it will be more tolerable in that Day for Sodom than for that city.

¹³"How horrible it will be to you, Chorazin! How horrible it will be to you, Bethsaida! For if the miraculous works had occurred in Tyre and Sidon, the ones having occurred in you*, they [would have] repented long ago, sitting in sackcloth and ashes. ¹⁴Nevertheless, it will be more tolerable for Tyre and Sidon in the judgment than for you*. ¹⁵And you, Capernaum, the one having been exalted as far as heaven, you will be brought down as far as the realm of the dead [Gr., *hades*]. ¹⁶The one hearing you* hears Me, and the one rejecting you* [or, regarding you* as nothing] rejects Me, and the one rejecting Me rejects the One having sent Me."

¹⁷Then the seventy returned with joy, saying, "Lord, even the demons are subjected to us in Your name." ¹⁸But He said to them, "I was watching Satan having fallen like lightning out of heaven. ¹⁹Listen! I give to you* the authority to be treading on serpents and scorpions and on all the power of the enemy, and nothing by any means shall injure you*. ²⁰Nevertheless, stop rejoicing in this, that the spirits are subjected to you*, but be rejoicing that your* names were written in the heavens."

²¹In that hour Jesus was very glad in the Spirit [or, in His spirit] and said, "I praise You, Father, Lord of heaven and of the earth, that You hid these [things]

from wise and intelligent [people] and revealed them to young children. Yes, Father, because in this way it became well-pleasing before You." ²²And turning to the disciples, He said, "All [things] were handed over to Me by My Father, and no one knows who the Son is except the Father, and who the Father is except the Son and to whom[ever] the Son shall be desiring to reveal [Him]." ²³And having turned to the disciples, He said privately, "Happy [are] the eyes, the ones seeing what you* see. ²⁴For I say to you*, that many prophets and kings desired to see what you* see, and did not see, and to hear what you* hear, and did not hear."

²⁵And look! A certain lawyer stood up, testing Him and saying, "Teacher, [by] having done what, will I inherit eternal life?" ²⁶But He said to him, "What has been written in the Law? How do you read [it]?" ²⁷Then answering, he said, *" 'You will love [the] LORD your God with your whole heart* [fig., *your entire inner self*] *and with your whole soul and with your whole strength and with your whole understanding,' and 'your neighbor as yourself.'"* [Deut 6:5; Lev 19:18] ²⁸Then He said to him, "You answered correctly. Do this and you will live." ²⁹But that one wanting to be justifying himself [or, to be declaring himself righteous], said to Jesus, "And who is my neighbor?"

³⁰Then having taken up [the word] [fig., replying], Jesus said, "A certain man was going down from Jerusalem to Jericho and encountered robbers, who having both stripped him and having inflicted wounds, they went away, having left [him] as it turned out half dead. ³¹Now by a coincidence, a certain priest was going down on that road, and having seen him, he passed by on the opposite side [of the road]. ³²Then likewise also a Levite having been at the place, having come and seen, passed by on the opposite side.

³³"But a certain Samaritan, being on a journey, came by him, and having seen him, he was moved with compassion. ³⁴And having approached, he bandaged his wounds, pouring on oil and wine. Then having placed him on his own beast [of burden], he brought him to an inn and took care of him. ³⁵And on the next day, when he departed, having taken out two denarii [i.e., two days' wages], he gave [them] to the innkeeper and said to him, 'Take care of him, and whatever you spend besides, in my coming again, I will pay back to you.'

³⁶"So which of these three do you suppose to have become a neighbor of the one having fallen among the robbers?" ³⁷Then he said, "The one having done the mercy with him [fig., having shown him mercy]." Then Jesus said to him, "Be going, and you be doing likewise."

³⁸Now it happened, as they [were] going, that He entered into a certain village. Then a certain woman, by name Martha, welcomed Him into her house. ³⁹And to this [woman] was a sister [fig., she had a sister] being called Mary, who also having seated herself beside the feet of Jesus, was listening to His word. ⁴⁰But Martha was being distracted about much service, and coming up, she said, "Lord, You are concerned that my sister has been leaving me alone to be serving, are You not? Then tell her, that she should help along with me." ⁴¹But answering, Jesus said to her, "Martha, Martha, you are anxious and disquieted about many [things], ⁴²but of one [thing] there is need. But Mary chose the good part, which will not be taken away from her."

11 And it happened, while He [was] praying in a certain place, when He [had] finished, a certain one of His disciples said to Him, "Lord, teach us to pray, just as also John taught his disciples." ²Then He said to them, "Whenever you* are praying, be saying:

Our Father, the [One] in the heavens, let Your name be regarded as holy; Let Your kingdom come; let Your will be done, as in heaven, [so] also on the earth.
³Each day be giving us the bread sufficient for the day.
⁴And forgive us our sins, for also we ourselves forgive every[one] being indebted to us.
And do not lead us into temptation, but deliver us from evil [or, from the evil [one]]."

⁵And He said to them, "Which of you* will have a friend and will go to him at midnight and say to him, 'Friend, lend me three loaves of bread, ⁶since a friend came to me from a journey, and I do not have what I would set before him;' ⁷and that [one] answering from within shall say, 'Stop causing me troubles! The door has already been shut, and my young children are with me in bed. I am not able, having gotten up, to give to you.' ⁸I say to you*, even if he will not give to him, having gotten up, because of him being a friend, yet because of his shameless persistence, having gotten up, he will give to him as much as he needs. ⁹And I say to you*, be asking, and it will be given to you*; be seeking, and you* will find; be knocking, and it will be opened to you*. ¹⁰For every[one] asking receives, and the one seeking finds, and to the one knocking it will be opened. ¹¹"Now which father [among] you*, [if] his son will ask [for] a loaf of bread, he will not give to him a stone, will he? Or also [if he asks for] a fish, he will not give to him a serpent instead of a fish, will he? ¹²Or also if he asks [for] an egg, he will not give to him a scorpion, will he? ¹³If you* then being evil know [how] to be giving good gifts to your* children, how much more will the Father of heaven [fig., your* heavenly Father] give [the] Holy Spirit to the ones asking Him?"

¹⁴And He was casting out a demon, and it was mute. Then it happened, the demon having gone out, the mute [person] spoke, and the crowds marveled. ¹⁵But some of them said, "By Beelzebul [i.e. a Philistine deity, used as a name for the devil], ruler of the demons, He casts out demons." ¹⁶But others, testing [Him], were seeking a sign from Him from heaven. ¹⁷But knowing their thoughts, He said to them, "Every kingdom having been divided against itself is laid waste, and a house [divided] against a house falls. ¹⁸So if Satan also was divided against himself, how will his kingdom be made to stand? Because you* say [that] I am casting out demons by Beelzebul. ¹⁹But if I cast out demons by Beelzebul, by whom do your* sons [fig., disciples] cast [them] out? For this reason they will be your* judges. ²⁰But if I cast out demons by the finger of God, in that case, the kingdom of God came upon you*. ²¹When the strong [man] having been fully armed is guarding his own palace, his possessions

are in peace [fig., undisturbed]. ²²But when the [one] stronger than he, having come upon [him], overcomes him, he takes away his complete suit of armor in which he had relied on, and he distributes his spoils. ²³The [one] not with Me is against Me, and the [one] not gathering with Me scatters.

²⁴"When the unclean [or, defiling] spirit goes out from the person, it goes through waterless places seeking rest, and not finding [any], it says, 'I will return to my house from where I came out.' ²⁵And having come, it finds [it] having been swept and having been put in order. ²⁶Then it goes and takes along seven different spirits more evil [than] itself. And having come, they dwell there, and the last [state] of that person becomes worse [than] the first."

²⁷Now it happened, while He [was] saying these [things], a certain woman from the crowd having raised [her] voice, said to Him, "Happy [is] the womb, the one having carried You, and [the] breasts [from] which You nursed!" ²⁸But He said, "But rather, happy [are] the ones hearing the word of God and keeping [fig., obeying] [it]!"

²⁹Now [as] the crowds gathered even more, He began to be saying, "This generation is evil. It seeks a sign, and a sign will not be given to it, except the sign of Jonah the prophet. ³⁰For just as Jonah became a sign to the Ninevites, so also will the Son of Humanity be to this generation. [see Jonah 1:17] ³¹[The] Queen of [the] South will be raised up in the judgment with the men of this generation and will condemn them, because she came from the ends of the earth to hear the wisdom of Solomon. [see 1Kings 10:1-29] And listen! [One] greater than Solomon [is] here! ³²Men, Ninevites, will rise up in the judgment with this generation and will condemn it, because they repented at [or, because of] the proclamation of Jonah. [see Jonah 3:5] And listen! [One] greater than Jonah [is] here!

³³"But no one having lit a lamp puts [it] in a hidden place [or, a cellar] nor under the basket, <u>but</u> on the lampstand, so that the one coming in shall be seeing the light. ³⁴The lamp of the body is the eye. Therefore, when your eye is healthy, your whole body is also full of light. But when it is bad, your body is also dark. ³⁵Therefore, be watching out lest the light, the [one] in you, is darkness. ³⁶So if your whole body is full of light, not having any part darkened, the whole will be full of light, like when the lamp by its brightness shall be giving you light."

³⁷Now while [He was] speaking, a certain Pharisee was asking Him that He should dine with him. So having entered, He reclined [to eat]. ³⁸But the Pharisee having seen, marveled that He was not first baptized [or, ceremonially washed] before the meal. ³⁹Then the Lord said to him, "Now you*, the Pharisees, make the outside of the cup and of the wooden platter clean, but the inside of you* is full of violent greed and wickedness. ⁴⁰Fools! The One having made the outside also made the inside, did He not? ⁴¹Nevertheless, give the [things] being [or, what is] inside [as] charitable gifts. Then listen! All things are clean to you*.

⁴²"<u>But</u> how horrible it will be to you*, the Pharisees! Because you* tithe [i.e. give a tenth of] the mint and the rue [i.e. a scented herb] and every vegetable, and you* pass by [fig., overlook] the justice and the love of God. These [things] it is necessary to do, and those not to be neglecting. ⁴³How horrible it will be to you*, the Pharisees! Because you* love the first seats [fig., most important places] in

the synagogues and the greetings in the marketplaces. ⁴⁴How horrible it will be to you*, scribes and Pharisees, hypocrites! Because you* are like the unmarked tombs, and the people walking about above do not know [it]."

⁴⁵Then answering, one of the lawyers says to Him, "Teacher, by saying these [things] You also insult us." ⁴⁶But He said, "How horrible it will be to you* also, the lawyers! Because you* burden the people with hard to carry [fig., difficult] burdens, and you* yourselves do not touch the burdens with one of your* fingers.

⁴⁷"How horrible it will be to you*! Because you* build the tombs of the prophets, but your* fathers killed them. ⁴⁸Consequently, you* bear witness to and approve of the works of your* fathers, because they indeed killed them, but you* build their tombs! ⁴⁹For this reason the wisdom of God also said, I will send to them prophets and apostles, and [some] of them they will kill, and [some] they will persecute, ⁵⁰so that the blood of all the prophets, the [blood] being shed from the laying of the foundation of the world, shall be charged against this generation, ⁵¹from the blood of Abel to the blood of Zacharias, the one having perished between the altar and the house [of God]. [see Gen 4:8; 2Chr 24:20,21] Yes, I say to you*, it will be charged against this generation.

⁵²"How horrible it will be to you*, the lawyers! For you* took away the key of knowledge. You* yourselves did not enter, and you* hindered the ones entering in."

⁵³Now while He [was] speaking these [things] to them, the scribes and the Pharisees began to be terribly hostile towards [Him] and to be attacking Him with questions concerning many things, ⁵⁴lying in wait for Him, seeking to catch something out of His mouth [fig., to catch Him in something He might say], so that they should bring charges against Him.

12 At which time [fig., Meanwhile], when the countless thousands of the crowd had been gathered together, so as to be trampling on one another, He began to be saying to His disciples first [of all], "You* yourselves be watching out for the leaven [or, yeast] of the Pharisees, which is hypocrisy [or, insincerity]. ²But nothing has been concealed which will not be revealed, and hidden which will not be made known. ³Because whatever you* said in the darkness will be heard in the light, and what you* spoke to the ear in private rooms will be proclaimed on the housetops.

⁴"Now I say to you*, My friends, do not be afraid of the ones killing the body, and after these [things] are not having anything further to do. ⁵But I will show to you* whom you* should fear: fear the [One, who] after [having] killed is having authority to cast into hell [Gr., *gehenna*]. Yes, I say to you*, fear this [One]! ⁶Five sparrows are sold [for] two assars [i.e. copper coins worth about an hour's wage], are they not? And not one of them has been forgotten before God. ⁷But even the hairs of your* head have all been numbered. Therefore, stop fearing. You* are worth more than many sparrows!

⁸"Now I say to you*, all who shall confess Me before the people, the Son of Humanity also will confess with him before the angels of God. ⁹But the one having

denied [or, disowned] Me before the people will be denied before the angels of God. ¹⁰And all who will speak a word against the Son of Humanity, it will be forgiven to him; but to the one having spoken against [or, having blasphemed] the Holy Spirit, it will not be forgiven.

¹¹"Now when they shall be bringing you* before the synagogues and the rulers and the authorities, stop being anxious how or what you* are to speak in your* defense, or what you* should say. ¹²For the Holy Spirit will teach you* in that very hour what it is necessary to say."

¹³Then someone from the crowd said to Him, "Teacher, tell my brother to divide the inheritance with me." ¹⁴But He said to him, "Man, who appointed Me a judge or a divider [or, an arbitrator] over you*?" ¹⁵Then He said to them, "Be watching out for and be guarding yourselves against covetous desire [or, greed], because not in the abounding of his possessions is his life [fig., a person's life does not consist of the abundance of his possessions]."

¹⁶So He spoke an allegory to them, saying, "The field of a certain rich man brought forth well [fig., produced a bountiful harvest]. ¹⁷And he was pondering within himself, saying, 'What shall I do, because I do not have where I will gather [fig., room to store] my harvest?' ¹⁸And he said, 'This I will do: I will tear down my barns, and I will build larger ones, and there I will gather together [fig., store] all my crops and my goods. ¹⁹And I will say to my soul, "Soul, you have many goods laid up for many years, be resting [or, be taking it easy], eat, drink, [and] be celebrating!"' ²⁰But God said to him, 'Fool! This night they are demanding your soul from you. Now what you prepared, to whom will it be [fig., belong]?' ²¹In the same way [is] the one storing up [earthly riches] for himself and [who] is not rich toward God."

²²Then He said to His disciples, "For this reason I say to you*, stop being anxious [about] your* life, what you* shall eat, and [about] the body, what you* shall wear. ²³The life is more [than] nourishment, and the body [is more than] clothing. ²⁴Be considering the ravens, for they do not sow nor reap, to which there is no [fig., which do not have] storeroom nor barn, and God provides for them. How much more valuable you* are than the birds! ²⁵But which of you* [by] being anxious is able to add one cubit [about 18 inches or 45 centimeters] to his height? ²⁶So if you* are not able [to do] a very little [thing], why are you* anxious [about] the rest?

²⁷"Consider the lilies, how do they grow? They do not labor nor do they spin. But I say to you*, not even Solomon in all his glory was arrayed like one of these. ²⁸But if God clothes in such a manner the grass in the field, being [here] today and tomorrow is thrown into a furnace, how much more [will He clothe] you*, [O you*] of little faith? ²⁹And you*, stop seeking what you* shall eat or what you* shall drink, and stop being upset. ³⁰For all these [things] the nations of the world seek after, but your* Father knows that you* have need of these [things]. ³¹Nevertheless, be seeking the kingdom of God, and all these [things] will be added to you*.

³²"Stop being afraid, little flock, because your* Father was delighted to give to you* the kingdom. ³³Sell your* possessions and give charitable gifts. Make for

yourselves money bags [which] are not wearing out, an inexhaustible treasure in the heavens, where a thief does not come near nor does a moth destroy. ³⁴For where your* treasure is, there your* heart [fig., inner desire] will be also.

³⁵"Let your* waist be wrapped around [with a belt] [fig., Prepare yourselves], and [keep] the lamps burning. ³⁶And you* [are to be] like people waiting for their lord, when he returns from the marriage festivities, so that having come and knocked, immediately they shall open to him. ³⁷Happy [are] those slaves, whom the lord having come will find keeping watch. Positively, I say to you*, he will wrap [a belt] around himself and have them recline [to eat], and having come alongside, he will serve them. ³⁸And if he comes in the second watch [i.e. between 9:00 p.m. and midnight], [or] he even comes in the third watch [i.e. between midnight and 3:00 a.m.], and he finds [them] so, happy are those slaves.

³⁹"But know this, that if the master of the house had known what hour the thief [was] coming, he would have kept watch and would not have allowed [the walls of] his house to be dug through. ⁴⁰Therefore, you* also become ready, because the Son of Humanity is coming at the hour you* do not think [fig., expect]."

⁴¹Now Peter said to Him, "Lord, do You speak this allegory to us, or also to all?" ⁴²Then the Lord said, "Who then is the faithful and wise steward, whom the lord will put in charge over his household servants to give [them their] food allowance at [the right] time? ⁴³Happy [is] that slave, whom his lord having come, will find so doing. ⁴⁴Truly I say to you*, he will put him in charge over all his possessions. ⁴⁵But if that slave says in his heart, 'My lord is delaying to be coming,' and he begins to be beating the slave-boys and the slave-girls and to be eating and to be drinking and to be getting drunk, ⁴⁶the lord of that slave will come in a day in which he does not expect [him], and in an hour which he does not know, and he will cut him in two [fig., punish him severely], and he will appoint his portion with the unbelievers.

⁴⁷"So that slave, the one having known his lord's will and not having prepared nor having done according to his will, will be repeatedly beaten with many [lashes]. ⁴⁸But the one not having known, and having done [things] worthy of a beating, will be repeatedly beaten with few [lashes]. So to every[one] to whom much was given, much will be demanded from him, and to whom they entrusted much, all the more they will ask of him.

⁴⁹"I came to cast fire to the earth, and how I wish that it was already kindled! ⁵⁰But I have a baptism to be baptized [with], and how distressed I am until it is completed! ⁵¹Do you* think that I came to give peace on the earth? Not at all, I say to you*, but rather division! ⁵²For from now [on] five in one house will have been divided: three against two and two against three. ⁵³A father will be divided against a son and a son against a father, a mother against a daughter and a daughter against a mother, a mother-in-law against her daughter-in-law and a daughter-in-law against her mother-in-law." [see Micah 7:6]

⁵⁴Then He also said to the crowds, "Whenever you* see the cloud rising from [the] west, immediately you* say, 'A shower is coming,' and so it happens. ⁵⁵And whenever [you* see] a south wind blowing, you say*, 'It will be scorching heat [fig., It will be a hot day],' and so it happens. ⁵⁶Hypocrites! You know [how]

to be interpreting the face of the earth and of the sky, but how [is it] you* are not interpreting this time? ⁵⁷But why do you* not even judge of yourselves the righteous [thing] [fig., what is righteous]?

⁵⁸"For as you* are going with your opponent [in a lawsuit] to a ruler [or, magistrate], on the way give work [fig., make every effort] to have been released from [fig., to make a settlement with] him, lest he drag you to the judge, and the judge hand you over to the court officer, and the court officer throw you into prison. ⁵⁹I say to you, by no means shall you come out from there until you pay back even the last lepton [i.e. a small copper coin worth 1/1000th of an ounce or 0.025 grams of silver]."

13 Now some [people] were showing up at that very time reporting to Him about the Galileans whose blood Pilate mixed with their sacrifices. ²And answering, Jesus said to them, "Do you* think that these Galileans were sinners more than all the [other] Galileans, because they have suffered such [things]? ³Not at all, I say to you*, but if you* are not repenting, you* will all likewise perish. ⁴Or those, the eighteen, on whom the lookout tower in Siloam fell and killed them, do you* think that these were debtors more [fig., worse sinners] than all the [other] people dwelling in Jerusalem? ⁵Not at all, I say to you*, but if you* are not repenting, you* will all likewise perish."

⁶Then He spoke this allegory: "A certain [man] had a fig tree having been planted in his vineyard, and he came looking for fruit on it and did not find [any]. ⁷Then he said to the vineyard-keeper, 'Look! Three years I [have] come looking for fruit in this fig tree and do not find [any]. Cut it down! Why does it even use up the ground?' ⁸But answering, he says to him, 'Lord, let it alone this year also, until which [time] I dig around it and put piles of manure [on it]. ⁹And if then it produces fruit [fine], but if not, in the coming [year] you will cut it down.'"

¹⁰Now He was teaching in one of the synagogues on the Sabbath. ¹¹And look! [There] was a woman having a spirit of infirmity eighteen years, and she [was] bent double and [was] not being able to straighten up to the completion [fig., at all]. ¹²But Jesus having seen her called [her] over and said to her, "Woman, you have been set free from your infirmity!" ¹³And He laid [His] hands on her, and immediately she was made erect and began glorifying God!

¹⁴But the synagogue leader answering (expressing indignation that Jesus healed on the Sabbath), began saying to the crowd, "There are six days in which it is necessary [for us] to be working. Therefore, on these [days] [be] coming [and] getting healed, and not on the day of the Sabbath." ¹⁵Then the Lord answered him and said, "Hypocrites! Does not each [one] of you* on the Sabbath untie his ox or donkey from the stall, and having led [it] away, give [it] water? ¹⁶But this [woman], being a daughter of Abraham, whom Satan indeed bound eighteen years, it was necessary [for her] to be released from this bond on the day of the Sabbath, was it not?" ¹⁷And when He said these [things] all the ones opposing Him were being put to shame, and the whole crowd was rejoicing over all the glorious [things], the ones being done by Him.

¹⁸Then He was saying, "What is the kingdom of God like? And to what will I compare it? ¹⁹It is like a grain of mustard [or, a mustard seed], which a man having taken, put into his garden, and it grew and became a large tree, and the birds of the sky nested in its branches." ²⁰Again He said, "To what will I compare the kingdom of God? ²¹It is like leaven [or, yeast], which a woman having taken, hid [or, mixed] into three satons [about 1.5 bushels or 36 liters] of wheat flour until it was all leavened."

²²And He was passing through according to [fig., through various] cities and villages teaching and making a journey to Jerusalem. ²³Now someone said to Him, "Lord, are the ones being saved few?" And He said to them, ²⁴Be striving to go in through the narrow gate, because many, I say to you*, will seek to enter and will not be able. ²⁵From whatever [time] the Master of the house is risen up and shuts the door, and you* begin to have stood outside and to be knocking at the door, saying, 'Lord, Lord, open to us,' and answering, He will say to you*, 'I do not know you*, where you* are from.'

²⁶"Then you* will begin to be saying, 'We ate and drank before You, and You taught in our open streets.' ²⁷And He will say, 'I say to you*, I do not know you*, where you* are from. Depart from Me, all you* workers of unrighteousness!' ²⁸In that place [there] will be weeping and gnashing of teeth, when you* see Abraham and Isaac and Jacob and all the prophets in the kingdom of God, but you* yourselves being thrown out outside! ²⁹And they will come from east and west and north and south, and they will recline [to eat] in the kingdom of God. ³⁰And listen! [There] are last [ones] who will be first, and [there] are first [ones] who will be last."

³¹On that very day some Pharisees approached, saying to Him, "Get out and be going from here, for Herod wants to kill You." ³²And He said to them, "Having gone, say to this fox, 'Look! I am casting out demons and performing healings today and tomorrow, and the third [day] I am being perfected.' ³³Nevertheless, it is necessary [for] Me to be traveling today and tomorrow and the following [day], because it is not possible for a prophet to perish outside of Jerusalem.

³⁴"Jerusalem, Jerusalem, the [city] killing the prophets and stoning the ones having been sent to her! How often I wanted to gather together your children [by] which manner [fig., just as] a hen [gathers] her brood [of chicks] under her wings, and you* did not want [to]. ³⁵Look! Your* house is being left to you* desolate. But, I say to you*, by no means shall you* see Me until [the time] comes when you* shall say, *'Having been blessed [is] the One coming in [the] name of [the] LORD.'"* [Psalm 118:26]

14And it happened, when He went into [the] house of one of the rulers of the Pharisees on a Sabbath to eat bread, that they were watching Him closely. ²And look! A certain man was dropsical [i.e. having swollen arms and legs] before Him. ³And answering, Jesus spoke to the lawyers and Pharisees, saying, "Is it lawful to be healing on the Sabbath?" ⁴But they were silent. And having taken hold of [him], He healed him and let [him] go. ⁵And replying to them, He said, "A son or ox of which of you* will fall into a well, and he will not immediately draw it up on the day of the Sabbath?" ⁶And they were not able to answer Him back regarding these things.

⁷Then He began telling an allegory to the ones having been called, noticing how they were choosing the first couches [fig., places of honor], saying to them, ⁸"Whenever you are invited by someone to marriage festivities, do not recline [to eat] on the first couch [fig., the place of honor], lest a more honorable [person than] you has been invited by him; ⁹and having come, the one having invited you and him, he will say to you, 'Give [your] place to this [person],' and then you begin with shame to be taking the last place. ¹⁰But whenever you are invited, having gone, recline [to eat] in the last place, so that whenever the one having invited you comes, he shall say to you, 'Friend, move up higher.' Then [there] will be glory for you before the ones reclining [to eat] with you. ¹¹Because every[one] exalting himself will be humbled, and the one humbling himself will be exalted."

¹²Then He also began saying to the one having invited Him, "Whenever you prepare a lunch or a dinner, do not be calling your friends nor your brothers nor your relatives nor rich neighbors, lest they also invite you back, and [that] shall be your repayment. ¹³But whenever you prepare a banquet, be inviting poor [people], crippled [people], lame [people], [and] blind [people], ¹⁴and you will be happy [or, blessed], because they do not have [anything] to repay to you, for it will be repaid to you in the resurrection of the righteous."

¹⁵Then one of the ones reclining [to eat] with [Him], having heard these things, said to him, "Happy [or, Blessed] [is he] who will eat dinner in the kingdom of God." ¹⁶But He said to him, "A certain man prepared a great banquet, and he invited many; ¹⁷and he sent his slave at the hour of the banquet to say to the ones having been invited, 'Be coming, because all [things] are now ready.' ¹⁸And they all began with one [accord] to be excusing themselves. The first said to him, 'I bought a field, and I have a need to go out and to see it. I beg of you, be having me having been excused.' ¹⁹And another said, 'I bought five yoke of oxen, and I am going to test them. I beg of you, be having me having been excused.' ²⁰And another said, 'I married a wife, and for this reason I am not being able to come.'

²¹"And that slave having come, reported these [things] to his lord. Then the master of the house, having been enraged, said to his slave, 'Go out quickly into the open streets and alleys of the city and bring in here the poor and crippled and lame and blind.' ²²And the slave said, 'Lord, it has been done as you commanded, and still there is room.' ²³And the lord said to the slave, 'Go out into the roads and [along the] fences, and compel [them] to come in, so that my house shall be filled. ²⁴For I say to you*, none of those men, the ones having been invited, will taste of my banquet,' for many are called, but few chosen."

²⁵Now large crowds were going along with Him, and having turned around, He said to them, ²⁶"If anyone comes to Me and does not hate his father and mother and wife and children and brothers and sisters, and in addition even his own life, he is not able to be My disciple. ²⁷And whoever does not carry his cross and come after Me is not able to be My disciple.

²⁸"For which of you*, the one wanting to build a lookout tower, does not first, having sat down, calculate the cost, whether he has the [resources] for [its]

completion? ²⁹Lest perhaps, after he has laid a foundation, and not being able to finish, all the ones watching begin to be ridiculing him, ³⁰saying, 'This man began to be building and was not able to finish.'

³¹"Or what king going to engage another king in battle, does not, having sat down, first consider if he is able with ten thousand [soldiers] to encounter the one with twenty thousand [soldiers] coming against him? ³²But if not, while he is still far away, having sent a delegation, he asks the [terms] for peace. ³³So likewise, every[one] of you* who does not give up all his own possessions is not able to be My disciple.

³⁴"The salt [is] good, but if the salt becomes tasteless, with what will it be seasoned? ³⁵It is fit neither for soil nor for a manure pile—they throw it out. The one having ears to be hearing, let him be hearing [or, be paying attention]."

15 Now all the tax collectors and the sinners were coming near to Him, to be hearing Him. ²And the Pharisees and the scribes began protesting, saying, "This One welcomes sinners and eats with them!"

³So He told this allegory to them, saying, ⁴"'What man from [among] you*, having a hundred sheep and having lost one of them, does not leave behind the ninety-nine in the wilderness and go after the one having been lost until he finds it? ⁵And having found [it], he puts [it] on his own shoulders rejoicing. ⁶And having come into his house, he calls together his friends and his neighbors, saying to them, 'Rejoice with me, because I found my sheep, the one having been lost!' ⁷I say to you*, in the same way [there] will be [more] joy in heaven over one sinner repenting than over ninety-nine righteous [people] who have no need of repentance.

⁸"Or what woman having ten drachmas [each worth about 1/8 of an ounce or 3.5 grams of silver], if she loses one drachma, does not light a lamp and sweep the house and search carefully until which [time] she finds [it]? ⁹And having found [it], she calls together her female friends and her female neighbors, saying, 'Rejoice with me, for I found the drachma which I lost!' ¹⁰In the same way, I say to you*, joy takes place in the presence of the angels of God over one sinner repenting."

¹¹And He said, "A certain man had two sons. ¹²And the younger of them said to the father, 'Father, give to me the share of the wealth falling [by inheritance] to [me].' And he divided to them his livelihood [or, his property]. ¹³And not many days after, having gathered all together, the younger son went on a journey to a distant country, and there he squandered his wealth, living recklessly. ¹⁴Then when he had spent all, a severe famine occurred throughout that country, and he began to be having need. ¹⁵And having gone, he was joined to [or, hired out to] one of the citizens of that country, and he sent him to the farms to be feeding pigs. ¹⁶And he was longing to fill his stomach from the carob pods which the pigs were eating, and no one was giving [anything] to him.

¹⁷"But having come to himself, he said, 'How many of my father's hired workers have an abundance of bread, but I am perishing with hunger! ¹⁸Having risen, I will go to my father and will say to him, "Father, I [have] sinned against

heaven and before you, [19]and I am no longer worthy to be called your son; make me as one of your hired workers.'" [20]And having risen, he went to his father.

"But he still being a long distance away, his father saw him and was moved with compassion; and having ran, he fell on his neck [fig., embraced him] and affectionately kissed him. [21]Then the son said to him, 'Father, I [have] sinned against heaven and before you, and I am no longer worthy to be called your son.' [22]But the father said to his slaves, 'Bring out the first [fig., best] long robe and clothe him, and give [him] a ring for his hand and sandals for his feet. [23]And having brought the fatted calf, slaughter [it], and having eaten, let us celebrate; [24]because this son of mine was dead and came back to life, and he had been lost and was found!' And they began to be celebrating.

[25]"Now his older son was in a field. And while coming, he approached the house [and] heard music and dancing. [26]And having summoned one of the slave boys, he began inquiring what these [things] might be [fig., meant]. [27]Then he said to him, 'Your brother has come, and your father slaughtered the fatted calf, because he received him back being in good health.' [28]But he was enraged and would not go in. So his father having come out began pleading with him.

[29]"But answering, he said to the father, 'Listen! So many years I am serving as a slave to you, and I never transgressed your command, yet you never gave me a young goat so that I could celebrate with my friends. [30]But when this son of yours, the one having devoured your livelihood with prostitutes came, you slaughtered the fatted calf for him!'

[31]"Then he said to him, 'Child, you are always with me, and all my [things] are yours. [32]But it was necessary to celebrate and to be glad, because this your brother was dead and came back to life, and had been lost and was found.'"

16

Now He was also saying to His disciples, "A certain man was rich, who had a steward, and this [steward] was accused to him as squandering his possessions. [2]And having called him, he said to him, 'What [is] this I hear about you? Give the account of your stewardship, for you will no longer be able to continue being steward.' [3]And the steward said within himself, 'What shall I do, since my lord is taking the stewardship away from me? I am not able to be digging. I am ashamed to be begging. [4]I knew [fig., have figured out] what I will do, so that when I am removed from the stewardship, they shall welcome me into their houses.'

[5]"And having summoned each one of his lord's debtors, he began saying to the first, 'How much do you owe to my lord?' [6]And he said, 'A hundred baths [about 800 gallons or 3000 liters] of oil.' And he said to him, 'Take your bill, and having sat down, quickly write fifty.' [7]Next to another he said, 'Now you, how much do you owe?' And he said, 'A hundred kors [or, homers; about 1000 bushels or 30 metric tons] of wheat.' And he says to him, 'Take your bill, and write eighty.'

[8]"And the lord highly praised the unrighteous steward because he did wisely [or, acted shrewdly], because the sons [and daughters] of this age are wiser [or, more shrewd] in their own generation than the sons [and daughters] of the light. [9]And I say to you*, make friends for yourselves by means of the worldly wealth

of unrighteousness, so that whenever you* fail, they shall welcome you* into the eternal tabernacles.

[10]"The one faithful in a very little [thing] [is] also faithful in much, and the one unrighteous in a very little [thing] is also unrighteous in much. [11]Therefore, if you* were not faithful in the unrighteous worldly wealth, who will entrust to you* the true? [12]And if you* were not faithful in the [thing] belonging to another, who will give to you* your* own property? [13]No household servant is able to be serving as a slave to two masters, for either he will hate the one and love the other, or he will be devoted to one and despise the other. You* are not able to be serving as a slave to God and to worldly wealth."

[14]Now the Pharisees also were hearing all these things, being lovers of money, and they began sneering at Him. [15]And He said to them, "You* are the ones justifying yourselves [or, declaring yourselves righteous] before the people, but God knows your* hearts, because the exalted [thing] among people [is] an abomination before God. [16]The Law and the Prophets [were] until John, since that time the Gospel of the kingdom of God is being proclaimed, and every[one] is forcing his way into it. [17]But it is easier [for] the heaven and the earth to pass away than [for] one tittle [i.e., a stroke of a letter] of the Law to fall.

[18]"Every[one] divorcing his wife and marrying another commits adultery, and every[one] marrying the one having been divorced from a husband commits adultery.

[19]"Now a certain man was rich and was dressing himself in a purple garment and fine linen, lavishly celebrating every day. [20]But [there] was a certain poor man, by name Lazarus, who had been placed at his gate, covered with sores [21]and longing to be fed from the crumbs, the ones falling from the table of the rich [man], but even the dogs, coming, were licking his ulcerated sores. [22]Now it happened, the poor man died, and he was carried away by the angels to the bosom of Abraham. Then the rich [man] also died and was buried. [23]And in the realm of the dead [Gr. *hades*], having lifted up his eyes, being in torments, he sees Abraham from a distance, and Lazarus in his bosom. [24]And having cried out, he said, 'Father Abraham, be merciful to me, and send Lazarus, so that he shall dip the tip of his finger in water and cool off my tongue, because I am in agony in this flame.'

[25]"But Abraham said, 'Child, remember that you received your good [things] in your life, and Lazarus likewise the bad [things], but now here he is comforted, but you are in agony. [26]And besides all these [things], between us and you* a great chasm has been fixed, in order that the ones wanting to cross over from here to you* are not able, nor can the [ones] from there cross over to us.' [27]Then he said, 'Then I beg you, father, that you send him to the house of my father—[28]for I have five brothers—in order that he should urgently warn them, so that they also shall not come to this place of torment.' [29]Abraham says to him, 'They have Moses and the Prophets; let them hear [or, pay attention to] them.' [30]But he said, 'No, father Abraham! But if someone goes to them from [the] dead, they will repent.' [31]But he said to him, 'If they do not hear Moses and the Prophets, neither will they be persuaded if someone rises from [the] dead.'"

17 Now He said to the disciples, "It is impossible for the stumbling blocks not to come, but how horrible it will be [to the one] through whom they come! ²It [would have been] better for him if a donkey millstone [i.e., a huge millstone turned by a donkey] [had been] put round about his neck, and he had been thrown into the sea, than that he should cause one of these little ones to stumble [fig., to sin].

³"Be watching yourselves! Now if your brother [fig., friend, neighbor, or compatriot] sins against you rebuke him, and if he repents forgive him. ⁴And if he sins against you seven times in the day, and returns seven times in the day, saying, 'I repent,' you will forgive him."

⁵And the apostles said to the Lord, "Add to us [or, Increase our] faith!" ⁶But the Lord said, "If you* have faith like a grain of mustard [or, a mustard seed], you* could say to this mulberry tree, 'Be uprooted and be planted in the sea,' and it would [have] obeyed you*.

⁷"Now which of you* having a slave plowing or tending [sheep], who having come in from the field, will immediately say [to him], 'Having come beside [me], recline [to eat]?' ⁸But will he not say to him, 'Prepare what I shall eat, and having wrapped [your belt] around yourself, serve me, until I eat and drink, and after these [things] you will eat and drink'? ⁹He does not have gratitude [for] that slave because he did the [things] having been instructed, does he? I think not. ¹⁰In the same way you* also, whenever you* do all the [things] having been instructed to you*, say, 'We are worthless slaves, because we have [only] done what we are obligated to do.'"

¹¹And it happened, while He [was] traveling to Jerusalem, that He was passing through between Samaria and Galilee. ¹²And as He [was] entering into a certain village, ten leprous men [or, men with a skin disease] met Him, who stood at a distance. ¹³And they lifted up [their] voice, saying, "Jesus, Master! Be merciful to us!" ¹⁴And having seen [them], He said to them, "Having gone, show yourselves to the priests." And it happened, while they [were] going, they were cleansed!

¹⁵But one of them, having seen that he was healed, returned, glorifying God with a loud voice. ¹⁶And he fell on [his] face at His feet, giving thanks to Him. And he was a Samaritan. ¹⁷Then answering, Jesus said, "The ten were cleansed, were they not? But where [are] the nine? ¹⁸Were not [any] found returning to give glory to God, except this foreigner?" ¹⁹And He said to him, "Having gotten up, go. Your faith has cured you."

²⁰Now having been questioned by the Pharisees when the kingdom of God is coming, He answered them and said, "The kingdom of God does not come with observation; ²¹neither will they say, 'Look here!' or 'Look there!' For listen! The kingdom of God is within [or, among] you*."

²²Then He said to His disciples, "Days will come when you* will long to see one of the days of the Son of Humanity, and you* will not see [it]. ²³And they will say to you*, 'Look here!' or 'Look there!' Do not go away, nor run after [them]. ²⁴For just as the lightning, the one flashing from the [one part] under heaven, shines to the [other part] under heaven, so will the Son of Humanity be in His day.

²⁵But first it is necessary [for] Him to suffer many [things] and to be rejected by this generation.

²⁶"And just as it happened in the days of Noah, so will it be also in the days of the Son of Humanity: ²⁷They were eating, they were drinking, they were marrying, [and] they were being given in marriage, until which day that Noah entered into the ark, and the flood came and destroyed [them] all. [see Gen 6:5-8, 7:1-24] ²⁸Likewise also, as it happened in the days of Lot: they were eating, they were drinking, they were buying, they were selling, they were planting, [and] they were building; ²⁹but [on the] day which Lot went out from Sodom, He rained fire and sulfur [or, brimstone] from heaven and destroyed [them] all. [see Gen 19:1-38] ³⁰According to these [things] [fig., In the same way] it will be in [the] day which the Son of Humanity is revealed. ³¹In that day, [the one] who will be on the housetop and his goods in the house, he must not come down to take them away. And the [one] in the field, likewise, he must not turn back for the [things left] behind. ³²Be remembering the wife of Lot! [see Gen 19:26]

³³"Whoever seeks to save his life will lose it, and whoever loses it will preserve it. ³⁴I say to you*, in that night there will be two [people] on one bed: one will be taken and the other will be left. ³⁵Two [women] will be grinding at the same [place]: one will be taken and the other will be left." ³⁷And answering, they say to Him, "Where, Lord?" Then He said to them, "Where the body [is], there will the vultures be gathered together."

18 Now He was also telling an allegory to them to [show] that it is necessary to always be praying and not to continue becoming discouraged, ²saying, "A certain judge was in a certain city, [who was] not fearing God and not respecting humanity. ³Now a widow was in that city, and she was coming to him, saying, 'Give justice to me against my opponent [in a lawsuit].' ⁴And he did not want [to] for a time, but after these [things] he said in himself, 'Even though I do not fear God and do not respect humanity, ⁵yet because this widow is causing me trouble, I will give justice to her, so that [she will] not be wearing me out by coming to [the] end [fig., coming continually].'"

⁶Then the Lord said, "Hear [or, Pay attention to] what the unrighteous judge says. ⁷But shall not God surely execute justice for His chosen ones, the ones crying out to Him day and night? And is He [not] waiting patiently by them? ⁸I say to you*, He will execute justice for them with quickness. Nevertheless, the Son of Humanity having come, will He find faith on the earth?"

⁹Now He spoke this allegory to some, the ones having confidence in themselves that they are righteous, and despising [or, looking down on] the rest: ¹⁰"Two men went up to the temple to pray: the one a Pharisee and the other a tax collector. ¹¹The Pharisee having stood, was praying these [words] to himself [or, having stood by himself, was praying these [words]]: 'God, I thank You that I am not just like the rest of people: swindlers, unrighteous, adulterers, or even as this tax collector. ¹²I fast twice in the week; I tithe all [things], as many as I acquire.'

¹³"And the tax collector, having stood at a distance, was not even willing to lift up his eyes to heaven, but he was beating on his chest, saying, 'God be propitious

[or, merciful] to me, the sinner!' ¹⁴I say to you*, this [one] went down to his house having been justified [or, declared righteous], rather than in fact that [other one]. For every[one] exalting himself will be humbled, but the one humbling himself will be exalted."

¹⁵And they were also bringing the babies to Him, so that He would be touching them, but the disciples having seen, rebuked them. ¹⁶But Jesus having summoned them, said, "Allow the young children to be coming to Me, and stop forbidding them, for of such is the kingdom of God. ¹⁷Positively, I say to you*, whoever does not receive the kingdom of God like a young child shall by no means enter into it."

¹⁸And a certain ruler questioned Him, saying, "Good Teacher, having done what will I inherit eternal life?" ¹⁹But Jesus said to him, "Why do you call Me good? No one [is] good except One—God. ²⁰The commandments you know: *'You shall not commit adultery; You shall not murder; You shall not steal; You shall not give false testimony; Honor your father and your mother.'"* [Exod 20:12-16; Deut 5:16-20] ²¹But he said, "All these I myself obeyed from my youth." ²²So having heard these [things], Jesus said to him, "Yet one [thing] is lacking to you: all [things]—as many as you have—sell and distribute to [the] poor, and you will have treasure in heaven. And come! Be following Me!" ²³But having heard these [things], he became deeply grieved, for he was extremely rich.

²⁴Then Jesus having seen him, having become deeply grieved, said, "How with difficulty will the ones having possessions [or, riches] enter into the kingdom of God! ²⁵For it is easier [for] a camel to enter through the eye of a needle than [for] a rich [person] to enter into the kingdom of God." ²⁶So the ones having heard, said, "Then who is able to be saved?" ²⁷Then He said, "The [things] impossible with people are possible with God!"

²⁸Now Peter said, "Listen! We left all and followed You." ²⁹So He said to them, "Positively, I say to you*, [there] is no one who left house or parents or brothers or wife or children for the sake of the kingdom of God, ³⁰who shall not certainly receive back many times more in this time, and in the coming age eternal life."

³¹Then having taken the twelve aside, He said to them, "Listen! We are going up to Jerusalem, and all the [things] having been written through the prophets about the Son of Humanity will be fulfilled. ³²For He will be handed over to the Gentiles and will be ridiculed and will be mistreated and will be spit on, ³³and having scourged [Him], they will kill Him. And on the third day He Himself will rise again." ³⁴And they understood none of these [things], and this saying had been hidden from them, and they were not knowing [or, comprehending] the [things] being said.

³⁵Now it happened, as He [was] drawing near to Jericho, a certain blind man was sitting beside the road begging. ³⁶So having heard a crowd traveling through [the city], he began inquiring what this might be. ³⁷Then they told him that Jesus the Nazarene is passing by. ³⁸And he shouted, saying, "Jesus, Son of David! Be merciful to me!" ³⁹And the ones going ahead of [Him] began warning him that he should be silent, but all the more he kept crying out, "Son of David! Be merciful to me!"

⁴⁰So Jesus having stood still, He commanded him to be brought to Him. Now when he drew near, He questioned him, ⁴¹saying, "What do you desire [that] I do for you?" Then he said, "Lord, that I receive [my] sight!" ⁴²And Jesus said to him,

"Receive [your] sight! Your faith has cured you." ⁴³And immediately he received [his] sight! And he began following Him, glorifying God. And having seen, all the people gave praise to God.

19And having entered, He was passing through Jericho. ²And look! [There was] a man by name being called Zaccheus, and he was a tax collection superintendent, and he was rich. ³And he was trying to see Jesus, who He is, and he was not able [to] because of the crowd, for he was small in stature. ⁴And having run ahead in front of [the crowd], he went up into a sycamore tree, so that he should see Him, because He was about to be passing by that [way]. ⁵And as Jesus came up to the place, having looked up, He saw him and said to him, "Zaccheus, having hurried, come down, for it is necessary [for] Me to stay in your house today." ⁶And having hurried, he came down and welcomed Him rejoicing.

⁷And having seen, they all began protesting, saying, "He went in to lodge with a sinful man!" ⁸Now Zaccheus having stood, said to the Lord, "Listen! The half of my possessions, Lord, I give to the poor, and if I defrauded anyone of anything, I give back four times as much." ⁹Then Jesus said to him, "Today salvation came to this house, because he also is a son of Abraham. ¹⁰For the Son of Humanity came to seek and to save the lost."

¹¹Now while they [were] hearing these [things], again He spoke an allegory, because of His being near Jerusalem, and [because] they [were] thinking that the kingdom of God is about to immediately appear. ¹²Therefore, He said, "A certain man of noble birth went on to a distant country to receive a kingdom for himself and to return. ¹³So having called ten of his own slaves, he gave to them ten minas [each worth about 12.5 ounces or 350 grams of silver] and said to them, 'Do business until I come.' ¹⁴But his citizens were hating him and sent a delegation after him, saying, 'We do not want this [man] to reign over us.' ¹⁵And it happened, when he returned [from] having received the kingdom, he then commanded these slaves to be called to him, to whom he gave the money, so that he should know who gained what by trading.

¹⁶"So the first came, saying, 'Lord, your mina earned ten minas.' ¹⁷And he said to him, 'Well done, good slave! Because you were faithful in a very little [thing], be having authority over ten cities.' ¹⁸And the second came, saying, 'Lord, your mina made five minas.' ¹⁹Then he said also to this [one], 'And you, be over five cities.' ²⁰And another came, saying, 'Lord, look—your mina, which I had been storing away in a handkerchief! ²¹For I was fearing you, because you are a stern man. You take up what you did not lay down and reap what you did not sow.'

²²"Then he says to him, 'Out of your mouth [fig., By your own words] I will judge you, evil slave! You knew that I am a stern man, taking up what I did not lay down and reaping what I did not sow. ²³And why did you not give my money to a [money changer's] table [fig., a bank], and having come, I might [have] collected it with interest?' ²⁴And to the ones having stood by he said, 'Take the mina away from him, and give [it] to the one having the ten minas.' ²⁵(And they said to him, 'Lord, he has ten minas!') ²⁶'For I say to you*, to every one having, [more] will be given, but from the one not having, even what he has will be taken away from

him. ²⁷Nevertheless, those enemies of mine, the ones not having wanted me to reign over them, bring [them] here and execute [them] before me.'"

²⁸And having said these [things], He was traveling ahead [of His disciples], going up to Jerusalem. ²⁹And it happened, as He drew near to Bethsphage and Bethany, to the mountain, the one being called Of Olives, He sent two of His disciples, ³⁰having said, "Go into the village opposite [you*], in which entering you* will find a colt [or, a young donkey] having been bound, on which no person ever sat, having untied it, bring [it]. ³¹And if anyone asks you*, 'Why are you* untying [it]?' thus you* will say to him, 'The Lord has need of it.'" ³²So the ones having been sent, having gone away, found [everything] just as He said to them. ³³But as they are untying the colt, its owners said to them, "Why are you* untying the colt?" ³⁴Then they said, "The Lord has need of it."

³⁵And they brought it to Jesus. And having thrown their own coats on the colt, they placed Jesus on it. ³⁶Now as He [was] going, they were spreading their coats on the road. ³⁷Then He having now drawn near to the descent of the Mount of Olives, the whole crowd of the disciples began rejoicing [and] to be praising God with a loud voice for all [the] miraculous works which they saw, ³⁸saying, *"'Having been blessed [is] the One coming [as] King in [the] name of [the] LORD!'* [Psalm 118:26] Peace in heaven and glory in [the] highest!" ³⁹And some of the Pharisees from the crowd said to Him, "Teacher, rebuke Your disciples!" ⁴⁰And answering, He said to them, "I say to you*, if these shall be silent, the stones will cry out!"

⁴¹And as He drew near, having seen the city, He wept over it, ⁴²saying, "If [only] you knew, even you, at least in this your day, the [things] for your peace! But now they were hid from your eyes. ⁴³Because days will come upon you, and your enemies will throw up a barricade around you and will surround you and will hem you in on every side, ⁴⁴and they will level you to the ground and your children within you, and they will not leave in you a stone on a stone, because you did not know the time of your visitation."

⁴⁵And having entered into the temple, He began to throw out the ones selling and buying in it, ⁴⁶saying to them, "It has been written, *'My house is a house of prayer.'* [Isaiah 56:7] But you* made it a *'hideout for robbers!'*" [Jer 7:11]

⁴⁷And He was teaching daily in the temple. But the chief priests and the scribes were seeking to destroy Him, also the leading [men] of the people. ⁴⁸And they could not find [out] what they should do, for all the people were hanging on His [words] as they [were] hearing [Him].

20And it happened, on one of those days, as He [was] teaching the people in the temple and proclaiming the Gospel, the priests and the scribes, with the elders, approached [Him] ²and spoke to Him, saying, "Tell us by what authority You are doing these [things]? Or who is the one having given this authority to You?" ³And answering, He said to them, "I also will ask you* one word [or, one thing], and tell Me: ⁴The baptism of John—was it from heaven or from people?" ⁵And they debated among themselves, saying, "If we say, 'From heaven,' He will say, 'Why did you* not believe him?' ⁶But if we say, 'From people,' all the people will stone us, for they have been persuaded John is a prophet." 7And they answered, "We do not know from where [it was]." 8And Jesus said to them, "Neither do I tell you* by what authority I am doing these [things]."

9Then He began to be telling the people this allegory: "A man planted a vineyard and leased it to vineyard keepers and went on a journey [for] a long time. 10And at [harvest] time, he sent a slave to the vineyard keepers, so that they should give to him from the fruit of the vineyard. But the vineyard keepers having repeatedly beat him, sent [him] away empty-handed. 11And again he sent another slave, but that [one] also, having repeatedly beaten [him] and having treated [him] shamefully, they sent [him] away empty-handed. 12And he again sent a third, and this [one] also, having wounded, they threw [him] out. 13So the owner of the vineyard said, 'What shall I do? I will send my son—the beloved—perhaps having seen this [one], they will respect [him].'

14"But having seen him, the vineyard keepers reasoned among themselves, saying, 'This is the heir. Come, let us be killing him, so that the inheritance shall become ours!' 15And having thrown him outside of the vineyard, they killed [him]. Therefore, what will the owner of the vineyard do to them? 16He will come and will destroy these vineyard keepers and will give the vineyard to others."

But having heard, they said, "Absolutely not!" 17Then having looked with care upon them, He said, "What then is this [which] has been written: *'A stone which the ones building rejected, this [one] became for [the] head of a corner?'* [Psalm 118:22] 18Every[one] having fallen on that stone will be broken to pieces, but on whomever it falls, it will crush him." 19And the chief priests and the scribes sought to lay hands on Him in that very hour, and they were afraid, for they knew that He spoke this allegory against them.

20And having watched [Him] closely, they sent spies, pretending themselves to be righteous, so that they should seize on His word [fig., catch Him in some statement] in order to hand Him over to the rule and the authority of the governor. 21And they questioned Him, saying, "Teacher, we know that You say and teach correctly, and You do not accept a face [fig., show favoritism], but You teach the way of God in truth. 22Is it lawful for us to give tribute [or, a tax] to Caesar or not?"

23But having perceived their craftiness, He said to them, "Why do you* test Me? 24Show to Me a denarius [i.e., a Roman, silver coin]. Whose image and inscription does it have?" Then answering, they said, "Caesar's." 25Then He said to them, "So render the [things] of Caesar to Caesar and the [things] of God to God." 26And they were not able to seize on His saying [fig., catch Him in some statement] before the people, and having marveled at His answer, they kept silent.

27Then some of the Sadducees, the ones denying that [there] is a resurrection, having come to [Him], questioned Him, 28saying, "Teacher, Moses wrote to us: if anyone's brother dies, having a wife, and this [man] dies childless, that his brother should take the wife and raise up seed [fig., offspring] for his brother. [Deut 25:5] 29Now [there] were seven brothers. And the first having taken a wife, died childless. 30And the second took the wife, and this [man] died childless.

³¹And the third took her in the same way; then in the same way also the seven. And they left no children, and they died. ³²But last of all the woman also died. ³³So in the resurrection, of which of them does she become wife? For the seven had her [as] wife."

³⁴And answering, Jesus said to them, "The sons [and daughters] of this age marry and are given in marriage. ³⁵But the ones being counted worthy to attain that age and the resurrection, the [resurrection] from [the] dead, neither marry nor are given in marriage. ³⁶For neither are they able to die any more, for they are like angels, and they are sons [and daughters] of God, being sons [and daughters] of the resurrection. ³⁷But that the dead are raised, even Moses revealed at The Bush, when he calls [the] Lord, *'the God of Abraham and the God of Isaac and the God of Jacob.'* [Exod 3:6] ³⁸Now He is not [the] God of dead [people], but of living [people], for all are alive to Him."

³⁹Then answering, some of the scribes said, "Teacher, You spoke well." ⁴⁰So they no longer dared to be asking Him anything.

⁴¹Then He said to them, "How [is it that] they say the Christ [is] to be David's Son? ⁴²Even David himself says in a scroll of [the] Psalms, *'The LORD said to my Lord, "Be sitting at My right hand, ⁴³until I make Your enemies Your footstool."'* [Psalm 110:1] ⁴⁴So David calls Him 'Lord,' and how is He his Son?"

⁴⁵Now all the people hearing, He said to His disciples, ⁴⁶"Be watching out for [or, Beware of] the scribes, the ones desiring to be walking about in long robes and affectionately loving greetings in the marketplaces and [the] first seats [fig., most important places] in the synagogues and [the] first couches [fig., places of honor] at the banquets, ⁴⁷the ones devouring the houses of the widows [fig., illegally cheating widows' out of their property], and in pretence [or, with a false show] are long [in] praying. These will receive more severe judgment [or, condemnation]."

21 Now having looked up, He saw the rich [people] putting their offerings into the treasury [fig., collection boxes]. ²Then He saw also a certain poor widow putting [in] there two lepta [or, two very small copper coins]. ³And He said, "Truly I say to you*, this poor widow put [in] more [than] all. ⁴For all these out of their abundance [or, surplus] put into the offerings for God, but this [woman] out of her poverty, all her livelihood which she was having, she put [in]."

⁵And while some [were] saying about the temple, that it has been adorned with beautiful stones and dedicated offerings, He said, ⁶"These [things] which you* are looking at—days will come in which a stone will not be left on a stone, which will not be torn down." ⁷Then they questioned Him, saying, "Teacher, so when will these [things] be? And what [will be] the sign when these [things] are about to be happening?"

⁸So He said, "Be watching [that] you* are not led astray [fig., deceived]. For many will come in My name, saying, 'I Am!,' and 'The time has drawn near!' Therefore, do not go after them. ⁹But when you* hear of wars and rebellions, do not be terrified, for it is necessary [for] these [things] to happen first, but the end [is] not immediately." ¹⁰Then He was saying to them, "Nation will be raised up against nation and kingdom against kingdom. ¹¹And [there] will be great earthquakes in

[various] places and famines and plagues, and [there] will be dreadful events and great signs from heaven.

¹²"But before all these [things], they will lay their hands on you* and persecute [you*], handing [you*] over to synagogues and prisons, being brought before kings and governors [or, rulers] for My name's sake. ¹³And it will lead to [an opportunity] to you* for a testimony. ¹⁴So put [it] in your* hearts [fig., make up your* minds] not to be preparing beforehand to speak in your* own defense, ¹⁵for I will give to you* a mouth and wisdom which all the ones opposing you* will not be able to refute nor to resist. ¹⁶But you* will be betrayed even by parents and relatives and friends and brothers, and they will put [some] of you* to death. ¹⁷And you* will be continually hated by all because of My name. ¹⁸And a hair from your* head shall by no means perish. ¹⁹In [or, By] your* patient endurance acquire your* souls.

²⁰"But when you* see Jerusalem having been surrounded by armies, then know that her desolation [or, desecration] has drawn near. ²¹Then the [ones] in Judea must be fleeing into the mountains, and the [ones] in her midst must depart, and the [ones] in the fields must not come into her. ²²Because these are days of vengeance, to be fulfilled all the [things] having been written. ²³But how horrible it will be to the ones having in the womb [fig., who are pregnant] and to the ones nursing [babies] in those days! For [there] will be great distress on the land and wrath among this people. ²⁴And they will fall by [the] mouth [fig., edge] of the sword, and they will be led captive into all the nations. And Jerusalem will be continually trampled down by [the] Gentiles until the times of [the] Gentiles are fulfilled.

²⁵"And [there] will be signs in [the] sun and moon and stars, and on the earth distress of nations with perplexity [at the] roaring of [the] sea and waves; [cp. Isaiah 34:4; Joel 2:10; 2:31] ²⁶people fainting [or, ceasing to breathe] from fear and [the] expectation of the [things] coming upon the inhabited earth, for the powers of the heavens will be shaken. ²⁷And then they will see '*the Son of Humanity coming in a cloud*' with power and great glory! [Dan 7:13] ²⁸But when these [things] are beginning to happen, straighten up and lift up your* heads, because your* redemption is drawing near."

²⁹And He spoke an allegory to them: "See the fig tree and all the trees; ³⁰when they [have] already sprouted [leaves], having seen, you* know for yourselves that the summer is already near. ³¹In this way also when you* see these [things] happening, be knowing that the kingdom of God is near!

³²"Positively, I say to you*, this generation [or, race] shall by no means pass away until all [things] happen. ³³The heaven and the earth will pass away, but My words shall by no means pass away.

³⁴"But be watching out for yourselves, lest your* hearts be weighed down with hangovers and drunkenness and anxieties over [things] pertaining to everyday life, and that day come on you* suddenly [or, unexpectedly]. ³⁵For it will come as a snare on all the ones sitting [fig., living] on [the] face of all the earth. ³⁶Therefore, be staying alert in every season, imploring [in prayer] that you* shall be counted

worthy to escape all the [things] about to be happening and to stand before the Son of Humanity."

³⁷Now [during] the days He was teaching in the temple, but [during] the nights, going out, He would spend the night on the mount, the one being called Of Olives. ³⁸And all the people would rise very early in the morning [to come] to Him in the temple to hear Him.

22 Now the Feast of Unleavened Bread, the one being called Passover, was approaching. ²And the chief priests and the scribes were seeking how they could execute Him, for they were fearing the people.

³Then Satan entered into Judas, the one being surnamed Iscariot, being of the number of the twelve. ⁴And having gone away, he conferred with the chief priests and the captains [of the temple guard] [about] how he should betray Him to them. ⁵And they were glad and agreed to give him money [or, silver]. ⁶And he consented, and he began seeking a convenient moment to betray Him to them, away from a crowd.

⁷Then the day of the [Feast of] Unleavened Bread came, in which it was necessary [for] the Passover [or, Paschal Lamb] to be sacrificed. ⁸And He sent Peter and John, saying, "Having gone, prepare the Passover for us, so that we shall eat." ⁹So they said to Him, "Where do You desire [that] we will prepare [it]?" ¹⁰Then He said to them, "Listen! When you* have entered into the city, a man carrying a pitcher of water will meet you*; follow him into the house which he enters. ¹¹And you* will say to the master [or, owner] of the house, 'The Teacher says to you, "Where is the guest room, where I shall eat the Passover with My disciples?"' ¹²And that one will show to you* a large, upstairs room, having been furnished. There prepare [it]." ¹³Then having gone away, they found [everything] just as He had said to them, and they prepared the Passover.

¹⁴And when the hour came, He reclined [to eat], and the twelve apostles with Him. ¹⁵And He said to them, "I desired with desire [fig., I earnestly desired] to eat this Passover with you* before I suffer. ¹⁶For I say to you*, no longer by any means shall I eat of it until which [time] it shall be fulfilled in the kingdom of God." ¹⁷And having taken a cup, having given thanks, He said, "Take this and divide [it] among yourselves. ¹⁸For I say to you*, by no means shall I drink of the fruit of the grapevine until which [time] the kingdom of God comes."

¹⁹And having taken bread, having given thanks, He broke [it] and gave [it] to them, saying, "This is My body, the [one] being given on your* behalf; be doing this in remembrance of Me." ²⁰And in the same manner [He took] the cup after [they] ate, saying, "This cup [is] the New Covenant in My blood, the [blood] being poured out on your* behalf.

²¹"Nevertheless, look! The hand of the one betraying Me [is] with Mine on the table! ²²And indeed the Son of Humanity is going according to the [thing] having been determined. Nevertheless, how horrible it will be to that man through whom He is betrayed!" ²³And they began to discuss among themselves which of them then it might be, the one about to be doing this [thing].

²⁴Then a dispute also occurred among them, [as to] which of them seems to be greater. ²⁵But He said to them, "The kings of the nations [or, the Gentiles] exercise lordship over them, and the ones exercising authority over them are called benefactors. ²⁶But you* [shall] not [be acting] in this way, but the greatest among you* must become like the youngest, and the one leading like the one serving. ²⁷For who is greater, the one reclining [to eat] or the one serving? It is the one reclining [to eat], is it not? But I am in your* midst as the One serving. ²⁸Now you* are the ones having remained with [or, having stood by] Me in My trials. ²⁹And I covenanted to you*, just as My Father covenanted to Me, a kingdom, ³⁰so that you* shall be eating and drinking at My table, and you* will sit on thrones judging the twelve tribes of Israel."

³¹Then the Lord said, "Simon, Simon, listen! Satan himself asked for you* to sift [you*] like wheat. ³²But I implored [in prayer] for you, so that your faith shall not fail; and you, when having returned, strengthen your brothers." ³³But he said to Him, "Lord, I am ready to go with You both to prison and to death!" ³⁴But He said, "I say to you, Peter, by no means shall a rooster crow today before you will deny three times to have known Me."

³⁵And He said to them, "When I sent you* without money bag and traveler's bag and sandals, you* did not lack anything, did you*?" Then they said, "Nothing." [see Luke 10:3-7] ³⁶Then He said to them, "But now, the one having a money bag must take [it] up, and likewise also a traveler's bag. And the one not having [a sword] will sell his coat and will buy a sword. ³⁷For I say to you*, it is still necessary [for] this, the [saying] having been written, to be fulfilled in Me, *'And He was counted with lawless [ones],'* for also the [things] concerning Me have an end [fig., a fulfillment]." [Isaiah 53:12] ³⁸Then they said, "Lord, look! Here [are] two swords." Then He said to them, "It is sufficient."

³⁹And having gone out, He went according to [His] custom to the Mount of Olives, and His disciples also followed Him. ⁴⁰So having come to the place, He said to them, "Be praying not to enter into temptation." ⁴¹And He was withdrawn from them about a stone's throw. And having placed the knees [fig., having knelt down], He began praying, ⁴²saying, "Father, if You are willing to take this cup away from Me—nevertheless, not My will, but Yours be done." ⁴³Then an angel from heaven appeared to Him, strengthening Him.

⁴⁴And having been in agony, He was [even] more fervently praying. Then His sweat became like great drops of blood falling on the ground. ⁴⁵And having gotten up from the prayer, having come to the disciples, He found them sleeping from the sorrow. ⁴⁶And He said to them, "Why are you* sleeping? Get up! Be praying, so that you* shall not enter into temptation."

⁴⁷Now while He [was] still speaking, look!, a crowd, and the one being called Judas, one of the twelve, was going before them. And he approached Jesus to kiss Him. ⁴⁸But Jesus said to him, "Judas, are you betraying the Son of Humanity with a kiss?"

⁴⁹Now the ones around Him, having seen the [thing] going to happen, said to Him, "Lord, will we strike with a sword?" ⁵⁰And a certain one of them struck the slave of the high priest and cut off his right ear. ⁵¹But answering, Jesus said, "Stop

this!" And having touched his ear, He healed him. ⁵²Then Jesus said to the chief priests and captains of the temple guard and elders having come against Him, "Have you* come out with swords and clubs as [you* would] against a robber [or, an insurrectionist]? ⁵³When I [was] daily being with you* in the temple, you* did not stretch your* hands against Me [fig., you* did not arrest Me]. But this is your* hour and the power of darkness!"

⁵⁴Then having arrested Him, they led and brought Him into the house of the high priest. But Peter was following at a distance. ⁵⁵Now they having kindled a fire in the middle of the courtyard, and having sat down together, Peter was sitting in [the] middle of them. ⁵⁶Then a certain slave-girl, having seen him sitting by the firelight, and having looked intently at him, said, "This [man] also was with Him!" ⁵⁷But he denied [or, disowned] Him, saying, "Woman, I do not know Him." ⁵⁸And after a short [while], another [person] having seen him, was saying, "You also are [one] of them!" But Peter said, "Man, I am not!"

⁵⁹And about an hour having passed, a certain other [person] was insisting, saying, "Upon truth [fig., Certainly] this [man] also was with Him, for he is also a Galilean." ⁶⁰But Peter said, "Man, I do not know what you are saying!" And immediately, while he [was] still speaking, a rooster crowed. ⁶¹And the Lord, having turned around, looked attentively at Peter. And Peter remembered the word of the Lord, how He said to him, "Before a rooster crows, you will deny [or, disown] Me three times." [see Luke 22:34] ⁶²And having gone outside, Peter wept bitterly.

⁶³And the men, the ones holding Jesus prisoner, began ridiculing Him, repeatedly beating [Him]. ⁶⁴And having blindfolded Him, they kept striking Him on the face and kept questioning Him, saying, "Prophesy, who is the one having struck You?" ⁶⁵And many other things, blaspheming, they were saying to Him.

⁶⁶And when it became day, the council of the elders of the people, chief priests and scribes, were gathered together, and they led Him up to their own High Council [or, Sanhedrin], saying, ⁶⁷"If You are the Christ, tell us." But He said to them, "If I tell you*, by no means shall you* believe. ⁶⁸And if I also question [you*], by no means shall you* answer Me or release [Me]. ⁶⁹From now [on], '*the Son of Humanity will be sitting at [the] right hand* of the power *of God!*'" [Psalm 110:1] ⁷⁰Then they all said, "Are You then the Son of God?" So He said to them, "You say [it], because I am!" ⁷¹Then they said, "What need do we still have of testimony? For we heard [it] ourselves from His mouth."

23 And having risen, the whole multitude of them led Him to Pilate. ²Then they began to be accusing Him, saying, "We found this One misleading the nation and forbidding to give tribute [or, tax] to Caesar, saying [that] He Himself is Christ, a king." ³So Pilate questioned Him, saying, "Are You the King of the Jews?" But answering Him, He said, "You say [it]." ⁴Then Pilate said to the chief priests and the crowds, "I find no fault at all in this Man."

⁵But they kept insisting, saying, "He shakes up [fig., incites] the people, teaching throughout the whole of Judea, having begun from Galilee to here." ⁶Now having heard Galilee [mentioned], Pilate asked if the Man is a Galilean.

⁷And having known that He is from the jurisdiction of Herod, he sent Him to Herod, he also being in Jerusalem in those days.

⁸Now having seen Jesus, Herod was exceedingly glad, for he was desiring for a long [time] to see Him because of hearing many [things] about Him, and he was hoping to see some miraculous sign done by Him. ⁹So he began questioning Him with many words, but He answered him nothing. ¹⁰Now the chief priests and the scribes had stood vehemently accusing Him. ¹¹Then Herod with his soldiers, having despised Him [or, having treated Him with contempt] and having ridiculed [Him], having put an elegant robe around Him, sent Him back to Pilate. ¹²But both Pilate and Herod became friends with one another on that very day, for previously they were being hostile towards one another.

¹³Now Pilate having summoned the chief priests and the rulers and the people, ¹⁴said to them, "You brought this Man to me as misleading the people [or, inciting the people to riot]. And listen! Having examined [Him] in your* presence, I found in this Man no cause at all [for the] charges which you* are bringing against Him. ¹⁵But neither [did] Herod, for I sent you* to him. And look! Nothing deserving of death has been done by Him. ¹⁶Therefore, after having [Him] scourged, I will release [Him]." ¹⁷(Now he had a necessity to be releasing one [prisoner] to them at [the] feast). ¹⁸But they all shouted together, saying, "Be taking away this One, but release to us Barabbas!" ¹⁹(who had been thrown into prison for a certain insurrection having occurred in the city, and [for] murder).

²⁰So again Pilate addressed [them], wanting to release Jesus. ²¹But they kept shouting, saying, "Crucify! Crucify Him!" ²²Now a third time he said to them, "But what evil did this [Man] do? I did not find [any] cause for death [fig., grounds for the death penalty] in Him. Therefore, after having Him scourged, I will release [Him]." ²³But they kept insisting with loud voices demanding [for] Him to be crucified. And their voices and the [ones] of the chief priests began prevailing. ²⁴So Pilate pronounced sentence [for] their demand to be done. ²⁵Then he released the one having been thrown into the prison for insurrection and murder, [for] whom they kept demanding. But he handed Jesus over to their will.

²⁶And as they led Him away, having taken hold of Simon, a certain Cyrenian coming from [the] country, they put the cross on him, to be carrying [it] behind Jesus. ²⁷Now a large crowd of the people was following Him, and women who also were beating their breasts [fig., were mourning] and were lamenting Him.

²⁸But Jesus having turned to them, said, "Daughters of Jerusalem, stop weeping for Me. Instead, be weeping for yourselves and for your* children. ²⁹For listen! Days are coming in which they will say, 'Happy [are] the barren [or, women incapable of having children], and [the] wombs which did not give birth, and [the] breasts which did not nurse.' ³⁰Then they will begin '*to be saying to the mountains, "Fall on us," and to the hills, "Cover us."*' [Hosea 10:8] ³¹For if they do these [things] in the green tree [or, while the tree is green], what shall happen in the dry?"

³²Now they were also leading others, two criminals, with Him to be executed. ³³And when they came to the place, the one being called Skull, there they crucified Him and the criminals, one on [His] right hand and one on [the] left. ³⁴But Jesus

was saying, "Father, forgive them, for they do not know what they are doing." Then dividing His garments, they cast a lot.

[35]And the people had stood looking on. Then the rulers also began sneering with them, saying, "He saved others, let Him save Himself, since this is the Christ, the Chosen One of God!" [36]Now the soldiers also began ridiculing Him, approaching and offering wine vinegar to Him, [37]and saying, "Since You are the King of the Jews, save Yourself!"

[38]Now an inscription also had been written over Him in Greek and Roman [or, Latin] and Hebrew [or, Aramaic] letters: "This is the King of the Jews."

[39]Then one of the criminals having been hanged began deriding Him, saying, "Since You are the Christ, save Yourself and us!" [40]But answering, the other [one] began rebuking him, saying, "Do you not even now fear God, since you are in the same judgment [or, condemnation]? [41]And we indeed [are suffering] justly, for we are receiving back [things] worthy of what we did, but this [Man] did nothing wrong." [42]And he was saying to Jesus, "Remember me, Lord, when You come in Your kingdom." [43]And Jesus said to him, "Positively, I say to you, today you will be with Me in Paradise."

[44]Now it was about the sixth hour [i.e., 12:00 noon], and darkness came over the whole land until the ninth hour [i.e., 3:00 p.m.]. [45]And the sun was darkened, and the veil [or, curtain] of the sanctuary was torn in the middle. [46]And having called out with a loud voice, Jesus said, "Father, into Your hands I will commit [or, will entrust] My spirit." And having said these [things], He breathed His last.

[47]Now the centurion having seen the [thing] having happened, glorified God, saying, "Certainly, this Man was righteous!" [48]And all the crowds, the ones having gathered to this sight [or, for this spectacle], watching the [things] having happened, beating their breasts, began returning [home]. [49]But all His acquaintances had stood at a distance, and the women, the ones having followed Him from Galilee, seeing these things.

[50]And look! A man by name [of] Joseph, being a member of the High Council [or, the Sanhedrin], a good and righteous man [51](this one had not consented to their plan and action), from Arimathea, a city of the Jews, who indeed also was himself waiting for [or, expecting] the kingdom of God, [52]having approached Pilate, this one requested for himself the body of Jesus. [53]And having taken it down, he wrapped it in linen cloth and placed it in a tomb cut out of rock, where no one was yet lying. [54]And [that] day was a preparation [day]—[the] Sabbath was drawing near.

[55]Now the women who had accompanied Him out of Galilee, having followed closely, observed the tomb and how His body was placed. [56]Then having returned [home], they prepared spices and ointments [or, perfumes]. And on the Sabbath indeed they rested, according to the commandment [see Exod 20:8-10].

24 Now on [the] first [day] of the week [i.e. Sunday], at early dawn, they came [or, went] to the tomb, carrying the spices which they prepared, and some [others] with them. [2]But they found the stone having been rolled away from the tomb. [3]And having entered, they did not find the body of the Lord Jesus. [4]And it happened, while they [were] being thoroughly perplexed about this, and look!, two men stood by them in dazzling robes.

[5]Then they having become terrified and having bowed the face to the ground, they said to them, "Why are you* seeking the living among the dead? [6]He is not here, but He was raised! Remember how He spoke to you*, being yet in Galilee, [7]saying, 'It is necessary [for] the Son of Humanity to be betrayed into [the] hands of sinful men and to be crucified and on the third day to rise again?'" [cp. Luke 9:22,44] [8]And they remembered His words.

[9]And having returned from the tomb, they told all these [things] to the eleven and to all the rest. [10]Now it was Mary the Magdalene [or, Mary, a woman from Magdala] and Joanna and Mary [the mother] of James and the rest with them, who were telling these [things] to the apostles. [11]And their words seemed before them [fig., in their view] like nonsense [or, idle tales], and they were refusing to believe them. [12]But Peter having gotten up, ran to the tomb, and having stooped down, he sees the linen strips lying alone. And he went away to himself [fig., to his own home] wondering about the [thing] having happened.

[13]And look! Two of them were traveling on that very day to a village to which [was] the name Emmaus [at a] distance [of] sixty stadia [about 7.7 miles or 12.2 kilometers] from Jerusalem. [14]And they were conversing with one another about all these [things which] had happened. [15]And it happened, while they [were] conversing and discussing, that Jesus Himself, having drawn near, began going along with them. [16]But their eyes were being held [or, restrained] [so as] not to know [or, recognize] Him. [17]Then He said to them, "What [are] these words which you* are exchanging with one another as you* are walking, and [why] are you* gloomy?"

[18]So one to whom [was the] name Cleopas, answering, said to Him, "Are You alone living as a stranger [in] Jerusalem that You do not know the [things] having happened in it in these days?" [19]And He said to them, "What [things]?"

Then they said to Him, "The [things] about Jesus the Nazarene, who was a Man, a Prophet, powerful in deed and word before God and all the people, [20]how also the chief priests and our rulers handed Him over to a judgment of death, and they crucified Him. [21]But we were hoping that He is the One about to be redeeming Israel. But besides even all these [things], today brings this third day from which [time] these [things] happened. [22]But also some women from our [group] astonished us, having come early in the morning to the tomb, [23]and not having found His body, they came saying also to have seen a vision of angels, who say He is living. [24]And some of the [ones] with us went to the tomb and found [it] in the same way, just as the women said, but Him they did not see."

[25]And He said to them, "O foolish [ones] and slow of heart to be believing in all which the prophets spoke! [26]It was necessary [for] the Christ to suffer these [things] and to enter into His glory, was it not?" [27]And having begun with Moses and with all the prophets, He began interpreting for them in all the Scriptures the [things] about Himself.

[28]And they drew near to the village where they were going, and He gave the impression that [He was] going farther. [29]And they persuaded Him, saying, "Stay

with us, for it is [getting] towards evening, and the day has declined." And He went in to stay with them. ³⁰And it happened, while He [was] reclining [to eat] with them, having taken the bread, He bestowed a blessing upon [it], and having broken [it], He began giving [it] to them. ³¹Then their eyes were opened, and they knew [or, recognized] Him, and He became invisible from their [sight]. ³²And they said to one another, "Our heart was burning within us as He was speaking to us on the road and as He was opening up the Scriptures to us, was it not?"

³³And having gotten up that very hour, they returned to Jerusalem, and they found the eleven having been gathered together, and the [ones] with them, ³⁴saying, "The Lord was indeed raised, and He was seen by Simon!" ³⁵And they began describing their experiences on the road, and how He was made known to them in the breaking of the bread.

³⁶Now while they [were] telling these [things], Jesus Himself stood in [the] middle of them and says to them, "Peace to you*." ³⁷But having been startled and having become terrified, they were thinking [they were] seeing a spirit. ³⁸And He said to them, "Why have you* been frightened? And why do doubts arise in your* hearts? ³⁹See My hands and My feet, that I am I Myself. Handle Me and see, because a spirit does not have flesh and bones, just as you* see I have."

⁴⁰And having said this, He showed His hands and His feet to them. ⁴¹Then while they [were] refusing to believe from the joy, and marveling, He said to them, "Do you* have anything edible here?" ⁴²So they gave to Him a piece of a broiled fish and a honeycomb from a beehive. ⁴³And having taken, He ate before them.

⁴⁴Then He said to them, "These [are] the words which I spoke to you*, being still with you*, that it is necessary [for] all the things to be fulfilled, the ones having been written in the Law of Moses and [the] Prophets and [the] Psalms about Me." ⁴⁵Then He opened up their mind[s] to be understanding the Scriptures.

⁴⁶And He said to them, "Thus it has been written, and thus it was necessary [for] the Christ to suffer and to rise from [the] dead the third day, ⁴⁷and [for] repentance and forgiveness of sins to be proclaimed in His name to all the nations, beginning from Jerusalem. ⁴⁸Now you* are witnesses of these [things]. ⁴⁹And listen! I am sending the Promise of My Father upon you*. But you* [are to] sit [fig., wait] in the city of Jerusalem until which [time] you* are clothed with power from on high."

⁵⁰Then He led them outside as far as Bethany, and having lifted up His hands, He bestowed a blessing upon them. ⁵¹And it happened, while He [was] bestowing a blessing upon them, He parted from them and was being taken up into heaven. ⁵²And they, having prostrated themselves in worship before Him, returned to Jerusalem with great joy, ⁵³and they were through all [fig. continually] in the temple, praising and blessing God. So be it!

The Gospel According to
John

1 In the beginning was the Word [fig., the Expression of [Divine] Logic], and the Word was with [fig., in communion with] God, and the Word was God [fig., was as to His essence God]. ²This One was in the beginning with God. ³All [things] came to be through Him, and without Him not even one thing came to be which has come to be. ⁴In Him was life, and the life was the Light of the people. ⁵And the Light shines in the darkness, and the darkness did not apprehend it.

⁶There came a man having been sent from God, [the] name to him [fig., whose name] [was] John. ⁷This one came for a testimony, so that he should testify concerning the Light, so that all should believe through him. ⁸That one was not the Light, but [he came] so that he should testify concerning the Light. ⁹He was the true Light which enlightens every person coming into the world. ¹⁰He was in the world, and the world came to be through Him, and the world did not know Him. ¹¹He came to His own, and His own did not receive Him. ¹²But as many as received Him, He gave to them authority to become children of God—to the ones believing [or, trusting] in His name, ¹³who were begotten, not from [or, by] bloods, nor from a will of [the] flesh, nor from [the] will of a man, but from God.

¹⁴And the Word [fig., the Expression of [Divine] Logic] became flesh and tabernacled among us, and we beheld His glory, glory as of an only-begotten [or, uniquely-begotten] from [the] Father, full of grace and truth. ¹⁵John testifies concerning Him and has cried out, saying, "This was [the One concerning] whom I said, 'The One coming after me before me has come to be, for He was before me.'" ¹⁶And out of His fullness we all received, even grace in place of grace. ¹⁷For the law was given through Moses: grace and truth came to be through Jesus Christ. ¹⁸No one has seen God at any time. The only-begotten [or, unique] Son, the One in the bosom of the Father, that One explained [Him] [or, made [Him] known].

¹⁹And this is the testimony of John, when the Jews sent from Jerusalem priests and Levites, so that they should question him, "You, who are you?" ²⁰And he confessed and did not deny, and confessed, "I am not the Christ ["the Anointed One"]." ²¹And they questioned him, "What then? Are you Elijah?" And he says, "I am not."—"Are you the Prophet?" And he answered, "No." ²²So they said to him, "Who are you, so that we shall give an answer to the ones sending us? What do you say concerning yourself?" ²³He said, "I [am] *a voice shouting in the wilderness: "Make straight the way of [the]* LORD,"' just as Isaiah the prophet said." [Isaiah 40:3, LXX]

²⁴And the ones having been sent were from the Pharisees. ²⁵And they questioned him and said to him, "Why then do you baptize [or, immerse, and throughout book], if you are not the Christ nor Elijah nor the Prophet?" ²⁶John answered them saying, "I baptize in water [or, with water, and throughout book], but He has stood in the midst of you* whom you* do not know. ²⁷He is the One

coming after me, who has come to be before me, of whom I am not worthy that I untie the strap of His sandal." ²⁸These things took place in Bethany, beyond the Jordan [River], where John was baptizing.

²⁹The next day he sees Jesus coming towards him and says, "Look! The Lamb of God, the One taking away the sin of the world! ³⁰This is [the One] concerning whom I said, 'After me comes a Man, who has come before me, because He was before me.' ³¹And I did not know Him. However, so that He should be revealed to Israel, for this reason I came in water baptizing."

³²And John testified, saying, "I have seen the Spirit coming down as a dove out of heaven, and He remained upon Him. ³³And I did not know Him; but the One having sent me to baptize in water, that [One] said to me, 'Upon whomever you see the Spirit coming down and remaining upon Him, this is the One baptizing in [or, with] [the] Holy Spirit.' ³⁴And I have seen and have testified that this is the Son of God."

³⁵The next day again John had stood and two of his disciples. ³⁶And having looked attentively at Jesus walking about, he says, "Look! The Lamb of God!" ³⁷And the two disciples heard him speaking, and they followed Jesus. ³⁸But Jesus having been turned and having beheld them following, says to them, "What do you* seek?" But they said to Him, "Rabbi (which [is], being interpreted, Teacher), where are You staying?" ³⁹He says to them, "Be coming and see." They came and saw where He stayed, and they stayed with Him that day. It was about [the] tenth hour [i.e. 4:00 p.m. Jewish time or 10:00 a.m. Roman time].

⁴⁰Andrew, the brother of Simon Peter, was one of the two having heard from John and having followed Him. ⁴¹This one finds first his own brother Simon and says to him, "We have found the Messiah!" (which is, being translated, Christ). ⁴²And he brought him to Jesus. Having looked attentively at him, Jesus says, "You are Simon, the son of Jonah; you will be called Cephas" (which is interpreted, Peter).

⁴³The next day He wanted to go out to Galilee. And Jesus finds Philip and says to him, "Be following Me!" ⁴⁴And Philip was from Bethsaida, of the city of Andrew and Peter. ⁴⁵Philip finds Nathanael and says to him, "[The One about] whom Moses wrote in the Law and the prophets we have found—Jesus the Son of Joseph, who [is] from Nazareth." ⁴⁶And Nathanael said to him, "Is anything good able to be [fig., to come] out of Nazareth?" Philip said to him, "Be coming and see."

⁴⁷Jesus saw Nathanael coming towards Him, and He says concerning him, "Look! Truly an Israelite in whom [there] is no deceit [or, treachery]!" ⁴⁸Nathanael says to him, "From where do You know me?" Jesus answered and said to him, "Before Philip called you, while you were under the fig tree, I saw you." ⁴⁹Nathanael answered and says to Him, "Rabbi, You are the Son of God! You are the King of Israel!" ⁵⁰Jesus answered and said to him, "Because I said to you, 'I saw you under the fig tree,' you believe; greater things than these you will see." ⁵¹And He says to him, "Most positively, I say to you*, from now [on] you* will see heaven [or, the sky] having been opened, and the angels of God ascending and descending upon the Son of Humanity."

2And on the third day a marriage took place in Cana of Galilee, and the mother of Jesus was there. ²Now Jesus also was called, and His disciples, to the marriage feast. ³And when [the] wine had fallen short, the mother of Jesus says to Him, "They have no wine." ⁴Jesus says to her, "What [concern is that] to Me and to you, woman? My hour is not yet come." ⁵His mother says to the servants, "Whatever He says to you*, do."

⁶Now [there] were standing there six water-jugs of stone according to the purification [rites] of the Jews, each containing two or three measures [about 18-27 gallons or 80-120 liters]. ⁷Jesus says to them, "Fill the water-jugs with water." And they filled them up to the brim. ⁸And He says to them, "Now draw [it] out and be carrying [it] to the head steward." And they carried [it]. ⁹But when the head steward tasted the water having become wine and knew not from where [it] is [from] (but the servants knew, the ones having drawn the water), the head steward calls the bridegroom ¹⁰and says to him, "Every person first puts out the good wine, and when they have drunk freely, then the inferior. You have kept the good wine until now!"

¹¹This beginning of the signs Jesus did in Cana of Galilee, and He revealed His glory, and His disciples believed [or, trusted] in Him. ¹²After this He went down to Capernaum, He and His mother and His brothers and His disciples. And there they stayed not many days.

¹³And the Passover of the Jews was near, and Jesus went up to Jerusalem. ¹⁴And He found in the temple the ones selling oxen and sheep and doves, and the money changers sitting [there]. ¹⁵And having made a whip out of small cords, He cast out all [of them] out of the temple, both the sheep and the oxen. And He poured out the coins of the money changers and He overturned the tables. ¹⁶And He said to the ones selling the doves, "Take these things from here! Stop making the house of my Father a house of trade!" ¹⁷Then His disciples remembered that it is written, *"The zeal of Your house will consume Me."* [Psalm 69:9]

¹⁸But the Jews answered and said to Him, "What sign do You show to us, that these things You do?" ¹⁹Jesus answered and said to them, "Destroy this temple, and in three days I will raise it up!" [cp. Matt 26:61; Mark 14:58] ²⁰Then the Jews said, "This temple was built [in] forty and six years, and You will raise it up in three days?" ²¹But that [One] spoke concerning the temple of His body. ²²So when He was raised from [the] dead, His disciples remembered that He said this. And they believed the Scripture and the word which Jesus said.

²³Now when He was in Jerusalem at the Passover, at the feast, many believed [or, trusted] in His name, watching the signs which He was doing. ²⁴But Jesus Himself was not trusting Himself to them, on account of Him knowing all [people] ²⁵and because He did not need that any should testify concerning humanity, for He Himself was knowing what was in humanity.

3Now there was a man from the Pharisees, Nicodemus [was] his name, a ruler of the Jews. ²This one came to Him by night and said to Him, "Rabbi, we know that You have come [as] a teacher from God, for no one is able to be doing these signs which You are doing unless God is with him." ³Jesus answered and said to him, "Most positively, I say to you, unless someone is born from above [or, born again], he is not able to see the kingdom of God." ⁴Nicodemus says to Him, "How is a person able to be born, being old? He is not able to enter into the womb of his mother a second time and to be born, is he?"

⁵Jesus answered, "Most positively, I say to you, unless someone is born from water and Spirit, he is not able to enter into the kingdom of God. ⁶The [thing] having been born from the flesh is flesh, and the [thing] having been born from the Spirit is spirit. ⁷Stop marveling that I said to you, 'It is necessary [for] you* to be born from above [or, born again].' ⁸The Spirit breathes where He desires, and you hear His voice, but you do not know from where He comes and where He goes. [or, The wind blows where it wishes, and you hear its sound, but you do not know from where it comes and where it goes.] In this manner [or, Like this] is every[one] having been born from the Spirit."

⁹Nicodemus answered and said to Him, "How are these things able to happen?" ¹⁰Jesus answered and said to him, "You are the teacher of Israel, and you do not know these things! ¹¹Most positively, I say to you, We speak [of] what We know, and We testify [of] what We have seen, and you* do not receive Our testimony. ¹²If I said to you* the earthly [things] and you* do not believe [or, do not accept [them] as true], how if I should say to you* the heavenly [things] will you* believe?

¹³"And no one has ascended into heaven, except the One having descended from heaven—the Son of Humanity, the One being in heaven. ¹⁴And just as Moses lifted up the serpent in the wilderness, so it is necessary [for] the Son of Humanity to be lifted up, ¹⁵so that every[one] believing [or, trusting] in Him shall not perish, but shall be having eternal life."

¹⁶For God so loved the world that He gave His only-begotten [or, unique] Son, so that every[one] believing [or, trusting] in Him shall not perish, but shall be having eternal life! ¹⁷For God did not send His Son into the world so that He should judge the world, but so that the world shall be saved through Him. ¹⁸The one believing [or, trusting] in Him is not judged, but the one not believing already has been judged, because he has not believed in the Name of the only-begotten [or, unique] Son of God.

¹⁹Now this is the judgment, that the Light has come into the world, and people loved the darkness rather than the Light, for their works were evil. ²⁰For every[one] practicing wicked [things] hates the Light and does not come towards the Light, so that his works shall not be exposed. ²¹But the one doing the truth comes towards the Light, so that his works shall be revealed, that they have been done in God.

²²After these things Jesus and His disciples came into the land of Judea, and there He was staying with them and was baptizing. ²³But John was also baptizing in Aenon, near to Salem, because [there] was many waters [or, much water] in that place. And they were coming and were being baptized—²⁴for John had not yet been cast into the prison.

²⁵Therefore, [there] occurred a dispute from the disciples of John with a Jew concerning purification [rites]. ²⁶And they came to John and said to him, "Rabbi, [He] who was with you beyond the Jordan, to whom you have testified, look!, this One is baptizing, and all are coming to Him!" ²⁷John answered and said, "A person is not able to be receiving anything unless it has been given to him from heaven. ²⁸You* yourselves testify that I said, 'I myself am not the Christ', but 'I have been sent before that One.' ²⁹The one having the bride is [the] bridegroom, but the friend of the bridegroom, the one standing and hearing him, rejoices with joy because of the voice of the bridegroom. Therefore, [in] this my joy has been fulfilled. ³⁰It is necessary [for] that One to be increasing, but [for] me to be becoming less [or, to be decreasing]."

³¹The One coming from above is above all; the one being from the earth is from the earth and speaks from the earth; the One coming from heaven is above all. ³²And what He has seen and heard, this He testifies, and no one receives His testimony. ³³The one receiving His testimony [has] certified that God is true. ³⁴For [He] whom God sent speaks the sayings of God, for God does not give the Spirit by measure.

³⁵The Father loves the Son and has given all [things] into His hand. ³⁶The one believing [or, trusting] in the Son has eternal life, but the one refusing to believe the Son will not see life, but the wrath of God abides on him.

4 So when the Lord knew that the Pharisees heard that Jesus is making and baptizing more disciples than John, ²(although Jesus Himself was not baptizing, but His disciples), ³He left Judea and went away into Galilee. ⁴And it was necessary [for] Him to be passing through Samaria.

⁵Then He comes to a city of Samaria, being called Sychar, near the place which Jacob gave to Joseph his son. ⁶Now a well of Jacob was there. So Jesus, having grown weary from the journey, was sitting thus by the well. It was about the sixth hour [i.e. 12:00 noon Jewish time or 6:00 p.m. Roman time]. ⁷A woman comes from Samaria to draw water.

Jesus says to her, "Give Me to drink." ⁸(for His disciples had gone away into the city, so that they should buy food.) ⁹So the Samaritan woman says to Him, "How is it that You, being a Jew, ask to drink from me, being a Samaritan woman?" (for Jews do not associate with Samaritans).

¹⁰Jesus answered and said to her, "If you knew the free gift of God and who is the One saying to you, 'Give Me to drink,' you would have asked Him, and He would have given you living water." ¹¹The woman says to Him, "Lord, You do not even have a vessel to draw with, and the well is deep; from where then do You have this living water? ¹²You are not greater than our father Jacob, who gave us this well, and [he] himself drank out of it, and his sons and his cattle, are You?"

¹³Jesus answered and said to her, "Every[one] drinking of this water will thirst again. ¹⁴But whoever drinks of the water which I will give to him will by no means thirst into the age [fig., ever thirst again]! But the water which I will give to him will become in him a well of water springing up to eternal life!" ¹⁵The

woman says to Him, "Lord, give this water to me so that I shall not be thirsting nor coming to this place to be drawing."

¹⁶Jesus says to her, "Be going, call your husband and come to this place." ¹⁷The woman answered and said, "I do not have a husband." Jesus says to her, "Correctly you said, 'I do not have a husband.' ¹⁸For five husbands you had, and [the one] whom you now have is not your husband; this you have said truly."

¹⁹The woman says to him, "Lord, I perceive that You are a prophet. ²⁰Our fathers prostrated themselves in worship in this mountain, and you* say, 'In Jerusalem is the place where it is necessary to be prostrating in worship.'" ²¹Jesus says to her, "Woman, be believing Me, that an hour is coming when neither in this mountain nor in Jerusalem will you* prostrate yourselves in worship before the Father. ²²You* prostrate yourselves in worship before what you* do not know; we prostrate ourselves in worship before what we know, because salvation is from the Jews. ²³But an hour is coming and now is when the true worshipers will prostrate themselves in worship before the Father in spirit and truth, for indeed the Father is seeking such to be prostrating themselves in worship before Him. ²⁴God [is] Spirit [fig., [is] as to His essence Spirit], and it is necessary [for] the ones prostrating themselves in worship before Him to be prostrating in worship in spirit and truth."

²⁵The woman says to Him, "I know that Messiah is coming, the one being called Christ, when that One comes He will tell us all things." ²⁶Jesus says to her, "I am [He], the One speaking to you."

²⁷And upon this [or, at this [point]] His disciples came, and they were marveling that He was speaking with a woman, although no one said, "What are You seeking?" or "Why are You speaking with her?" ²⁸Then the woman left her water-jug and went away into the city. And she says to the people, ²⁹"Come! See a Man who told me all [things]—as many as I did. This is not the Christ, is it?" ³⁰They went out from the city and were coming towards Him. ³¹But in the meantime His disciples were asking Him, saying, "Rabbi, eat." ³²But He said to them, "I have food to eat which you* do not know." ³³So the disciples said to one another, "Someone has not brought Him [something] to eat, has he?"

³⁴Jesus says to them, "My food is that I should be doing the will of the One having sent Me and should finish His work. ³⁵Do you* not say, 'It is yet four months and the harvest comes?' Listen! I say to you*, lift up your* eyes and see the fields, that they are already white to harvest. ³⁶And the one reaping receives a reward and gathers fruit to eternal life, so that both the one sowing and the one reaping shall rejoice together. ³⁷For in this the word is true, 'One is the one sowing and another is the one reaping.'" [cp. Judges 6:3,4; Micah 6:15] ³⁸I sent you* to be reaping what you* have not labored [for]; others have labored, and you* have entered into their labor."

³⁹Now from that city many of the Samaritans believed [or, trusted] in Him, because of the word of the woman testifying, "He told me all [things]—as many as I did." ⁴⁰So when the Samaritans came to Him, they kept asking Him to remain with them, and He remained there two days. ⁴¹And many more believed because of His word. ⁴²And so they were saying to the woman, "No longer do we believe

because of your speech, for we ourselves have heard and know that this is truly the Savior of the world—the Christ!"

⁴³But after the two days He went out from there and went away into Galilee. ⁴⁴For Jesus Himself testified that a prophet does not have honor in his hometown. ⁴⁵So when He came into Galilee, the Galileans received Him, having seen all [things] which He did in Jerusalem at the feast, for they also went to the feast.

⁴⁶So Jesus came again to Cana of Galilee, where He made the water wine. And [there] was a certain royal official whose son was sick in Capernaum. ⁴⁷This one, having heard that Jesus is coming out of Judea to Galilee, went away to Him and kept asking Him that He come down and heal his son, for he was about to die. ⁴⁸So Jesus said to him, "Unless you* see signs and wonders you* shall by no means believe." ⁴⁹The royal official says to Him, "Lord, come down before my young child dies!" ⁵⁰Jesus says to him, "Be going; your son lives!" And the man believed [or, trusted in] the word which Jesus said to him and was going.

⁵¹But already as he was going down, his slaves met him and reported, saying, "Your child lives!" ⁵²So he inquired of them the hour in which he got better. And they said to him, "Yesterday at the seventh hour [i.e. 1:00 p.m. Jewish time or 7:00 p.m. Roman time] the fever left him." ⁵³Then the father knew that [it was] in that hour in which Jesus said to him, "Your son lives!" And he himself believed, and his whole house. ⁵⁴This again [is the] second sign Jesus did, having come out of Judea to Galilee.

5 After these things [there] was the feast of the Jews, and Jesus went up to Jerusalem. ²Now [there] is in Jerusalem by the sheep[gate] a pool, the one being called in Hebrew Bethesda, having five porticoes [or, covered walkways]. ³In these were lying a great multitude of ones being sick, blind, lame, [and] withered, waiting for the moving of the water. ⁴For at a set time an angel would be descending into the pool and would be stirring up the water, then the first [one] having stepped in after the troubling of the water became well of whatever disease he was being held.

⁵Now [there] was a certain man there having the infirmity thirty-eight years. ⁶Jesus having seen this one lying [there] and having known that a long time he had already [been there], He says to him, "Do you wish to become well?" ⁷The one being sick answered Him, "Lord, I [do] not have a person that, whenever the water is stirred up, he should put me into the pool, but while I am coming another descends before me." ⁸Jesus says to him, "Get up! Take up your cot, and be walking about." ⁹And immediately the man became well and took up his cot and began walking about! But it was a Sabbath on that day.

¹⁰Therefore the Jews were saying to the one having been healed, "It is a Sabbath! It is not lawful for you to take up your cot." ¹¹He answered them, "The One having made me well, that [One] said to me, 'Take up your cot, and be walking about.'" ¹²So they questioned him, "Who is the Person, the One saying to you, 'Take up your cot, and be walking about?'" ¹³But the one having been healed did not know who He is, for Jesus left unnoticed, a crowd being in that place.

¹⁴After these things, Jesus finds him in the temple and said to him, "Look! You have become well! No longer be sinning, lest something worse should happen to you." ¹⁵The man went away and told the Jews that it is Jesus, the One making him well.

¹⁶And for this reason the Jews were persecuting Jesus and were seeking to kill Him, because He was doing these things on a Sabbath. ¹⁷But Jesus answered them, "My Father is working until now, and I am working." ¹⁸Therefore, for this reason, all the more the Jews were seeking to kill Him, because not only was He breaking the Sabbath, but He also called God His own Father, making Himself equal to God.

¹⁹So Jesus answered and said to them, "Most positively, I say to you*, the Son is not able to be doing anything of Himself unless He sees the Father doing [it], for whatever He is doing, these also the Son likewise does. ²⁰For the Father affectionately loves the Son and shows to Him all which He Himself does, and greater works than these He will show to Him, so that you* shall be marveling. ²¹For even as the Father raises the dead [ones] and makes alive, so also the Son makes alive whom He wills. ²²For neither does the Father judge anyone, but He has given all judgment to the Son, ²³so that all shall be honoring the Son just as they honor the Father. The one not honoring the Son does not honor the Father who sent Him. ²⁴Most positively, I say to you*, the one hearing My word and believing [or, trusting] the One having sent Me has eternal life and does not come into judgment, but has passed from death into life!

²⁵"Most positively, I say to you*, an hour is coming and now is when the dead [ones] will hear the voice of the Son of God, and those having heard will live. ²⁶For even as the Father has life in Himself, so He gave also to the Son to be having life in Himself. ²⁷And He gave also to Him authority to be making judgment, because He is [the] Son of Humanity. ²⁸Stop marveling at this, because an hour is coming in which all those in the tombs will hear His voice, ²⁹and they will come forth: the ones having done the good [things] into a resurrection of life, but the ones having practiced the wicked [things] into a resurrection of judgment. ³⁰I am not able to be doing anything of Myself. Just as I hear I judge, and My judgment is righteous, because I do not seek My will but the will of the Father having sent Me.

³¹"If I testify concerning Myself, My testimony is not true. ³²Another is the One testifying concerning Me, and I know that the testimony is true which He testifies concerning Me. ³³You* have sent to John, and he has testified to the truth. ³⁴But I do not receive testimony from a man, but these things I say so that you* shall be saved. ³⁵That one was the burning and shining lamp, but you* were pleased to be very glad for an hour [or, for a while] in his light.

³⁶"But I have the testimony greater than John's, for the works which the Father gave to Me that I should finish them, the works themselves which I am doing, they testify concerning Me that the Father has sent Me. ³⁷And the Father having sent Me, [He] Himself has testified concerning Me. Neither have you* heard His voice at any time nor have you* seen His form. ³⁸And you* [do] not have His word remaining in you*, because whom that One sent, this One you* do not believe. ³⁹You* search the Scriptures, because you* think in them to be having

eternal life, and these they are which testify concerning Me. ⁴⁰And you* are not willing to come to Me so that you* shall have life.

⁴¹"I do not receive glory from people. ⁴²<u>But</u> I have known you*, that you* do not have the love of God in yourselves. ⁴³<u>I</u> have come in the Name of My Father, and you* do not receive Me. If another comes in his own name, that one you* will receive. ⁴⁴How are <u>you</u>* able to believe, while receiving glory from one another, and the glory that [is] from God alone you* do not seek? ⁴⁵Stop thinking that <u>I</u> will accuse you* before the Father; the one accusing you* is Moses, in whom you* have hoped [or, have trusted in]. ⁴⁶For if you* were believing Moses, you* would have been believing Me, for that one wrote concerning Me. ⁴⁷But if the writings of that one you* do not believe, how will you* believe My sayings?"

6After these things Jesus departed to the other side of the Sea of Galilee (that [is], of Tiberias). ²And a large crowd was following Him, because they were seeing His signs which He was doing upon the ones being sick. ³But Jesus went up into the mountain, and He was sitting there with His disciples.

⁴Now the Passover was near, the feast of the Jews. ⁵Then Jesus, having lifted up His eyes and having seen that a large crowd is coming to Him, says to Philip, "From where shall we buy loaves of bread, so that these shall eat?" ⁶(But this He said testing him, for He Himself knew what He was about to be doing.) ⁷Philip answered Him, "Two hundred denarii [i.e., 200 days' wages] [worth] of loaves of bread are not sufficient for them that each of them shall receive some little [piece]."

⁸One of His disciples, Andrew, the brother of Simon Peter, says to Him, ⁹"There is one little boy here who has five barley loaves and two fish, <u>but</u> these— what are they to so many?" ¹⁰But Jesus said, "Make the people to recline."

Now there was much grass in the place. So they reclined (the men in number about five thousand). ¹¹Then Jesus took the loaves of bread, and having given thanks, He distributed to the disciples, and the disciples to the ones reclining, likewise also of the fish, as much as they wanted! ¹²And when they were satisfied, He says to His disciples, "Gather together the broken pieces of bread having been leftover, so that nothing shall be lost." ¹³So they gathered together and filled twelve handbaskets with broken pieces of bread from the five barley loaves which were left over by the ones having eaten.

¹⁴Therefore, the people having seen the sign Jesus did, said, "This is truly the Prophet, the One coming into the world!" ¹⁵Then Jesus, having known that they are about to come and to take Him by force so that they should make Him king, withdrew into the mountain Himself alone.

¹⁶But when evening came, His disciples went down to the sea. ¹⁷And having stepped into the boat, they began going over the sea to Capernaum. And it had already become dark, and Jesus had not come to them. ¹⁸And the sea was being stirred up by a strong blowing wind. ¹⁹Then having rowed about twenty-five or thirty stadia [about three or four miles or five or six kilometers], they watched Jesus walking about on the sea and coming near the boat. And they were afraid. ²⁰But He says to them, "<u>I</u> Am! Stop being afraid!" ²¹So they were willing to receive

Him into the boat, and immediately the boat came to be on the land to which they were going.

²²The next day, the crowd which was standing on the other side of the sea, having seen that [there] was no other small boat there except that one which His disciples stepped into, and that Jesus did not enter with His disciples into the small boat, but His disciples went away alone ²³(but other small boats came from Tiberias, near the place where they ate the bread, the Lord having given thanks), ²⁴so when the crowd saw that Jesus is not there, nor His disciples, they themselves stepped into the boats and came to Capernaum seeking Jesus. ²⁵And having found Him on the other side of the sea, they said to Him, "Rabbi, when have You come here?"

²⁶Jesus answered them and said, "Most positively, I say to you*, you* seek Me, not because you* saw signs, but because you* ate of the loaves of bread and were satisfied. ²⁷Stop working [for] the food that perishes by itself, but [be working for] the food that remains to eternal life, which the Son of Humanity will give to you*, for God the Father has set [His] seal [on] Him." ²⁸Therefore, they said to Him, "What shall we be doing so that we shall be working the works of God?" ²⁹Jesus answered and said to them, "This is the work of God, that you* be believing [or, trusting] in Him whom that One sent."

³⁰So they said to Him, "What sign then do You do so that we shall see and believe You? What are You working? ³¹Our fathers ate the manna in the wilderness, just as it has been written, *'He gave to them bread out of heaven to eat.'"* [Exod 16:4; Neh 9:15; Psalm 78:24] ³²So Jesus said to them, "Most positively, I say to you*, Moses has not given to you* the bread out of heaven, but My Father gives to you* the true bread out of heaven. ³³For the bread of God is the One coming down out of heaven and giving life to the world."

³⁴Then they said to Him, "Lord, always give to us this bread." ³⁵But Jesus said to them, "I am the bread of life! The one coming to Me shall by no means hunger, and the one believing [or, trusting] in Me will by no means thirst at any time! ³⁶But I said to you* that you* have both seen Me, and you* do not believe. ³⁷All that the Father gives to Me will come to Me, and the one coming to Me I shall by no means cast out. ³⁸Because I have come down out of heaven, not so that I shall be doing My will, but the will of the One having sent Me. ³⁹And this is the will of the Father having sent Me, that out of all which He has given to Me I will not lose [any of] it, but I will raise it up on the last day. ⁴⁰And this is the will of the One having sent me, that every[one] looking on the Son and believing [or, trusting] in Him shall be having eternal life, and I will raise him up on the last day."

⁴¹Therefore, the Jews were grumbling about Him, because He said, "I am the bread having come down out of heaven." ⁴²And they said, "Is this not Jesus, the Son of Joseph, whose father and mother we know? How then says this One, "I have come down out of heaven?" ⁴³So Jesus answered and said to them, "Stop grumbling with one another. ⁴⁴No one is able to come to Me unless the Father having sent Me draws [or, drags] him, and I will raise him up on the last day. ⁴⁵It has been written in the prophets, *'And they will all be taught of God.'* [Isaiah 54:13, LXX] Therefore, every[one] hearing from the Father and having learned comes to Me. ⁴⁶Not that anyone has seen the Father, except the One being from

God, He has seen the Father. ⁴⁷Most positively, I say to you*, the one believing in Me has eternal life.

⁴⁸"I am the bread of life! ⁴⁹Your* fathers ate the manna in the wilderness, and they died. ⁵⁰This is the bread which comes down out of heaven, so that anyone shall eat from it and shall not die. ⁵¹I am the living bread, the One having come down from heaven. If anyone eats from this bread he will live into the age [fig., forever], and indeed the bread which I will give is My flesh, which I will give on behalf of the life of the world."

⁵²Therefore, the Jews began fighting [fig., arguing angrily] with one another, saying, "How is this One able to give to us His flesh to eat?" ⁵³So Jesus said to them, "Most positively, I say to you*, unless you* eat the flesh of the Son of Humanity and drink His blood, you* do not have life in yourselves. ⁵⁴The one eating My flesh and drinking My blood has eternal life, and I will raise him up on the last day. ⁵⁵For My flesh truly is food, and My blood truly is drink. ⁵⁶The one eating My flesh and drinking My blood remains in Me, and I in him. ⁵⁷Just as the living Father sent Me, and I live because of the Father, also the one feeding on Me, that one will also live because of Me. ⁵⁸This is the bread having come down out of heaven, not as your* fathers ate the manna and died. The one eating this bread will live into the age [fig., forever]!" ⁵⁹These things He said in a synagogue, teaching in Capernaum.

⁶⁰Therefore, many from His disciples having heard, said, "This word is harsh. Who is able to be hearing it?" ⁶¹But Jesus, knowing in Himself that His disciples are grumbling about this, said to them, "Does this cause you* to stumble [fig, offend you*]? ⁶²Then [what] if you* shall be watching the Son of Humanity ascending where He was before? ⁶³The Spirit is the One giving life; the flesh does not accomplish [or, benefit] anything. The words which I have spoken to you* are spirit and are life! ⁶⁴But there are some of you* who do not believe." For Jesus knew from [the] beginning who they are, the ones not believing, and who is the one [who] will be betraying Him. ⁶⁵And He said, "For this reason I have said to you*, 'No one is able to come to Me unless it has been given to him from My Father.'"

⁶⁶From this [time] many went away of His disciples to the things behind and were no more walking about with Him. ⁶⁷So Jesus said to the twelve, "You* do not also want to be going away, do you*?" ⁶⁸Then Simon Peter answered Him, "Lord, to whom will we go? You have [the] words of eternal life. ⁶⁹And we have come to believe and have come to know that You are the Christ, the Son of the living God!"

⁷⁰Jesus answered them, "I Myself chose you*, the twelve, did I not? And one of you* is a devil!" ⁷¹Now He spoke of Judas Iscariot, [son] of Simon, for this one was about to be betraying Him, being one of the twelve.

7 And Jesus was walking about after these things in Galilee, for He was not wanting to be walking in Judea because the Jews were seeking to kill Him. ²But the feast of the Jews was near, the Feast of Tabernacles. ³So His brothers said to Him, "Depart from here and be going into Judea, so that Your disciples also will watch Your works which You are doing. ⁴For no one does anything in secret and

himself seeks to be in public. If You do these things, show Yourself to the world." [5]For His brothers were not believing in Him.

[6]So Jesus says to them, "My time is not yet present; but your* time is always ready. [7]The world is not able to be hating you*, but Me it hates because I testify concerning it that its works are evil. [8]You* go up to this feast; I am not yet going up to this feast because My time has not yet been fulfilled." [9]And having said these things to them, He remained in Galilee. [10]But when His brothers went up, then also He Himself went up to the feast, not openly, but as in secret.

[11]So the Jews were seeking Him at the feast and said, "Where is that One?" [12]And there was much grumbling [or, whispering] concerning Him among the crowds. Some indeed said, "He is good." Others said, "No, but He is leading the crowd astray [fig., deceiving the crowd]." [13]Though no one was speaking freely about Him on account of the fear of the Jews.

[14]But now in the middle of the feast Jesus went up into the temple and began teaching. [15]And the Jews were marveling, saying, "How does this One know letters, not having learned?" [or, "How is this One learned, not having been educated?"] [16]Therefore, Jesus answered them and said, "My teaching is not mine, but of the One having sent Me. [17]If anyone is willing to be doing His will, he will know concerning such teaching, whether it is from God or [whether] I speak from Myself. [18]The one speaking from himself seeks his own glory, but the One seeking the glory of the One having sent Him, this One is true, and unrighteousness is not in Him. [19]Has not Moses given to you* the Law? And not one of you* does the Law. Why are you* seeking to kill Me?" [20]The crowd answered and said, "You have a demon! Who seeks to kill You?"

[21]Jesus answered and said to them, "One work I did, and you* all marvel [or, are amazed]! [22]For this reason Moses has given to you* circumcision—not that it is from Moses, but from the fathers—and on a Sabbath you* circumcise a man. [23]If a man receives circumcision on a Sabbath so that the Law of Moses is not broken, [why] are you* very angry with Me that I made a man entirely well on a Sabbath? [24]Stop judging according to appearance, but be judging the righteous judgment."

[25]So some from the people of Jerusalem said, "This is [the One] whom they are seeking to kill, is it not? [26]And look! He speaks freely, and they say nothing to Him. Perhaps the rulers truly knew [or, came to know] that this One is truly the Christ? [27]But this One—we know from where He is. But when the Christ shall come, no one knows from where He is."

[28]Then Jesus cried out in the temple, teaching and saying, "You* both know Me and you* know from where I am. And of Myself I have not come, but the One having sent Me is true [or, dependable], whom you* do not know. [29]I know Him because I am from Him, and that One sent Me."

[30]So they were seeking to seize Him, but no one laid a hand on Him because His hour had not yet come. [31]But many out of the crowd believed [or, trusted] in Him and said, "When the Christ shall come, He will not do more signs [than] these which this One did, will He?" [32]The Pharisees heard the crowd muttering these

things concerning Him, and the Pharisees and the chief priests sent attendants so that they should take Him.

[33]Therefore Jesus said, "Yet a little time I am with you*, and [then] I am going away to the One having sent Me. [34]You* will seek Me and will not find [Me], and where I am, you* are not able to be coming." [35]Then the Jews said among themselves, "Where is this One about to be going that we will not find Him? He is not about to be going to the Dispersion [i.e. the scattered Jews among the Greeks] and to be teaching the Greeks, is He? [36]What is this word which He said, 'You* will seek Me and will not find [Me], and where I am, you* are not able to come?'"

[37]But on the last [day], the great day of the feast, Jesus had stood and cried out, saying, "If anyone is thirsting, let him come to Me and be drinking. [38]The one believing [or, trusting] in Me, just as the Scripture said, 'Out of his belly [or, innermost being] will flow rivers of living water." [no specific OT reference, but for general idea see Isaiah 55:1; 58:11; Ezek 47:1; Joel 3:18; Zech 13:1; 14:8] [39]But this He said concerning the Spirit, which [or, whom] the ones believing in Him were about to be receiving, for [the] Holy Spirit was not yet [given], because Jesus was not yet glorified.

[40]Therefore, many from the crowd having heard the word were saying, "This One is truly the Prophet." [41]Others were saying, "This is the Christ." Others were saying, "But the Christ is not coming out of Galilee, is He? [42]The Scripture said the Christ is coming from the seed of David and from Bethlehem, the village where David was, did it not?" [Psalm 132:11; Jer 23:5; 1Sam 16:1,13; Micah 5:2] [43]So a division arose among the crowd because of Him. [44]But some out of them were wanting to seize Him, but no one laid his hands on Him.

[45]Then the attendants came to the chief priests and Pharisees. And those [religious rulers] said to them, "Why did you* not bring Him?" [46]The attendants answered, "Never in such a manner spoke a person like this Person!" [47]Therefore, the Pharisees answered to them, "You* have not also been led astray [fig., been deceived], have you*? [48]No one from the rulers believed in Him nor from the Pharisees, have they? [49]But this crowd, the one not knowing the Law, is accursed."

[50]Nicodemus, the one having come to Him by night, says to them, being one of them, [51]"Our Law does not judge the person unless it hears from him first and knows what he does, does it?" [52]They answered and said to him, "You are not also out of Galilee, are you? Search and see that a prophet has not been raised out of Galilee." [53]And each one departed to his house.

8 But Jesus departed to the Mount of Olives. [2]Then at dawn He came again to the temple, and all the people were coming. And having sat down, He began teaching them.

[3]But the scribes and the Pharisees bring to Him a woman having been caught in adultery. And having set her in the middle [of them], [4]they say to Him, "Teacher, this woman was caught in the very act—committing adultery! [5]Now in the Law, Moses commanded us that such be stoned. Therefore, You, what do You say?"

6But this they said, testing Him, so that they should be having [something] to accuse Him. But Jesus, having stooped down, began writing into the ground with His finger, not taking notice.

7But when they continued asking Him, having straightened Himself back up, He said to them, "The sinless [one] of you*, let him first cast the stone at her." 8And again having stooped down, He was writing into the ground. 9But they having heard, and by the conscience being convicted, began going out one by one, having begun from the older [ones]. And Jesus was left alone, and the woman being in the midst.

10Now Jesus having straightened Himself back up and having seen no one but the woman, said to her, "Where are those accusers of yours? Did no one condemn you?" 11And she said, "No one, Lord." So Jesus said, "Neither do I judge you. Be going, and no longer be sinning."

12Then again Jesus spoke to them, saying, "I am the Light of the world! The one following Me shall by no means walk around in the darkness, but shall have the Light of life! 13So the Pharisees said to Him, "You are testifying concerning Yourself! Your testimony is not true!" 14Jesus answered and said to them, "Even if I am testifying concerning Myself, My testimony is true, because I know from where I came and where I am going. But you* do not know from where I come and where I am going. 15You* judge according to the flesh; I am not judging anyone. 16But even if I judge, My judgment is true, because I am not alone, but I and the Father having sent Me. 17And also in your* Law it has been written that the testimony of two persons is true. [Deut 19:15] 18I am the One testifying concerning Myself, and the Father having sent Me is testifying of Me."

19Therefore, they were saying to Him, "Where is Your father?" Jesus answered, "You* neither know Me nor My Father. If you* knew Me, you* would also know My Father." 20These sayings Jesus spoke in the treasury [fig., in the area where collection boxes were located], teaching in the temple, and no one seized Him, because His hour had not yet come.

21Then Jesus said again to them, "I am going away, and you* will seek Me, and in your* sin you* will die; where I am going, you* are not able to come." 22So the Jews were saying, "Surely He will not kill Himself, will He?—because He says, 'Where I am going, you* are not able to come?'" 23And He said to them, "You* are from below; I am from above. You* are from this world; I am not from this world. 24Therefore, I said to you*, 'you* will die in your sins,' for unless you* believe that I Am, you* will die in your* sins."

25So they were saying to Him, "You, who are You?" And Jesus said to them, "Just what I [have been] speaking to you* even [from] the beginning. 26Many [things] I have to be speaking concerning you* and to be judging; but the One having sent Me is true, and what I heard from Him, these things I say to the world." 27They did not understand that [about] the Father He spoke to them.

28Then Jesus said to them, "When you* lift up the Son of Humanity then you* will know that I Am, and from Myself I do nothing, but just as My Father taught Me, these things I speak. 29And the One having sent Me is with Me; the Father did not leave Me alone, because I always do the things pleasing to Him." ³⁰While speaking these things, many believed [or, trusted] in Him.

³¹So Jesus was saying to the Jews having believed [or, trusted] in Him, "If you* remain in My word, truly you* are My disciples. ³²And you* will know the truth, and the truth will set you* free!" ³³They answered Him, "We are seed [fig., descendents] of Abraham, and to no one have we at any time been enslaved. How can You say, 'You* will become free?'"

³⁴Jesus answered them, "Most positively, I say to you*, that every one committing [or, practicing] sin is a slave of sin. ³⁵But the slave does not remain in the house into the age [fig., forever]: the Son remains into the age [fig., forever]. ³⁶Therefore, if the Son makes you* free, you* will be free indeed! ³⁷I know that you* are seed [fig., descendents] of Abraham, but you* seek to kill Me, because My word does not find a place in you*. ³⁸I am speaking what I have seen with My Father, and therefore you* are doing what you* have seen with your* father."

³⁹They answered and said to Him, "Our father is Abraham." Jesus says to them, "If you* were children of Abraham, you* would be doing the works of Abraham. ⁴⁰But now, you* seek to kill Me—a Man who has spoken to you* the truth which I heard from God—this Abraham did not do. ⁴¹You* do the works of your* father." Then they said to Him, "We have not been born out of sexual sin; we have one Father—God!"

⁴²So Jesus said to them, "If God were your* father, you* would love Me, for I came forth and am come from God. For I have not come from Myself, but that One sent Me. ⁴³Why do you* not understand My speech? Because you* are not able to be hearing My word. ⁴⁴You* are from the [or, your*] father the Devil, and the desires of your* father you* want to be doing. That one was a murderer from [the] beginning, and he has not stood in the truth, because truth is not in him. When he is speaking falsehood, out of his own he speaks, because he is a liar, and the father of it. ⁴⁵But because I speak the truth, you* are not believing Me. ⁴⁶Who out of you* convicts Me concerning sin? But if I am speaking truth, why are you* not believing Me? ⁴⁷The one being from God, the words of God he hears [or, pays attention to], for this reason you* do not hear, because you* are not from God."

⁴⁸Then the Jews answered and said to Him, "We say rightly that You are a Samaritan and You have a demon, do we not?" ⁴⁹Jesus answered, "I have no demon, but I am honoring My Father, and you* are dishonoring Me. ⁵⁰But I do not seek My own glory; [there] is One seeking and judging. ⁵¹Most positively, I say to you*, if anyone keeps My word, he shall by no means see death into the age [fig., forever]!" ⁵²Then the Jews said to Him, "Now we have known that You have a demon. Abraham died, and the prophets, and You say, 'If anyone keeps My word, he shall by no means taste of death into the age [fig., forever]!' ⁵³You are not greater than our father Abraham, who died, are You? And the prophets died. Whom are You making Yourself [out to be]?"

⁵⁴Jesus answered, "If I glorify Myself, My glory is nothing; My Father is the One glorifying Me, [of] whom you* say, 'He is our God.' ⁵⁵And you* have not known Him, but I know Him; and if I should say that I do not know Him, I will be

like you*—speaking falsely. <u>But</u> I know Him, and I keep His word. ⁵⁶Abraham, your* father, was very glad that he should see My day, and he saw and rejoiced."

⁵⁷So the Jews said to Him, "You do not yet have fifty years [fig., You are not yet fifty years old], and You have seen Abraham?" ⁵⁸Jesus said to them, "Most positively, I say to you*, before Abraham came to be, <u>I</u> Am!" [cp. Exod 3:14] ⁵⁹Therefore, they took up stones that they should cast on Him. But Jesus was hidden. And He went out from the temple, having passed through [the] middle of them, and so He passed by.

9And passing by, He saw a man blind from birth. ²And His disciples asked Him, saying, "Rabbi, who sinned, this one or his parents, that he should be born blind?" ³Jesus answered, "Neither this one sinned nor his parents, <u>but</u> [this happened] so that the works of God should be revealed in him. ⁴It is necessary [for] Me to be working the works of the One having sent Me while it is day; night is coming when no one is able to be working. ⁵As long as I am in the world, <u>I</u> am [the] Light of the world."

⁶Having said these things, He spit on the ground and made mud from the saliva and rubbed the mud on the eyes of the blind man. ⁷And He said to him, "Be going away; be washing in the pool of Siloam" (which, is interpreted, "Having Been Sent"). So he went away and washed, and he came seeing! ⁸Therefore, the neighbors and those seeing him previously that he was blind, were saying, "This is the one sitting and begging, is it not?" ⁹Others were saying, "This is he." But others, "He is like him." That one kept saying, "<u>I</u> am [he]."

¹⁰So they were saying to him, "How were your eyes opened?" ¹¹That one answered and said, "A Man being called Jesus made mud and rubbed my eyes and said to me, 'Be going away to the pool of Siloam and be washing.' And having gone away and having washed, I received sight!" ¹²So they said to him, "Where is that One?" He says, "I do not know."

¹³They bring him to the Pharisees, the one formerly blind. ¹⁴Now it was a Sabbath when Jesus made the mud and opened his eyes. ¹⁵So again the Pharisees also were asking him how he received sight. And that one said to them, "He put mud on my eyes, and I washed, and I see!" ¹⁶Then some of the Pharisees were saying, "This Man is not from God because He does not keep the Sabbath." Others were saying, "How is a sinful person able to be doing such signs?" And a division was among them. ¹⁷They say to the blind one again, "You, what do you say concerning Him, because He opened your eyes?" So he said, "He is a prophet."

¹⁸Then the Jews did not believe concerning him that he was blind and received sight, until which [time] they called the parents of him, the one having received sight. ¹⁹And they asked them, saying, "Is this your son, whom you* say that he was born blind? How then does he now see?" ²⁰So his parents answered them and said, "We know that this is our son and that he was born blind. ²¹But how he now sees, we do not know, or who opened his eyes, we do not know. He is of age, ask him. He will speak concerning himself." ²²These things his parents said because they were afraid of the Jews, for the Jews had already agreed together

that if anyone shall confess Him [as the] Christ, he should be expelled from the synagogue. ²³For this reason his parents said, "He is of age, ask him."

²⁴So a second time they called the man who was blind. And they said to him, "Be giving glory to God; we know that this Man is a sinner!" ²⁵Then that one answered and said, "If He is a sinner, I do not know; one [thing] I do know, that being blind, now I see!" ²⁶But they said to him again, "What did He do to you? How did He open your eyes?" ²⁷He answered them, "I told you* already and you* did not hear; why do you* again want to be hearing? You* do not want to become His disciples, do you*?" ²⁸They insulted him and said, "You are that [One's] disciple, but we are Moses' disciples! ²⁹We know that God has spoken to Moses, but this One—we do not know from where He is."

³⁰The man answered and said to them, "Indeed, in this is a marvelous [thing], that you* do not know from where He is—and He opened my eyes! ³¹But we know that God does not hear sinners, but if anyone is God-fearing [or, devout] and is doing His will, this one He hears. ³²From the age [fig., Since the beginning of time] it was not heard that anyone opened [the] eyes of one having been born blind. ³³If this One were not from God, He would not be able to be doing anything." ³⁴They answered and said to him, "You were totally born in sins, and you are teaching us!" And they cast him outside.

³⁵Jesus heard that they cast him outside. And having found him, He said to him, "Do you believe [or, trust] in the Son of God?" ³⁶That one answered and said, "And who is He, Lord, so that I shall believe in Him?" ³⁷And Jesus said to him, "You have both seen Him and the One speaking with you—that One is He." ³⁸And he said, "I believe, Lord!" And he prostrated himself in worship before Him.

³⁹And Jesus said, "For judgment I came into this world, so that the ones not seeing shall be seeing, and the ones seeing shall become blind." ⁴⁰And those of the Pharisees who were with Him heard these things, and they said to Him, "We are not also blind, are we?" ⁴¹Jesus said to them, "If you* were blind, you* would not have sin, but now you* say, 'We see.' Therefore, your* sin remains.

10 "Most positively, I say to you*, the one not entering through the door into the fold of the sheep, but climbing up some other way, that one is a thief and a robber. ²But the one entering through the door is shepherd of the sheep. ³To this one the doorkeeper opens. And the sheep hear his voice, and his own sheep he calls by name, and he leads them out. ⁴And whenever he brings out his own sheep, he goes before them, and the sheep follow him, because they know his voice. ⁵But a stranger they will by no means follow, but they will flee from him, because they do not know the voice of strangers." ⁶This illustration Jesus spoke to them, but those ones did not understand what the things were which he was speaking to them.

⁷Therefore, Jesus said again to them, "Most positively, I say to you*, I am the door of the sheep! ⁸All, as many as came, are thieves and robbers, but the sheep did not hear them. ⁹I am the door. If anyone enters through Me, he will be saved, and he will come in and will go out and will find pasture. ¹⁰The thief does not

come except so that he should steal and kill and destroy. I came so that they shall have life, and they shall have [it] abundantly!

11"I am the good shepherd! The good shepherd lays down His life on behalf of the sheep. 12But the hired worker, not being also a shepherd, whose own the sheep are not, watches the wolf coming and leaves the sheep and flees, and the wolf seizes them and scatters the sheep. 13Now the hired worker flees because he is a hired worker and is not concerned about the sheep.

14"I am the good shepherd, and I know My [own], and I am known by My [own]. 15Just as the Father knows Me, and I know the Father, and I lay down My life on behalf of the sheep. 16And other sheep I have which are not from this fold. These also it is necessary [for] Me to bring, and My voice they will hear. And they will become one flock, one shepherd. 17For this reason the Father loves Me, because I lay down My life, so that I shall take it [up] again. 18No one takes it from Me, but I lay it down of Myself; I have authority to lay it down, and I have authority to take it [up] again. This command I received from My Father."

19So [there] again came to be division among the Jews because of these words. 20But many of them were saying, "He has a demon and is raving mad; why do you hear Him [or, pay attention to Him]?" 21Others were saying, "These are not the sayings of [one] being demon-possessed [or, oppressed by a demon]. A demon is not able to open [the] eyes of blind [people], is it?"

22Now the Feast of Dedication [i.e. Hanukkah] took place in Jerusalem, and it was winter. 23And Jesus was walking about in the temple in the Portico of Solomon. 24Then the Jews surrounded Him and said to Him, "How long do You hold our soul in suspense? If You are the Christ, tell us plainly."

25Jesus answered them, "I told you*, and you* do not believe; the works which I do in the Name of My Father, these testify concerning Me. 26But you* do not believe, because you* are not of My sheep, just as I said to you*. 27My sheep hear My voice, and I know them, and they follow Me. 28And I give to them eternal life, and they shall by no means perish into the age [fig., forever]! And no one will pluck them out of My hand. 29My Father who has given [them] to Me is greater than all, and no one is able to be plucking [them] out of the hand of My Father. 30I and the Father are one!"

31Therefore, the Jews again took up stones so that they should stone Him. 32Jesus answered to them, "Many good works I showed to you* from my Father. On account of which work of them do you* stone Me?" 33The Jews answered Him, saying, "Concerning a good work we do not stone You, but for blasphemy, and because You, being a human being, are making Yourself God."

34Jesus answered them, "Has it not been written in your* Law, 'I said, you* are gods?' [Psalm 82:6] 35If He called those ones "gods" to whom the word of God came (and the Scripture is not able to be broken), 36[why of] whom the Father sanctified and sent into the world, do you* say, 'You blaspheme,' because I said, 'I am God's Son?' 37If I am not doing the works of My Father, do not believe Me. 38But if I am doing [them], even if you* do not believe Me, be believing the works, so that you* shall know and believe that the Father [is] in Me, and I [am] in Him." ³⁹Therefore, they were seeking again to seize Him, and He went out from their hand.

⁴⁰And He went away again beyond the Jordan [River] to the place where John was first baptizing, and He remained there. ⁴¹And many came to Him and were saying, "John indeed did no sign. But all [things], as many as John said concerning this One were true." ⁴²And many in that place believed [or, trusted] in Him.

11 Now [there] was a certain one being sick, Lazarus from Bethany, of the village of Mary and her sister Martha. ²And it was Mary, the one anointing the Lord with ointment and wiping His feet with her hair, whose brother Lazarus was being sick. ³So the sisters sent to Him, saying, "Lord, listen! [He] whom You affectionately love is sick."

⁴But Jesus having heard, said, "This sickness is not to death, but [it is] for the glory of God, so that the Son of God shall be glorified through it!" ⁵Now Jesus was loving Martha and her sister and Lazarus. ⁶So when He heard that he is sick, then indeed He remained in the place in which He was two days. ⁷Then after this, He says to the disciples, "We shall be going again to Judea."

⁸The disciples say to Him, "Rabbi, [just] now the Jews were seeking to stone You, and You are going there again?" ⁹Jesus answered, "Are [there] not twelve hours in the day? If anyone shall be walking about in the day, he does not stumble, because he sees the light of this world. ¹⁰But if anyone shall be walking about in the night, he stumbles, because the light is not in him."

¹¹These [things] He said, and after this He says to them, "Lazarus our friend has fallen asleep, but I am going so that I shall wake him up." ¹²Then His disciples said, "Lord, if he has fallen asleep, he will be cured." ¹³But Jesus had spoken concerning his death, but those ones thought that He is speaking concerning the resting of sleep. ¹⁴So then Jesus said to them plainly, "Lazarus has died. ¹⁵And I rejoice for your* sake that I was not there, so that you* shall believe. But we shall be going to him." ¹⁶Therefore, Thomas, the one being called Didymus ["Twin"], said to his fellow-disciples, "Let us also go so that we shall die with Him."

¹⁷So having come, Jesus found him four days already having [been] in the tomb. ¹⁸Now Bethany was near Jerusalem, about fifteen stadia away [about 1.7 miles or 2.75 kilometers]. ¹⁹And many of the Jews had come to the [women] around Martha and Mary, so that they should comfort them concerning their brother.

²⁰Then Martha, when she heard that Jesus is coming, met Him. But Mary was sitting in the house. ²¹So Martha said to Jesus, "Lord, if You were here my brother would not have died. ²²But even now I know that whatever You ask of God, God will give to You." ²³Jesus says to her, "Your brother will rise again." ²⁴Martha says to Him, "I know that he will rise again, in the resurrection on the last day." ²⁵Jesus said to her, "I am the Resurrection and the Life! The one believing in Me, even if he dies, he will live! ²⁶And every[one] living and believing [or, trusting] in Me shall by no means die into the age [fig., forever]! Do you believe this [or, Are you convinced of this]?" ²⁷She says to Him, "Yes, Lord, I have believed [or,

am convinced] that You are the Christ, the Son of God, the One coming into the world."

[28]And having said these things, she went away and called Mary her sister privately, saying, "The Teacher is present and is calling you." [29]Then that one, when she heard, rises up quickly and comes to Him. [30]Now Jesus had not yet come to the village, but He was in the place where Martha met Him. [31]Therefore, the Jews, the ones being with her in the house and comforting her, having seen Mary that she rose up quickly and went out, followed her, saying, "She is going off to the tomb so that she should weep there."

[32]So Mary, when she came where Jesus was, having seen Him, fell to His feet, saying to Him, "Lord, if You were here my brother would not [have] died." [33]Then Jesus, when He saw her weeping, and the Jews having come with her weeping, was deeply moved in His spirit and stirred Himself up [or, was disturbed]. [34]And He said, "Where have you* laid him?" They say to Him, "Lord, be coming and see." [35]Jesus wept. [36]So the Jews said, "Look how He was affectionately loving him!" [37]But some of them said, "This One, the One having opened the eyes of the blind man, He was able to do [something] so that also this one would not have died, was He not?"

[38]So Jesus, again being deeply moved in Himself, comes to the tomb. Now it was a cave, and a stone was lying upon it. [39]Jesus says, "Take away the stone." Martha, the sister of the one having died, says to Him, "Lord, already he stinks, for it is the fourth day [since he died]." [40]Jesus says to her, "I said to you that if you believe you will see the glory of God, did I not?" [41]Then they took away the stone from where the one having died was lying. And Jesus lifted His eyes upwards and said, "Father, I give thanks to You because You heard Me. [42]Now, I knew that You always hear Me, but because of the crowd, the ones having stood around, I said [it], so that they shall believe [or, shall be convinced] that You sent Me."

[43]And having said these things, with a loud voice He cried out, "Lazarus, come out!" [44]And the one having died came out, [his] feet and hands having been bound with grave-clothes, and his face had been wrapped around with a facecloth. Jesus says to them, "Loose him, and allow [him] to be going."

[45]Therefore, many of the Jews, the ones having come to Mary and having seen what Jesus did, believed [or, trusted] in Him. [46]But some of them went away to the Pharisees and told them what Jesus did. [47]Therefore, the chief priests and the Pharisees gathered together a High Council [or, Sanhedrin] and said, "What are we doing? For this Person is performing many signs! [48]If we leave Him in this way, all will believe [or, trust] in Him, and the Romans will come and will take away both our place and nation."

[49]But a certain one of them, Caiaphas, being high priest of that year, said to them, "You* do not know anything, [50]nor do you* take into account that it is advantageous for us that one person should die on behalf of the people, and the whole nation shall not perish." [51]But this he said not from himself, but being high priest of that year, that one prophesied that Jesus was about to be dying on behalf of the nation. [52]And not on behalf of that nation only, but so that He shall

also gather together into one the children of God, the ones having been scattered abroad.

⁵³So from that day they plotted among themselves so that they should kill Him. ⁵⁴Therefore, Jesus was no more freely walking about among the Jews, but He went away from there to the countryside near the wilderness, to a city being called Ephraim. And there He stayed with His disciples.

⁵⁵But the Passover of the Jews was near. And many went up to Jerusalem out of the countryside before the Passover so that they should purify themselves. ⁵⁶So they were seeking Jesus and were speaking one with another, having stood in the temple, "What do you* think, that He shall not at all come to the feast?" ⁵⁷Now both the chief priests and the Pharisees had given a command that if anyone knew where He is, he should report [it], in order that they should seize Him.

12 So six days before the Passover, Jesus came to Bethany, where Lazarus was, the one having died, whom He raised from [the] dead. ²So they made Him dinner there, and Martha was serving. But Lazarus was one of the ones reclining [to eat] with Him.

³Then Mary, having taken a litra [about 12 ounces or 340 grams] of very valuable, pure spikenard ointment, anointed the feet of Jesus and wiped His feet with her hair. And the house was filled from the fragrance of the ointment. ⁴Therefore one of His disciples (Judas Iscariot, [son] of Simon, the one about to betray Him) says, ⁵"Why was not this ointment sold for three hundred denarii [i.e., 300 days' wages] and given to poor [people]?" ⁶Now he said this, not because he was concerned about the poor, but because he was a thief and [was] holding the money-bag and was carrying off [fig., stealing] the [things] being put in. ⁷Then Jesus said, "Allow her (or, Let her alone); she has kept it for the day of My burial preparation. ⁸For the poor you* always have with yourselves, but Me you* do not always have."

⁹So a large crowd of the Jews knew that He is there. And they came, not because of Jesus only, but so that they should also see Lazarus, whom He raised from the dead. ¹⁰Now the chief priests plotted that they should also kill Lazarus, ¹¹because on account of him many of the Jews were going away and were believing [or, trusting] in Jesus.

¹²The next day a large crowd, the one having come to the feast, having heard that Jesus is coming to Jerusalem, ¹³took the branches of the palm trees and went out to meet Him and began crying out, "We praise You [Gr., *Hosanna*]! *'Blessed [is] the One coming in [the] name of [the] LORD'*—[the] King of Israel!" [Psalm 118:26] ¹⁴Now Jesus having found a young donkey, sat on it, just as it has been written, ¹⁵*"Stop being afraid, daughter of Zion. Look! Your King is coming, sitting on a donkey's colt."* [Zech 9:9] ¹⁶But these things His disciples did not understand at first, but when Jesus was glorified, then they remembered that these things had been written about Him, and these things they did to Him.

¹⁷Then the crowd, the ones being with Him, were testifying that he called Lazarus out of the tomb and raised him from the dead. ¹⁸For this reason also the crowd met Him, because they heard He had done this sign. ¹⁹Therefore, the

Pharisees said among themselves, "You* see that you* are not accomplishing anything. Look! The world went away after Him!"

²⁰Now [there] were some Greeks from the ones going up so that they should prostrate themselves in worship at the feast. ²¹Then these [Greeks] came to Philip, the [one] from Bethsaida of Galilee, and were asking him, saying, "Lord [or, Sir], we desire to see Jesus." ²²Philip comes and tells Andrew, and again Andrew and Philip tell Jesus.

²³But Jesus answered them, saying, "The hour has come that the Son of Humanity shall be glorified. ²⁴Most positively, I say to you*, unless the grain of wheat, having fallen to the earth, dies, it remains alone. But if it dies, it brings forth much fruit. ²⁵The one affectionately loving his life will lose it, and the one hating his life in this world will keep it to eternal life. ²⁶If anyone shall be serving Me, let him be following Me, and where I am, there also My servant shall be. And if anyone shall be serving Me, the Father will honor him.

²⁷"Now has My soul been disturbed, and what shall I say—Father, save Me from this hour? But on account of this [reason] I came to this hour. ²⁸Father, glorify Your name." Then came a voice out of heaven, "I both glorified [it], and again I will glorify [it]!" ²⁹Then the crowd, having stood and heard, were saying it had thundered. Others were saying, "An angel has spoken to Him." ³⁰Jesus answered and said, "Not for My sake has this voice come, but for your* sakes.

³¹"Now is [the] judgment of this world; now the ruler of this world will be cast out. ³²And I, if I am lifted up from the earth, I will draw [or, drag] all to Myself." ³³But this He was saying signifying by what sort of death He was about to die. ³⁴The crowd answered Him, "We heard out of the Law that the Christ remains into the age [fig., forever], and [so] how do You say, 'It is necessary [for] the Son of Humanity to be lifted up?' Who is this—'the Son of Humanity?'"

³⁵So Jesus said to them, "Yet a little time is the Light with you*. Be walking about as long as you* have the Light, so that darkness does not overpower you*. And the one walking about in the darkness does not know where he is going. ³⁶As long as you* have the Light, be believing [or, trusting] in the Light, so that you* shall become sons [and daughters] of Light." These things Jesus spoke, and having gone away, He was hid from them. [cp. Luke 24:16; John 7:30; 8:59; 10:39]

³⁷But [although] He had done so many signs before them, they were not believing [or, trusting] in Him, ³⁸so that the word of Isaiah the prophet should be fulfilled, which he said, *"Lord, who believed our report [or, accepted our report as true]? And the arm [fig., power] of [the] LORD—to whom was it revealed?"* [Isaiah 53:1, LXX] ³⁹On account of this they were not able to be believing [or, to be convinced], because again Isaiah said, ⁴⁰*"He has blinded their eyes and hardened their heart [fig., made them stubborn], so that they shall not see with their eyes and understand with the heart and be turned [or changed], and I should heal them."* [Isaiah 6:10] ⁴¹These things Isaiah said when he saw His [i.e. Jesus'] glory and spoke about Him. [Isaiah 6:1-8]

⁴²Nevertheless, still also out of the rulers many believed [or, trusted] in Him, but because of the Pharisees they were not confessing [Him publicly], so that they

should not be expelled from the synagogue. [43]For they loved the glory of people more than the glory of God.

[44]But Jesus cried out and said, "The one believing [or, trusting] in Me does not believe in Me but in the One having sent Me! [45]And the one looking upon Me, looks upon the One having sent Me. [46]I have come as Light to the world, so that every[one] believing [or, trusting] in Me shall not remain in the darkness.

[47]"And if anyone hears My sayings and does not believe [them] [or, does not accept [them] as true], I do not judge Him, for I did not come so that I should judge the world, but so that I should save the world. [48]The one rejecting Me [or, regarding Me as nothing] and not receiving My sayings has one judging him—the word which I spoke, that will judge him on the last day. [49]Because I spoke not from Myself, but the Father having sent Me, He gave Me a command what I should say and what I should speak. [50]And I know that His command is eternal life. Therefore, what I speak, just as the Father has said to Me, so I speak."

13 Now before the feast of the Passover, Jesus knowing that His hour has come, that He should depart out of this world to the Father, having loved His own, the ones in the world, to [the] end He loved them. [2]And dinner having taken place, the Devil already having put into the heart of Judas Iscariot, [son] of Simon, that he should betray Him, [3]Jesus (knowing that the Father has given all [things] to Him, into His hands, and that He came forth from God, and He is going to God) [4]rises up from the dinner and lays down His garments, and having taken a towel, He tied [it] around Himself.

[5]Next He puts water into the foot basin and began to be washing the feet of His disciples and to dry [them] with the towel with which He had tied around Himself. [6]Then He comes to Simon Peter. And that one says to Him, "Lord, You are washing my feet?" [7]Jesus answered and said to him, "What I am doing you do not know now, but you will know after these things." [8]Peter says to Him, "By no means shall You wash my feet—into the age [fig., forever]!"

Jesus answered him, "Unless I wash you, you have no part with Me." [9]Simon Peter says to Him, "Lord, not my feet only, but also the hands and the head!" [10]Jesus says to him, "The one having been bathed does not have need except to wash his feet, but he is altogether clean. And you* are clean, but not all [of you*]." [11]For He knew the one betraying Him; on account of this He said, "You* are not all clean."

[12]So when He washed their feet and took His garments, and having reclined [at the table] again, He said to them, "Do you* understand what I have done to you*? [13]You* call Me, 'The Teacher' and 'The Lord,' and you* say correctly, for I am. [14]If then I washed your* feet—the Lord and the Teacher—you* also ought to be washing one another's feet. [15]For an example I gave to you*, so that just as I did to you*, you* also should be doing. [16]Most positively, I say to you*, a slave is not greater than his lord, nor a messenger [or, an apostle] greater than the one having sent him. [17]If these things you* know, happy [or, blessed] are you* if you* shall be doing them.

¹⁸"I do not speak concerning all of you*. I know whom I chose for Myself, but so that the Scripture shall be fulfilled, *'The one eating the bread with Me lifted up his heel against Me.'* [Psalm 41:9] ¹⁹From now on I am telling you* before it happens, so that when it happens you* shall believe [or, shall be convinced] that I Am! ²⁰Most positively, I say to you, the one receiving whomever I send, receives Me, and the one receiving Me, receives the One having sent Me."

²¹These things having said, Jesus was troubled in the [or, His] spirit and testified and said, "Most positively, I say to you* that one of you* will betray Me." ²²Therefore, the disciples began looking one at another, themselves being perplexed concerning whom He speaks.

²³Now there was reclining [at the table] one of His disciples on the bosom of Jesus, whom Jesus was loving. ²⁴So Simon Peter motioned to this one to inquire who it might be, concerning whom He speaks. ²⁵Then that one, having leaned back thus on the breast of Jesus, says to Him, "Lord, who is it?" ²⁶Jesus answers, "That one it is to whom I, having dipped the piece of bread, will give [it]." And having dipped the piece of bread, He gives [it] to Judas Iscariot, [son] of Simon. ²⁷And after the piece of bread, then Satan entered into that one.

Then Jesus says to him, "What you are doing—do [it] quickly!" ²⁸But none of the ones reclining [at the table] knew for what [reason] He said this to him. ²⁹For some were thinking, since Judas was holding the money-bag, that Jesus says to him, "Buy what we have need of for the feast," or that he should give something to the poor. ³⁰Then having received the piece of bread, that one immediately went out. And it was night.

³¹When he went out, Jesus says, "Now was the Son of Humanity glorified, and God was glorified in Him! ³²If God was glorified in Him, God will also glorify Him in Himself, and immediately He will glorify Him.

³³"Little children [or, [My] dear children], yet a little while longer I am with you*. You* will seek Me, and just as I said to the Jews, 'Where I am going away, you* are not able to come.' To you* also now I say [it]. ³⁴A new commandment I give to you*, that you* shall be loving one another just as I loved you*, that you* also shall be loving one another. ³⁵By this all will know that you* are My disciples, if you* shall be having love for one another."

³⁶Simon Peter says to Him, "Lord, where are You going away [to]?" Jesus answered him, "Where I am going away, you are not able now to follow me, but later you will follow Me." ³⁷Peter says to Him, "Lord, why am I not able to follow You now? I will lay down my life for You!" ³⁸Jesus answered him, "You will lay down your life for Me? Most positively, I say to you, by no means shall a rooster crow until you deny Me three times.

14 "Stop letting your* heart be troubled! You* believe [or, trust] in God, be believing also in Me. ²In the house of My Father are many dwelling places, but if not [fig., if it were not so], I would have told you*. I am going to prepare a place for you*. ³And if I go, I shall prepare a place for you*. I am coming again, and I will receive you* to Myself, so that where I am you* also shall be. ⁴And where I am going you* know, and the way you* know."

⁵Thomas says to Him, "Lord, we do not know where You are going. And how are we able to know the way?" ⁶Jesus says to him, "I am the Way and the Truth and the Life! No one comes to the Father except through [or, by means of] Me! ⁷If you* had known Me, you* also would have known My Father, and from now on you* know Him and have seen Him."

⁸Philip says to Him, "Lord, show to us the Father, and it is sufficient for us." ⁹Jesus says to him, "[For] so long a time am I with you*, and you have not known Me, Philip? The one having seen Me has seen the Father, and how do you say, 'Show to us the Father?' ¹⁰Do you not believe [or, Are you not convinced] that I [am] in the Father and the Father is in Me? The sayings which I speak to you*, I do not speak from Myself, but the Father abiding in Me, Himself does the works. ¹¹Be believing Me that I [am] in the Father and the Father [is] in Me, but if not [fig., or else] be believing Me because of the works themselves.

¹²"Most positively, I say to you*, the one believing [or, trusting] in Me, the works which I do that one also will do, and greater [things] than these he will do, because I am going to My Father. ¹³And whatever you* ask in My name, this I will do, so that the Father is glorified in the Son. ¹⁴If you* ask Me anything in My name, I will do [it].

¹⁵"If you* are loving Me, keep My commandments. ¹⁶And I will ask the Father, and another Counselor [or, Helper] He will give to you*, so that He shall dwell with you* into the age [fig., forever]— ¹⁷the Spirit of the truth, whom the world is not able to receive, because it does not look upon [or, watch [for]] Him, nor knows Him. But you* know Him, because He dwells with you* and will be in you.*

¹⁸"I will not leave you* bereaved; I am coming to you*. ¹⁹Yet a little while longer and the world no longer looks upon Me. But you* are looking upon Me. Because I live, you* also will live. ²⁰In that day you* will know that I [am] in My Father, and you* in Me, and I in you*. ²¹The one having My commandments and keeping them, that one is the one loving Me. And the one loving Me will be loved by My Father, and I will love him and will reveal Myself to him."

²²Judas says to him (not Iscariot), "Lord, and what has happened that You are about to be revealing Yourself to us and not to the world?" ²³Jesus answered and said to him, "If anyone is loving Me, My word he will keep. And My Father will love him, and We will come to him and will make [Our] dwelling place with him. ²⁴The one not loving Me does not keep My words, and the word which you* hear [or, pay attention to] is not Mine, but of the Father, the One having sent Me. ²⁵These things I have spoken to you*, [while] dwelling with you*. ²⁶But the Counselor [or, Helper], the Holy Spirit, whom the Father will send in My name, that One will teach you* all [things] and will cause you* to remember all [things] which I said to you*.

²⁷"Peace I leave to you*. My peace I give to you*; not as the world gives I give to you*. Stop letting your* heart be troubled, and stop letting it be afraid. ²⁸You heard that I said to you*, 'I am going away, and I am coming to you*.' If you* were loving Me, you* would have rejoiced because I said 'I am going to the Father,' because My Father is greater than I. ²⁹And now I have said [it] to you* before it happens, so that when it happens, you* shall believe [or, have confidence [in Me]]. ³⁰I will no longer talk much with you*, for the ruler of the world is

coming, and he does not have anything in Me. ³¹But so that the world shall know that I love the Father, and just as the Father gave Me command so I am doing, be rising up. Let us be going from here.

15 "I am the true grapevine, and My Father is the vineyard keeper. ²Every branch in Me not bearing fruit, He takes it away [or, lifts it up]; and every [branch] bearing fruit, He prunes clean, so that it shall be bearing more fruit. ³Already you* are pruned clean because of the word which I have spoken to you*. ⁴Abide in Me, and I in you*. Just as the branch is not able to be bearing fruit by itself unless it shall be abiding in the vine, so neither you*, unless you* shall be abiding in Me.

⁵"I am the vine; you* [are] the branches. The one abiding in Me, and I in him, this one bears much fruit, because apart from Me you* are not able to be doing anything. ⁶If anyone does not abide in Me, he was thrown out as the branch and was withered. And they gather them and cast [them] into the fire, and they are burned. ⁷If you* abide in Me, and My sayings abide in you*, you* will ask whatever you* desire, and it will happen to you*. ⁸In this was My Father glorified, that you* shall be bearing much fruit, and you* will become My disciples.

⁹"Just as the Father loved Me, I also loved you*; abide in My love. ¹⁰If you* keep My commandments, you* will abide in My love; just as I have kept the commandments of My Father, and I abide in His love. ¹¹These things I have spoken to you* so that My joy shall abide in you*, and your* joy shall be made full.

¹²"This is My commandment, that you* shall be loving one another just as I loved you*. ¹³Greater love has no one than this, that someone lays down his life on behalf of his friends. ¹⁴You* are My friends, if you* are doing whatever I command you*. ¹⁵No longer do I call you* slaves, because the slave does not know what his lord does. But I have called you* friends because all which I heard from My Father, I made known to you*. ¹⁶You* did not choose Me, but I chose you* and appointed you*, so that you* shall be going away and bearing fruit, and your* fruit shall be abiding, so that whatever you* ask of the Father in My name, He shall give to you*. ¹⁷These things I command you*, so that you* shall be loving one another.

¹⁸"If the world hates you*, you* know that it has hated Me before you*. ¹⁹If you* were from the world, the world would be affectionately loving its own. But because you* are not from the world, but I chose you* out of the world, for this reason the world hates you*. ²⁰Be remembering the word which I said to you*, 'A slave is not greater than his lord.' If they persecuted Me, they will also persecute you*. If My word they kept, yours* also they will keep. ²¹But they will do all these things to you* on account of My name, because they do not know the One having sent Me.

²²"If I did not come and did not speak to them, they would not have sin, but now they have no excuse for their sin. ²³The one hating Me, also hates My Father. ²⁴If I did not do among them the works which no other has done, they would not have sin, but now they have both seen and have hated both Me and My Father. ²⁵But [this happened] so that the word shall be fulfilled, the one having been written in their Law, *'They hated Me without a cause.'* [Psalm 69:4]

²⁶"But when the Counselor [or, Helper] comes, whom I will send to you* from the Father, the Spirit of the truth, who proceeds from the Father, that One will testify concerning Me. ²⁷And you* also testify [or, be testifying], because you* are with Me from the beginning.

16"These things I have spoken to you*, so that you* shall not be caused to stumble [fig., be offended]. ²They will make you* be expelled from the synagogue, but an hour is coming that every[one] having killed you* shall think [he is] offering sacred service to God. ³And these things they will do because they did not know the Father nor Me. ⁴But these things I have spoken to you* so that when the hour comes, you* shall be remembering them, that I said to you*. But these things I did not say to you* from the beginning, because I was with you*.

⁵"But now I am going away to the One having sent Me, and none of you* asks Me, 'Where are You going?' ⁶But because these things I have said to you*, sorrow has filled your heart. ⁷But I speak the truth to you*. It is advantageous for you* that I go away. For if I do not go away, the Counselor [or, Helper] will not come to you*, but if I go, I will send Him to you*. ⁸And having come, that One will convict the world concerning sin and concerning righteousness and concerning judgment: ⁹concerning sin indeed because they do not believe [or, trust] in Me, ¹⁰and concerning righteousness because I am going away to My Father, and you* no longer look upon Me, ¹¹and concerning judgment because the ruler of this world has been judged.

¹²"I still have many things to be saying to you*, but you* are not able to be bearing [them] now. ¹³But when that One shall come—the Spirit of the truth—He will guide you* into all the truth. For He will not speak from Himself, but as many things as He hears He will speak, and He will announce to you* the coming [things]. ¹⁴That One will glorify Me, because He will take from [what is] Mine and will announce [it] to you*. ¹⁵All [things], as many as the Father has, are Mine, for this reason I said, 'He takes from [what is] Mine and will announce [it] to you*.' ¹⁶A little while and you* are not looking upon Me, and again, a little while and you* will see Me, because I am going away to the Father."

¹⁷Therefore, [some] of His disciples said to one another, "What is this which He says to us, 'A little while, and you* are not looking upon Me, and again, a little while and you* will see Me,' and 'Because I am going away to the Father?'" ¹⁸Then they said, "What is this which He says, 'The little while?' We do not know what He is saying."

¹⁹So Jesus knew that they were desiring to be asking Him. And He said to them, "Concerning this you* inquire one with another, because I said, 'A little while, and you* are not looking upon Me, and again, a little while and you* will see Me?' ²⁰Most positively, I say to you*, that you* will weep and you* will lament, but the world will rejoice. You* will be sorrowful, but your* sorrow will become [fig., will turn] into joy. ²¹The woman, whenever she shall be giving birth, has sorrow, because her hour came. But when she gives birth to the young child, no longer does she remember the anguish, on account of the joy that a person was

born into the world. ²²So also you* now indeed have sorrow. But I will see you* again, and your* heart will rejoice, and your* joy no one takes from you*.

²³"And in that day you* will not ask Me anything. Most positively, I say to you*, that as many [things] as you* ask the Father in My name, He will give to you*. ²⁴Until now you* asked nothing in My name. Be asking and you* will receive, so that your* joy shall be filled.

²⁵"These things in figures of speech I have spoken to you*; but an hour is coming when no longer in figures of speech will I speak to you*, but I will tell you* plainly about the Father. ²⁶In that day, you* will request for yourselves in My name. And I do not say to you* that I will ask the Father on behalf of you*. ²⁷For the Father Himself affectionately loves you*, because you* have affectionately loved Me, and you* have believed [or, have accepted as true] that I came forth from God. ²⁸I came forth from the Father and have come into the world. Again I am leaving the world and am going to the Father."

²⁹His disciples say to Him, "Listen! Now You are speaking plainly, and You are not even speaking one figure of speech. ³⁰Now we know that You know all, and we do not have need that anyone should be questioning You. By this we believe [or, are convinced] that You came forth from God."

³¹Jesus answered them, "Now are you* believing [or, convinced]? ³²Listen! An hour is coming, and now has come, that you* shall be scattered, each to his own [home], and you* shall leave Me alone. Yet I am not alone, because the Father is with Me. ³³These things I have spoken to you*, so that in Me you* shall be having peace [or, freedom from anxiety]. In the world you* have tribulation, but be taking courage, I have overcome the world!"

17 Jesus spoke these things. And He lifted up His eyes to heaven and said, "Father, the hour has come: glorify Your Son, so that Your Son shall also glorify You. ²Just as You gave to Him authority [over] all flesh, so that every[one] You have given to Him, He will give to them eternal life. ³Now this is eternal life: that they shall be knowing You, the only true God, and Jesus Christ whom You sent. ⁴I glorified You on the earth. I finished the work which You have given to Me that I should do. ⁵And now You glorify Me, Father, with Yourself with the glory which I had with You before the world [came] to be.

⁶"I made Your name known to the people whom You have given to Me out of the world. They were Yours, and You have given them to Me, and Your word they have kept. ⁷Now they have known [or, have come to understand] that all [things], as many as You have given to Me, are from You. ⁸Because the sayings which You have given to Me, I have given to them. And they received [them], and they truly knew [or, came to understand] that I came forth from You. And they believed that You sent Me.

⁹"I ask concerning them; I do not ask concerning the world, but concerning [those] whom You have given to Me, because they are Yours. ¹⁰And all [which are] Mine are Yours, and Yours [are] Mine, and I have been glorified in them. ¹¹And I am no longer in the world, yet these are in the world, and I am coming to You. Holy Father, keep them in Your name, which You have given to Me, so that they

shall be one just as We [are]. [12]When I was with them in the world, I was keeping them in Your name. [Those] whom You have given to Me I guarded, and none of them was destroyed [or, lost] except the son of destruction [or, the one destined to be lost], so that the Scripture should be fulfilled. [13]But now I am coming to You, and I speak these things in the world, so that they shall be having My joy fulfilled [or, made complete] in themselves.

[14]"I have given to them Your word. And the world hated them, because they are not of the world, just as I am not of the world. [15]I do not ask that You take them out of the world, but that You keep them out of evil [or, from the evil [one]]. [16]They are not of the world, just as I am not of the world. [17]Sanctify them in Your truth; Your word is truth. [18]Just as You sent Me into the world, I also sent them into the world. [19]And I sanctify Myself on behalf of them, so that they also shall have been sanctified in truth.

[20]"But not concerning these only do I ask, but also concerning the ones believing [or, trusting] in Me through their word, [21]so that they all shall be one. Just as You, Father, [are] in Me and I [am] in You, so that they also shall be one in Us, so that the world shall be believing [or, shall be convinced] that You sent Me. [22]And the glory which You have given to Me I have given to them, so that they shall be one just as We are one. [23]I in them and You in Me, so that they shall have been perfected into one, and so that the world shall be knowing that You sent Me, and You loved them just as You loved Me.

[24]"Father, [those] whom You have given to Me, I desire that where I am they also shall be with Me, so that they shall be looking upon My glory which You gave to Me, because You loved Me before [the] laying of the foundation of [the] world. [25]O righteous Father! Indeed the world did not know You. But I knew You, and these knew [or, came to know] that You sent Me. [26]And I made Your name known to them, and I will make [it] known, so that the love [with] which You loved Me shall be in them and I in them."

18These things having said, Jesus went out with His disciples beyond the ravine of Kidron, where [there] was a garden, into which He entered, and His disciples. [2]But Judas also, the one having betrayed Him, knew the place, because Jesus frequently gathered there with His disciples. [3]Then Judas, having taken the detachment [of soldiers] and attendants from the chief priests and Pharisees, comes there with lanterns and torches and weapons.

[4]So Jesus, knowing all the [things] coming upon Him, having gone out, said to them, "Whom are you* seeking?" [5]They answered Him, "Jesus the Nazarene." Jesus says to them, "I Am!" Now also Judas, the one having betrayed Him, stood with them. [6]So when He said to them, "I Am!," they stepped backward and fell to the ground. [7]Therefore, He again questioned them, "Whom are you* seeking?" And they said, "Jesus the Nazarene." [8]Jesus answered, "I said to you*, 'I Am!' If then you* are seeking Me, allow these to be going away," [9]so that the word should be fulfilled which He said, "[Those] whom You have given to Me, I did not lose even one of them." [John 17:12]

¹⁰Then Simon Peter, having a sword, drew it and struck the high priest's slave and cut off his right ear. Now the name of the slave was Malchus. ¹¹So Jesus said to Peter, "Put your sword into the sheath! The cup which the Father has given to Me, shall I not surely drink it?"

¹²Then the detachment [of soldiers] and the commanding officer [or, the Chiliarch] and the attendants of the Jews arrested Jesus and bound Him. ¹³And they led Him away to Annas first, for he was [the] father-in-law of Caiaphas, who was high priest that year. ¹⁴Now Caiaphas was the one having advised the Jews that it is advantageous [for] one person to perish on behalf of the people. [see John 11:49,50]

¹⁵And Simon Peter was following Jesus, and the other disciple. Now that disciple was known to the high priest and entered with Jesus into the courtyard of the high priest. ¹⁶But Peter had stood at the gate outside. Therefore, the other disciple who was known to the high priest went out and spoke to the female doorkeeper, and he brought in Peter.

¹⁷Then the slave-girl, the female doorkeeper, said to Peter, "You are not also of the disciples of this Man, are you?" He says, "I am not." ¹⁸Now the slaves and the [courtyard] attendants had stood [there], having made a charcoal fire, because it was cold, and they were warming themselves. Now Peter was with them, having stood [there], also warming himself.

¹⁹Then the high priest questioned Jesus concerning His disciples and concerning His teaching [or, doctrine]. ²⁰Jesus answered him, "I have spoken publicly to the world; I always taught in a synagogue and in the temple, where the Jews are always coming together, and I spoke nothing in secret. ²¹Why are you questioning Me? Question the ones having heard what I spoke to them. Listen! These ones know what I said."

²²So when He had said these things, one of the attendants having stood by gave a slap with the hand [or, a blow with a club] to Jesus, saying, "Are You answering the high priest in this way?" ²³Jesus answered him, "If I spoke wrongly [or, with wrong motives], testify concerning the wrong, but if rightly, why do you beat Me?" ²⁴Annas sent Him, having been bound, to Caiaphas the high priest.

²⁵Now Simon Peter was standing and warming himself. So they said to him, "You are not also of His disciples, are you?" Then that one denied [it] and said, "I am not." ²⁶One of the slaves of the high priest, being a relative of him whose ear Peter cut off, says, "I saw you in the garden with Him, did I not?" ²⁷Then Peter again denied [it]. And immediately a rooster crowed. [cp. John 13:38]

²⁸Then they lead Jesus from Caiaphas to the Fortified Palace [or, Praetorium, and in 18:33; 19:9]. Now it was morning. And they themselves did not enter into the Fortified Palace, so that they should not be defiled, but so that they shall eat the Passover. ²⁹Therefore, Pilate went out to them and said, "What accusation do you* bring against this Man?" ³⁰They answered and said to him, "If this One were not an evil doer [or, criminal], we would not have handed Him over to you." ³¹So Pilate said to them, "You* take Him yourselves and judge Him according to your* law." Then the Jews said to him, "It is not lawful for us to put anyone to death,"

[32](so that the word of Jesus should be fulfilled which He said, signifying by what sort of death He was about to die). [see John 12:32,33]

[33]Therefore, Pilate entered into the Fortified Palace again and called Jesus and said to Him, "Are You the King of the Jews?" [34]Jesus answered him, "Do you say this from yourself, or did others say [it] to you about Me?" [35]Pilate answered, "I am not a Jew, am I? Your nation and the chief priests handed You over to me. What did You do?" [36]Jesus answered, "My kingdom is not of this world. If My kingdom were of this world, My attendants would be fighting, so that I should not be handed over to the Jews, but now My kingdom is not from here."

[37]Then Pilate said to Him, "So then, You are a king?" Jesus answered, "You say that I am a king. For this [reason] I have been born, and for this [reason] I have come into the world, so that I should testify to the truth. Every[one] being of the truth hears My voice." [38]Pilate says to Him, "What is truth?"

And having said this, he again went out to the Jews and says to them, "I find no [grounds for] an accusation [or, no guilt; and in 19:4,6] in Him. [39]But [there] is a custom to you* [or, you* have a custom], that I release to you* one [person] at the Passover. So do you* desire [that] I release to you* the King of the Jews?" [40]Therefore, they all cried out again, saying, "Not this One, but Barabbas!" Now Barabbas was a robber [or, an insurrectionist].

19 So then Pilate took Jesus and flogged [Him]. [2]And the soldiers having woven a wreath [or, crown] out of thorns, placed [it] on His head, and they put a purple garment around Him. [3]And they kept saying, "Hail! The King of the Jews!" And they kept giving Him slaps with the hand [or, blows with a club].

[4]Then Pilate again went outside and says to them, "Listen! I bring Him outside to you*, so that you* shall know [or, shall come to understand] that in Him I find no [grounds for] an accusation." [5]So Jesus went outside wearing the thorny wreath [or, crown] and the purple garment. And he [i.e. Pilate] says to them, "Look! The Man!" [6]Therefore, when the chief priests and the attendants saw Him, they cried out [or, shouted], saying, "Crucify! Crucify Him!" Pilate says to them, "You* take Him and crucify [Him], for I find no [grounds for] an accusation in Him." [7]The Jews answered him, "We have a law, and according to our law He ought to die, because He made Himself [out to be] God's Son."

[8]So when Pilate heard this word, he was [even] more afraid. [9]And he entered into the Fortified Palace again and says to Jesus, "Where are You from?" But Jesus gave no answer to him. [10]Therefore, Pilate says to Him, "You are not speaking to me, are You? You do know that I have authority to crucify You, and I have authority to release You, do You not?" [11]Jesus answered, "You would have no authority at all against Me unless it had been given to you from above. For this reason, the one having betrayed Me to you has greater sin."

[12]From this [point] Pilate kept seeking to release Him. But the Jews kept crying out [or, shouting], saying, "If you release this One, you are not a friend of Caesar! Every[one] making himself a king speaks against [or, opposes] Caesar."

[13]So Pilate, having heard this word, brought Jesus outside and sat down on the judgment seat at a place being called Pavement, but in Hebrew Gabbatha. [14]Now

it was [the] preparation [day] of the Passover, and [it was] about the sixth hour [i.e. 12:00 noon Jewish time or 6:00 a.m. Roman time]. And he says to the Jews, "Look! Your* king!" [15]But they cried out [or, shouted], "Take [Him] away! Take [Him] away! Crucify Him!" Pilate says to them, "Shall I crucify your* king?" The chief priests answered, "We have no king except Caesar." [16]Therefore, he then handed Him over to them so that He should be crucified.

And they took Jesus and led [Him] away. [17]And carrying His cross, He went out to a place being called Place of a Skull, which is called in Hebrew Golgotha, [18]where they crucified Him, and with Him two others, [one] on this side and [one] on that side, and Jesus in the middle.

[19]But Pilate also wrote an inscription and put [it] on the cross. Now [on] it had been written, "Jesus the Nazarene, the King of the Jews." [20]So many of the Jews read this inscription because the place where Jesus was crucified was near to the city, and it had been written in Hebrew [or, Aramaic], in Greek, [and] in Roman [or, Latin]. [21]Therefore, the chief priests of the Jews were saying to Pilate, "Stop writing, 'The King of the Jews,' but 'That One said, "I am King of the Jews."'" [22]Pilate answered, "What I have written, I have written."

[23]Then the soldiers, when they crucified Jesus, took His garments and made four parts, to each soldier a part, also the tunic. Now the tunic was seamless, from the top woven through [the] whole [fig., woven into one piece]. [24]So they said to one another, "Let us not tear it, but let us cast a lot for it, whose it will be," so that the Scripture should be fulfilled, which says, *"They themselves divided My garments among themselves, and they cast a lot upon My clothing."* [Psalm 22:18] Therefore indeed the soldiers did these things.

[25]Now [there] stood by the cross of Jesus His mother and His mother's sister, Mary [the wife] of Cleopas, and Mary the Magdalene [or, Mary, a woman from Magdala]. [26]Then Jesus, having seen His mother and the disciple having stood by whom He was loving, He says to His mother, "Woman, look!, your son." [27]Next He says to the disciple, "Look! Your mother." And from that hour the disciple took her into his own [home].

[28]After this, Jesus having seen that all had now been finished, so that the Scripture should be fulfilled, says, "I am thirsty." [see Psalm 22:15] [29]Now a vessel full of wine vinegar was sitting [there]. And they, having filled a sponge with wine vinegar and having put [it] around a hyssop [branch], brought [it] to His mouth. [see Psalm 69:21] [30]So when Jesus received the wine vinegar, He said, "It has been finished!" And having bowed His head, He gave up His spirit.

[31]Therefore, the Jews, so that the bodies should not remain on the cross on the Sabbath, since it was the preparation [day] (for the day of that Sabbath was a great [one]), asked Pilate that their legs be broken, and they be taken away. [32]So the soldiers came and indeed they broke the legs of the first [man] and of the other [one] having been crucified with Him. [33]But having come to Jesus, when they saw He had already died, they did not break His legs. [34]But one of the soldiers pierced His side with a spear, and immediately blood and water came out.

[35]And the one having seen has testified, and his testimony is true. And that one knows that he speaks true [things], so that you* also shall believe [or, be

convinced]. ³⁶For these things happened, so that the Scripture should be fulfilled, *"Not a bone of Him will be broken."* [Exod 12:46; Numb 9:12; Psalm 34:20] ³⁷And again a different Scripture says, *"They will look on [Him] whom they pierced."* [Zech 12:10]

³⁸Now after these things Joseph, the one from Arimathea—being a disciple of Jesus, but having been concealed [or, but secretly] because of the fear of the Jews—asked Pilate that he should take away the body of Jesus. And Pilate permitted [him]. So he came and took away the body of Jesus. ³⁹And Nicodemus also came, the one having earlier come to Jesus by night, bringing a mixture of myrrh and aloes, about one hundred litra [about 75 pounds or 34 kilograms]. ⁴⁰So they took the body of Jesus and wrapped it with linen strips with the spices, just as [the] custom is for the Jews to be preparing for burial. ⁴¹Now [there] was in the place where He was crucified a garden, and in the garden a new tomb in which no one had yet been buried. ⁴²So there, on account of the preparation [day] of the Jews, because the tomb was near, they buried Jesus.

20Now on the first [day] of the week [i.e. Sunday], Mary the Magdalene goes [or, comes] early in the morning ([there] being yet darkness) to the tomb, and she sees the stone having been taken away from the tomb. ²Therefore, she runs and goes to Simon Peter and to the other disciple whom Jesus was affectionately loving, and she says to them, "They took away the Lord out of the tomb, and we do not know where they laid Him!"

³So Peter went out, and the other disciple, and they began going to the tomb. ⁴Now the two were running together, and the other disciple ran ahead more quickly than Peter and came first to the tomb. ⁵And having stooped down, he sees the linen strips lying, although he did not enter. ⁶Then Simon Peter comes, following him, and he entered into the tomb. And he looks upon the linen strips lying [there], ⁷and the facecloth which was on His head not lying with the linen strips, but apart, having been rolled up in one place.

⁸So then the other disciple, the one having come first to the tomb, also entered, and he saw and believed [or, was convinced]. ⁹For they did not yet know the Scripture, that it is necessary [for] Him to rise again from [the] dead. ¹⁰So the disciples went away again to themselves [fig., to their own homes].

¹¹Now Mary was standing outside facing the tomb, weeping. Then, as she was weeping, she stooped down into the tomb. ¹²And she looks upon two angels in white sitting, one at the head and one at the feet where the body of Jesus had been lying. ¹³And they say to her, "Woman, why are you weeping?" She says to them, "Because they took away my Lord, and I do not know where they put Him."

¹⁴And these things having said, she was turned to the [things] behind and sees Jesus having stood [there], but she did not know that it is Jesus. ¹⁵Jesus says to her, "Woman, why are you weeping? Whom do you seek?" That one, supposing that He is the gardener, says to Him, "Lord [or, Sir], if You carried Him away, tell me where You put Him, and I will take Him away."

¹⁶Jesus says to her, "Mary!" That one, having been turned, says to Him, "Rabbouni!" (which is saying, "Teacher"). ¹⁷Jesus says to her, "Stop holding [or,

clinging to] Me, for I have not yet ascended to My Father. But be going to My brothers, and say to them, 'I am ascending to My Father and your* Father, and [to] My God and your* God.'" [18]Mary the Magdalene comes reporting to the disciples that she has seen the Lord, and these things He said to her.

[19]So it being evening on that day, the first [day] of the week, and the doors having been shut [or, locked] where the disciples were assembled, because of the fear of the Jews, Jesus came and stood in the middle [of them] and says to them, "Peace to you*!" [20]And having said this, He showed His hands and side to them. Therefore, the disciples rejoiced, having seen the Lord. [21]So Jesus said to them again, "Peace to you*. Just as the Father has sent Me, I also send you*." [22]And having said this, He breathed on [them] and says to them, "Receive [the] Holy Spirit. [23]If any of you* forgive their sins, they have been forgiven to them; if any of you* retain [their sins], they have been retained."

[24]But Thomas, one of the twelve, the one being called Didymus, was not with them when Jesus came. [25]So the other disciples said to him, "We have seen the Lord!" But he said to them, "Unless I see in His hands the mark of the nails, and I put my finger into the mark of the nails, and I put my hand into His side, by no means shall I believe [or, be convinced]."

[26]And after eight days, His disciples were again inside, and Thomas with them. Jesus comes, the doors having been shut, and He stood in the middle [of them] and said, "Peace to you*!" [27]Then He says to Thomas, "Be bringing your finger here and see My hands, and be bringing your hand and put [it] into My side, and become not unbelieving, but believing!" [28]And Thomas answered and said to Him, "My Lord and my God!" [29]Jesus says to him, "Because you have seen Me, you have believed [or, have been convinced]; happy [or, blessed] [are] the ones not having seen yet having believed."

[30]Now indeed many other signs Jesus also did in the presence of His disciples which have not been written in this scroll. [31]But these have been written so that you* shall believe [or, be convinced] that Jesus is the Christ, the Son of God, and so that believing you* shall be having life in His name.

21 After these things Jesus revealed Himself again to the disciples on the sea of Tiberias. Now He revealed Himself in this manner: [2][There] were together Simon Peter and Thomas, the one being called Didymus, and Nathanael from Cana of Galilee and the [sons] of Zebedee and two others of His disciples. [3]Simon Peter says to them, "I am going away to be fishing." They say to him, "We are also going with you." They went out and immediately stepped into the boat, and on that night they caught nothing. [4]Now morning already having come, Jesus stood at the shore, although the disciples did not know that it is Jesus.

[5]So Jesus says to them, "Young children [or, [My] dear children], you* do not have any fish, do you*?" They answered to Him, "No." [6]But He said to them, "Cast the net on the right side of the boat, and you* will find [some fish]." So they cast and were no longer able to drag it [in] as a result of the large number of fish. [7]Therefore, that disciple whom Jesus was loving says to Peter, "It is the Lord!" So Simon Peter, having heard that it is the Lord, tied his outer coat around himself

(for he was naked [or, poorly dressed]), and he cast himself into the sea. ⁸But the other disciples came by the small boat (for they were not far from the land, <u>but</u> about two hundred cubits away [about 100 yards or 90 meters], dragging the net of the fish.

⁹So when they disembarked onto the land, they notice a charcoal fire lying [there], and fish lying on [it], and bread. ¹⁰Jesus says to them, "Bring [some] from the fish which you* now caught." ¹¹Simon Peter went up and dragged the net onto the land, full of large fish, one hundred fifty-three. And although there were so many, the net was not torn. ¹²Jesus says to them, "Come, eat breakfast." But none of the disciples were daring to inquire of Him, "Who are You?" knowing that it is the Lord. ¹³Then Jesus comes and takes the bread and gives [it] to them, and the fish likewise. ¹⁴This [is] now a third time Jesus was revealed to His disciples, having been raised from [the] dead.

¹⁵So when they ate breakfast, Jesus says to Simon Peter, "Simon, [son] of Jonah, do you love Me more than these?" He says to Him, "Yes, Lord; <u>You</u> know that I affectionately love You." He says to him, "Feed My lambs."

¹⁶He says to him again a second time, "Simon, [son] of Jonah, do you love Me?" He says to Him, "Yes, Lord; <u>You</u> know that I affectionately love You." He says to him, "Tend My sheep."

¹⁷He says to him the third time, "Simon, [son] of Jonah, do you affectionately love Me?" Peter was grieved that He said to him the third time, "Do you affectionately love Me?" And he said to Him, "Lord, <u>You</u> know all. <u>You</u> know that I affectionately love You." Jesus says to him, "Feed My sheep.

¹⁸"Most positively, I say to you, when you were younger, you were fastening a belt on yourself and were walking about where you would desire. But when you become old, you will stretch out your hands, and another will fasten a belt on you and will lead [you] where you do not desire." ¹⁹But this He said signifying by what sort of death he will glorify God. And having said this, He says to him, "Be following Me!"

²⁰And Peter, having been turned around, sees the disciple whom Jesus was loving following, who also reclined in the dinner on His breast and said, "Lord, who is the one betraying You?" [John 13:25] ²¹Peter having seen this one, says to Jesus, "Lord, but what [about] this one?" ²²Jesus says to him, "If I want him to be remaining until I come, what [is that] to you? <u>You</u> be following Me!" ²³Therefore, this word went out among the brothers [and sisters], "That disciple does not die." Yet Jesus did not say to him, "He does not die," <u>but</u> "If I want him to be remaining until I come, what [is that] to you?"

²⁴This is that disciple, the one testifying concerning these things and having written these things, and we know that his testimony is true. ²⁵But there are also many other things—as many as Jesus did—which, if they should be written one by one, not even the world itself I suppose would have room for the scrolls being written. So be it!

The Acts
of the Apostles

1 The first word [or,account] indeed I made concerning all [things], O Theophilus, which Jesus began both to be doing and to be teaching, [see Luke 1:1-3] ²until the day [in] which He was taken up [into heaven], having commanded by [the] Holy Spirit the apostles whom He chose, ³to whom also He presented Himself living after His suffering, by many convincing proofs, appearing to them during forty days and speaking the [things] concerning the kingdom of God.

⁴And being assembled together, He gave strict orders to them not to be departing from Jerusalem, but to be waiting for the promise of the Father, "Which," [He said,] "You heard from Me; [Luke 24:49] ⁵because John indeed baptized [or, immersed, and throughout book] in [or, with] water, but you* will be baptized in [or, with] [the] Holy Spirit after not many [of] these days [fig., in a few days]." [Matt 3:11; Mark 1:8; Luke 3:16]

⁶So indeed, having come together, they began questioning Him, saying, "Lord, are You restoring the kingdom to Israel at this time?" ⁷But He said to them, "It is not yours* to know times or seasons which the Father placed in His own authority, ⁸but you* will receive power, the Holy Spirit having come upon you*, and you* will be witnesses to Me both in Jerusalem and in all Judea and Samaria, and as far as [the] end of the earth."

⁹And having said these [things], while they [were] looking, He was lifted up, and a cloud took Him from their eyes [fig., sight]. ¹⁰And as they were looking intently into heaven [or, at the sky] as He [was] going, then look!, two men had stood by them in white robes, ¹¹who also said, "Men, Galileans, why have you* stood looking attentively into heaven? This Jesus, the One having been taken up from you* into heaven, will come in the same manner [in] which manner you* saw Him going into heaven."

¹²Then they returned to Jerusalem from the mount being called Of Olives, which is near Jerusalem, a Sabbath day's journey [away] [i.e. the distance which Jews could travel on the Sabbath without breaking the Law, which was 2000 paces, or about half a mile or 800 meters.]. ¹³And when they entered [Jerusalem], they went up into the upstairs room where they were staying: both Peter and James, and John and Andrew, Philip and Thomas, Bartholomew and Matthew, James [the son] of Alphaeus and Simon the Zealot, and Judas [the son; or, the brother] of James. [cp. Jude 1:1] ¹⁴These all were continuing with one mind in prayer and petition, together with [the] women and Mary the mother of Jesus and with His brothers.

¹⁵And in these days, Peter having risen up in [the] middle of the disciples, said (and [the] crowd of names [fig., the number of people] at the same [place] was about a hundred and twenty), ¹⁶"Men, brothers [fig., fellow believers, friends, or compatriots, and elsewhere in book], it was necessary [for] this Scripture to be fulfilled which the Holy Spirit foretold by the mouth of David concerning Judas

(the one having become a guide to the ones having arrested Jesus), [17]because he had been numbered with us and obtained [or, was chosen to have] the share in this ministry."

[18](This one indeed then acquired a field by [the] payment of [his] unrighteousness, and having fallen headfirst, he burst open in the middle and all his inward parts were poured out. [19]And it became known to all the ones living in Jerusalem, with the result that that place is called, in their own language [i.e. Aramaic], *Akel Dama*, that is, Field of Blood.)

[20]"For it has been written in a scroll of [the] Psalms: *'Let his residence become desolate, and let no [one] be dwelling in it'*; and *'Let another take his position of overseer.'* [Psalm 69:25; 109:8] [21]Therefore, it is necessary of the men having accompanied us in every time in which the Lord Jesus came in and went out among us—[22]having begun from the baptism [or, immersion, and throughout book] of John until the day which He was taken up from us—[for] one of these to become a witness with us of His resurrection."

[23]And they put forward two: Joseph, the one being called Barsabas, who was surnamed Justus, and Matthias. [24]And having prayed, they said, "You Lord, knower of the hearts of all [people], disclose which one of these two You chose [25]to receive the share of this ministry and apostleship, from which Judas turned aside to go to his own place." [26]And they gave [fig., cast] their lots, and the lot fell on Matthias, and he was numbered with the eleven apostles.

2 And when the Day of Pentecost [had] come, they were all with one mind at the same [place]. [2]And suddenly [there] came from heaven a sound like a violent rushing wind, and it filled the whole house where they were sitting. [i.e. possibly the temple, cp. Luke 19:45-46; Acts 7:47] [3]And [there] appeared to them tongues as of fire distributing themselves, and [one] sat on each one of them. [4]And they were all filled of [or, with] [the] Holy Spirit, and they began to be speaking with different tongues [fig., foreign languages], just as the Spirit was giving them to be declaring boldly.

[5]Now [there] were Jews dwelling in Jerusalem, devout men from every nation of the [ones] under heaven. [6]Now this sound having occurred, the crowd came together and was bewildered, because they were each one hearing them speaking in his own language.

[7]Then they themselves were all being amazed and were marveling, saying to one another, "Listen! All these [who] are speaking are Galileans, are they not? [8]And how [is it that] we each hear in our own language in which we were born? [9]Parthians and Medes and Elamites, and the ones dwelling in Mesopotamia, also in Judea and Cappadocia, Pontus and Asia, [10]also Phrygia and Pamphylia, Egypt and the parts of Libya, the [one] along Cyrene, and the visiting Romans, both Jews and proselytes [i.e. converts to Judaism], [11]Cretes and Arabians, we are hearing them speaking in our tongues [fig., languages] the marvelous [deeds] of God!"

[12]So they themselves were all amazed and thoroughly perplexed, saying another to another [or, to one another], "What might this want to be [fig., What

does this mean]?" [13]But others mocking, were saying, "They have been filled with sweet wine!"

[14]But Peter having stood up with the eleven, lifted up his voice and declared boldly to them, "Men, Jews, and all the ones dwelling in Jerusalem, let this be known to you*, and listen carefully to my words. [15]For these are not drinking, as you* suppose, for it is the third hour of the day [i.e. 9:00 a.m.]. [16]But this is the [thing] having been spoken by the prophet Joel:

> [17]*And it will be in the last days* (says God), *[that] I will pour out of My Spirit upon all flesh* [fig., *all of humanity*]; *and your* sons and your* daughters will prophesy, and your* young men will see visions, and your* old men will dream dreams.* [18]*And even upon My slave-men and upon My slave-women, in those days I will pour out of My Spirit, and they shall prophesy.* [19]*And I will give* [fig., *show*] *wonders in heaven* [or, *in the sky*] *above and signs on the earth beneath—blood and fire and vapor of smoke.* [20]*The sun will be turned into darkness and the moon into blood before the great and glorious Day of [the]* LORD *comes.* [21]*And it will be [that] every[one] who himself shall call on the name of [the]* LORD *will be saved!* [Joel 2:28-32]

[22]"Men, Israelites! Pay attention to these words! Jesus the Nazarene, a Man having been attested by God among you* by miraculous works and wonders and signs which God did through Him in your* midst, just as you* yourselves also know—[23]this One, handed over by the having been designated plan and foreknowledge of God, you* having taken by lawless hands, having crucified, you* executed; [24]whom God raised up, having loosed the pains of death, because it was not possible [for] Him to continue being held by it. [25]For David says in regard to Him:

> *I myself was foreseeing the* LORD *through all* [fig. *continually*] *before me, because He is at my right hand, so that I shall not be shaken.* [26]*For this reason my heart celebrated and my tongue was very glad, and yet my flesh also will rest on hope* [or, *confident expectation*]; [27]*because You will not abandon my soul to the realm of the dead* [Gr., *hades*], *nor will You give* [fig., *allow*] *Your Holy One to see corruption.* [28]*You made known to me [the] ways of life; You will make me full of gladness with Your face* [fig., *presence*]. [Psalm 16:8-11]

[29]"Men, brothers! It is possible [for me] to speak with confidence to you* concerning the patriarch David, that he both came to the end [of his life] and was buried, and his tomb is with us until this day. [30]Therefore, being a prophet and knowing that God vowed to him with an oath, from [the] fruit of his reproductive organs according to [the] flesh [fig., from one of his descendents], to raise up the Christ [or, the Messiah, and throughout book] to sit on his throne, [31]having foreseen [this], he spoke concerning the resurrection of the Christ, that 'His soul

was not left in the realm of the dead [Gr., *hades*]*, nor did* His flesh *see corruption.'* [Psalm 16:10] ³²This Jesus God raised up, of which we are all witnesses!

³³"Therefore, having been exalted to the right hand of God, and having received the promise of the Holy Spirit from the Father, He poured out this which you* now see and hear. ³⁴For David did not ascend into the heavens, but he says himself: *'The* LORD *said to my Lord, "Sit at My right hand,* ³⁵*until I put Your enemies [as] Your footstool for Your feet."'* [Psalm 110:1] ³⁶Therefore, let all the house of Israel know securely [fig., without a doubt] that God made Him both Lord and Christ—this Jesus whom you* crucified!"

³⁷Now having heard, they were pierced through to the heart [fig., were greatly distressed], and they said to Peter and to the rest of the apostles, "What will we do, men, brothers?" ³⁸Then Peter was saying to them, "Repent, and let each of you* be baptized in the name of Jesus Christ, to [or, for; or, because of] [the] forgiveness of sins, and you* will receive the free gift of the Holy Spirit. ³⁹For the promise is to you* and to your* children and to all the [ones] far off, as many as [the] Lord our God shall call to Himself." ⁴⁰And with many other words he was urgently warning and urging [them], saying, "Be saved from this perverse generation!" ⁴¹So then, the ones having gladly received his word were baptized, and about three thousand souls were added on that day.

⁴²Now they were continuing in the teaching of the apostles and in fellowship, and in the breaking of the bread and in prayers. ⁴³Then fear came to be in every soul, and many wonders and signs were taking place through the apostles. ⁴⁴Now all the ones believing were at the same [place], and they were having all [things] in common. ⁴⁵And they were selling their possessions and their belongings, and they were distributing them to all, to the extent which anyone was having need.

⁴⁶And continuing daily with one mind in the temple, and breaking bread at every house, they were sharing food with great happiness and simplicity of heart [fig., generosity], ⁴⁷praising God and having favor with all the people. So the Lord was daily adding the ones being saved to the Assembly [or, Church, and throughout book].

3 Now Peter and John were going up at the same [time] to the temple at the hour of prayer, the ninth [hour] [i.e. 3:00 p.m.]. ²And a certain man being lame from his mother's womb was being carried, whom they were laying every day at the gate of the temple, the [gate] being called Beautiful, [in order for him] to be asking [for] a charitable gift from the ones entering into the temple, ³who having seen Peter and John about to be entering into the temple, began asking [for] a charitable gift.

⁴But Peter, having looked intently toward him, along with John, said, "Look at us!" ⁵So he began fixing his attention on them, expecting to receive something from them. ⁶But Peter said, "Silver and gold do not belong to me [fig., I do not have silver and gold], but what I do have, this I give to you: in the name of Jesus Christ the Nazarene, get up and be walking about!"

⁷And having taken hold of him by the right hand, he raised [him] up. Then immediately his feet and ankles were strengthened. ⁸And jumping up, he stood

and began walking about! And he entered with them into the temple, walking about and jumping and praising God! [9]And all the people saw him walking about and praising God. [10]And they were knowing [or, recognizing] him, that this was the one sitting at the Beautiful Gate of the temple [begging] for a charitable gift; and they were filled with wonder and amazement at the [thing] having happened to him.

[11]Now while the lame [man] having been healed [was] holding on to Peter and John, all the people ran together to them in the Portico [or, covered walkway], the one being called Solomon's, utterly astonished. [12]But Peter having seen [this], he replied to the people, "Men, Israelites! Why do you* marvel at this? Or why do you* look so intently on us, as if by our own power or piety we have made him to be walking about?

[13]"The God of Abraham and Isaac and Jacob, the God of our fathers, glorified His Servant Jesus, whom you* indeed handed over and denied [or, disowned] Him to [the] face of [fig., in the presence of] Pilate, he having given judgment to be releasing [Him]. [14]But you* denied [or, disowned] the Holy and Righteous One, and demanded a man, a murderer, to be graciously granted to you*; [15]but you* killed the Prince of Life, whom God raised from [the] dead, of which we are witnesses. [16]And on the basis of faith in His name, this one whom you* see and know, His name made [him] strong. And the faith, the [one] by Him, gave to him this perfect health in the presence of you* all.

[17]"And now, brothers [and sisters], I know that according to ignorance you* did [it], as indeed [did] also your* rulers. [18]But what [things] God announced beforehand by [the] mouth of all His prophets, [that] the Christ [would] suffer, He fulfilled in this manner. [19]Therefore, repent and turn back [to God] in order for your* sins to be blotted out, in order that times of refreshing shall come from [the] face [fig., presence] of the Lord [20]and [that] He shall send the One having been appointed for you*—Jesus Christ, [21]whom it is necessary [for] heaven indeed to receive until [the] times of restoration of all [things] of which God spoke by [the] mouth of all His holy prophets from [the earliest] age.

[22]"For Moses indeed said to the fathers:

> *[The]* LORD *our God will raise up for you* a Prophet like to me from your* brothers; Him you* will hear [or, pay attention to] in all [things], as many [things] as He shall speak to you*. [23]And it will be [that] every soul who does not hear [or, pay attention to] that Prophet will be utterly destroyed [or, completely cut off] from the people.* [Deut 18:15,18,19]

[24]"Now also all the prophets from Samuel and the succeeding ones, as many as spoke, also announced these days. [25]You* are sons [and daughters] of the prophets and of the covenant which God covenanted to our fathers, saying to Abraham, *'And in your Seed all the families of the earth will be blessed.'* [Gen 22:18; 26:4; 28:14; cp. Gal 3:16] [26]To you* first, God, having raised up His Servant Jesus, sent Him, blessing you* by the turning away of each one from your* wicked ways."

*4*Now while they [were] speaking to the people, the priests and the captain of the temple guard and the Sadducees came up to them, ²being greatly disturbed because they [were] teaching the people and preaching in Jesus the resurrection of the dead. ³And they laid hands on them and put [them] in custody for [fig., until] the next day, for it was already evening. ⁴But many of the ones hearing the word believed, and the number of the men came to be about five thousand.

⁵Now it happened on the next day, their rulers and elders and scribes were gathered together in Jerusalem, ⁶and Annas the high priest and Caiaphas and John and Alexander and as many as were of high priestly descent. ⁷And having placed them in the middle [of them], they began inquiring, "By what power or in what kind of name did you* do this?"

⁸Then Peter, having been filled with [the] Holy Spirit, said to them: "Rulers of the people and elders of Israel, ⁹if we today are being examined concerning an act of kindness [done] to a sick man, by what [means] this [man] has been cured, ¹⁰let it be known to you* all and to all the people of Israel that by the name of Jesus Christ the Nazarene, whom you* crucified, whom God raised from [the] dead, by Him has this [man] stood before you* healthy! ¹¹This is, *'The stone, the one having been rejected by you* the builders, which has became [the] head of a corner.'* [Psalm 118:22] ¹²And [there] is no salvation in any other, for neither [is there] a different name, the One having [or, which has] been given among people by which it is necessary [for] us to be saved!"

¹³And observing the confidence of Peter and John, and having perceived that they are uneducated and untrained men, they began marveling, and they were recognizing them that they were with Jesus. ¹⁴Then seeing the man having stood with them, the one having been healed, they had nothing to say against [them]. ¹⁵But having commanded them to go away outside of the High Council [or, Sanhedrin, and throughout book], they began conferring with one another, ¹⁶saying, "What will we do to these men? For indeed, that a recognizable sign has taken place through them [is] evident to all the ones living in Jerusalem, and we are not able to deny [it]. ¹⁷But so that it shall not spread further among the people, let us ourselves threaten them with a threat [fig., severely threaten them] to no longer be speaking in this name to any person." ¹⁸And having summoned them, they gave strict orders to them not to be speaking at all nor to be teaching in the name of Jesus.

¹⁹But answering, Peter and John said to them, "Whether it is righteous before God to listen to you* rather than God, you* judge. ²⁰For we are not able not to [or, we cannot but] be speaking [about] what we saw and heard." ²¹So having threatened [them] further, they released them, finding nothing [as to] how they themselves will punish them, because of the people, because all were glorifying God for the [thing] having taken place. ²²For the man was more than forty years old on whom this sign of the healing had taken place.

²³And being released, they went to their own [people] and reported as many [things] as the chief priests and the elders said to them. ²⁴And having heard, with one mind they lifted up a voice to God and said, "Master, You [are] the God, the One having *'made the heaven and the earth and the sea and all the [things] in*

them,' [Exod 20:11] [25]who by [the] mouth of David Your servant, said, *'Why did [the] Gentiles rage, and [the] people think about empty* [fig., *plot futile*] *[things]?* [26]*The kings of the earth stood up* [or, *took a stand*]*, and the rulers were gathered on the same against the* LORD *and against His Christ.'* [Psalm 2:1,2]

[27]"For truly [there] were gathered together against Your Holy Servant Jesus, whom You anointed, both Herod and Pontius Pilate, along with [the] Gentiles and [the] people of Israel, [28]to do as many [things] as Your hand and Your plan predestined to occur. [29]And now, Lord, take notice of their threats, and grant to Your slaves to be speaking Your word with all confidence, [30]by the stretching out of Your hand, for healing and signs and wonders to take place through the name of Your Holy Servant Jesus."

[31]And when they had implored [God in prayer], the place was shaken in which they had been gathered together; and they were all filled with [the] Holy Spirit, and they were speaking the word of God with confidence.

[32]Now the heart and the soul of the congregation of the ones having believed was one, and not one [of them] was saying [that] any of their belongings to be [or, was] his own, but all things were common [property] to them. [33]Now with great power the apostles kept giving the testimony of the resurrection of the Lord Jesus, and great grace was on them all. [34]For [there] was not any needy [person] among them, for as many as were owners of lands or houses, selling [them], would bring the proceeds of the [property] being sold [35]and would place them at the feet of the apostles; then they would distribute to each to the extent [which] anyone was having need.

[36]Now Joses, the one having been surnamed Barnabas by the apostles (which is, having been translated, Son of Encouragement), a Levite, a Cyprian by race, [37]a field being his, having sold [it], brought the money and placed [it] at the feet of the apostles.

[5]But a certain man, Ananias by name, with Sapphira his wife, sold a piece of property, [2]and kept back [part] of the proceeds for himself, his wife also having become aware of [it], and having brought a certain part, he placed [it] at the feet of the apostles. [3]But Peter said, "Ananias, why did Satan fill your heart [for] you to lie to the Holy Spirit and [for] you to keep back [part] of the price of the proceeds of the piece of property for yourself? [4]While it [was] remaining [unsold], was it not remaining yours, and having been sold, was it not in your authority? Why [is it] that you put this thing in your heart? You did not lie to people but to God!"

[5]Then Ananias hearing these words, having fallen down, expired [or, emitted his last breath]! And great fear came to be on all the ones hearing these [things]. [6]Then having risen, the young men wrapped him up, and having carried [him] out, they buried [him].

[7]Now it happened, [after] an interval of about three hours, that his wife came in, not knowing the [thing] having taken place. [8]Then Peter answered her, "Tell me whether [for] so much you yourself sold the piece of property?" Then she said, "Yes, [for] so much." [9]Then Peter said to her, "Why [is it] that it was agreed by you to test the Spirit of [the] Lord? Look! The feet of the ones having buried your

husband [are] at the door, and they will carry you out!" ¹⁰Then immediately she fell down at his feet and expired [or, emitted her last breath]! And the young men having come in, found her dead, and having carried [her] out, they buried [her] beside her husband. ¹¹And great fear came to be on all the Assembly and on all the ones having heard these [things].

¹²Now through the hands of the apostles many signs and wonders were taking place among the people, and they were all of one mind in the Portico of Solomon. ¹³But of the rest no one was daring to be joining himself to them, but the people were magnifying them [fig., were holding them in high esteem]. ¹⁴And more than ever believing [ones] were being added to the Lord, crowds of both men and women, ¹⁵with the result that [they were] bringing out the sick and laying [them] on cots and mats along the open streets, so that when Peter came [by] at least his shadow should overshadow someone of them. ¹⁶Now also the crowds from the cities all around were gathering to Jerusalem, bringing sick [people] and [people] being harassed by unclean [or, defiling] spirits, who were all being healed.

¹⁷But having risen, the high priest and all the [ones] with him (the sect being of the Sadducees) were filled with jealousy. ¹⁸And they laid their hands on the apostles and put them in public custody. ¹⁹But during the night an angel of [the] Lord opened the doors of the prison, and having brought them out, he said, ²⁰"Go, and having stood, be speaking in the temple to the people all the words of this life." ²¹So having heard, they entered into the temple at daybreak and began teaching.

But the high priest and the [ones] with him having arrived, they summoned the High Council and the entire council of the elders of [fig., who rule over] the sons [and daughters] of Israel, and they sent [their attendants] to the jail to have them brought. ²²But the attendants having arrived did not find them in the prison. So having returned, they reported, ²³saying, "Indeed, we found the jail having been shut with all security and the guards having stood before the doors, but having opened we found no one inside."

²⁴So when both the [high] priest and the captain of the temple guard, and the chief priests heard these words, they were greatly perplexed concerning them [as to] what might come of this. ²⁵Then having come, someone reported to them, "Look! The men whom you* put in the prison are in the temple, having stood and teaching the people!" ²⁶So the captain [of the temple guard], having gone away with attendants, brought them, [but] not with force, so that they should not be stoned, for they were fearing the people.

²⁷So having brought them, they set [them] in the High Council [chambers]. And the high priest questioned them, ²⁸saying, "We gave strict orders to you* not to be teaching in this name, did we not? And look! You* have filled Jerusalem with your* teaching, and you* intend to bring on us the blood of this Man!"

²⁹But answering, Peter and the apostles said, "It is necessary to be obeying God rather than people! ³⁰The God of our fathers raised up Jesus, whom you* murdered, having hanged [Him] on a tree [or, a cross]. ³¹This One God has exalted to His right hand [as] Prince and Savior, to give repentance to Israel and forgiveness of sins. ³²And we are His witnesses of these matters, and also the Holy Spirit, whom God gave to the ones obeying Him."

³³But hearing, they were cut through [fig., infuriated] and began plotting to execute them. ³⁴But someone in the High Council having gotten up, a Pharisee, by name Gamaliel, a teacher of the Law, [considered] honorable by all the people, commanded [the attendants] to put the apostles outside [for] some short [time].

³⁵And he said to them, "Men, Israelites, be watching yourselves concerning these men, what you* are about to be doing. ³⁶For before these days Theudas rose up, claiming himself to be someone, to whom was joined a number of men, about four hundred, who was executed, and all, as many as were obeying him were dispersed, and it came to nothing. ³⁷After this, Judas the Galilean rose up in the days of the registration [or, census] and drew away [or, incited to revolt] a considerable [number of] people after him. That one also perished, and all, as many as were obeying him, were scattered. ³⁸And [as for] the present [matter], I say to you*, keep away from these men and let them alone, because if the plan or this work is of people [fig., human origins], it will be overthrown; ³⁹but if it is of God, you* are not able to overthrow it, lest you* [may] even be found [to be] fighting against God."

⁴⁰And they were persuaded by him; and having summoned the apostles, having repeatedly beaten [them], they gave strict orders [to them] not to be speaking in the name of Jesus, and [then] they released them. ⁴¹So they indeed departed from the face [fig., presence] of the High Council, rejoicing that they were counted worthy to be dishonored on behalf of the name of Jesus. ⁴²And every day in the temple and in every house, they were not ceasing [from] teaching and proclaiming the Gospel [or, Good News, and throughout book] of Jesus the Christ.

*6*And in these days, the disciples increasing [in number], there came to be a complaint from the Hellenists [fig., Greek-speaking Jews] towards the Hebrews [fig., Aramaic-speaking Jews], because their widows were being overlooked in the daily service [fig., distribution of food]. ²So the twelve having summoned the congregation of the disciples, said, "It is not desirable [for] us, having left the word of God, to be serving tables. ³Therefore, brothers [and sisters], look for seven men from [among] you*, being well spoken of, full of [the] Holy Spirit and wisdom, whom we shall appoint over this need [or, necessity]. ⁴But we will give ourselves continually to prayer and to the ministry of the word."

⁵And the word was pleasing before the whole congregation. And they chose Stephen, a man full of faith and of [the] Holy Spirit, and Philip and Prochorus and Nicanor and Timon and Parmenas and Nicolaus, a proselyte [i.e. convert to Judaism] from Antioch, ⁶whom they set before the apostles. And having prayed, they laid [their] hands on them.

⁷And the word of God kept spreading, and the number of the disciples kept being increased greatly in Jerusalem, and a large crowd of the priests were becoming obedient to the faith.

⁸Now Stephen, full of faith and of power, was performing wonders and great signs among the people. ⁹But [there] rose up some of the [ones] from the synagogue, the ones being called Freed Slaves, both of [the] Cyrenians and of [the] Alexandrians, and of the [ones] from Cilicia and Asia, disputing with Stephen.

¹⁰And they were not being able to resist the wisdom and the spirit with which he was speaking. ¹¹Then they secretly bribed men [to be] saying, "We have heard him speaking blasphemous words against Moses and God!"

¹²And they incited the people and the elders and the scribes, and having come up [to him], they dragged him away and brought [him] to the High Council. ¹³And they put [forward] false witnesses, saying, "This man does not cease from speaking blasphemous words against the holy place [i.e. the temple] and the Law! ¹⁴For we have heard him saying that this Jesus the Nazarene will tear down this place and will change the customs which Moses handed down to us." ¹⁵And looking intently at him, all the ones sitting in the High Council saw his face like [the] face of an angel.

7Then the high priest said, "Do you so hold these [things]?" ²But he said, "Men, brothers and fathers, pay attention! The God of glory appeared to our father Abraham, being in Mesopotamia, before he lived in Haran, ³and said to him, *'Go out from your [native] land and from your relatives, and come into a land which I shall show to you.'* [Gen 12:1]

⁴"Then having come out from the land of [the] Chaldeans, he settled in Haran; and from there, after the death of his father, He relocated him to this land in which you* now live. ⁵And He gave him no inheritance in it, not even a stride of a foot [worth of land], and [yet] He promised to give it to him for a possession and to his seed [fig., offspring] after him, no child being to him [fig., though he had no child].

⁶"And God spoke in this way: that his seed [fig., offspring] will be a stranger in a foreign land, and they will enslave it [i.e., his seed] and will oppress [it] four hundred years. [Gen 15:12] ⁷*'And the nation to which they shall serve as slaves I will judge,'* said God; *'and after these [things] they will come out and will sacredly serve Me in this place.'* [Gen 15:14; Exod 3:12] ⁸And He gave to him a covenant of circumcision, and in this way he fathered Isaac and circumcised him on the eighth day; and Isaac [fathered] Jacob, and Jacob the twelve patriarchs.

⁹"And the patriarchs having become jealous, sold Joseph into Egypt; and [yet] God was with him, ¹⁰and delivered him out of all his afflictions and gave to him favor and wisdom before Pharaoh, king of Egypt, and he appointed him [as] a ruler over Egypt and all his house.

¹¹"Then a famine came on the whole land of Egypt and Canaan, and great affliction, and our fathers were not finding food. ¹²But Jacob having heard grain being in Egypt, sent our fathers out first. ¹³And on the second [visit] Joseph made himself known to his brothers, and Joseph's race [or, family] became known to Pharaoh. ¹⁴Then having sent [word], Joseph summoned his father Jacob and all the relatives, seventy-five souls [fig., persons] in [all]. ¹⁵So Jacob went down into Egypt and came to the end [of his life], he and our fathers. ¹⁶And they were transferred into Shechem and were laid in the tomb which Abraham bought for a sum of money from the sons of Hamor, the [father] of Shechem.

¹⁷"Now as the time of the promise was drawing near, [about] which God made an oath to Abraham, the people increased and were multiplied in Egypt, ¹⁸until which

[time] *'a different king arose, who had not known Joseph.'* [Exod 1:8] [19]This [king] having cunningly taken advantage of our race, oppressed our fathers to be making their babies exposed, for [them] not to be staying alive, [20]in which time Moses was born, and he was beautiful to God, who was brought up three months in the house of his father. [21]But being placed outside, the daughter of Pharaoh took him up and brought him up as a son for herself. [22]And Moses was educated in all [the] wisdom of the Egyptians, and he was mighty in words and deeds.

[23]"Now when forty years were fulfilled to him [fig., When he was forty years old], it entered his heart to visit his brothers [and sisters], the sons [and daughters] of Israel. [24]And having seen someone being treated unjustly, he defended [him] and did justice to [fig., avenged] the one being oppressed by striking the Egyptian. [25]Now he was assuming his brothers [and sisters] to be understanding that God [was] giving deliverance to them through his hand, but they did not understand.

[26]"And the next day he appeared to them as they [were] fighting, and he [tried to] reconcile them to peace, saying, 'Men, you* are brothers! Why are you* injuring one another?' [27]But the one injuring his neighbor pushed him away, saying, *'Who appointed you a ruler and a judge over us? [28]You do not want to kill me [in the] manner which you killed the Egyptian yesterday, do you?'* [Exod 2:14] [29]Then Moses fled at this word, and he became a stranger in [the] land of Midian, where he fathered two sons.

[30]"And forty years having been fulfilled [fig., after another forty years had passed], [the] Angel of [the] Lord appeared to him in the wilderness of Mount Sinai, in a flame of fire in a bush. [31]Then Moses having seen, began marveling at the sight. Now as he [was] approaching to look [more] closely, [the] voice of [the] Lord came to him: [32] *'I [am] the God of your fathers; the God of Abraham and the God of Isaac and the God of Jacob.'* [Exod 3:6,15] Then Moses having become trembling [fig., terrified] did not dare to look closely.

> [33]*Then the LORD said to him, "Untie the sandal[s] from your feet, for the place on which you have stood is holy ground. [34]Having seen I saw [fig., I have certainly seen] the oppression of My people, the [ones] in Egypt, and I heard their groaning, and I came down to deliver them. And now come, I will send you to Egypt."* [Exod 3:5,7,8,10]

[35]"This Moses, whom they refused, saying, *'Who appointed you a ruler and a judge?'*—this [man] God sent [as] a ruler and a liberator by [the] hand of [the] Angel, the One having appeared to him in the bush. [36]This [man] led them out, having performed wonders and signs in [the] land of Egypt and in [the] Red Sea and in the wilderness [for] forty years. [37]This is the Moses, the one having said to the sons [and daughters] of Israel, *'[The] LORD our God will raise up for you* a Prophet like to me from your* brothers.'* [Deut 18:15] [38]This is the one having been in the assembly in the wilderness with the Angel, the One speaking to him on Mount Sinai, and [with] our fathers, who received a living word to give to us; [39]to whom our fathers did not want to become obedient, but they pushed [him] aside and in their heart turned back to Egypt, [40]saying to

Aaron, *'Make for us gods who will go before us, for this Moses who led us out from the land of Egypt, we do not know what has happened to him.'* [Exod 32:1]

[41]"And in those days they made a calf and brought a sacrifice to the idol and began celebrating in the works of their hands. [42]So God turned away and gave them over to be sacredly serving the host of heaven [i.e. the sun, moon, planets, and stars], just as it has been written in a scroll of the prophets:

> *You* did not offer slaughtered animals and sacrifices to Me [for] forty years in the wilderness, O house of Israel, did you*?* [43]*You* also took along the tabernacle of Moloch* [i.e. the Canaanite-Phoenician sun god] *and the star of your god Remphan* [i.e. the Egyptian name for the Roman god Saturn], *the images which you* made to be prostrating yourselves in worship before them. And I will relocate you* beyond Babylon.* [Amos 5:25-27, LXX]

[44]"The tabernacle of the testimony was with our fathers in the wilderness, just as the One speaking to Moses gave instructions [to him] to make it according to the pattern which he had seen, [45]which also our fathers having received in turn, brought [it] in with Joshua while [taking] possession of the [land of the] nations which God drove out from [the] face [fig., presence] of our fathers, until the days of David, [46]who found favor before God and requested to find a dwelling place for the God of Jacob. [47]But Solomon built a house for Him. [48]But the Most High does not dwell in temples made with human hands, just as the prophet says, [49]*'Heaven [is] My throne, but the earth [is] a footstool for My feet. What kind of house will you* build for Me?'* says [the] LORD, *'Or what [is] My place of rest?* [50]*My hand made all these [things], did it not?'* [Isaiah 66:1,2]

[51]"O stiff-necked and uncircumcised in heart and in ears [fig., O stubborn and obstinate people]! You* are always resisting the Holy Spirit—like your* fathers, also you*! [52]Which of the prophets did your* fathers not persecute? And they killed the ones having announced beforehand about the coming of the Righteous One, of whom now you* have become betrayers and murderers, [53]who received the Law as [the] ordinances of angels and [yet] did not keep [it]."

[54]Now hearing these [things], they were cut through to their hearts [fig., they were infuriated], and they began gnashing their teeth at him. [55]But being full of [the] Holy Spirit, having looked intently into heaven, he saw [the] glory of God, and Jesus having stood at [the] right hand of God. [56]And he said, "Look! I see the heavens having been opened and the Son of Humanity having stood at [the] right hand of God!" [57]But they, having cried out with a loud voice, covered their ears and rushed on him with one mind.

[58]And having driven [him] outside of the city, they began stoning [him]. And the witnesses laid their cloaks down at the feet of a young man being called Saul. [59]And they kept on stoning Stephen as he [was] calling on [the Lord] and saying, "Lord Jesus, receive my spirit!" [60]Then having placed the knees [fig., having knelt down], he cried out with a loud voice, "Lord, do not hold this sin against them!" And having said this, he fell asleep [fig., died].

169

8Now Saul was giving approval to his murder. Then in that day a great persecution took place on the assembly, the one in Jerusalem, and all were scattered throughout the regions of Judea and Samaria, except the apostles. ²(Now devout men prepared Stephen for burial, and they themselves made loud wailing over him.) ³But Saul began making havoc of the assembly—entering every house, dragging off both men and women, handing them over to prison.

⁴So indeed, the ones having been scattered went about proclaiming the Gospel [of] the word. ⁵Now Philip having gone down to a city of Samaria began preaching the Christ to them. ⁶And the crowds with one mind were paying close attention to the [things] being spoken by Philip, as they [were] hearing and seeing the signs which he was performing. ⁷For many of the ones having unclean [or, defiling] spirits, [the spirits] were coming out, shouting with a loud voice; and many having been paralyzed and lame were healed. ⁸And [there] was great joy in that city.

⁹But a certain man, by name Simon, was previously in the city practicing magic and astonishing the nation of Samaria, claiming himself to be someone great, ¹⁰to whom they were paying close attention, from [the] least to [the] greatest, saying, "This [man] is the great power of God!" ¹¹Now they were paying close attention to him because of the considerable time he had astonished them with magical acts. ¹²But when they believed Philip as he [was] proclaiming the Gospel of the [things] concerning the kingdom of God and the name of Jesus Christ, both men and women were baptized. ¹³Then Simon himself also believed. And having been baptized, he was continuing with Philip; and observing signs and miraculous works taking place, he himself was amazed.

¹⁴Now the apostles in Jerusalem having heard that Samaria had received the word of God sent Peter and John to them, ¹⁵who, having come down, prayed concerning them in order that they shall receive [the] Holy Spirit—¹⁶for He had not yet fallen upon any of them, but they had only been baptized in the name of Christ Jesus. ¹⁷Then they began laying hands on them, and they were receiving [the] Holy Spirit. ¹⁸Now Simon having observed that the Holy Spirit is given through the laying on of the hands of the apostles, he offered money to them, ¹⁹saying, "Give this power to me also, so that on whomever I shall lay the hands he shall receive [the] Holy Spirit."

²⁰But Peter said to him, "May your silver be with you in perdition [fig., hell], because you thought to be acquiring the free gift of God through money! ²¹[There] is neither part nor portion for you in this matter, for your heart is not right before God. ²²Therefore, repent from this your wickedness, and implore God, if perhaps the intention of your heart will be forgiven you. ²³For I perceive you [as] being in the gall of bitterness and bond of unrighteousness." ²⁴But answering, Simon said, "<u>You*</u> implore [in prayer] to the Lord on my behalf, in order that nothing of what you have spoken shall come upon me."

²⁵So they indeed having solemnly testified and having spoken the word of the Lord turned back to Jerusalem, and they themselves proclaimed the Gospel in many villages of the Samaritans.

²⁶Now an angel of [the] Lord spoke to Philip, saying, "Get up and go toward [the] south on the road, the one going down from Jerusalem to Gaza." (This is a desert [road]). ²⁷And having gotten up, he went. And look! A man, an Ethiopian, an eunuch [i.e., a man incapable of having sex], a court official of Candace the queen of [the] Ethiopians, who was over all her treasury, who had come to Jerusalem to prostrate himself in worship, ²⁸and he was returning and sitting in his chariot, and he was reading aloud the prophet Isaiah.

²⁹Then the Spirit said to Philip, "Approach and be joined to this chariot." ³⁰So Philip having run up, heard him reading aloud the prophet Isaiah, and he said, "So do you understand what you are reading?" ³¹Then he said, "For how could I unless someone guides me?" And he invited Philip, having come up, to sit with him.

³²Now the passage of the Scripture which he was reading aloud was this:

He was led as a sheep to slaughter, and as a lamb before the one shearing it [is] silent, so He does not open His mouth. ³³In His humiliation His justice was taken away, but who will describe His generation? Because His life is taken away from the earth. [Isaiah 53:7,8, LXX]

³⁴So answering, the eunuch said to Philip, "I ask you, about whom does the prophet say this? About himself or about some other [person]?" ³⁵Then Philip, having opened his mouth and having begun from this Scripture, proclaimed the Gospel [about] Jesus to him.

³⁶Now as they were traveling down the road, they came upon some water. And the eunuch said, "Look! Water! What prevents me [from being] baptized?" ³⁸And he commanded the chariot to stand still. And they both went down into the water, both Philip and the eunuch, and he baptized him. ³⁹Now when they came up out of the water, [the] Spirit of [the] Lord caught Philip up, and the eunuch no longer saw him, for he began going his way rejoicing. ⁴⁰But Philip was found at Azotus, and passing through, he was proclaiming the Gospel to all the cities until he came to Caesarea.

9Now Saul, still breathing threat[s] and murder [fig., murderous threats] against the disciples of the Lord, having gone to the high priest, ²requested letters from him to Damascus, to the synagogues, in order that if he should find any being of the Way, both men and women, having been bound, he should bring them to Jerusalem. ³Now as he [was] traveling, he came to be approaching Damascus, and suddenly a light from heaven [or, the sky] flashed around him. ⁴And having fallen on the ground, he heard a voice saying to him, "Saul, Saul, why are you persecuting Me?"

⁵Then he said, "Who are You, Lord?" And the Lord said, "I am Jesus, whom you are persecuting! ⁶But get up and enter into the city, and it will be told to you what it is necessary [for] you to be doing." ⁷But the men, the ones traveling with him, had stood speechless, indeed hearing the voice but seeing no one. ⁸Then Saul got up from the ground, and [although] his eyes had been opened, he saw no one.

So leading him by the hand, they brought [him] into Damascus. [9]And he was three days not seeing, and he neither ate nor drank.

[10]Now [there] was a certain disciple in Damascus, by name Ananias, and the Lord said to him in a vision, "Ananias!" So he said, "Here I [am], Lord!" [11]Then the Lord [said] to him, "Having risen, go to the street, the one being called Straight, and look in [the] house of Judas for [a man] by name of Saul of Tarsus. For listen! He is praying. [12]And he saw in a vision a man by name Ananias coming in and laying a hand on him, in order that he should regain [his] sight."

[13]But Ananias answered, "Lord, I have heard from many about this man, how many wicked [things] he did to Your holy ones [or, saints, and throughout book] in Jerusalem. [14]And here he has authority from the chief priests to bind all the ones calling on Your name." [15]But the Lord said to him, "Be going, because this one is a chosen vessel to Me to bear My name before Gentiles and kings and the sons [and daughters] of Israel. [16]For I will show to him how many [things] it is necessary [for] him to suffer for the sake of My name."

[17]And Ananias went away and entered into the house; and having laid his hands on him, he said, "Saul, brother, the Lord, the One appearing to you on the road in which you were coming, has sent me in order that you shall regain [your] sight and shall be filled with [the] Holy Spirit." [18]And immediately [there] fell off from his eyes [something] like scales, and he regained [his] sight! And having gotten up, he was baptized. [19]And having received food, he was strengthened.

Then Saul was with the disciples in Damascus several days. [20]And immediately in the synagogues he began preaching the Christ, that this One is the Son of God. [21]But all the ones hearing were amazed and said, "This is the one having destroyed the ones calling on this name in Jerusalem, is it not? And he has come here for this [purpose], so that having been bound, he should bring them to the chief priests." [22]But Saul all the more was being empowered, and he was confounding the Jews, the ones dwelling in Damascus, proving that this [Jesus] is the Christ.

[23]Now when many days were fulfilled [fig., after many days], the Jews plotted among themselves to execute him. [24]But their plot became known to Saul. And they were watching the gates closely both day and night, in order that they should execute him. [25]But the disciples having taken him by night, they let [him] down through [an opening in] the [city] wall, lowering [him] in a large basket.

[26]Then Saul, having arrived in Jerusalem, was attempting to be joined to the disciples, and they all were fearing him, not believing that he is a disciple. [27]But Barnabas having taken him, brought [him] to the apostles and described to them how on the road he saw the Lord and that He spoke to him, and how in Damascus he was speaking boldly in the name of Jesus. [28]And he was with them at Jerusalem, coming in and speaking boldly in the name of the Lord Jesus, [29]and he was speaking and disputing with the Hellenists [fig., Greek-speaking Jews]. But they were attempting to execute him, [30]but the brothers [and sisters] having found out, brought him down to Caesarea and sent him off to Tarsus.

[31]Then indeed the assemblies throughout the whole of Judea and Galilee and Samaria were having peace, being edified; and going on [or, living] in the fear of the Lord and in the comfort of the Holy Spirit, they were being multiplied. [32]Now

it happened, as Peter [was] passing through all [those regions], he came down also to the holy ones, the ones living [in] Lydda. ³³Then he found there a certain man, Aeneas by name, lying on a cot for eight years, who had been paralyzed. ³⁴And Peter said to him, "Aeneas, Jesus the Christ heals you! Get up and make your bed yourself!" And immediately he got up! ³⁵And all the ones living [in] Lydda and Sharon saw him, and they turned to the Lord.

³⁶Now in Joppa [there] was a certain female disciple, by name Tabitha, (which, being translated, is being called Dorcas); this [woman] was full of good works and charitable giving which she was doing. ³⁷Then it happened in those days, having been sick, she died. So having washed her [body], they laid her in an upstairs room. ³⁸Now Lydda being close to Joppa, the disciples having heard that Peter is in it [i.e. Lydda], sent [messengers] to him urging [him] not to delay to come over to them. ³⁹So Peter having gotten up, went with them, whom having arrived, they brought [him] into the upstairs room. And all the widows stood by him weeping and showing tunics and cloaks, as many as Dorcas used to make while being with them.

⁴⁰But Peter having sent them all outside, having placed the knees [fig., having knelt down], prayed; and having turned to the body, he said, "Tabitha, get up!" Then she opened her eyes, and having seen Peter, she sat up! ⁴¹Then having given her [his] hand, he lifted her up; and having called the holy ones and the widows, he presented her living. ⁴²Now it became known throughout all of Joppa, and many believed on the Lord. ⁴³And it happened, [that] he stayed many days in Joppa, with a certain Simon a tanner [i.e. a person who converts animal hides into leather].

10Now [there] was a certain man in Caesarea, by name Cornelius, a centurion of a garrison [of soldiers], the one being called Italian [fig., a captain of the Italian Regiment], ²devout and fearing God [i.e. a worshipper of the one true God, but not a full convert to Judaism, also called "God-worshiping"] together with all his house, and doing [or, giving] many charitable gifts to the people and imploring God through all [fig. continually].

³About [the] ninth hour of the day [i.e. 3:00 p.m.] he saw clearly in a vision an angel of God having come to him and having said to him, "Cornelius!" ⁴Then having looked intently at him and having become terrified, he said, "What is it, Lord?" So he said to him, "Your prayers and your charitable gifts [have] ascended as a memorial before God. ⁵And now send men to Joppa and summon Simon, the one being called Peter. ⁶This [man] is staying as a guest with a certain Simon a tanner, whose house is by [the] sea." ⁷So when the angel, the one speaking to Cornelius, left, having summoned two of his household servants and a devout soldier [from among] the ones waiting on him continually, ⁸and having explained everything to them, he sent them to Joppa.

⁹Now the next day, as these are traveling and approaching the city, Peter went up on the housetop to pray, about [the] sixth hour [i.e. 12:00 noon]. ¹⁰But he became very hungry and was desiring to eat; but while they [were] preparing [a meal], a trance fell on him, ¹¹and he observes heaven [or, the sky] having been

opened, and a certain object like a great sheet descending to him, having been tied at [the] four corners and being lowered on the ground, ¹²in which were all the four-footed animals of the earth and the wild beasts and the reptiles and the birds of heaven [or, of the air]. ¹³And a voice came to him: "Having gotten up, Peter, slaughter and eat!" ¹⁴But Peter said, "Most certainly not, Lord! Because never did I eat any[thing] common [fig., ritually impure] or unclean [or, which defiles]." ¹⁵And a voice [came] again a second time to him: "What God [has] cleansed, by all means stop calling common [fig., ritually impure]!" ¹⁶Now this was done three times, and again the object was taken up into heaven.

¹⁷Now as Peter was thoroughly perplexed in himself what the vision which he saw might be [fig., mean], then look!, the men, the ones having been sent from Cornelius, having found by inquiry the house of Simon, stood at the gate. ¹⁸And having called, they were asking whether Simon, the one being called Peter, is staying here as a guest. ¹⁹Now as Peter [was] pondering about the vision, the Spirit said to him, "Listen! Men are seeking you. ²⁰But having gotten up, go down and go with them, doubting nothing [fig., without hesitation], because I have sent them."

²¹So Peter having gone down to the men, said, "Listen! I am [the one] whom you* are seeking. What [is] the reason for which you* are here?" ²²Then they said, "Cornelius, a centurion, a righteous man and fearing God, and well spoken of by [the] whole nation of the Jews, was divinely directed by a holy angel to summon you to his house and to hear words from you." ²³So having invited them in, he received [them] as guests. Then the next day Peter went away with them, and some of the brothers from Joppa went with him.

²⁴And the next day they entered into Caesarea. Now Cornelius was waiting for them, having called together his relatives and close friends. ²⁵Then when it happened [that] Peter entered, Cornelius having met him, having fallen at [his] feet, prostrated himself in worship before [him]. ²⁶But Peter raised him up, saying, "Stand up! I myself am also a person." ²⁷And talking with him, he went in and finds many [people] having gathered. ²⁸And he said to them, "You* know how it is unlawful for a man, a Jew, to be associating with or to be visiting one of another race, and [yet] God showed to me to be calling no one common or unclean [or, defiled]. ²⁹And so, without even raising any objection, I came, having been summoned. So I ask for what reason did you summon me?"

³⁰And Cornelius said, "From [the] fourth day [fig., Four days ago], I was fasting until this hour, and [at] the ninth hour [i.e. 3:00 p.m.] praying in my house. And listen! A man stood before me in a shining robe! ³¹And he said, 'Cornelius, your prayer was heard and your charitable gifts are remembered before God. ³²Therefore, send [men] to Joppa and summon Simon, who is called Peter. This [man] is staying as a guest in [the] house of Simon, a tanner by the sea, who having arrived, will speak to you.' ³³So I sent for you at once, and you did well, having arrived. Now then, we all are present before God to hear all the [things] having been commanded to you by God."

³⁴Then Peter having opened his mouth, said, "Truly, I comprehend that God is not One to accept faces [fig., to be prejudice], ³⁵but in every nation the one fearing

Him and working righteousness is acceptable to Him. ³⁶The word which He sent to the sons [and daughters] of Israel, proclaiming the Gospel of peace through Jesus Christ—this One is Lord of all—³⁷[that word] you* know, the word having taken place throughout the whole of Judea, having begun from Galilee, after the baptism which John preached—³⁸Jesus who [is] from Nazareth—how God anointed Him with the [the] Holy Spirit and power, who went about doing good and healing all the ones being oppressed by the Devil, because God was with Him.

³⁹"And we are witnesses of all [things] which He did, both in the country of the Jews and in Jerusalem; whom they also executed, having hanged [Him] on a tree [or, a cross]. ⁴⁰This One God raised up on the third day and gave Him to become visible, ⁴¹not to all the people, but to witnesses, the ones having been chosen beforehand by God, to us who ate together and drank together with Him after He rose from [the] dead. ⁴²And He gave strict orders to us to preach to the people and to solemnly testify that He is the One having been designated by God [to be] Judge of living [ones] and of dead [ones]. ⁴³To this One all the prophets bear witness [that] through His name every[one] that is believing [or, trusting] in Him receives forgiveness of sins."

⁴⁴While Peter [was] still speaking these words, the Holy Spirit fell upon all the ones hearing the word. ⁴⁵And the believing ones from the circumcision were astonished, as many as came with Peter, because the free gift of the Holy Spirit had been poured out on the Gentiles also. ⁴⁶For they were hearing them speaking with tongues [fig., other languages] and magnifying God. Then Peter answered, ⁴⁷"Surely no one is able to forbid the water, can he, [for] these not to be baptized who received the Holy Spirit just as we also [did]?" ⁴⁸And he commanded them to be baptized in the name of the Lord. Then they urgently asked him to stay several days.

11 Now the apostles and the brothers [and sisters], the ones being throughout Judea, heard that the Gentiles also [had] received the word of God. ²And when Peter came up to Jerusalem, the [ones] from [the] circumcision were taking issue with him, ³saying, "To men having foreskin [fig., who are uncircumcised] you went in and ate with them!"

⁴But Peter having begun, began explaining to them [everything] in consecutive order saying, ⁵"I was in [the] city of Joppa praying, and in a trance I saw a vision: a certain object like a great sheet coming down, being lowered by four corners out of heaven [or, the sky], and it came to me, ⁶at which having looked intently, I was considering [it], and I saw the four-footed animals of the earth and the wild beasts and the reptiles and the birds of heaven [or, the air]. ⁷Then I heard a voice saying to me, 'Having gotten up, Peter, slaughter and eat!' ⁸But I said, 'Most certainly not, Lord! Because never did any[thing] common [fig., ritually impure] or unclean [or, which defiles] enter into my mouth.' ⁹But a voice out of heaven answered to me a second [time], 'What God cleansed, by all means stop calling common [fig., ritually impure]!' ¹⁰Now this happened three times, and again all [things] were drawn up to heaven.

[11]"And listen! Immediately, three men stood before the house in which I was [staying], having been sent from Caesarea to me. [12]Then the Spirit said to me to go with them doubting nothing [fig., without hesitation]. Now these six brothers also went with me, and we entered into the house of the man. [13]And he reported to us how he saw the angel having stood in his house and saying to him, 'Send men to Joppa and summon Simon, the one being called Peter, [14]who will speak words by which you will be saved, you and all your house.'

[15]"Now when I began to be speaking, the Holy Spirit fell on them, even as [He] also [did] on us in [the] beginning. [16]Then I remembered the word of [the] Lord, how He used to say, 'John indeed baptized in [or, with] water, but you* will be baptized in [or, with] [the] Holy Spirit.' [Acts 1:5] [17]Since then God gave the same free gift to them as also to us, having believed on [or, trusted in] the Lord Jesus Christ, now who was I [to be] able to forbid God?" [18]So having heard these [things], they were silent, and they began glorifying God, saying, "In that case, God also gave to the Gentiles repentance to life!"

[19]Then indeed the ones having been scattered because of the affliction [or, persecution], the one having occurred over Stephen, passed through as far as Phoenicia and Cyprus and Antioch, speaking the word to no one except to Jews only. [20]But some of them were male Cyprians and Cyrenians, who having entered into Antioch, began speaking to the Hellenists [fig., Greek-speaking Jews], proclaiming the Gospel of the Lord Jesus. [21]And [the] hand of [the] Lord was with them, and a large number having believed turned to the Lord.

[22]Then the word about them was heard in the ears of the assembly, the [one] in Jerusalem, and they sent out Barnabas to pass through as far as Antioch, [23]who having arrived and having seen the grace of God, was glad, and began encouraging [them] all with purpose of [or, a resolute] heart [fig., with steadfast devotion] to be continuing with [fig., remaining loyal to] the Lord, [24]because he was a good man and full of [the] Holy Spirit and of faith. And a considerable crowd was added to the Lord.

[25]Then Barnabas departed for Tarsus to look for Saul. [26]And having found [him], he brought him to Antioch. So it happened [that for] a whole year they were gathered together with the assembly and taught a considerable crowd. And the disciples were first called Christians in Antioch.

[27]Now in those days prophets came from Jerusalem to Antioch. [28]Then one of them, by name Agabus, having stood up, signified [or, foretold] by the Spirit [of] a great famine being about to happen over all the inhabited earth—which also [or, then] occurred during [the reign of] Claudius Caesar. [29]Then the disciples, just as anyone was prospering, each of them determined to send [a contribution] for ministry [fig., relief] to the brothers [and sisters] dwelling in Judea, [30]which they also did, having sent to the elders by [the] hand of Barnabas and Saul.

12 Now about that time Herod the king put his hands to mistreat [or, persecute] some of the [ones] from the assembly. [2]Then he executed James the brother of John with [the] sword. [3]And having seen that it is pleasing to the Jews, he proceeded to arrest Peter also (now [at that time] were the Days of the Unleavened

Bread [i.e. Passover]), ⁴whom also having seized, he put in prison, having handed [him] over to four four-man squads of soldiers to be guarding him, intending after the Passover to bring him [before] the people. ⁵Therefore, Peter indeed was being kept in the prison, but fervent [or, constant] prayer was being made by the assembly to God on his behalf.

⁶Now when Herod was about to be bringing him out, on that night Peter was sleeping between two soldiers, having been bound with two chains, and guards in front of the door were watching over the prison. ⁷And look! An angel of [the] Lord stood by [him], and a light shined in the prison cell. Then having struck the side of Peter, he raised him up, saying, "Get up with quickness!" And his chains fell off from [his] hands. ⁸And the angel said to him, "Wrap [a belt] around yourself, and tie on your sandals." So he did so. And he says to him, "Put your cloak on yourself, and be following me."

⁹And having gone out, he was following him, and he did not know that it is real, the [thing] taking place by the angel, but was thinking he is seeing a vision. ¹⁰Now having passed by [the] first and second guard, they came to the iron gate, the one leading into the city, which opened by itself to them. And having gone out, they went along one street, and immediately the angel departed from him. ¹¹And Peter having come to himself, said, "Now I know truly that [the] Lord sent forth His angel and delivered me out of [the] hand of Herod and all the expectation of the people of the Jews."

¹²And having become aware of [this], he came to the house of Mary, the mother of John, the one being called Mark, where a considerable [number] had been gathering together and [were] praying. ¹³So Peter having knocked at the door of the porch, a slave-girl came to answer, by name Rhoda. ¹⁴And having recognized the voice of Peter, because of [her] joy she did not open the gate, but having run in, she announced [that] Peter has stood before the gate.

¹⁵But they said to her, "You are raving mad!" But she kept insisting, holding [it to be] so. Then they said, "It is his angel." ¹⁶But Peter was continuing knocking, so having opened, they saw him and were astonished. ¹⁷Then having motioned to them with the hand to be keeping silent, he described to them how the Lord led him out of the prison. Then he said, "Report these [things] to James and to the brothers [and sisters]." And having gone out, he went to another place.

¹⁸Now day having come, [there] was no small [fig., a great] disturbance among the soldiers [as to] what then became of Peter. ¹⁹Then Herod having searched for him and not having found [him], having examined the guards, commanded [them] to be led away [to be executed]. And having gone down from Judea to Caesarea, he was staying [there].

²⁰Now Herod was very angry [or, was quarreling angrily] with [the] Tyrians and Sidonians, but they came to him with one mind. And having won over Blastus, the [one] over the bedroom of the king [fig., the king's personal attendant], they began asking for peace, because of their country being provided with food from the king's [country]. ²¹So on an appointed day, Herod having put a royal robe on himself and having sat down on the judgment seat [or, his throne], began making a speech to them. ²²Then the populace began shouting, "[The] voice of a god and

not of a man!" ²³So immediately an angel of [the] Lord struck him, because he did not give glory to God. And having been eaten by worms, he expired [or, emitted his last breath]!

²⁴But the word of God kept growing and kept being multiplied. ²⁵Now Barnabas and Saul returned to Jerusalem, having fulfilled the ministry [or, their mission], having taken along also John, the one being called Mark.

13 Now [there] were some prophets and teachers in the assembly being in Antioch: both Barnabas and Simon (the one being called Niger), and Lucius the Cyrenian and Manaen (foster-brother of Herod the ruler of the quadrant [or, the tetrarch]) and Saul. ²Now while they [were] ministering to the Lord and fasting, the Holy Spirit said, "Set apart to Me Barnabas and Saul for the work which I have called them to." ³Then having fasted and having prayed and having laid their hands on them, they sent [them] away.

⁴So these [two] indeed having been sent out by the Holy Spirit, went down to Seleucia. Then from there they sailed to Cyprus. ⁵And having come to be [fig., having arrived] in Salamis, they began preaching the word of God in the synagogues of the Jews. Now they also had John [i.e. Mark] [as] an assistant.

⁶Then having crossed over the island as far as Paphos, they found a certain learned astrologer [or, Magus], a false prophet, a Jew, whose name [was] Bar-Jesus, ⁷who was with Sergius Paulus, the governor of the providence [or, the proconsul], an intelligent man. This one having summoned for Barnabas and Saul, sought to hear the word of God. ⁸But Elymas the learned astrologer (for so is his name translated) was opposing them, seeking to turn the governor of the providence away from the faith.

⁹But Saul (the [one] also [called] Paul), having been filled of [or, with] [the] Holy Spirit and having looked intently on him, ¹⁰said, "O [one] full of all deceit and all lack of principles, son of [the] Devil, enemy of all righteousness, you will not cease distorting the straight ways of [the] Lord, will you? ¹¹And now, listen! [The] hand of [the] Lord [is] on you, and you shall be blind, not seeing the sun until a season [has passed]." Then immediately a mist and darkness fell on him, and going [fig., groping] about, he was seeking ones who would lead [him] by the hand. ¹²Then the governor of the providence having seen the [thing] having taken place, believed, being astonished at the teaching of the Lord.

¹³Now having set sail from Paphos [with] the ones about [him] [fig., with his companions], Paul came to Perga of Pamphylia. But John [i.e. Mark] having departed from them returned to Jerusalem. ¹⁴But they having gone on from Perga, arrived at Antioch of Pisidia, and having gone into the synagogue on the Sabbath day, they sat down. ¹⁵Now after the reading aloud of the Law and of the Prophets, the synagogue leaders sent to them, saying, "Men, brothers, if [there] is a word in you* of exhortation to the people, be speaking [it]."

¹⁶Then Paul having gotten up and having motioned with his hand, said, "Men, Israelites, and the ones fearing God, pay attention! ¹⁷The God of this people chose our fathers and exalted the people [fig., made the people prosper] during their sojourning in the land of Egypt, and with an uplifted arm He led them out

from it. [18]And [for] about a forty-year time He put up with their conduct in the wilderness. [19]And having brought down [fig., conquered] seven nations in [the] land of Canaan, He distributed their land to them as an inheritance.

[20]"And after these things, [for] about four hundred and fifty years, He gave judges until [the time of] Samuel the prophet. [21]And then they asked for a king, and God gave to them Saul [the] son of Kish, a man from [the] tribe of Benjamin, [for] forty years. [22]And having removed him, He raised up to them David for king, to whom also having testified, He said, '*I found David* the [son] of Jesse, [to be] *a man in accordance with My heart*, who will do all My will.' [1Sam 13:14; Psalm 89:20]

[23]"God, from this one's seed [fig., offspring] according to [His] promise, [has] brought to Israel salvation, [24]John [the Baptist] having previously preached before [the] face of His entrance [fig, before His coming] a baptism of repentance to Israel. [25]Now as John was completing the course [of his ministry], he said, 'Whom do you* suppose me to be? I am not [He]. But listen! One is coming after me, of whom I am not worthy to untie the sandal of [His] feet.' [Mark 1:7; John 1:20,27]

[26]"Men, brothers, sons of [the] family of Abraham and the ones among you* fearing God, to you* the word of this salvation was sent. [27]For the ones living in Jerusalem and their rulers, having failed to understand this One and the voices of the prophets, the ones being read aloud every Sabbath, having condemned [Him], they fulfilled [these things]. [28]And [although] having found no cause for [putting Him to] death, they asked Pilate [for] Him to be executed. [29]Now when they fulfilled all the [things] having been written concerning Him, having taken [Him] down from the tree [or, the cross], they laid Him in a tomb. [30]But God raised Him from [the] dead, [31]who appeared for many days to the ones having come up together with Him from Galilee to Jerusalem, who are His witnesses to the people.

[32]"And we proclaim [to] you* the Gospel, [which is] the promise having been made to the fathers, [33]that God has fulfilled this [promise] for us their children, having raised up Jesus, as it also has been written in the second Psalm, '*You are My Son; today I have begotten You.*' [Psalm 2:7] [34]And that He raised Him up from [the] dead, no longer being about [fig., subject] to return to corruption, He has said in this way, '*I will give to you* the holy [and] trustworthy [promises] of David.*' [Isaiah 55:3] [35]And so He says in another [Psalm], '*You will not give* [fig., allow] *Your Holy One to see corruption.*' [Psalm 16:10]

[36]"For David indeed, having served his own generation by the counsel [or, plan] of God, fell asleep [fig., died], and he was added to [fig., buried with] his fathers and saw corruption. [37]But [He] whom God raised up did not see corruption. [38]Therefore, let it be known to you*, men, brothers, that through this One the forgiveness of sins is proclaimed to you*, [39]and from all [the things] from which you* were not able to be justified [or, declared righteous] by the Law of Moses, in this One every[one] believing is justified!

[40]"Therefore, be watching lest [there] come on you* the [thing] having been spoken in the prophets, [41]'*Look, [you*] scoffers, and marvel and perish! Because I*

work a work in your* days which you* shall by no means believe, even if someone shall be describing [it] to you*in detail.'" [Hab 1:5]

⁴²Then they [i.e. Paul and Barnabas] having gone out from the synagogue of the Jews, the Gentiles began pleading with [them] for [these] words to be spoken to them on the next Sabbath. ⁴³Now the synagogue having been dismissed, many of the Jews and of the God-worshiping proselytes followed Paul and Barnabas, who, speaking to [them], were persuading them to be continuing in the grace of God.

⁴⁴And on the coming [fig., next] Sabbath, almost all the city was gathered together to hear the word of God. ⁴⁵But the Jews, having seen the crowds, were filled with jealousy and began objecting to the [things] spoken by Paul, objecting and blaspheming. ⁴⁶But speaking boldly, Paul and Barnabas said, "It was necessary [for] the word of God to be spoken to you* first, but since you* push it away [fig., reject it] and do not judge yourselves worthy of eternal life, listen!, we turn to the Gentiles. ⁴⁷For in this manner has the Lord commanded us, *'I have placed you as a light for [the] Gentiles, for you to be for salvation as far as [the] end of the earth.'"* [Isaiah 49:6]

⁴⁸Now the Gentiles hearing [this], they began rejoicing and glorifying the word of the Lord, and as many as had been appointed to eternal life believed. ⁴⁹So the word of the Lord was spreading abroad throughout the whole region. ⁵⁰But the Jews incited the God-worshiping women and the prominent [women] and the first [fig., leading] [men] of the city, and they stirred up persecution against Paul and Barnabas, and they drove them out from their borders. ⁵¹But they having shaken off the dust of their feet against them, came to Iconium. ⁵²Now the disciples were being filled of [or, with] joy and [the] Holy Spirit.

14Now it happened in Iconium [that] they entered by the same [way] into the synagogue of the Jews, and they spoke in such a manner [that] a large number of both Jews and Greeks believed. ²But the refusing to believe Jews stirred up and embittered the souls of the Gentiles against the brothers [and sisters]. ³Therefore, they indeed stayed [there] a considerable time speaking boldly in the Lord, the One testifying to the word of His grace, giving signs and wonders to be taking place by their hands. ⁴But the populace of the city was divided, and some were with the Jews, but some with the apostles. ⁵Now when an attempt took place by both the Gentiles and [the] Jews, with their rulers, to mistreat and to stone them, ⁶having become aware of [it], they fled to the cities of Lycaonia, Lystra, and Derbe, and the surrounding region. ⁷And there they kept proclaiming the Gospel.

⁸And a certain man in Lystra, powerless in the feet, was sitting, lame from [the] womb of his mother, who had never walked. ⁹This [man] heard Paul speaking, who, having looked intently on him and having seen that he had faith to be healed, ¹⁰said with a loud voice, "Stand up properly on your feet!" And he began leaping and walking!

¹¹So the crowds having seen what Paul did, raised their voice, saying in Lycaonian, "The gods, having become like men, came down to us!" ¹²And they began calling Barnabas Zeus [i.e. the supreme Greek god] and Paul Hermes [i.e.

the messenger of the Greek gods], since he was the leader of the word [fig,. the chief speaker]. [13]Then the priest of Zeus, the one being before their city, having brought oxen and wreaths [of flowers] to the gates, together with the crowds, [was] intending to be sacrificing [them to Paul and Barnabas].

[14]But the apostles Barnabas and Paul having heard, having torn their robes, rushed into the crowd, crying out [15]and saying, "Men, why are you* doing these [things]? We also are human, like in every way to you*, proclaiming the Gospel [in order for] you* to be turning from these useless [things] to the living God, who made the heaven and the earth and the sea and all the [things] in them, [16]who in the past generations allowed all the nations to be going in their own ways; [17]and yet He did not leave Himself without witness, doing good, giving rains to you* from heaven and fruitful seasons, satisfying our hearts [fig., inner desires] with food and gladness." [18]Even [with] saying these [things], they scarcely restrained the crowds from sacrificing to them.

[19]Then Jews came from Antioch and Iconium, and having persuaded the crowds and having stoned Paul, they dragged [him] outside of the city, having supposed him to have died. [20]But the disciples having surrounded him, having risen, he entered into the city, and the next day he went away with Barnabas to Derbe.

[21]And having proclaimed the Gospel to that city and having made many disciples, they returned to Lystra and Iconium and Antioch, [22]strengthening the souls of the disciples, encouraging [them] to be continuing firm in the faith, and [saying], "Through many afflictions it is necessary [for] us to enter into the kingdom of God." [23]And having elected by raising of hands [fig., having appointed by votes] elders for them in every assembly, having prayed with fastings, they commended them to the Lord in whom they had believed.

[24]And having passed through Pisidia, they came to Pamphylia. [25]And having spoken the word in Perga, they went down to Attalia. [26]And from there they sailed to Antioch, from where they had been handed over [or, committed] by the grace of God for the work which they [had] completed. [27]So having arrived and having gathered the assembly together, they reported as many things as God did with them, and that He opened a door of faith to the Gentiles. [28]Then they were staying there not a little [fig., a long] time with the disciples.

15 And certain [men] having come down from Judea began teaching the brothers, "Unless you* are circumcised [according to] the custom of Moses, you* are not able to be saved." [2]Therefore, [there] having occurred not a little [fig, a serious] conflict and debate with Paul and Barnabas against them, they arranged for Paul and Barnabas and certain others of them to be going up to the apostles and elders to Jerusalem about this point of disagreement. [3]So they indeed having been sent on their journey by the assembly, were passing through Phoenicia and Samaria, describing in detail the conversion of the Gentiles, and they were causing great joy to all the brothers [and sisters]. [4]Now having arrived at Jerusalem, they were received by the assembly and the apostles and the elders, and they reported as many things as God did with them.

⁵But some of the ones having believed from the sect of the Pharisees stood up, saying, "It is necessary to be circumcising them and to be giving strict orders [to them] to be keeping the Law of Moses." ⁶So the apostles and the elders were gathered together to see about this matter.

⁷Now much debate having taken place, having risen up, Peter said to them, "Men, brothers, you* know that from former days God chose among us [for] the Gentiles to hear the word of the Gospel through my mouth and to believe. ⁸And the heart-knowing God testified to them by having given the Holy Spirit to them, just as also to us, ⁹and also distinguished nothing between us and them, having purified [or, purged] their hearts by faith. ¹⁰Now therefore, why are you* testing God [by trying] to put a yoke on the neck of the disciples, which neither our fathers nor we were able to bear? ¹¹But we believe [we are] saved through the grace of the Lord Jesus, according to which manner they also [are]."

¹²Then all the multitude kept silent, and they were listening to Barnabas and Paul explaining how many signs and wonders God did among the Gentiles through them.

¹³Now after they became silent, James answered, saying, "Men, brothers, listen to me. ¹⁴Simon [i.e. Peter] explained how God first visited [them] to take out of [the] Gentiles a people for His name. ¹⁵And with this the words of the prophets agree, just as it has been written:

>¹⁶*After these [things] I will return, and I will rebuild the tabernacle of David, the one having fallen down, and the [things] having been torn down from it I will rebuild, and I will restore it, ¹⁷in order that the remaining peoples* [i.e. non-Jews] *shall diligently seek the LORD, even all the Gentiles on whom My name has been called on them, says the LORD, the One doing all these things.* [Amos 9:11,12, LXX]

¹⁸"Known from [the] ages [fig., from eternity] to God is all His works.

¹⁹"For this reason, I judge not to be troubling the [ones] turning to God from the Gentiles, ²⁰but to write instructions to them to be abstaining from the pollutions of the idols and from sexual sin and from the strangled [animal] and from blood. ²¹For Moses from ancient generations has in every city the ones preaching him, being read aloud in the synagogues every Sabbath."

²²Then it seemed good to the apostles and the elders, with the whole assembly, having chosen men from them, to send to Antioch with Paul and Barnabas, Judas (the one being called Barsabbas) and Silas, leading men among the brothers, ²³having written by their hand these [things]:

The apostles and the elders and the brothers, to the brothers [and sisters], the [ones] from the Gentiles, in Antioch and Syria and Cilicia, greetings!

²⁴Since we heard that some having gone out from us disturbed you* with words, unsettling your* souls, saying [for you*] to continue being circumcised and to be keeping the Law, to whom we did not give [such]

orders, ²⁵it seemed good to us, having come to be of one mind, to send to you* having been chosen men, with our beloved Barnabas and Paul, ²⁶men having given up their souls [or, lives] for the sake of the name of our Lord Jesus Christ. ²⁷Therefore, we have sent Judas and Silas, and they are telling [you*] the same [things] by [the spoken] word.

²⁸For it seemed good to the Holy Spirit and to us to lay no more burden on you*, except [for] these necessary things: ²⁹to be abstaining from [meat] sacrificed to idols and from blood and from [anything] strangled and from sexual sin. From which keeping yourselves, you* will do well. Farewell!

³⁰So indeed, having been sent off, they went to Antioch; and having gathered the congregation together, they delivered the letter. ³¹Then having read [it] aloud, they rejoiced over the encouragement. ³²And Judas and Silas, also being prophets themselves, encouraged and strengthened the brothers [and sisters] with a lengthy message. ³³So having spent time [there], they were sent away with [a blessing] of peace [or, with a greeting] from the brothers [and sisters] to the apostles. ³⁵But Paul and Barnabas were staying in Antioch, teaching and proclaiming the Gospel of the word of the Lord, with many others also.

³⁶Then after some days, Paul said to Barnabas, "Having returned now, we should visit our brothers [and sisters] in every city in which we have preached the word of the Lord, [to see] how they have [it] [fig., how they are doing]." ³⁷And Barnabas decided to take along John, the one being called Mark. ³⁸But Paul was not considering it good to take this [one] along with [them], the one having withdrawn from them at Pamphylia and not having gone with them to the work. [Acts 13:13]

³⁹So [there] came to be a sharp disagreement, with the result that they were separated from one another, and Barnabas, having taken Mark, sailed away to Cyprus. [cp. 2Tim 4:11] ⁴⁰But Paul, having chosen Silas, went out, having been handed over [fig., committed] to the grace of God by the brothers [and sisters]. ⁴¹So he was passing through Syria and Cilicia, strengthening the assemblies.

16 Then he came to Derbe and Lystra. And look! A certain disciple was there, by name Timothy, a son of a certain believing Jewish woman but of a Greek father, ²who was well spoken of by the brothers [and sisters] in Lystra and Iconium. ³Paul wanted this [one] to go out with him, and having taken [him], he circumcised him because of the Jews, the ones in those places, for they all knew his father, that he was a Greek. ⁴Now as they were traveling through the cities, they were delivering to them the decrees to be keeping, the ones having been decided [on] by the apostles and the elders, the [ones] in Jerusalem. ⁵So the assemblies were indeed being strengthened in the faith and were increasing in number every day.

⁶Now having passed through Phrygia and the region of Galatia, having been forbidden by the Holy Spirit to speak the word in Asia, ⁷having gone toward Mysia, they were trying to be going to Bithynia, and the Spirit did not allow them.

⁸So having passed by Mysia, they came down to Troas. ⁹And a vision appeared to Paul during the night: a certain man of Macedonia was standing, pleading with him and saying, "Having crossed over to Macedonia, help us!" ¹⁰So when he saw the vision, immediately we sought to go out to Macedonia, concluding that the Lord had summoned us to preach the Gospel to them.

¹¹Therefore, having set sail from Troas, we sailed a straight course to Samothrace, and on the next [day] to Neapolis, ¹²and from there to Philippi, which is a first [fig., prominent] city of the district of Macedonia, a [Roman] colony. Then we were staying in that very city [for] several days. ¹³And on the Sabbath day we went forth outside of the city, by a river, where prayer was customarily to be [fig., made]; and having sat down, we began speaking to the women having assembled.

¹⁴And a certain woman by name Lydia, a dealer of purple fabrics of [the] city of Thyatira, worshiping God, was listening, whose heart the Lord opened to be paying close attention to the [things] being spoken by Paul. ¹⁵Now when she was baptized, and her household, she pleaded with us, saying, "Since you* have judged me to be faithful to the Lord, having entered into my house, remain." And she persuaded us.

¹⁶Then it happened as we [were] going to prayer, a certain slave-girl having a spirit of Python [i.e., in Greek mythology, a giant snake which guarded the oracle at Delphi; fig., having a fortune-telling spirit] met us, who brought much profit to her masters by fortune-telling. ¹⁷This [girl], having closely followed Paul and us, kept crying out, saying, "These men are slaves of the Most High God, who declare to us [the] way of salvation!" ¹⁸Now she was doing this for many days. But Paul having been greatly annoyed and having turned, said to the spirit, "I command you in the name of Jesus Christ to come out from her!" And it came out that very hour [or, moment]!

¹⁹But her masters having seen that the hope [or, expectation] of their profit was gone, having taken hold of Paul and Silas, dragged [them] to the marketplace before the rulers. ²⁰And having brought them to the magistrates, they said, "These men, being Jews, are throwing our city into confusion, ²¹and they are proclaiming customs that are not lawful for us, being Romans, to be receiving nor to be doing."

²²And the crowd rose up together against them, and the magistrates having torn their garments from them, began ordering [the rod-bearers] to be beating [them] with rods. ²³And having laid many blows on them, they threw [them] into prison, having given strict orders to the jailor to be keeping them securely, ²⁴who having received such an order, put them into the inner prison and fastened their feet in the stocks.

²⁵But about midnight Paul and Silas [were] praying [and] were singing hymns to God, and the prisoners were listening to them. ²⁶Then suddenly a great earthquake occurred, with the result that the foundations of the jail were shaken, and immediately all the doors were opened, and all of the chains were unfastened! ²⁷Then the jailor having become aroused from sleep and having seen the doors of the prison having been opened, having drawn a sword, was about to be killing

himself, supposing the prisoners to be escaping. [28]But Paul cried out with a loud voice, saying, "Do nothing harmful to yourself, for we are all here!"

[29]Then having asked for a light [fig., torch], he rushed in. And having become trembling [with fear], he fell down before Paul and Silas. [30]And having brought them out, he said, "Sirs, what is it necessary [for] me to be doing so that I shall be saved?" [31]So they said, "Believe on the Lord Jesus Christ, and you will be saved, you and your house!" [32]And they spoke the word of the Lord to him and to all the [ones] in his house. [33]And having taken them in that hour of the night, he washed off their wounds, and he was immediately baptized, himself and all the [ones] of his [house]. [34]And having brought them into his house, he set food before [them]. And he was being very glad, with his whole house, he having believed in God.

[35]Now having become day, the magistrates sent the rod-bearers, saying, "Release those men." [36]So the jailor reported these words to Paul, "The magistrates have sent so that you* shall be released. Now therefore, having come out, be going in peace." [37]But Paul said to them, "Having repeatedly beaten us publicly, uncondemned men being Romans, they threw [us] into prison. And now they are forcing us out secretly? No indeed! But having come themselves, let them lead [us] out!" [38]Then the rod-bearers reported these words to the magistrates, and they were afraid, having heard that they are Romans. [39]And having come, they pleaded with them, and having led [them] out, they kept asking [them] to go out from the city. [40]So having come out from the prison, they entered to [the house of] Lydia, and having seen the brothers [and sisters], they comforted them and departed.

17 Now having traveled through Amphipolis and Apollonia, they came to Thessalonica, where the synagogue of the Jews was. [2]Then according to the custom with Paul, he went in to them, and for three Sabbaths he reasoned with them from the Scriptures, [3]opening up and placing before [them] [fig., explaining and demonstrating] that it was necessary [for] the Christ to suffer and to rise again from [the] dead, and [saying], "This [One] is the Christ—Jesus, whom I am proclaiming to you*." [4]And some of them believed and were joined with Paul and Silas, both a large number of the God-worshiping Greeks and not a few [fig., a large number] of the first [fig., prominent] women.

[5]But the Jews, the ones refusing to believe, having taken along some evil men of the marketplace loiters and having formed a mob, began setting the city in an uproar, and having come upon the house of Jason, they were seeking to bring them to the mob. [6]But not having found them, they began dragging Jason and some brothers [and sisters] to the city officials [or, politarchs], shouting, "The ones having upset the inhabited earth, these are also present in this place, [7]whom Jason has welcomed; and these all act contrary to the decrees of Caesar, saying another to be king, Jesus." [8]So they stirred up the crowd and the city officials hearing these things. [9]And having taking a security bond [or, bail] from Jason and the rest, they released them.

[10]Then the brothers [and sisters] immediately during the night sent both Paul and Silas away to Berea, who having arrived, went into the synagogue of the Jews. [11]Now these were more noble-minded [than] the [ones] in Thessalonica,

who received the word with all [fig., great] eagerness, every day examining the Scriptures [to see] if these things might be so. [12]Therefore, many of them indeed believed, and not a few [fig., and a large number] of the prominent Greek women and men.

[13]But when the Jews from Thessalonica found out that also in Berea the word of God was declared by Paul, they came there also, agitating the crowds. [14]And then immediately the brothers [and sisters] sent Paul away to be going as though by the sea, but both Silas and Timothy were remaining there. [15]So the ones escorting Paul brought him as far as Athens, and having received a command for Silas and Timothy that they should come to him as quickly [as possible], they departed.

[16]But while Paul [was] waiting for them in Athens, his spirit was being provoked within him, observing the city being full of idols. [17]Therefore indeed, he began reasoning in the synagogue with the Jews and with the God-worshiping [Greeks] and in the marketplace every day with the [people] coming by. [18]Then also some of the Epicurean and the Stoic philosophers began disputing with him, and some were saying, "What does this seed picker [fig., babbler] wish to be saying?" But others [said], "He seems to be a proclaimer of strange deities," because he was proclaiming the Gospel of Jesus and the resurrection [Gr., *anastasia*] to them [i.e. they mistook Jesus to be just another god and *Anastasia* to be the name of Jesus' goddess wife].

[19]And having taken him, they brought [him] to the Areopagus [i.e. where the Athenian court met], saying, "Are we able to know what this new teaching [is], the one being spoken by you? [20]For you are bringing some startling [things] to our ears. So we wish to know what these [things] might be [fig., mean]." [21](Now all Athenians and the foreigners visiting [there] were spending their time for nothing other than to be saying and to be hearing something new.)

[22]So Paul having stood in [the] middle of the Areopagus, said, "Men, Athenians, I perceive you* as [being] extremely fearful of the gods in all things. [23]For passing through and contemplating your* objects of worship, I found also an altar on which had been inscribed: 'To an unknown God.' Therefore, [the One] whom you* are practicing piety [towards] [or, worshiping] without knowing, this One I proclaim to you*.

[24]"The God, the One having made the world [or, universe] and all the [things] in it, this One being Lord of heaven and of earth does not dwell in temples made with human hands, [25]nor is He served by [the] hands of people, [as if] needing something, [since] He is giving to all life and breath with respect to [fig., in] all [things]. [26]And He made from one blood every nation of human beings to be living on all the face of the earth, having designated times having been appointed [for them] and the boundaries of their habitation, [27][in order for them] to be seeking the Lord, if perhaps they might grope for Him and find [Him], and yet He is not far from each one of us. [28]'For in Him we live and move and are [fig., exist],' as also some of your* poets have said, 'For we are also His offspring' [i.e. quoting Epimendes (c. 600 B.C.) and Aratus of Cilia (c. 270 B.C.), respectively].

[29]"Therefore, being offspring of God, we ought not to be thinking the Divine Nature to be similar to gold or silver or stone, an image [shaped by] humanity's

skill and imagination. [30]Therefore indeed, [these] times of ignorance having overlooked, God is now giving strict orders to all people everywhere to be repenting, [31]because He set a day in which He is about to be judging the inhabited earth in righteousness by a Man whom He designated, having given assurance to all by having raised Him from [the] dead!"

[32]But having heard of [the] resurrection of [the] dead, some indeed began mocking, but others said, "We will hear you again concerning this." [33]And so Paul went out from their midst. [34]But some men having been joined to him, believed, among whom [were] also Dionysius the Areopagite [i.e. one of the 12 members of the Athenian court] and a woman by name Damaris and others with them.

*18*Then after these [things], Paul having departed out of Athens, came to Corinth. [2]And having found a certain Jew by name Aquila, of Pontus by race [or, a native of Pontus], recently having come from Italy, and Priscilla his wife (because of Claudius ordering all the Jews to depart out of Rome), he came to them. [3]And because of being of the same trade, he stayed with them and was working, for they were tent-makers [by] trade. [4]Now he was reasoning in the synagogue every Sabbath, and he was persuading Jews and Greeks.

[5]Now when both Silas and Timothy came down from Macedonia, Paul was held completely by the Spirit, solemnly testifying to the Jews [that] Jesus [is] the Christ. [6]But when they set themselves in opposition against [him] and [were] blaspheming, having shaken [the dust] off [of his] clothes, he said to them, "Your* blood [be] on your* head! I am clean. From now [on] I will go to the Gentiles!"

[7]And having departed from there, he went to [the] house of a certain [man] by name Justus, worshiping God, whose house was being next door to the synagogue. [8]Then Crispus the synagogue leader believed in the Lord together with his whole house, and many of the Corinthians, hearing, were believing and were being baptized. [9]Then the Lord said to Paul by means of a vision in the night, "Stop being afraid, but be speaking and do not be silent; [10]because I am with you, and no one will set on [fig., attack] you to harm you, because [there] are many people [belonging] to Me in this city." [11]And he settled [there] a year and six months teaching the word of God among them.

[12]But Gallio being proconsul [i.e. the Roman military commander] of Achaia, the Jews rose up with one mind against Paul and brought him to the judgment seat, [13]saying, "This [man] persuades men to worship God contrary to the Law." [14]Now Paul being about to be opening [his] mouth, Gallio said to the Jews, "If indeed then it was some misdeed or a wicked crime, O Jews, according to reason I would put up with you*. [15]But since it is a point of disagreement concerning words and names and the law according to you* [fig., your* own law], you* will look [to it] yourselves, [for] I am not willing to be a judge of these [things]." [16]And he drove them away from the judgment seat. [17]Then all the Greeks [who] had taken Sosthenes the synagogue leader began beating [him] before the judgment seat, and none of these [things] was a concern to Gallio.

[18]So Paul still having remained [there] a considerable [number of] days, having said good-bye to the brothers [and sisters], began setting sail for Syria,

and Priscilla and Aquila [were] with him, having cut off the hairs [of his] head in Cenchrea, for he had [taken] a vow. [19]Then he arrived at Ephesus and left those [two] there, but <u>he</u> having entered into the synagogue, reasoned with the Jews.

[20]Now they having asked [him] to remain for a longer time with them, he did not consent. [21]<u>But</u> he said good-bye to them, saying, "It is necessary [for] me by all means to keep the coming feast at Jerusalem, but I will return again to you*, God willing." And he set sail from Ephesus. [22]And having gone down to Caesarea, having gone up and having greeted the assembly, he went down to Antioch. [23]And having spent some time [there], he went out, passing through in order the Galatian region and Phrygia, strengthening all the disciples.

[24]Now a certain Jew, Apollos by name, an Alexandrian by race [or, a native of Alexandria], an educated man [or, a man skilled in speech], being mighty in the Scriptures, arrived at Ephesus. [25]This [man] had been instructed [in] the way of the Lord, and boiling [fig., being fervent] in his spirit [or, in the Spirit], he was speaking and teaching accurately the [things] concerning the Lord, knowing only the baptism of John. [26]And this [man] began to be speaking boldly in the synagogue. But Aquila and Priscilla having heard of him, they took him aside and explained to him the way of God more accurately.

[27]Now when he wanted to cross over into Achaia, having encouraged [him], the brothers [and sisters] wrote to the disciples [there] to welcome him, who, having arrived, greatly assisted the ones having believed by grace [or, by the grace [of God]]. [28]For he was powerfully refuting the Jews publicly, demonstrating by the Scriptures Jesus to be the Christ.

19 Now it happened, while Apollos was in Corinth, Paul having passed through the interior regions, came to Ephesus, and having found certain disciples, [2]he said to them, "Did you* receive [the] Holy Spirit, having believed?" But they said to him, "<u>But</u> we did not even hear whether there is a Holy Spirit." [3]And he said to them, "Into what then were you* baptized?" So they said, "Into John's baptism." [4]Then Paul said, "John indeed baptized with a baptism of repentance, saying to the people that they should believe in the One coming after him, that is, in the Christ—Jesus!" [5]So they having heard were baptized in the name of the Lord Jesus. [6]And Paul having laid [his] hands on them, the Holy Spirit came upon them, and they began speaking with tongues [fig., other languages] and prophesying. [7]Now [there] were [in] all about twelve men.

[8]Now having gone into the synagogue, he kept speaking boldly, for three months reasoning and persuading the [things] concerning the kingdom of God. [9]But when some were hardened [fig., became stubborn] and were refusing to believe, speaking against the Way before the populace, having departed from them, he took away the disciples, every day reasoning in the school of a certain Tyrannus. [10]Now this took place for two years, with the result that all the ones living in Asia heard the word of the Lord Jesus, both Jews and Greeks.

[11]And God was performing miraculous works, not the ones having happened, [fig., God was performing extraordinary miraculous works] through the hands of Paul, [12]with the result that even handkerchiefs or aprons from his skin [were]

being brought to the ones being sick, and the diseases [were] departing from them, and the evil spirits [were] going out from them.

[13]But some of the traveling about [or, itinerant] Jewish exorcists attempted to be naming the name of the Lord Jesus over the ones having evil spirits, saying, "We adjure you* by Jesus, whom Paul preaches." [14]Now [there] were some sons of Sceva, a Jewish high priest, seven [who were] doing this thing. [15]But answering, the evil spirit said, "Jesus I know, and Paul I am acquainted with—but you*, who are you*?" [16]And the man in whom was the evil spirit, leaping on them and having overpowered them, prevailed against them, with the result that they fled out of that house naked and wounded.

[17]Then this became known to all, both Jews and Greeks, the ones living in Ephesus, and fear fell on them all, and the name of the Lord Jesus was being magnified. [18]And many of the ones having believed were coming, confessing and disclosing their [sinful] actions. [19]Then a considerable [number] of the ones having practiced the magical arts, having collected their scrolls, began burning [them] before all. And they added up the prices of them and found [it totaled] five ten-thousands [i.e., 50,000] pieces of silver. [20]So with power the word of God was increasing and prevailing.

[21]Now when these things were accomplished, Paul was compelled by the Spirit [or, resolved in his spirit], having gone through Macedonia and Achaia, to be traveling to Jerusalem, saying, "After me to be there [fig., After I have been there], it is necessary [for] me also to see Rome." [22]Then having sent to Macedonia two of the ones serving him [fig., two of his assistants], Timothy and Erastus, he himself stayed [for] a time in Asia.

[23]But about that time [there] occurred no small [fig., a great] disturbance about the Way. [24]For a certain silversmith, Demetrius by name, making silver shrines of Artemis [i.e. the Greek goddess of fertility], was bringing to the craftsmen no small [fig., a great] profit, [25]whom he having gathered together, and the laborers with such [trades], said [to them], "Men, you* know that from this trade is our prosperity. [26]And you* see and hear that not only in Ephesus, but almost in all Asia, this Paul, having persuaded, turned away a considerable crowd, saying that they are not gods, the [things] coming to be by [human] hands. [27]So not only is this part to us [fig., is our business] in danger to come into disrepute, but also the temple of the great goddess Artemis [is] to be accounted for nothing, and also her magnificence is about to be pulled down, whom all Asia and the inhabited earth worships." [28]Now having heard and having become full of rage, they began crying out, saying, "Great [is] Artemis of [the] Ephesians!"

[29]And the whole city was filled with the confusion, and they rushed with one mind into the amphitheater, having dragged along Gaius and Aristarchus, Macedonians, traveling companions of Paul. [30]Now when Paul [was] intending to enter into the mob, the disciples were not allowing him. [31]Then also some of the officials of the providence of Asia, being his friends, having sent to him, were urging [him] not to present himself in the amphitheater.

[32]So indeed some were crying out [one thing and] some another [thing], for the assembly had been confused, and the majority did not know for what reason

they had come together. [33]Now [some] from the crowd induced Alexander, the Jews having put him forward. Then Alexander, having motioned with his hand, was intending to be making a defense to the populace. [34]But having known [or, having recognized] that he is a Jew, one voice came from [them] all for about two hours, crying out, "Great [is] Artemis of the Ephesians!"

[35]But the city clerk having quieted the crowd, says, "Men, Ephesians, for what person is [there] who does not know [about] the city of the Ephesians being [the] temple guardian of the great goddess Artemis and of the [image] fallen down from Zeus? [i.e., probably a meteorite that was worshiped as an image of Artemis] [36]So these things being undeniable, it is necessary [for] you* to have been quieted and to be doing nothing rash. [37]For you* brought these men, [who are] neither temple-robbers nor [ones] blaspheming your* goddess. [38]If then indeed Demetrius and the craftsmen with him have a word [fig., complaint] against anyone, courts are held and [there] are governors of the providence [available]. Let them bring charges against one another. [39]But if you* seek after anything concerning other [matters], it will be set free [fig., be settled] in the lawful assembly. [40]For we also are in danger of being accused of a riot concerning today, [there] being no cause [for it], on account of which we will not be able to give an account of this uproar." [41]And having said these [things], he dismissed the assembly.

20Now after the ceasing of the commotion, Paul having summoned the disciples, having embraced [them], went out to go to Macedonia. [2]So having gone through those regions, and having encouraged them with many words, he came to Greece. [3]And having made [fig., stayed] [there] three months, a plot having been [formed] against him by the Jews, being about to set sail for Syria, a decision came about [fig., was made] to be returning through Macedonia.

[4]Now accompanying him as far as Asia were: Sopater a Berean, and Aristarchus and Secundus of [the] Thessalonians, and Gaius a Derben, and Timothy, and [the] Asians Tychicus and Trophimus. [5]These [men] having gone ahead were waiting for us in Troas. [6]Then we set sail after the Days of the Unleavened Bread [i.e. Passover] from Philippi and came to them to Troas within five days, where we stayed seven days.

[7]Now on the first [day] of the week [i.e. Sunday], the disciples having been gathered together to break bread, Paul began holding a discussion with them, being about to be departing the next day, and he kept prolonging the word [fig., discussion] until midnight. [8]And a considerable [number] of lamps were in the upstairs room where we had been gathered together.

[9]Then a certain young man by name Eutychus, sitting in the window, being overcome by a deep sleep, Paul discussing for a long [time, the young man] having been overcome by sleep, fell down from the third story and was taken up dead. [10]But Paul, having gone down, fell on him. And having embraced [him], he said, "Stop being so upset, for his soul [or, life] is in him!" [11]So having gone [back] up, and having broken bread and having tasted and having talked for a long time, until daylight, thus he departed. [12]And they brought the boy living, and they were comforted not moderately [fig., greatly].

¹³But <u>we</u> having gone ahead to the ship, set sail for Assos, from there intending to take Paul on board, for so it had been arranged, since he [was] intending to travel by land. ¹⁴Now when he met with us at Assos, having taken him on board, we came to Mitylene. ¹⁵And from there having set sail, the following [day] we arrived opposite Chios, then the next [day] we approached Samos, and having stayed in Trogyllium, the following day we came to Miletus. ¹⁶For Paul decided to sail by Ephesus, in order that [it] would not happen to him to [have to] spend time in Asia, for he was hurrying, if it was possible for him to be in Jerusalem on the Day of Pentecost.

¹⁷Now from Miletus, having sent to Ephesus, he summoned the elders of the assembly. ¹⁸Then when they came to him, he said to them, "<u>You*</u> know from [the] first day from which I set foot in Asia how I was with you* all the time, ¹⁹serving as a slave to the Lord with all humility and many tears and trials, the [trials] having happened to me by the plots of the Jews; ²⁰how I did not keep back any of the [things] benefiting [you*, but I] declared to you* and taught you* publicly and in every house, ²¹solemnly testifying both to Jews and to Greeks [about] repentance toward God and faith toward our Lord Jesus.

²²"And now, listen! <u>I</u>, having been bound in the spirit [or, by the Spirit], am traveling to Jerusalem, not knowing the [things that] will be happening to me in it, ²³except that the Holy Spirit solemnly testifies in every city, saying that chains and afflictions await me. ²⁴But I make myself an account of nothing [or, of no account], neither do I hold my life precious to myself, so [as] to complete my course with joy and the ministry which I received from the Lord Jesus, to solemnly testify [to] the Gospel of the grace of God.

²⁵"And now, listen! <u>I</u> know that you* will no longer see my face, you* all among whom I went about preaching the kingdom of God. ²⁶For this reason, I testify to you* on this very day that I [am] innocent from the blood of all [people]. ²⁷For I did not keep back [anything, but I] declared to you* all the counsel [or, the entire plan] of God. ²⁸Therefore, continue being on guard for yourselves and for all the flock, in which the Holy Spirit placed you* [as] overseers, to be shepherding [fig., serving as pastors in] the Assembly of the Lord and God, which He acquired through His own blood. ²⁹For <u>I</u> know this, that after my departure vicious wolves will come into you*, not sparing the flock; ³⁰and from among you* yourselves men will arise, speaking [things] having been perverted [in order] to be drawing away the disciples after them. ³¹For this reason, keep watching, remembering that [for] three years, night and day, I did not cease warning each one with tears.

³²"And now, I entrust you*, brothers [and sisters], to God and to the word of His grace, the one being able to build [you*] up and to give to you* an inheritance among all the ones having been sanctified. ³³I coveted no one's silver or gold or clothes. ³⁴You* yourselves know that these hands provided for my necessities and for the [ones] with me. ³⁵I showed you* all [things] [or, in every way] that by laboring in this way it is necessary [for us] to be helping the ones being sick and to be keeping in mind the words of the Lord Jesus, that He Himself said, "It is more blessed to be giving than to be receiving."

³⁶And having said these [things], having placed his knees [fig. having knelt down], he prayed with them all. ³⁷Then [there] was considerable weeping by all, and having fallen on the neck of Paul, they were affectionately kissing him, ³⁸being deeply distressed most of all over the word which he had spoken, that they are about to be seeing his face no longer. Then they were accompanying him to the ship.

21 Now it happened, when we set sail, having withdrawn from them, having sailed a straight course, we came to Cos; then the next [day] to Rhodes, and from there to Patara. ²And having found a ship crossing over to Phoenicia, having boarded, we set sail. ³Now having come in sight of Cyprus, and having left [or, passed] it on the left, we kept sailing to Syria and came down to Tyre, for there the ship was unloading its cargo. ⁴And having found disciples, we stayed there seven days, who kept saying to Paul through the Spirit not to be going up to Jerusalem.

⁵But when it came about [for] us to [have] completed the days, having gone out, we were going, all [of them] accompanying us, with [their] wives and children, as far as [the] outside of the city. And having placed the knees [fig., having knelt down] on the shore, we prayed. ⁶And having embraced one another, we went on board into the ship, but they returned to their own [homes].

⁷Now <u>we</u> having completed the voyage from Tyre arrived at Ptolemais, and having embraced the brothers [and sisters], we remained with them one day. ⁸Then the next [day] the ones about Paul [fig., Paul's traveling companions], having gone out, came to Caesarea, and having entered into the house of Philip the evangelist, the one being of the seven, we stayed with him. [cp. Acts 6:5] ⁹Now to this [man] were daughters, four virgins prophesying.

¹⁰So while we [were] staying [there] several more days, a certain prophet by name Agabus came down from Judea. ¹¹And having come to us and having taken the belt of Paul and having bound his feet and hands, he said, "These [things] says the Holy Spirit, 'The man whose belt this is, in this way the Jews in Jerusalem will bind [him], and they will hand [him] over into [the] hands of [the] Gentiles.'"

¹²Now when we heard these [things], both we and the local residents began pleading with [Paul] not to be going up to Jerusalem. ¹³And Paul answered, "What are you* doing weeping and breaking my heart? For <u>I</u> am ready not only to be bound <u>but</u> also to die at Jerusalem on behalf of the name of the Lord Jesus." ¹⁴But he not being persuaded, we were silent, saying, "The will of the Lord be done." ¹⁵Then after these days, having prepared, we began going up to Jerusalem. ¹⁶And also [some] of the disciples from Caesarea went along with us, bringing [us] to a certain Mnason, a Cyprian, an early disciple, with whom we would stay as guests.

¹⁷Now we having come to be [fig., having arrived] in Jerusalem, the brothers [and sisters] received us gladly. ¹⁸Then on the next [day] Paul had gone in with us to James, and all the elders were present. ¹⁹And having embraced them, he began reporting one by one each of [the things] which God did among the Gentiles through his ministry.

²⁰So having heard, they began glorifying the Lord, having said to him, "You see, brother, how many thousands there are of Jews having believed, and all are zealots for the Law. ²¹But they are informed about you, that you are teaching apostasy from Moses to all Jews among the Gentiles, saying [for] them not to be circumcising their children nor to be walking [fig., conducting themselves] [according to] the customs. ²²What then is [to be done]? It is certainly necessary [for] the congregation to come together, for they will hear that you have come.

²³"Therefore, do this which we say to you: [there] are four men with us having a vow on themselves; ²⁴these having taken, be purified with them and pay their expenses for them, so that they shall shave the head, and all may know that [the things] of which they have been informed about you are nothing, but you are keeping in line with [fig., living in conformity with] and you yourself are keeping the Law. ²⁵But concerning the ones having believed of [the] Gentiles, we wrote, having judged [that they need] to be observing no such [thing], except to be keeping themselves both [from] the [meat] sacrificed to idols and [from] blood and [from anything] strangled and [from] sexual sin."

²⁶Then Paul, having taken the men on the following day, having been purified with them, had gone into the temple announcing the completion of the days of the purification, until which [time] the offering was offered on behalf of each one of them.

²⁷Now when the seven days were about to be coming to an end, the Jews from Asia having seen him in the temple began stirring up all the crowd, and they laid their hands on him, ²⁸crying out, "Men, Israelites, help! This is the man, the one teaching all [people] everywhere against the people and the Law and this place! And further, he also brought Greeks into the temple and has defiled this holy place!" ²⁹(For they had seen Trophimus the Ephesian in the city with him, whom they were assuming that Paul brought into the temple.) ³⁰And all the city was moved [fig., aroused], and [there] was a rushing together of the people, and having taken hold of Paul, they began dragging him outside of the temple, and immediately the doors were shut.

³¹Now as they [were] seeking to kill him, a report came up to the commanding officer [or, Chiliarch] of the garrison [of soldiers] that all Jerusalem had been stirred up, ³²who at once, having taken along soldiers and centurions, ran down to them. Then [the people] having seen the commanding officer and the soldiers, they stopped beating Paul. ³³Then the commanding officer, having come near, took hold of him and ordered [him] to be bound with two chains, and he began inquiring who he might be and what it is he had been doing.

³⁴But among the crowd some were shouting [one thing and] some another [thing], but not being able to know the certainty [or, to learn the facts] because of the commotion, he ordered him to be brought into the barracks. ³⁵But when he [i.e. Paul] came to be at the stairs, it happened [that] he [was] being carried by the soldiers because of the violence of the crowd. ³⁶For the crowd of people kept following, crying out, "Take him away!"

³⁷And Paul being about to be brought into the barracks says to the commanding officer, "Is it permitted for me to speak to you?" Then he said, "Do you know

Greek? ³⁸So you are not the Egyptian, the one having incited a riot before these days and having led the four thousand men of the assassins into the desert, are you?" ³⁹But Paul said, "I indeed am a man, a Jew of Tarsus of Cilicia, a citizen of no insignificant [fig., an important] city. Now I implore you, permit me to speak to the people." ⁴⁰So he having given him permission, Paul having stood on the stairs, motioned with his hand to the people. Now a great silence having taken place, he began addressing them in the Hebrew dialect, saying:

22"Men, brothers and fathers, now pay attention to my defense to you*." ²Now they having heard that in the Hebrew dialect he was speaking to them, they gave [him] even more silence.

And he says, ³"I indeed am a man, a Jew, having been born in Tarsus of Cilicia, but having been brought up in this city at the feet of Gamaliel, having been educated according to the exactness of the ancestral Law, being a zealot for God, just as you* all are today; ⁴[I] who persecuted this Way to death, binding and handing over to prisons both men and women, ⁵as also the high priest testifies to me, and all the council of the elders; from whom also having received letters to the brothers, I began traveling to Damascus to bring even the ones being there having been bound to Jerusalem, so that they should be punished.

⁶"But it happened to me, as I [was] traveling and approaching Damascus, about noon, suddenly a great light out of heaven [or, the sky] flashed around me. ⁷And I fell to the ground and heard a voice saying to me, 'Saul, Saul, why are you persecuting Me?' ⁸So I answered, 'Who are You, Lord?' And He said to me, 'I am Jesus the Nazarene, whom you are persecuting.' ⁹Now the ones being with me indeed saw the light and became terrified, but they did not hear the voice of the One speaking to me. ¹⁰So I said, 'What shall I do, Lord?' Then the Lord said to me, 'Having gotten up, be going into Damascus, and there it will be told to you concerning all [things] which have been appointed for you to do.' ¹¹Now when I was not seeing clearly because of the glory of that light, being led by the hand by the ones being with me, I came to Damascus.

¹²"Then a certain Ananias, a devout man according to the Law, being testified to [or, well-spoken of] by all the Jews living [there], ¹³having come to me and having stood by [me], said to me, 'Saul, brother, regain [your] sight!' And at that very hour [or, moment] I looked up at him [or, I regained [my] sight [and saw] him]! ¹⁴Then he said, 'The God of our fathers handpicked you beforehand to know His will and to see the Righteous [One] and to hear a voice from His mouth. ¹⁵For you will be His witness to all people of what you have seen and heard. ¹⁶And now, why are you delaying? Having gotten up, get yourself baptized, and get yourself washed [fig., purified] [of] your sins, you [or, sins by you] yourself calling on the name of the Lord.' [cp. Acts 2:21]

¹⁷"Now it happened to me, having returned to Jerusalem, and while I [was] praying in the temple, I came to be in a trance, ¹⁸and I saw Him saying to me, 'Hurry, and go out with quickness from Jerusalem, because they will not accept your witness about Me.' ¹⁹And I said, 'Lord, they know that I was imprisoning and repeatedly beating in each synagogue the ones believing on You. ²⁰And when

the blood of your witness Stephen was being shed, I myself also had stood by and [was] giving approval to his murder, guarding the cloaks of the ones executing him.' [see Acts 7:57-8:1] ²¹And He said to me, 'Go, because I will send you far away to [the] Gentiles.'"

²²And they were listening to him until this word, and they raised their voice, saying, "Take such a [man] away from the earth, for it was not fitting [for] him to be living!" ²³Now while they [were] crying out and throwing off their cloaks and tossing dust into the air, ²⁴the commanding officer ordered him to be brought into the barracks, having said [for him] to be interrogated with scourges, so that he should know for what cause they were shouting against him in this way.

²⁵But as he [i.e. one of the interrogators] stretched him out with the straps, Paul said to the centurion having stood by, "Is it lawful for you* to be scourging a man [who is] a Roman and uncondemned?" ²⁶Now the centurion having heard [this], having approached the commanding officer, reported, saying, "Watch what you are about to be doing, for this man is a Roman." ²⁷Then the commanding officer having approached, said to him, "Tell me, are you a Roman?" And he said, "Yes." ²⁸And the commanding officer answered, "I acquired this citizenship with a large sum of money." But Paul said, "But indeed I have been born [a Roman citizen]."

²⁹So immediately, the ones about to be interrogating him withdrew from him; and the commanding officer also was afraid, having learned that he is a Roman and because he had bound him. ³⁰Now the next day, wanting to know the certainty [or, facts] [as to] why he is being accused by the Jews, he released him from the bonds and ordered the chief priests and their whole High Council to come, and having brought Paul down, he set [him] by them.

23 Then Paul having looked intently at the High Council, said, "Men, brothers, I in all good conscience have lived to God until this day." ²But the high priest Ananias commanded the ones having stood by him to be striking his mouth. ³Then Paul said to him, "God is about to be striking you, [you] wall having been whitewashed! And do you sit judging me according to the Law, and violating the Law, order me to be struck?" ⁴But the ones having stood by said, "Do you insult the high priest of God?" ⁵And Paul said, "I did not know, brothers, that he is high priest, for it has been written, *'You will not speak evil of a ruler of your people.'"* [Exod 22:28]

⁶But Paul having perceived that the one part is Sadducees but the other Pharisees, cried out in the High Council, "Men, brothers, I am a Pharisee, a son of a Pharisee; concerning [the] hope [or, confident expectation] and resurrection of [the] dead I am being judged!" ⁷Now he having said this, there occurred a dispute [instigated by] the Pharisees, and the group was divided. ⁸For Sadducees indeed say there is no resurrection nor angel nor spirit, but Pharisees confess both the [things] [fig., all these things].

⁹Then [there] occurred a loud outcry. And the scribes of the Pharisees' party having gotten up, began protesting vehemently, saying, "We find nothing evil in this man! But if a spirit spoke to him, or an angel, let us not be fighting against

God." [10]Now a great dispute having occurred, the commanding officer having been afraid lest Paul be torn apart by them, ordered the detachment of soldiers to go down and to take him away by force from [the] middle of them and to be bringing [him] into the barracks. [11]But on the following night, the Lord having stood by him said, "Take courage Paul, for as you solemnly testified [about] the [things] concerning Me at Jerusalem, in the same way it is necessary [for] you also to testify at Rome."

[12]Then day having come, some of the Jews having formed a conspiracy, bound themselves by a curse saying [they would] neither eat nor drink until they kill Paul. [13]Now they were more than forty, the ones having formed this conspiracy, [14]who having approached the chief priests and the elders said, "With a curse we invoked a curse on ourselves to taste nothing until we kill Paul. [15]Now you*, therefore, together with the High Council, suggest to the commanding officer that tomorrow he should bring him down to you* as being about to be determining more accurately the [things] concerning him. But we, before he approaches, are ready to execute him."

[16]But the son of Paul's sister having heard of the ambush, having arrived and having entered into the barracks, reported [this] to Paul. [17]Then Paul having summoned one of the centurions, said, "Lead this young man to the commanding officer, for he has something to report to him." [18]So he indeed having taken him, brought him to the commanding officer and says, "The prisoner Paul, having summoned me, asked [me] to bring this young man to you, having something to say to you."

[19]So the commanding officer having taken him by the hand and having stepped aside, began inquiring privately, "What is it which you have to report to me?" [20]Then he said, "The Jews agreed to ask you, in order that tomorrow you should bring Paul down to the High Council as being about to be inquiring something more accurately concerning him. [21]You, therefore, do not be persuaded by them, for more than forty men of them lie in ambush for him, who invoked a curse on themselves not to eat nor to drink until they execute him, and now they are ready, waiting for the promise from you."

[22]Therefore, the commanding officer indeed let the young man go, having given strict orders [to him], "Tell no one you revealed these [things] to me." [23]And having summoned a certain two of the centurions, he said, "Prepare two hundred soldiers, in order that that they should go to Caesarea, and seventy horsemen and two hundred spearmen at the third hour of the night; [24]also provide animals, so that having placed Paul on [them], they should bring [him] safely to Felix the governor," [25]having written a letter containing this content:

[26]Claudius Lysias, to the most excellent governor Felix, greetings.

[27]This man having been arrested by the Jews and being about to be executed by them, having come with the detachment of soldiers, I rescued him, having learned that he is a Roman. [28]But wanting to know the cause for which they were accusing him, I brought him down to their High Council, [29]whom I found being accused concerning points

of disagreement [about] their law, [but] having no accusation worthy of death or chains. ³⁰Then a plot having been revealed to me against this man [was] about to happen by the Jews, at once I sent [him] to you, having also given strict orders to the accusers to be saying the [things] against him before you. Farewell.

³¹So indeed the soldiers according to [things] having been instructed to them, having taken up Paul, brought him during the night to Antipatris. ³²But the next day, having allowed the horsemen to travel with him, they returned to the barracks, ³³who having entered into Caesarea and having delivered the letter to the governor, also presented Paul to him. ³⁴Now the governor having read [it] and having inquired from what province he is and having learned that [he is] from Cilicia, ³⁵said, "I will give you a hearing when your accusers also arrive." And he also ordered him to be continually guarded in the Fortified Palace [or, Praetorium] of Herod.

24 Now after five days the high priest Ananias came down, with the elders and a certain attorney [named] Tertullus, who made known to the governor [the charges] against Paul.

²So he [i.e. Paul] having been called, Tertullus began to be accusing [him], saying [to the governor], "Since we are attaining great peace by you, and successes are [fig., prosperity is] coming about for this nation through your foresight, ³both in every [way] and everywhere we welcome it, most excellent Felix, with all thankfulness. ⁴But so that I do not detain you for more [fig., any longer], I beg you to hear us briefly in your kindness. ⁵For we having found this man [to be] a pest and [one] stirring up a discord [among] all the Jews throughout the inhabited earth and a ringleader of the sect of the Nazarenes, ⁶who also was trying to desecrate the temple, whom also we arrested, ⁸from whom you will be able, having examined [him] yourself, to learn about all these [things] of which <u>we</u> accuse him." ⁹Then the Jews also joined in the attack, asserting to be holding these [things] in this way.

¹⁰But Paul answered, the governor having motioned for him to be speaking, "Knowing [that] you being a judge to this nation for many years, the more confidently I speak in my defense the [things] concerning myself, ¹¹you being able to ascertain that [there] are not more [than] twelve days to me from which [time] I went up to be prostrating myself in worship in Jerusalem, ¹²and neither in the temple did they find me disputing with anyone or causing an uprising of the crowd, nor in the synagogues nor in the city. ¹³Nor are they able to prove [against] me [the things] concerning which they are now accusing me.

¹⁴"But I confess this to you, that according to the Way which they call a sect, in this way I sacredly serve the ancestral God, believing all the [things] according to the Law and having been written in the prophets, ¹⁵having hope [or, confident expectation] in God, which even they themselves are waiting for, [that there is] about to be a resurrection of [the] dead, both of righteous [ones] and of

unrighteous [ones]. [16]Now in this I am engaging myself, having through all [fig. always] a blameless conscience before God and people.

[17]"Now after many years I arrived, being about to give charitable gifts to my nation, and offerings, [18]in which some Jews from Asia found me [occupied] in the temple, having been purified, not with a crowd nor with a commotion, [19]whom it is necessary to be present before you and to be making an accusation, if they might have anything against me. [20]Or let these themselves say what misdeed they found in me in my having stood before the High Council, [21]or [is it] concerning this one voice, in which I cried out, having stood among them, 'Concerning [the] resurrection of [the] dead I am being judged by you* today.'" [see Acts 23:6]

[22]Now having heard these [things], Felix adjourned them, having learned more accurately the [things] concerning the Way, saying, "When Lysias the commanding officer comes down, I will decide the [things] regarding you*," [23]having also given instructions to the centurion to be guarding Paul, and [for him] to be having [some] freedom, and to be forbidding none of his own [people] to be providing for [him] or to be coming to him.

[24]Now after several days, Felix having arrived with Drusilla his wife (she being Jewish), he sent for Paul and heard him concerning the faith in Christ. [25]But while he [was] reasoning about righteousness and self-control and the judgment, the one being about to happen, Felix having become terrified, answered, "For the present be going, but having time, I will call for you." [26]And at the same time also hoping that money will be given to him by Paul, in order that he should release him. And so, frequently sending for him, he was talking with him. [27]But two years having been completed, Felix received a successor, Porcius Festus. And Felix wishing to lay favors on the Jews, left Paul having been bound.

25 Festus then, having set foot in the province, after three days went up to Jerusalem from Caesarea. [2]Then the high priest and the first [fig., leading] men of the Jews made known to him [the charges] against Paul, and were appealing to him, [3]requesting a favor against him, that he would summon him to Jerusalem, forming an ambush to execute him along the way. [4]Then indeed Festus answered [that] Paul is being kept in Caesarea, but [that he] himself is about to be going out [to Caesarea] with quickness. [5]"Therefore, the powerful [or, prominent] [ones] among you," he says, "having come down together, if there is anything in this man, let them accuse him."

[6]Then having stayed among them more than ten days, having gone down to Caesarea, the next day having sat on the judgment seat, he ordered Paul to be brought. [7]So he having arrived, the Jews having come down from Jerusalem stood around [him], and they are bringing many weighty charges against Paul, which they were not able to prove, [8][while he was] speaking in his own defense, "Neither in regard to the Law of the Jews, nor in regard to the temple, nor in regard to Caesar did I commit any sin." [9]But Festus wishing to lay on the Jews a favor, answering Paul, said, "Are you willing, having gone up to Jerusalem, there to be judged before me concerning these [charges]?"

[10]But Paul said, "I have stood at the judgment seat of Caesar, where it is necessary [for] me to be judged; in nothing did I wrong the Jews, as you also know very well. [11]For if indeed I am doing wrong and have done anything worthy of death, I do not refuse to die. But if [there] is nothing [to the things] of which these are accusing me, no one is able to give me as a favor to them. I appeal to Caesar!" [12]Then Festus, having conferred with the council, answered, "You have appealed to Caesar; you will go before Caesar!"

[13]Then some days having passed, Agrippa the king and Bernice arrived in Caesarea, having greeted Festus. [14]So while he was staying there many days, Festus laid before the king the [things] concerning Paul, saying, "There is a certain man having been left by Felix [as] a prisoner, [15]about whom, me having been [or, while I was] in Jerusalem, the chief priests and the elders of the Jews informed [me], asking for punishment against him; [16]to whom I answered that it is not a custom with Romans to be giving [as] a favor any person to destruction even before the one being accused may have [fig., may meet] the accusers face to face and may receive an opportunity for defense concerning the charge.

[17]"Therefore, they having assembled here, I having made no delay, on the next [day] having sat on the judgment seat, ordered the man to be brought; [18]concerning whom the accusers having stood up, began bringing against [him] no accusation of [the things] which I was supposing, [19]but some points of disagreement concerning their own religion they had against him, and concerning a certain Jesus having died, whom Paul asserted to be living. [20]Now I myself being perplexed regarding the investigation concerning this was asking if he might be willing to be going to Jerusalem, and there to be judged concerning these [charges]. [21]But Paul having appealed [for] him to be kept for the decision of His Majesty the Emperor, I ordered him to be kept until which [time] I should send him to Caesar." [22]Then Agrippa said to Festus, "I also was wishing to hear the man myself." So he said, "Tomorrow you will hear him."

[23]Therefore, the next day, Agrippa and Bernice having come with great pomp and having entered into the auditorium together with both the commanding officers and the men being according to prominence [fig., the prominent men] of the city, and Festus having ordered, Paul was brought [in].

[24]And Festus said, "King Agrippa and all men being present with us, you* see this [man] concerning whom all the populace of the Jews appealed to me, both in Jerusalem and here, yelling [that it is] not fitting [for] him to be living any longer. [25]But I having found him to have done nothing worthy of death, and this one himself also having appealed to His Majesty the Emperor, I decided to be sending him, [26]concerning whom I do not have anything certain to write to [my] lord. For this reason, I brought him out before you*, and especially before you, king Agrippa, in order that the preliminary hearing having taken place, I should have something to write. [27]For it seems to me irrational, sending a prisoner, not also to signify the charges against him."

26 Now Agrippa said to Paul, "It is permitted for you to be speaking on behalf of yourself." Then Paul having stretched out his hand, began speaking in his own defense: ²"Concerning all things of which I am accused by Jews, king Agrippa, I have considered myself fortunate [or, blessed] being about to be speaking in my own defense before you today; ³especially knowing you are an expert in all [things] in relation to Jews, both customs [or, morals] and points of disagreement. For this reason, I implore you to patiently hear me.

⁴"So then indeed, my way of life from youth, the one having taken place from [the] beginning among my [own] nation in Jerusalem, all the Jews know; ⁵knowing already [about] me from the beginning, if they are willing to testify, that according to the most accurate [or, strictest] sect of our religion, I lived [as] a Pharisee. ⁶And now for the hope [or, confident expectation] of the promise having been made by God to the fathers, I have stood being judged, ⁷[the promise] to which our twelve tribes sacredly serving in earnestness night and day hope [or, confidently expect] to attain, concerning which hope [or, confident expectation], king Agrippa, I am being accused by [the] Jews. ⁸Why is it judged incredible with you* if God raises [the] dead?

⁹"Therefore I indeed thought to myself [for] it to be necessary [for me] to do many [things] against the name of Jesus of Nazareth, ¹⁰which also I did in Jerusalem; and many of the holy ones I locked up in prison, having received the authority from the chief priests, and when they [were] being executed, I cast a pebble [fig., my vote] against [them]. ¹¹And punishing them often in all the synagogues, I was compelling [them] to be blaspheming, and being exceedingly enraged against them, I was persecuting [them] even as far as outer [fig., foreign] cities.

¹²"In which [pursuits] also traveling to Damascus with authority and commission from the chief priests, ¹³in [the] middle of [the] day, O king, I saw on the way a light from heaven more than the brightness of the sun shining around me and the ones traveling with me. ¹⁴Then we all having fallen to the ground, I heard a voice speaking to me and saying in the Hebrew dialect, 'Saul, Saul, why are you persecuting Me? [It is] difficult for you to be kicking against [the] goads [i.e. pointed sticks used to drive livestock].'

¹⁵"So I said, 'Who are You, Lord?' And He said, 'I am Jesus whom you are persecuting. ¹⁶But get up and stand on your feet; because for this [reason] I appeared to you, to handpick you [as] a servant and a witness both of what you saw and of what I will appear [fig., will reveal] to you, ¹⁷delivering you from the [Jewish] people and [from] the Gentiles, to whom I am sending you, ¹⁸to open their eyes [in order] to turn [them] back from darkness [i.e., falsehood and unrighteousness] to light [i.e., truth and righteousness] and [from] the authority of Satan to God, [in order for] them to receive forgiveness of sins and an inheritance among the ones having been sanctified by faith in Me.'

¹⁹"For which reason, king Agrippa, I was not disobedient to the heavenly vision, ²⁰but first to the [ones] in Damascus and to the [ones] in Jerusalem and into all the region of Judea and to the Gentiles, preaching [for them] to be repenting and to be turning to God, doing works worthy of repentance. ²¹Because of these things the Jews having arrested me in the temple were attempting to murder [me]. ²²Therefore, having obtained help from God, until this day I have stood testifying

both to small and to great, saying nothing except what both the Prophets and Moses spoke of [as] being about to be taking place, ²³that the Christ is subject to suffering, that [being the] first from [the] resurrection of the dead, He is about to be proclaiming light to the [Jewish] people and to the Gentiles."

²⁴Now while he [was] speaking these [things] in his own defense, Festus said with a loud voice, "You are raving mad, Paul! The many writings [fig., Your great learning] is driving you to madness!" ²⁵But he says, "I am not raving mad, most excellent Festus, but I boldly declare words of truth and of soundness of mind. ²⁶For the king knows about these [things], before whom also speaking boldly I speak, for I am not persuaded [that] any of these [things] are escaping His notice, for this has not been done in a corner. ²⁷Do you believe the prophets, king Agrippa? I know that you believe!" ²⁸Then Agrippa said to Paul, "With little [effort] you are persuading me to become a Christian?" ²⁹But Paul said, "I would have wished to God, both with little [effort] and with much [effort], not only you but also all the ones hearing me today to become such as I also am, except for these chains."

³⁰And he having spoken these [things], the king stood up, and the governor and Bernice and the ones sitting with them. ³¹And having stepped aside, they began speaking to one another, saying, "This man is doing nothing worthy of death or of chains." ³²Then Agrippa said to Festus, "This man was able to have been released if he had not appealed to Caesar."

27 Now when it was decided [for] us to set sail for Italy, they were handing over both Paul and some other prisoners to a centurion by name Julius, of the garrison [of soldiers] of His Majesty the Emperor [or, of the Imperial Regiment]. ²So having boarded an Adramyttium ship about to be sailing to the places [or, ports] along [the coast of] Asia, we set sail, Aristarchus, a Macedonian of Thessalonica, being with us. ³And the next [day] we docked at Sidon, and Julius having treated Paul considerately, permitted [him], having gone to his friends, to receive care. ⁴And from there, having set sail, we sailed under the sheltered side of Cyprus, because of the winds being against [us].

⁵And having sailed across the open sea along [the coast of] Cilicia and Pamphylia, we landed at Myra of Lycia. ⁶And there the centurion having found an Alexandrian ship sailing to Italy, he put us aboard in it. ⁷Now sailing slowly [for] a considerable [number of] days and with difficulty having come to be down from Cnidus, the wind not allowing us to go further, we sailed under the sheltered side of Crete, down from Salmone. ⁸And sailing past it with difficulty, we came to a certain place being called Fair Havens, near to which was the city [of] Lasea.

⁹Now a considerable [amount] of time having passed and the voyage already being dangerous, because of the Fast [i.e., Yom Kipper, which occurs in late September to early October] also already having passed, Paul began recommending, ¹⁰saying to them, "Men, I perceive that with damage and great loss, not only of the cargo and of the ship, but also of our lives, the voyage is about to be." ¹¹But the centurion was being persuaded by the helmsman and the captain more than the [words] being spoken by Paul.

¹²Now the harbor being unsuitable to spend the winter in, the majority part gave counsel to sail from there also, if perhaps they might be able, having arrived at Phenice, [there] to spend the winter, [which is] a harbor of Crete looking [fig., opening] to [the] southwest and to [the] northwest. ¹³Now a south wind having blown gently, having thought to have taken hold of [fig., to have achieved] the plan, having taken up anchor, they began sailing along Crete.

¹⁴But not long after a typhoon-like wind rushed down from it [i.e., Crete]—the [wind] being called Euroclydon ["southeast wind"]. ¹⁵So the ship having been dragged off [course] and not being able to be facing into the wind, having given up [to it], we were being carried along. ¹⁶Then having run under the sheltered side of a certain small island being called Clauda, with difficulty we were able to become in command of the lifeboat, ¹⁷which having taken up, they began using supports, fastening ropes around the ship, and fearing lest they run aground in the [sandbanks of] Syrtes, having let down the sea anchor, in this way we were being carried along.

¹⁸So we being violently storm-tossed, the following [day] they began making a jettison [of cargo]. ¹⁹And on the third [day] with our own hands we threw [overboard] the rigging of the ship [i.e. the ropes and chains used to support and work the mast and sails of the ship]. ²⁰Now neither sun nor stars appearing for many days, and no small [fig., a terrible] storm pressing on [us], from then on all hope of our being saved was being abandoned.

²¹But [after there] being a lack of appetite [for] a long [time], then Paul having stood in [the] middle of them, said, "It was being necessary indeed, O men, having followed my advice, not to be setting sail from Crete and to spare this damage and loss. ²²And now I am urging you* to be taking courage, for [there] will be no loss of life among you*, but [only] of the ship. ²³For [there] stood by me this night an angel of God, whose I am, and to whom I sacredly serve, ²⁴saying, 'Stop being afraid Paul! It is necessary [for] you to stand before Caesar. And listen! God has graciously granted to you all the ones sailing with you.' ²⁵For this reason, be keeping up [your*] courage, men! For I believe God, that in this way it will be, according to what manner it has been spoken to me. ²⁶But it is necessary [for] us to run aground on a certain island."

²⁷Now when the fourteenth night came, we being driven about in the Adriatic Sea, in [the] middle of the night, the sailors were suspecting some land to be approaching to them. ²⁸And having taken a sounding, they found [the water to be] twenty fathoms [deep] [about 120 feet or 37 meters], then having gone a little farther, and again having taken a sounding, they found [it to be] fifteen fathoms [about 90 feet or 28 meters]. ²⁹And fearing lest perhaps we should run aground on rocky places, having thrown out four anchors from [the] stern, they began praying [or, wishing] for day to come. ³⁰But as the sailors [were] trying to flee from the ship, and having let down the lifeboat into the sea, pretending like they [were] about to spread out anchors from the bow, ³¹Paul said to the centurion and to the soldiers, "If these [men] do not remain in the ship you* [will] not be able to be saved!" ³²Then the soldiers cut off the ropes of the lifeboat and allowed it to fall off.

³³Now until which [time] it was about to be day, Paul was encouraging all to partake of food, saying, "Today [is the] fourteenth day you* continue waiting without appetite for food, having taken nothing. ³⁴For this reason, I encourage you* to take [some] food, for this is for your* salvation [or, survival], for not a hair from the head of [any of] you* will fall."

³⁵And having said these [things], and having taken bread, he gave thanks to God before all, and having broken [it], he began to be eating. ³⁶Then all having become encouraged, they also took [some] food. ³⁷Now we were all the souls in the ship, two hundred [and] seventy-six. ³⁸So having enough of the food, they began lightening the ship, throwing out the wheat into the sea.

³⁹Now when it became day, they could not recognize the land. But they noticed a certain bay having a beach, into which they decided, if possible, to beach the ship. ⁴⁰And having cut away the anchors, they were leaving [them] in the sea, at the same time having loosed the ropes of the rudders and having hoisted up the foresail to the blowing [wind], they began heading for the shore.

⁴¹But having fallen into a place where two seas meet [fig., having struck a sand bar; or, having encountered cross-currents], they ran the vessel aground. And the bow indeed having stuck fast remained immovable, but the stern began being broken up by the force of the waves. ⁴²Now the soldiers' plan was that they should be killing the prisoners, lest anyone having swam away, should escape. ⁴³But the centurion wanting to bring Paul safely through, kept them from [their] intention. And he commanded the ones being able to be swimming, having jumped overboard first, to get to the land, ⁴⁴and the rest [should follow], some indeed on boards and others on some of the [parts] of the ship. And in this way it came about [for] all to be brought safely through to the land.

28And having been brought through safely, then they knew [or, learned] that the island is called Malta. ²Now the non-Greek natives were showing us the kindness not having been ordinary [fig., extraordinary kindness], for having kindled a fire, they received us all, because of the rain, the one having arrived, and because of the cold. ³But Paul having gathered together a number of dry sticks and having laid [them] on the fire, a viper having come out of the heat fasten on his hand.

⁴And when the non-Greek natives saw the animal hanging from his hand, they said to one another, "Certainly this man is a murderer, whom, having been brought through safely out of the sea, Dike [i.e., the goddess of justice] did not allow to live." ⁵He then indeed, having shaken off the animal into the fire, suffered nothing harmful. ⁶But they were expecting him to be about to be swelled up, or to be suddenly falling down dead. But they expecting [it for] a long [time], and seeing nothing harmful happening to him, changing [their] minds, began saying he is a god.

⁷Now in the [areas] around that place were pieces of lands [belonging] to the first [fig., leading] [man] of the island, by name Publius, who, having welcomed us, he courteously entertained [us] as guests [for] three days. ⁸But it happened, the father of Publius, suffering attacks of fever and dysentery [i.e., an intestinal

infection], [was] lying down, to whom Paul having entered and having prayed, having laid [his] hands on him, healed him. [9]So this having happened, also the rest [of] the ones having sicknesses on the island were coming and were being healed, [10]who also honored us with many honors, and when we [were] setting sail, they themselves put [on board] the [things] for the need [fig., which we needed].

[11]So after three months, we were brought in an Alexandrian ship [which] had spent the winter on the island, marked by [the] Dioscuri [i.e. twin Roman gods regarded as patrons of sailors]. [12]And having docked at Syracuse, we stayed [there] three days. [13]From there having sailed around, we arrived at Rhegium, and after one day, a south wind having sprung up, the second [day] we came to Puteoli, [14]where having found brothers [and sisters], we were invited to stay with them seven days, and in this manner we came to Rome. [15]And from there, the brothers [and sisters] having heard the [things] concerning us, came out for a meeting with us, as far as Appii Forum and Three Taverns, whom Paul having seen, having given thanks to God, took courage. [16]Now when we came to Rome, the centurion handed the prisoners over to the camp commander, but Paul was permitted to stay by himself, with the soldier guarding him.

[17]Then it happened after three days, Paul called together the ones being the first [fig., leading] [men] of the Jews. So they having come together, he said to them: "Men, brothers, I having done nothing against the people or the ancestral customs, [yet] I was handed over [as] a prisoner from Jerusalem into the hands of the Romans, [18]who having examined me were wanting to release [me] because of [there] being no cause in me for [putting me to] death. [19]But the Jews having objected to [it], I was compelled to appeal to Caesar, not as having anything [of which] to accuse my nation. [20]For this reason, therefore, I requested to see you* and to speak with [you*], for because of the hope [or, confident expectation] of Israel I am bound with this chain."

[21]Then they said to him, "We neither received letters concerning you from Judea, nor having arrived, did any of the brothers report or speak anything evil concerning you. [22]But we consider it fitting to hear from you what you think, for indeed concerning this sect it is known to us that it is objected to everywhere."

[23]So having appointed for him a day, many came to him at [his] lodging place, to whom he was explaining, solemnly testifying [to] the kingdom of God and persuading them of the [things] concerning Jesus, both from the Law of Moses and the Prophets, from early morning until evening. [24]And some indeed were being persuaded by the [things] being spoken, but others were refusing to believe.

[25]So being in disagreement with one another, they began leaving, Paul having spoken one [parting] word, "The Holy Spirit spoke rightly through Isaiah the prophet to our fathers, [26]saying:

Go to this people and say, "With hearing you* will hear, and by no means shall you* understand; and seeing you* will see, and by no means shall you* perceive. [27]For the heart of this people [has] become dull [or, insensitive], and they heard heavily with the ears [fig., they are hard of hearing], and they closed their eyes, lest they see with the eyes, and they *hear with the ears, and they understand with the heart, and they turn back, and I would heal them."* [Isaiah 6:9,10, LXX]

²⁸"Therefore, let it be known to you* that the salvation of God was sent to the Gentiles, and these will hear [it]." ²⁹And he having said these [things], the Jews went away, having much debate among themselves.

³⁰Now Paul remained [for] an entire two year period in his own rented quarters, and he was receiving all the ones coming in to him, ³¹preaching the kingdom of God and teaching the [things] concerning the Lord Jesus Christ with all confidence, without hindrance.

The Epistle of Paul the Apostle to the

Romans

*1*Paul, a slave of Jesus Christ, a called apostle, having been separated [or, appointed] to the Gospel [or, Good News, and throughout book] of God, ²which He promised beforehand through His prophets in [the] Holy Scriptures, ³concerning His Son, the One having come from [the] seed of David according to [the] flesh, ⁴the [One] having been designated Son of God with power according to [the] Spirit of holiness, by [the] resurrection from [the] dead, Jesus Christ our Lord, ⁵through whom we received grace and apostleship for obedience of faith among all the nations on behalf of His name, ⁶among whom you* also are called of Jesus Christ:

⁷To all the ones being in Rome, beloved of God, called holy ones [or, saints, and throughout epistle]: Grace to you* and peace from God our Father and [the] Lord Jesus Christ!

⁸First indeed I thank my God through Jesus Christ for all of you*, that your* faith is being proclaimed in the whole world. ⁹For God is my witness, whom I sacredly serve in my spirit in the Gospel of His Son, how I constantly make mention of you*, ¹⁰always imploring in my prayers, if in some way now at last I will succeed, by the will of God, to come to you*. ¹¹For I long to see you*, so that I should impart some spiritual gift to you*, for you* to be established, ¹²now that is [for me] to be comforted [or, encouraged] together among you*, through faith in one another, both yours* and mine.

¹³But I do not want you* to be unaware, brothers [and sisters], that frequently I myself intended to come to you* (and was prevented until the present), so that I should have some fruit also among you*, just as also among the other Gentiles. ¹⁴I am a debtor [fig., under obligation] both to Greeks and to foreigners, both to wise and to foolish. ¹⁵So the [situation] concerning me [is this: I am] eager to proclaim the Gospel also to you*, the [ones] in Rome.

¹⁶For I am not ashamed of the Gospel of Christ, for it is [the] power of God to salvation to every[one] believing, both to [the] Jew first and to [the] Greek. ¹⁷For [the] righteousness of God is revealed in it from faith to faith, just as it has been written, *"But the [one] righteous by faith will live* [or, *the righteous will live by faith*]." [Hab 2:4]

¹⁸For the wrath of God is revealed from heaven upon all impiety [or, ungodliness] and unrighteousness of people, [upon] the ones suppressing the truth in unrighteousness. ¹⁹For this reason, the [thing] known of God is revealed among [or, within] them, for God revealed [it] to them. ²⁰For from [the] creation of [the] world His invisible [attributes] are plainly seen, being understood by the [things] made, both His eternal power and divinity, so that they are without excuse.

²¹For this reason, having known God, they did not glorify [Him] as God nor did they give thanks, but they were given over to deception in their thought processes [or, they became futile in their speculations], and their foolish heart

was darkened. [22]Professing to be wise, they were made fools, [23]and exchanged the glory of the incorruptible God for a likeness of an image of corruptible people and of birds and of four-footed animals and of reptiles.

[24]And so God also gave them over in the lusts of their hearts to impurity [or, immorality], to the dishonoring of their bodies among themselves; [25]who exchanged the truth of God for the lie [or, changed the truth of God into a lie], and worshipped and sacredly served the creation rather than the One having created, who is blessed into the ages [fig., forever]. So be it!

[26]For this reason God gave them over to dishonorable, lustful passions, for even their females exchanged the natural use for the [use] against nature, [27]and likewise also the males having left the natural use of the female were inflamed in their craving for one another; males with males committing shameful behavior and receiving back in themselves the penalty which was fitting [for] their deception [or, perversion].

[28]And just as they did not think it was worthwhile to be having [or, keeping] God in [their] true knowledge [or, consciousness], God gave them over to a disapproved [fig. debased] mind to be doing the [things] not proper, [29]having been filled with all unrighteousness, sexual sin, wickedness, covetous desire [or, greed], malice; full of envy, murder, bitter conflict, deceit [or, treachery], maliciousness; gossips, [30]back-biters, God-haters, insolent persons, arrogant boasters, schemers of evil [things], disobedient to parents, [31]foolish, untrustworthy, without natural affection, unforgiving, unmerciful; [32]who having known the righteous judgment of God, that the ones practicing such things are deserving of death, not only are doing them, <u>but</u> they are also approving of the ones practicing [them].

2For this reason, you are without excuse [or, defense], O person, every[one] judging, for in what you judge [or, pass sentence on] the other, you condemn yourself, for the same [things] you, the one judging, are practicing! [2]But we know that the judgment of God is according to truth upon the ones practicing such [things]. [3]But do you think this, O person (the one judging the ones practicing such things yet doing them), that <u>you</u> will escape the judgment of God? [4]Or do you despise [or, think lightly of] the riches of His goodness and tolerance and patience, failing to understand [or, disregarding] that the kindness of God leads you to repentance?

[5]But according to your hardness [fig., obstinacy] and impenitent heart, you are storing up for yourself wrath in [the] day of wrath and of revelation and of [the] righteous judgment of God, [6]who *"will render to each [person] according to his works,"* [Psalm 62:12; Prov 24:12] [7]to the [ones] on the one hand [who] by perseverance of good work seek glory and honor and incorruptibility [or, immortality], eternal life; [8]but on the other hand to the [ones who are] selfishly ambitious and [who are] refusing to believe the truth, but obey unrighteousness, anger and wrath, [9]affliction and distress upon every soul of a person, the one working the evil, both of Jew first and of Greek; [10]but glory and honor and peace to every [one who] works the good, both to Jew first and to Greek. [11]For [there] is no accepting of faces [fig., prejudice] with God.

[12]For as many as sinned without [the] Law will also perish without [the] Law; and as many as sinned in [the] Law will be judged by means of [the] Law. [13]For the hearers of the Law [are] not righteous before God, but the doers of the Law will be justified [or, declared righteous]. [14]For when nations [or, Gentiles], the ones not having [the] Law, by nature are doing the [things] of the Law, these not having [the] Law are a law to themselves; [15]who show the work of the Law written in their hearts, their conscience also bearing witness with [them], and among themselves their thoughts accusing or even defending [them], [16]in [the] day when God will judge the secrets of the people according to my Gospel through Jesus Christ.

[17]Listen! You call yourself a Jew and rest [or, rely] on the Law and boast in God, [18]and you know His will and approve the essential [things] [or, the [things] of greater value], being instructed out of the Law, [19]and are confident [that] you yourself are a guide of blind ones, a light to the [ones] in darkness, [20]an instructor of foolish ones, a teacher of young children, having the form of the knowledge and of the truth in the Law. [21]Therefore, the one teaching another, you teach yourself, do you not? The one preaching not to steal, do you steal? [22]The one saying not to be committing adultery, do you commit adultery? The one detesting the idols, do you rob temples [or, commit sacrilege]? [23]You who boast [or, pride yourselves] in [the] Law, do you dishonor God through the transgression of the Law? [24]For *"The name of God is blasphemed among the nations because of you*,"* just as it has been written. [Isaiah 52:5, LXX]

[25]For indeed circumcision profits [or, is of value] if you practice [the] Law, but if you are a transgressor of [the] Law, your circumcision has become uncircumcision. [26]So if the uncircumcision [i.e. a Gentile] is keeping the righteousness of the Law, his uncircumcision will be regarded as circumcision, will it not? [27]And the uncircumcision by nature [or, the one physically uncircumcised] [who] fulfills the Law will judge you, the one [who] in spite of [having] letter and circumcision [are] a transgressor of [the] Law. [28]For he is not a Jew, the one in the open [fig., who is so outwardly], neither [is] circumcision in the open [fig., outwardly] in flesh; [29]but a Jew [is] the one in the secret [fig., who is so inwardly], and circumcision [is] of [the] heart, in spirit, not in letter, whose praise is not from people, but from God.

3 What then [is] the advantage of the Jew? Or what [is] the benefit of circumcision? [2]Much in every way! For indeed first that they were entrusted with the oracles of God. [3]For what if some were unfaithful [or, refused to believe]? Their unfaithfulness [or, unbelief] will not make the faithfulness of God useless, will it? [4]Absolutely not! But let God become true, but every person a liar! Just as it has been written, *"In order that You shall be justified* [or, *declared righteous*] *in Your words and prevail in Your being judged."* [Psalm 51:4, LXX]

[5]But if our unrighteousness demonstrates God's righteousness, what will we say? God, the One inflicting the wrath, is not unrighteous, is He? (I speak according to human [standards].) [6]Absolutely not! Otherwise [or, In that case], how will God judge the world? [7]For if the truth of God by my lie [or, deceitfulness] abounded to

His glory, why am I still also judged as a sinner? [8]And [why] not [say] (just as we are slandered and just as some imply us to be saying), "Let us do evil [things] so that good [things] shall come?" whose condemnation is deserved.

[9]What then? Are we [any] better? Certainly not! For we previously charged [that] both Jews and Greeks are all under sin, [10]just as it has been written:

[There] is not a righteous [person], not even one. [11][There] is not [one] understanding; there is not [one] diligently seeking after God. [12]All turned aside, together they became unprofitable; [there] is not [one] doing kindness [or, what is right], [there] is not so much as one. [Psalm 14:1-3; 53:1-3; Eccl 7:20]

[13]*Their throat [is] a grave having been opened; with their tongues they deceived; [the] venom of poisonous snakes [is] under their lips.* [Psalm 5:9; 140:3]

[14]*Whose mouth is full of cursing and bitterness.* [Psalm 10:7]

[15]*Their feet [are] swift to shed blood.* [16]*Ruin and misery [are] in their ways.* [17]*And [the] way of peace they did not know.* [Isaiah 59:7,8]

[18]*[There] is no fear of God before their eyes.* [Psalm 36:1]

[19]Now we know that as many [things] as the Law says, it speaks to the [ones] in the Law, so that every mouth shall be stopped [fig., silenced] and all the world shall become answerable to God. [20]Therefore, by works of [the] Law not will all flesh [or, will no flesh] be justified [or, declared righteous] before Him, for by means of [the] Law is [the] full [or, true] knowledge of sin.

[21]But now apart from [the] Law has the righteousness of God been revealed, being testified to by the Law and the Prophets, [22]but the righteousness of God [is] through faith [or, trust] in Jesus Christ to all and upon all the ones believing, for there is no difference [or, distinction]. [23]For all sinned and fall short of the glory of God, [24]being justified [or, declared righteous] freely by His grace through the redemption [or, setting free], the [one] in Christ Jesus, [25]whom God Himself put forward publicly [as] a mercy seat [or, propitiation] through faith in His blood, for a demonstration of His righteousness, because of the passing over of the sins having previously occurred in the tolerance of God, [26]for a demonstration of His righteousness in the present time, for Him to be righteous and justifying the [one] [or, declaring the [one] righteous] [who has] faith in Jesus.

[27]Where then [is] the boasting? It was excluded. By what law? Of works? Not at all, but by a law of faith. [28]Therefore, we maintain [that] a person is justified [or, declared righteous] by faith apart from works of [the] Law. [29][Is He] the God of Jews only, but not also of Gentiles? Yes, also of Gentiles, [30]since [there is] one God who will justify [or, will declare righteous] [the] circumcision by faith and [the] uncircumcision through faith. [31]So do we nullify [the] Law through faith? Absolutely not! But we establish [the] Law.

4 What then will we say [that] Abraham our father to have found according to [the] flesh? [2]For if Abraham was justified [or, declared righteous] by works, he

has [grounds for] boasting—but not before God. [3]For what does the Scripture say? *"But Abraham believed God, and it was accounted to him for righteousness."* [Gen 15:6] [4]But to the one working, the reward [or, his wage] is not accounted [or, considered] according to grace, but according to debt. [5]But to the one not working, but [who] believes on the One justifying the impious [or, trusts in the One declaring the godless righteous], his faith is accounted for righteousness.

[6]Just as David also speaks of the happiness [or, blessing] of the person to whom God accounts [or, considers] righteousness apart from works, [7]*"Happy* [or, *Blessed] [are they] whose lawless deeds were forgiven and whose sins were covered. [8]Happy [is] a man to whom the* LORD *shall by no means account* [or, *impute] sin."* [Psalm 32:1,2]

[9]So [is] this happiness upon the circumcision, or also upon the uncircumcision? For we say, *"His faith was accounted to Abraham for righteousness."* [Gen 15:6] [10]How then was it accounted? He being in circumcision or in uncircumcision? Not in circumcision, but in uncircumcision! [11]And he received a sign of circumcision, a seal [fig., proof] of the righteousness of the faith, the [faith while] in the uncircumcision, for him to be a father of all the ones believing through uncircumcision [or, although uncircumcised], for the righteousness to also be accounted to them; [12]and a father of circumcision to the [ones] not of circumcision only, but to the ones keeping in line with [fig., following in] the footsteps of the faith of our father Abraham, the [faith he had while] in the uncircumcision.

[13]For not by means of [the] Law [was] the promise to Abraham or to his seed [fig., descendents], [for] him to be the heir of the world, but by means of the righteousness of faith. [14]For if the [ones who are] of [the] Law [are] heirs, faith has been made empty [or, has been deprived of power], and the promise has been nullified. [15]For the Law produces wrath, for where [there] is no law, neither [is there] transgression.

[16]For this reason [it is] of faith, that [it should be] according to grace, for the promise to be secure to all the seed [fig., descendents], not to the [one] of the Law only, but also to the [one] of [the] faith of Abraham, who is father of all of us [17](just as it has been written, *"I have appointed you [as] a father of many nations"*) in the presence of God, whom he believed, the One giving life to the dead [ones] and calling the [things] not existing as existing. [Gen 17:5]

[18]Who against [or, beyond] hope [or, confident expectation] believed in hope [or, confident expectation], for him to become *"a father of many nations"* according to the [word] having been spoken, *"So will your seed* [fig., *descendents] be."* [Gen 15:5] [19]And not having been weak in faith, he did not consider his own body, already having become dead (being about a hundred years old), and the deadness [fig., barrenness] of the womb of Sarah; [20]yet, he did not waver [or, hesitate] at the promise of God in unbelief, but he was strengthened in his faith, having given glory to God, [21]and having been fully convinced that what He had promised He is able also to do. [22]And so, *"it was accounted to him for righteousness."* [Gen 15:6]

[23]But it was not written on his account alone, *"it was accounted to him,"* [24]but also on account of us, to whom it is about to be accounted [or, imputed], to the

ones believing on [or, trusting in] the One having raised up Jesus our Lord from [the] dead, ²⁵who was handed over because of our transgressions and was raised up because of our justification [or, our [being] declared righteous].

5Therefore, having been justified [or, declared righteous] by faith, we have peace toward God through our Lord Jesus Christ, ²through whom also we have the access [or, privilege to enter] by faith into this grace in which we have stood, and we boast [or, rejoice] in the hope [or, confident expectation] of the glory of God! ³But not only [this], <u>but</u> we also boast [or, take pride] in afflictions, knowing that affliction produces patient endurance, ⁴and patient endurance proven character, and proven character hope [or, confident expectation], ⁵and hope [or, confident expectation] does not disappoint [us], because the love of God has been poured out in our hearts by [the] Holy Spirit, the One having been given to us.

⁶For Christ, while we were still weak [or, helpless], at the right time, died on behalf of the impious [or, ungodly]. ⁷For scarcely [or, only rarely] will anyone die on behalf of a righteous [person]; for perhaps someone even dares [or, might be prepared] to die on behalf of the good [person]. ⁸But God demonstrates His own love to us, [in] that us still being sinners [or, while we were still sinners], Christ died on our behalf!

⁹Much more then, having been justified [or, declared righteous] now by His blood, we will be saved from the wrath through Him. ¹⁰For if, being enemies, we were reconciled to God through the death of His Son, much more, having been reconciled, we will be saved by His life. ¹¹But not only [this], <u>but</u> we also boast [or, rejoice] in God, through our Lord Jesus Christ, through whom we now received the reconciliation.

¹²For this reason, even as through one man sin entered into the world, and through sin death; and thus death passed through [or, extended] to all people, for that [or, because] all sinned; ¹³for until [the] Law sin was in the world, but sin is not accounted [or, imputed] [there] not being law [or, when [there] is no law]. ¹⁴<u>But</u> death reigned from Adam until Moses, even on the ones not having sinned according to the likeness of Adam's transgression, who is a type of the coming One.

¹⁵<u>But</u> not as the offense so also [is] the gracious gift; for if by the offense of the one [man] the many died, much more the grace of God and the free gift by grace of the one Man Jesus Christ abounded to the many. ¹⁶And not as through one [man] having sinned [is] the gift; for on the one hand the judgment from one [offense resulted] in condemnation, on the other hand the gracious gift from many offences [resulted] in justification [or, a declared righteousness]. ¹⁷For if by the offense of the one [man] death reigned through the one, much more the ones receiving the abundance of the grace and of the free gift of the righteousness in life will reign through the one [Man], Jesus Christ.

¹⁸So, consequently, as through one offense [judgment came] to all people [resulting] in condemnation, so also [the gift came] through one righteous deed to all people [resulting] in justification [or, a declared righteousness] of life. ¹⁹For even as through the disobedience of the one man, the many were constituted [or,

caused to be] sinners, so also through the obedience of the one [Man], the many will be constituted righteous. ²⁰But [the] Law entered alongside so that the offense should abound, but where sin abounded, grace super-abounded, ²¹so that even as sin reigned by death, so also grace reigns through righteousness to eternal life, through Jesus Christ our Lord!

6What then will we say? Do we continue in sin so that grace shall abound? ²Absolutely not! We who died to sin, how will we still live in it? ³Or do you* fail to understand that we, as many as were baptized [or, immersed] into Christ Jesus, were baptized into His death? ⁴Therefore, we were buried together with Him through the baptism [or, immersion] into death, so that even as Christ was raised up from [the] dead through the glory of the Father, so also we should walk about [fig., conduct ourselves] in newness of life.

⁵For if we have become planted together [fig., united] [with Him] in the likeness of His death, certainly we also will be [in the likeness] of the resurrection; ⁶knowing this, that our former person was crucified together [with Him], so that the body of sin shall be made useless [or, pass away], [so that] we [are] no longer to be serving as a slave to sin. ⁷For the one having died has been justified [or, set free] from sin. ⁸But if we died with Christ, we believe that we will also live together with Him, ⁹knowing that Christ, having been raised up from [the] dead, no longer dies; death no longer exercises lordship over Him. ¹⁰For what [death] He died, He died once [and] for all [fig., once and never again] to sin, but what [life] He lives, He lives to God. ¹¹So also you*, be considering yourselves to be dead indeed to sin, but living to God in Jesus Christ our Lord.

¹²Therefore, stop letting sin reign in your* mortal body to be obeying it in its lusts [or, evil desires], ¹³and stop presenting your* body parts [as] instruments of unrighteousness to sin, but present yourselves to God as living from [the] dead, and your* body parts [as] instruments of righteousness to God. ¹⁴For sin will not exercise lordship over you*, for you* are not under law, but under grace.

¹⁵What then? Will we sin because we are not under law, but under grace? Absolutely not! ¹⁶You* do know, do you* not, that to whom you* present yourselves [as] slaves for obedience, you* are slaves to whom you* obey, whether of sin to death, or of obedience to righteousness? ¹⁷But thanks [be] to God, that you* were slaves of sin, but were obedient from [the] heart to the pattern of teaching to which you* were committed. ¹⁸But having been freed from sin, you* became servants to righteousness.

¹⁹I speak in human terms, because of the weakness of your* flesh, for even as you* presented your* body parts [as] slaves to impurity [or, immorality] and to lawlessness [resulting] in [more] lawlessness, so now present your* members [or, body parts] [as] slaves to righteousness [resulting] in sanctification. ²⁰For when you* were slaves of sin, you* were freed [from] righteousness. ²¹So what fruit were you* having then, in which [things] you* are now ashamed? For the end of those [things is] death. ²²But now, having been freed from sin, but having been enslaved to God, you* have your* fruit [resulting] in sanctification, and the

outcome [is] eternal life! ²³For the wages of sin [is] death, but the gracious gift of God [is] eternal life in Christ Jesus our Lord!

7Do you* fail to understand, brothers [and sisters] (for I speak to [ones] knowing [the] Law), that the Law is lord of [or, has power over] the man as long a time [as] he is living? ²For the married woman has been bound by law to the living husband, but if the husband dies, she has been released from the law of the husband. ³So, consequently, the husband being alive, she will be called an adulteress if she becomes [joined] to a different man; but if the husband dies, she is free from the law, [so as] not to be an adulteress, having become [joined] to another man.

⁴Accordingly, brothers [and sisters], <u>you*</u> also were made dead to the Law through the body of Christ, for you* to become [joined] to another, to the One having been raised up from [the] dead, so that we should bear fruit to God. ⁵For when we were in the flesh, the passions of the sins, the ones [aroused] through the Law, were working in our body parts [in order] to bear fruit to death. ⁶But now we were released from the Law, having died in [that] by which we were held, with the result that we serve as slaves in newness of spirit [or, of [the] Spirit] and not in oldness of letter.

⁷What then will we say? [Is] the Law sin? Absolutely not! <u>But</u> I did not know sin except through [the] Law. For also I had not known covetousness unless the Law had said, *"You will not covet."* [Exod 20:17; Deut 5:21] ⁸But that sin having received an opportunity through the commandment, produced in me all covetousness, for apart from [the] Law, sin is dead. ⁹But <u>I</u> was once living apart from [the] Law, but the commandment having come, sin came back to life, but <u>I</u> died. ¹⁰And the commandment, the [one meant] for life, was found by me, this [one to be] for death. ¹¹For sin having received an opportunity through the commandment deceived me, and through it put [me] to death. ¹²Accordingly, the Law indeed [is] holy, and the commandment holy and righteous and good.

¹³So has the good become to me death? Absolutely not! <u>But</u> sin, so that it should appear sin, through the good, produces death to me, so that sin becomes utterly sinful through the commandment. ¹⁴For we know that the Law is spiritual, but <u>I</u> am fleshly, having been sold as a slave under sin [fig., having been enslaved to sin]. ¹⁵For what I do, I do not understand; for what I do not desire [or, will], this I practice, <u>but</u> what I hate, this I do. ¹⁶But if what I do not desire, this I do, I agree with the Law that [it is] good. ¹⁷But now [it is] no longer <u>I</u> [who] produces it, <u>but</u> the sin dwelling in me. ¹⁸For I know that [there] does not dwell in me, that is in my flesh, [any] good; for the [ability] to be desiring is present with me, but the [ability] to be producing the good I do not find. ¹⁹For what good I desire, I do not do, <u>but</u> what evil I do not desire, this I practice. ²⁰But if what <u>I</u> do not desire, this I do, [it is] no longer <u>I</u> [who] produces it, <u>but</u> the sin dwelling in me.

²¹Consequently, I find the law to me, the one desiring to be doing the good, that with me the evil is present. ²²For I delight in the Law of God according to my inner being. ²³But I discover a different law in my body parts, warring against the law of my mind and capturing me by the law of the sin, the one being in my

members. [24][What] a wretched person I [am]! Who will deliver me out of the body of this death? [25]I thank God through Jesus Christ our Lord; so consequently, I myself on the one hand with the mind serve as a slave to the Law of God, on the other hand with the flesh, [the] law of sin.

8Consequently, [there is] now no condemnation to the [ones] in Christ Jesus, [who] do not walk about [fig., conduct themselves] according to [the] flesh, but according to [the] Spirit [or, to spirit, and possibly elsewhere in 8:2-15]. [2]For the law of the Spirit of the life in Christ Jesus set me free from the law of sin and of death. [3]For the [thing] impossible [for] the Law [to do] in that it was weak through the flesh, God [did], having sent His own Son in the likeness of sinful flesh, and concerning sin, condemned sin in the flesh, [4]so that the righteous requirement of the Law should be fulfilled in us, the [ones] not walking about [fig., conducting ourselves] according to [the] flesh, but according to [the] Spirit.

[5]For the ones according to [the] flesh set their minds on the [things] of the flesh, but the [ones] according to [the] Spirit, the things of the Spirit. [6]For the mind-set [or, the way of thinking] of the flesh [is] death, but the mind-set of the Spirit [is] life and peace. [7]Because the mind-set of the flesh [is] hostile towards God, for it is not subject to the law of God, nor indeed is it able [to be]. [8]Now the ones being in [the] flesh are not able to please God.

[9]But you* are not in [the] flesh but in [the] Spirit, since [the] Spirit of God dwells in you*; but if anyone does not have [the] Spirit of Christ, this one is not His. [10]But if Christ [is] in you*, on the one hand the body [is] dead because of sin, on the other hand the Spirit [is] life because of righteousness. [11]But if the Spirit of the One having raised up Jesus from [the] dead dwells in you*, the One having raised up Christ from [the] dead will also give life to your* mortal bodies through His Spirit indwelling in you.*

[12]So, consequently, brothers [and sisters], we are debtors [fig., under obligation], not to the flesh to be living according to the flesh. [13]For if you* live according to [the] flesh, you* are about to die; but if by [the] Spirit you* put to death the deeds of the body, you* will live.

[14]For as many as are led by [the] Spirit of God, these are the sons [and daughters] of God. [15]For you* did not receive a spirit of slavery again for fear, but you* received [the] Spirit of adoption [i.e., the formal and legal declaration that we are His children] in which we cry out, "Dad [Gr. *Abba*], Father!" [16]The Spirit Himself testifies with our spirit that we are children of God! [17]Now if children, also heirs—heirs on the one hand of God, joint-heirs on the other hand with Christ, since we suffer together, so that we shall also be glorified together.

[18]For I consider that the sufferings of the present time [are] not worthy [to be compared] with the glory about to be revealed in us! [19]For the earnest expectation of the creation eagerly awaits the revelation of the sons [and daughters] of God. [20]For the creation was subjected to futility, not of its will, but because of the One having subjected [it] in hope [or, confident expectation], [21]because even the creation itself will be set free from the slavery of the corruption into the liberty

of the glory of the children of God. ²²For we know that all the creation groans together and labors together in birth-pains until now.

²³But not only [this], <u>but</u> even ourselves, having the first-fruit of the Spirit, <u>we</u> also ourselves groan within ourselves, eagerly awaiting adoption—the redemption of our body! ²⁴For in hope [or, confident expectation] we were saved, but hope being looked at is not hope; for what anyone looks at, why also does he hope for [or, confidently expect] [it]? ²⁵But if what we do not look at we hope for [or, confidently expect], with patient endurance we eagerly wait for [it].

²⁶So in the same manner also, the Spirit helps our weaknesses; for what we will pray for, as it is necessary [for us], we do not know, <u>but</u> the Spirit Himself makes intercession on our behalf with inexpressible groanings. ²⁷Now the One searching the hearts knows what [is] the mind-set of the Spirit, because according to God He intercedes on behalf of [the] holy ones.

²⁸But we know that to the ones loving God all things work together for good, to the ones being called according to [His] purpose. ²⁹Because whom He foreknew, He also predestined [to be] conformed to the image of His Son, for Him to be the first-born among many brothers [and sisters]. ³⁰Now whom He predestined, these He also called; and whom He called, these He also justified [or, declared righteous]; but whom He justified, these He also glorified.

³¹What then will we say about these [things]? Since God [is] for us [or, on our side], who [is] against us? ³²The [One] who indeed did not spare His own Son, <u>but</u> [who] handed Him over on behalf of us all, how will He not also with Him graciously give to us all [things]? ³³Who will bring a charge against [the] chosen ones of God? God [is] the One justifying [or, declaring righteous]. ³⁴Who [is] the one condemning? Christ [is] the One having died, but rather also, having been raised up, who is also at [the] right hand of God, who also intercedes on our behalf.

³⁵Who will separate us from the love of Christ? [Will] affliction or distress or persecution or famine or nakedness or peril or sword? ³⁶Just as it has been written, *"For Your sake we are being put to death the whole day; we were accounted as sheep for slaughter."* [Psalm 44:22] ³⁷<u>But</u> in all these [things] we are completely victorious through the One having loved us. ³⁸For I have been persuaded that neither death nor life nor angels nor rulers nor powers nor [things] present nor things about to be ³⁹nor height nor depth nor any other created [thing] will be able to separate us from the love of God, the [one] in Christ Jesus our Lord!

9I speak truth in Christ, I do not lie, my conscience testifies with me in [the] Holy Spirit, ²that great sorrow is with me and unceasing pain in my heart, ³for I could wish I myself to be accursed [Gr., *anathema*] from Christ on behalf of my [Jewish] brothers [and sisters], my fellow citizens according to [the] flesh, ⁴who are Israelites, whose [is] the adoption and the glory and the covenants [or, the ordinances of the covenant] and the law-giving and the sacred service and the promises, ⁵of whom [are] the fathers and out of whom [is] the Christ [or, the Messiah] (the [ancestral descent] according to [the] flesh), the One being over all God blessed into the ages [fig., forever]! So be it!

⁶But it is not possible that the word of God has failed. For all the [ones] of Israel, these [are] not Israel; ⁷nor [are they] all children because they are seed [fig., descendents] of Abraham, <u>but</u> *"by Isaac will your seed [fig., descendents] be named."* [Gen 21:12] ⁸That is, the children of the flesh, these [are] not children of God, <u>but</u> the children of the promise are counted for seed [fig., descendents]. ⁹For this [is] the word of promise, *"At this time I will come, and [there] will be to Sarah a son."* [Gen 18:10,14]

¹⁰But not only [this], <u>but</u> also Rebecca, having conceived [twins] by one [man], Isaac our father ¹¹(for they having not yet been born, neither having done anything good nor wicked, so that the purpose of God according to [His] choice [or, election] should be remaining, not of works, <u>but</u> of the One calling), ¹²it was said to her, *"The greater [or, older] will serve as a slave to the lesser [or, younger]."* [Gen 25:23] ¹³Just as it has been written, *"Jacob I loved, but Esau I hated."* [Mal 1:2,3]

¹⁴What then will we say? [There is] not unrighteousness with God, is there? Absolutely not! ¹⁵For to Moses He says, *"I will show mercy to whomever I show mercy, and I will have compassion on whomever I have compassion."* [Exod 33:19] ¹⁶So, consequently, [it is] not of the one desiring [or, willing], nor of the one running, <u>but</u> of the One showing mercy—God! ¹⁷For the Scripture says to Pharaoh, *"For this very [reason] I raised you up, in order that I should show in you My power, and in order that My name shall be proclaimed far and wide in all the land."* [Exod 9:16] ¹⁸So, consequently, [to] whom He wills He shows mercy, but whom He wills He hardens [fig., makes stubborn].

¹⁹You will say then to me, "Why does He still find fault? For who has [ever] stood up against [or, resisted] His purpose?" ²⁰But rather, O human, who are <u>you</u>, the one answering back to God? The thing formed will not say to the one having formed [it], "Why did you make me like this?" will it? ²¹The potter has [the] right [over] the clay to make out of the same lump on the one hand one vessel to honor, on the other hand one to dishonor, does he not? ²²So [what] if God, desiring to show His wrath and to make His power known, endured with much patience vessels of wrath having been prepared for destruction, ²³and so that He should make known the riches of His glory on vessels of mercy, which He prepared beforehand for glory, ²⁴even us whom He called not only from Jews, <u>but</u> also from Gentiles?

²⁵As also in Hosea He says, *"I will call the [one] not My people, 'My people;' and the [one] not beloved, 'Beloved.' ²⁶And it will be in the place where it was said to them, 'You [are] not My people,' in that place they will be called sons [and daughters] of the living God."* [Hosea 2:23; 1:10]

²⁷But Isaiah cries out concerning Israel, *"If the number of the sons [and daughters] of Israel are as the sand of the sea, the remnant will be saved. ²⁸For He is finishing and abruptly ending [the] matter in righteousness, because [the] matter having been ended abruptly will [the] LORD do on the land."* [Isaiah 10:22,23, LXX]

²⁹And just as Isaiah had foretold, *"Unless [the]* LORD *of Armies* [fig., LORD *Almighty] left us a seed, we would have become as Sodom, and we would have been made like Gomorrah."* [Isaiah 1:9, LXX]

³⁰What then will we say? That Gentiles, the ones not pursuing righteousness attained righteousness, but a righteousness by faith. ³¹But Israel, pursuing a law of righteousness, did not arrive at a law of righteousness. ³²Why? Because [they did] not [pursue it] by faith, but as though [it was] by works of [the] Law; for they stumbled at the stone of stumbling. ³³Just as it has been written, *"Look! I place in Zion a stone of stumbling and a rock of offence; and every one believing on* [or, *trusting in] Him will not be put to shame."* [Isaiah 8:14; Isaiah 28:16, LXX]

*10*Brothers [and sisters], indeed the desire of my heart and my petition, the [one] to God on behalf of Israel, is for salvation. ²For I testify about them that they have a zeal for God, but not according to full [or, true] knowledge. ³For failing to understand the righteousness of God and seeking to establish their own righteousness, they did not submit to the righteousness of God. ⁴For Christ [is the] end of [the] law for righteousness to everyone believing.

⁵For Moses writes [about] the righteousness, the [one] by the Law, *"The person having done them* [i.e. all the commandments of the Law] *will live by them."* [Lev 18:5] ⁶But the righteousness by faith speaks in this way, *"You shall not say in your heart, 'Who will ascend to heaven?'"* [Deut 30:12] (that is, to bring Christ down) ⁷or, *"Who will descend into the bottomless pit* [or, *abyss]?"* [Deut 30:13] (that is, to bring Christ up from [the] dead). ⁸But what does it say? *"The word is near you, in your mouth and in your heart"* [Deut 30:14]—that is, the word of the faith which we are preaching, ⁹that if you confess with your mouth [the] Lord Jesus [or, [that] Jesus [is] Lord], and believe in your heart that God raised Him from [the] dead, you will be saved! ¹⁰For with the heart it is believed to righteousness, and with the mouth it is confessed to salvation.

¹¹For the Scripture says, *"Every one believing on* [or, *trusting in] Him will not put to shame."* [Isaiah 28:16, LXX] ¹²For there is no difference [or, distinction] [between] both Jew and Greek, for the same [Lord is] Lord of all, being rich [fig., giving generously] to all the ones calling on Him. ¹³For every[one], *"who himself shall call on the name of [the]* LORD *will be saved!"* [Joel 2:32]

¹⁴How then will they call on [Him] in whom they did not believe? But how will they believe [on Him] of whom they did not hear? But how will they hear apart from one preaching? ¹⁵But how will they preach unless they be sent? Just as it has been written, *"How beautiful [are] the feet of the ones proclaiming the Gospel of peace, of the ones proclaiming the Gospel of the good [things]!"* [Isaiah 52:7; Nahum 1:15] ¹⁶But they were not all obedient to the Gospel, for Isaiah says, *"Lord, who believed our report?"* [Isaiah 53:1, LXX] ¹⁷So, consequently, faith [is] by hearing, but hearing through [the] word of God.

¹⁸But I say, did they never at all hear? On the contrary, *"Their voice went out to all the earth, and their words to the ends of the inhabited earth."* [Psalm 19:4] ¹⁹But I say, did Israel never at all know? First Moses says, *"I will provoke you**

to jealousy by [that which is] not a nation; by an unintelligent nation I will anger you*." [Deut 32:21] ²⁰So Isaiah is very bold [or, speaks out fearlessly] and says, *"I was found by the ones not seeking Me; I became known [or, clearly evident] to the ones not inquiring after [or, desiring to know] Me."* [Isaiah 65:1] ²¹But to Israel He says, *"The whole day I stretched out My hands to a people refusing to believe and being obstinate."* [Isaiah 65:2, LXX]

11 I say then, God did not push away [fig., reject] His people, did He? Absolutely not! For I also am an Israelite, of [the] seed of Abraham, of [the] tribe of Benjamin. ²God did not push away [fig., reject] His people whom He foreknew. Or do you* not know in [the passage about] Elijah what the Scripture says? How he pleads with God concerning Israel, saying, ³*"LORD, they killed Your prophets, and they tore down Your altars; and I was left alone, and they seek my life."* [1Kings 19:10]

⁴But what does the divine answer say to him? *"I left [or, kept] for Myself seven thousand men who did not bend a knee [fig., kneel down] to Baal."* [1Kings 19:18] ⁵In the same way then also in the present time [there has] been a remnant according to [God's] choice [or, election] of grace [or, [God's] gracious choice]. ⁶But if by grace, [it is] no longer of works, otherwise [or, in that case] grace no longer becomes grace; but if by works, it is no longer grace, otherwise [or, in that case] work is no longer work.

⁷What then? What Israel seeks, this it did not obtain, but the chosen ones [or, elect] did obtain, but the rest were hardened.

⁸Just as it has been written, *"God gave to them a spirit of deep sleep, eyes not to be seeing, and ears not to be hearing, to this very day,"* [Deut 29:4; Isaiah 29:10]

⁹And David says, *"Let their table become for a snare and for a trap and for a stumbling block [or, offense] and for a recompense [or, retribution] to them. ¹⁰Let their eyes be darkened not to be seeing, and their back be bent down through all [fig., continually]."* [Psalm 69:22,23, LXX]

¹¹I say then, they did not stumble so that they should fall, did they? Absolutely not! But by their transgression salvation [came] to the Gentiles to arouse them to jealousy. ¹²But if their transgression [is the] riches of [the] world, and their failure [the] riches of [the] Gentiles, how much more their fullness!

¹³For I speak to you*, the Gentiles, to the degree that I am indeed an apostle of Gentiles, I glorify my ministry, ¹⁴if in some way I arouse [those of] my flesh to jealousy and save some of them. ¹⁵For if the casting away [fig., rejection] of them [means] reconciliation of [the] world, what [will] their acceptance [be] if not life from [the] dead?

¹⁶But if the first portion [of dough is] holy, the lump [will be] also; and if the root [is] holy, the branches [will be] also. ¹⁷But if some of the branches were broken off, and you being a wild olive tree, were grafted in among them and

became a fellow-partaker of the root and of the fatness of the olive tree, [18]stop being arrogant towards the branches. But if you are arrogant, [remember] you do not sustain the root, but the root [sustains] you!

[19]You will say then, "Branches were broken off, so that I should be grafted in." [20]Rightly [said]! They were broken off by unbelief, but you have stood by your faith. Stop being conceited, but be fearing. [21]For if God did not spare the natural branches, perhaps neither will He spare you. [22]Therefore, look at [or, consider] [the] goodness and severity of God: on the one hand upon the ones having fallen, severity; on the other hand upon you, kindness, if you remain in the goodness; otherwise, you also will be cut off.

[23]But also those, if they do not remain in unbelief, will be grafted in, for God is able to again graft them in. [24]For if you, the [one] by nature of the wild olive tree, were cut out, and contrary to nature, were grafted into a cultivated olive tree, how much more will these, the natural ones, be grafted into their own olive tree?

[25]For I do not desire [for] you* to be unaware, brothers [and sisters], of this secret [or, mystery], so that you* shall not be wise in your* own conceits, that hardness in part [fig., partial stubbornness] has happened to Israel until the fullness of the Gentiles comes in. [26]And so all Israel will be saved, just as it has been written, *"The One delivering will come out of Zion, and He will turn away impiety [or, ungodliness] from Jacob;* [27]*and this [is] the covenant from Me with them, when I take away their sins."* [Isaiah 59:20,21; 27:9, LXX] [28]On the one hand according to the Gospel [they are] enemies on your* account, on the other hand according to His choice [or, election] [they are] beloved on account of the fathers. [29]For the gracious gifts and the calling of God [are] irrevocable.

[30]For even as you* also at one time disobeyed God due to unbelief, but you* were shown mercy by their refusal to believe, [31]so also these now refused to believe by the mercy shown to you*, so that they also should be shown mercy. [32]For God confined all in unbelief leading to disobedience, so that He should show mercy to all.

[33]O [the] depth of [the] riches of both [the] wisdom and knowledge of God! How inscrutable [are] His judgments and unfathomable His ways! [34]For *"who knew [the] mind of [the] LORD? Or who became His counselor [or, adviser]?"* [Isaiah 40:13, LXX; Jer 23:18] [35]Or *"who first gave to Him, and it will be given back to Him again?"* [Job 41:11] [36]Because of Him and through Him and to Him [are] all [things]; to Him [be] the glory into the ages [fig., forever]! So be it!

12 Therefore, I call on [or, plead with] you*, brothers [and sisters], through the compassions of God, to present your* bodies a living sacrifice, holy, acceptable to God [which is] your* intelligent, sacred service. [2]And [you* are] to stop conforming yourselves to this age, but [are] to continue being transformed by the renewal of your* mind, in order for you* to be proving what [is] the good and acceptable and perfect will of God.

[3]For I say, through the grace, the one having been given to me, to every[one] being among you*, stop thinking too highly of yourselves beyond what it is necessary to be thinking, but be thinking [so as] to be thinking sensibly, to each as

God apportioned a measure of faith. [4]For just as we have many body parts in one body, but all the body parts do not have the same function, [5]so we, the many, are one body in Christ, but parts each one of one another.

[6]Now we have spiritual gifts of various kinds according to the grace, the one having been given to us: whether prophecy, according to the proportion of the faith; [7]whether ministry, in the ministry; whether the one teaching, in the teaching; [8]whether the one exhorting [or, encouraging], in the exhortation [or, encouragement]; the one sharing, with generosity; the one leading, with diligence; the one showing mercy, with cheerfulness.

[9][Let] love [be] sincere; be abhorring the evil; be clinging to the good. [10][Be] warmly devoted to one another with brotherly love [fig., affection for fellow-believers], giving preference to one another in honor, [11]not lagging in diligence, boiling [fig., being fervent] in spirit [or, in the Spirit], serving as a slave to the Lord, [12]rejoicing in the hope [or, confident expectation], enduring in affliction, persevering in prayer, [13]contributing to the needs of the holy ones, pursuing hospitality.

[14]Be blessing the ones persecuting you*; be blessing, and stop cursing. [15][You* are] to be rejoicing with rejoicing [ones] and to be weeping with weeping [ones]. [16]Be having the same mind towards one another. Stop having the high [things] in mind, <u>but</u> be associating with the lowly [or, the ones of humble circumstances]. Stop becoming wise in your* own conceit, [17]repaying to no one evil for evil, having regard for good [things] before all people.

[18]If possible, the [thing] of you* [fig., as much as it depends on you*], be living in peace with all people, [19]not avenging yourselves, beloved, <u>but</u> give place to [fig., make room for] the wrath [of God], for it has been written, *"Vengeance [is] Mine, I will repay,"* says [the] Lord. [Deut 32:35] [20]*"So if your enemy is hungering, be feeding him; if he thirsts, be giving him to drink; for doing this, you will heap coals of fire on his head."* [Prov 25:21,22, LXX] [21]Stop being overcome by evil, <u>but</u> be overcoming evil with good.

13 Let every soul be submitting to higher [or, governing] authorities, for [there] is no authority except from God, but the existing authorities have been appointed by God. [2]Accordingly, the one setting himself in opposition to the [governing] authority has resisted God's ordinance, and the ones having resisted will receive judgment to themselves. [3]For the ones ruling are not a terror of good works, <u>but</u> of evil [works]. So do you want not to be fearing the [governing] authority? Be doing good, and you will have praise [or, approval] from it [i.e. the ruling authority]. [4]For it is a servant of God to you for good. But if you are doing evil, be fearing, for it does not bear the sword without reason. For.it is a servant of God, an avenger for wrath to the one doing evil. [5]For this reason, it is necessary to be subjecting oneself, not only because of wrath, <u>but</u> also because of your conscience.

[6]Then, for this reason, you* also pay taxes, for they are public servants of God attending continually [or, devoting themselves] to this very thing. [7]Therefore, pay to all the [things] due [to them]: to the one the tax the tax, to the one the

custom [or, tribute] the custom, to the one the fear the fear, to the one the honor the honor.

[8]Be owing to no one anything, except to be loving one another; for the one loving the other [or, the different [one]] has fulfilled [the] law. [9]For, *"You will not commit adultery; You will not murder; You will not steal; You will not covet."* And if [there is] any other command, it is summed up in this word, in this: *"You will love your neighbor as yourself."* [Exod 20:12-16; Deut 5:16-20; Lev 19:18] [10]Such love does not bring about evil [or, harm] to the neighbor. Therefore such love [is] the fulfillment of [the] law.

[11]And [do] this, knowing the time, that [it is] already the hour for us to be awakened out of sleep, for our salvation [is] now nearer than when we [first] believed. [12]The night is advanced [or, almost gone], but the day has drawn near; therefore, let us take off [fig., cease from] the deeds of the darkness, and let us put on [or, clothe ourselves with] the armor of the light. [13]As in daytime, let us walk about [fig., conduct ourselves] properly; not in drunken orgies and drunkennesses, not in promiscuities and flagrant sexual immorality, not in strife [or, bitter conflict] and jealous rivalry. [14]But put on [or, clothe yourselves with] the Lord Jesus Christ, and stop making provision for the flesh, for [its] desires [or, lusts].

*14*Now be receiving the one being weak in the faith, not for disputes over opinions. [2]One believes [it is permissible] to eat all [things], but the one being weak eats [only] vegetables. [3]Stop letting the one eating despise [or, look down on] the one not eating; and stop letting the one not eating judge the one eating, for God [has] accepted him. [4]Who are you, the one judging another's household servant? To his own master he stands or falls; but he will be made to stand, for God is able to make him stand. [5]One indeed judges [or, considers] a day [to be] above [another] day, but another judges every day [to be alike]; be letting each be fully convinced in his own mind.

[6]The one honoring [or, observing] the day, to [the] Lord he honors [it], and the one not honoring the day, to [the] Lord he does not honor [it]. And the one eating, to [the] Lord he eats, for he gives thanks to God; and the one not eating, to [the] Lord he does not eat, and he gives thanks to God. [7]For none of us lives to himself, and none dies to himself. [8]For both if we live, to the Lord we live, and if we die, to the Lord we die. So both if we live and if we die, we are the Lord's. [9]Because for this [reason] Christ also died and rose and lives, so that He should exercise lordship over both dead [ones] and living [ones].

[10]But why do you judge your brother [fig., fellow believer, and throughout chapter]? Or also, why do you despise [or, look down on] your brother? For we will all stand before the judgment seat of Christ. [11]For it has been written, *"[As] I live, says [the] LORD, every knee will bow to Me, and every tongue will confess to God."* [Isaiah 45:23, LXX; cp. Phil 2:10,11] [12]So, consequently, each of us will give an account concerning himself to God. [13]Therefore, let us no longer be judging one another, but rather, judge [or, determine] this, not to be putting a stumbling-stone before your brother, or an offence [or, an occasion for sin].

221

¹⁴I know and have been persuaded in [the] Lord Jesus that nothing [is] unclean by means of itself, except to the one considering anything to be unclean, to that one [it is] unclean. ¹⁵But if on account of food your brother is distressed, you are no longer walking about [fig., conducting yourself] according to love; stop ruining with your food that one on behalf of whom Christ died. ¹⁶So stop letting your good be slandered [or, be spoken of as evil]. ¹⁷For the kingdom of God is not eating and drinking, but righteousness and peace and joy in [the] Holy Spirit. ¹⁸For the one serving as a slave to Christ in these [things] [is] acceptable to God and approved by people. ¹⁹So, consequently, let us be pursuing the [things] of peace and the [things] of building up [or, edifying] one another.

²⁰Stop tearing down the work of God for the sake of food. All [things] indeed [are] clean, but [they are] evil to the person eating with offense [fig., eating something that cause someone else to sin]. ²¹[It is] good not to eat meat nor to drink wine nor [to do anything] by which your brother is caused to stumble [fig., to sin] or is made to fall [fig., is offended] or becomes weak. ²²You have faith? Be having [it] to yourself before God. Happy is the one not judging [or, condemning] himself in what he approves [of]. ²³But the one doubting, if he eats, has been condemned, because [it is] not of faith. Now all which [is] not of faith is sin.

²⁴Now to the One able to establish you* according to my Gospel and the proclamation of Jesus Christ, according to [the] revelation of [the] secret [or, mystery] in eternal times having been kept silent, ²⁵but now having been made known [or, disclosed], and through prophetic Scriptures, according to [the] commandment of the eternal God, having been made known to all the nations for obedience of faith, ²⁶to [the] only wise God, through Jesus Christ, to whom [be] glory into the ages [fig., forever]! So be it!

15 But we, the strong, ought to be enduring the infirmities of the weak and not to be pleasing ourselves. ²Let each one of us be pleasing the neighbor for good, toward edification. ³For even Christ did not please Himself, but just as it has been written, *"The insults [or, reproaches] of the ones insulting You fell on Me."* [Psalm 69:9] ⁴For as many [things] as were previously written, were previously written for our instruction, so that through the patient endurance and through the encouragement of the Scriptures we shall be having hope [or, confident expectation]. ⁵Now [may] the God of patient endurance and of encouragement give to you* to be having the same mind [or, to be like-minded] among one another, according to Christ Jesus, ⁶so that with one mind, with one mouth [fig., in unison], you* shall be glorifying the God and Father of our Lord Jesus Christ.

⁷For this reason, be receiving one another, just as also Christ received you*, to [the] glory of God. ⁸Now I say Christ Jesus has become a servant of [the] circumcision on behalf of the truth of God, in order to confirm the promises to the fathers, ⁹and the Gentiles to glorify God on behalf of mercy.

Just as it has been written, *"For this reason I Myself will confess [or, will give praise] to You among Gentiles, and I will sing praise to Your name."* [2Sam 22:50]

¹⁰And again it [or, he] says, *"Celebrate, [O] Gentiles, with His people!"* [Deut 32:43]

¹¹And again, *"Be praising the LORD, all you* Gentiles; and highly praise Him, all you* peoples!"* [Psalm 117:1]

¹²And again, Isaiah says, *"[There] will be the root* [or, *shoot*; fig., *descendent] of Jesse, and the One rising up to rule Gentiles* [or, *nations*], *Gentiles will hope on* [or, *trust in] Him."* [Isaiah 11:10, LXX]

¹³Now may the God of hope [or, confident expectation] fill you* with all joy and peace [or, freedom from anxiety] in the believing, in order for you* to be abounding in hope in [the] power of [the] Holy Spirit.

¹⁴Now I have been persuaded, my brothers [and sisters], I myself also concerning you*, that you* yourselves also are full of goodness [or, generosity], having been filled with all knowledge, being able also to be instructing others. ¹⁵So rather boldly I wrote to you*, brothers [and sisters], in part, as reminding you* again, because of the grace, the one having been given to me by God, ¹⁶in order for me to be a temple [or, public] servant of Jesus Christ to the Gentiles, serving the Gospel of God as a priest, so that the offering up of the Gentiles becomes acceptable, sanctified by [the] Holy Spirit.

¹⁷Therefore, I have a [reason for] boasting in Christ Jesus, [in] the [things] pertaining to God. ¹⁸For I will not dare to be speaking anything of [the things] which Christ did not accomplish through me, towards [the] obedience of [the] Gentiles, by word and by deed, ¹⁹in [the] power of signs and wonders, in [the] power of [the] Spirit of God, with the result that I, from Jerusalem and all around, as far as Illyricum, have fully preached the Gospel of Christ. ²⁰And so I ambitiously strive [or, count it an honor] to be proclaiming the Gospel, not where Christ was named [or, heard of], so that I shall not be building on another's foundation; ²¹but just as it has been written, *"To whom it was not told concerning Him, they will see; and those who have not heard, will understand."* [Isaiah 52:15]

²²And so I have often been prevented from coming to you*. ²³But now, no longer having place in these regions, and having a longing to come to you* for many years, ²⁴when I shall be traveling to Spain, I will come to you*; for I hope [or, expect] while passing through to see you* and to be helped by you* on my journey from there, when first I am satisfied for a while by your* [company].

²⁵But now, I am traveling to Jerusalem, ministering to [or, serving] the holy ones. ²⁶For Macedonia and Achaia were pleased [or, thought it good] to make a certain contribution for the poor of the holy ones, the [ones] in Jerusalem. ²⁷For they were pleased [or, thought it good], and they are indebted to them, for if the Gentiles shared in the [things] pertaining to the spirit, they ought also to minister to them in the [things] pertaining to the flesh. ²⁸Therefore, having finished this and having sealed this fruit to them, I will go away through you*, to Spain. ²⁹But I know that coming to you*, I will come in [the] fullness of [the] blessing of the Gospel of Christ.

³⁰Now I call on [or, plead with] you*, brothers [and sisters], through our Lord Jesus Christ, and through the love of the Spirit, to strive together with me in prayers

on behalf of me to God, ³¹that I be delivered from the ones refusing to believe in Judea, and that my ministry, the [one] for Jerusalem, becomes acceptable to the holy ones, ³²so that I shall come to you* in joy by [the] will of God and shall be refreshed together with you*. ³³Now the God of peace [be] with you* all. So be it!

16 Now I commend to you* Phoebe our sister, being a servant [or, deaconess] of the assembly [or, church], the [one] in Cenchrea, ²so that you* shall receive [or, welcome] her in [the] Lord in a manner worthy of holy ones and assist her in whatever matter she shall be having need of you*, for indeed she became a helper of many, and of me myself.

³Greet Prisca [i.e., Priscilla] and Aquila, my co-workers in Christ Jesus, ⁴who for the sake of my life risked their own neck[s], to whom not only I give thanks, but also all the assemblies of the Gentiles, ⁵and [greet] the assembly [or, church] at their house. Greet Epaenetus, my beloved, who is [the] first-fruit of Achaia to Christ. ⁶Greet Mary, who labored much for us. ⁷Greet Andronicus and Junia, my relatives [or, close companions] and my fellow-prisoners, who are well-known by [or, among] the apostles, who also have been in Christ before me. ⁸Greet Amplias, my beloved in [the] Lord. ⁹Greet Urbanus, our co-worker in Christ, and Stachys, my beloved.

¹⁰Greet Apelles, the approved in Christ. Greet the [ones] of the [household] of Aristobulus. ¹¹Greet Herodion, my relative [or, close companion]. Greet the [ones] of the [household] of Narcissus, the ones being in [the] Lord. ¹²Greet Tryphaena and Tryphosa, the ones laboring in [the] Lord. Greet Persis, the beloved, who labored much in [the] Lord. ¹³Greet Rufus, the chosen one in [the] Lord, and his mother and mine. ¹⁴Greet Asyncritus, Phlegon, Hermas, Patrobas, Hermes, and the brothers [and sisters] with them. ¹⁵Greet Philologus and Julia, Nereus and his sister, and Olympas, and all the holy ones with them. ¹⁶Greet one another with a holy kiss. The assemblies [or, churches] of Christ greet you*.

¹⁷Now I call on [or, plead with] you*, brothers [and sisters], to be watching out for [or, to be keeping a close eye on] the [ones] causing divisions [or, discords] and the stumbling blocks contrary to the teaching which you* learned, and turn away from them. ¹⁸For such do not serve as a slave to our Lord Jesus Christ, but their own belly [fig., bodily desires], and through smooth talk and flattery, they deceive the hearts of the innocent [or, unsuspecting]. ¹⁹For your* obedience became known to all. Therefore, I am rejoicing over you*, but I want you* on the one hand to be wise [as] to the good, on the other hand innocent [as] to the evil.

²⁰Now the God of peace will crush Satan under your* feet with quickness. The grace of our Lord Jesus Christ [be] with you*.

²¹Timothy, my co-worker, greets you*, and Lucius and Jason and Sosipater, my relatives [or, close companions]. ²²I Tertius (the one having written this epistle) greet you* in [the] Lord. ²³Gaius greets you*, my host and of the whole assembly; Erastus greets you*, the treasurer of the city, and Quartus the brother.

²⁴The grace of our Lord Jesus Christ [be] with you* all. So be it!

The First Epistle of Paul the Apostle to the
Corinthians

1 Paul, a called apostle of Jesus Christ by [the] will of God, and Sosthenes the brother, ²To the assembly [or, church, and throughout epistle] of God, the one being in Corinth, to the ones having been sanctified [or, made holy] in Christ Jesus, called holy ones [or, saints, and throughout epistle], with all the ones calling on the name of our Lord Jesus Christ in every place, both theirs and ours: ³Grace to you* and peace from God our Father and [the] Lord Jesus Christ!

⁴I give thanks to my God always concerning you* because of the grace of God, the one having been given to you* in Christ Jesus, ⁵that in every[thing] you* were enriched in Him, in [or, with] all word [or, discourse] and all knowledge, ⁶just as the testimony of Christ was confirmed in you*, ⁷with the result that you* are not falling short [or, lacking] in any spiritual gift, eagerly waiting for the revelation of our Lord Jesus Christ, ⁸who also will confirm [or, sustain] you* to the end, blameless in the day of our Lord Jesus Christ. ⁹God [is] faithful, by whom you* were called into [the] fellowship of His Son, Jesus Christ our Lord.

¹⁰Now I am calling on [or, pleading with] you*, brothers [and sisters], through the name of our Lord Jesus Christ, that you* all shall be speaking the same [thing] [fig., shall be in agreement], and [there] shall not be divisions among you*, but you* shall have been perfected in the same mind and in the same judgment [or, purpose]. ¹¹For it was clearly shown to me concerning you*, my brothers [and sisters], by the [members] of Chloe's [household], that [there] are quarrels among you*. ¹²Now I say this, that each of you* are saying, "I indeed am of Paul," "But I of Apollos," "But I of Cephas [i.e. Peter]," "But I of Christ."

¹³Has Christ been divided? Paul was not crucified for you*, was he? Or were you* baptized [or, immersed, and throughout epistle] into the name of Paul? ¹⁴I give thanks to God that I baptized none of you*, except Crispus and Gaius, ¹⁵lest anyone should say that I baptized into my name. ¹⁶Now I baptized also the household of Stephanas. Beyond that I do not know whether I baptized any other [or, anyone else].

¹⁷For Christ did not send me to be baptizing, but to be proclaiming the Gospel [or, Good News, and throughout book]; not in wisdom of word [or, cleverness of speech], so that the cross of Christ would not be made of no effect [or, be deprived of its power]. ¹⁸For the word of the cross indeed is foolishness to the ones perishing, but to us, the ones being saved, it is [the] power of God! ¹⁹For it has been written, *"I will destroy the wisdom of the wise, and the intelligence of the intelligent I will bring to nothing."* [Isaiah 29:14, LXX]

²⁰Where [is the] wise? Where [is the] scribe? Where [is the] skillful debater of this age? God made the wisdom of this world foolish, did He not? ²¹For since in the wisdom of God the world through its wisdom did not know God, it pleased God through the foolishness of the proclamation [or, the message being preached] to save the ones believing. ²²Since also Jews ask for a sign, and Greeks

seek wisdom, ²³but we proclaim Christ having been crucified, to Jews indeed a stumbling block and to Greeks foolishness, ²⁴but to them, the ones called, both to Jews and to Greeks, Christ the power of God and the wisdom of God. ²⁵Because the foolishness of God is wiser than people, and the weakness of God is stronger than people.

²⁶For you* see your* calling, brothers [and sisters], that [there are] not many wise according to [the] flesh, not many powerful, not many noble [or, of high social status]; ²⁷but God chose the foolish [things] of the world, so that He should be humiliating the wise; and God chose the weak [things] of the world, so that He should be humiliating the strong; ²⁸and God chose the insignificant [things] of the world and the [things] having been despised [or, looked down on], and the [things] not being [fig., which are considered nothing at all], so that He should nullify the [things] being [fig., which are considered most important], ²⁹in order that all flesh shall not [or, no flesh shall] boast before God. ³⁰But by Him you* are in Christ Jesus, who became to us wisdom from God, and righteousness and sanctification and redemption, ³¹so that, just as it has been written, *"The one boasting, let him be boasting in [the] LORD."* [Jer 9:24]

2 And when I came to you*, brothers [and sisters], I came not according to superiority of speech or of wisdom declaring to you* the testimony of God. ²For I decided [or, determined] not to know any[thing] among you*, except Jesus Christ, and this One having been crucified! ³And I was with you* in weakness and in fear and in much trembling. ⁴And my word [or, message] and my proclamation [were] not in persuasive words of human wisdom, but in demonstration of [the] Spirit and of power, ⁵so that your* faith should not be in [the] wisdom of people, but in the power of God!

⁶But we speak wisdom among the perfect [or, mature], but wisdom not of this age, nor of the rulers of this age, the ones being destroyed. ⁷But we speak [the] wisdom of God in a secret, the [wisdom] having been hidden, which God predestined before the ages for our glory, ⁸which none of the rulers of this age knew; for if they had known, they would not have crucified the Lord of glory. ⁹But just as it has been written, *"What [things] an eye did not see and an ear did not hear and did not enter into the heart of humanity,* [fig., *no person thought could happen*], *which [things] God prepared for the ones loving Him."* [Isaiah 64:4] ¹⁰But God revealed [them] to us through His Spirit. For the Spirit searches all [things], even the depths of God.

¹¹For who among people knows the [things] of the person, except the spirit of the person, the [one] in him? In the same way also no one knows the [things] of God, except the Spirit of God. ¹²But we did not receive the spirit of the world, but the Spirit, the [One] from God, so that we should know the [things] having been graciously given to us by God; ¹³which [things] also we speak, not in words taught by human wisdom, but in [words] taught by [the] Holy Spirit, interpreting spiritual [things] by spiritual [words] [or, combining spiritual [ideas] with spiritual [words]].

[14]But a natural [or, unspiritual] person does not receive the [things] of the Spirit of God, for they are foolishness to him, and he is not able to know [them], because they are spiritually examined. [15]But the spiritual [one] indeed examines all [things], but he himself is examined by no one. [16]*"For who knew [the] mind of [the] LORD? Who will instruct Him?"* But we have the mind of Christ. [Isaiah 40:13, LXX; Jer 23:18]

3And I, brothers [and sisters], was not able to speak to you* as to spiritual [people], but as to fleshly [people], as to young children in Christ. [2]I gave you* milk to drink and not solid food, for you* were not yet able [to receive it]. Indeed, neither are you* now yet able, [3]for you* are still fleshly. For whereas [there are] among you* jealous rivalry and strife and divisions [or, discords], you* are fleshly and are walking about [fig., conducting yourselves] according to human [standards], are you* not? [4]For whenever someone says, "I indeed am of Paul," but a different [one], "I of Apollos," you* are fleshly, are you* not?

[5]Who then is Paul? But who [is] Apollos? But rather [they are] servants through whom you* believed, and to each [one] as the Lord gave. [6]I planted; Apollos watered, but God was causing growth. [7]So then, neither the one planting is anything, nor the one watering, but the One causing growth—God! [8]Now the one planting and the one watering are one, but each will receive his own reward, according to his own labor. [9]For we are God's co-workers, God's field; you* are God's building.

[10]According to the grace of God, the one having been given to me, like a wise, expert builder, I have laid a foundation, but another is building on [it]. But let each be watching [or, be taking care] how he builds on [it]. [11]For no one is able to lay another foundation besides the one laid, which is Jesus Christ.

[12]Now if anyone builds on this foundation gold, silver, precious stones, wood, hay, straw, [13]the work of each will become evident, for the Day will make [it] clear, because it is revealed in fire, and the work of each, the fire will prove what kind it is. [14]If the work of anyone remains which he built on [it], he will receive a reward. [15]If the work of anyone will be burned up, he will suffer loss; but he himself will be saved, but so as through fire.

[16]You* know that you* are a temple of God, and the Spirit of God dwells in you*, do you* not? [17]If anyone destroys the temple of God, this one God will destroy; for the temple of God is holy, which you* are.

[18]Stop letting anyone deceive himself. If anyone seems to be wise among you* in this age, let him become foolish, so that he shall become wise. [19]For the wisdom of this world is foolishness with God. For it has been written, *"[He is] the One trapping the wise [ones] in their craftiness."* [Job 5:13] [20]And again, *"[The] LORD knows the thought processes of the wise [ones], that they are futile [or, useless]."* [Psalm 94:11] [21]So then, let no one be boasting in people. For all [things] are yours*, [22]whether Paul or Apollos or Cephas [i.e. Peter] or [the] world or life or death or [things] present or [things] about to be. All [things] are yours*, [23]but you* [are] Christ's, and Christ [is] God's.

4Let a person be considering us in this way, as attendants of Christ and stewards of [the] secrets [or, mysteries] of God. ²Now furthermore, what is required among the stewards [is] that one be found faithful. ³But to me it is as an insignificant [thing] that I should be examined by you* or by [any] human day [fig., human court], but I do not even examine myself. ⁴For I have been conscious of nothing against myself [fig., my conscience is clear]; but I have not been justified [or, acquitted] by this, but the One examining me is [the] Lord. ⁵So then, stop judging anything before the time, until the Lord comes, who will both bring to light the hidden [things] of the darkness and will reveal the counsels [or, intentions] of the hearts, and then the praise will come to each from God.

⁶Now these [things], brothers [and sisters], I transformed [fig., applied] to myself and to Apollos for your* sakes, so that in us you* shall learn not to be thinking beyond what has been written, so that you* shall not become conceited one on behalf of one against the other. ⁷For who makes you to differ [or, who is regarding you to be superior]? Now what do you have which you did not receive? But if you also received, why are you boasting as though not having received?

⁸Already you* have been filled! Already you* grew rich! You* reigned [or, became like a king] without us! And O that indeed you* did reign, so that we also should reign together [or, live together as kings] with you*! ⁹For I think that God displayed us, the apostles, last, as sentenced to death, because we have become a spectacle to the world and to angels and to people. ¹⁰We [are] fools because of Christ, and you* [are] wise in Christ! We [are] weak, but you* [are] strong! You* [are] esteemed, but we [are] despised!

¹¹Until the present time we both hunger and thirst, and we wear ragged clothing and are beaten with fists [fig., are harshly treated] and wander about without a home, ¹²and labor, working with [our] own hands. Being insulted we bless, being persecuted we ourselves endure [it], ¹³being defamed we speak words of encouragement; we have become like garbage of the world, scum of all until now.

¹⁴I am not writing these [things] [to be] shaming you, but as my beloved children I am warning [or, instructing] [you*]. ¹⁵For although you* shall be having countless tutors in Christ, but not many fathers; for in Christ Jesus through the Gospel I became your* father. ¹⁶ Therefore, I am calling on [or, pleading with] you*, continue becoming imitators of me. ¹⁷For this reason I sent Timothy to you*, who is my child, beloved and faithful in [the] Lord, who will remind you* of my ways, the [ones] in Christ, just as I teach everywhere in every assembly.

¹⁸Now some became conceited, as though I were not coming to you*. ¹⁹But I will come to you* soon, if the Lord wills, and I will know not the word of the ones having become conceited, but the power. ²⁰For the kingdom of God [is] not in word, but in power. ²¹What do you* desire? Shall I come to you* with a rod, or in love and in a spirit of gentleness?

5Sexual sin is actually heard of [or, reported] among you*, and such sexual sin which is not even named [or, known] among the Gentiles, that someone is having the wife of his father! ²And you* have become conceited and did not at all rather grieve, so that he should be expelled from the midst of you*, the one having done this deed! ³For I indeed, as being absent as to the body, but being present in the spirit, have already judged the one having committed this, as being present.

⁴In the name of our Lord Jesus Christ, when you* are gathered together and my spirit [is with you*], with the power of our Lord Jesus Christ, ⁵hand over such a one to Satan for destruction of the flesh, so that the spirit shall be saved in the Day of the Lord Jesus. ⁶Your* boasting [is] not good! You* know that a little leaven [or, yeast] leavens the whole lump [of dough] [or, causes the whole lump [of dough] to rise], do you* not?

⁷Clean out the old leaven [or, yeast], so that you* shall be a new lump, just as you* are unleavened [or, made without yeast], for also Christ our Passover [or, Paschal Lamb] was sacrificed on our behalf. ⁸So then we should be keeping the feast, not with old leaven [or, yeast], nor with leaven of evil and wickedness, but with unleavened [bread] of integrity and truth.

⁹I wrote to you* in the epistle not to be associating with sexual sinners; ¹⁰yet [I did] not at all [mean] with the sexual sinners of this world, or with the covetous or swindlers or idolaters . In that case you* then [would] be obligated to go out of the world! ¹¹But now, I wrote to you* not to be associating with anyone being named a brother [fig., fellow believer, and elsewhere in book] if he is a sexual sinner or covetous or an idolater or a slanderer [or, an abusive person] or a drunkard or a swindler, not even to eat with such a person. ¹²For what [is it] to me to also judge the ones outside? You* judge the ones within, do you* not? ¹³But God judges the ones outside. *"And you* will expel the evil [one] from among yourselves."* [Deut 17:7; 19:19]

6Does any of you* dare [or, presume], having a dispute with the other, to be going to court [or, to be suing] before the unrighteous and not before the holy ones? ²You* know that the holy ones will judge the world, do you* not? And if the world is judged by you*, are you* unworthy [or, incapable] of the smallest court [cases]? ³You* know that we will judge angels, do you* not? Why not then the things pertaining to everyday life? ⁴If then indeed you* have law courts [for] things pertaining to everyday life, the ones having been despised [or, of little esteem] in the assembly, these you* cause to sit [fig., appoint as judges]? ⁵I speak to your* shame. So [is there] not among you* one wise [person], not even one, who will be able to discern [or, settle a dispute] in the midst of his brothers [and sisters]? ⁶But a brother goes to court against a brother, and this before unbelievers!

⁷Already, therefore, it is altogether a failure for you*, that you* have judgments [or, lawsuits] against one another. Why not rather be letting yourselves be treated unjustly? ⁸But you* act unjustly, and you* defraud, and these [things to] brothers [and sisters]!

⁹You* know that unrighteous [ones] will not inherit [the] kingdom of God, do you* not? Stop being led astray [fig., being deceived]; neither sexual sinners, nor idolaters, nor adulterers, nor passive partners in male-male sex, nor active partners in male-male sex, ¹⁰nor covetous [ones], nor thieves, nor drunkards, nor slanderers [or, abusive persons], nor swindlers will inherit [the] kingdom of God.

[11]And these some of you* were! But you* yourselves were washed [fig., purified], but you* were sanctified, but you* were justified [or, declared righteous] in the name of the Lord Jesus and in [or, by] the Spirit of our God! [12]All [things] are lawful to me, but all [things] are not advantageous [or, beneficial]. All [things] are lawful to me, but I will not be controlled by anything. [13]The foods for the stomach, and the stomach for the foods. But God will make both this [stomach] and these [foods] useless. So the body [is] not for sexual sin, but for the Lord, and the Lord for the body. [14]Now God both raised up the Lord and will raise us up through His power. [15]You* know that your* bodies are members of Christ, do you* not? So having taken the members of Christ, shall I make [them] members of a prostitute? Absolutely not! [16]You* know that the one joined to the prostitute is one body [with her], do you* not? For He says, *"They will be—the two—into one flesh* [or, *The two will become one flesh*]" [Gen 2:24, LXX]. [17]But the one joined to the Lord is one spirit [with Him].

[18]Be fleeing sexual sin! Every sin, whichever a person commits, is outside of the body, but the one committing sexual sin sins against his own body. [19]You* know, do you* not, that your* body is a temple of the Holy Spirit in you*, which you* have from God, and [that] you* are not your* own? [20]For you* were bought [fig., redeemed] with a price. Therefore, glorify God in your* body and in your* spirit, which are God's.

7 Now concerning [the things] of which you* wrote to me: [it is] good for a man not to be touching a woman [sexually]. [2]But because of such sexual sins, let each man have his own wife, and let each woman have her own husband. [3]Let the husband be rendering the affection being owed to the wife, and likewise also the wife to the husband. [4]The wife does not have control [or, authority] over her own body, but the husband; and, likewise also the husband does not have control over his own body, but the wife. [5]Stop depriving one another, except by mutual consent for a time, so that you* shall be devoting yourselves to [or, having free time for] fasting and prayer; and again to the same be coming together, lest Satan be tempting you* because of your* lack of self-control. [6]But this I say as a concession, not as a command. [7]For I desire all people to be even as myself. But each has his own gracious gift from God, one indeed in this manner, but another in that.

[8]Now I say to the unmarried [ones] and to the widows, it is good for them if they remain even as I [am]. [9]But if they are not exercising self-control, let them marry; for it is better to marry than to continue being inflamed [with lust].

[10]Now to the ones having married I am giving strict orders [or, am instructing] (not I, but the Lord) [i.e. Jesus commented on this subject during His earthly ministry]: do not let a wife separate from a husband. [11]But even if she is separated, let her be remaining unmarried or let her be reconciled to the husband. And stop letting a husband divorce a wife. [see Matt 19:3-9]

[12]But to the rest I speak (not the Lord) [i.e. Jesus did not comment on this subject during His earthly ministry]: if any brother has an unbelieving wife, and she is willing to be living with him, stop letting him divorce her. [13]And a woman

who has an unbelieving husband, and <u>he</u> is willing to be living with her, stop letting her divorce him. [14]For the unbelieving husband has been sanctified [or, set apart to God] by the wife, and the unbelieving wife has been sanctified by the husband; for otherwise indeed your* children are unclean [or, defiled], but now they are holy [or, set apart to God]. [15]But if the unbelieving [spouse] separates himself, let him be separating himself; the brother or the sister has not been bound in such [cases], but God has called us in peace. [16]For how do you know, O wife, whether you will save the husband? Or how do you know, O husband, whether you will save the wife?

[17]Otherwise, as God distributed to each, as the Lord has called each, in this manner let him be walking about [fig., conducting himself]; and in this manner I instruct in all the assemblies. [18]Was anyone called having been circumcised? Stop letting him become uncircumcised. Was anyone called in uncircumcision? Stop letting him be circumcised. [19]Circumcision is nothing, and uncircumcision is nothing, <u>but</u> [what matters is] keeping [the] commandments of God. [20]Each [one] in the calling in which he was called, in this let him remain.

[21]Were you called [as] a slave? Stop letting it be a concern to you, <u>but</u> if also you are able to become free, rather make use of [it]. [22]For the [one] in the Lord having been called [as] a slave is [the] Lord's freedman. Likewise also the free person having been called is a slave of Christ. [23]You* were bought [or, redeemed] with a price; stop becoming slaves of people. [24]Each [one] in [the circumstance] in which he was called, brothers [and sisters], in this [circumstance] let him remain with God.

[25]Now concerning the virgins, I do not have a commandment of [or, from] [the] Lord [i.e. Jesus did not comment on this subject during His earthly ministry], but I give an opinion as one having been shown mercy from [the] Lord to be faithful [or, trustworthy]. [26]So I consider this to be good because of the present distress, that [it is] good for a man to be in this manner: [27]Have you been bound to a wife? Stop seeking to be loosed [or, divorced]. Have you been loosed from a wife? Stop seeking a wife. [28]But even if you do marry, you did not sin; and if the virgin marries, she did not sin. But such will have tribulation in the flesh, and <u>I</u> [am trying to] spare you*.

[29]But this I say, brothers [and sisters], the time has been shortened; from now on, it is that even the ones having wives should be as not having, [30]and the ones weeping as not weeping, and the ones rejoicing as not rejoicing, and the ones buying as not possessing, [31]and the ones making use of this world as not making full use of [it], for the form of this world is passing away.

[32]But I want you* to be free from anxiety; the unmarried [man] is anxious for [or, concerned about] the [things] of the Lord, how he will please the Lord. [33]But the married [man] is anxious for [or, concerned about] the [things] of the world, how he will please the wife. [34]The wife and the virgin have been distinguished [or, have different interests]: the unmarried [woman] is anxious for [or, concerned about] the [things] of the Lord, so that she should be holy both in body and in spirit, but the married [woman] is anxious for [or, concerned about] the [things] of the world, how she will please the husband. [35]Now this I say for your* own profit

[or, benefit], not so that I should cast a noose [fig., a restriction] on you*, <u>but</u> for the proper behavior and devotion to the Lord, without distraction.

³⁶Now if anyone thinks [he is] acting shamefully [or, behaving improperly] towards his virgin, if she is past marriageable age [or, if his passions are strong], and it is obligated to happen, what he desires let him do; he does not sin. Let them marry. ³⁷But [he] who has stood steadfast [fig., is convinced] in his heart, not having necessity, and has authority [or, control] over his own desire, and this he has determined in his heart, to be keeping his own virgin, he does well. ³⁸Accordingly, also the one giving in marriage [or, getting married] does well, but the one not giving in marriage [or, not getting married] does better.

³⁹A wife has been bound by [the] law as long as her husband lives, but if also the husband sleeps [fig., dies], she is free to be married to whomever she desires, only in [the] Lord. ⁴⁰But she is happier if she remains in this manner, according to my opinion. And I think <u>I</u> also to be having [the] Spirit of God.

8Now concerning the [meat] sacrificed to idols, we know that we all have knowledge: such knowledge causes conceit, but love builds up [fig., edifies]. ²And if anyone thinks to know anything, he has not yet known anything just as it is necessary [for him] to know. ³But if anyone loves God, this one has been known by Him. ⁴So concerning the eating of the [meat] sacrificed to idols, we know that an idol [is] nothing in the world, and that [there is] no other God except for one. ⁵For even if they are called "gods," whether in heaven or on earth (just as there are gods many and lords many), ⁶<u>but</u> to us [there is] one God, the Father, of whom [are] all [things], and we [exist] for Him; and one Lord Jesus Christ, through whom [are] all [things], and we [exist] through Him.

⁷<u>But</u> this knowledge [is] not in all [people], but some with consciousness [or, awareness] of the idol until now, eat [it] as [meat] sacrificed to an idol, and their conscience, being weak, is defiled. ⁸But food does not present [or, commend] us to God, for neither if we eat do we excel [or, are we better off]; nor if we do not eat do we fall short [or, are we inferior]. ⁹But be watching out [or, be aware] lest this right [or, privilege] of yours* becomes a stumbling block to the ones being weak.

¹⁰For if anyone sees you, the one having knowledge, in an idol's temple reclining [to eat], will not his conscience, being weak, be emboldened to be eating the [things] sacrificed to idols? ¹¹And the brother being weak will perish because of your knowledge, for the sake of whom Christ died. ¹²But sinning in this manner in regard to the brothers [and sisters], and beating [fig., wounding] their conscience, being weak, in regard to Christ you* sin. ¹³For this very reason, if food causes my brother to stumble [fig., to sin], I shall never at all eat flesh into the age [fig., forever], so that I do not cause my brother to stumble.

9I am an apostle, am I not? I am free, am I not? I have seen Jesus Christ our Lord, have I not? You* are my work in [the] Lord, are you* not? ²If to others I am not an apostle, <u>but</u> yet doubtless I am to you*. For you* are the seal [fig. proof] of my apostleship in [the] Lord. ³My defense to the ones examining me is this: ⁴Do we never at all have a right to eat and to drink? ⁵Do we never at all have a right to be taking along [or, traveling around with] a sister, a wife, as also the other apostles and the brothers of the Lord and Cephas [i.e. Peter]? ⁶Or do only I and Barnabas not have a right not to be working?

⁷Who ever serves as a soldier at his own expense? Who plants a vineyard and does not eat of the fruit of it? Or [who] tends a flock and does not eat of the milk of the flock? ⁸I do not speak these things according to human [standards], do I? Or the Law also says these [things], does it not? ⁹For it has been written in the Law of Moses, *"You will not muzzle an ox while it is threshing [the chaff from the grain]."* [Deut 25:4] God does not care for the oxen, does He? ¹⁰Or does He certainly say [this] for our sakes? For our sakes it was written, that in hope [or, confident expectation] ought the one plowing to be plowing, and the one threshing in hope [ought] to partake of his hope.

¹¹If _we_ sowed to you* the spiritual [things, is it] a great [thing] if _we_ reap material [things] from you*? ¹²If others partake of this right over you*, we [do] more, [do] we not? But we did not make use of this right, _but_ we put up with [or, endure] all [things] so that we shall not give any hindrance to the Gospel of Christ.

¹³You* know that the ones performing the sacred [work] of the temple eat from the temple, [and] the ones serving at the altar have a share from the altar, do you* not? ¹⁴In the same way also, the Lord gave instructions to the ones proclaiming the Gospel to be living from the Gospel. [cp. Matt 10:10; Luke 10:7]

¹⁵But _I_ have used none of these [things]. Now I did not write these [things] so that it should become in this way in my [case], for [it is] good for me rather to die than that anyone makes my [grounds for] boasting empty. ¹⁶For if I proclaim the Gospel, it is not [grounds for] me to be boasting, for necessity lays on me; but how horrible it is to me if I do not proclaim the Gospel! ¹⁷For if I do this willingly [or, voluntarily], I have a reward; but if unwillingly, I have been entrusted with a stewardship [fig., responsibility]. ¹⁸What then is my reward? That proclaiming the Gospel, I present the Gospel of Christ without charge, not to make full use of [or, exploit] my authority in the Gospel.

¹⁹For being free from all [people], I made myself a servant to all [people], so that I should win the more. ²⁰And I became to the Jews as a Jew, so that I should win Jews; to the [ones] under law as under law, so that I should win the [ones] under law; ²¹to the [ones] without law as without law (not being without law to God, _but_ subject to law to Christ), so that I should win the [ones] without law. ²²I became to the weak as weak, so that I should win the weak. I have become all [things] to all [people], so that I should by all means [or, certainly] save some. ²³Now this I do because of the Gospel, so that I shall become a fellow-partaker of it.

²⁴You* know that the ones running in a stadium, all indeed run, but one receives the prize, do you* not? In the same way, be running, so that you* shall obtain [or, win]. ²⁵But everyone competing exercises self-control in all [things]. Now these indeed [compete] so that they shall receive a corruptible victor's wreath, but we an incorruptible [one]! ²⁶So _I_ run in this manner, not as without a goal. In this manner I fight, not as repeatedly beating air. ²⁷But _I_ beat my body black and blue [fig., keep my body under control] and bring [it] into slavery [fig., make it ready to serve], lest, having preached to others, I myself become disqualified.

10Now I do not want you* to be unaware, brothers [and sisters], that all our fathers were under the cloud, and all passed through the sea, ²and all were baptized into Moses in the cloud and in the sea, ³and all ate the same spiritual food, ⁴and all drank the same spiritual drink, for they were drinking of a spiritual rock following [them]; but that rock was Christ. ⁵But God was not well pleased with the majority of them, for they were struck down in the wilderness.

⁶So these [things] became examples for us, for us not to be passionately desiring evil things, just as those also desired. ⁷Neither continue becoming idolaters, just as some of them, just as it has been written, *"The people sat down to eat and to drink, and stood up to be playing."* [Exod 32:6] ⁸Neither shall we be committing sexual sin, just as some of them committed sexual sin, and twenty-three thousand fell in one day. [see Numb 25:1-9] ⁹Neither shall we be tempting [or, testing] Christ, just as also some of them tempted, and perished by the serpents. [see Numb 21:5,6] ¹⁰Nor be grumbling, just as also some of them grumbled, and they perished by the destroyer. [see Numb 14:27-30] ¹¹Now all these [things] happened to those [people as] examples, and they were written for our instruction, to whom the end of the ages came.

¹²So then, let the one thinking to be standing [or, who thinks he is standing], be watching, lest he falls. ¹³No temptation has taken hold of you*, except a human [one] [or, [one] characteristic of humanity]. But God [is] faithful, who will not allow you* to be tempted beyond what you* are able [or, capable of], but with the temptation He will also make the way out, for your* being able to endure [it].

¹⁴For this very reason, my beloved, be fleeing from idolatry. ¹⁵I am speaking as to wise [ones]; you* judge what I am saying. ¹⁶The cup of the blessing which we bless, it is [the] fellowship of [or, a sharing in] the blood of Christ, is it not? The bread which we break, it is [the] fellowship of the body of Christ, is it not? ¹⁷Because we, the many, are one bread, one body, for we all partake of the one bread. ¹⁸Be watching Israel according to [the] flesh. The ones eating the sacrifices are participants in the altar, are they not?

¹⁹So what am I saying? That an idol is anything or that [meat] sacrificed to an idol is anything? ²⁰But [I am saying that] what the Gentiles sacrifice, they sacrifice to demons and not to God. And I do not want you* to become participants of the demons. ²¹You* are not able to be drinking [the] cup of [the] Lord and [the] cup of demons; you* are not able to be partaking of [the] table of [the] Lord and of [the] table of demons. ²²Or do we provoke the Lord to jealousy? We are not stronger than He, are we?

²³All [things] are lawful for me, but all [things] are not advantageous [or, beneficial]. All [things] are lawful for me, but all [things] do not build up [fig., edify]. ²⁴Let no one be seeking his own [concern], but each the [concern] of the other. ²⁵Whatever is sold in the meat-market, eat, examining nothing, for the sake of the conscience. ²⁶*"For the earth [is] the LORD's and its fullness."* [Psalm 24:1; 50:12; 89:11] ²⁷But if someone of the unbelieving invite you*, and you* want to go, eat all the [food] set before you*, examining nothing, for the sake of the conscience. ²⁸But if someone says to you*, "This is [meat] sacrificed to an idol,"

stop eating [it], for the sake of that one having made [it] known and his conscience, *"for the earth [is] the LORD's and its fullness."*

²⁹Now I say conscience, not of yourself, but the [conscience] of the other. For why [is it] that my liberty is judged by another's conscience? ³⁰If I partake with thankfulness, why am I being defamed concerning what I give thanks for?

³¹So whether you* eat or drink, or whatever you* do, be doing all [things] for the glory of God. ³²Continue becoming without offence both to Jews and to Greeks, and to the Assembly [or, Church] of God, ³³just as I also try to please all [people] in all [things], not seeking my own profit, but the [profit] of the many, so that they shall be saved.

11 Continue becoming imitators of me, just as I also [am] of Christ. ²Now I highly praise you*, brothers [and sisters], because you* have remembered me in all [things], and you* keep [or, hold firmly to] the handed down teachings [or, traditions] just as I handed [them] down to you*.

³Now I want you* to know that the head of every man is Christ, but [the] head of a woman [is] the husband, but [the] head of Christ [is] God. ⁴Every man praying or prophesying, having [something] on [his] head dishonors his head. ⁵But every woman praying or prophesying with the head uncovered [or, unveiled] dishonors her own head, for it is one and the same with having had herself shaved.

⁶For if a woman is not covered [or, veiled], let her also have her hair cut off, but if [it is] disgraceful [or, shameful] for a woman to have her hair cut off or to be having herself shaved, be letting her be covered [or, veiled]. ⁷For indeed a man ought not to be having the head covered, being [the] image and glory of God, but a woman is [the] glory of a man. ⁸For man is not from woman, but woman from man. [see Gen 2:21-23] ⁹For also man was not created for the sake of the woman, but woman for the sake of the man. [see Gen 2:18] ¹⁰For this reason, the woman ought to be having [a symbol of] authority on her head, because of the angels.

¹¹Nevertheless, neither [is] man apart from [fig., independent of] woman, nor woman apart from man, in [the] Lord. ¹²For even as the woman [is] from the man, so also the man [is] by the woman, but all such [things are] from God. ¹³Judge among you* yourselves: is it fitting [or, proper] for an uncovered [or, unveiled] woman to be praying to God? ¹⁴Does not even nature itself teach you* that if a man indeed is wearing long hair, it is a dishonor to him? ¹⁵But a woman, if she is wearing long hair, it is a glory to her, because her hair has been given in place of a covering. ¹⁶But if anyone seems to be contentious, we do not have such a custom, neither [do] the assemblies of God.

¹⁷Now giving strict orders [about] this, I do not highly praise [or, commend] [you*], because you* come together not for the better, but for the worse. ¹⁸For first indeed [when] you* come together in an assembly, I hear of divisions being among you*, and to some extent I believe [it]. ¹⁹For it is necessary [for] heretical sects also to be among you*, so that the approved [ones] become evident among you*. ²⁰So [when] you* come together at the same [place], it is not to eat [the] Lord's Supper. ²¹For in the eating each one takes his own supper first, and one is hungry, and another is drunk. ²²Why? Do you* not have houses to be eating and

to be drinking in? Or do you* despise the Assembly of God and disgrace the ones not having? What shall I say to you*? Shall I highly praise [or, commend] you* in this? I do not highly praise [you*]!

²³For I received from the Lord what I also handed down to you*, that the Lord Jesus in the night in which He was betrayed took bread, ²⁴and having given thanks, He broke [it] and said, "Take, eat; this is My body, the [one] being broken on behalf of you*. Be doing this in remembrance of Me." ²⁵And in the same manner [He took] the cup after [they] ate, saying, "This cup is the New Covenant in My blood. Be doing this, as often as you* drink [it], in remembrance of Me." ²⁶For as often as you* shall be eating this bread and drinking this cup, you* proclaim the death of the Lord, until He comes.

²⁷So then, whoever eats this bread or drinks the cup of the Lord unworthily [or, in a careless manner], he will be guilty of the body of the Lord and of the blood of the Lord. ²⁸But let a person be examining himself, and in this manner let him be eating of the bread and let him be drinking of the cup. ²⁹For the one eating and drinking unworthily [or, in a careless manner], eats and drinks judgment to himself, not discerning [or, correctly judging] the body of the Lord. ³⁰For this reason, many among you* [are] sick [or, weak] and infirm [or, ill], and many are fallen asleep [fig., have died]. ³¹For if we had discerned [or, correctly judged] ourselves, we would not have been judged. ³²But being judged by [the] Lord, we are disciplined [or, chastened], so that we shall not be condemned with the world.

³³So then, my brothers [and sisters], [when] you* come together to eat, be waiting for one another. ³⁴So if anyone is hungry, let him eat at home, so that you* shall not be coming together for judgment. But the rest [or, the remaining things], whenever I come, I will give instructions.

*12*Now concerning the spiritual [gifts], brothers [and sisters], I do not want you* to be lacking understanding. ²You* know that when you* were Gentiles [or, pagans], you* were being led to the mute idols, being carried away. ³For this reason, I make known to you* that no one speaking by [the] Spirit of God, says "Jesus [is] accursed" [Gr., *anathema*], and no one is able to say "Jesus [is] Lord," except by [the] Holy Spirit.

⁴Now [there] are varieties of spiritual [gifts], but the same Spirit. ⁵And [there] are varieties of ministries, and the same Lord. ⁶And [there] are varieties of divine workings [or, activities], but the same God is the One supernaturally working all such [things] in all. ⁷But to each [one] has been given the manifestation of the Spirit for the advantage [of all] [or, for the common good].

⁸For to one has been given a word of wisdom by the Spirit, but to another a word of knowledge according to the same Spirit, ⁹but to a different [one] faith by the same Spirit, but to another spiritual gifts of healings by the same Spirit, ¹⁰but to another divine workings of miraculous works, but to another prophecy, but to another discernment of spirits, but to a different [one] [various] kinds of tongues [fig., languages, and throughout epistle], but to another interpretation [or,

translation] of tongues. [11]But the one and the same Spirit supernaturally works all these [things], distributing to each just as He intends.

[12]For just as the body is one and has many body parts, but all the body parts of the one body, being many, are one body, in the same manner also [is] Christ. [13]For also by one Spirit we all were baptized into one body, whether Jews or Greeks, whether slaves or free persons, and we were all given to drink into one Spirit. [14]For also the body is not one body part, but many. [15]If the foot should say, "Because I am not a hand, I am not of the body," it is not, because of this, not of the body. [16]And if the ear should say, "Because I am not an eye, I am not of the body," it is not, because of this, not of the body.

[17]If the whole body [were] an eye, where [would be] the hearing? If [the] whole [were] hearing, where [would be] the sense of smell? [18]But now God set the body parts each one of them in the body, just as He willed. [19]But if all the [parts] were one body part, where [would be] the body? [20]But now indeed [there are] many body parts, but one body. [21]Now the eye is not able to say to the hand, "I have no need of you," nor again the head to the feet, "I have no need of you*."

[22]But by much more [or, to a greater degree] the parts of the body which seem to be weaker are necessary. [23]And which [parts] of the body we consider to be less honorable, to these we put around [fig., bestow] greater honor, and our unpresentable [parts] have greater presentability [fig., are treated with greater modesty], [24]but our presentable [parts] do not have [such a] need; but God arranged the body, having given greater honor to the [part] lacking [apparent importance], [25]so that there shall not be divisions in the body, but that the body parts shall have the same concern for one another. [26]And if one part suffers, all the parts suffer with [it]; if one part is glorified, all the parts rejoice with [or, congratulate] [it].

[27]Now you* are [the] body of Christ and parts from [each] part [fig., individually parts of it]. [28]And indeed [those] whom God set in the Assembly [are]: first apostles, second prophets, third teachers, next miraculous powers, next spiritual gifts of healings, helpers, leaders [or, administrators], [various] kinds of tongues.

[29]All [are] not apostles, are they? All [are] not prophets, are they? All [are] not teachers, are they? All [are] not [workers of] miraculous powers, are they? [30]All do not have spiritual gifts of healings, do they? All do not speak in tongues, do they? All do not interpret [or, translate], do they? [31]But be earnestly desiring the better spiritual gifts. And yet I show to you* a far better way.

13 If I speak with the tongues of people and of angels, but I do not have love, I have become [as] brass sounding or a cymbal tinkling. [2]And if I am having [the gift of] prophecy and know all secrets [or, mysteries] and all knowledge, and if I am having all faith so as to be removing mountains, and have not love, I am nothing. [3]And if I dole out all my possessions, and if I hand over my body so that I shall be burned, but am not having love, I am not at all benefited.

[4]Love waits patiently; it acts kindly. Love does not envy [or, is not jealous]; love does not boast; it does not become haughty. [5]It does not behave disgracefully; it does not seek its own [things]; it is not provoked [or, irritated]; it does not keep a record of evil. [6]It does not rejoice over unrighteousness, but it rejoices with the

truth. ⁷It puts up with all [things], believes all, hopes [or, confidently expects] all, endures all.

⁸Love never fails. But if [there be] prophecies, they will become useless; if tongues, they will cease by themselves; if knowledge, it will become useless. ⁹Now we know by part, and we prophesy by part. ¹⁰But when the perfect [or, complete] comes, then the [thing] by part [fig., which is partial] will become useless. ¹¹When I was a child, I was speaking as a child, I was thinking as a child, I was reasoning as a child; but when I have become a man, I have put away the [things] of the child. ¹²For we now see by means of a mirror by reflection [fig., indirectly], but then face to face; now I know in part, but then I will know fully, just as I also was known.

¹³But now these three remain: faith, hope [or, confident expectation], [and] love—but [the] greatest of these [is] love.

14 Be pursuing love, yet be seeking earnestly the spiritual [gifts], but rather that you* shall be prophesying. ²For the one speaking in a tongue does not speak to people <u>but</u> to God, for no one understands [him], but in [his] spirit [or, by [the] Spirit] he speaks secrets [or, mysteries]. ³But the one prophesying to people speaks edification and exhortation [or, encouragement] and comfort. ⁴The one speaking in a tongue edifies himself, but the one prophesying edifies [the] assembly. ⁵Now I want you* all to be speaking with tongues, but more that you* shall be prophesying. For the one prophesying [is] greater than the one speaking with tongues, unless he interprets [or, translates], so that the assembly receives edification.

⁶But now, brothers [and sisters], if I come to you* speaking with tongues, what will I benefit you*, unless I speak to you* either with a revelation or with knowledge or with prophesy or with teaching? ⁷Likewise, the lifeless [things] give a sound, whether flute or harp. If it is not giving a difference in the sounds, how will the [music] played on a flute or the [music] played on a harp be known [or, be distinguished]? ⁸For if a trumpet also gives an indistinct sound, who will prepare himself for battle? ⁹In the same way, you* also, if you* do not give intelligible speech by means of the tongue, how will the [thing] spoken be known? For you* will be speaking into air.

¹⁰[There] are, it may be [fig., perhaps], so many kinds of sounds in the world, and none of them without meaning. ¹¹So if I do not know the power [fig., meaning] of the sound, I will be to the one speaking [as] a foreigner, and the one speaking [will be] to me [as] a foreigner. ¹²In the same way, <u>you*</u> also, since you* are zealous of spiritual [gifts], for the building up [or, edification] of the assembly, be seeking so that you* shall be abounding.

¹³For this very reason, the one speaking in a tongue, let him be praying that he shall be interpreting [or, translating]. ¹⁴For if I am praying in a tongue, my spirit prays, but my mind [or, understanding] is unfruitful. ¹⁵What then is it? I will pray with the spirit, but I will also pray with the mind [or, understanding]; I will sing praises with the spirit, but I will also sing praises with the mind [or, understanding]. ¹⁶Otherwise, if you bless with the spirit, how will the one occupying the place of the unlearned say the "So be it!" at your giving of thanks, since he does not know

238

[or, understand] what you are saying? [17]For you indeed are rightly giving thanks, but the other is not built up [or, edified].

[18]I give thanks to my God [that] I speak in tongues more than all of you*. [19]But in an assembly I desire to speak five words by means of my understanding, so that I shall also instruct others, rather than countless [or, ten thousand] words in a tongue.

[20]Brothers [and sisters], stop being young children in your* understanding, but continue being as a child in evil, but continue becoming perfect [or, complete] in your* understanding. [21]In the Law it has been written, *"By ones speaking different tongues and by different lips [fig., speech] I will speak to this people, and not even in this manner will they hear Me,"* says [the] Lord. [Isaiah 28:11,12; Deut 28:49] [22]So then tongues are for a sign, not to the ones believing, but to the unbelieving ones; but prophesy [is] not for the unbelieving ones, but for the ones believing.

[23]Therefore, if the whole assembly comes together to the same [place] and all are speaking in tongues, and unlearned [ones] or unbelievers come in, they will say that you* are raving mad, will they not? [24]But if all are prophesying, and someone comes in, an unbeliever or an unlearned [one], he is convicted by all, he is called to account by all. [25]And in this way, the secrets of his heart become revealed, and in this way, having fallen on [his] face, he will prostrate himself in worship before God, declaring [or, acknowledging] that God truly is among you*.

[26]What then is it, brothers [and sisters]? Whenever you* shall be coming together, each [one] of you* has a psalm, has a teaching, has a tongue, has a revelation, has an interpretation [or, a translation]. Be letting all [things] be for building up [or, edification]. [27]If anyone speaks in a tongue, [let it be] by two or [at] the most by three, and [each] in turn, and let one be interpreting [or, translating]. [28]But if [there] is not an interpreter [or, translator], let him keep silent in an assembly, but let him speak to himself and to God.

[29]Now let two or three prophets speak, and let the others pass judgment. [30]But if [something] is revealed to another sitting [there], let the first keep silent. [31]For you* are able, one by one, all to be prophesying, so that all shall be learning, and all shall be continually encouraged. [32]And [the] spirits of prophets are subject to prophets. [33]For God is not of disorder but of peace, as in all the assemblies of the holy ones. [or, The final phrase could instead be the first phrase of the next paragraph.]

[34]Let your* women be keeping silent in the assemblies, for it has not been permitted to them to be speaking, but to be subjecting themselves, just as also the Law says. [35]But if they desire to learn anything, let them be questioning their own husbands at home, for it is disgraceful [or, shameful] [for] women to be speaking in an assembly.

[36]Or did the word of God go out from you*? Or did it come to you* alone? [37]If anyone thinks [that he] is a prophet or spiritual, let him acknowledge what I write to you*, that they are commandments of [the] Lord. [38]But if anyone fails to understand, let him be failing to understand. [39]Accordingly brothers [and sisters], be earnestly desiring to be prophesying; and stop forbidding [or, preventing] to be speaking in tongues. [40]Be letting all [things] be done properly and according to order.

15Now I make known to you*, brothers [and sisters], the Gospel, the one I have proclaimed to you*, which also you* received, in which also you* have stood, ²through which also you* are saved, if you* hold fast to which word [or, that word which] I proclaimed the Gospel to you*, unless you* believed thoughtlessly [or, without reason].

³For I handed down [or, delivered] to you* first what also I received, that Christ died on behalf of our sins according to the Scriptures, ⁴and that He was buried, and that He had been raised on the third day according to the Scriptures, ⁵and that He appeared to Cephas [i.e. Peter], then to the twelve. ⁶Afterwards, He appeared to over five hundred brothers [and sisters] at once, of whom the greater part remain until now, but some also fell asleep [fig., have died]. ⁷Afterwards, He appeared to James, then to all the apostles.

⁸But last of all, as though to the [one] untimely born, He appeared also to me. ⁹For I am the least of the apostles, who am not worthy to be called an apostle, because I persecuted the Assembly of God. ¹⁰But by God's grace I am what I am! And His grace, the [one] towards me, did not become in emptiness [fig. was not without purpose], but I labored more than they all, yet not I, but the grace of God, the [one] with me. ¹¹So whether I or they, in this manner we preach, and in this manner you* believed.

¹²But if Christ is preached that He has been raised from [the] dead, how are some among you* saying that [there] is no resurrection of [the] dead? ¹³But if [there] is no resurrection of [the] dead, neither has Christ been raised. ¹⁴But if Christ has not been raised, in that case, our proclamation [is] empty [fig. without purpose], and your* faith also [is] empty. ¹⁵And we also are found [to be] false witnesses of God, because we testified of God that He raised up Christ, whom He did not raise if indeed [the] dead are not raised. ¹⁶For if [the] dead are not raised, neither has Christ been raised. ¹⁷But if Christ has not been raised, your* faith is futile [or, worthless]; you* are still in your* sins! ¹⁸In that case, also, the ones having fallen asleep [fig., having died] in Christ perished. ¹⁹If in this life only we have been hoping [or, have been having confident expectation] in Christ, we are of all people most pitiful.

²⁰But now Christ has been raised from [the] dead! He became the first-fruits of the ones having fallen asleep [fig., having died]. ²¹For since by means of a man death [came], also by means of a Man [is] [the] resurrection of [the] dead.

²²For just as in Adam all die, in the same way also in Christ all will be given life. ²³But each in his own order, Christ [the] first-fruit, afterwards the [ones] of Christ at His Arrival [or, Coming]. ²⁴Then the end, when He shall hand over the kingdom to God, even [the] Father, when He shall abolish every ruler and every authority and power. ²⁵For it is necessary [for] Him to be reigning until He shall put all the enemies under His feet. ²⁶[The] last enemy being abolished [is] death. ²⁷For *"He put all [things] in subjection under His feet."* [Psalm 8:6] But when He says that all [things] have been subjected, [it is] evident that [this is] except for the One subjecting all the [things] to Him. ²⁸Now when all the [things] are subjected

to Him, then the Son also Himself will be subjected to the One having subjected all the [things] to Him, so that God shall be the all in all.

²⁹Otherwise, what will they do, the ones being baptized on behalf of the dead, if [the] dead are not raised at all? Why are they also baptized on behalf of the dead? ³⁰Why also are _we_ in danger every hour? ³¹[I affirm] by my boasting [or, pride] in you* which I have in Christ Jesus our Lord, I die daily [or, every day I am in danger of death]. ³²If according to [or, If from] human [motives] I fought with wild beasts in Ephesus, what [is] the benefit to me if the dead are not raised? *"Let us eat and drink, for tomorrow we die!"* [Isaiah 22:13]

³³Stop being led astray [fig., being deceived]: "Evil associations corrupt good habits [or, morals]" [i.e. a quote from the Grecian philosopher Menander]. ³⁴Become sober rightly [fig., Come to your* senses as you* ought], and stop sinning; for some have a lack of knowledge of God. I say [this] to your* shame.

³⁵_But_ someone will say, "How are the dead raised? And with what kind of body do they come?" ³⁶Fool! What _you_ sow is not given life unless it dies. ³⁷And what you sow, you do not sow what the body is going to be, _but_ bare grain; it may be of wheat or of some of the remaining [grains]. ³⁸But God gives to it a body just as He willed, and to each of the seeds its own body.

³⁹All flesh [is] not the same flesh, _but_ [there is] one [flesh] of people, but another flesh of animals, but another of fish, but another of birds. ⁴⁰And [there are] heavenly [or, celestial] bodies, and earthly bodies, _but_ one [is] the glory of the heavenly, but another the [glory] of the earthly. ⁴¹[There is] one glory of [the] sun, and another glory of [the] moon, and another glory of [the] stars, for [one] star differs from [another] star in glory.

⁴²In the same way also [is] the resurrection of the dead. It is sown in corruption, it is raised in incorruption. ⁴³It is sown in dishonor, it raised in glory; it is sown in weakness, it is raised in power. ⁴⁴It is sown a natural body, it is raised a spiritual body; [there] is a natural body, and [there] is a spiritual body.

⁴⁵In the same way also it has been written, *"The first man Adam became a living soul."* [Gen 2:7] The last Adam [became] for a life-giving spirit. ⁴⁶_But_ the spiritual [is] not first, _but_ the natural, afterwards the spiritual. ⁴⁷The first man [is] out of the earth, earthy [or, made of dust]; the second Man [is the] Lord from heaven. ⁴⁸Of what sort [is] the earthy [one], such also [are] the earthy [ones]; of what sort [is] the heavenly [One], such also [will be] the heavenly [ones]. ⁴⁹And just as we bear the image of the earthy [one], we also shall bear the image of the heavenly [One].

⁵⁰Now this I say, brothers [and sisters], that flesh and blood is not able to inherit [the] kingdom of God, nor does the corruption [or, perishable] inherit the incorruption [or, imperishable]. ⁵¹Listen! I tell you* a secret [or, mystery]. We indeed will not all sleep [fig., die], but we will all be changed [or, be transformed], ⁵²in a moment, in a blinking of an eye, in the last trumpet. For the trumpet will sound, and the dead will be raised incorruptible [or, imperishable], and _we_ will be changed [or, transformed]! ⁵³For it is necessary [for] this corruptible to put on incorruption, and this mortal to put on immortality. ⁵⁴Now when this corruptible shall put on incorruption, and this mortal shall put on immortality, then will happen

the word, the one having been written, *"Death was swallowed up into victory."* [Isaiah 25:8] ⁵⁵ *"O Death, where [is] your sting? O realm of the dead* [Gr., *hades*], *where [is] your victory?"* [Hosea 13:14]

⁵⁶Now the sting of death [is] sin, but the power of sin [is] the Law. ⁵⁷But thanks [be] to God, the One giving us the victory through our Lord Jesus Christ! ⁵⁸So then, my beloved brothers [and sisters], continue becoming steadfast, unmovable, abounding in the work of the Lord at all times, knowing that your* labor is not empty [fig., not without results] in [the] Lord.

16 Now concerning the collection, the [one] for the holy ones, just as I gave instructions to the assemblies of Galatia, in the same way also you* must be doing. ²On every first [day] of [the] week [i.e. every Sunday], let each one of you* be putting aside [something], storing up [or, saving] whatever he shall be prospering, so that when I come, at that time, collections shall not be taking place. ³But whenever I arrive, [those] whomever you* approve by [your*] letters, these I will send to carry your* gracious gift to Jerusalem. ⁴But if it be fitting for me also to be going, they will go with me.

⁵Now I will come to you* when I pass through Macedonia, for I am passing through Macedonia. ⁶But with you*, perhaps, I will stay, or even will spend the winter, so that you* shall help me on my journey wherever I am going. ⁷For I do not want to see you* now in passing, but I hope [or, expect] to remain some time with you*, if the Lord shall be permitting. ⁸But I will remain in Ephesus until Pentecost. ⁹For a door has been opened to me [that is] great and effective, and many [are] in opposition [or, are hostile].

¹⁰Now if Timothy comes, be seeing that he becomes without fear with you*, for he works [or, performs] the work of [the] Lord, even as I. ¹¹Therefore, let no one despise [or, look down on] him, but help him journey in peace, so that he shall come to me, for I am expecting him with the brothers.

¹²Now concerning Apollos our brother, I encouraged him greatly that he should come to you* with the brothers. And it was not at all [his] will that he should come now, but he himself will come when he finds the time [or, the opportunity].

¹³Keep watching! Be standing firm in the faith. Be acting like a man [fig., Be brave]. Continue becoming strengthened. ¹⁴Let all your* [deeds] be taking place in love.

¹⁵Now I urge you*, brothers [and sisters] (you* know the household of Stephanas, that it is [the] first-fruit of Achaia, and they appointed [or, devoted] themselves to the ministry to the holy ones), ¹⁶so that you* also shall be subjecting yourselves to such [people] and to everyone working together and laboring. ¹⁷Now I rejoice over the arrival of Stephanas and Fortunatus and Achaicus, because these filled up [fig., supplied] the [thing] lacking [on] your* [part] [or, [in] your* absence]. ¹⁸For they refreshed my spirit and yours*. Therefore, be acknowledging [or, be giving recognition to] such [people].

¹⁹The assemblies of Asia greet you*; Aquila and Priscilla greet you* much [fig., warmly] in [the] Lord, with the assembly in their house. ²⁰All the brothers [and sisters] greet you*. Greet one another with a holy kiss.

²¹The greeting of [me] Paul with my hand. ²²If anyone does not affectionately love the Lord Jesus Christ, let him be accursed [Gr., *anathema*]! The Lord has come [or, O Lord come – Gr., *maranatha*]! ²³The grace of the Lord Jesus Christ [be] with you*. ²⁴My love [is] with you* all in Christ Jesus. So be it!

The Second Epistle of Paul the Apostle to the
Corinthians

1 Paul, an apostle of Jesus Christ by [the] will of God, and Timothy the brother, to the assembly [or, church] of God, the one being in Corinth, with all the holy ones [or, saints, and throughout epistle], the ones being in all Achaia: ²Grace to you* and peace from God our Father and [the] Lord Jesus Christ!

³Blessed [be] the God and Father of our Lord Jesus Christ, the Father of compassions and God of all comfort, ⁴the One comforting us in all our affliction, for our being able to be comforting the ones in every affliction by means of the comfort with which we are comforted ourselves by God. ⁵Because just as the sufferings of Christ abound to us, in the same manner our comfort also abounds through Christ.

⁶Now if we experience hardship [or, are afflicted], [it is] for the sake of your* comfort and salvation, the one being effective in [the] patient endurance of the same sufferings which we also are suffering; and our hope [or, confident expectation] [is] steadfast concerning you*. If we are comforted, [it is] for the sake of your* comfort and salvation, ⁷knowing that even as you* are sharers of the sufferings, in the same manner also [you* will share] of the comfort.

⁸For we do not want you* to continue being unaware, brothers [and sisters], concerning our affliction, the one having happened to us in Asia, that to an extraordinary degree we were burdened beyond [our] strength, with the result that we despaired even of life. ⁹But we ourselves have had in ourselves the sentence of death, so that we shall not be relying on ourselves, but on God, the One raising the dead, ¹⁰who delivered us from so great a death and is delivering [us], in whom we have hoped [or, have confidently expected] that even yet He will deliver; ¹¹you* also joining in helping on our behalf by your* petition, so that thanks is given by many persons on our behalf [for] the gracious gift [given] to you*, through [the prayers of] many.

¹²For our boasting is this: the testimony of our conscience, that in sincerity and integrity of God, not in fleshly wisdom, but in grace of God, we conducted ourselves in the world, but especially toward you*. ¹³For we do not write other [things] to you*, but [things] which you* either read [in public worship] or also acknowledge [or, understand], and I hope [or, confidently expect] that also until [the] end you* will acknowledge [these things], ¹⁴just as also you* acknowledged us in part, that we are your* [grounds for] boasting, even as also you* [are] ours, in the day of the Lord Jesus.

¹⁵And in this confidence I was intending to come to you* before, so that you* would be having a second grace [or, benefit], ¹⁶and to pass by way of you* to Macedonia, and again from Macedonia to come to you*, and to be helped by you* on my journey to Judea. ¹⁷Therefore, deciding this, I did not use the lightness [fig., do it lightly], did I? Or [the things] which I decided, do I decide according to [the] flesh, so that there shall be with me the Yes, yes, and the No, no? ¹⁸But God [is]

faithful, that our word to you* became not Yes and No. ¹⁹For the Son of God, Jesus Christ, the One having been preached among you* by us—by me and Silvanus and Timothy—did not become Yes and No, <u>but</u> in Him it has become Yes. ²⁰For as many promises as [are] of God, in Him [are] the Yes, and in Him the Amen, for glory to God through us. ²¹Now the One inwardly strengthening you* with us into Christ and having anointed us [is] God, ²²the One also having sealed us and having given the down payment [or, guarantee] of the Spirit in our hearts.

²³Now <u>I</u> call on God [for] a witness to my soul, that sparing you* [or, in order to spare you*], I came no more to Corinth. ²⁴Not that we exercise lordship over your* faith, <u>but</u> we are co-workers with your* joy, for you* have stood firm by faith.

2But I determined this within myself, not to come again in sorrow to you*. ²For if <u>I</u> make you* sorrowful, then who is the one cheering me up, except the one being made sorrowful by me? ³And I wrote to you* this same [thing], lest having come, I shall be having sorrow from [those] of whom it was necessary [for] me to be having joy, having confidence in you* all, that my joy is [the joy] of you* all. ⁴For out of much affliction and distress of heart I wrote to you* through many tears, not so that you* would be made sorrowful, <u>but</u> so that you* would know the love which I have especially toward you*.

⁵Now if anyone has caused sorrow, he has not caused sorrow to me, <u>but</u> in part, that I would not be burdening you* all. ⁶Sufficient to such a one [is] this punishment, the [one punished] by the majority, ⁷so that on the contrary, you* [ought] rather to forgive and to comfort, lest such a one be swallowed up by the excessive sorrow. ⁸For this reason, I call on [or, plead with] you* to confirm [your*] love to him. ⁹Because, for this [reason] also I wrote, so that I shall know your* character, whether you* are obedient in all [things]. ¹⁰And to whom you* forgive anything, I also [forgive]. For I also, if I have forgiven anything, to whom I have forgiven [it], for your* sakes, in [the] face [fig., presence] of Christ, [I forgave it], ¹¹so that we shall not be taken advantage of by Satan, for we are not unaware of his schemes.

¹²And having come to Troas for the Gospel [or, Good News, and throughout book] of Christ, and a door having been opened to me in [the] Lord, ¹³I have not had rest in my spirit, [because] I did not find Titus my brother, <u>but</u> having said good-bye to them, I departed for Macedonia.

¹⁴Now thanks [be] to God, the [One] leading us at all times in triumph in Christ and revealing through us the fragrance of His knowledge in every place, ¹⁵for we are a sweet fragrance of Christ to God among the ones being saved and among the ones perishing; ¹⁶to some a fragrance of death to death, but to others, a fragrance of life to life. And who is sufficient [or, adequate] for these [things]? ¹⁷For we are not as the rest, adulterating the word of God for financial gain, <u>but</u> as out of integrity, <u>but</u> as from God, we speak in the presence of God, in Christ.

3Are we beginning again to be commending ourselves?—unless we need, as some [do], letters of recommendation to you*, or [letters] of recommendation from you*. ²You* are our letter, having been written in our hearts, being known and being read by all people; ³being made known that you* are [the] letter of Christ having been ministered [or, cared for] by us, having been written not with ink, <u>but</u> with [the] Spirit of [the] living God, not in tablets [made of] stone, <u>but</u> in fleshy tablets of hearts.

⁴And such confidence [or, trust] we have by means of Christ toward God. ⁵Not that we are sufficient in ourselves to consider anything as [coming] from ourselves, <u>but</u> our sufficiency [is] from God, ⁶who also made us sufficient [or, capable] [to be] servants of a new covenant, not of letter <u>but</u> of spirit; for the letter kills, but the spirit makes alive [or, gives life].

⁷Now if the ministry of death, having been engraved in letters in stones, came in glory, with the result that the sons [and daughters] of Israel were not able to look intently upon the face of Moses because of the glory of his face, the [glory which was] passing away, ⁸how will the ministry of the Spirit not be more in glory [or, be more glorious]? ⁹For if the ministry of condemnation [had] glory, by much more the ministry of righteousness abounds [or, excels] in glory. ¹⁰For even the [thing] having been glorified has not been glorified, in this respect, because of the surpassing glory [fig., the glory which is superior to it]. ¹¹For if the [thing] passing away [was] with glory, by much more the [thing] remaining [is] in glory [or, [is] glorious].

¹²Having therefore such a hope [or, confident expectation], we use great boldness in [our] speech, ¹³and [are] not like Moses, [who] was putting a veil on his own face, so that the sons [and daughters] of Israel [could] not look intently at the end of the [glory which was] passing away. ¹⁴But their minds were hardened [fig., were made stubborn], for until this day the same veil remains not having been unveiled [fig., remains unlifted] during the reading aloud of the Old Covenant, which in Christ passes away [fig., is removed]. ¹⁵<u>But</u> until today, when Moses is read aloud [in their synagogue], a veil lies on their heart. ¹⁶But whenever [a person] turns to [the] Lord, the veil is taken away. ¹⁷Now the Lord is the Spirit; and where the Spirit of [the] Lord [is], there [is] liberty. ¹⁸But <u>we</u> all, with a face having been unveiled, ourselves beholding as in a mirror [fig., contemplating] the glory of [the] Lord, are being transformed to the same image, from glory to glory, just as by [the] Spirit of [the] Lord.

4 For this reason, having this ministry, just as we received mercy, we do not become discouraged. ²<u>But</u> we ourselves renounced the hidden things of shame, not walking about [fig., conducting ourselves] in craftiness, nor distorting the word of God, <u>but</u> we commend ourselves by the disclosure of the truth to every conscience of people, before God. ³But even if our Gospel has been hidden, it has been hidden among the ones perishing, ⁴among whom the god of this age blinded the minds of the unbelieving, in order for the illumination of the Gospel of the glory of Christ not to shine on them, who is the image of God. ⁵For we do not preach ourselves, <u>but</u> Christ Jesus [as] Lord, and ourselves your* slaves for the sake of Jesus. ⁶Because God [is] the One having said [for] light to shine out of

darkness, who shined in our hearts to [give] the illumination of the knowledge of the glory of God in [the] face of Jesus Christ. [see Gen 1:2-4]

⁷But we have this treasure in clay vessels [fig., fragile containers], so that the excellency [or, extraordinary quality] of the power should be of God and not from us; ⁸in every[thing] experiencing hardship [or, being afflicted], <u>but</u> not being crushed [fig., overwhelmed with difficulties]; being perplexed, <u>but</u> not experiencing despair; ⁹being persecuted, but not being abandoned; cast down, but not being destroyed; ¹⁰at all times carrying about in the body the putting to death of the Lord Jesus, so that also the life of Jesus would be revealed in our body. ¹¹For always <u>we</u>, the ones living, are being handed over to death for the sake of Jesus, so that also the life of Jesus would be revealed in our mortal flesh. ¹²So then, death indeed is working in us, but life in you*.

¹³But having the same spirit of faith, according to the [word] having been written, *"I believed, therefore, I spoke"* [Psalm 116:10]—<u>we</u> also believe, and so we speak, ¹⁴knowing that the One having raised up the Lord Jesus will also raise us up by means of Jesus and will present [us] with you*. ¹⁵For all the [things are] for your* sakes, so that grace having increased [or, having spread] through the many should cause thanksgiving to abound to the glory of God.

¹⁶For this reason, we do not become discouraged, <u>but</u> even if our outward person [fig., body] is decaying, yet the inward [person] is being renewed day by day. ¹⁷For the momentary light matter of our affliction [fig., our insignificant affliction] is producing for us an eternal weight of glory more and more [fig., far beyond all comparison]! ¹⁸We are not looking at the [things] being seen, <u>but</u> to the [things] not being seen; for the [things] being seen [are] temporary, but the [things] not being seen [are] eternal.

5 For we know that if our earthly house of this tent is [fig., our bodies are] torn down, we have a building from God, a house not made with human hands, eternal in the heavens. ²For also in this [body] we groan, longing to clothe ourselves with our habitation, the one from heaven. ³If indeed also having clothed ourselves, we will not be found naked. ⁴For the ones being in the tent [fig., who are alive] groan, being burdened, seeing we do not desire to strip ourselves <u>but</u> to clothe ourselves, so that the mortal [body] shall be swallowed up by life. ⁵Now the One having prepared us for this same [thing is] God, the One having given to us the down payment [or, guarantee] of the Spirit.

⁶Therefore, being confident at all times and knowing that being at home in the body we are away from the Lord—⁷for by faith we walk about [fig., conduct ourselves], not by sight—⁸but we are confident and prefer rather to be away from the body and to be at home with the Lord! ⁹And so we ambitiously strive, whether being at home or being away from home, to be acceptable [or, pleasing] to Him. ¹⁰For it is necessary [for] all of us to appear before the judgment seat of Christ, so that each one shall receive the things [done] through the body, according to the [things] which he did, whether good or wicked.

¹¹Knowing, therefore, the fear of the Lord, we persuade people, but we have been revealed to God. And I hope [or, confidently expect] to also have been

revealed in your* consciences. [12]For we are not commending ourselves again to you, but we are giving an opportunity to you* of boasting on our behalf, so that you* shall have [an answer] for the ones boasting in appearance and not in heart. [13]For if we were out of [our] senses, [it was] for God; if we are of sound mind, [it is] for you*. [14]For the love of Christ compels us, having judged [or, concluded] this: that since One died on behalf of all, consequently, these all died. [15]And He died on behalf of all, so that the ones living should no longer be living to themselves, but to the One having died and having been raised on behalf of them.

[16]Therefore, from now on we know no one according to [the] flesh; and even if we have known Christ according to [the] flesh, but now no longer do we know [Him thus]. [17]Therefore, if anyone [is] in Christ, [he is] a new creation; the old [things] passed away, look!, all [things] have become new. [18]And all these [things are] of God, the One having reconciled us to Himself through Jesus Christ and having given to us the ministry of that reconciliation, [19]how that God was in Christ reconciling [the] world to Himself, not imputing their transgressions to them and having put in [or, having committed to] us the word of that reconciliation.

[20]Therefore, we serve as ambassadors on behalf of Christ, as though God [were] appealing through us: we implore [you*] on behalf of Christ, be reconciled to God! [21]For the One not having known sin, He made sin on our behalf, so that we shall become [the] righteousness of God in Him.

6Now working together [with Him] we also call on [or, plead with] [you* that] you* do not receive the grace of God in emptiness [fig., without results]—[2]for He says, *"In an acceptable time I heard you, and in a day of salvation I helped you."* [Isaiah 49:8]

Listen! Now [is the] acceptable time. Listen! Now [is the] day of salvation— [3]in nothing giving any cause of offence, so that the ministry shall not be blamed [or, discredited], [4]but in every[thing] commending ourselves as God's servants, in much patient endurance, in afflictions, in hardships, in distresses, [5]in beatings, in imprisonments, in riots, in labors, in sleepless nights, in [days] without food, [6]in purity, in knowledge, in patience, in kindness, in [the] Holy Spirit, in sincere love, [7]in [the] word of truth, in [the] power of God, through the weapons of righteousness, on the right and on the left; [8]through glory and dishonor, through evil report [or, slander] and good report [or, good reputation], [regarded] as deceivers and [yet] true; [9]as being unknown and [yet] as being well-known, as dying and [yet], look!, we live, as being chastened and [yet] not being put to death; [10]as being sorrowful but always rejoicing, as poor but making many rich, as having nothing and [yet] possessing all [things].

[11]Our mouth has opened [fig., We have spoken freely] to you*, O Corinthians, our heart has been opened wide [fig., we have great affection for you*]. [12]You* are not restricted by us, but you* are restricted by your* [own] bowels [fig., affections]. [13]Now [in] the same exchange [fig., in return for the same] (as to children I say [it]), you* also be opened wide [fig., have the same affections for us].

[14]Stop being unequally yoked [fig., mismatched] with unbelievers; for what partnership [is there] for righteousness and lawlessness? And what fellowship [is

there] for light with darkness? ¹⁵And what agreement [or common ground] [is there for] Christ with Belial [i.e., the devil]? Or what part [is there for] a believer with an unbeliever [fig., what do a believer and an unbeliever have in common]? ¹⁶And what harmony [is there for the] temple of God with idols?

For you* are a temple of the living God, just as God said, *"I will dwell in them and will walk about* [fig., *live] among [them], and I will be their God, and they will be a people to Me [or, My people]."* [Lev 26:12; Jer 32:38; Ezek 37:27] ¹⁷For this reason, *"Come out from [the] midst of them and be separated,"* says [the] Lord. *"And stop touching [any] unclean* [or, *defiling] [thing*; or, *person],"* and I will receive you*. [Isaiah 52:11; Ezek 20:34,41] ¹⁸*"And I will be to you* for a Father, and you* will be to Me for sons and daughters, says [the] L*ORD* Almighty."* [2Sam 7:14; Isaiah 43:6; Jer 31:9]

7 Therefore, having these promises, beloved, let us cleanse [or, purge] ourselves from every pollution [or, defilement] of flesh and of spirit, perfecting holiness in [the] fear of God.

²Make room for us [in your* hearts]. We wronged no one [or, we treated no one unjustly]; we corrupted no one; we took advantage of no one. ³I do not speak for [your*] condemnation [or, to condemn [you*]], for I have said before that you* are in our hearts for [us] to die together and to live together. ⁴Great [is] my boldness [or, confidence] towards you*; great [is] my boasting on your* behalf. I have been filled with comfort; I overflow with joy in all our afflictions.

⁵For even when we came to Macedonia our flesh had no rest at all, but in every[thing] we [were] experiencing hardship [or, being afflicted]—outside [were] fights [fig., angry arguments], within [were] fears. ⁶But God, the One comforting the downcast [or, the ones of humble circumstances], comforted us by the arrival of Titus; ⁷but not only in his arrival, but also by the encouragement with which he was comforted over you*, reporting to us your* longing desire, your* mourning, your* zeal on behalf of me, with the result that I rejoiced [even] more.

⁸Because even if I caused you* sorrow by my letter, I do not regret [it], even if I did regret [it]. For I see that the letter, even if for an hour [or, for a while], caused you* sorrow. ⁹I now rejoice, not because you* were caused sorrow, but because you* were caused sorrow to repentance; for you* were caused sorrow toward God, so that in nothing you* would suffer loss from us. ¹⁰For the sorrow according to God [fig., godly sorrow] produces repentance to salvation, free from regret, but the sorrow of the world produces death.

¹¹For this very thing, your* being caused to sorrow according to God [fig., in a godly manner], look how much diligence it produced in you*! [And not only this], but [also] defense [fig., an eagerness to defend yourselves], but [also] indignation, but [also] fear, but [also] longing desire, but [also] zeal, but [also] avenging [of wrong]! In every[thing] you* demonstrated yourselves to be pure in this matter. ¹²So even if I wrote to you*, [it was] not for the sake of the one having done wrong nor for the sake of the one having been wronged, but for the sake of your* diligence on our behalf to be revealed to you* before God. ¹³For this reason we have been comforted.

So in your* comfort we rejoiced all the more over the joy of Titus, that his spirit had been refreshed by you* all. ¹⁴Because if I have boasted anything to him concerning you*, I was not put to shame, <u>but</u> we spoke as all things to you* in truth, so also our boasting before Titus became truth. ¹⁵And his bowels [fig., affections] are especially [or, all the more] toward you*, remembering the obedience of you* all, how with fear and trembling you* received him. ¹⁶I rejoice that in every[thing] I am confident in [or, about] you*.

8Now we make known to you*, brothers [and sisters], the grace of God, the one having been given in the assemblies [or, churches, and throughout epistle] of Macedonia: ²that in a great trial of affliction, the abundance of their joy and their extremely deep poverty overflowed to the riches of their generosity. ³Because I testify [that] according to [their] ability and above [their] ability [they gave] of their own accord, ⁴imploring us with much urging [for] the grace and the fellowship of the ministry [which is] to the holy ones—⁵and not just as we hoped [or, expected], <u>but</u> they themselves gave first to the Lord and to us through [the] will of God, ⁶so that we urged Titus, that just as he began previously, so also he should finish to you* also this grace.

⁷<u>But</u> even as you* abound in every[thing]—in faith and in word and in knowledge and in all diligence and in your* love for us—[see] that also in this grace you* are abounding. ⁸I do not speak [this] as a command, <u>but</u> by means of the diligence of others, I am also proving the genuineness of your* love. ⁹For you* know the grace of our Lord Jesus Christ, that being rich, for your* sake, He became poor, so that <u>you*</u> by that poverty should become rich.

¹⁰And I give [my] opinion in this [matter]: for this is advantageous for you*, who began previously a year ago not only to do [this], <u>but</u> also to be desiring [to do it]. ¹¹And now also finish to do [it], in order that even as [there was] the eagerness to be desiring [it], so also [have] the [desire] to finish [it], from [the ability which you*] are having. ¹²For if the eagerness is present, according as anyone shall be having, [it is] acceptable, not according as he does not have.

¹³For [this is] not so that others [have] relief, but for you* affliction, ¹⁴<u>but</u> by [way of] equality; at the present time your* abundance for their lack, so that also their abundance shall be for your* lack, in order that there shall be equality; ¹⁵just as it has been written, *"The [one who gathered] much did not have too much; and the [one who gathered] little had no lack."* [Exod 16:18]

¹⁶Now thanks [be] to God, the One giving the same diligence [or, earnest care] concerning you* in the heart of Titus. ¹⁷Because indeed he accepted my appeal, but being more diligent, he went forth to you* of [his] own accord. ¹⁸And we sent along with him the brother, whose praise in [things of] the Gospel [is] [spread] through all the assemblies; ¹⁹and not only [this], <u>but</u> also having been elected by a raising of hands [fig., having been appointed by a vote] by the assemblies [as] our fellow-traveler with this grace [or, gift], the one being ministered [or, administered] by us, to the glory of the Lord Himself and [to show] our eagerness; ²⁰trying to guard against this, lest anyone finds fault with us in this generous gift,

the one being ministered [or, administered] by us; [21]providing [or, having regard] [for] honorable [things], not only before [the] Lord, but also before people.

[22]And we sent along with them our brother, whom we often proved [as] being eager in many [things], but now [being] much more diligent by his great confidence [or, trust], the [one] toward you*. [23]If [anyone inquires] about Titus, [he is] my partner and co-worker towards you*; or if [anyone inquires about] our brothers, [they are] apostles [or, messengers] of [the] assemblies, a glory to Christ. [24]Therefore, show to them proof of your* love and of our boasting on your* behalf in [the] face [fig., presence] of the assemblies.

*9*For indeed concerning the ministry, the [one] to the holy ones, it is unnecessary for me to write to you*. [2]For I know your* eagerness, which I boast concerning you* to [the] Macedonians, that Achaia has been prepared since last year, and the zeal from you* [or, your* zeal] stirred up the majority. [3]But I sent the brothers, so that our boasting about you* is not made empty in this matter, so that, just as I said, you* shall have been prepared; [4]lest perhaps [some] Macedonians come with me and find you* unprepared, we should be put to shame (that we say not you* [fig., not to mention you*]) in this confidence of boasting. [5]Therefore, I considered [it] necessary to urge the brothers, so that they should go before to you* and prepare in advance your* blessing having been previously announced, that this [would] be ready, thus as a blessing [or, bountiful gift] and not as grudgingly given.

[6]Now [I say] this: the one sowing sparingly, will also reap sparingly; and the one sowing in blessings [fig., bountifully], will also reap in blessings [fig., bountifully]. [7][Let] each one [give] just as he decides in his heart, not from sorrow [fig., reluctantly] or from necessity [fig., under compulsion], for God loves a cheerful giver. [8]And God [is] able to cause all grace to abound to you*, so that in every[thing] always having all sufficiency, you* shall abound to every good work, [9]just as it has been written, *"He scattered abroad* [fig., *gave generously]; He gave to the poor. His righteousness endures into the age* [fig., *forever]."* [Psalm 112:9]

[10]Now the One supplying seed to the sower and bread for food, may He supply and multiply your* seed and increase the fruits of your* righteousness; [11]in every[thing] being enriched to all generosity, which is producing through us thanksgiving to God. [12]Because the ministry [or, administration] of this sacred service not only is supplying the needs of the holy ones but is also overflowing through many thanksgivings to God, [13][while] through the proof of this ministry they are glorifying God for the obedience of your* confession to the Gospel of Christ and [for the] generosity of the fellowship to them and to all, [14]and their petition [to God] on your* behalf, longing for you* because of the surpassing grace of God upon you*. [15]And thanks [be] to God for His indescribable gift!

*10*Now I, Paul, myself plead with you* by the gentleness and kindness of Christ; [I] who according to face [fig., in presence] indeed [am] humble [or, servile] among you*, but being absent, act boldly toward you*. [2]Now I implore [you*], that when I am present I [need] not to act boldly with the confidence with which I am considering [or, planning] to be bold against some, the ones considering us as walking about [fig., conducting ourselves] according to [the] flesh. ³For [though] walking about [fig., conducting ourselves] in [the] flesh, we do not wage war [fig., struggle against evil forces] according to [the] flesh.

⁴For the weapons of our warfare [are] not fleshly <u>but</u> powerful in God for [the] tearing down of strongholds [or, fortresses], ⁵tearing down misleading arguments and every high place [fig., arrogance] lifting itself up against the knowledge of God, and bringing every thought into captivity to the obedience of Christ, ⁶and being in readiness to punish every disobedience, whenever your* obedience is completed.

⁷You* are looking at [things] according to [their outward] face [fig., appearance]. If anyone has persuaded himself [that he] is Christ's, let him again consider this in himself, that just as he [is] Christ's, so also we [are] Christ's. ⁸For even if also I boast something further concerning our authority, which the Lord gave to us for edification and not for tearing you* down, I will not be ashamed, ⁹so that I shall not seem as if I would terrify you* through my letters. ¹⁰Because "His letters indeed," he says, "[are] weighty and strong, but his bodily presence weak, and his speech having been despised [fig., amounts to nothing]." ¹¹Let such [a person] consider this: that such as we are in word, by letters, being absent, such also, being present, [we are] in deed.

¹²For we do not dare to classify or to compare ourselves with any of the ones commending themselves; <u>but</u> they, measuring themselves by themselves and comparing themselves with themselves, do not understand. ¹³But <u>we</u> will not at all boast in the immeasurable [things] [fig., excessively], <u>but</u> after the measure of the sphere [of influence] which the God of measure appointed to us to reach even as far as you*.

¹⁴For we are not overextending ourselves, as if not reaching to you*, for even as far as you* we came with the Gospel of Christ; ¹⁵not boasting in the immeasurable [things] [fig., excessively] in other people's labors, but having hope [or, confident expectation], [that as] your* faith increases, to be enlarged to abundance [or, greatly] by you*, according to our sphere [of influence], ¹⁶to proclaim the Gospel in the [regions] beyond you*, [and] not to boast in regard to the [things] prepared [fig., the work already done] in another's sphere [of influence]. ¹⁷But *"the one boasting, let him boast in [the] LORD."* [Jer 9:24] ¹⁸For the one commending himself is not approved, <u>but</u> [the one] whom the Lord commends.

11O that you* would put up with me [in] a little of my foolishness [or, boastful folly]! <u>But</u> indeed you* are putting up with me. ²For I am jealous [or, zealous] for you* with [the] jealousy [or, zeal] of God, for I betrothed you* [or, promised you* as a bride] to one husband, to present [you* as] a pure virgin to Christ. ³But I am afraid, lest perhaps, as the serpent deceived Eve in his craftiness, so your* minds shall be corrupted from the sincerity [or, single-hearted devotion], the [one] in [or, to] Christ.

⁴For if indeed the one coming [to you*] preaches another Jesus whom we did not preach, or you* receive a different Spirit [or, spirit] which you* did not

receive, or a different gospel which you* did not accept, you* may well [or, would readily] put up [with it]! ⁵For I consider [myself] to have fallen short in nothing [compared] to those "super-apostles." ⁶But even if [I am] unskilled in word [or, speech], yet not in knowledge, but in every [way] we have been made known to you* in all [things].

⁷Or did I commit sin [by] humbling myself so that you* should be exalted, because I freely proclaimed the Gospel of God to you*? ⁸I robbed other assemblies, having taken wages [from them] for your* ministry. ⁹And being present with you* and having been in need, I was not a [financial] burden to anyone, for the brothers supplied my need, having come from Macedonia. And in everything I kept myself from being a burden to you*, and I will keep [myself]. ¹⁰[The] truth of Christ is in me, because this boasting in regard to me will not be stopped in the regions of Achaia. ¹¹Why? Because I do not love you*? God knows! ¹²But what I am doing, I also will do, so that I shall cut off the opportunity of the ones desiring an opportunity, so that in what they boast they shall be found just as we also [are].

¹³For such [ones are] false apostles, deceitful laborers, transforming themselves into [or, disguising themselves as] apostles of Christ. ¹⁴And no wonder! For even Satan transforms himself into [or, disguises himself as] an angel of light. ¹⁵Therefore, [it is] not a great thing if also his servants are transformed [or, disguised] as servants of righteousness, whose end will be according to their works.

¹⁶Again I say, let no one consider me to be a fool; but if [you* do], at least receive me as a fool, so that I also shall boast a little something [fig., in a small way]. ¹⁷What I speak, I speak not according to [the] Lord, but as in foolishness, in this confidence of boasting. ¹⁸Since many boast according to the flesh, I also will boast. ¹⁹For gladly you*, being [so] wise, put up with the fools. ²⁰For you* put up with [it] if someone enslaves [fig., takes advantage of] you*, if someone devours [you*], if someone takes away [from you*], if someone exalts himself, if someone repeatedly slaps you* in the face [fig., insults you*]. ²¹According to shame I speak, how that we were [too] weak [for that]!

But in whatever anyone is bold, in foolishness I say [it], I also am bold. ²²Hebrews [fig., Jewish by heritage] are they? I also! Israelites are they? I also! Seed of Abraham are they? I also! ²³Servants of Christ are they? (As out of my mind I speak), I even more [so]: in labors far more, in beatings many more times, in prisons more frequently, in deaths frequently [or, frequently [in danger of] death]. ²⁴Five times I received forty [lashes] less one from Jews. ²⁵Three times I was beaten with rods, once was I stoned, three times I was shipwrecked, I have spent a night and a day in the deep; ²⁶frequently on journeys, in dangers of rivers, dangers of robbers, dangers from [my] race, dangers from Gentiles, dangers in a city, dangers in a desolate place [or, uninhabited region], dangers in sea, dangers among false brothers [and sisters] [fig., ones only pretending to be believers]; ²⁷in labor and toil, frequently in sleepless nights, in hunger and thirst, frequently without food, in cold and nakedness [or, without sufficient clothing]. ²⁸Apart from these external [things], the burden on me daily: my anxiety for all the assemblies.

²⁹Who is weak, and I am not weak? Who is caused to stumble [fig., to sin], and I do not burn [with anger]?

³⁰If it is necessary to boast, I will boast about the [things] of my weakness. ³¹The God and Father of the Lord Jesus Christ, the One being blessed into the ages [fig. forever], knows that I am not lying! ³²In Damascus the official of Aretas the king was guarding the city of the Damascenes, desiring to arrest me, ³³and I was let down in a basket through a window in the wall and escaped out of his hands. [see Acts 9:25]

12To be boasting surely is not profitable for me, for I will come to visions and revelations of [the] Lord. ²I know a man in Christ, fourteen years ago—whether in body I do not know, or outside the body I do not know, God knows—such a one being carried off to [the] third heaven. ³And I know such a man—whether in body or outside the body, I do not know, God knows—⁴that he was carried off into Paradise and heard inexpressible [or, sacred] words, which it is not permissible for a person to speak. ⁵Concerning such a one I will boast, but concerning myself I will not boast, except in my weaknesses. ⁶For if I desire to boast, I will not be a fool, for truth I will speak; but I refrain [from this], lest anyone considers me above what he sees me [to be] or hears something from me.

⁷And so that I should not be puffed up with pride by the exceeding greatness of the revelations, a thorn in the flesh was given to me, a messenger [or, angel] of Satan, so that it should be beating me with its fists [fig., treating me harshly], so that I should not be puffed up with pride. ⁸Concerning this, three times I pleaded with the Lord that it depart from me. ⁹And He said to me, "My grace is sufficient for you, for My power is perfected in weakness." Therefore, gladly I will rather boast in my weakness, so that the power of Christ should rest upon me. ¹⁰For this reason, I delight in weaknesses, in insults, in troubles, in persecutions, in distresses on behalf of Christ; for whenever I am weak, then I am strong.

¹¹I have become a fool by boasting; you* compelled me! For I ought to be commended by you*. For in nothing did I fall short of those "super-apostles"— even if I am nothing. ¹²Indeed the signs of the apostle were performed among you* with all perseverance, in signs and wonders and miraculous works. ¹³For what is [there in] which you* were inferior to the rest [of the] assemblies, except that I myself was not a [financial] burden to you*? Forgive me this injustice!

¹⁴Listen! A third time I am ready to come to you*, and I will not be your* [financial] burden. For I do not seek the [things] of you*, but you*! For the children ought not to store up [or, save] for the parents, but the parents for the children. ¹⁵And I gladly will spend and be entirely spent for the sake of your* souls, even if, loving you* more so, less I am loved. ¹⁶But be [that as it may], I did not burden you, but being crafty, I took you* with deceit! ¹⁷[By] anyone whom I have sent to you*, I did not take advantage of you* through him, did I? ¹⁸I urged Titus, and I sent the brother with [him]. Titus did not take advantage of you*, did he? We walked about [fig., conducted ourselves] in the same Spirit, did we not? [We walked] in the same footsteps, did we not?

¹⁹Again, do you* think that we are defending ourselves to you*? Before God in Christ we are speaking. But [we do] all the things, beloved, for the sake of your* up-building [or, edification]. ²⁰For I am afraid lest, having come, I find you* not such as I desire; and I am found by you* such as you* do not desire, lest perhaps [there be] quarrels, jealousies, angry outbursts, rivalries, slanders, gossipings, conceits, rebellions [or, disorders]; ²¹lest again having come, my God will humble me in regard to you*, and I will mourn [for] many of the ones having sinned previously and not having repented concerning the impurity [or, immorality] and sexual sin and flagrant sexual immorality which they practiced.

13This [will be the] third time I am coming to you*. *"By [the] mouth of two or three witnesses every word will be established."* [Deut 19:15] ²I have previously said as being present [or, when I was present] the second time, and also now being absent I say [it] in advance [or, forewarn], I write to the ones having sinned previously and to all the rest, that if I come again I will not spare [you*], ³since you* are seeking proof of Christ speaking in me, who is not weak toward you*, but is strong in you*. ⁴For even since [or, For although] He was crucified out of weakness, yet He lives by [the] power of God. For we also are weak in Him, yet we will live with Him by [the] power of God toward you*.

⁵Be testing yourselves, if you* are in the faith; be examining yourselves. You* yourselves know that Jesus Christ is in you*, do you* not?—unless you* fail to meet the test. ⁶But I hope [or, confidently expect] that you* will know that we do not fail to meet the test. ⁷Now I pray before God that you* do not do any evil, not so that we should appear approved, but so that you* should do the good [thing], but [or, though] we shall [seem] as failing to meet the test. ⁸For we are not able [to do] anything against the truth, but for the sake of the truth. ⁹For we rejoice when we are weak, but you* are strong. And this also we pray for: your* maturity! ¹⁰For this reason these things, being absent, I write, so that being present, I shall not deal sharply [with you*], according to the authority which the Lord gave to me for building up [or, edifying] and not for tearing down.

¹¹Finally, brothers [and sisters], be rejoicing [or, farewell]! Be striving for perfection. Continue being comforted. Be thinking the same [thing] [fig., be in agreement]. Be living at peace, and the God of love and peace will be with you*.

¹²Greet one another with a holy kiss. ¹³All the holy ones greet you*.

¹⁴The grace of the Lord Jesus Christ and the love of God and the fellowship of the Holy Spirit [be] with you* all! So be it!

The Epistle of Paul the Apostle to the
Galatians

*1*Paul, an apostle (not from people [or, human [authority]] nor by a person, <u>but</u> by Jesus Christ, and God [the] Father, the One having raised Him from [the] dead) ²and all the brothers [and sisters] with me, to the assemblies [or, churches] of Galatia: ³Grace to you* and peace from God [the] Father and our Lord Jesus Christ, ⁴the One having given Himself for our sins, in order that He should deliver us out of the present evil age, according to the will of our God and Father, ⁵to whom [be] the glory into the ages of the ages [fig., forever and ever]! So be it!

⁶I marvel [or, am amazed] that you* are so quickly turning away [or, apostatizing] from the One having called you* in [or, by] the grace of Christ to a different gospel, ⁷which is not another [Gospel], except there are some, the ones having disturbed you* and desiring to distort the Gospel [or, Good News, and throughout book] of Christ.

⁸<u>But</u> even if we or an angel out of heaven shall himself be proclaiming a gospel to you* besides [or, contrary to] what we proclaimed to you*, let him be accursed [Gr., *anathema*]! ⁹As we have forewarned and now say again, if anyone shall be proclaiming a gospel to you* besides [or, contrary to] what you* received, let him be accursed! ¹⁰For am I now persuading [or, seeking the approval of] people or God? Or am I seeking to be pleasing people? For if I am still trying to please people, I would not be Christ's slave.

¹¹But I make known to you*, brothers [and sisters], the Gospel, the one having been proclaimed by me, that it is not according to humanity [or, human [standards]]. ¹²For neither did I receive it from humanity [or, human [origins]], nor was I taught [it], <u>but</u> [I received it] through a revelation of Jesus Christ.

¹³For you* heard of my former conduct in Judaism, that I was excessively persecuting the Assembly [or, Church] of God and trying to destroy it. ¹⁴And I was advancing in Judaism above many contemporaries [or, beyond many of my own age] among my race, being far more a zealot for the handed down teachings [or, traditions] of my forefathers. ¹⁵But when God, the One having separated [or, appointed] me from [the] womb of my mother and having called [me] by His grace, was well pleased ¹⁶to reveal His Son in me, so that I should be proclaiming the Gospel [of] Him among the nations, I did not immediately confer with [or, ask advice from] flesh and blood [fig., any human being]; ¹⁷nor did I go up to Jerusalem to the [ones who were] apostles before me, <u>but</u> I went away to Arabia and returned again to Damascus.

¹⁸Then after three years I went up to Jerusalem to visit with Peter and stayed with him fifteen days. ¹⁹But I did not see [any] other of the apostles, except James, the brother of the Lord. ²⁰(Now the [things] I am writing to you*, listen!, before God I am not lying.) ²¹Then I came to the regions of Syria and of Cilicia. ²²But I was unknown by face [or, personally] to the assemblies [or, churches] of Judea, the [ones] in Christ. ²³But only they kept hearing, "The one having persecuted us

at one time is now proclaiming the Gospel—the faith which at one time he was trying to destroy!" ²⁴And they were glorifying God in [or, because of] me.

2Then after fourteen years I again went up to Jerusalem with Barnabas, having taken along also Titus. ²Now I went up because of a revelation, and I presented to them the Gospel which I preach among the nations, but privately to the ones highly regarded, lest somehow I should be running or did run for nothing. ³But not even Titus, the one with me, being a Greek, was compelled to be circumcised. ⁴But [it was] because of the false brothers [and sisters] brought in under false pretenses, who sneaked in to spy out our liberty which we have in Christ Jesus, so that they should enslave us, ⁵to whom not even for an hour [or, moment] did we yield in subjection, so that the truth of the Gospel should remain with you*.

⁶But from the ones highly regarded to be something—whatever kind they were then, it makes no difference to me; God does not accept [the] face of a person [fig., God does not show prejudice]—for the ones highly regarded contributed nothing to me, ⁷but, on the contrary, having seen that I have been entrusted [with] the Gospel for the uncircumcision [i.e. non-Jews], just as Peter [was with the Gospel] for the circumcision [i.e. Jews] ⁸(for the One having supernaturally worked in Peter in [his] apostleship to the circumcision, also supernaturally worked in me with respect to the Gentiles), ⁹and having known the grace, the one having been given to me, James and Cephas [i.e., Peter] and John, the ones highly regarded to be pillars, gave to me and to Barnabas [the] right hand of fellowship, so that we indeed [should go] to the Gentiles, but they to the circumcision [i.e. Jews]. ¹⁰[They] only [asked] that we should be remembering [or, continue to remember] the poor [ones], which indeed I was eager to do this very [thing].

¹¹But when Peter came to Antioch, I opposed him to [his] face, because he had been condemned. ¹²For before certain [ones] came from James, he was eating with the Gentiles, but when they came, he began drawing back and separating himself, fearing those from [the] circumcision [i.e. legalist Jews]. ¹³And the other Jews also joined him in hypocrisy, with the result that even Barnabas was carried away by their hypocrisy [or, insincerity].

¹⁴But when I saw that they [were] not walking uprightly [fig., not behaving in a consistent manner] with reference to the truth of the Gospel, I said to Peter in the presence of all, "If you, being a Jew, live like a Gentile and not like a Jew, why do you compel the Gentiles to live according to Jewish customs? ¹⁵We [who are] Jews by nature and not sinners of the Gentiles, ¹⁶having known that a person is not justified [or, declared righteous] by works of [the] Law but by means of faith in Jesus Christ, we also believed in Christ Jesus, so that we shall be justified by faith in Christ and not by works of [the] Law, because all flesh will not [or, no flesh will [at] all] be justified by works of [the] Law!"

¹⁷But if while seeking to be justified [or, declared righteous] in Christ, we ourselves also are found [to be] sinners, in that case, [is] Christ a servant of sin? Absolutely not! ¹⁸For if what I tore down, these [things] I build up again, I show [or, prove] myself to be a transgressor. ¹⁹For I through [the] Law died to [the] Law, so that I should live to God.

257

²⁰I have been crucified with Christ, but no longer do I live, but Christ lives in me! But [that] which I now live in [the] flesh, I live by faith in the Son of God, the One having loved me and having given Himself [or, having handed Himself over] for me! ²¹I do not regard the grace of God as nothing [or, nullify the grace of God], for if righteousness [is] through [the] Law, in that case, Christ died for nothing [or, needlessly].

*3*O foolish Galatians! Who bewitched you* [so as] not to be obeying the truth, before whose eyes Jesus Christ was publicly portrayed among you* [as] having been crucified? ²This only I want to learn from you*: did you* receive the Spirit by works of [the] Law or by hearing with faith? ³Are you* so foolish? Having begun in [or, by] [the] Spirit, are you* now being completed [or, perfected] in [or, by] [the] flesh? ⁴Did you* endure so many things for nothing—if indeed [it was] really for nothing? ⁵Therefore, the One supplying the Spirit to you* and supernaturally working miraculous powers [or, miracles] among you*, [is He doing so] by works of [the] Law or by hearing with faith?

⁶Just as *"Abraham believed [or, trusted] God and it was accounted to him for righteousness."* [Gen 15:6] ⁷Consequently, be knowing that the [ones justified] by faith, these are sons [and daughters] of Abraham. ⁸Now the Scripture having foreseen that God justifies [or, declares righteous] the nations by faith, proclaimed the Gospel beforehand to Abraham, [saying], *"All the nations will be blessed in you."* [Gen 12:3] ⁹Therefore, the [ones justified] by faith are blessed with the faithful [or, believing] Abraham.

¹⁰For as many as are [trying to be justified] by works of [the] Law are under a curse, for it has been written, *"Under a curse* [fig., *Condemned by God*] *[is] every[one] not remaining in* [fig., *carefully obeying*] *all the [things] having been written in the Scroll of the Law to do them."* [Deut 27:26] ¹¹Now that no one is justified [or, declared righteous] before God by [the] Law is evident, because *"The [one] righteous by faith will live* [or, *"The righteous will live by faith*]*."* [Hab 2:4] ¹²But the Law is not by faith, but *"The person having done them* [i.e. all the commandments of the Law] *will live by them."* [Lev 18:5] ¹³Christ redeemed us [or, set us free] from the curse of the Law, having become a curse on our behalf—for it has been written, *"Under a curse* [fig., *Condemned by God*] *[is] every[one] hanging upon a tree"*— [Deut 21:23] ¹⁴so that the blessing of Abraham shall come to the Gentiles in Christ Jesus, so that we shall receive the promise of the Spirit through faith.

¹⁵Brothers [and sisters], I speak according to human [standards]; likewise, a covenant having been put into effect [by] a person, no one regards [it] as nothing [or, makes [it] void] or adds to [it]. ¹⁶But the promises were spoken to Abraham and to his Seed. He does not say, "And to seeds," as by many, but as by One, *"And to your Seed,"* which is Christ. [Gen 12:7; 13:15] ¹⁷Now this I say: the Law having come four hundred and thirty years later does not nullify a covenant previously confirmed by God to Christ, so as to make the promise of no effect [or, to cancel the promise]. ¹⁸For if the inheritance [comes] by [the] Law, [it is] no longer by promise, but God has graciously given [it] to Abraham by means of promise.

¹⁹Why then the Law? It was added on account of transgressions, until the Seed should come to whom it had been promised, having been set in order [or, ordained] by means of angels by [the] hand of a mediator [i.e. Moses]. ²⁰But the mediator is not for one [i.e., for only one party], but God is one [i.e., God is the only active party in the promise; or, the one and same God that gave the Law made the promise]. ²¹Therefore, [is] the Law against the promises of God? Absolutely not! For if a law [had been] given which was able to make alive, [then] righteousness would indeed be by law. ²²But the Scripture confined all under sin, so that the promise shall be given by faith in Jesus Christ to the ones believing.

²³But before faith came, we were being guarded [or, being kept in protective custody] under [the] Law, having been confined to the faith about to be revealed. ²⁴Therefore, the Law has became our tutor [to lead us] to Christ, so that by faith we shall be justified [or, declared righteous]. ²⁵But since faith has come, we are no longer under a tutor. ²⁶For you* are all sons [and daughters] of God by means of faith in Christ Jesus. ²⁷For as many as were baptized [or, immersed] into Christ put on [or, clothed themselves with] Christ. ²⁸There is no Jew nor Greek, there is no slave nor free, there is no male and female, for you* are all one in Christ Jesus. ²⁹Now since you* [are] Christ's, consequently, you* are seed [fig., descendents] of Abraham and heirs according to promise.

4 Now I say, for as much time as [or, while] the heir is a minor, he does not differ at all from a slave, although he is lord [or, owner] of all, ²but he is under guardians and trustees until the appointed time of the father. ³In the same way we also, when we were minors, we were under the rudimentary elements [or, basic teachings] of the world, having been enslaved. ⁴But when the fullness [or, completion] of the time came, God sent forth His Son, having been born of a woman, having been born under [the] Law, ⁵so that He should redeem [or, set free] the [ones] under [the] Law, so that we shall receive the adoption [or, the formal and legal declaration that we are His children]. ⁶Now because you* are sons [and daughters], God sent forth the Spirit of His Son into your* hearts, crying out, "Dad [Gr. *Abba*], Father!" ⁷Therefore, you are no longer a slave, but a son, and if a son, also an heir of God through Christ!

⁸But at that time indeed, not having known God, you* were serving as slaves to the [ones] not being by nature gods. ⁹But now, having known God, but rather having been known by God, how is it that you* are turning back again to the weak and poor [fig., worthless], rudimentary elements [or, basic teachings] to which once more you* desire again to be serving as a slave? ¹⁰You* yourselves carefully observe days and months and seasons and years! ¹¹I fear for you*, lest somehow I labored over you* for nothing [or, without results].

¹²Brothers [and sisters], I implore you*, continue becoming like me, because I also [am] like you*. You* wronged me [in] nothing [or, You* did not mistreat me at all]. ¹³Now you* know that because of a weakness [or, an infirmity] of the flesh I proclaimed the Gospel to you* the first time. ¹⁴And my trial, the [one] in my flesh, you* did not look down on nor reject with contempt, but as an angel of God you* received me—as Christ Jesus [Himself]. ¹⁵What then was your happiness

[or, blessing]? For I testify to you* that, if possible, having gouged out your* eyes, you* would have given [them] to me. [16]Therefore, have I become your* enemy by speaking the truth to you*?

[17]They [i.e., the false brothers and sisters] are zealous for you* [or, are trying to win you* over], [but] not rightly [or, for no good]; <u>but</u> they want to exclude us, so that you* shall be zealous for [or, be eagerly seeking] them. [18]But [it is] good to be zealous in [or, to be setting your heart on] good at all times, and not only in my being present with you*. [19]My little children, for whom once more I am going through labor pains [fig., am suffering greatly] until Christ is formed in you*. [20]But I want to be present with you* now and to change my tone, because I myself am perplexed about you*.

[21]Be telling me, the ones desiring to be under [the] Law, do you* not pay attention to the [the] Law? [22]For it has been written that Abraham had two sons, one by the slave-woman and one by the free-woman. [Gen 16:2-4,15; 21:1-3] [23]<u>But</u> the [one] by the slave-woman has been born according to [the] flesh, but the [one] by the free-woman through the promise, [24]which [things] speak allegorically. For these are two covenants: one indeed from Mount Sinai giving birth to [children] into slavery, which is Hagar. [25]For this Hagar is Mount Sinai in Arabia and stands corresponding to the present Jerusalem and serves as a slave with her children. [26]But the Jerusalem above is the free-woman, which is mother of us all. [27]For it has been written, *"Celebrate, O barren woman, the one not giving birth; break forth and shout, the one not experiencing labor pains, because many [are] the children of the desolate [or, forsaken] [woman]—more than [those] of the one having the husband."* [Isaiah 54:1] [28]Now <u>we</u>, brothers [and sisters], just like Isaac, are children of promise.

[29]<u>But</u> just as at that time, the one having been born according to [the] flesh was persecuting the [one] according to the spirit, so [it is] also now. [30]<u>But</u> what does the Scripture say? *"Cast out the slave-woman and her son, for by no means shall the son of the slave-woman inherit [or, be a heir] with the son of the free-woman."* [Gen 21:10] [31]Consequently, brothers [and sisters], we are not a slave-woman's children, <u>but</u> the free-woman's.

5Therefore, in the freedom in which Christ set you* free, be standing firm, and stop letting yourselves be subjected again to a yoke of slavery. [2]Listen! <u>I</u>, Paul, say to you* that if you* are circumcised, Christ will not benefit you* at all. [3]Now I testify again to every man being circumcised, that he is a debtor [fig., he is under obligation] to do the whole Law. [4]You* were cut off from Christ, you* who are justified [or, declared righteous] by [the] Law! You* fell away from His grace! [5]For <u>we</u>, by [the] Spirit, by faith, eagerly wait for [the] hope [or, confident expectation] of righteousness. [6]For in Christ Jesus neither circumcision has any power [or, avails anything] nor uncircumcision, <u>but</u> faith working through love.

[7]You* were running [fig., exerting yourselves] well. Who hindered you* [so as] not to be obeying the truth? [8]This persuasion [or, enticement] [is] not from the One calling you*. [9]A little leaven [or, yeast] leavens the entire lump [of dough] [or, causes the entire lump [of dough] to rise]. [10]<u>I</u> have placed [my] confidence

in you* in [the] Lord, that you* will think in no other way [or, will be intent on nothing else]. But the one disturbing you* will bear the judgment, whoever he should be. ¹¹But I, brothers [and sisters], if I am still preaching circumcision, why am I still being persecuted? In that case, the stumbling block [or, offense] of the cross has been done away with [or, has been abolished]. ¹²O that the ones agitating you* would also castrate themselves!

¹³For you* were called to freedom, brothers [and sisters]; only [do] not [turn] that freedom into an opportunity to [satisfy] the flesh, but by means of love be serving as slaves to one another. ¹⁴For the entire Law is fulfilled in one word, in this [commandment], *"You will love your neighbor as yourself."* [Lev 19:18] ¹⁵But if you* bite and devour one another, be watching out [that] you* are not consumed [fig., ruined] by one another.

¹⁶But I say, be walking about [fig., conducting yourselves] in [or, by] [the] Spirit, and you* shall by no means fulfill [or, carry out] the lust of [the] flesh. ¹⁷For the flesh lusts contrary to the Spirit, and the Spirit contrary to the flesh. Now these are hostile to one another, so that what you* should be desiring, these [things] you* are not doing. ¹⁸But since you* are led by [the] Spirit, you* are not under [the] Law.

¹⁹Now the works of the flesh are evident, which are: adultery, sexual sin, impurity [or, immorality], flagrant sexual immorality, ²⁰idolatry, witchcraft, hostilities [or, feuds], quarrels, jealous rivalries, angry outbursts, selfish ambitions, divisions [or, discords], heretical sects, ²¹envies [or, jealousies], murders, drunkennesses, drunken orgies, and the [things] like these; which I forewarn you*, just as I also warned [you*] before that the ones practicing such [things] will not inherit [the] kingdom of God.

²²But the fruit of the Spirit is: love, joy, peace [or, freedom from anxiety], patience, kindness, goodness [or, generosity], faith, ²³gentleness [or, considerateness], [and] self-control. Against such there is no law. ²⁴Now the [ones who are] Christ's [have] crucified the flesh with its passions and its desires [or, lusts]. ²⁵Since we live in [or, by] [the] Spirit, let us also be keeping in line with [fig., be living in conformity with] the Spirit. ²⁶Let us not continue becoming conceited, provoking [or, irritating] one another, envying one another!

6 Brothers [and sisters], even if a person shall be overtaken in any transgression, you*, the spiritual [ones], be restoring such a one in a spirit of humility, watching out for yourself, lest you also be tempted. ²Be bearing the burdens of one another, and in this way fill up [or, fig., obey] the law of Christ. ³For if anyone considers [himself] to be something—being nothing [or, when he is nothing]—he deceives himself. ⁴But let each [person] be examining his own work, and then he will have with respect to himself alone the [grounds for] boasting and not with respect to the other [person]. ⁵For each will bear his own load.

⁶Now let the one being instructed in the word be contributing to [or, sharing with] the one instructing in all good things [or, be sharing in all good things with the one instructing].

⁷Stop being led astray [fig., being deceived]: God is not mocked! For whatever a person shall be sowing, this also he will reap. ⁸Because the one sowing to his own flesh from the flesh will reap corruption [fig., moral ruin], but the one sowing to the Spirit from the Spirit will reap eternal life. ⁹Now let us not become discouraged [or, weary] in the doing of good, for at the proper time we will reap, not being discouraged [or, if we do not get discouraged]. ¹⁰So, consequently, as we have opportunity, let us be working the good [thing] to all, but especially to the [ones] of the household of the faith.

¹¹See with what large letters I wrote to you* with my own hand! ¹²As many as want to make a good showing [or, impression] in [the] flesh, these compel [or, urge] you* to be circumcised, only so that they shall not be getting persecuted for the cross of Christ. ¹³For not even the ones having been circumcised are themselves keeping the Law, but they want for you* to be getting circumcised, so that they should boast in your* flesh. ¹⁴But for me, [I will] absolutely not boast except in the cross of our Lord Jesus Christ, by means of whom to me [the] world has been crucified and I to the world. ¹⁵For in Christ Jesus neither does circumcision have any power [or, avail anything] nor uncircumcision, but a new creation! ¹⁶And as many as are keeping in line with this measuring rod [fig., following this standard], peace upon them and mercy and on the Israel of God!

¹⁷Finally, let no one give me hardships, for I bear the scars [or, ownership brand marks] of the Lord Jesus in my body.

¹⁸The grace of our Lord Jesus Christ [be] with your* spirit, brothers [and sisters]! So be it!

The Epistle of Paul the Apostle to the
Ephesians

1 Paul, an apostle of Jesus Christ by [the] will of God, to the holy ones [or, saints, and throughout epistle], the [ones] being in Ephesus and faithful in Christ Jesus: ²Grace to you* and peace from God our Father and [the] Lord Jesus Christ!

³Blessed [be] [or, Worthy of praise [is]] the God and Father of our Lord Jesus Christ, the One having blessed us with every spiritual blessing in the heavenlies [or, heavenly [realms]] in Christ, ⁴just as He chose us in Him before [the] laying of the foundation of [the] world, so that we shall be holy and unblemished [fig., without fault] before Him, in love, ⁵having predestined us to [the] adoption [or, the formal and legal declaration that we are His children] by means of Jesus Christ to Himself, according to the good pleasure of His will, ⁶to [the] praise of the glory [or, splendor] of His grace [or, of His glorious grace], by which He bestowed grace upon [or, showed kindness to] us in the Beloved, ⁷in whom we have the redemption by means of His blood, the forgiveness of transgressions, according to the riches [fig., abundance] of His grace, ⁸which He made to abound toward [or, lavished on] us in all wisdom and insight [or, intelligence], ⁹having disclosed to us the secret [or, mystery, and throughout book] of His will, according to His good pleasure which He Himself purposed [or, planned] in Him, ¹⁰with respect to the administration of the fullness [or, completion] of the times, to gather together [or, to unify] all [things] in Christ, the [things] in the heavens and the things on the earth, ¹¹in Him in whom also we were appointed by lot [or, obtained an inheritance], having been predestined according to the purpose [or, plan] of the One supernaturally working all [things] according to the counsel [or, intention] of His will, ¹²for us to be to [the] praise of His glory, the ones having been the first to hope in Christ, ¹³in whom you* also, having heard the word of the truth, the Gospel [or, Good News, and throughout book] of your* salvation, in whom also having believed [or, having trusted], you* were sealed with the Holy Spirit of the promise, ¹⁴who is [the] down payment [or, guarantee] of our inheritance, with respect to the redemption of His acquired possession, to the praise of His glory!

¹⁵For this reason, I also, having heard of the faith of each of you* in the Lord Jesus and your* love for all the holy ones, ¹⁶do not cease from giving thanks for you*, making mention of you* in my prayers, ¹⁷so that the God of our Lord Jesus Christ, the Father of glory [or, splendor], shall give to you* a spirit of wisdom and revelation in the full [or, true] knowledge of Him, ¹⁸the eyes of your* heart having been enlightened, for you* to know what is the hope [or, confident expectation] of His calling and what [are] the riches [or, abundance] of the glory [or, splendor] of His inheritance in the holy ones ¹⁹and what [is] the surpassing greatness of His power to us, the ones believing, according to the supernatural working of the might of His strength, ²⁰which He supernaturally worked in Christ, having raised Him from the dead and seated [Him] at His right hand in the heavenlies [or,

heavenly [realms]], [21]far above all rule and authority and power and lordship [or, dominion] and every name having been named, not only in this age, <u>but</u> also in the one coming. [22]And He put all things in subjection under His feet and gave Him [to be] head over all [things pertaining] to the Assembly [or, Church, and throughout epistle], [23]which is His body, the fullness of the One filling all in all.

2And <u>you*</u> being dead in transgressions and sins, [2]in which at one time you* walked about [fig., conducted yourselves] according to the age [fig., the practices] of this world, according to the ruler of the authority of the air, of the spirit of the one now supernaturally working in the sons [and daughters] of disobedience; [3]among whom also <u>we</u> at one time lived in the lusts of our flesh, doing the desires of the flesh and of the thoughts [fig., senses], and we were by nature children of wrath, as also the others. [4]But God, being rich [fig., abundant] in mercy, because of His great love [with] which He loved us, [5]even while we were dead in transgressions, made us to live together with Christ (by grace you* have been saved), [6]and He raised [us] up together and seated [us] together in the heavenlies [or, heavenly [realms]] in Christ Jesus, [7]so that He should show in the ages, the ones coming, the surpassing riches [fig., abundance] of His grace in kindness toward us in Christ Jesus!

[8]For by grace you* have been saved, through faith, and this [is] not from you*; [it is] the gift of God, [9]not by works, so that no one shall boast. [10]For we are His workmanship, having been created in Christ Jesus for good works, which God prepared beforehand so that we should walk about [fig., conduct ourselves] in them.

[11]For this reason, be remembering that you* at one time [were] the Gentiles in [the] flesh, the ones called Uncircumcision by the ones called Circumcision, performed by human hands in [the] flesh—[12]that you* were at that time apart from [or, without] Christ, having been separated from [or, a foreigner to] the citizenship [fig., community] of Israel and strangers to [fig., excluded from] the covenants of the promise, having no hope [or, confident expectation] and without God in the world. [13]But now, in Christ Jesus, <u>you*</u>, the ones at one time being far away, became near by the blood of Christ.

[14]For He is our peace, the One having made them both one and having broken down the dividing wall of the fence [fig., the separation], [15]having done away with [or, having annulled] the hostility in His flesh, the law of the commandments in ordinances, so that from the two He should create in Himself into one new person [or, humanity], making peace, [16]and reconcile them both in one body to God by means of the cross, having put to death the hostility by it [or, in Himself]. [17]And having come, He Himself proclaimed the Gospel [of] peace to you*, to the [ones] far away and to the [ones] near. [18]Because by means of Him we both have the access [or, privilege to enter] by one Spirit to the Father.

[19]So, consequently, you* are no longer strangers and foreigners, but fellow-citizens with the holy ones and [members] of the household of God, [20]having been built on the foundation of the apostles and prophets, Jesus Christ Himself being [the] cornerstone, [21]in whom [the] entire building having been joined together

is growing into a holy temple in [the] Lord, ²²in whom also <u>you*</u> are being built together into a habitation for God in the Spirit.

3 For this reason, <u>I</u>, Paul, the prisoner of Christ Jesus on behalf of the Gentiles— ²if indeed you* heard of the stewardship of the grace of God, the one having been given to me for you*, ³that by revelation He disclosed to me the secret, just as I wrote before briefly, ⁴with reference to which you* are able, when reading [it], to understand my insight in the secret of Christ, ⁵which in different generations was not disclosed to the sons [and daughters] of people, as it was now revealed to His holy apostles and prophets by [the] Spirit, ⁶[that] the Gentiles [are] to be joint-heirs and joint-members of the same body and joint-partakers of His promise in Christ by means of the Gospel, ⁷of which I became a servant [or, minister] according to the free gift of the grace of God, the one having been given to me according to the supernatural working of His power.

⁸To me, the very least of all [the] holy ones, was given this grace, to proclaim the Gospel among the Gentiles, the unfathomable riches of Christ, ⁹and to enlighten all [as to] what [is] the administration of the secret, the one having been hidden from the ages in God, the One having created all things through Jesus Christ, ¹⁰so that the many-sided [or, manifold] wisdom of God should be revealed now through the Assembly to the principalities and the authorities in the heavenlies [or, heavenly [realms]], ¹¹according to [the] purpose [or, plan] of the ages, which He made in Christ Jesus our Lord, ¹²in whom we have the boldness [or, joyful sense of freedom] and the access [or, privilege to enter] in confidence by means of faith in Him. ¹³For this reason, I ask [you*] to stop becoming discouraged because of my afflictions on behalf of you*, which is your* glory.

¹⁴Because of this, I bow my knees towards the Father of our Lord Jesus Christ, ¹⁵from whom every family in [the] heavens and on earth is named, ¹⁶so that He shall grant to you*, according to the riches [fig., abundance] of His glory, to be strengthened with power by means of His Spirit in the inner being, ¹⁷[in order for] Christ to dwell in your* hearts by means of faith, having been firmly established and founded in love, ¹⁸so that you* shall be fully able to comprehend with all the holy ones what [is] the width and length and depth and height ¹⁹and to know the love of Christ [which] surpasses knowledge, so that you* shall be filled to all the fullness of God.

²⁰Now to the One being able above all [things] to do infinitely more than what we ask or think, according to the power, the [one] supernaturally working in us, ²¹to Him [be] the glory in the Assembly in Christ Jesus, to all the generations of the age of the ages [fig., forever and ever]! So be it!

4 Therefore, <u>I</u>, the prisoner in [the] Lord, call on [or, plead with] you* to walk about [fig., conduct yourselves] in a manner worthy of the calling with which you* were called, ²with all humility and gentleness [or, considerateness], with patience, yourselves putting up with one another in love, ³being eager [or, diligent] to be keeping the unity of the Spirit in the bond of peace: ⁴one body and one Spirit, just as also you* were called in one hope [or, confident expectation] of your*

calling; ⁵one Lord, one faith, one baptism [or, immersion], ⁶one God and Father of all, who [is] over all and through all and in us all.

⁷But to each one of us was given grace according to the measure of the free gift of Christ. ⁸For this reason, He [or, it] says, *"When He ascended on high, He led captive a group of captives and gave gifts to people."* [Psalm 68:18] ⁹Now this, *"He ascended,"* what is it [fig., what does it mean] except that He also descended first into the lower parts of the earth? ¹⁰The One having descended, He is also the One having ascended far above all the heavens, so that He should fill all [things].

¹¹And He gave some [to be] apostles, and some [to be] prophets, and some [to be] evangelists, and some [to be] shepherds [or, pastors] and teachers, ¹²for the purpose of the equipping of the holy ones for [the] work of service, for [the] building up [fig., edifying] of the body of Christ, ¹³until we all arrive [fig., attain] to the unity of the faith and of the full [or, true] knowledge of the Son of God, to a perfect [or, mature] man, to [the] measure [fig., extent] of [the] maturity of the fullness of Christ, ¹⁴so that we shall no longer be young children, being tossed about by waves and being carried about from place to place by every wind of teaching [or, doctrine], by the cunning of people, in craftiness, for the purpose of the trickery of deception. ¹⁵But speaking the truth in love, we shall increase to Him [in] all [things], who is the head, Christ, ¹⁶from whom the entire body being joined together and united by means of the supply of every joint [or, by what every joint supplies], according to the working of the measure of each individual part, causing the growth of the body for the building up of itself in love.

¹⁷So this I say, and I insist in the Lord: you* are no longer to be walking about [fig., conducting yourselves] just as also the rest of [the] Gentiles are walking about [fig. conducting themselves] in the futility of their mind, ¹⁸having been darkened in the understanding, being [in the state of] having been separated from [or, a foreigner to] the life of God, because of the ignorance, the one being in them, because of the hardness of their heart [fig., stubbornness of their inner self], ¹⁹who, having become callous, they gave themselves over to flagrant sexual immorality for the pursuit of all impurity, with covetous desire [or, greed]. ²⁰But you* did not so learn Christ.

²¹Since indeed you* heard Him and in Him were taught, just as truth is in Jesus, ²²you* [are] to put off [or, be done with], with respect to your former manner of life, the old [or, former] person, the one being corrupt according to the desires [or, lusts] of deception, ²³but [you* are] to be continually renewed in the spirit of your* mind ²⁴and to put on the new person, the one having been created according to God in righteousness and holiness of [or, dedication to] the truth.

²⁵For this reason, you* yourselves having put off falsehood, *"Be speaking truth each one with his neighbor"* [Zech 8:16]—because we are members one of another. ²⁶*"Continue being enraged, and stop sinning."* [Psalm 4:4] Stop letting the sun go down on your* angry mood, ²⁷and stop giving place [fig., an opportunity] to the Devil. ²⁸The one stealing let him no longer be stealing, but rather let him be laboring, working the good [thing] with his hands, so that he shall be having [something] to be sharing with the one having need.

²⁹Stop letting any rotten [fig., harmful] word come out of your* mouth, <u>but</u> if anything [fig., what] [is] useful for building up [fig., edifying] of the need [fig., as needed], so that it shall give grace to the ones hearing. ³⁰And stop grieving the Holy Spirit of God, by whom you* were sealed [or, secured] for [the] day of redemption. ³¹Let all bitterness and rage and anger and clamor [or, angry shouts of dissatisfaction] and slander be removed from you*, [along] with all malice. ³²But continue becoming kind to one another, compassionate, forgiving one another, just as also God in Christ forgave us.

5Therefore, continue becoming imitators of God, as beloved children, ²and be walking about [fig., conducting yourselves] in love, as also Christ loved us and gave Himself [or, handed Himself over] on our behalf, [as] an offering and a sacrifice to God for an odor of a sweet smell [or, a sweet-smelling aroma].

³But sexual sin and all impurity [or, immorality] or covetous desire [or, greed], stop letting it even be named among you*, as is fitting for holy ones, ⁴also [neither] indecent behavior [or, obscene speech] and foolish [or, idle] talk nor coarse joking [or, vulgar talk]—the [things] not fitting—<u>but</u> rather thanksgiving. ⁵For this you* are knowing: that every sexual sinner or unclean [or, impure] [person] or covetous person, who is an idolater, does not have an inheritance in the kingdom of Christ and of God. ⁶Let no one be deceiving [or, misleading] you* with empty [fig., foolish] words, for because of these [things] the wrath of God is coming upon the sons [and daughters] of disobedience. ⁷Therefore, stop becoming joint-partakers with them.

⁸For you* were at one time darkness, but now [you* are] light in [the] Lord; as children of light be walking about [fig., conducting yourselves] ⁹(for the fruit of the Spirit [is] in all goodness [or, generosity] and righteousness and truth), ¹⁰proving [or, discovering] what is acceptable to the Lord. ¹¹And stop participating in the unfruitful works of the darkness, but instead, even be exposing [them]. ¹²For it is disgraceful even to speak of the [things] being done by them in secret. ¹³But all the [things] exposed by the light are revealed, for every[thing] revealed is light. ¹⁴For this reason, He [or, it] says, "Be waking up, the one sleeping, and arise from the dead, and Christ will shine on you."

¹⁵Therefore, be watching how carefully you* are walking about [fig., conducting yourselves], not as unwise <u>but</u> as wise, ¹⁶redeeming [fig., making the best use of] the time, because the days are evil. ¹⁷For this reason, stop becoming foolish, <u>but</u> be understanding what [is] the will of the Lord. ¹⁸And stop getting drunk with wine, in which is reckless behavior, <u>but</u> continue being filled with [the] Spirit, ¹⁹speaking to yourselves in psalms and hymns and spiritual songs, singing and making melody in your* heart to the Lord, ²⁰giving thanks always for all [things] in [the] name of our Lord Jesus Christ to the God and Father, ²¹being subject [or, being submissive] to one another in the fear of Christ.

²²The wives, be subjecting [or, submitting] yourselves to your* own husbands, as to the Lord, ²³because [the] husband is head of the wife, as also Christ [is] head of the Assembly, and <u>He</u> is [the] Savior of the body. ²⁴<u>But</u> even as the Assembly

is subjected [or, submitted] to Christ, so also the wives [should be] to their own husbands in everything.

²⁵The husbands, be loving your* own wives, just as also Christ loved the Assembly and gave Himself [or, handed Himself over] on her behalf, ²⁶so that He should sanctify her, having cleansed [or, purged] [her] with the bathing of the water by [the] word, ²⁷so that He should present her to Himself, the glorious [or, splendid] Assembly, not having spot [or, blemish] nor wrinkle, nor any of such things, but so that she should be holy and unblemished.

²⁸In the same way ought the husbands to be loving their own wives as their own bodies. The one loving his own wife loves himself. ²⁹For no one ever hated his own flesh, but he nourishes and cherishes it, just as also the Lord [does] the Assembly, ³⁰because we are members of His body, from His flesh and from His bones. ³¹*"For this reason, a man will leave behind his father and mother and will be joined to* [or, *united with*] *his wife. And they will be—the two—into one flesh* [or, *And the two will become one flesh*]." [Gen 2:24, LXX]

³²This secret is great, but I am speaking with respect to Christ and to the Assembly. ³³Nevertheless, you* also, let each one individually, be loving his own wife as himself in this manner, but the wife, that she should be respecting her husband.

6 The children, be obeying your* parents in [the] Lord, for this is righteous. ²*"Be honoring your father and mother,"* which is the first commandment with a promise, ³*"so that it shall be well with you, and you will be long-lived on the earth."* [Exod 20:12, LXX; Deut 5:16]

⁴And the fathers, stop provoking your* children [or, stop making your* children resentful], but be nourishing them in [the] discipline and instruction of [the] Lord.

⁵The slaves, be obeying the masters according to [the] flesh, with fear and trembling, in sincerity of your* heart, as to Christ, ⁶not with eye-service as people-pleasers, but as slaves of Christ, doing the will of God from [the] soul [fig., wholeheartedly], ⁷serving with goodwill [or, wholehearted zeal] as to the Lord and not to people, ⁸knowing that whatever good [thing] each one does, this he will receive back from the Lord, whether a slave or a free [person].

⁹And the masters, be doing the same [things] to them, giving up threatening, knowing that also your* own Master is in [the] heavens, and [there] is no accepting of faces [fig., prejudice] with Him.

¹⁰Finally my brothers [and sisters], continue becoming strong in [the] Lord and in the might of His strength. ¹¹Put on the full armor of God in order [for] you* to be able to stand firm against the tricks [or, cunning schemes] of the Devil. ¹²Because our struggle is not against blood and flesh, but against the rulers, against the authorities, against the world-rulers of the darkness of this age, against the spiritual [forces] of the wickedness in the heavenlies [or, heavenly [realms]].

¹³For this reason, take up the full armor of God, so that you* shall be able to resist in the day of evil, and having accomplished [or, overcome] everything, to stand firm. ¹⁴Therefore, stand firm, *"having wrapped your waist around with*

truth," and *"having put on the breastplate of righteousness,"* [Isaiah 11:5; 59:17] [15]and having *"put on your feet as shoes the preparation of the Gospel of peace,"* [Isaiah 52:7] [16]above all [or, in addition to all [these things]], having taken up the shield of faith, by which you* will be able to extinguish all the arrows, the ones having been set on fire, [fig., the flaming arrows] of the evil [one], [17]and to receive [or, take] *"the helmet of salvation,"* and the sword of the Spirit, which is the word of God, [Isaiah 59:17; 49:2; Hos 6:5] [18]through all prayer and petition praying in every season in [the] Spirit, and with respect to this same [thing] [or, to this same [end]], be staying alert in all perseverance and supplication for all the holy ones, [19]and on my behalf, so that to me shall be given a word [or, speech] in [the] opening of my mouth, in boldness [or, confidence], to declare the secret of the Gospel, [20]for the sake of which I serve as an ambassador [or, a representative] [bound] in a chain, so that in it I should speak boldly, as it is necessary [for] me to speak.

[21]Now so that you* shall also know the [things] with reference to me [fig., my circumstances], what I am doing, Tychicus will disclose to you* all things, the beloved brother and faithful servant [or, deacon] in [the] Lord, [22]whom I sent to you* for this very [purpose], so that you* shall know the things concerning us, and that he shall comfort [or, encourage] your* hearts.

[23]Peace to the brothers [and sisters] and love with faith from God [the] Father and [the] Lord Jesus Christ. [24]Grace [be] with all the ones loving our Lord Jesus Christ in incorruptibility [or, with an incorruptible [love]]! So be it!

The Epistle of Paul the Apostle to the
Philippians

1 Paul and Timothy, slaves of Jesus Christ, To all the holy ones [or, saints] in Christ Jesus, the ones being in Philippi, with [the] overseers and servants [or, deacons]: ²Grace to you* and peace from God our Father and [the] Lord Jesus Christ.

³I give thanks to my God upon every remembrance of you*, ⁴always, in my every petition on behalf of all of you*, making petition with joy, ⁵because of your* fellowship in [or, contribution to] the Gospel [or, Good News, and throughout book] from [the] first day until now, ⁶having been confident [or, persuaded] of this very [thing], that the One having begun a good work in you* will complete [or, perfect] [it] until [the] day of Christ Jesus; ⁷just as it is right for me to be thinking this about all of you*, because I hold you* in my heart, both in my bonds [fig., imprisonment] and in the defense and confirmation of the Gospel, all of you* being fellow-partakers with me of grace. ⁸For God is my witness, how I long for you* all with the bowels [fig., affections] of Jesus Christ.

⁹And this I pray, that your* love be overflowing yet more and more in full [or, true] knowledge and with all insight [or, capacity for understanding], ¹⁰for the purpose of your* discerning the things differing, so that you* shall be pure and blameless—to the day of Christ, ¹¹having been filled with fruits of righteousness [which are] through Jesus Christ, to [the] glory and praise of God.

¹²Now I want you* to be knowing, brothers [and sisters], that the [things] with reference to me [fig., my circumstances] have come rather for [the] progress of the Gospel, ¹³with the result that my bonds have become known [as being] in Christ in the entire fortified palace and to all the rest, ¹⁴and the majority of the brothers [and sisters] in [the] Lord, having gained confidence by my bonds [fig., imprisonment], are all the more bold to be fearlessly speaking the word. ¹⁵Some indeed even because of envy and strife [or, rivalry], but some also because of goodwill [or, good motives] are preaching Christ. ¹⁶The [former ones] indeed proclaim Christ out of selfish ambition [or, self-interest], not sincerely [or, of pure motives], supposing to be causing me to be experiencing distress in my bonds, ¹⁷but the [latter ones] out of love, knowing that I stand [or, am appointed] for [the] defense of the Gospel.

¹⁸What then? Nevertheless, in every way, whether in pretense [or, with a false motive] or in truth [or, with a right motive], Christ is proclaimed, and in this I rejoice, indeed also I will rejoice. ¹⁹For I know that this will lead to deliverance for me, through your* petition and [the] provision of the Spirit of Christ Jesus, ²⁰according to my earnest expectation [or, eager longing] and hope [or, confident expectation], that in nothing I will be ashamed, <u>but</u> with all boldness [or, confidence], as always, also now Christ will be magnified [or, highly praised] in my body, whether by means of [my] life or by means of [my] death.

²¹For to me to be living [is] Christ and to die gain. ²²But if [I am] to be living in [the] flesh, this [will mean] to me fruit from labor [or, fruitful labor]. And what will I choose [or, prefer]? I do not know. ²³But I am hard-pressed by the two, having the desire to depart and to be with Christ, [which is] far better, ²⁴but to be remaining in the flesh is more necessary for your* sake. ²⁵And having become convinced of this, I know that I will remain and will continue with you* all, for your* progress and joy in the faith, ²⁶so that your* boasting shall be abounding in Christ Jesus in [or, because of] me by means of my arrival again to you.

²⁷Only be conducting yourselves in a manner worthy of the Gospel of Christ, so that, whether having come and having seen you* or being absent, I shall hear the [things] concerning you* [fig., hear about you*], that you* are standing firm in one spirit, with one soul, striving together for the faith of the Gospel. ²⁸And stop being intimidated in any way by the ones being in opposition, which to them indeed is a demonstration [or, sign] of destruction, but to you* of salvation, and this from God. ²⁹Because to you* it was graciously granted for Christ's sake not only to believe in Him, <u>but</u> also to be suffering for His sake, ³⁰having the same conflict, such as you* saw in me and are now hearing [is] in me.

2 Therefore, if [there is] any encouragement in Christ, if any comfort of love, if any fellowship of spirit, if any bowels [fig., affections] and mercies, ²fulfill my joy [or, make my joy complete], that you* shall be thinking the same [thing] [fig., you* are being like-minded], having the same love, united in spirit, thinking the one [thing] [fig., intending the same purpose], ³[doing] nothing according to selfish ambition or empty [or, groundless] conceit, <u>but</u> with humility be regarding one another [as] being better than yourselves. ⁴Stop being concerned each one about the [interests; or, concerns] of themselves, <u>but</u> each one also [about] the [interests] of others.

⁵Indeed, be letting the frame of mind [or, attitude] be in you* which [was] also in Christ Jesus, ⁶who existing in the nature of God, did not consider being equal to God something to be held onto, ⁷<u>but</u> He emptied Himself, having taken the nature of a slave, having come to be in the likeness of people, ⁸and having been found in appearance as a person, He humbled Himself, having become obedient to the point of death—even of death of a cross. ⁹And so God highly exalted Him [or, put Him in the most important position] and gave to Him a Name, the [Name] above every name, ¹⁰so that at the name of Jesus every knee shall bow, of heavenly [ones] and of earthly [ones] and of [ones] under the earth, ¹¹and every tongue [fig., person] shall confess that Jesus Christ [is] Lord to [the] glory of God [the] Father! [cp. Isaiah 45:23]

¹²So then, my beloved, just as you* always obeyed, not as in my presence only, <u>but</u> now much more in my absence, be working out your* own salvation with fear and trembling, ¹³for God is the One supernaturally working in you* both to be desiring and to be supernaturally working for the sake of His good pleasure.

¹⁴Be doing all things without complaints and arguments, ¹⁵so that you* shall become blameless and innocent children of God, unblemished in [the] midst of

271

a crooked and having been perverted generation, among whom you* shine like stars in the universe, ¹⁶holding firmly to [or, offering] the word of life, as my right to boast in [the] day of Christ, that I did not run [fig., exert myself] in vain, nor did I labor in vain. ¹⁷But even if I am being poured out as a drink offering on the sacrifice and sacred service of your* faith, I rejoice, and I rejoice together with you* all. ¹⁸And in the same [manner], you* also are to be rejoicing and are to be rejoicing together with me.

¹⁹But I hope [or, trust] in [the] Lord Jesus to soon send Timothy to you*, so that I also shall be encouraged, having learned the things concerning you* [fig. your* circumstances]. ²⁰For I have no one with the same attitude, who will be genuinely concerned about the [things] concerning you*. ²¹For they all seek the [things] of themselves [fig., their own interests], not the [things] of Christ Jesus. ²²But you* know his proven character, that as a child to a father, he served as a slave with me concerning the Gospel. ²³Therefore, this [one] indeed I hope [or, expect] to send immediately, as soon as I ascertain the [things] concerning me [fig., my circumstances]. ²⁴But I have placed [my] confidence in [the] Lord that I myself also will soon come.

²⁵And I considered [it] necessary to send to you* Epaphroditus, my brother and fellow-worker and fellow-soldier, but your* apostle and public servant to my need, ²⁶since he was longing for you* all, and being distressed, because you* heard that he was sick. ²⁷For indeed he was sick nearly to death, but God showed him mercy, but not him only, but also me, so that I would not have sorrow upon sorrow. ²⁸Therefore, I sent him as quickly as possible [or, with great urgency], so that having seen him again you* shall rejoice, and I shall be relieved of sorrow. ²⁹Therefore, be receiving [or, be welcoming] him in [the] Lord, with all joy, and be holding such [ones] in honor, ³⁰because he came near to the point of death on account of the work of Christ, having shown disregard for his life, so that he shall fill up [fig., supply] your* deficiency of sacred service to me.

3 [As to] the rest [or, Finally], my brothers [and sisters], be rejoicing in [the] Lord. For me to be writing the same [things] to you* indeed is not tiresome, but for you* [it is] a safeguard. ²Be watching out for [or, Beware of] the dogs! Be watching out for the evil laborers! Be watching out for the mutilation [or, false circumcision]! ³For we are the [true] circumcision, the [ones] sacredly serving in [or, by] the Spirit of God and boasting in Christ Jesus and not having placed trust [or, having confidence] in [the] flesh, ⁴although I have trust [or, confidence] also in [the] flesh.

If any other [person] supposes to have trust [or, confidence] in flesh, I even more: ⁵circumcision on the eighth day, from the nation of Israel, of the tribe of Benjamin, a Hebrew of Hebrews [fig., a pure-blooded Jew], with respect to [the] law a Pharisee, ⁶with respect to zeal persecuting the Assembly [or, Church], with respect to righteousness, the [one] that is in [the] law, having become blameless.

⁷But whatever [things] were gains to me, these I have considered loss for the sake of Christ. ⁸But indeed, therefore, I also consider all [things] to be loss for the sake of the surpassing excellency of the knowledge of Christ Jesus my Lord, for

the sake of whom I suffered loss of all [things], and I consider them to be garbage, so that I shall gain Christ ⁹and be found in Him, not having my righteousness, the [righteousness] from [the] Law, but the [righteousness] by means of faith in Christ, [which is] the righteousness from God on the basis of faith; ¹⁰[so as] to know Him and the power of His resurrection and the fellowship of His sufferings, being conformed to His death, ¹¹if in some way I shall arrive [fig., attain] to the resurrection of the dead. ¹²Not that I already obtained or have already been perfected, but I press forward, if also I shall lay hold of [that] for which I also was laid hold of by Christ Jesus. ¹³Brothers [and sisters], I do not consider myself to have laid hold, but forgetting indeed one [thing], the [things] behind, but reaching out to the [things] ahead. ¹⁴I press forward toward [the] goal, for the prize of the upward calling of God in Christ Jesus.

¹⁵Therefore, as many as [are] mature, let us be thinking this [or, be having this attitude], and if [in] anything you* think otherwise [or, have a different attitude], this also God shall reveal to you*. ¹⁶Nevertheless, in regards to what we [have] attained, [let us] be keeping in line with [fig., be following] [the] same standard, to be thinking the same [thing] [or, to be having the same attitude].

¹⁷Join [others] in becoming imitators of me, brothers [and sisters], and be keeping a close eye on the ones walking about [fig., conducting themselves] in this manner, just as you* have us [for] a pattern. ¹⁸For many walk about [fig., conduct themselves] of whom frequently I was speaking to you*, but now also weeping I speak [of] the enemies of the cross of Christ, ¹⁹whose end [is] destruction, whose god [is] the belly [fig., their appetite] and [whose] glory [is] in their shame, who set their minds on the [things] of the earth. ²⁰For our citizenship exists in [the] heavens, from where also we eagerly await a Savior, [the] Lord Jesus Christ, ²¹who will transform the body of our humble state for it to become similar in form to the body of His glory, according to the supernatural working [or, energy] [by which] He also is able to subject all [things] to Himself.

4 So then, my beloved and longed for brothers [and sisters], my joy and victor's wreath [or, crown], in this way be standing firm in [the] Lord, beloved. ²I urge Euodia and I urge Syntyche to be thinking the same [thing] [fig., to be in agreement] in [the] Lord. ³Yes, I ask you also, genuine co-worker [or, loyal Syzygus], be assisting these [women] who strove together with me in the Gospel, with Clement also, and the others, my co-workers, whose names [are] in [the] Scroll of Life.

⁴Be rejoicing in [the] Lord always! I will say again, be rejoicing! ⁵Let your* gentleness [or, considerateness] be known to all people. The Lord [is] near! ⁶Stop being anxious about anything, but in every[thing] by prayer and by petition, with thanksgiving, be letting your* requests be made known to God. ⁷And the peace of God, the [peace] surpassing all understanding, will guard [or, protect] your* hearts and your* thoughts in Christ Jesus.

⁸[As to] the rest [or, Finally], brothers [and sisters], as many things as are true, as many as [are] worthy of respect [or, honorable], as many as [are] righteous, as many [things] as are pure, as many as [are] acceptable [or, lovely], as many as

[are] commendable, if [there is] any virtue [or, moral excellence], and if any[thing] deserving to be praised, be meditating on [or, be thinking about] these things. ⁹What [things] you* both learned and received, and heard and saw in me, these [things] be practicing, and the God of peace will be with you*.

¹⁰But I rejoiced in the [Lord] greatly, that now at last you* revived thinking on behalf of me [fig., were again concerned about me], for which indeed you* were thinking [fig., concerned] but lacked opportunity. ¹¹Not that I speak in respect to need, for I [have] learned to be content in whatever [state] I am. ¹²I know both [how] to be living in humble circumstances, and I know [how] to be living in abundance; in every [place] and in all [circumstances] I have learned the secret of being filled and [of] being hungry, both to be living in abundance and to be having need. ¹³I am capable of [doing] all [things] through Christ, the [One] strengthening me.

¹⁴Nevertheless, you* did well, having shared with [me] in my affliction [or, hardship]. ¹⁵Now you* also know, Philippians, that in [the] beginning of the Gospel, when I went out from Macedonia, no assembly [or, church] shared with me in [the] matter [of] giving and receiving, except you* only; ¹⁶because even in Thessalonica, both once and twice [fig., again and again] you* sent [something] for my need. ¹⁷Not that I seek the gift, but I seek the fruit [which is] increasing in your* account. ¹⁸But I am receiving back all [things], and I am overflowing! I have been filled, having received from Epaphroditus the [things] from you*, a fragrant aroma, an acceptable sacrifice, acceptable to God. ¹⁹Now my God will fully supply all your* need [or, your* every need] according to His riches [fig., abundance] in glory in Christ Jesus!

²⁰Now to our God and Father [be] the glory into the ages of the ages [fig., forever and ever]! So be it!

²¹Greet every holy one [or, saint] in Christ Jesus; the brothers [and sisters] with me greet you*. ²²All the holy ones [or, saints] greet you*, but especially the [ones] from Caesar's household.

²³The grace of the Lord Jesus Christ [be] with you* all. So be it!

The Epistle of Paul the Apostle to the
Colossians

1 Paul, an apostle of Jesus Christ by [the] will of God, and Timothy the brother, ²To the holy ones [or, saints, and throughout epistle] and faithful brothers [and sisters] in Christ in Colosse: Grace to you* and peace from God our Father and [the] Lord Jesus Christ!

³We give thanks to the God and Father of our Lord Jesus Christ, always praying for you*, ⁴having heard of your* faith in Christ Jesus and the love [which you* have] towards all the holy ones, ⁵because of the hope [or, confident expectation], the one laid up for you* in the heavens, which you* heard of before in the word of the truth of the Gospel [or, Good News], ⁶coming to you*, just as also in all the world, and is bearing fruit and growing, just as [it is] also in you*, from [the] day which you* heard and knew the grace of God in truth; ⁷just as you* also learned from Epaphras, our beloved fellow-slave, who is a faithful [or, trustworthy] servant of Christ on your* behalf, ⁸the one having also declared [or, made clear] to us your* love in [the] Spirit.

⁹For this reason, we also, from [the] day which we heard, do not cease from praying on your* behalf and asking that you* be filled with the full [or, true] knowledge of His will in all wisdom and spiritual understanding [or, insight], ¹⁰[in order for] you* to walk about [fig., conduct yourselves] in a manner worthy of the Lord to please [Him] in all [respects], bearing fruit [fig., being effective] in every good work and increasing in the full [or, true] knowledge of God, ¹¹being empowered with all power according to the might of His glory, for all perseverance and patience, with joy, ¹²giving thanks to the Father, the One having qualified us for the portion of [or, to share in] the inheritance of the holy ones in the light, ¹³who rescued us out of the dominion of the darkness and transferred [us] into the kingdom of the Son of His love, ¹⁴in whom we have redemption, the forgiveness of sins, ¹⁵who is [the] image of the invisible God, first-born of [fig., existing before] all creation; ¹⁶because by Him all [things] were created, the [ones] in the heavens and the [ones] on the earth, the visible [things] and the invisible [things], whether thrones or dominions or rulers or authorities; all such things have been created through Him and for Him, ¹⁷and He is before all [things] and all [things] are held together by Him.

¹⁸And He is the head of the body, the Assembly [or, Church, and throughout epistle]; who is [the] beginning, [the] first-born from the dead, so that He shall be having preeminence in all [things]; ¹⁹because in Him all the fullness [of the Godhead] was pleased to dwell, ²⁰and through Him to reconcile all [things] to Himself, having made peace through the blood of His cross, through Him, whether the [things] on the earth or the [things] in the heavens.

²¹And you* at one time having been alienated and enemies in the mind by your* evil works, yet now He reconciled [you*] ²²in the body of His flesh through His death, to present you* holy and unblemished [fig., without fault] and free

275

from reproach before Him, ²³since indeed you* are continuing in the faith, having been firmly established and steadfast, and are not being shifted away from the hope [or, confident expectation] of the Gospel [or, Good News] which you* heard, the one having been preached in all the creation under heaven, of which I, Paul, became a servant.

²⁴Now I rejoice in my sufferings on your* behalf, and I am filling up [or, completing] the [things] lacking of the afflictions of Christ in my flesh for His body, which is the Assembly, ²⁵of which I became a servant [or, minister] according to the stewardship of God, the one having been given to me for you*, to fulfill the word of God, ²⁶the secret [or, mystery, and throughout book], the one having been hidden from the ages and from the generations, but now was revealed to His holy ones, ²⁷to whom God willed to make known what [is] the riches of the glory of this secret among the nations [or, the Gentiles], who is Christ in you*, the hope [or, confident expectation] of glory; ²⁸whom we proclaim, warning every person and teaching every person in [or, with] all wisdom, so that we shall present every person perfect [or, complete] in Christ Jesus, ²⁹for which also I labor, striving according to His supernatural working, the one supernaturally working in me in power.

2 For I want you* to know how great a struggle I have concerning you* and the ones in Laodicea and as many as have not seen my face in [the] flesh [fig., have not met me personally], ²that their hearts shall be comforted [or, encouraged], having been united in love, and [attaining] to all [the] riches [fig., abundance] of the full assurance of understanding, to the full [or, true] knowledge of the secret of both God the Father and of Christ, ³in whom are hidden all the treasures of wisdom and knowledge.

⁴Now this I say so that no one shall be deceiving you* with persuasive speech. ⁵For even though I am absent in the flesh, but I am with you* in the spirit, rejoicing and looking at [or, considering] your* [good] order and the steadfastness of your* faith in Christ. ⁶Therefore, as you* received Christ Jesus the Lord, [so] be walking about [fig, be conducting yourselves] in Him, ⁷having been rooted [fig., firmly established] and having been built up in Him and being established [or, strengthened] in the faith, just as you* were taught, abounding in it with thanksgiving.

⁸Be watching out lest anyone will be carrying you* away as spoils of war [fig., taking control of you*] through philosophy [or, human wisdom] and empty deception, according to the traditions of people, according to the rudimentary elements [or, basic teachings] of the world and not according to Christ. ⁹Because in Him dwells all the fullness of the Godhead [or, Deity] bodily, ¹⁰and you* have been made full [or, have been completed] in Him, who is the Head of every rule and authority, ¹¹in whom you* also were circumcised with a circumcision done without human hands, by the putting off of the body of the sins of the flesh by the circumcision of Christ, ¹²having been buried together with Him in baptism [or, immersion], in which you* also were raised together [with Him] through faith in the supernatural working of God, the One having raised Him from the dead.

¹³And you*, being dead in your* transgressions and the uncircumcision of your* flesh, He made you* alive together with Him, having forgiven you* all transgressions, ¹⁴having blotted out [or, canceled] the handwritten record of debts in the ordinances against us, which was contrary to us, and He has taken it out of the way, having nailed it to the cross; ¹⁵having disarmed the rulers and the authorities, He publicly disgraced them, having triumphed over them by it [i.e. the cross].

¹⁶Therefore, stop letting anyone judge you* in eating or in drinking or with regard to a feast or of a new moon [festival] or of Sabbaths, ¹⁷which are a shadow of the coming [things], but the body [is] of Christ. ¹⁸Stop letting anyone decide against you* [fig., judge you* as not being worthy], delighting in [false] humility and religious worship of the angels, basing his authority on [things] he has not seen, being conceited without cause by the mind of his flesh, ¹⁹and not holding fast to the head, from whom the entire body, by means of the joints and ligaments being supplied and being knit together, grows [with] the growth of God.

²⁰Since you* died with Christ from the rudimentary elements [or, basic teachings] of the world, why as living in the world are you* submitting to regulations? ²¹"You* yourselves should not handle nor should you* taste nor should you* touch," ²²which [things] are all for corruption with the using, according to the commandments and teachings of people, [cp. Isaiah 29:13] ²³which are indeed having a reputation of wisdom in self-imposed religion and [false] humility and severe discipline [or, non-indulgence] of [the] body, [but which are] not of any value against indulgence of the flesh.

3 Therefore, since you* were raised together with Christ, be seeking the [things] above, where Christ is, sitting at [the] right hand of God. ²Be setting your* minds on the [things] above, not [on] the [things] on the earth. ³For you* died, and your* life has been hid with Christ in God. ⁴Whenever Christ, [who is] our life, is revealed, then also we will be revealed with Him in glory!

⁵Therefore, put to death your* members, the ones on the earth: sexual sin, impurity [or, immorality], lustful passion, evil desire, and the covetous desire [or, greed], which is idolatry, ⁶because of which [things] the wrath of God is coming upon the sons [and daughters] of disobedience, ⁷in which you* also at one time walked about [fig., conducted yourselves], when you* were living in them. ⁸But now you* yourselves also put off [fig., cease from] all these [things]: anger, rage, malice, blasphemy, [and] obscene language out of your* mouth.

⁹Stop lying to one another, having put off the old [or, former] person with his practices, ¹⁰and having put on the new [person], the [one] being renewed in full [or, true] knowledge according to [the] image of the One having created him, ¹¹where there is not Greek and Jew, circumcision and uncircumcision, foreigner, Scythian, slave, free person, but Christ [is] all [things] and in all [things].

¹²Therefore, put on as chosen [or, elect] ones of God, holy and beloved, bowels [or, hearts] of compassion, kindness, humility, gentleness [or, considerateness], patience, ¹³putting up with one another and forgiving each other, if anyone shall be having a complaint against anyone, just as Christ also forgave you*, so also

[should] you* [forgive]. ¹⁴But above all these [things put on] love, which is [the] bond of perfection. ¹⁵And let the peace of God be exercising control in your* hearts, to which also you* were called in one body, and become thankful.

¹⁶Let the word of Christ be richly [or, abundantly] dwelling in you*, in all wisdom, teaching and admonishing each other, in psalms and hymns and spiritual songs, singing with grace [or, gratitude] in your* hearts to the Lord. ¹⁷And every[thing], whatever you* shall be doing in word or in deed, [be doing] all [things] in [the] name of [the] Lord Jesus, giving thanks to the God and Father through Him.

¹⁸The wives, be subjecting [or, submitting] yourselves to your* own husbands, as is fitting in [the] Lord. ¹⁹The husbands, be loving your* wives, and stop becoming bitter towards them. ²⁰The children, be obeying your* parents with respect to all [things], for this is well-pleasing in [the] Lord. ²¹The fathers, stop making your* children resentful, so that they shall not continue becoming discouraged.

²²The slaves, be obeying with respect to all [things] your* masters according to [the] flesh, not in eye-service as people-pleasers, <u>but</u> in sincerity of heart, fearing God. ²³And every[thing], whatever you* shall be doing, be working from [your*] soul [fig., heartily] as to the Lord and not to people, ²⁴knowing that from [the] Lord you* will receive the recompense of the inheritance, for to the Lord Christ you* are serving as a slave. ²⁵But the one doing wrong [or, acting unjustly] will receive back what he did wrong [or, did unjustly], and there is no accepting of faces [fig., partiality].

4 The masters, be providing the just [thing] [fig., justice] and equality [or, fairness] to the slaves, knowing that <u>you*</u> also have a Master in [the] heavens.

²Be continuing earnestly in prayer; be staying alert in it with thanksgiving, ³praying at the same time also concerning us, that God opens to us a door for the word, to speak the secret of Christ (on account of which I have also been bound), ⁴that I shall reveal it [or, make it clear], as it is necessary [for] me to speak.

⁵Be walking about [fig., Be conducting yourselves] with wisdom toward the [ones] outside, redeeming [or, making the best use of] the time. ⁶[Let] your* word always [be] in grace, having been seasoned with salt, [in order for you*] to know how it is necessary [for] you* to be answering each one.

⁷All the [things] with reference to me [fig., All my circumstances] Tychicus will make known to you*, the beloved brother and faithful servant [or, deacon] and fellow-slave in [the] Lord, ⁸whom I sent to you* for this very thing, so that he shall know the things concerning you* [fig., your* circumstances] and comfort your* hearts, ⁹with Onesimus, the faithful and beloved brother, who is [one] of you*. They will make known to you* all the [things happening] here.

¹⁰Aristarchus greets you*, my fellow-prisoner, and Mark, the cousin of Barnabas (concerning whom you* received instructions; if he comes to you*, receive him), ¹¹and Jesus, the one called Justus, [of] the ones of [the] circumcision, these [are the] only co-workers for the kingdom of God who became [or, proved to be] a comfort to me.

¹²Epaphras greets you*, the [one] from you* [or, [who is one] of you*], a slave of Christ, always striving earnestly on your* behalf in his prayers, so that you* shall stand perfect and having been fulfilled [or, completed] in all [the] will of God. ¹³For I testify [concerning] him that he has much zeal on your* behalf and [for] the [ones] in Laodicea and the [ones] in Hierapolis.

¹⁴Luke, the beloved physician, greets you*, and Demas. ¹⁵Greet the brothers [and sisters] in Laodicea, and [also] Nymphas and the assembly in his house.

¹⁶And when this epistle is read aloud before you*, cause that it shall also be read aloud in the assembly of the Laodiceans, and you* should also read aloud the [epistle] from Laodicea. ¹⁷And say to Archippus, "Be seeing to the ministry which you received in [the] Lord, so that you shall be fulfilling it."

¹⁸The greeting by the hand of me, Paul; be remembering my bonds [fig., imprisonment]. Grace [be] with you*. So be it!

The First Epistle of Paul the Apostle to the
Thessalonians

1 Paul and Silvanus and Timothy, To the assembly [or, church] of [the] Thessalonians in God [the] Father and [the] Lord Jesus Christ: Grace to you* and peace from God our Father and [the] Lord Jesus Christ!

²We give thanks to God always concerning you* all, making mention of you* in our prayers, ³constantly remembering your* work of faith and labor of love and patient endurance in the hope [or, confident expectation] of our Lord Jesus Christ, in [the] presence of our God and Father, ⁴knowing brothers [and sisters], having been loved by God, your* election [or, [God's] choosing of you*].

⁵Because our Gospel [or, Good News, and throughout book] did not come to you* in word only, but also in power and in [the] Holy Spirit and in much assurance [or, with full conviction], even as you* know of what sort we became among you* for your* sake. ⁶And you* became imitators of us and of the Lord, having received the word in much affliction [or, during a great trial], with [the] joy of [the] Holy Spirit, ⁷with the result that you* became examples to all the ones believing in Macedonia and Achaia.

⁸For the word of the Lord has sounded forth from you*, not only in Macedonia and in Achaia, but also in every place your* faith toward God has gone out, with the result that we have no need to be saying anything. ⁹For they themselves report about us what kind of entrance we had to you*, and how you* turned to God from the idols, to be serving as a slave to [the] living and true God, ¹⁰and to be waiting expectantly for His Son from the heavens, whom He raised from the dead—Jesus—the One rescuing us from the coming wrath.

2 For you* yourselves know, brothers [and sisters], our entrance to you*, that it did not become empty [fig., it was not without results]. ²But having suffered previously and having been mistreated (as you* know) in Philippi, we were bold in our God to speak to you* the Gospel of God in much conflict [or, amid much opposition].

³For our exhortation [was] not by deception, nor from an impure [motive], nor in treachery [or, deceit]. ⁴But just as we have been approved by God to be entrusted with the Gospel, so we speak, not as pleasing people, but God, the One examining our hearts. ⁵For at no time did we come with a word of flattery [fig., with flattering speech], as you* know, nor with a pretext for greed [fig., nor were we secretly desiring profit] (God [is our] witness!), ⁶nor seeking glory from people, neither from you* nor from others, being able [or, [even] though we were able] to be burdensome as Christ's apostles.

⁷But we became gentle in your* midst, just as a nursing mother is cherishing her own children. ⁸In this way, longing for [or, dearly loving] you*, we were delighted to impart to [or, share with] you* not only the Gospel of God, but also our own souls, because you* have become beloved to us.

⁹For you* remember, brothers [and sisters], our labor and toil, working night and day [so as] not to be a [financial] burden to any of you*, we proclaimed the Gospel of God to you*. ¹⁰You* [are] witnesses and [so is] God, how devoutly [or, in a godly manner] and righteously and blamelessly we became [fig., proved to be] to you*, the ones believing, ¹¹even as you* know how each one of you*, as a father his own children, we [were] exhorting you* and comforting [you*] ¹²and imploring [you*], in order for you* to walk about [fig., conduct yourselves] in a manner worthy of God, the One calling you* into His own kingdom and glory.

¹³For this reason also, we constantly give thanks to God, that having received [the] word of God [which you*] heard from us, you* accepted [it], not [as the] word of a person, but just as it truly is, [the] word of God, which also supernaturally works in you*, the ones believing. ¹⁴For you* became imitators, brothers [and sisters], of the assemblies [or, churches] of God, the ones being in Judea in Christ Jesus, because you* suffered the same [things], even you*, from your* own fellow-citizens, just as also they [did] from the Jews, ¹⁵the ones both having put to death the Lord Jesus and their own prophets and having persecuted us, and they are not pleasing God, and [are] against all people, ¹⁶forbidding us to speak to the Gentiles so that they should be saved, in order to always fill up [the measure of] their sins, but the wrath [of God] came upon them to [the] end [fig., in full measure].

¹⁷But we, brothers [and sisters], having been separated from you* for [the] time of an hour [fig., for a short while]—in face [fig., presence], not in heart—were especially eager with great desire to see your* face. ¹⁸For this reason, we wanted to come to you* (indeed I, Paul), both once and twice [fig., time and again], and [yet] Satan hindered us. ¹⁹For what [is] our hope [or, confident expectation] or joy or victor's wreath [or, crown] of rejoicing? [It is] even you* in the presence of our Lord Jesus at His Arrival [or, Coming, and throughout book], is it not? ²⁰For you* are our glory and joy.

3 For this reason, when we could no longer endure [it], we thought [it] best to be left in Athens alone, ²and we sent Timothy (our brother and a servant [or, deacon] of God and our co-worker in the Gospel of Christ) to establish [fig., strengthen] you* and to encourage you* concerning your* faith, ³[that] no one be disturbed by these afflictions [or, trials], for you* yourselves know that we are appointed for this. ⁴For even when we were with you*, we kept telling you* in advance [or, forewarning you*] that we are about to be experiencing hardships [or, to be afflicted], just as also it happened, and you* know [it]. ⁵For this reason also, when I could no longer endure [it], I sent to know [or, to learn about] your* faith, lest somehow the one tempting [or, the tempter] had tempted you*, and our labor came to be in emptiness [fig., for nothing].

⁶But now Timothy having come to us from you* and having declared good news to us [regarding] your* faith and love, and that you* have a good remembrance of us always, longing to see us, just as we also [long to see] you*. ⁷For this reason, we were encouraged, brothers [and sisters], in regard to you*, in all our affliction and distress, by means of your* faith. ⁸Because now we live,

since <u>you*</u> stand firm in [the] Lord. ⁹For what thanksgiving are we able to give in return to God concerning you*, for all the joy with which we rejoice because of you* in the presence of our God, ¹⁰imploring [in prayer] most earnestly night and day in order to see your* face and to perfect the [things] lacking in your* faith?

¹¹Now [may] our God and Father Himself and our Lord Jesus Christ direct our way to you*. ¹²And [may] the Lord cause you* to increase and to abound in love to one another and to all [people], even as we also [do] for you*, ¹³in order to establish your* hearts [as being] blameless in holiness before our God and Father at the Arrival of our Lord Jesus Christ with all His holy ones [or, saints].

4[As to the] rest [or, Finally] then brothers [and sisters], we ask and call on [or, plead with] you* in [the] Lord Jesus, just as you* received from us how it is necessary [for] you* to be walking about [fig., conducting yourselves] and to be pleasing God, so that you* shall be abounding [or, be excelling] still more. ²For you* know what instructions we gave you* through [or, by [the authority of]] the Lord Jesus.

³For this is the will of God, your* sanctification: [for] you* yourselves to be abstaining from sexual sin, ⁴[for] each of you* to know how to be acquiring his own vessel [fig., wife] in sanctification and honor, ⁵not in lustful passion of desire, just as also the Gentiles, the ones not knowing God, ⁶[so as] not to do wrong and take advantage of his brother [fig., fellow believer] in this matter, because the Lord [is the] avenger concerning all these [things], just as also we forewarned you* and solemnly testified. ⁷For God did not call us to impurity [or, immorality], <u>but</u> in sanctification. ⁸Therefore, the one rejecting [this] [or, regarding [this] as nothing] does not reject a person, <u>but</u> God, the One having also given His Holy Spirit to you*.

⁹Now concerning brotherly love [fig., affection for fellow-believers], you* have no need of [my] writing to you*, for <u>you*</u> yourselves are taught by God to be loving one another. ¹⁰For indeed you* do practice it toward all the brothers [and sisters], the [ones] in all Macedonia, but we call on [or, plead with] you*, brothers [and sisters], to be increasing [even] more ¹¹and to be ambitiously striving to be living a quiet life and to be doing your* own [things] [fig., to be minding your* own business] and to be working with your* own hands, just as we gave strict orders to [or, commanded] you*, ¹²so that you* shall be walking about [fig., conducting yourselves] properly toward the outsiders [fig., unbelievers] and have need of nothing.

¹³But we do not want you* to continue being unaware, brothers [and sisters], concerning the ones having fallen asleep [fig., who have died], so that you* shall not be sorrowing just as also the rest, the ones not having hope [or, confident expectation]. ¹⁴For since we believe that Jesus died and rose again, so also God will bring the ones having fallen asleep through [fig., having died in] Jesus with Him.

¹⁵For this we say to you* by [the] word of [the] Lord, that <u>we</u>, the ones living, the ones being left to the Arrival of the Lord, by no means shall precede the ones having fallen asleep [fig., who have died]. ¹⁶Because the Lord Himself with a shout of command, with [the] voice of an archangel and with [the] trumpet of God, will descend from heaven, and the dead in Christ will rise first, ¹⁷then <u>we</u>,

the ones living, the ones being left, will be caught up together with them in [the] clouds to a meeting of the Lord in [the] air, and so we will always be with [the] Lord! [18]Therefore, be comforting one another with these words.

5Now concerning the times and the seasons, brothers [and sisters], you* have no need [of] my writing to you*. [2]For you* yourselves accurately know that the Day of [the] Lord comes in this manner: as a thief in [the] night. [3]For when they say, "Peace and safety!" then destruction comes upon them suddenly, even as the birth-pains [come upon] the one having in [the] womb [fig., who is pregnant], and by no means shall they escape.

[4]But you*, brothers [and sisters], are not in darkness, so that the Day should overtake you* as a thief. [5]You* all are sons [and daughters] of light and sons [and daughters] of day; we are not of night nor of darkness. [6]So, consequently, let us not be sleeping as also the rest, but let us keep watching and be sober [or, clear-headed]. [7]For the ones sleeping sleep at night, and the ones getting drunk get drunk at night.

[8]But we, being [of the] day, let us be sober [or, clear-headed], having put on [the] breastplate of faith and of love, and [as] a helmet, [the] hope [or, confident expectation] of salvation. [9]Because God did not appoint us to wrath, but to [the] obtaining of salvation through our Lord Jesus Christ, [10]the One having died on our behalf, so that whether we are awake [fig,. are alive] or are sleeping [fig., have died], we shall live together with Him. [11]For this reason, be comforting one another and be building up [or, edifying] one the one [fig., each one the other], just as also you* are doing.

[12]And we request of you*, brothers [and sisters], to know [fig., appreciate] the ones laboring among you* and leading [or, caring for] you* in [the] Lord and instructing you*, [13]and to regard them very highly in love because of their work. Be living at peace among yourselves. [14]Now we urge you*, brothers [and sisters], be warning the disorderly [or, lazy] [ones]; be encouraging the discouraged [ones]; be supporting the sick [ones]; continue being patient toward all. [15]See [that] no one repays evil for evil, but always be pursuing the good, both for one another and for all.

[16]Be rejoicing always! [17]Be constantly praying. [18]In every[thing] be giving thanks. For this [is the] will of God in Christ Jesus for you*.

[19]Stop extinguishing [fig., stifling] the Spirit. [20]Stop despising [or, rejecting] prophecies. [21]But be examining all [things]; be holding fast [to] the good. [22]Be abstaining from every form of evil.

[23]Now may the God of peace Himself sanctify you* completely, and may your* spirit and soul and body be preserved complete, without blame at the Arrival of our Lord Jesus Christ! [24]The One calling you* [is] faithful, who also will do [this].

[25]Brothers [and sisters], be praying for us. [26]Greet all the brothers [and sisters] with a holy kiss. [27]I adjure you* [or, place you* under an oath] [by] the Lord, [for] this letter to be read aloud to all the holy brothers [and sisters].

[28]The grace of our Lord Jesus Christ [be] with you*! So be it!

The Second Epistle of Paul the Apostle to the
Thessalonians

1 Paul and Silvanus and Timothy, To the assembly [or, church] of [the] Thessalonians in God our Father and [the] Lord Jesus Christ: ²Grace to you* and peace from God our Father and [the] Lord Jesus Christ!

³We ought to be giving thanks to God always for you*, brothers [and sisters], just as it is fitting, because your* faith grows abundantly, and the love of each one of you* all for one another increases, ⁴with the result that we ourselves are boasting of you* in the assemblies [or, churches] of God about your* perseverance and faith in all your* persecutions and afflictions which you* endure, ⁵[which is] evidence of the righteous judgment of God, for you* to be counted worthy of the kingdom of God, for the sake of which also you* suffer, ⁶since [it is] a righteous [thing] with God to repay with affliction the ones afflicting you* ⁷and [to repay] with relief to you*, the ones being afflicted, along with us in the revelation of the Lord Jesus from heaven, with [the] angels of His power [or, His powerful angels], ⁸in a fire of flame [or, a flaming fire], giving [fig., inflicting] vengeance on the ones not knowing God and to the ones not obeying the Gospel [or, Good News] of our Lord Jesus, ⁹who will suffer divine justice, eternal ruin, from [the] face [fig., presence] of the Lord and from the glory of His strength, ¹⁰when He comes to be glorified in [or, among] His holy ones [or, saints] in that Day and to be marveled at among all the ones having believed, because our testimony to you* was believed.

¹¹For which we also pray always concerning you*, that our God considers you* worthy of the calling and fulfills all [the] good pleasure of [or, every desire for] [His] goodness [or, generosity] and [the] work of faith in power, ¹²in order that the name of our Lord Jesus is glorified in you*, and you* in Him, according to the grace of our God and of [the] Lord Jesus Christ [or, of our God and Lord, Jesus Christ].

2 Now we request of you*, brothers [and sisters], in regard to the Arrival [or, Coming] of our Lord Jesus Christ and of our gathering together to Him, ²for you* not to be quickly shaken in mind nor to be disturbed, neither by spirit nor by word nor by letters as [written] by us, as [if] that Day of Christ has arrived. ³Let no one deceive you* by any means, because [that Day will not come] unless the apostasy comes first, and the man of sin is revealed, the son of destruction [or, the one destined to be lost], ⁴the one being in opposition [or, being hostile] and puffing himself up with pride over every[thing] being called god or [every] object of worship, with the result that he sits down in the sanctuary of God as God, displaying himself that he is God.

⁵You* do remember that, being yet with you*, I said these things to you*, do you* not?

⁶And now, you* know the [thing] restraining, for him to be revealed in his own time. ⁷For the secret [or, mystery] of lawlessness is already supernaturally working, only the one [or, the One] now restraining [will continue to do so] until he [or, He] comes [or, appears] out of [the] midst. ⁸And then the lawless [one] will be revealed, whom the Lord will consume with the breath of His mouth and will destroy by the appearance of His Arrival [or, Coming], ⁹of whom is his [i.e., the lawless one's] arrival according to [the] supernatural working of Satan, in all power and signs and wonders of deceit [fig., counterfeit miracles], ¹⁰and in all deception of the unrighteousness among the ones perishing, because they did not receive the love of the truth for them to be saved. ¹¹And for this reason God will send to them a supernatural working of deception, for them to believe the lie, ¹²so that they shall be judged, all the ones not having believed the truth, <u>but</u> the ones having delighted in unrighteousness.

¹³But <u>we</u> ought to be giving thanks to God always concerning you*, brothers [and sisters], having been loved by [the] Lord, that God chose you* from [the] beginning for salvation, by sanctification of [the] Spirit and faith [in] the truth, ¹⁴to which He called you* through our Gospel [or, Good News] to [the] obtaining of [the] glory of our Lord Jesus Christ. ¹⁵So, consequently, brothers [and sisters], be standing firm and be holding [or, keeping] the handed down teachings which you* were taught, whether by word or by our letter. ¹⁶Now may our Lord Jesus Christ Himself, and our God and Father, the One having loved us and having given eternal comfort and good hope [or, confident expectation] by grace, ¹⁷comfort your* hearts and establish you* in every good word and work.

3[As to] the rest [or, Finally], be praying, brothers [and sisters], concerning us, that the word of the Lord shall be running [fig., spreading rapidly] and shall continue being glorified, just as also [it has been] with you*, ²and that we shall be delivered from the perverse and wicked people, for the faith [is] not of all. ³But faithful is the Lord, who will establish you* and will guard [you*] from evil [or, from the evil [one]]. ⁴And we have confidence in [the] Lord concerning you*, that [about] what we give strict orders to you*, both you* are doing and will do. ⁵Now may the Lord direct your* hearts into the love of God and into the patient endurance of Christ.

⁶Now we give strict orders to you*, brothers [and sisters], in [the] name of our Lord Jesus Christ, to be withdrawing yourselves from every brother walking about [fig., conducting themselves] in idleness and not according to the handed down teaching which they received from us. ⁷For you* yourselves know how it is necessary to be imitating us, because we did not live in idleness among you*, ⁸nor did we eat bread from anyone without paying, <u>but</u> [we were] working in labor and in toil, night and day, so as not to be a financial burden to any of you*; ⁹not because we do not have authority [or, the right], <u>but</u> so that we should give ourselves [as] a pattern to you*, for [you*] to be imitating us. ¹⁰For even when we were with you*, [about] this we had given strict orders to you*, that if anyone is not willing to be working neither let him be eating!

¹¹For we hear [that] some walk about [fig., conduct themselves] among you*
in idleness, not working at all, <u>but</u> being busybodies. ¹²Now to such [persons] we
give strict orders and exhort by our Lord Jesus Christ, that working with quietness,
they should be eating their own bread. ¹³But <u>you*</u>, brothers [and sisters], do not
become discouraged [in] [or, weary [of]] doing what is good.

¹⁴Now if anyone does not obey our word in this letter, be taking note of this
[one] and stop associating with him, so that he shall be ashamed. ¹⁵Yet do not
consider [him] as an enemy, <u>but</u> be admonishing [him] as a brother.

¹⁶Now may the Lord of peace Himself give to you* through all [fig. continually]
peace in every way [or, circumstance]. The Lord [be] with you* all!

¹⁷The greeting by my hand, Paul, which is a sign in every letter; in this way I
write. ¹⁸The grace of our Lord Jesus Christ [be] with you* all! So be it!

The First Epistle of Paul the Apostle to
Timothy

1 Paul, an apostle of Jesus Christ according to [the] command of God our Savior and of [the] Lord Jesus Christ our hope [or, confident expectation], ²To Timothy, a genuine child in [the] faith: Grace, mercy, [and] peace from God our Father and Christ Jesus our Lord!

³Just as I urged you to remain in Ephesus while I traveled to Macedonia, so that you should give strict orders to certain [ones] to stop teaching a different [or, heretical] doctrine ⁴and to stop paying attention to myths and endless genealogies, which cause disputes rather than [furthering the] administration [or, plan] of God, the [one] in faith. ⁵But the end [or, goal] of the command is love out of a pure heart and a good conscience and a sincere faith, ⁶from which certain [ones], having strayed [or, deviated] from, were turned aside to futile discourse, ⁷desiring to be teachers of the Law, not understanding neither what they are saying, nor concerning what they confidently assert.

⁸But we know that [the] Law [is] good, if anyone makes use of it lawfully, ⁹knowing this: that law is not laid down for a righteous [person] but for lawless and insubordinate [persons], for ungodly [ones] and for sinners, for unholy [ones] and for profane [or, worldly] [ones], for killers of fathers and for killers of mothers, for murderers, ¹⁰for sexual sinners, for participants in male-male sex, for slave dealers [or, kidnappers], for liars, for perjurers, and if anything else is in opposition to sound teaching, ¹¹according to the Gospel [or, Good News] of the glory of the blessed God, [with] which I was entrusted.

¹²And I give thanks to the One having empowered me—Christ Jesus our Lord—that He considered me faithful, having put [me] into the ministry, ¹³the one formerly being a blasphemer and a persecutor and an insolent person, but I was shown mercy, because failing to understand, I did [it] in unbelief; ¹⁴but the grace of our Lord overflowed with faith and love, the [grace which is] in Christ Jesus.

¹⁵Trustworthy [is] the word and worthy of all acceptation, that Christ Jesus came into the world to save sinners, of whom I am first [fig., the foremost of all]. ¹⁶But for this reason I was shown mercy, so that in me first [fig., as the foremost of all] Jesus Christ should demonstrate all His patience, as a pattern for the ones about to be believing on [or, trusting in] Him to life eternal. ¹⁷Now to the King of the ages [fig., the King eternal], immortal, invisible, [the] only wise God, [be] honor and glory into the ages of the ages [fig., forever and ever]! So be it!

¹⁸This command I entrust to you, [my] child Timothy, according to the previously made prophesies concerning you, so that in them you war the good warfare [fig., struggle against evil forces], ¹⁹having faith and a good conscience, which certain [ones] having pushed away [fig., rejected], suffered shipwreck concerning the faith, ²⁰of whom are Hymenaeus and Alexander, whom I handed over to Satan, so that they shall be taught not to be blaspheming.

2 Therefore, I urge first of all [for] petition to be continually made, prayers, intercessions, [and] thanksgivings, on behalf of all people: ²on behalf of kings and the ones being in positions of authority, so that we should lead a tranquil and peaceful life in all godliness and dignity. ³For this [is] good and acceptable before God our Savior, ⁴who desires all people [or, peoples] to be saved and to come to a full [or, true] knowledge of the truth. ⁵For [there is] one God and one Mediator [between] God and people, a Person, Christ Jesus, ⁶the One having given Himself [as] a ransom on behalf of all, the testimony in its own times, ⁷in regard to which I was put [or, appointed] [as] a preacher and apostle (I am telling [the] truth in Christ, I am not lying), [as] a teacher of Gentiles in faith and truth.

⁸Therefore, I want men to be praying in every place, lifting up holy hands, without wrath and dissension [or, doubting]. ⁹In the same manner also [I want] the women to be adorning themselves in sensible apparel [or, behavior], with modesty and decency [or, self-control], not with braided hair [or, elaborate hairstyles] or gold or pearls or very costly clothing, ¹⁰<u>but</u> with good works, which is fitting [or, proper] for women professing godliness.

¹¹Let a woman be learning in quietness with all submission. ¹²But I do not permit a woman to be teaching, nor to be exerting dominance over a man, <u>but</u> to be in quietness. ¹³For Adam was formed first, then Eve. ¹⁴And Adam was not deceived, but the woman, having been deceived, has come to be in transgression. ¹⁵But she will be saved through the bearing of children, if they remain in faith and love and sanctification, with decency [or, self-control].

3 Trustworthy [is] the word: If anyone aspires to [the] position of overseer [Gr. *episkope*], he desires a good work. ²Therefore, it is necessary [for] the overseer to be blameless [or, above reproach], a husband of one wife [fig., a one-wife kind of man], temperate, self-controlled, sensible, a friend of strangers [or, hospitable], skillful at teaching, ³not addicted to wine, not violent [or, quarrelsome], not greedy for dishonest gain, <u>but</u> gentle [or, considerate], peaceable, not a lover of money; ⁴leading his own house well, having children in submission with all dignity ⁵(but if someone does not know [how] to lead his own house, how can he take care of an assembly [or, church] of God?), ⁶not a new convert, lest having been swollen up with pride he should fall into [the] judgment of the Devil. ⁷And it is necessary [for] him also to have a good testimony from the [ones] outside [fig., unbelievers], lest he fall into disgrace and a snare of the Devil.

⁸In the same manner, deacons [are to be] worthy of respect, not double-tongued, not being given to much wine, not greedy for dishonest gain, ⁹holding the secret [or, mystery] of the faith in a pure conscience. ¹⁰But let these also first be tested, then let them be serving as a deacon, being beyond reproach. ¹¹In the same manner, women [or, [their] wives] [are to be] worthy of respect, not slanderous, temperate, faithful in all [things]. ¹²Let deacons be husbands of one wife [fig., one-wife kind of men], leading their children well and their own houses. ¹³For the ones having served well as a deacon obtain to themselves a good standing and much boldness [or, confidence] in faith, the [one] in Christ Jesus.

¹⁴These [things] I write to you, hoping [or, expecting] to come to you soon. ¹⁵But if I delay, [I write] so that you shall know how it is necessary to be conducting yourself in [the] house of God, which is [the] Assembly [or, Church] of the living God, [the] pillar and foundation of the truth. ¹⁶And confessedly, great is the secret [or, mystery] of godliness: God was revealed in [the] flesh, justified [or, shown to be righteous] in spirit [or, by [the] Spirit], seen by angels, preached among [the] nations [or, Gentiles], believed on in [the] world, taken up in glory!

4Now the Spirit explicitly says that in latter times some will fall away [or, apostatize] from the faith, paying attention to deceitful spirits and teachings of demons, ²in hypocrisy [or, insincerity] of liars, having been seared in their own conscience, ³forbidding to be marrying, [commanding] to be abstaining from foods which God created for receiving with thanksgiving by the [ones who are] faithful and have acknowledged the truth. ⁴Because every[thing] created by God [is] good, and nothing [is to be] rejected, [if] being received with thanksgiving. ⁵For it is sanctified through [the] word of God and prayer.

⁶[By] instructing the brothers [and sisters] [in] these things, you will be a good servant [or, deacon] of Jesus Christ, being nourished by the words of the faith and of the good teaching, which you have carefully followed. ⁷But be refusing to pay attention to the profane [or, worldly] and old wives' tales, but be exercising yourself to godliness. ⁸For bodily exercise is beneficial for a few [things], but godliness is beneficial for all [things], having promise of the present life and of the coming [life]. ⁹Trustworthy [is] the word and worthy of all acceptation. ¹⁰Because, for this [reason] we both labor and are insulted [or, denounced], because we have placed our hope on [or, have trusted in] the living God, who is [the] Savior [or, Preserver] of all people, especially of believers.

¹¹Be giving strict orders [concerning] these [things] and be teaching [them]. ¹²Stop letting anyone look down on your youth, but continue becoming an example for the ones believing—in word, in conduct, in love, in spirit, in faith, [and] in purity. ¹³Until I come, be giving attention to the reading aloud [of the Scriptures], to the exhortation [or, encouragement], [and] to the teaching. ¹⁴Stop disregarding the spiritual gift in you, which was given to you through prophecy, with laying on of the hands of the council of the elders.

¹⁵Be thinking about [or, Be practicing] these [things]; be in these things, so that your progress shall be evident to all. ¹⁶Be paying close attention to yourself and to the teaching; be continuing in them, for by doing this you will save [or, preserve safe and unharmed] both yourself and the ones hearing you.

5Do not sharply rebuke an older man, but be appealing [to him] as a father, younger men as brothers, ²older women as mothers, younger women as sisters, with all purity.

³Be honoring widows, the [ones] really [being] widows. ⁴But if any widow has children or grandchildren, let them be learning first to be practicing piety in regard to their own house and to be giving payments back [or, making repayments] to the parents, for this is acceptable before God. ⁵But the [one who is] really a

widow and having been left alone has placed her hope on [or, has trusted in] God and continues in petitions and in prayers night and day. 6But the one living in self-indulgence, living has died. 7And be giving strict orders [concerning] these [things], so that they shall be blameless [or, above reproach]. 8But if anyone does not provide for his own and especially his household, he has denied the faith and is worse than an unbeliever.

9Stop letting a widow be enrolled [who is] less than sixty years [old, and only if] she has been [the] wife of one husband [fig., a one-husband kind of woman], 10being testified to in [or, being approved by] good works, if she brought up children, if she entertained strangers [or, showed hospitality], if she washed holy ones' [or, saints'] feet, if she relieved [the ones] experiencing hardship [or, being afflicted], if she dedicated herself to every good work.

11But be refusing [to enroll] younger widows, for whenever they are drawn away by sensual desires [in disregard] of Christ, they desire to marry, 12having judgment [or, condemnation], because they set aside their first [pledge of] faith. 13And also at the same time, they learn [to be] idle, going about the houses, but not only idle, but also idle accusers [or, babblers] and busybodies, speaking the [things] they ought not. 14Therefore, I want younger [women] to be marrying, to bearing children, to be managing their homes, [and] to be giving no occasion to the one being in opposition [or, to the enemy] for reproach. 15For already some were turned aside after Satan.

16If any believing man or believing woman has widows, let [that one] be supporting them, and stop burdening the assembly [or, church], so that it can support the [ones who are] really widows.

17Be letting the elders having ruled well be counted worthy of double honor, especially the ones laboring in word and teaching. 18For the Scripture says, *"You will not muzzle an ox treading out [grain],"* and *"The laborer [is] worthy of his pay."* [Deut 25:4; Luke 10:7] 19Stop receiving an accusation against an elder, unless on [the basis of] two or three witnesses. 20The ones sinning, be rebuking before all, so that the others shall also be having fear. 21I strongly urge [you*] before God and [the] Lord Jesus Christ [or, the God and Lord, Jesus Christ,] and the chosen angels [or, elect messengers], that you observe these [things] without prejudgment [or, prejudice], doing nothing by partiality.

22Be laying hands quickly on no one, nor be sharing [or, participating] in sins of others. Be keeping yourself pure. 23No longer be drinking water [only], but be using a little wine, because of your stomach and your frequent infirmities.

24The sins of some people are quite evident, preceding [them] to judgment, and some also follow after. 25In the same manner also the good works [of some] are quite evident, and the [ones] having [fig., which are] otherwise are not able to be kept secret.

6As many as are slaves under a yoke, let them be considering their own masters worthy of all honor, so that the name of God and the teaching shall not be continually blasphemed. 2And the ones having believing masters, stop letting them despise [them], because they are brothers [and sisters], but rather let them be serving as slaves, because they are believers and beloved, the ones receiving benefit. Be teaching and exhorting these [things].

³If anyone teaches a different [or, heretical] doctrine and does not consent to sound words, the [ones] of our Lord Jesus Christ, and to the teaching according to godliness, ⁴having been swollen up with pride, knowing nothing, but obsessing about disputes and quarrels about words [fig., petty controversies], from which comes envy [or, jealousy], strife [or, bitter conflict], blasphemies, evil suspicions, ⁵constant arguing of people having been corrupted in the mind and having been deprived of the truth, supposing godliness to be a means of gain. Be withdrawing from such people.

⁶But godliness with contentment is great gain. ⁷For we brought nothing into the world, [and it is] certain that neither are we able to carry anything out! ⁸But having food and clothing, with these [things] we will be content. ⁹But the ones desiring to be growing rich fall into temptation and a snare and many foolish and harmful desires, which sink people into ruin and destruction. ¹⁰For the love of money is a root of all evils, of which some by longing for [it] went astray [or, wandered away] from the faith and pierced themselves through with many sorrows.

¹¹But you, O man of God, be fleeing from these [things], and be pursuing righteousness, godliness, faith, love, patient endurance, [and] gentleness [or, considerateness]. ¹²Be fighting the good fight of the faith. Be taking hold of eternal life, to which you were called and confessed the good confession before many witnesses.

¹³I am giving strict orders to you before God, the One giving life to all [things], and [before] Christ Jesus, the One having testified before Pontius Pilate the good confession, ¹⁴[for] you to keep the commandment spotless [and] blameless [or, above reproach] until the Appearing of our Lord Jesus Christ, ¹⁵which He will reveal in His own times, the blessed and only Sovereign, the King of the ones being kings and Lord of the ones exercising lordship, ¹⁶the only One having immortality, dwelling in unapproachable light, whom no one of people saw nor is able to see, to whom [is] honor and eternal might [or, dominion]! So be it!

¹⁷Be giving strict orders to the [ones] rich in the present age to stop being conceited and to stop placing their hope on [or, trusting in] the uncertainty of riches, but in the living God, the One giving to us all [things] richly for enjoyment, ¹⁸to be doing good, to be growing rich in good works, [and] to be generous, ready to share, ¹⁹treasuring [or, storing] up for themselves a good foundation for the coming [time], so that they shall take hold of eternal life.

²⁰O Timothy, guard the deposit entrusted to you, avoiding the profane [or, worldly] empty babblings and contradictions of the so-called knowledge, ²¹which some [by] professing strayed concerning [or, deviated from] the faith.

Grace [be] with you! So be it!

The Second Epistle of Paul the Apostle to
Timothy

1 Paul, an apostle of Jesus Christ by [the] will of God, according to [the] promise of life, the [one] in Christ Jesus, ²To Timothy, beloved child: Grace, mercy, [and] peace from God [the] Father and Christ Jesus our Lord!

³I thank God, whom I sacredly serve [as my] forefathers [did] with a pure conscience, as I have unceasing remembrance concerning you in my petitions night and day, ⁴longing to see you, having remembered your tears, so that I shall be filled with joy, ⁵taking [fig., calling to] remembrance the sincere faith within you, which dwelt first in your grandmother Lois and in your mother Eunice, and I have been persuaded that [is] also in you. ⁶For which cause I remind you to be rekindling the spiritual gift of God, the [one] in you through the laying on of my hands. ⁷For God did not give us a spirit of cowardice, but of power and of love and of a sound mind [or, of self-discipline].

⁸Therefore, you shall not be ashamed of the testimony of our Lord nor of me His prisoner, but endure hardship along with [me in] the Gospel [or, Good News, and throughout book] according to [the] power of God, ⁹the One having saved us, having called [us] with a holy calling, not according to our works, but according to His own purpose and grace, the one having been given to us in Christ Jesus before eternal times [or, before time began], ¹⁰but having been revealed now through the appearance of our Savior Jesus Christ, on the one hand having abolished death, on the other hand having brought to light life and immortality through the Gospel, ¹¹to which I was appointed a preacher and an apostle and a teacher of Gentiles. ¹²For which cause also I suffer these [things], but I am not ashamed; for I know in whom I have believed, and I have been persuaded that He is able to guard [what] I have entrusted to Him until that Day!

¹³Be holding [the] pattern [or, standard] of sound words which you heard from me, in faith and love, the [one] in Christ Jesus. ¹⁴Guard the good thing entrusted to you through [the] Holy Spirit, the One dwelling in us.

¹⁵You know this, that they turned away from me, all the [ones] in Asia, of whom are Phygellus and Hermogenes. ¹⁶May the Lord grant mercy to the house of Onesiphorus, because he frequently refreshed me and was not ashamed of my chain; ¹⁷but having been in Rome, he very diligently sought and found me. ¹⁸May the Lord grant to him to find mercy from [the] Lord in that Day! And you know very well [in] how many [ways] he served in Ephesus.

2 Therefore, you, my child, continue being empowered in the grace, the [one] in Christ Jesus. ²And what you heard from me through many witnesses, these [things] be committing to trustworthy people, who will be competent also to teach others. ³Therefore, you endure hardship as a good soldier of Jesus Christ. ⁴No one serving as a soldier entangles [himself] with the affairs of [civilian] life, so he shall please the one having enlisted him. ⁵And if anyone shall be competing [as an athlete], he is not awarded the victor's wreath, unless he competes lawfully [or, according to the rules]. [6]It is necessary [for] the laboring [or, hard-working] vineyard keeper [or, farmer] to be partaking of the fruits [or, crops] first. [7]Be considering what I am saying, for the Lord may give you understanding [or, insight] in all [things].

[8]Be remembering Jesus Christ having been raised from [the] dead, of [the] seed of David, according to my Gospel, [9]in which I endure hardship [even] to the point of chains as a criminal, but the word of God has not been bound. [10]For this reason I endure all [things], for the sake of the chosen ones [or, the elect], so that they also shall obtain salvation, the [one] in Christ Jesus, with eternal glory.

[11]Trustworthy [is] the word: For if we died with [Him], we will also live with [Him]. [12]If we endure, we will also reign with [Him]; if we deny [or, disown] [Him], that One will also deny us. [13]If we are unfaithful, that One remains faithful; He is not able to deny Himself.

[14]Remind [them] of these things, urgently warning [them] before the Lord, not to be quarreling about words [or, wrangling over the meanings of terms] [which is] useful for nothing [except] for the ruin of the ones hearing. [15]Be eager [or, diligent] to present yourself approved to God [as] a worker with no need to be ashamed, cutting straight [fig., teaching accurately; or, interpreting correctly] the word of truth. [16]But be avoiding profane [or, worldly] empty babblings, for they will advance to more impiety [or, ungodliness] [fig., will go from bad to worse], [17]and their word will spread like gangrene, of whom are Hymenaeus and Philetus, [18]who strayed concerning [or, deviated from] the truth, saying the resurrection to have already occurred, and they overturn [or, upset] the faith of some. [19]Nevertheless, [the] foundation of God has stood firm, having this seal [fig., inscription], "[The] Lord knew the ones being His," and "Let every one naming the name of [the] Lord depart from unrighteousness." [cp. Numb 16:5 (LXX); Nahum 1:7; Isaiah 52:11]

[20]Now in a great [fig., wealthy] house [there] are not only vessels of gold and of silver, but also of wood and of clay, and some indeed for honor, but some for dishonor. [21]Therefore, if anyone cleanses himself from these [things], he will be a vessel for honor, having been consecrated and beneficial to the Master, having been prepared for every good work.

[22]But be fleeing the youthful lusts! But be pursuing righteousness, faith, love, [and] peace with the ones calling on the Lord out of a pure heart. [23]But be avoiding the foolish and stupid disputes, knowing that they cause fights [fig., angry arguments]. [24]And it is necessary [for] a servant of [the] Lord not to be fighting [fig., arguing angrily], but to be gentle towards all, skillful at teaching, tolerant [or, patient when wronged], [25]in gentleness [or, humility] instructing the ones opposing, [if] perhaps God shall grant to them repentance [leading] to a full [or, true] knowledge [or, an acknowledging] of the truth, [26]and they regain their senses [and escape] from the Devil's snare, having been captured alive to [do] that one's will.

3But know [or, realize] this, that in [the] last days perilous times will come. [2]For people will be lovers of themselves [or, self-centered], lovers of money, arrogant boasters, proud, blasphemers, disobedient to parents, ungrateful, ungodly, [3]without natural affection [or, heartless], unwilling to be at peace with others [or, unforgiving], slanderous, lacking in self control, fierce, not loving what is good, [4]traitors, headstrong [or, reckless], having been swollen up with pride, lovers of pleasure more than lovers of God, [5]having an outward form of godliness, but having denied its power. And be [or, Be also] keeping away from these [people].

[6]For of these [people] are the ones worming into houses and leading captive little [fig., gullible] women, having been weighed down with sins, being led away with various lusts, [7]always learning and never able to come to a full [or, true] knowledge of truth. [8]And even as Jannes and Jambres stood up against Moses, so also are these standing themselves up against the truth, people having been corrupted in the mind, disapproved concerning the faith. [9]But they will not advance any further, for their folly will be evident to all, just as theirs [i.e., Jannes' and Jambres'] also became.

[10]And _you_ have carefully followed my teaching, manner of life, purpose, faith, patience, love, perseverance, [11]persecutions, [and] sufferings, such as happened to me in Antioch, in Iconium, [and] in Lystra. What persecutions I endured! And the Lord rescued me out of [them] all! [12]And indeed, all the ones desiring to be living in a godly manner in Christ Jesus will be persecuted. [13]But evil people and impostors will advance to the worse [fig., will go from bad to worse], leading astray [fig., deceiving] and being led astray [fig., being deceived].

[14]But _you_, be remaining in the [things] you learned and were entrusted with, knowing from whom you learned [them], [15]and that from childhood you know the Sacred Writings, the ones being able to make you wise to salvation through faith, the [one] in Christ Jesus. [16]All Scripture [is] God-breathed and [is] beneficial for teaching [or, doctrine], for verification [or, reproof], for correcting faults, for instruction in righteousness [or, the behavior that God requires], [17]so that the person of God shall be fully qualified [or, perfectly fit], having been completely equipped for every good work.

4Therefore, I strongly urge [you] before God and the Lord Jesus Christ, the One being about to be judging [the] living and [the] dead at His appearing and His kingdom. [2]Preach the word! Be ready in season [and] out of season [fig., whether the time is favorable or not], convict, rebuke, [and] encourage, with all patience and teaching. [3]For there will be a time when they themselves will not put up with sound teaching, _but_ according to their own lusts they will heap up teachers to themselves, itching in the ear [fig., craving to hear what they want to hear], [4]and on the one hand they will turn away the ear from the truth, on the other hand they will be turned aside to myths. [5]But _you_, be sober [or, clear-headed] in all [things]; endure hardship; do the work of an evangelist; completely fulfill your ministry.

[6]For _I_ am already being poured out as a drink offering, and the time of my departure has arrived. [7]I have fought the good fight; I have finished the course [or, race]; I have kept the faith. [8]Finally, [there] is laid up for me the victor's

wreath [or, crown] of righteousness which the Lord, the Righteous Judge, will give to me in that Day, but not only to me, but also to all the ones having loved His appearing.

⁹Be eager [or, diligent] to come to me quickly. ¹⁰For Demas abandoned me, having loved the present age, and traveled to Thessalonica, Crescens to Galatia, Titus to Dalmatia. ¹¹Only Luke is with me. Having picked up Mark, be bringing [him] with yourself, for he is useful to me for ministry [or, service]. [cp. Acts 15:36-40] ¹²But Tychicus I sent to Ephesus. ¹³When you come, bring the cloak which I left in Troas with Carpus, and the scrolls, especially the parchments.

¹⁴Alexander the coppersmith showed to me many evils [fig., did me much harm]. May the Lord repay him according to his works, ¹⁵whom you also [must] be guarding yourself against, for he greatly stood up against [or, resisted] our words.

¹⁶At my first defense no one stood with [or, supported] me, but all abandoned me. May it not be counted against them! ¹⁷But the Lord stood by me and gave me strength, so that through me the proclamation shall be completely fulfilled and all the nations shall hear, and I was rescued out of [the] mouth of a lion. ¹⁸And the Lord will rescue me from every evil work and will save [or, preserve] [me] for His heavenly kingdom, to whom [be] the glory into the ages of the ages [fig., forever and ever]! So be it!

¹⁹Greet Prisca [i.e. Priscilla] and Aquila, and Onesiphorus' household. ²⁰Erastus stayed in Corinth, but I left Trophimus sick in Miletus. ²¹Be eager [or, diligent] to come before winter. Eubulus greets you, and Pudens and Linus and Claudia and all the brothers [and sisters].

²²The Lord Jesus Christ [be] with your spirit. Grace [be] with you*! So be it!

The Epistle of Paul the Apostle to
Titus

1 Paul, a slave of God and an apostle of Jesus Christ, according to [the] faith of [the] chosen ones of God and [the] full [or, true] knowledge of [the] truth, the [one] according to godliness, ²in [the] hope [or, confident expectation] of eternal life, which the incapable of lying God promised before eternal times [or, before time began], ³but in its own times [fig., at the proper time] He revealed His word in [the] proclamation which I was entrusted with according to [the] command of God our Savior,

⁴To Titus, a genuine child according to [our] common faith: Grace, mercy, [and] peace from God [the] Father and [the] Lord Jesus Christ our Savior!

⁵On account of this I left you in Crete, so that you should set in order the things lacking and appoint [or, set up] elders [Gr. *presbuteros*] in every city, as I commanded you—⁶if anyone is beyond reproach, [the] husband of one wife [fig., a one-wife kind of man], having faithful [or, believing] children, not under accusation of reckless living or insubordinate. ⁷For it is necessary [for] the overseer [Gr. *episkope*] to be beyond reproach, as God's steward, not self-willed [or, stubborn], not quick-tempered, not addicted to wine, not violent [or, quarrelsome], not greedy for dishonest gain, ⁸but a friend of strangers [or, hospitable], loving what is good [or, tireless in activities prompted by love], sensible, righteous, holy, [and] self-controlled, ⁹holding firmly to the trustworthy word according to the teaching, so that he shall be able also to encourage [others] in the sound teaching and to convince the ones speaking against [it].

¹⁰For there are also many [who are] insubordinate, idle-talkers, and deceivers, especially the [ones] of the circumcision, ¹¹whose mouth it is necessary to be silencing, who overturn [or, upset] whole households, teaching what is not necessary, for the sake of dishonest gain. ¹²A certain one of them, a prophet of their own, said, "Cretans [are] always liars, evil beasts, [and] lazy bellies [fig., gluttons]!" [i.e. a quote from Epimendes, c. 600 B.C.] ¹³This testimony is true; for which cause rebuke them sharply, so that they shall be sound in the faith, ¹⁴not paying attention to Jewish myths and commandments of people, turning themselves away from the truth. ¹⁵All things indeed [are] pure to the pure, but to the ones having been defiled and unbelieving nothing [is] pure, but both their mind and their conscience [are] defiled. ¹⁶They profess to know God, but they deny [Him] in their works, being detestable and disobedient and disqualified for every good work.

2 But you, be speaking what is fitting [or, proper] [for] sound teaching [or, doctrine].

²Older men [are] to be temperate, worthy of respect, sensible, sound in the faith, in love, in patient endurance.

³Older women, in the same manner, in demeanor [are to be] reverent, not slanderous, not having been enslaved to much wine, teaching what is good, ⁴so that they shall be training the young women to be lovers of [their] husbands, lovers of [their] children, ⁵sensible, pure, keepers of [their own] homes, good, being subject to their own husbands, so that the word of God shall not be blasphemed.

⁶The younger men, in the same manner, be encouraging [them] to be thinking sensibly, ⁷showing yourself concerning all things [or, in all respects] [to be] an example of good works, in your teaching [showing] integrity, dignity, incorruptibility, ⁸sound [in] word, above criticism, so that the [one] from the opposition [fig., an enemy] shall be ashamed, having nothing evil to be saying concerning us.

⁹Slaves [are] to continue being subject to their own masters in all [things], to be serving well, not talking back, ¹⁰not pilfering, but showing all good faith, so that they shall adorn the teaching [or, doctrine] of God our Savior in all things [or, in every respect].

¹¹For the saving grace of God was revealed to all people, ¹²teaching us that having denied impiety [or, ungodliness] and worldly desires, we shall live soberly [or, sensibly] and righteously and in a godly manner in the present age, ¹³waiting for the blessed hope [or, confident expectation] and appearance of the glory of our great God and Savior Jesus Christ, ¹⁴who gave Himself on our behalf, so that He shall redeem us from all lawlessness and purify for Himself a people as His own special possession, zealous of good works.

¹⁵Be speaking these [things], and be exhorting and rebuking with all authority. Let no one be disregarding you!

3Remind them to continue being subject to rulers and authorities, to be obeying, to be ready for every good work, ²to be speaking evil of [or, slandering] no one, to be peaceable, gentle [or, considerate], showing all gentleness to all people.

³For we also were once foolish, disobedient, being led astray [fig., deceived], serving as slaves to lusts and various passions [or, desires for pleasure], living in malice and envy [or, jealousy], hateful, hating one another. ⁴But when the kindness and the love for humanity of God our Savior appeared ⁵(not by means of works, the [ones] in righteousness which we did, but according to His mercy), He saved us, through a bathing of regeneration and a renewing of [the] Holy Spirit, ⁶whom He poured out upon us richly, through Jesus Christ our Savior, ⁷so that having been justified [or, declared righteous] by that One's grace, we shall become heirs according to [the] hope [or, confident expectation] of eternal life.

⁸Trustworthy [is] the word, and I want you to be confidently asserting concerning these [things], so that they, the ones having believed God, shall be concentrating on devoting themselves to good works. These are the good and beneficial [or, valuable] things to people. ⁹But be avoiding foolish controversies and genealogies and quarrels and fights [fig., angry arguments] about law, for they are unprofitable and futile.

[10]Be rejecting a divisive [or, heretical] person after a first and second warning, [11]knowing that such [a person] has been corrupted and is sinning, being self-condemned.

[12]Whenever I send Artemas or Tychicus to you, be eager [or, diligent] to come to me to Nicopolis, for I have decided to spend the winter there. [13]Eagerly help Zenas the lawyer and Apollos on their journey, so that nothing shall be lacking to them. [14]And let our [people] also be learning to be concentrating on good works for urgent needs, so that they shall not be unfruitful.

[15]All the [ones] with me greet you. Greet the ones affectionately loving us in faith. Grace [be] with all of you*! So be it!

The Epistle of Paul the Apostle to
Philemon

¹Paul, a prisoner of Christ Jesus, and Timothy the brother, To Philemon our beloved [brother] and co-worker, ²and to the beloved Apphia and to Archippus our fellow-soldier and to the assembly [or, church] in your house: ³Grace to you* and peace from God our Father and [the] Lord Jesus Christ!

⁴I give thanks to my God, always making mention of you in my prayers, ⁵hearing of your love and faith which you have toward the Lord Jesus and for all the holy ones [or, saints], ⁶in order that the fellowship of your faith shall become effective in the full [or, true] knowledge of every good [thing], the [good] in us in [or, for] Christ Jesus. ⁷For I have much thankfulness and comfort [or, encouragement] over your love, because the bowels [fig., hearts] of the holy ones [or, saints] have been refreshed through you, brother.

⁸For this reason, having much boldness [or, confidence] in Christ to be commanding you [to be doing] the proper [thing], ⁹[yet] on account of love I rather appeal, being such a one as Paul, an old man, but now also a prisoner of Jesus Christ. ¹⁰I appeal to you concerning my child, whom I fathered in my bonds, Onesimus ["useful"], ¹¹the one once useless to you, but now useful to me and to you, whom I sent back. ¹²Now you receive him (that is, my own bowels [fig., my very heart]), ¹³whom I wished to be keeping to myself, so that he should minister to [or, serve] me on your behalf in the bonds of the Gospel [or, Good News]. ¹⁴But I wanted to do nothing without your consent, so that your good [deed] shall not be as by necessity, but by a voluntary [action].

¹⁵For perhaps for this reason he departed for an hour [fig, for a while], so that you shall be having him eternally, ¹⁶no longer as a slave, but above a slave, a beloved brother, especially to me, but how much more to you, both in [the] flesh and in [the] Lord. ¹⁷Therefore, since you have fellowship with me, receive him as me. ¹⁸But since he wronged you or owes [something], be charging this to me [or, to my account]. ¹⁹I, Paul, wrote [this] with my [own] hand. I will repay—lest I say to you [fig., not to mention] that you owe even yourself to me! ²⁰Yes, brother, may I have profit of you [or, let me benefit from you] in [the] Lord. Refresh my bowels [fig., heart] in [the] Lord.

²¹Having been confident of your obedience, I wrote to you, knowing that even more than what I say you will do. ²²But at the same time also be preparing for me a lodging [or, guest room], for I hope [or, expect] that through your* prayers I will be graciously given to you*.

²³Epaphras greets you (my fellow-prisoner in Christ Jesus), ²⁴[as do] Mark, Aristarchus, Demas, [and] Luke, my co-workers!

²⁵The grace of our Lord Jesus Christ [be] with your* spirit! So be it!

The Epistle to the
Hebrews

1 In many parts [or, Bit by bit] and in various ways in time past, God having spoken to the fathers by the prophets, in these last days He spoke to us by [His] Son, ²whom He appointed heir of all [things], through whom also He made the ages [fig., universe]; ³who being [the] outshining of His glory and [the] exact expression of His essence, and sustaining all the [things] by the word of His power, having Himself made by Himself a purification [or, purgation] of our sins, sat down at [the] right hand of the Majesty on high, ⁴having become so much better than the angels, as He has inherited a more excellent name than they.

⁵For to which of the angels did He ever say, *"You are My Son; today I have begotten You?"* and again, *"I will be to Him for a father, and He will be to Me for a Son?"* [Psalm 2:7; 2Sam 7:14; 1Chr 17:13]
⁶Now again when He brings the Firstborn [fig., the Pre-existent One] into the inhabited earth, He says, *"And let all [the] angels of God prostrate themselves in worship before Him."* [Deut 32:43, LXX; Psalm 97:7, LXX]
⁷And on the one hand to the angels He says, *"The One making His angels spirits, and His public [or, temple] servants a flame of fire."* [Psalm 104:4]
⁸On the other hand to the Son [He says], *"Your throne, O God, [is] into the age of the age [fig., forever and ever]; a scepter of integrity [is] the scepter of Your kingdom. ⁹You loved righteousness and hated lawlessness; for this reason God, your God anointed You with [the] oil of great happiness above Your companions."* [Psalm 45:6,7]
¹⁰And, *"You, LORD, in [the] beginning laid the foundation of the earth, and the heavens are works of Your hands. ¹¹These will perish, but You remain; and all [things] will become old like a garment, ¹²and You will roll them up like a cloak, and they will be changed. But You are the same, and Your years will not come to an end."* [Psalm 102:25-27]
¹³But to which of the angels did He ever say, *"Sit at My right hand, until I put Your enemies [as] Your footstool?"* [Psalm 110:1]

¹⁴They are all spirits of spiritual service being sent out to render service for the sake of the ones being about to be inheriting salvation, are they not?

2 For this reason it is necessary [for] us to pay much closer attention to the [things] having been heard, lest we drift away. ²For since the word having been spoken through angels became legally valid, and every transgression and disobedience received a just reward, ³how will we escape having disregarded so great a salvation? Which having received a beginning [by] being spoken by the Lord, was confirmed to us by the ones having heard, ⁴God adding further testimony both with signs and wonders and with various miraculous powers and distributions [fig., gifts] of [the] Holy Spirit, according to His will.

⁵For He did not subject to angels the coming inhabited earth, concerning which we are speaking. ⁶But someone somewhere solemnly testified, saying:

> *What is humanity* [or, *man*], *that You remember him, or [the] son of humanity, that You look after him?* ⁷*You made him only a little lower* [or, *only for a short while lower*] *than [the] angels. You awarded him the victor's wreath [of]* [or, *crowned him with*] *glory and honor.* ⁸*You put all [things] in subjection under his feet.* [Psalm 8:4-6]

For in the subjecting to him all [things], He left nothing unsubjected to him. But now we do not yet see all [things] having been subjected to him. ⁹But we see Jesus, the One having been made only a little lower [or, only for a short while lower] than [the] angels because of the suffering of death, having been awarded the victor's wreath [of] [or, having been crowned with] glory and honor, in order that by [the] grace of God He should taste [fig., experience] death on behalf of all.

¹⁰For it was fitting for Him, because of whom [are] all [things], and through whom [are] all [things], having brought many sons [and daughters] to glory, to make the Originator of their salvation perfect through sufferings. ¹¹For both the One sanctifying and the ones being sanctified [are] all of one [Father], for which reason He is not ashamed to be calling them brothers [and sisters], ¹²saying, *"I will proclaim Your name to my brothers [and sisters]; in [the] midst of [the] assembly I will sing praise to You."* [Psalm 22:22] ¹³And again, *"I will have put trust in Him."* [2Sam 22:3, LXX; Isaiah 8:17, LXX] And again, *"Look! I and the young children whom God gave to Me."* [Isaiah 8:18]

¹⁴Therefore, since the young children have shared of flesh and blood, He Himself also likewise shared in the same, so that through death He should destroy [or, render powerless] the one having the power of death, that is, the Devil, ¹⁵and release those, as many as [due to] a fear of death, throughout all their life, were subjects of slavery. ¹⁶For surely He does not take hold of [fig., give aid to] angels, but He takes hold of [fig., gives aid to] [the] seed of Abraham. ¹⁷Therefore, it was necessary [for] Him to become like His brothers [and sisters] in all [respects], so that He should become a merciful and faithful High Priest [in] the [things pertaining] to God, [in order] to make propitiation [or, an appeasing sacrifice] for the sins of the people. ¹⁸For He Himself having been tempted in what He suffered, He is able to help the ones being tempted.

3 Therefore, holy brothers [and sisters], sharers of [the] heavenly calling, consider the Apostle and High Priest of our profession—Christ Jesus—²being faithful to the One having appointed Him, as also Moses [was] in all his house. ³For this One has been counted worthy of more glory than Moses, to the degree that the one having built the house has more honor than [the house] itself. ⁴For

every house is built by someone, but the One having built all [things is] God.
⁵And Moses on the one hand as a trusted servant [was] faithful in all his house,
for a testimony of those things which would be spoken [later], ⁶on the other hand
Christ as a Son over His [own] house, whose house we are, if indeed we hold
fast the confidence [or, joyful sense of freedom] and the boasting of the hope [or,
confident expectation] firm to [the] end.

⁷For this reason, just as the Holy Spirit says:

> *Today if you* hear His voice, ⁸stop hardening your* hearts* [fig.,
> *becoming stubborn*] *as in the rebellion, in the day of the testing in the
> wilderness, ⁹where your* fathers tested Me; they tried Me and saw
> My works [for] forty years. ¹⁰For this reason, I was angry with that
> generation, and said, "They are always being led astray* [fig., *being
> deceived*] *in* [*their*] *heart, and these did not know My ways." ¹¹So in My
> anger I took an oath: "They will not enter into My rest."* [Psalm 95:7-
> 11]

¹²Be watching, brothers [and sisters], lest [there] will be in any of you* an evil
heart of unbelief [which] falls away from the living God. ¹³But be encouraging
one another daily, while it is being called "Today," lest any of you* be hardened
[fig., are made stubborn] by [the] deception of sin. ¹⁴For we have become sharers
of Christ, if indeed we hold fast the beginning of [our] assurance until the end,
¹⁵[while] it is being said, *"Today if you* hear His voice, stop hardening your*
hearts as in the rebellion."* [Psalm 95:7,8]

¹⁶For who having heard rebelled? But it was not all the ones having come out
of Egypt through Moses, was it? ¹⁷Now with whom was He angry forty years?
[It was] the ones having sinned, whose corpses fell in the wilderness, was it not?
¹⁸And to whom did He take an oath [that they] would not enter into His rest, if not
to the ones having refused to believe? ¹⁹And [so] we see that they were not able to
enter because of unbelief.

4Therefore, since a promise has been left [fig., remains] to enter into His rest,
let us fear lest anyone of you* seems to have come short. ²For we also have
had the Gospel [or, Good News] proclaimed [to us], even as they; but the word
[which they] heard was of no use to them, it not having been mixed with faith
by the ones having heard. ³For we, the ones having believed, enter into that rest,
just as He has said, *"So in My anger I took an oath: 'They will not enter into My
rest'"* [Psalm 95:11]—His works were done from [the] laying of the foundation of
[the] world. ⁴For He has said somewhere concerning the seventh [day] thus, *"And
God rested on the seventh day from all His works."* [Gen 2:2] ⁵And in this [place]
again, *"They will not enter into My rest."* [Psalm 95:11]

⁶Therefore, since it remains for some to enter into it, and the ones having first
heard the Gospel [or, Good News] did not enter in because of disobedience due to
unbelief, ⁷again He designates a certain day, "Today," saying in David, after such
a long time just as it has been said, *"Today if you* hear His voice, stop hardening*

your* hearts [fig., *becoming stubborn*]." [Psalm 95:7,8] ⁸For if Joshua had given them rest, He [i.e., God] would not have spoken concerning another day after these [things]. ⁹So there remains a Sabbath rest for the people of God. ¹⁰For the one having entered into His rest, also [has] rested himself from his works, even as God [rested] from His own [works]. ¹¹Therefore, let us be eager [or, diligent] to enter into that rest, lest anyone falls in the same example of disobedience due to unbelief.

¹²For the word of God [is] living and effective and sharper than every double-edged sword, and [is] penetrating as far as [the] division of both soul and spirit, of both joints and marrow, and [is] able to discern [the] thoughts and intentions of the heart. ¹³And no created thing is able to be hidden before Him, but all [things are] naked and have been exposed to His eyes to whom we [must give] an account.

¹⁴Therefore, having a great High Priest [who] has passed through the heavens—Jesus, the Son of God—let us be holding fast our confession. ¹⁵For we do not have a High Priest [who is] unable to sympathize with our weaknesses, but [One] having been tried in all [respects] in the same way [we are, yet] without sin. ¹⁶Therefore, let us be approaching with confidence [or, a joyful sense of freedom] to the throne of grace, so that we shall receive mercy and find grace for well-timed help.

5For every high priest being taken from [among] people is appointed on behalf of people in the [things pertaining] to God, so that he shall offer both gifts and sacrifices on behalf of sins, ²being able to be dealing gently [with] the ones failing to understand and being led astray [fig., being deceived], since he himself is also being subject to weakness. ³And because of this [weakness] he must, just as for the people, in the same manner also for himself, to be offering [sacrifices] for sins. ⁴And no one takes the honor to himself, but [he receives it] when being called by God, just as also Aaron [was].

⁵In the same way also Christ did not glorify Himself to become High Priest, but the One having said to Him, *"You are My Son, Today I have begotten You."* [Psalm 2:7] ⁶Just as He also says in another [place], *"You [are] a Priest into the age* [fig., *forever*] *according to the order of Melchisedek;"* [Psalm 110:4] ⁷who in the days of His flesh having offered up with loud crying and tears both prayers and petitions to the One being able to be saving Him from death, and having been heard due to His godly fear [or, piety], ⁸although being a Son, He learned obedience from what He suffered. ⁹And having been made perfect, He became to all the ones obeying Him [the] source of eternal salvation, ¹⁰having been designated by God [as] a High Priest *"according to the order of Melchisedek,"* ¹¹concerning which we have much to be saying [in] word, and [it is] difficult to explain since you* have become dull in the hearing [fig., slow to respond to spiritual things].

¹²For indeed, [though] you* ought to be teachers by this time, you* again have need [for someone] to be teaching you* what [are] the rudimentary elements [or, basic teachings] of the beginning of the oracles of God, and you* have become [ones] having need of milk and not of solid food. ¹³For everyone partaking of milk [is] inexperienced in [the] word of righteousness, for he is a young child.

¹⁴But solid food is for [the] mature, for the ones having, because of practice, their powers of discernment having been trained to discern [between] both good and evil.

6For this reason, having left the subject of the beginning [principles] of Christ, let us continue being moved to maturity, not laying again a foundation of repentance from dead [fig., utterly useless] works and of faith toward God, ²of [the] teaching of baptisms [or, doctrine of immersions] and of [the] laying on of hands and of [the] resurrection of the dead and of eternal judgment. ³And this we shall do, only if God shall be permitting.

⁴For [it is] impossible for the ones once having been enlightened and having tasted of [fig., experienced] the heavenly free gift and having became sharers of [the] Holy Spirit ⁵and having tasted [fig., experienced] [the] good word of God and the powers of the coming age, ⁶and having fallen away, to be renewing [them] again to repentance, having crucified again to themselves the Son of God and having publicly disgraced [Him].

⁷For [the] ground, the one drinking the frequently coming upon it rain and yielding vegetation suitable for those on account of whom indeed it is cultivated, receives a blessing from God; ⁸but [if] producing thorn plants and thistles [it is] worthless and on the verge of being cursed, whose end [is] for burning.

⁹But we have been convinced concerning you*, beloved, the better [things] and having [fig., those accompanying] salvation, even though we are speaking in this way. ¹⁰For God is not unjust to forget your* work and labor of love which you* yourselves showed toward His name, having served the holy ones [or, saints] and [still] serving [them]. ¹¹But we desire [for] each of you* to be showing the same diligence to the full assurance of the hope [or, confident expectation] to [the] end, ¹²so that you* do not become sluggish, but imitators of the ones [who] through faith and patient endurance [are] inheriting the promises.

¹³For when God made a promise to Abraham, since He was having no one greater to take an oath by, He took an oath by Himself, ¹⁴saying, *"Surely blessing I will bless you, and multiplying I will multiply you."* [Gen 22:17] ¹⁵And so, having waited patiently, he obtained the promise.

¹⁶For people indeed take an oath by the greater, and with them the oath [given] as confirmation [is] an end of every dispute, ¹⁷in which God wanting to show even more [clearly] to the heirs of the promise the unchangeable nature of His purpose, guaranteed [it] by an oath, ¹⁸so that through two unchangeable things, in which [it is] impossible for God Himself to lie, we shall be having a strong encouragement, the ones having fled for refuge to take hold of the hope [or, confident expectation] being set before [us], ¹⁹which [hope] we have as an anchor of the soul, both sure and secure, and having entered into the inner side of the veil [of the temple], ²⁰where Jesus, [the] Forerunner, entered on our behalf having become a High Priest *"into the age [fig., forever] according to the order of Melchisedek."* [Psalm 110:4].

7For this Melchisedek, king of Salem, priest of God Most High, the one having met Abraham while returning from the defeat of the kings and having blessed him, ²to whom also Abraham divided a tenth of all [the spoils] ([his name] first on the one hand being interpreted "king of righteousness," and on the other hand, "king of Salem," which is, "king of peace"), ³without father, without mother, without genealogy, having neither beginning of days nor end of life, but having been made like to the Son of God, remains a priest continually.

⁴But notice how great this one [was], to whom even Abraham the patriarch gave a tenth out of the best of the spoils. ⁵And indeed the ones receiving the priesthood from the sons of Levi have a commandment to be collecting tithes from the people according to the Law, that is, [from] their brothers [and sisters], even though they have come out from the reproductive organs of Abraham [fig., they have descended from Abraham].

⁶But the one not having [his] descent traced from them has received tithes from Abraham, and he has blessed the one having the promises. ⁷But without any dispute, the lesser is blessed by the better. ⁸And here on the one hand dying [fig., mortal] men receive tithes, there on the other hand [it is] being witnessed that he lives. ⁹And as a word to say [fig., so to speak], through Abraham even Levi, the one receiving tithes, has paid tithes. ¹⁰For he was still in the reproductive organs of his father when Melchisedek met him.

¹¹Therefore, if indeed perfection was through the Levitical priesthood (for the people under it had received the Law) what further need [was there] for a different priest to be arising according to the order of Melchisedek and not to be called according to the order of Aaron? ¹²For the priesthood being changed, of necessity [there] also takes place a change of law. ¹³For [He] about whom these [things] are being said has shared of [fig., belongs to] a different tribe, from which no one has officiated at the altar. ¹⁴For [it is] evident that our Lord has arisen out of Judah, regarding which tribe Moses spoke nothing concerning priesthood.

¹⁵And it [i.e. this change in law] is yet even more evident since a different Priest arises according to the likeness of Melchisedek, ¹⁶who has come not according to [the] law of a worldly commandment, but according to [the] power of an endless life. ¹⁷For He testifies, *"You [are] a Priest into the age* [fig., *forever*] *according to the order of Melchisedek."* [Psalm 110:4]

¹⁸For on the one hand an annulment comes about of [the] proceeding commandment because of its weakness and uselessness ¹⁹(for nothing was made perfect [by] the Law), on the other hand [there is the] bringing in of a better hope [or, expectation] through which we draw near to God.

²⁰And to the degree that [it was] not without [the] taking of an oath ²¹(for on the one hand the ones without taking an oath [have] become priests, on the other hand the One with taking an oath through the One saying to Him, *"[The] LORD took an oath, and will not change His mind, 'You [are] a Priest into the age* [fig., *forever] according to the order of Melchisedek),'"* [Psalm 110:4] ²²by so much Jesus has become [the] guarantee of a better covenant.

²³And on the one hand many have become priests because they are being prevented by death from continuing, ²⁴on the other hand the One because of His

remaining into the age [fig., forever] has the priesthood permanently. ²⁵Therefore, He is also being able to be saving to the [very] end [fig., completely] the ones coming through Him to God, [since] He is always living to be making the intercession on their behalf.

²⁶For such a High Priest was fitting for us: holy, innocent, undefiled, having been separated from the sinners and having become higher [than] the heavens, ²⁷who does not have a daily need like the high priests to be first offering up sacrifice on behalf of His own sins then for the [sins] of the people; for this He did once [and] for all [fig., once and never again], having offered up Himself. ²⁸For the Law appoints men having weakness [as] high priests, but the word of the oath, the [one] after the Law, [appoints] the Son having been perfected into the age [fig., forever].

8 Now [this is the] main point about the [things] being said: we have such a High Priest who sat down at [the] right hand of the throne of the Majesty in the heavens, ²a Minister of the holy [places] [fig., the sanctuary] and of the true tabernacle, which the Lord pitched and not humanity [fig., and not by human hands]. ³For every high priest is appointed to be offering both gifts and sacrifices. Therefore, [it is] necessary for this One also to be having something which He should offer. ⁴For indeed if He were on earth, He would not be a priest, there being the priests, the ones offering the gifts according to the Law, ⁵who sacredly serve a copy and shadow of the heavenly [things], just as Moses had been divinely warned, being about to be erecting the tabernacle, *"See,"* for He says, *"you will make all [things] according to the pattern, the one having been shown to you in the mountain."* [Exod 25:40] ⁶But now He has obtained a far superior sacred service, to the degree that He is also Mediator of a better covenant, which has been enacted on better promises.

⁷For if that first [covenant] was faultless, a place would not have been sought for a second. ⁸For finding fault with them [i.e. the people], He says:

> *Listen! [The] days are coming, says [the]* Lord, *and I will establish a new covenant over the house of Israel and over the house of Judah,* ⁹*not according to the covenant which I made with their fathers, in [the] day of My having taken [them] by their hand to bring them out of [the] land of Egypt, because they did not continue in My covenant, and I disregarded them, says [the]* Lord.
>
> ¹⁰*Because this [is] the covenant which I will covenant with the house of Israel after those days, says [the]* Lord, *giving My laws into their mind, and I will inscribe them on their hearts, and I will be to them for a God, and they will be to Me for a people.* ¹¹*And by no means shall they teach each his fellow-citizen, and each his brother [and sister], saying, "Know the* Lord," *because all will know Me from [the] least of them to [the] greatest.* ¹²*For I will be merciful to their unrighteousness, and their sins and their lawlessness deeds I shall by no means remember anymore. [Jer 31:31-34 (verse 32, LXX)]*

¹³By the saying "new," He has made the first obsolete. Now the one becoming obsolete and growing old [is] on the verge of disappearing.

9Then indeed even the first [covenant] had ordinances of sacred service and the earthly sanctuary. ²For a tabernacle was prepared: the first [part] in which [were] both the lampstand and the table, and the loaves of bread of the presentation [fig., the consecrated bread], which is called "Holy [Place]" [fig., the outer sanctuary]; ³and after the second veil [was] a tabernacle which is being called "Holy of Holies" [fig., the inner sanctuary], ⁴having a golden, incense altar and the ark of the covenant having been overlaid on all sides with gold, in which [were the] golden pot having the manna and the rod of Aaron, the one having budded, and the tablets of the covenant, ⁵and above it [were the] cherubim of the glory overshadowing the mercy-seat [or, the place of forgiveness] concerning which we are not now [able] to be speaking in detail.

⁶Now these [things] having been prepared in this way, on the one hand the priests through all [fig. always] enter into the first tabernacle performing the sacred services, ⁷on the other hand once in the year, the high priest [enters] alone into the second [sanctuary], not without blood, which he offers on behalf of himself and the sins of the people committed in ignorance. ⁸The Holy Spirit making this clear, that not yet has been revealed the way into the Holy [Places], the first tabernacle still standing, ⁹which [was] a symbol for the present time, according to which both gifts and sacrifices are offered, [which] are not being able, in regard to conscience, to make perfect the one performing the sacred service, ¹⁰[since they are concerned] only with food and drinks and various baptisms [or, ceremonial washings] and ordinances of [the] flesh [or, regulations for the body] being imposed until a time of reformation.

¹¹But Christ having appeared [as] High Priest of the good [things] coming, through the greater and more perfect tabernacle not made with human hands (that is, not of this creation), ¹²and not through [the] blood of goats and calves, but through His own blood, entered in once [and] for all [fig., once and never again] into the Holy [Places], having secured eternal redemption. ¹³For if the blood of bulls and goats and ashes of a heifer [i.e. a young cow] sprinkling the ones having been defiled sanctifies to the purifying of the flesh, ¹⁴how much more will the blood of Christ (who through [the] eternal Spirit offered Himself unblemished to God) purify [or, purge] your* conscience from dead works for [you*] to be sacredly serving the living God?

¹⁵And for this reason He is Mediator of a new covenant, in order that (a death having occurred for redemption of the transgressions under the first covenant) the ones having been called shall receive the promise of the eternal inheritance. ¹⁶For where [there is] a covenant [or, a will, and through verse 17], it is necessary [for proof of the] death of the one having made the covenant to be brought. ¹⁷For a covenant [is] valid over dead [people], since it is never in force while the one having made the covenant lives.

¹⁸Therefore, not even the first [covenant] has been inaugurated without blood. ¹⁹For when every commandment had been spoken according to [the] Law by Moses to all the people, having taken the blood of the calves and goats, with water and scarlet wool and hyssop [i.e., a small bush with aromatic leaves used for ceremonial sprinkling], he sprinkled both the scroll itself and all the people, ²⁰saying, *"This [is] the blood of the covenant which God commanded to you*."* [Exod 24:8] ²¹And likewise he sprinkled both the tabernacle and all the vessels of the sacred service with the blood. ²²And with blood almost all [things] are purified according to the Law, and without shedding of blood forgiveness does not come.

²³Therefore, [it was] indeed necessary [for] the copies of the [things] in the heavens to be continually purified with these, but the heavenly things themselves with better sacrifices than these. ²⁴For Christ did not enter into holy [places] made with human hands, [which are] copies of the true, <u>but</u> [He entered] into heaven itself, now to be revealed in the face [fig., presence] of God on our behalf; ²⁵nor [did He enter] so that He should offer Himself often, even as the high priest enters into the holy [places] every year with blood belonging to another; ²⁶otherwise, it would had been necessary [for] Him to suffer often from [the] laying of the foundation of [the] world. But now once for all [time], at [the] completion of the ages, He has been revealed to put away sin through His sacrifice.

²⁷And just as it is laid up [fig., destined] for people to die once, and after this [comes] judgment, ²⁸so also Christ, having been offered once to bear [or, take away] the sins of many, will appear a second time without [reference to] sin to [bring] salvation to the ones eagerly waiting for Him!

10For the Law having [only] a shadow of the good [things] coming, [and] not the very form of things, by the same sacrifices which they offer continually every year, they are never able to make the ones approaching perfect. ²Otherwise, they would cease to be continually offered, would they not, because the ones sacredly serving would no longer have conscience of sins, having once for all [time] been purified? ³<u>But</u> in those [sacrifices there is] a reminder of sins every year. ⁴For [it is] impossible [for the] blood of bulls and goats to be taking away sins.

⁵For this reason, entering into the world, He says:

> *Sacrifice and offering You did not desire, but a body You prepared for Me;* ⁶*in whole-burnt offerings* [or, *offerings which are entirely burned*] *and [sacrifices] concerning sin, You took no pleasure.* ⁷*Then I said, "Look! I have come (in a roll of a scroll it has been written concerning Me) to do Your will, O God."* [Psalm 40:6-8, LXX]

⁸[After] saying above, *"Sacrifice and offering and in whole-burnt offerings and [sacrifices] concerning sin You did not desire, nor took pleasure in"* (which according to the Law are offered), ⁹then He has said, *"Look! I have come to do Your will, O God."* He abolishes the first so that He shall establish the second, ¹⁰by

which will we have been sanctified, the [ones] through the offering of the body of Jesus Christ, once [and] for all [fig., once and never again]!

¹¹And indeed every priest has stood daily sacredly serving and repeatedly offering the same sacrifices, which are never able to take away sins. ¹²But He Himself, having offered one sacrifice for sins for all time, *"sat down at [the] right hand of God,"* ¹³waiting from that time onward *"until His enemies are put [as] a footstool for His feet."* [Psalm 110:1] ¹⁴For by one offering He has perfected for all time the ones being sanctified.

¹⁵But the Holy Spirit also testifies to us, for after having said before, ¹⁶*"This [is] the covenant which I will covenant with them after those days, says [the] LORD, putting My laws on their hearts, and I will inscribe them on their minds,"* ¹⁷[then He adds] *"And I shall by no means remember their sins and their lawless deeds any longer."* [Jer 31:33,34] ¹⁸Now where [there is] forgiveness of these [things, there is] no longer an offering concerning sin.

¹⁹Therefore, brothers [and sisters], having confidence [or, a joyful sense of freedom] for the entrance into the holy [places] by the blood of Jesus, ²⁰by a new and living way which He inaugurated for us, through the veil, that is, His flesh, ²¹and [having] a High Priest over the house of God, ²²let us be approaching with a true heart [fig., pure inner desire], in full assurance of faith, our hearts having been sprinkled [clean] [fig., purified] from an evil conscience and the body having been bathed with pure water.

²³Let us be holding fast the confession of the hope [or, confident expectation] without wavering, for the One having promised [is] faithful. ²⁴And let us be considering one another for [the] stimulation of love and of good works, ²⁵not abandoning [or, neglecting] the assembling together of ourselves, as [is the] habit of some, but encouraging [one another], and so much more as you* see the Day approaching.

²⁶For [if] we [are] deliberately sinning after the receiving [of] the full [or, true] knowledge of the truth, [there] no longer remains a sacrifice concerning sins, ²⁷but only a terrifying expectation of judgment and fiery indignation being about to be devouring the adversaries. ²⁸Anyone regarding as nothing [or, rejecting] [the] Law of Moses dies without mercies on [the testimony of] two or three witnesses. ²⁹By how much severer punishment do you* suppose will be counted worthy the one having trampled underfoot God's Son and having regarded [as] unclean the blood of the covenant by which he [or, it] was sanctified, and having outraged the Spirit of grace? ³⁰For we know the One having said, *"Vengeance [is] Mine; I will repay,"* says [the] Lord. And again, *"[The] LORD will judge His people."* [Deut 32:35,36] ³¹[It is] terrifying to fall into [the] hands of [the] living God!

³²But remember your* former days, in which having been enlightened you* endured a great contest of sufferings [or, a great struggle with sufferings], ³³partly on the one hand by being publicly exposed both to insults and to afflictions, partly on the other hand by having become sharers of the ones being treated in this way. ³⁴For indeed you* sympathized with [me] in my chains, and you* accepted the seizure of your* property with joy, knowing to be having for yourselves a better and lasting possession in [the] heavens.

³⁵Therefore, you* shall not throw off your* confidence [or, joyful sense of freedom], which has great reward. ³⁶For you* have need of patient endurance, so that having done the will of God, you* shall receive the promise. ³⁷*"For yet [in] a very little while, the One coming will come and will not delay.* ³⁸*But the [one] righteous by faith will live* [or, *the righteous will live by faith*]; *and if he draws back, My soul has no pleasure in him. "* [Hab 2:3,4] ³⁹But <u>we</u> are not of [the ones] shrinking back to destruction, <u>but</u> of [the ones having] faith to [the] preserving of [the] soul.

11 Now faith is [the] assurance [or, substance] of [things] being hoped for [or, being confidently expected], [the] confident assurance [or, proof] of things not seen. ²For by this the elders received approval. ³By faith we understand the ages [fig., universe] to have been prepared by a word of God, for the [things] being visible not to have come from the [things] being seen. [see Gen 1:1-27]

⁴By faith Abel offered to God a better sacrifice than Cain, through which he was testified to be righteous, God testifying concerning his gifts, and through it [i.e. his faith], having died, he himself still speaks. [see Gen 4:3-10] ⁵By faith Enoch was taken up [so as] not to see death, *"and he was not being found because God took him up;"* for before his removal he had been testified to [as] having been pleasing to God. [see Gen 5:21-24] ⁶But without faith [it is] impossible to please [Him], for it is necessary [for] the one approaching God to believe that He is and [that] He becomes a rewarder to the ones diligently seeking Him.

⁷By faith Noah, having been divinely warned concerning the [things] not yet being seen, having been moved with reverent fear, prepared an ark for [the] salvation of his household, by which he condemned the world and became a heir of the righteousness according to faith. [see Gen 6:13-22]

⁸By faith Abraham obeyed, having been called to go out to the place which he was about to be receiving for an inheritance, and he went out not knowing where he [was] going. [see Gen 12:1-7] ⁹By faith he lived as a stranger in [the] land of the promise, as a foreigner, having lived in tents with Isaac and Jacob, the joint-heirs of the same promise. [see Gen 12:8; 13:3] ¹⁰For he was looking forward to the city having the foundations, whose architect and builder [is] God.

¹¹By faith also Sarah herself received power for conception of seed, and she gave birth after [the child-bearing] time of life, since she regarded the One having promised [to be] faithful. [see Gen 18:11-14; 21:2] ¹²And so from one [man] were born, and in these [things] having been as good as dead, [as many descendents] *"as the stars of heaven in number and as innumerable as sand which [is] by the sea-shore."* [Gen 15:5; 22:17; 32:12]

¹³All these died according to faith, not having received the promises, <u>but</u> having seen them from a distance and having welcomed [them], and having confessed that they are strangers and sojourners on the earth. ¹⁴For the ones saying such [things] make it clear that they are seeking a homeland. ¹⁵And if indeed they had been remembering that [land] from which they went out, they might have had an opportunity to return. ¹⁶But now they long for a better, that is, a heavenly

[land]. For this reason, God is not ashamed of them, to be called their God, for He prepared a city for them.

¹⁷By faith Abraham, being tested, had offered up Isaac, the one having received the promises was offering up his uniquely-begotten [son], ¹⁸in regard to whom it was said, *"In Isaac your seed will be called* [fig, *your descendents will come through Isaac*]," [Gen 21:12] ¹⁹having taken into account that God [was] able to raise [him] up even from [the] dead, from where he indeed received [him] back in a figurative sense. [see Gen 22:1-12]

²⁰By faith concerning coming [things], Isaac blessed Jacob and Esau. [see Gen 27:27-40] ²¹By faith Jacob, [when he was] dying, blessed each of the sons of Joseph, and worshiped, [leaning] on the top of his staff. [see Gen 47:31, LXX; Gen 48:1-22] ²²By faith Joseph, coming to the end [of his life], made mention of the departure [Gr., *exodus*] of the sons [and daughters] of Israel and gave orders concerning his bones. [see Gen 50:24,25]

²³By faith Moses, having been born, was hid three months by his parents, because they saw the beautiful, young child and were not afraid of the decree of the king. [see Exod 2:2; 1:16] ²⁴By faith Moses, having become great, refused to be called a son of [the] daughter of Pharaoh, [see Exod 2:11-15] ²⁵having chosen rather to be sharing hardship with the people of God than to be having [the] temporary pleasure of sin, ²⁶having regarded the disgrace of Christ greater wealth than the treasures of Egypt, for he was looking away from all else to [fig., concentrating on] the reward. ²⁷By faith he left Egypt behind, not having been afraid of the rage of the king, for he persevered as seeing the Invisible One. [see Exod 10:28; 12:50-51] ²⁸By faith he had kept the Passover and the sprinkling of the blood, so that the one destroying the first-born would not touch them. [see Exod 12:21-28]

²⁹By faith they passed through the Red Sea as through dry [land], which the Egyptians having taken an attempt were swallowed [fig., drowned]. [see Exod 14:21-29] ³⁰By faith the walls of Jericho fell, having been encircled for seven days. [see Josh 6:1-20] ³¹By faith Rahab the prostitute did not perish with the ones having refused to believe, having received the spies with peace. [see Josh 2:9-21; 6:22,23]

³²And what more shall I say? For the time will run short [for] me [to be] describing fully about Gideon, both Barak and Samson, and Jephthah, both David and Samuel, and the prophets, ³³who through faith conquered kingdoms, brought about righteousness, obtained promises, stopped [the] mouths of lions, ³⁴extinguished [the] power of fire, escaped [the] mouth [fig., edge] of [the] sword, were made strong from weaknesses [or, infirmities], became mighty in battle, routed foreign armies. ³⁵Women received [back] their dead [ones] by resurrection.

But others were tortured, not accepting [their] release, so that they would obtain a better resurrection. ³⁶But others received trial of [fig., experienced] public ridicule and beatings with a whip, and in addition, chains and imprisonment. ³⁷They were stoned; they were sawn in two; they were tested; they were put to death by murder with a sword; they went about in sheepskins, in goatskins, being destitute, being afflicted, being ill-treated ³⁸(of whom the world was not worthy), wandering about in desolate places and [in] mountains and [in] caves and [in] the holes of the earth.

³⁹And all these, having received approval through [their] faith, did not receive the promise, ⁴⁰God having provided something better concerning us, that they should not be made perfect without us.

12 So therefore, <u>we</u> also having so great a cloud of witnesses surrounding us, having put off every impediment and the easily entangling sin, let us be running with patient endurance the contest having been set before us, ²looking with undivided attention to the Originator and Perfecter of [our] faith—Jesus—who, because of the joy being set before Him, endured a cross, having disregarded [the] shame, and has sat down at [the] right hand of the throne of God. ³For consider carefully the One having endured such hostility by the sinners against Himself, lest you* become weary in your* souls, being discouraged.

⁴You* did not yet resist to the point of [shedding] blood struggling against sin. ⁵And you* have forgotten completely the encouragement which reasons with you* as with sons [and daughters], *"My son [fig., child] stop thinking lightly of [the] discipline of [the] LORD, and stop becoming discouraged when being corrected by Him. ⁶For whom [the] LORD loves He disciplines, and He scourges [fig., punishes] every son [fig., child] whom He receives."* [Prov 3:11,12, LXX]

⁷[It is] for discipline [that] you* endure. God deals with you* as with sons [and daughters]; for what son [fig., child] is [there] whom a father does not discipline? ⁸But if you* are without discipline, of which all have become sharers, then you* are illegitimate children and not sons [and daughters]. ⁹Furthermore, we indeed have had fathers of our flesh [fig., earthly fathers] [as] discipliners, and we were respecting [them]. Will we not much rather be subjected to the Father of spirits, and we will live? ¹⁰For <u>they</u> indeed were disciplining [us] for a few days [fig., a short while] according to the [thing] seeming good to them, but He for [our] advantage, for [us] to be sharers of His holiness. ¹¹Now indeed, all discipline for the present does not seem to be joyful, <u>but</u> painful; but afterwards it yields [the] peaceful [or, free from worry] fruit of righteousness to the ones having been trained by it.

¹²For this reason brace up the having been weakened hands and the having been paralyzed knees, [cp. Isaiah 35:3] ¹³and make straight paths for your* feet, so that the lame [person] shall not be turned aside [or, the lame [limb] shall not be dislocated], but rather shall be healed. [cp. Prov 4:26, LXX]

¹⁴Be pursuing peace with all [people], and the holiness, without which no one will see the Lord, ¹⁵looking after [one another] lest anyone [be] falling short of the grace of God, lest any root of bitterness growing up shall be causing trouble, and through this many be defiled, ¹⁶lest anyone [be] a sexual sinner or a godless [person] like Esau, who in exchange for a single meal sold his birthright. [see Gen 25:27-34] ¹⁷For you* know that indeed afterwards, wishing to inherit the blessing, he was rejected, for he did not find a place for repentance, although having diligently sought it with tears. [see Gen 27:30-38]

¹⁸For you* have not come to a mountain being touched and having been burned with fire, and to blackness and to darkness and to a whirlwind, ¹⁹and to a sound of a trumpet and to a voice of words, which the ones having heard begged [for] a word not to be added to them. ²⁰For they could not bear the [thing] being commanded, *"If even an animal touches the mountain, it will be stoned."* [Exod 19:12,13] ²¹And so terrifying was the [thing] being made visible [fig., the sight] [that] Moses said, *"I am terrified, and trembling."* [Deut 9:19] ²²But you* have come to Mount Zion and to [the] city of [the] living God, to heavenly Jerusalem and to countless thousands of angels, ²³to [the] festive gathering and assembly [or, church] of first-born [ones] having been enrolled in heaven and to God, [the] Judge of all [people], and to [the] spirits of righteous [ones] having been made perfect, ²⁴and to [the] Mediator of a new covenant—Jesus—and to [the] blood of sprinkling, speaking a better [thing] than the [blood] of Abel.

²⁵Be seeing [that] you* do not refuse to listen to the One speaking. For if those [ones] did not escape, having refused the One warning [them] on earth, much more [shall we not escape], the ones turning away from the One [speaking] from heaven, ²⁶whose voice at that time shook the earth, but now He has promised, saying, *"Yet once [more] I am shaking not only the earth, but also the heaven."* [Haggai 2:6] ²⁷Now the [phrase] *"Yet once [more]"* clearly shows the removal of the [things] being shaken, as of [things] having been created, so that the [things] not being shaken shall remain.

²⁸For this reason, [since we are] receiving an unshakable kingdom, let us be having grace, through which we are sacredly serving God in an acceptable manner, with reverence and godly fear. ²⁹For indeed our God [is] a consuming fire [fig., [is] as to His essence consuming fire]. [Exod 24:17; Deut 4:24]

13 Be continuing [in] brotherly love [fig., affection for fellow-believers]. ²Stop being neglectful of hospitality, for by this some were unaware they had entertained angels! ³Be remembering the prisoners as having been imprisoned with [them], the ones having been ill-treated, as also being in [the] body yourselves. ⁴Marriage [is to be] honorable [or, respected] among all and the marriage bed undefiled, but sexual sinners and adulterers God will judge.

⁵[Your*] way of life [is to be] without [the] love of money, being content with the things present [fig., with what you* have], for He Himself has said, *"By no means shall I desert you, nor in any way shall I be abandoning you;"* [Deut 31:6,8; Josh 1:5] ⁶so that we [are] confident to be saying, *"[The] LORD [is] a helper to me, and I will not fear. What will humanity do to me?"* [Psalm 118:6]

⁷Be remembering the ones leading you*, who spoke to you* the word of God, of whom considering the outcome of [their] conduct, be imitating [their] faith. ⁸Jesus Christ [is] the same yesterday and today and into the ages [fig., forever]!

⁹Stop being carried away by varied and strange teachings, for [it is] good [for] the heart to continue being established by grace, not by foods, in which the ones having been walking about [in] [fig., having been occupied with] were not benefited. ¹⁰We have an altar from which the ones sacredly serving in the tabernacle have no right to eat.

¹¹For of which animals the blood is brought concerning sin into the holy [places] by the high priest, the bodies of these are burned outside the camp. [see Lev 4:11,12,21; 16:27] ¹²And so Jesus, so that He should sanctify the people through [His] own blood, suffered outside the gate. ¹³So let us be going out to Him outside the camp, bearing His disgrace. ¹⁴For we do not have here a lasting city, but we are seeking the coming [one].

¹⁵Therefore, through Him let us through all [fig. always] be offering up a sacrifice of praise to God, that is, [the] fruit of [our] lips [fig., our words], confessing [fig., giving thanks to] His name. ¹⁶But stop neglecting the doing of good and generosity, for with such sacrifices God is pleased. ¹⁷You* yourselves be obeying the ones leading you*, and be yielding [to them] [fig., be accepting their authority], for they are watching over your* souls as they will be giving an account, so that they shall be doing this with joy and not complaining with groans, for this [would be] detrimental to you*.

¹⁸Be praying concerning us, for we are confident that we have a good conscience, in all [things] desiring to be honorably conducting ourselves. ¹⁹But especially I urge [you*] to do this, so that I shall be restored to you* more quickly.

²⁰Now may the God of peace, the One having brought up from [the] dead the great Shepherd of the sheep by [the] blood of an eternal covenant—our Lord Jesus, ²¹equip you* in every good work in order to do His will, doing in you* the acceptable [thing] before Him, through Jesus Christ, to whom [is] the glory into the ages of the ages [fig., forever and ever]! So be it!

²²But I urge you*, brothers [and sisters], be listening carefully to this word of encouragement, for indeed through a few words [fig., briefly] I wrote to you*. ²³Be knowing [that] the brother Timothy has been released, with whom, if he is coming quickly, I will see you*.

²⁴Greet all the ones leading you* and all the holy ones [or, saints]. The [holy ones] from Italy greet you*.

²⁵Grace [be] with you* all! So be it!

The Epistle of

James

1 James, a slave of God and of [the] Lord Jesus Christ, To the Twelve Tribes who are in the dispersion [i.e. the scattering of Jews outside of Judea]: Greetings!

²Consider [it] all joy, my brothers [and sisters], whenever you* encounter various trials, ³knowing that the testing of your* faith produces patient endurance. ⁴But be letting that patient endurance have a perfect work [or, full effect], so that you* shall be perfect [or, mature] and complete—lacking in nothing. ⁵Now if any of you* lacks wisdom, let him be asking from God, the One giving generously to all and not denouncing [or, without criticizing], and it will be given to him. ⁶But let him be asking in faith, doubting nothing. For the one doubting has been likened to a wave of the sea, being driven by wind and tossed about. ⁷For let not that person be supposing that he will receive anything from the Lord. ⁸[That one is] a double-minded [or, an indecisive] man, unstable in all his ways.

⁹Now let the lowly brother [or, brother of humble circumstances] be rejoicing in his exaltation, ¹⁰but the rich [brother] in his humble state, because like a flower of grass he will pass away. ¹¹For the sun rose with scorching heat and dried up the grass, and its flower fell off, and the beauty of its appearance perished. So also the rich [person] in his journeys [fig., in his pursuits of business or wealth] will fade away!

¹²Happy [or, Blessed] [is the] man who endures temptation [or, testing], because having become approved, he will receive the victor's wreath [or, crown] of the life which the Lord promised to the ones loving Him.

¹³Let no one say, when tempted, "I am being tempted by God," for God is incapable of being tempted by evil, and He Himself tempts no one. ¹⁴But each one is tempted by his own lusts, being pulled away and enticed. ¹⁵Then that lust having conceived gives birth to sin; then that sin having become full-grown brings forth death. ¹⁶Stop being led astray [fig., being deceived], my beloved brothers [and sisters].

¹⁷Every good giving and every perfect gift is from above, coming down from the Father of lights, with whom there is no variation or shadow of turning. ¹⁸Having willed, He gave birth to us by [the] word of truth for the purpose of our being a kind of first-fruits of His creatures [or, out of His creation].

¹⁹So then, my beloved brothers [and sisters], let every person be swift to hear, slow to speak, [and] slow to anger, ²⁰for [the] anger of a man does not produce the righteousness of God. ²¹For this reason, you* yourselves having put aside all filthiness [fig., moral uncleanness] and abundance of evil, in humility receive the implanted word [within you*], which is able to save your* souls.

²²Now continue becoming doers of [the] word, and not hearers only, deceiving yourselves. ²³Because if anyone is a hearer of the word and not a doer, this one has been likened to a man observing his natural face in a mirror, ²⁴for he observed himself and has gone away, and immediately he forgot what kind of [person] he

was. ²⁵But the one having looked into [the] perfect law, the [law] of liberty, and having continued [in it], this one—not having become a forgetful hearer <u>but</u> a doer of work—this one will be happy in his doing.

²⁶If anyone thinks to be religious among you*, [and yet] does not bridle [fig., control] his tongue, <u>but</u> deceives his heart, the religion of this one [is] useless. ²⁷Pure and undefiled religion before [our] God and Father is this: to be caring for orphans and widows in their affliction [and] to be keeping oneself unspotted [fig., uncorrupted] by the world.

2 My brothers [and sisters], stop holding the faith of our Lord Jesus Christ, the [Lord] of Glory, with accepting of faces [fig., with a prejudiced attitude]. ²For if a man comes into your* synagogue with a gold ring, in elegant clothing, and there comes in also a poor [man] in filthy clothing, ³and you* look with care upon the one wearing the elegant clothing and say to him, "<u>You</u>, be sitting here, please [or, in this good seat]," and to the poor [man] you* say, "<u>You</u>, stand there," or, "Be sitting here under my footstool," ⁴and [so] did you* not make distinctions among yourselves and [so] became judges with evil thought processes [or, motives]?

⁵Pay attention, my beloved brothers [and sisters]: God chose the poor [ones] of the world [to be] rich [ones] in faith and heirs of the kingdom which He promised to the ones loving Him, did He not? ⁶But <u>you</u>* dishonored the poor one. The rich [ones] oppress you*, and <u>they</u> drag you* into [the] courts, do they not? ⁷<u>They</u> blaspheme the good Name by which you* were called, do they not?

⁸If you* indeed fulfill [the] royal Law according to the Scripture, *"You will love your neighbor as yourself,"* you* are doing well. [Lev 19:18] ⁹But if you* accept faces [fig., are prejudiced], you* are committing sin, being convicted by the Law as transgressors. ¹⁰For whoever will keep the whole Law yet will stumble in one [point] has become guilty of all. ¹¹For the One saying, *"You shall not commit adultery,"* also said, *"You shall not murder."* [Exod 20:14,13; Deut 5:18,17] But if you will not commit adultery, yet you will murder, you have become a transgressor of [the] Law.

¹²So be speaking and so be doing as ones about to be judged by [the] law of liberty. ¹³For the judgment [is] merciless to the one not having shown mercy. Mercy triumphs over judgment.

¹⁴What [is] the advantage, my brothers [and sisters], if someone is saying he has faith but is not having works? Such faith is not able to save him, is it? ¹⁵Now if a brother or sister is naked [or, poorly dressed] and is lacking of the daily food, ¹⁶yet any of you* says to them, "Be going away in peace; be keeping yourselves warm and well fed," but does not give to them the necessary [things] of the body, what [is] the advantage? ¹⁷So also faith, if it is not having works, is dead [fig., utterly useless] by itself.

¹⁸<u>But</u> someone will say, "<u>You</u> have faith and <u>I</u> have works." [But I say], "Show to me your faith [apart] from your works, and <u>I</u> will show to you my faith by means of my works." ¹⁹<u>You</u> believe [or, are convinced] that God is one; you do well. The demons also believe—and they shudder [with fear]!

²⁰But are you willing to recognize, O empty [fig., foolish] person, that such faith without such works is dead? ²¹Abraham our father, he was justified [or, shown to be righteous] by means of works, having offered Isaac his son upon the altar, was he not? [see Gen 22:9] ²²Do you see that his faith was working together with his works, and by means of the works his faith was perfected? ²³And [so] was fulfilled the Scripture, the one saying, *"But Abraham believed [or, trusted] God, and it was accounted to him for righteousness."* [Gen 15:6] And he was called a friend of God. [see Isaiah 41:8] ²⁴So you* see that a person is justified [or, shown to be righteous] by means of works and not by means of faith only.

²⁵So likewise also Rahab the prostitute was justified [or, shown to be righteous] by means of works, having welcomed the messengers and having sent [them] out by a different way, was she not? [see Josh 2:1-21; 6:17] ²⁶For as the body without the spirit is dead, so also one's faith without such works is dead.

3 Stop letting [so] many become teachers, my brothers [and sisters], knowing that we will receive greater judgment. ²For we all frequently stumble [fig., sin] [or, stumble [in] many [ways]]; if anyone does not stumble in word [fig., what he says], this one [is] a perfect [or, mature] man, able to bridle [fig., control] also his whole body.

³Consider the bits [i.e. mouthpieces of bridles] we put into the mouths of the horses for them to be obeying us—and we guide their whole body! ⁴Consider also the ships, being so great and being driven by fierce winds, are guided by a very small rudder, wherever the inclination of the helmsman shall be desiring.

⁵So also the tongue is a little body part, and [yet it] boasts greatly. Consider how great a forest a little fire sets ablaze! ⁶And the tongue [is] a fire, the world of unrighteousness. Thus the tongue is set among our body parts [and is] the [thing] polluting [or, defiling] our whole body and setting on fire the course of our existence—and being set on fire by hell [Gr., *gehenna*].

⁷For every species, both of wild animals and of birds, both of reptiles and sea creatures, is tamed and has been tamed by the human species. ⁸But no one among people is able to tame the tongue; [it is] an uncontrollable evil, full of deadly poison. ⁹With it we praise the God and Father, and with it we curse the people having been created according to the likeness of God.

¹⁰Out of the same mouth comes forth praise and cursing; my brothers [and sisters], these [things] ought not to be happening in this way. ¹¹The spring does not pour forth the sweet and the bitter [water] out of the same opening, does it? ¹²My brothers [and sisters], a fig tree is not able to make olives, is it? Or a grapevine figs? In the same way, no spring [is able] to produce salt and sweet water.

¹³Who [is] wise and knowledgeable among you*? Let him show by his good conduct [that] his works [are] in humility of wisdom. ¹⁴But if you* have bitter jealousy and selfish ambition in your* heart, stop boasting and lying against the truth. ¹⁵This is not the wisdom descending from above, but [is] earthly, physical [or, unspiritual], [and] demonic. ¹⁶For where jealousy and selfish ambition [are], there is rebellion and every wicked deed. ¹⁷But the wisdom from above is first indeed pure, then peaceful [or, free from worry], considerate, open to reason, full

of mercy and good fruits, impartial [or, free from prejudice] and sincere. ¹⁸Now the fruit of such righteousness is sown in peace by the ones making peace.

4From where [come] wars and fights [fig., quarrels and angry arguments] among you*? Is it not from here—out of your* passions [or, desires for pleasure], the ones waging war in your* body parts? ²You* desire [or, lust for], and you* do not have. You* murder and are jealous and are not able to obtain. You* fight and wage war [fig., argue angrily and quarrel]. But you* do not have because you* do not ask. ³You* ask, and you* do not receive, because you* ask wrongly [or, with wrong motives], so that you* should spend [it] on your* passions [or, desires for pleasure].

⁴Adulterers and adulteresses! Do you* not know that the friendship of the world is hostility towards God? So whoever wants to be a friend of the world is made an enemy of [or, is hostile towards] God. ⁵Do you* think that the Scripture speaks in vain [or, for no purpose]? Does the Spirit which [has] dwelt in us yearn to [the point of] envy? ⁶But He gives greater grace. For this reason, He says, *"God resists [or, sets Himself in opposition against] proud [people], but He gives grace to humble [people]."* [Prov 3:34, LXX]

⁷Therefore, be subjected to God, but stand up against [or, resist] the Devil, and he will flee from you*. ⁸Draw near to God, and He will draw near to you*. Cleanse [fig., Purify] [your*] hands, sinners! And purify [your*] hearts, double-minded [ones] [or, doubters]! ⁹Be miserable and mourn and weep! Let your* laughter be changed into mourning and [your*] joy into gloom. ¹⁰Be humbled [or, Humble yourselves] before the Lord, and He will exalt you*.

¹¹Stop speaking evil of [or, slandering] one another, brothers [and sisters]. The one speaking evil of a brother and judging his brother speaks evil of [the] Law and judges [the] Law. But if you judge [the] Law, you are not a doer of [the] Law but a judge. ¹²[There] is one Lawgiver, the One able to save and to destroy. But who are you who judges the other [or, the different [one]]?

¹³Now listen! The ones saying, "Today or tomorrow we shall travel into such and such a city and shall spend one year there, and we shall carry on business and shall make profit," ¹⁴[you*] who do not know the [events] of tomorrow. For what [is] your* life? For it will be a vapor, the one appearing for a little while, but then also vanishing. ¹⁵Instead, you* [ought] to be saying, "If the Lord wills, we shall live, and we also shall do this or that." ¹⁶But now you* boast in your* pretentious pride; all such boasting is evil.

¹⁷So to the one knowing to be doing good and not doing [it], to him it is sin.

5Now listen! The rich [ones], weep, wailing over your* miseries, the ones coming upon [you*]! ²Your* riches have rotted, and your* clothes have become moth-eaten. ³Your* gold and silver have corroded, and their rust will be for a testimony against you* and will consume your* flesh as fire. You* stored up [treasure] in [the] last days!

⁴Listen! The pay of the laborers, of the ones having cut down grain [in] your* fields, their [pay] having been kept back by you* cries out, and the shouts [or,

outcries] of the ones having reaped have entered into the ears of [the] Lord of Armies [fig., [the] Lord Almighty]. ⁵You* lived in luxury on the earth and were self-indulgent; you* nourished [fig., fattened] your* hearts as in a day of slaughter. ⁶You* condemned, you* murdered the righteous one; he does not resist you*.

⁷Therefore, wait patiently, brothers [and sisters], until the Arrival [or, Coming] of the Lord. Look! The farmer awaits the precious fruit of the earth, waiting patiently for it, until it receives [the] early and latter [or, autumn and spring] rain. ⁸You* also wait patiently. Establish [or, strengthen] your* hearts, because the Arrival of the Lord has drawn near. ⁹Stop complaining with groans against one another, brothers [and sisters], so that you* shall not be judged. Look! The Judge has stood before the door!

¹⁰Take [as] an example of suffering, my brothers [and sisters], and of patience, the prophets who spoke in the name of [the] Lord. ¹¹Indeed, we consider the ones enduring to be fortunate. You* heard of the patient endurance of Job and the outcome [brought about by the] Lord; observe that He is very compassionate and merciful.

¹²Now above all [else], my brothers [and sisters], stop taking oaths, neither [by] the heaven nor the earth nor any other oath. But let your* "Yes" be "Yes" and the "No" [be] "No," so that you* shall not fall into hypocrisy.

¹³Is anyone enduring hardship among you*? Let him be praying. Is any being cheerful? Let him be singing praises. ¹⁴Is anyone sick among you*? Let him summon the elders of the assembly [or, the church]. And let them pray over him, having anointed him with oil in the name of the Lord. ¹⁵And the prayer of faith will cure the one being ill, and the Lord will raise him up. And if he has committed sins, they will be forgiven to him.

¹⁶You* yourselves be confessing your transgressions to one another, and be praying for one another, in order that you* shall be healed [or, be restored]. [The] petition of a righteous [person] itself has very powerful [or, many supernatural] effects. ¹⁷Elijah was a person of like nature to us. And with prayer he prayed [for it] not to rain, and it did not rain upon the land [for] three years and six months. ¹⁸And again he prayed, and heaven [or, the sky] gave rain, and the land produced its fruit.

¹⁹Brothers [and sisters], if anyone among you* is led astray [fig., is deceived] from the truth, and someone turns him back, ²⁰let him be knowing that the one having turned back a sinner from the error of his way will save a soul from death and will cover a multitude of sins.

The First Epistle of
Peter

1 Peter, an apostle of Jesus Christ, To the chosen [or, elect] sojourners of the dispersion [i.e. the scattering of Jews outside of Judea] of Pontus, Galatia, Cappadocia, Asia, and Bithynia, ²according to [the] foreknowledge of God [the] Father, in sanctification of [the] Spirit, for obedience and sprinkling of [the] blood of Jesus Christ: May grace and peace be multiplied to you*!

³Blessed [be] the God and Father of our Lord Jesus Christ, the One according to His great mercy having regenerated us to a living hope [or, confident expectation], through [the] resurrection of Jesus Christ from [the] dead, ⁴into an inheritance [which is] incorruptible and undefiled and unfading, having been reserved in the heavens for you*, ⁵the ones being guarded by [the] power of God through faith for [the] salvation ready to be revealed in [the] last time; ⁶in which you* are very glad, [though] now [for] a little [while], if it is necessary, you* have been distressed by various trials, ⁷so that the genuineness of your* faith, [being] much more precious [than] gold, the [thing] perishing, but being approved through fire, shall be found to praise and honor and to glory in [the] revelation of Jesus Christ, ⁸whom not having known, you* love; in whom now not seeing but believing, you* are very glad with a inexpressible and glorious joy, ⁹receiving the end of your* faith, [the] salvation of [your*] souls.

¹⁰Concerning which salvation [the] prophets sought diligently and carefully searched, the [prophets] having prophesied concerning the grace, the one [coming] to you*, ¹¹searching for who or what time the Spirit of Christ in them was clearly showing, predicting the sufferings of Christ and the glory after these. ¹²To whom it was revealed that not to themselves but to you* they were serving these [things], which now were announced to you* by the ones having proclaimed the Gospel [or, Good News, and throughout book] to you* by [the] Holy Spirit having been sent from heaven, into which [things] angels desire to look.

¹³For this reason, having tied up at the waist the clothes of your* mind [fig., having prepared your* mind for action], being sober [or, clear-headed], place your* hope [or, trust] completely upon the grace being brought to you* at the revelation of Jesus Christ. ¹⁴As obedient children, not conforming yourselves [or, not allowing yourself to be conformed] to the former lusts [which you* had] in your* ignorance, ¹⁵but just as the One having called you* [is] holy, you* also become holy in all [your*] conduct, ¹⁶because it has been written, *"Continue becoming holy, because I am holy."* [Lev 11:44,45]

¹⁷And if you* call on the Father, the One judging impartially according to the work of each [one], conduct yourselves in fear [during] the time of your* sojourn [fig., life on earth], ¹⁸knowing that not with corruptible [things like] silver or gold were you* redeemed from your* futile way of life handed down by your* fathers, ¹⁹but with [the] precious blood of Christ, as of a lamb unblemished and spotless, ²⁰having been foreknown, on the one hand before [the] laying of [the] foundation

of the world, on the other hand having been revealed in [the] last times for the sake of you*, ²¹the ones through Him believing in God, the One having raised Him from [the] dead and having given glory to Him, in order that your* faith and hope [or, expectation] are in God.

²²Having [or, Since you* have] purified your* souls in obedience to the truth through [the] Spirit in sincere brotherly love [fig., affection for fellow-believers], love one another earnestly from a pure heart, ²³having been [or, because you* have been] regenerated [or, born again] not from corruptible seed <u>but</u> incorruptible, through [the] word of God [which is] living and remaining into the age [fig., forever]. ²⁴For *"All flesh [is] like grass, and all glory of humanity like [the] flower of grass; the grass withered, and its flower fell off, ²⁵but the word of [the]* LORD *remains into the age* [fig., *forever*]." [Isaiah 40:6-8, LXX] Now this is the word, the Gospel having been proclaimed to you*.

2Therefore, having put aside all malice and all deceit and hypocrisies and envies and all slanders, ²as newborn babies long for the spiritual, pure milk, so that you* shall grow by it, ³if indeed you* tasted [fig., experienced] that the Lord [is] gracious.

⁴To whom having approached [as to] a living stone, on the one hand having been rejected by people, on the other hand chosen [and] precious before God, ⁵and you* yourselves, as living stones, are being built up [into] a spiritual house, a holy priesthood, to offer up spiritual sacrifices acceptable to God through Jesus Christ.

⁶For this reason, it is contained in the Scripture, *"Look! I lay in Zion a stone, a cornerstone, chosen, precious, and the one believing on Him shall by no means be put to shame* [or, *be disappointed*]." [Isaiah 28:16, LXX] ⁷Therefore, the honor [is] to you*, the ones believing. But to the ones disobeying [or, refusing to believe], *"[The] stone which the builders rejected, this [one] became for [the] head of [the] corner* [or, *the chief cornerstone*]" [Psalm 118:22] ⁸and *"A stone of stumbling and a rock of offence,"* [Isaiah 8:14] who stumble at the word, refusing to believe, to which also they were appointed.

⁹But you* [are] *"a chosen race, a royal priesthood, a holy nation, a people [for God's own] possession,"* [Exod 19:5,6; Isaiah 43:20,21; 61:6] in order that you* shall proclaim the excellencies of the One having called you* out of darkness into His marvelous light, ¹⁰who at one time [were] not a people, but now [are] people of God; the ones not having found mercy, but now having found mercy.

¹¹Beloved, I urge [you*] as exiles and sojourners, to be abstaining from the fleshly lusts which wage war against the soul, ¹²having your* conduct good among the Gentiles, so that in what they speak against you* as evildoers, having seen your* good works, they shall glorify God in [the] day of visitation.

¹³Therefore, be subject to every human institution [or, authority] for the Lord's sake, whether to a king as [the one] having authority, ¹⁴or to governors as [the ones] having been sent by him for [the] punishment of evildoers, but [for the] praise of [the ones] doing good. ¹⁵For such is the will of God, doing good [in order] to be silencing the ignorance of the foolish people. ¹⁶[Live] as free

[persons], yet not using such freedom as a covering [or, excuse] for evil, <u>but</u> as slaves of God.

[17]Honor all [people]. Love the brotherhood [fig., community of believers]. You* yourselves be fearing God. Be honoring the king.

[18]The household servants, [continue] being subjected [or, submitted] with all fear to your* masters, not only to the good and gentle [or, considerate], <u>but</u> also to the crooked [or, harsh]. [19]For this [finds] favor [with God] [or, [is] admirable], if for the sake of conscience toward God someone endures sorrows, suffering unjustly. [20]For what credit [is it] if sinning and being beaten with fists [fig., being harshly treated], you* will endure [it]? <u>But</u> if doing good and suffering [for it], you* will endure [it]; this [finds] favor with [or, [is] admirable before] God.

[21]Because, for this [reason] you* were called, because Christ also suffered on our behalf, leaving behind an example for you*, so that you* should follow in His footsteps, [22]who *"Did not commit sin, nor was deceit found in his mouth,"* [Isaiah 53:9] [23]who being verbally abused, was not returning verbal insults, suffering, was not threatening, but was entrusting Himself to the One judging righteously; [24]who Himself carried our sins in His body on the tree [fig., cross], so that having died to sins, we shall live to righteousness; of whom *"by His wound[s] you* were healed."* [Isaiah 53:5] [25]For you* were like sheep being led astray, <u>but</u> now you* were turned back to the Shepherd and Overseer of your* souls.

*3*Likewise, the wives, [continue] being subjected [or, submitted] to your* own husbands, so that even if some are refusing to believe the word, through the conduct of their wives they will be won [for Christ] without a word, [2]having observed your* pure conduct with respect, [3]whose adornment must not be external, of braided hair [or, elaborate hairstyles] and of wearing of gold [jewelry] or of putting on of [elegant] clothing, [4]<u>but</u> [it must be] the hidden person of the heart, with the incorruptible [beauty] of the gentle and quiet spirit, which is very costly [fig., precious] before God.

[5]For in this way in times past also the holy women, the ones placing their hope on [or, trusting in] God were adorning themselves, being subjected [or, submitted] to their own husbands, [6]as Sarah was obedient to Abraham, calling him "lord," of whom you* became daughters, doing good, and not fearing any terror. [see Gen 18:12]

[7]The husbands, likewise, [continue] living with [your* wives] according to knowledge, as with a weaker vessel, with the feminine [one], showing respect, as also being joint-heirs of [the] grace of life, for your* prayers not to be hindered.

[8]And finally, all [of you* be of] one mind, sympathetic, loving [one another] as brothers [and sisters], compassionate, friendly; [9]not returning evil for evil, or insult for insult, but on the contrary, giving a blessing, knowing that for this [reason] you* were called, so that you* shall inherit a blessing. [10]For:

The one desiring to be loving life and to see good days must keep his tongue from evil, and his lips [are] not to speak deceit [or, treachery]. [11]*He must turn away from evil and do good; he must seek peace and pursue it. ¹²For [the] eyes of [the] LORD [are] upon [the] righteous, and His ears toward their petition, but [the] face of [the] LORD [is] upon [the ones] doing evil.* [Psalm 34:12-16]

¹³And who [is] the one harming you* if you* become imitators of the good? ¹⁴But even if you* suffer for the sake of righteousness, [you* are] happy [or, blessed]. But do not be afraid of their fear [fig., threats], nor be troubled. ¹⁵But sanctify [the] Lord God in your* hearts, and always [be] prepared with a defense to every[one] asking you* an account concerning the hope [or, confident expectation] in you*, with gentleness [or, considerateness] and respect, ¹⁶having a good conscience, so that in what they speak against you* as evildoers, they shall be ashamed, the ones slandering your* good conduct in Christ. ¹⁷For [it is] better to suffer [for] doing good, if the will of God might be willing [it], than [for] doing evil.

¹⁸For Christ also suffered once for sin for all [time, the] Righteous [One] on behalf of unrighteous [ones], so that He should bring you* to God, [Christ] having been put to death on the one hand in [the] flesh [or, by flesh], on the other hand having been made alive in [the] spirit [or, by [the] Spirit], ¹⁹in which [or, by whom] also having gone, He preached to the spirits in prison, ²⁰having formerly refused to believe, when the patience of God kept eagerly waiting in [the] days of Noah, while an ark was being prepared, in which a few, that is, eight souls, were saved through water; ²¹which [as] an antitype baptism [or, immersion] now also saves us (not [the] removal of [the] filth of [the] flesh, but an appeal to God for [or, a pledge to God from] a good conscience) through [the] resurrection of Jesus Christ, ²²who is at [the] right hand of God, having gone into heaven, angels and authorities and powers having been subjected to Him.

4 Therefore, Christ having suffered [or, since Christ suffered] on our behalf in [the] flesh, you* also arm yourselves with the same mind [or, attitude], because the one having suffered in [the] flesh has ceased from sin, ²so as to live the remaining time in [the] flesh no longer in the lusts of people, but in [the] will of God.

³For the time of life having past [is] sufficient for us to accomplish the desire of the Gentiles, having gone [fig., lived] in flagrant sexual immorality, lusts, drunkenness, drunken orgies, drinking parties, and unlawful [fig., abominable] idolatries; ⁴in which they are surprised [by] your* not running with [them] into the same excess of reckless living, speaking evil of [you*], ⁵who will give an account to the One being prepared to judge [the] living and [the] dead. ⁶Because for this [reason] the Gospel also was proclaimed to [the] dead, so that they shall be judged, on the one hand according to people in [the] flesh, on the other hand they shall live according to God in [the] spirit.

⁷But the end of all [things] has drawn near. Therefore, be sober [or, clear-headed] and be self-controlled in your* prayers. ⁸Now above all [be] having fervent love for one another, because such love will cover a multitude of sins. ⁹[Be] hospitable to one another, without complaints.

¹⁰Just as each [one] received a spiritual gift, [be] serving [with] it to one another, as good stewards of the manifold [or, widely varied] grace of God. ¹¹When someone speaks, [let him speak] as [the] oracles [or, inspired utterances] of God. When someone serves, [let him serve] as from [the] strength [or, ability] as God supplies, so that in all [things] God shall be glorified through Jesus Christ, to whom is the glory and the might [or, dominion] into the ages of the ages [fig., forever and ever]! So be it!

¹²Beloved, stop being surprised by the fiery ordeal [or, painful suffering] taking place among you* to try you*, as [though] a strange [thing] is happening to you*. ¹³But to the degree that you* are sharing in the sufferings of Christ, be rejoicing, so that also in the revelation of His glory you* shall rejoice, being very glad. ¹⁴When you* are being insulted for the name of Christ, [you* are] happy [or, blessed], for the Spirit of the glory and of God rests on you*. On the one hand according to them, He is being blasphemed, on the other hand according to you*, He is glorified.

¹⁵Be making sure none of you* suffer as a murderer, or a thief, or an evildoer, or as a meddler into other's affairs; ¹⁶but if as a Christian, stop being ashamed, but be glorifying God in this matter. ¹⁷For [it is] the time for the judgment to begin with the house of God; but if with us first, what [will be] the end of the ones refusing to believe the Gospel of God? ¹⁸And *"If the righteous [person] is scarcely* [or, *with difficulty is] saved, where will the ungodly and sinner appear* [fig., *what will become of the ungodly and sinner]?"* [Prov 11:31, LXX] ¹⁹So also the ones suffering according to the will of God, as to a trustworthy Creator, must be committing [or, entrusting] their souls in good doing.

5¹I encourage the elders among you* [as] a fellow-elder and a witness of the sufferings of Christ and a partaker of the glory about to be revealed: ²shepherd [fig., serve as a pastor over] the flock of God, the [one] among you*, overseeing not under compulsion, but willingly, nor with greediness for dishonest gain, but eagerly; ³nor as domineering over the [ones] allotted to your* care, but being examples to the flock. ⁴And when the Chief Shepherd appears, you* will receive the unfading victor's wreath [or, crown] of glory.

⁵Likewise, younger [people], be subjected [or, submitted] to [the] elders. And all [continue] being subjected to one another. Clothe yourselves with humility, for, *"God resists* [or, *sets Himself in opposition against] proud [people], but He give grace to humble [people]."* [Prov 3:34, LXX] ⁶Therefore, be humbled [or, humble yourselves] under the mighty hand of God, so that He shall exalt you* at [the proper] time, ⁷having cast all your* anxiety upon Him, for it is a concern to Him about you* [fig., for He cares for you*]!

⁸Be sober [or, Be clear-headed]; keep watch! Your* adversary [the] Devil walks about as a roaring lion seeking someone to devour, ⁹whom you* [are to] stand up against [or, resist], [being] steadfast in the faith, knowing the same sufferings are being experienced by your* brotherhood [fig., the community of believers] in [the] world. ¹⁰But may the God of all grace, the One having called us into His eternal glory in Christ Jesus, [after] you* have suffered [for] a little

while, Himself make you* perfect [or, fully adequate], strengthened, more able, [and] firmly established. ¹¹To Him [be] the glory and the might [or, dominion] into the ages of the ages [fig., forever and ever]! So be it!

¹²By Silvanus, the faithful brother as I consider [him], through [whom] I wrote a few [words], encouraging and testifying this to be [the] true grace of God in which you* have stood firm.

¹³Your [sister-assembly] in Babylon, chosen together with [you*], greets you*, and Mark my son [fig., disciple]. ¹⁴Greet one another with a kiss of love.

Peace to you* all, the [ones] in Christ Jesus! So be it!

The Second Epistle of
Peter

1 Simon Peter, a slave and an apostle of Jesus Christ, To the ones having obtained [or, having been chosen to have] an equally precious faith with us [or, a faith as valuable as ours] by [the] righteousness of our God and Savior Jesus Christ:

²May grace and peace be multiplied to you* in the full [or, true] knowledge of God and of Jesus our Lord, ³as [fig., seeing that] His divine power has given to us all the [things] pertaining to life and godliness through the full [or, true] knowledge of the One having called us by glory and moral excellence, ⁴through which the most precious and great promises have been given to us, so that through these you* shall become participants of a divine nature [or, sharers in [the] divine nature], having escaped from the corruption [that is] in [the] world by lust.

⁵But also [for] this very [reason], having applied all diligence, provide with your* faith moral excellence, and with moral excellence knowledge, ⁶and with knowledge self-control, and with self-control patient endurance, and with patient endurance godliness, ⁷and with godliness brotherly kindness [fig., affection for fellow-believers], and with brotherly kindness love. ⁸For [if] these [qualities] belong to you* and [are] abounding [or, increasing], it makes [you*] neither useless nor unfruitful in regard to the full [or, true] knowledge of our Lord Jesus Christ. ⁹For [the one] with whom these [qualities] are not present is blind, being shortsighted, having become forgetful of the cleansing [or, purgation] of his former sins.

¹⁰For this reason, rather, brothers [and sisters], be eager [or, diligent] to be making certain His calling and choice [or, election] of you*, for these [things] doing, you* shall by no means stumble at any time. ¹¹For in this way, the entrance into the eternal kingdom of our Lord and Savior Jesus Christ will be richly supplied to you*.

¹²For this reason, I will not neglect to be always reminding you* concerning these [things], although you* know [them] and have been established in the present truth. ¹³But I consider [it] right, as long as I am in this tent-like dwelling [fig., this body] to be waking [fig., stirring] you* up by way of reminder, ¹⁴knowing that the taking down of my tent-like dwelling [fig., that my death] is soon, even as also our Lord Jesus Christ made clear to me. [see John 21:18,19] ¹⁵But I will be eager [or, will make every effort] also to cause you* to be having at all times after my departure [Gr., *exodus*] a remembrance of these [things].

¹⁶For not having followed having been cleverly made-up myths, we made known to you* the power and Arrival [or, Coming] of our Lord Jesus Christ, <u>but</u> having become eyewitnesses of the magnificence of that One. ¹⁷For having received from God [the] Father honor and glory, such a voice being brought [fig., uttered] to Him by the Majestic Glory, "This is My Son—the Beloved—in whom <u>I</u> am well-pleased." [Matt 17:5] ¹⁸And this voice <u>we</u> heard, being brought [fig., uttered] out of heaven, being with Him on the holy mountain.

¹⁹And we have the prophetic word [made] more certain [or, confirmed], to which you* do well [to be] paying close attention to, as a lamp shining in a dark place, until [the] day dawns and a morning star arises in your hearts; ²⁰knowing this first, that no prophecy of the Scripture comes of private interpretation, ²¹for prophecy never came by [the] will of a person, but holy men of God spoke being moved along by [the] Holy Spirit.

2 But also false prophets came to be among the people, as also false teachers will be among you*, who will secretly bring in destructive, heretical sects, and denying the Master having redeemed them, bringing swift destruction upon themselves. ²And many will follow their flagrant sexually immoral ways, because of whom the way of truth will be blasphemed. ³And in covetous desire [or, greed], with fabricated words, they will exploit you*, for whom their judgment of old is not idle, and their destruction will not sleep.

⁴For if God did not spare angels having sinned, but having hurled [them] down to the deepest pit of gloom [Gr. *tartarus*], He delivered [them] to chains of thick darkness, being kept for judgment; ⁵and He did not spare the ancient world, but kept Noah, [the] eighth person [fig., with seven others], a preacher of righteousness, having brought a Flood upon the world of the ungodly, ⁶and having reduced [the] cities of Sodom and Gomorrah to ashes, He condemned [them] to destruction, having set [them as] an example to [the ones] being about to be acting in an ungodly way, ⁷and rescued righteous Lot, [who was] being distressed by the conduct in flagrant sexual immorality of the lawless [ones] ⁸(for by seeing and hearing, that righteous [man] living among them, day by day [his] righteous soul was being tormented with [their] unlawful works), ⁹[the] Lord knows [how] to be rescuing [the] godly out of temptation, but to be keeping [the] unrighteous being punished for [the] day of judgment, ¹⁰and especially the ones going after [fig., indulging] [the] flesh in lust of uncleanness [or, unclean desires] and despising authority. [They are] presumptuous [or, reckless], self-willed [or, stubborn], not trembling when they speak evil of glories [fig., angelic beings], ¹¹whereas angels, being greater in strength and power, do not bring a slanderous judgment against them before [the] Lord.

¹²But these, like irrational animals [guided by] natural instinct having been born for capture and destruction [fig., slaughter], speaking evil of [or, blaspheming in] [things] which they fail to understand, in their destruction they will be destroyed, ¹³receiving back a reward of unrighteousness, counting [it as] a pleasure [to be engaging in] self-indulgence in the day; [they are] spots and blemishes [fig., a disgrace], openly indulging in their deceitful ways while they feast with you*, ¹⁴having eyes full of adultery and unceasing in sin, enticing unstable souls, having a heart having been trained in covetous desire [or, greed], children of a curse [or, accursed children], ¹⁵having forsaken [the] right way, they went astray [fig., were deceived], having followed in the way of Balaam the [son] of Bosor, who loved [the] wages of unrighteousness, ¹⁶but he had a rebuke [for] his own iniquity: a mute donkey, having spoken in a person's voice, restrained the madness of the prophet.

¹⁷These [people] are wells without water, clouds being driven by a storm, for whom the thick gloom of the darkness [fig., the gloomy hell] has been reserved into [the] age [fig., forever]. ¹⁸For speaking swollen [fig., pompous] [words] of emptiness [or, nonsense], they entice with lusts of [the] flesh, with flagrant sexual immorality, the ones actually having escaped from the ones conducting themselves in deception, ¹⁹promising freedom to them, while they themselves are slaves of the corruption, for by whom anyone has been defeated, by this one also he has been enslaved.

²⁰For if having escaped from the pollutions of the world by the full [or, true] knowledge of the Lord and Savior Jesus Christ, yet again being entangled by these [pollutions], they are defeated; the final [state] has become worse for them than the first. ²¹For it would have been better for them not to have known the way of righteousness, than having known [it], to turn back from the holy commandment having been handed down to them. ²²But it has happened to them [according to] the [saying] of the true proverb, *"A dog turns back upon his own vomit,"* and, "A pig having bathed herself [turns back] to wallowing in mud." [Prov 26:11]

3 This [is] now, beloved, [the] second letter I am writing to you*, in which I am stirring up your* pure [or, sincere] mind by reminding [you*] ²to be mindful of the words having been previously spoken by the holy prophets and of the commandment of your* apostles of the Lord and Savior, ³knowing this first, that scoffers will come at [the] last of the days [or, at [the] end of time], going [fig., living] according to their own desires, ⁴and saying, "Where is the promise of His Arrival [or, Coming]? For since the fathers fell asleep [fig., died], all [things] continue in the same manner [as] from [the] beginning of creation."

⁵For this they willingly forget [or, ignore], that [the] heavens were from of old, and [the] earth having existed out of water and through water by the word of God, ⁶through which the then world, having been flooded by water, was destroyed. ⁷But the present heavens and the [present] earth having been stored up [or, reserved] for fire by His word are being kept for [the] day of judgment and of destruction of the godless people.

⁸But stop letting this one [fact] be forgotten [or, ignored] by you*, beloved, that one day with [the] Lord [is] as a thousand years, and a thousand years as one day. [see Psalm 90:4] ⁹The Lord is not slow concerning His promise, as some regard slowness; but He is waiting patiently towards us, not wanting any [of us] to be lost, but [for] all [of us] to make room for repentance.

¹⁰But the day of [the] Lord will come like a thief in [the] night, in which the heavens with a loud roar [or, with roaring speed] will pass away, and [the] elements being consumed by intense heat will be destroyed, and [the] earth and the works in it will be burned up. ¹¹Therefore, all these [things] being destroyed, what sort of [people] is it necessary [for] you* to be in holy behaviors and godly acts, ¹²waiting for and hastening to the arrival of the Day of God, by which [the] heavens being set on fire will be destroyed, and [the] elements being consumed by intense heat are melted? ¹³But we are waiting for a new heavens and a new earth according to His promise, in which righteousness dwells.

[14]For this reason, beloved, waiting for these [things], be eager [or, diligent] to be found by Him in peace, spotless and blameless. [15]And consider the patience of our Lord [to be] salvation, just as also our beloved brother Paul, according to the wisdom having been given to him, wrote to you*, [16]as also in all his letters, speaking in them concerning these [things], in which are some [things] difficult to be understood, which the untaught and unstable twist [fig., distort] to their own destruction, as [they do] also the rest of [the] Scriptures.

[17]You* therefore, beloved, knowing [this] beforehand, be guarding yourselves, lest, together with the deception of the lawless [ones] being led away, you* fall from your* own firm footing [or, steadfastness]. [18]But be increasing in [the] grace and knowledge of our Lord and Savior Jesus Christ. To Him [be] the glory both now and to [the] day of [the] age [fig, to eternity]! So be it!

329

The First Epistle of

John

1 What was from [the] beginning, what we have heard, what we have seen with our eyes, what we looked upon and our hands handled, concerning the Word of the life—²and the life was revealed, and we have seen and testify and declare to you* the eternal life, which was with the Father and was revealed to us—³what we have seen and have heard we declare to you*, so that you* also shall be having fellowship with us, and indeed our fellowship [is] with the Father and with His Son Jesus Christ. ⁴And these things we write to you*, so that our joy shall have been made full.

⁵And this is the message which we have heard from Him and announce to you*, that God is light [fig., is as to His essence light], and in Him [there] is no darkness at all. ⁶If we say, "We have fellowship with Him," and are walking about [fig., conducting ourselves] in the darkness [i.e., in falsehood and unrighteousness], we are lying and are not doing the truth. ⁷But if we are walking about in the light [i.e., in truth and righteousness], as He is in the light, we have fellowship with one another, and the blood of Jesus Christ His Son cleanses [or, purges] us from all sin.

⁸If we claim, "We do not have sin," we lead ourselves astray [fig., deceive ourselves], and the truth is not in us. ⁹If we are confessing our sins, He is faithful [or, trustworthy] and righteous that He shall forgive us our sins and cleanse [or, purge] us from all unrighteousness. ¹⁰If we claim, "We have not sinned," we make Him a liar, and His word is not in us.

2 My little children [or, My dear children], I am writing these things to you* so that you* do not sin. And if anyone does sin, we have a Counselor [or, an Advocate] with the Father, Jesus Christ, [the] righteous. ²And <u>He</u> is [the] propitiation [or, appeasing sacrifice] concerning our sins, but not concerning ours only, <u>but</u> also concerning the whole world's!

³And by this we know that we have come to know Him, if we are keeping His commandments. ⁴The one claiming, "I have come to know Him," and does not keep His commandments is a liar, and the truth is not in him. ⁵But whoever is keeping His word, in this one the love of God has truly been perfected; by this we know that we are in Him. ⁶The one claiming to be abiding in Him just as that [One] walked ought also in the same manner himself to be walking.

⁷Brothers [and sisters], I am not writing a new commandment to you*, <u>but</u> an old commandment which you* were having from the beginning—the old commandment is the word which you* heard from [the] beginning. ⁸Again, I am writing a new commandment to you*, which is true in Him and in you*, because the darkness is passing away, and the true light is already shining.

⁹The one claiming to be in the light and [yet is] hating his brother [fig., fellow believer, and elsewhere in book] is in the darkness until now. ¹⁰The one loving his

brother abides in the light, and [there] is not a stumbling block [or, no enticement to sin] in him. [11]But the one hating his brother, he is in the darkness and walks about in the darkness. And he does not know where he is going, because the darkness [has] blinded his eyes.

[12]I am writing to you*, little children, because your* sins have been forgiven you* on account of His name. [13]I am writing to you*, fathers, because you* have come to know the [One who is] from [the] beginning. I am writing to you*, young men, because you* have overcome the evil [one]. I am writing to you*, little children, because you* have come to know the Father. [14]I wrote to you*, fathers, because you* have come to know the [One who is] from [the] beginning. I wrote to you*, young men, because you* are strong, and the word of God abides in you*, and you* have overcome the evil [one].

[15]Stop loving the world and the [things] in the world. If anyone is loving the world, the love of the Father is not in him. [16]Because all that [is] in the world—the lust of the flesh and the lust of the eyes and the pretentious pride of life—is not from the Father, but is from the world. [17]And the world is passing away, and the lust of it, but the one doing the will of God remains into the age [fig., forever].

[18]Young children [or, Dear children], it is the last hour. And just as you* heard that the antichrist is coming, even now antichrists have become many [or, many antichrists have appeared], for which reason we know that it is the last hour. [19]They went out from us, but they were not of us, for if they were of us, they would have remained with us; but [they went out] so that they should be revealed that they are not all of us [or, they all are not of us]. [20]And you* have an anointing from the Holy [One], and you* know all [things].

[21]I did not write to you* because you* do not know the truth, but because you* know it, and because every lie is not from the truth. [22]Who is the liar, except the one denying that Jesus is the Christ [or, the Messiah]? This one is the antichrist, the one denying the Father and the Son. [23]Everyone denying the Son neither has the Father. [24]Therefore, what you* heard from [the] beginning, let [it] be abiding in you*.

If what you* heard from [the] beginning abides in you*, you* will also remain in the Son and in the Father. [25]And this is the promise which He promised us—eternal life! [26]These things I wrote to you* concerning the ones leading you* astray [fig., deceiving you*]. [27]And the anointing which you* received from Him abides in you*. And you* have no need that anyone should be teaching you*, but as that same anointing teaches you* concerning all [things], and is true and is not a lie, and just as it taught you*, you* will abide in Him.

[28]And now, little children, be abiding in Him, so that when He shall be revealed we shall be having confidence [or, a joyful sense of freedom] and shall not be ashamed before Him at His Arrival [or, Coming]. [29]If you* know that He is righteous, you* know [or, be knowing] that everyone practicing righteousness has been begotten from Him.

3 See what great love the Father has given to us, that we should be called children of God! For this reason the world does not know you*, because it did not know

Him. ²Beloved, we are now children of God, and it has not yet been revealed what we will be. But we know that when it [or, He] shall be revealed, we will be like Him, because we will see Him just as He is! ³And every one having this hope [or, confident expectation] in Him, purifies himself, just as that One is pure.

⁴Everyone practicing sin also practices lawlessness, and sin is lawlessness. ⁵And you* know that that One was revealed so that He should take away our sins, and sin is not in Him. ⁶Everyone abiding in Him is not sinning; every one sinning has not seen Him, nor has come to know Him.

⁷Little children [or, [My] dear children], let no one be leading you* astray [fig., be deceiving you*]. The one practicing righteousness is righteous, just as He is righteous. ⁸The one practicing sin is from the Devil, because the Devil [has been] sinning from [the] beginning. For this [reason] the Son of God was revealed, so that He should destroy the works of the Devil. ⁹Everyone having been begotten from God is not practicing sin, because His seed abides in him, and he is not able to be sinning, because he has been begotten from God. ¹⁰By this are revealed [who are] the children of God and the children of the Devil. Every one not practicing righteousness is not from God, and the one not loving his brother.

¹¹Because this is the message which you* heard from [the] beginning, that we should be loving one another: ¹²not as Cain—he was from the evil [one] and slew his brother. And for what reason did he slay him? Because his works were evil, but those of his brother [were] righteous. ¹³Stop marveling, my brothers [and sisters], if the world hates you*. ¹⁴We know that we have passed over from death to life, because we are loving the brothers [and sisters]. The one not loving his brother abides in death. ¹⁵Every one hating his brother is a murderer, and you* know that every murderer does not have eternal life abiding in himself.

¹⁶By this we have come to know love, because that One laid down His life on our behalf, and we ought to be laying down our lives on behalf of the brothers [and sisters]. ¹⁷But whoever shall be having the goods of the world and shall be seeing his brother having need and shuts up his bowels from him [fig., refuses to show him compassion], how does the love of God abide in Him? ¹⁸My little children, let us not be loving in word nor in the tongue, but in deed and in truth! ¹⁹And by this we know that we are of the truth, and we will assure our hearts [fig., consciences] before Him, ²⁰because if our heart [fig., conscience] is condemning [us], that God is greater than our heart, and He knows all things.

²¹Beloved, if our heart [fig., conscience] shall not be condemning [us], we have confidence [or, a joyful sense of freedom] before God. ²²And whatever we shall be asking, we receive from Him, because we keep His commandments and do the [things] pleasing before Him. ²³And this is His commandment, that we should believe in the name of His Son Jesus Christ, and we should be loving one another, just as He gave commandment. ²⁴And the one keeping His commandments abides in Him, and He in him; and by this we know that He abides in us, from the Spirit which He gave to us.

4 Beloved, stop believing [or, trusting] every spirit, but be testing the spirits [to see] if they are from God, because many false prophets have gone out into the

world. ²By this is known the Spirit of God: every spirit which confesses Jesus Christ [as] having come in [the] flesh is of God. ³And every spirit which does not confess Jesus Christ [as] having come in [the] flesh is not from God, and this is the [spirit] of the antichrist which you* heard that it is coming and now is already in the world.

⁴You* are from God, little children, and you* have overcome them, because greater is the One in you* than the one in the world! ⁵They are from the world; for this reason, they speak [as] from the world, and the world hears them. ⁶We are from God. The one knowing God hears us; [the one] who is not of God does not hear us. From this we know the spirit of truth and the spirit of deception [or, error].

⁷Beloved, let us be loving one another, because love is from God, and every one loving has been begotten from God and knows God. ⁸The one not loving did not know [or, come to know] God, because God is love [fig., is as to His essence love]. ⁹By this was the love of God revealed in us, because God has sent His only-begotten [or, unique] Son into the world, so that we should live through Him. ¹⁰In this is love, not that we loved God, but that He loved us and sent His Son [as] a propitiation [or, appeasing sacrifice] concerning our sins! ¹¹Beloved, if God so loved us, we also ought to be loving one another.

¹²No one has seen God at any time. If we are loving one another, God abides in us, and His love has been perfected in us. ¹³By this we know that we abide in Him, and He in us, because He has given to us of His Spirit. ¹⁴And we have seen and testify that the Father has sent the Son [as] Savior of the world! ¹⁵Whoever shall confess that Jesus is the Son of God, God abides in him, and he in God. ¹⁶And we have known [or, have come to know] and have believed [or, have been convinced of] the love which God has in us. God is love, and the one abiding in that love abides in God, and God abides in him.

¹⁷By this, love has been perfected [or, completed] with us, so that we shall be having confidence [or, a joyful sense of freedom] in the day of the judgment, because just as that One is, [so] also we are in this world. ¹⁸[There] is no fear in love, but perfect love casts out fear, because fear has punishment. But the one fearing has not been perfected in love. ¹⁹We love Him, because He first loved us.

²⁰If anyone says, "I love God," and shall be hating his brother, he is a liar; for the one not loving his brother whom he has seen, how is he able to be loving God whom he has not seen? ²¹And this [is] the commandment we have from Him, that the one loving God should also be loving his brother.

5Every one believing [or, who is convinced] that Jesus is the Christ [or, the Messiah] has been begotten from God, and every one loving the One having begotten loves also the one having been begotten from [or, by] Him. ²By this we know that we love the children of God, when we love God and are keeping His commandments. ³For this is the love of God, that we are keeping His commandments, and His commandments are not burdensome [or, difficult to obey].

⁴Because every one having been begotten from God overcomes the world, and this is the victory having overcome the world—our faith! ⁵Who is the one overcoming the world, if not the one believing [or, who is convinced] that Jesus is the Son of God?

⁶This is the One having come through water and blood—Jesus Christ; not by the water only, but by the water and the blood. And the Spirit is the One testifying, because the Spirit is the truth. ⁷Because three are the Ones testifying: ⁸the Spirit and the water and the blood, and the three are into the one [fig., agree as one].

⁹If we receive the testimony of people, the testimony of God is greater; because this is the testimony of God which He has testified concerning His Son. ¹⁰The one believing [or, trusting] in the Son of God has that testimony in him; the one not believing God, has made Him a liar, because he has not believed in the testimony which God has testified concerning His Son. ¹¹And this is the testimony, that God gave eternal life to us, and this life is in His Son. ¹²The one having the Son has such life; the one not having the Son of God does not have such life.

¹³These things I wrote to you*, the ones believing [or, trusting] in the name of the Son of God, so that you* shall know that you* have eternal life, and so that you* shall be believing [or, shall continue believing] in the name of the Son of God.

¹⁴And this is the confidence which we have before Him, that if we are asking anything according to His will, He hears us. ¹⁵And if we know that He hears us, whatever we ask, we know that we have the requests which we have requested from Him.

¹⁶If anyone sees his brother sinning a sin not [leading] to death, he will ask, and He will give to him life, to the ones sinning [a sin] not [leading] to death. [There] is a sin [leading] to death; not concerning that [sin] am I saying that he should urgently ask. ¹⁷Every unrighteousness is sin, and [there] is a sin not [leading] to death.

¹⁸We know that every one having been begotten from God is not sinning, but the one having been begotten from God keeps himself, and the evil [one] does not touch him. ¹⁹We know that we are from God, and the whole world lies in evil [or, in the evil [one]]. ²⁰Now we know that the Son of God [has] come, and He has given to us understanding, so that we shall know the true [One]. And we are in the true [One], in His Son, Jesus Christ. This One is the true God and eternal life!

²¹Little children [or, [My] dear children], guard yourselves from the idols! So be it!

The Second Epistle of
John

¹The Elder, To [the] chosen Kyria [or, elect lady] and to her children, whom I love in truth; and not I only, but also all the ones having come to know the truth, ²on account of the truth which abides in us and will be with us into the age [fig., forever]. ³Grace, mercy, [and] peace will be with us, from God [the] Father and from [the] Lord Jesus Christ, the Son of the Father, in truth and love.

⁴I greatly rejoiced that I have found [some] of your children walking about [fig., conducting themselves] in truth, just as we received a commandment from the Father. ⁵And now I urgently ask you, Kyria, not as writing to you a new commandment, but [the one] which we were having from the beginning, that we should be loving one another. ⁶And this is love, that we are walking about [fig, conducting ourselves] according to His commandments. This is the commandment, just as you heard from the beginning that you should be walking about in it.

⁷Because many deceivers entered into the world, the ones not confessing Jesus Christ [as] coming in [the] flesh; this is the deceiver and the antichrist. ⁸Be watching yourselves so that we do not lose what we worked for, but [that] we shall receive a full reward. ⁹Every one transgressing and not abiding in the teaching [or, doctrine] of Christ does not have God. The one abiding in the teaching [or, doctrine] of Christ, this one has both the Father and the Son. ¹⁰If anyone comes to you* and does not bring this teaching [or, doctrine], stop receiving him into [your] house, and stop saying to him, "Rejoice!" [or, stop greeting him]. ¹¹For the one saying to him, "Rejoice!" [or, the one greeting him] contributes to [or, shares in] his evil works.

¹²Having many [things] to be writing to you*, I did not intend [to do so] through a sheet of papyrus and ink, but I hope [or, expect] to come to you* and to speak mouth to mouth [fig., face to face], so that our joy shall have been filled.

¹³The children of your chosen [or, elect] sister greet you. So be it!

The Third Epistle of
John

[1]The Elder, To Gaius, the beloved [fig., my dear friend], whom I love in truth!
[2]Beloved [fig., Dear friend], concerning all [things] I am praying [or, wishing] [for] you to be having things going well and to be having good health, just as your soul is doing well. [3]For I rejoiced greatly when [some] of [the] brothers [and sisters] came and testified of the truth in you, just as you are walking about [fig., conducting yourself] in truth. [4]I have no greater joy [than] these [things], that I hear my children are walking about [fig., conducting themselves] in truth.

[5]Beloved, you* are acting faithfully [in] whatever you* perform for the brothers [and sisters] and for the strangers [6](who testified of your* love before [the] assembly [or, church]), [to] whom you* will do well, if you* have helped them on their journey in a manner worthy of God. [7]For they went out on behalf of the Name, receiving nothing from the Gentiles [or, unbelievers]. [8]Therefore, we ought to be receiving such [ones], so that we shall become co-workers to the truth.

[9]I wrote to the assembly [or, church], but Diotrephes, the one loving the first place [or, desiring to be the leader] among them, does not receive us [or, accept our authority]. [10]For this reason, if I come, I will remind [him of] his works which he is doing, making idle accusations against us with evil words. And not content with these things, neither does he welcome the brothers [and sisters], and he forbids the ones desiring [to do so] and casts [them] out of the assembly [or, church].

[11]Beloved, stop imitating the evil, but [be imitating] the good. The one doing good is from God; the one doing evil has not seen God. [12]Demetrius has been testified to [or, well spoken of] by all, and by the truth itself. And we also testify, and you* know that our testimony is true.

[13]I had many [things] to be writing, but I do not want to write to you through ink and pen. [14]But I hope [or, expect] soon to see you, and we will speak mouth to mouth [fig., face to face].

Peace to you! Our friends greet you. Be greeting our friends by name.

The Epistle of
Jude

¹Jude, a slave of Jesus Christ and a brother of James, To the called [ones], having been sanctified by God the Father and having been kept in Jesus Christ. ²May mercy and peace and love be multiplied to you*!

³Beloved, making all diligence [or, while I was making every effort] to be writing to you* concerning the common salvation, I had necessity to write to you* urging [you*] to be contending earnestly for the faith having been handed down once [and] for all [time] to the holy ones [or, saints]. ⁴For certain people wormed their way in, the ones having been marked out long ago for this judgment, godless [ones], perverting the grace of our God into flagrant sexual immorality and denying our only Master, God, and Lord—Jesus Christ [or, the only Master God and our Lord Jesus Christ].

⁵But I want to remind you*, you* knowing this once [and] for all, that the Lord having saved [or, delivered] a people out of [the] land of Egypt, afterward destroyed the ones not having believed. ⁶And angels, the ones not having kept their own domain, but having left their own habitation, He has kept under darkness in everlasting chains for [the] judgment of [the] great Day. ⁷Just as Sodom and Gomorrah and the cities around them, in a similar manner to these [angels], having indulged in sexual sin and having gone after different flesh [fig., having engaged in homosexual sex], are exhibited [as] an example of suffering [the] divine justice of eternal fire.

⁸Likewise indeed even these dreaming ones defile [the] flesh and regard authority as nothing [or, reject authority], blaspheme glories [fig., angelic beings]. ⁹But Michael the archangel, when contending with the Devil, he was arguing about the body of Moses, did not dare to bring a slanderous judgment, but he said, "May [the] Lord rebuke you!"

¹⁰But these indeed slander as many [things] as they do not know [or, understand], but as many [things] as they understand by natural instinct (like the irrational animals), by these they are destroyed [or, corrupted].

¹¹How horrible it will be to them! Because they traveled in [fig., followed] the way of Cain, and for pay they plunged into the deception of Balaam, and they perished in the rebellion of Korah.

¹²These are hidden rocks in the sea [fig., hidden dangers] in your* love-feasts [fig., fellowship meals], feasting together without fear, shepherding [fig., caring only for] themselves, clouds without water, being carried along by winds, late autumn [i.e., harvest season] trees without fruit, twice having died, having been uprooted, ¹³wild waves of [the] sea, splashing up their own shames like foam, wandering stars [fig., stars out of their orbits], for whom the thick gloom of the darkness [fig., the gloomy hell] has been reserved into [the] age [fig., forever].

¹⁴Now Enoch, [in] the seventh [generation] from Adam, also prophesied about these [people], saying, "Look! [The] Lord came with countless thousands

of His holy ones, ¹⁵to execute judgment upon all, and to convict all the ungodly ones among them concerning all their ungodly deeds which they committed in an ungodly way, and concerning all the harsh [words] which ungodly sinners spoke against Him." ¹⁶These are grumblers, complainers, going [fig., living] according to their lusts, and their mouth speaks swollen [fig., pompous] [words], admiring faces [fig., flattering people] for the sake of [gaining] an advantage.

¹⁷But you*, beloved, remember the words, the ones having been spoken previously by the apostles of our Lord Jesus Christ, ¹⁸that they were saying to you*, that in [the] last time there will be scoffers, going [fig., living] according to their own ungodly lusts. ¹⁹These are the ones causing divisions, worldly, not having [the] Spirit.

²⁰But you*, beloved, building yourselves up in your* most holy faith, praying in [the] Holy Spirit, ²¹keep yourselves in [the] love of God, waiting for [or, expecting] the mercy of our Lord Jesus Christ to eternal life. ²²And be having mercy on some, making a distinction [between persons], ²³but others be saving with fear, snatching [them] out of a fire, hating even the tunic [or, garment] having been polluted [or, defiled] by the flesh.

²⁴Now to the One being able to keep them from stumbling and to make [you*] stand in the presence of His glory unblemished [or, blameless], with great happiness— ²⁵to [the] only wise God our Savior, [be] glory and majesty, dominion and authority, both now and to all the ages [fig., forevermore]! So be it!

The Revelation
of Jesus Christ

1[The] revelation of Jesus Christ, which God gave to Him to show to His slaves what [things are] necessary to occur with quickness. And He made [it] known, having sent through His angel to His slave John, ²who testified to the word of God and to the testimony of Jesus Christ, as many [things] as he also saw.

³Happy [or, Blessed] is the one reading [to the assembly] and the ones hearing the words of the prophecy and keeping [or, obeying] the [things] having been written in it, for the time [is] near!

⁴John, To the seven assemblies [or, churches, and throughout book], the [ones] in Asia: Grace to you* and peace from God, the One being and the One [who] was and the One [who is] coming, and from the seven spirits which [are] [fig., the seven-fold Spirit who is] before His throne, ⁵and from Jesus Christ, the faithful witness, the first-born of the dead [ones] and the ruler of the kings of the earth.

To the One loving us and having bathed us from our sins in His blood. ⁶And He made us a kingdom, priests to His God and Father—to Him [be] the glory and the power into the ages of the ages [fig., forever and ever]! So be it!

⁷*"Look! He is coming with the clouds,"* [Dan 7:13] and *"every eye will see Him, even [the ones] who pierced Him, and all the tribes of the earth will beat their breasts* [fig., *mourn*] *because of Him."* [Zech 12:10] Yes indeed! So be it!

⁸"I am the Alpha and the Omega [i.e. the first and last letters of the Greek alphabet]," says [the] Lord God, "The One being and the One [who] was and the One [who is] coming—the Almighty."

⁹I, John, the [one being] your* brother and partner in the affliction and the kingdom and patient endurance in Jesus Christ, came to be in the island, the one being called Patmos, because of the word of God and because of the testimony of Jesus Christ. ¹⁰I came to be in spirit [or, in [the] Spirit] on the Lord's Day, and I heard behind me a great voice, like a trumpet-blast, ¹¹saying, "What you see, write in a scroll, and send [it] to the seven assemblies: to Ephesus and to Smyrna and to Pergamos and to Thyatira and to Sardis and to Philadelphia and to Laodicea."

¹²And there I turned around to be seeing the voice which was speaking with me. And having turned around, I saw seven golden lampstands, ¹³and in [the] middle of the seven lampstands [One] like [the] Son of Humanity [or, a son of humanity], having been clothed with a robe reaching to the feet and having been wrapped around at the chest with a golden belt [or, sash]. ¹⁴Now His head and His hair [were] white like white wool, like snow, and His eyes like a flame of fire. ¹⁵And His feet [were] like fine brass [or, burnished bronze] when it has been refined in a furnace, and His voice like [the] sound of many waters, ¹⁶and having seven stars in His right hand, and a sharp, double-edged sword proceeding out of His mouth, and His face [was] like the sun shining in its might.

¹⁷And when I saw Him, I fell at His feet as dead. And He placed His right [hand] on me, saying, "Stop being afraid! I am the First and the Last, ¹⁸and the

living One. And I became dead. And look! I am living into the ages of the ages [fig., forever and ever]. Amen! And I have the keys of death and of the realm of the dead [Gr., *hades*]. ¹⁹Therefore, write what [things] you saw, and what [things] are, and what [things] are about to be coming after these [things]. ²⁰The secret [or, mystery] of the seven stars which you saw on My right hand, and the seven golden lampstands: the seven stars are angels of the seven assemblies, and the seven lampstands are seven assemblies.

2"To the angel of the assembly in Ephesus write: 'These [things] says the One holding the seven stars in His right hand, the One walking about in [the] middle of the seven golden lampstands: ²I know your works and your labor and your patient endurance, and that you are not able to tolerate evil [people]. And you tested the ones saying themselves to be apostles [fig., who say they are apostles] and are not, and found them [to be] liars. ³And you have perseverance and [have] endured because of My name, and you did not grow weary.

⁴"But I have [this] against you, that you left your first love! ⁵Therefore, remember from where you have fallen, and repent, and do the first works; but if not [fig., or else] I am coming to you quickly, and I will remove your lampstand from its place, unless you repent. ⁶But this you have, that you hate the works of the Nicolaitans, which I also hate.

⁷'The one having an ear, let him hear [or, pay attention to, and throughout book] what the Spirit says to the assemblies. To the one overcoming, I will give to him to eat from the tree of life which is in the Paradise of My God.'

⁸"And to the angel of the assembly in Smyrna write: 'These [things] says the First and the Last, who became dead and lived [or, came to life]: ⁹I know your works and affliction and poverty (but you are rich), and the blasphemy of the ones saying themselves to be Jews [fig., who say they are Jews], and are not, but [are] a synagogue of Satan. ¹⁰Stop being afraid of what you are about to suffer. Listen indeed! The Devil is about to throw [some] of you* into prison, so that you* shall be tested, and you* will have affliction ten days. Continue being faithful until death, and I will give to you the victor's wreath [or, crown, and throughout book] of life.

¹¹'The one having an ear, let him hear what the Spirit says to the assemblies. The one overcoming shall by no means be harmed by the second death.'

¹²"And to the angel of the assembly in Pergamos write: 'These [things] says the One having the sharp, double-edged sword: ¹³I know your works and where you are dwelling, where the throne of Satan [is]. And you hold fast to My name, and you did not deny My faith in the days in which Antipas, My faithful witness [or, martyr], who was put to death beside you*, where Satan dwells.

¹⁴'But I have a few [things] against you, that you have there [some] holding to the teaching of Balaam, who taught Balak to throw a stumbling block before the sons [and daughters] of Israel and to eat [food] sacrificed to idols and to commit sexual sin. ¹⁵In the same way, you even have [some] holding to the teaching of the Nicolaitans likewise. ¹⁶Therefore repent! But if not [fig., Or else] I am coming to you quickly, and I will wage war against them with the sword of my mouth.

¹⁷'The one having an ear, let him hear what the Spirit says to the assemblies. To the one overcoming, I will give to him to eat of the manna, the one having been hidden, and I will give to him a white stone, and on the stone a new name having been written, which no one knows except the one receiving [it].'

¹⁸"And to the angel of the assembly in Thyatira write: 'These [things] says the Son of God, the One having His eyes like a flame of fire and His feet like fine brass [or, burnished bronze]: ¹⁹I know your works and love and service and faith, and your patient endurance, and your last works [are] greater [than] the first.

²⁰'But I have against you that you permit your woman Jezebel, she [who] calls herself a prophetess, to be teaching and to be leading My slaves astray [or, deceiving My slaves] to commit sexual sin and to eat [food] sacrificed to idols. ²¹And I gave to her time so that she should repent, and she was not willing to repent from her sexual sin. ²²Listen! I am throwing her on a bed [of sickness], and the ones committing adultery with her into great affliction, unless they repent of her works. ²³And I will kill her children with death, and all the assemblies will know that I am the One searching kidneys and hearts [fig., thoughts and inner selves], and I will give to you*, to each [one] according to your* works.

²⁴'Now I say to you*, to [the] rest in Thyatira, as many as do not have this teaching, who did not know the depths of Satan, as they say—I will not put on you* [any] other burden. ²⁵Nevertheless, what you* have, hold fast until I come.

²⁶'And the one overcoming and the one keeping My works until the end, *"I will give to him authority over the nations*; ²⁷*and he will shepherd* [or, *rule*] *them with an iron staff; they will be broken in pieces like the vessels of the potter,"* [Psalm 2:8,9] as I also have received [authority] from My Father. ²⁸And I will give to him the morning star.

²⁹'The one having an ear, let him hear what the Spirit says to the assemblies.'

3 "And to the angel of the assembly in Sardis write: 'These [things] says the One having the seven spirits [fig., the seven-fold Spirit] of God and the seven stars: I know your works, that you have a name that you live, and you are dead. ²Become watching [fig., Wake up], and strengthen the rest which you were about to be throwing out, for I have not found your works having been completed before My God. ³Therefore, be remembering how you have received and heard, and be keeping [it], and repent. Therefore, if you will not watch [fig., keep awake], I will come upon you like a thief, and you shall by no means know what hour I will come upon you. ⁴But you have a few names [fig., individuals] in Sardis who did not defile their garments, and they will walk about with Me in white, because they are worthy.

⁵'The one overcoming, this [one] will be clothed in white garments, and by no means will I blot out his name from the Scroll of Life, and I will confess his name before My Father and before His angels.

⁶'The one having an ear, let him hear what the Spirit says to the assemblies.'

⁷"And to the angel of the assembly in Philadelphia write: 'These [things] says the holy [One], the true [One], the One having the key of David, the One

opening and no one shuts it except the One opening, and no one opens. [8]I know your works. Look! I have set before you a door having been opened, which no one is able to shut it; because you have a little strength and kept My word and did not deny My name. [9]Listen! I am giving [those] of the synagogue of Satan, the ones saying themselves to be Jews [or, who say they are Jews], and are not, but are lying. Listen! I will make them so that they shall come and prostrate themselves in reverence before your feet, and they shall know that I loved you. [10]Because you kept the word of My patient endurance, I also will keep you from the hour of the trial, the one about to be coming upon the whole inhabited earth, to test the ones dwelling on the earth. [cp. John 17:15]

[11]"I am coming quickly! Be holding fast what you have, so that no one shall receive your victor's wreath. [12]The one overcoming, I will make him a pillar in the temple of my God, and by no means shall he go out any longer. And I will write on him the name of My God and the name of the city of My God, the new Jerusalem, which is descending out of heaven from my God, and [I will write on him] My new name.

[13]'The one having an ear, let him hear what the Spirit says to the assemblies.'

[14]"And to the angel of the assembly in Laodicea write: 'These [things] says the Amen, the Faithful and True Witness, the Beginning [or, Origin; or, Ruler] of the creation of God: [15]I know your works, that you are neither cold nor hot. O that you* were cold or hot! [16]So then, because you are lukewarm, and not hot nor cold, I am about to vomit you out of My mouth. [17]Because you say, "I am wealthy and have grown rich and have need of nothing," and you do not know that you are the wretched [one] and the miserable [one], and poor and blind and naked, [18]I advise you to buy from me gold having been refined by fire, so that you shall grow rich, and white garments, so that you shall be clothed and the shame of your nakedness shall not be revealed, so that you shall smear your eyes with eye-salve, so that you shall see. [19]As many as I affectionately love, I rebuke and discipline. Therefore, be zealous and repent!

[20]'Look! I have stood at the door, and I am knocking. If anyone hears My voice and opens the door, then I will come in to him and will dine with him, and he with Me. [21]The One overcoming, I will give to him to sit down with Me in My throne, as I also overcame and sat down with my Father in His throne.

[22]'The one having an ear, let him hear what the Spirit says to the assemblies.'"

4 After these things I saw, and look!, a door having been opened in heaven, and the first voice which I heard [was] like a trumpet-blast speaking with me, saying, "Come up here, and I will show to you what must occur after these [things]." [2]And immediately I came to be in spirit [or, in [the] Spirit].

And look! A throne was standing in heaven (and [Someone was] sitting on the throne), [3]similar in appearance to a jasper stone [i.e. a gem of varying colors] and to a sardius [or, carnelian; i.e. a red gem], and [there was] a rainbow around the throne, likewise [there was the] appearance of emeralds. [4]And around the throne [were] twenty-four thrones, and on the thrones the twenty-four elders [were] sitting, having been clothed in white garments, and on their heads [were] golden victor's wreaths. ⁵And from the throne proceed lightning flashes and voices and peals of thunder. And seven lamps of fire [were] burning before His throne, which are seven spirits [fig., which is [the] seven-fold Spirit] of God. ⁶And before the throne [was something] like a glassy sea like crystal [or, ice].

And in [the] center of the throne and around the throne [were] four living creatures full of [or, covered with] eyes in front and in back. ⁷And the first living creature [was] like a lion, and the second living creature [was] like a calf, and the third living creature having a face of a person, and the fourth living creature [was] like a flying eagle. ⁸And the four living creatures, each one having six wings apiece covered with eyes around and within, and they do not have rest day and night, saying, "Holy, holy, holy [is] [the] Lord God, the Almighty, the One [who] was and the One being and the One [who is] coming!"

⁹And whenever the living creatures ascribe glory and honor and thanksgiving to the One sitting on the throne, the One living into the ages of the ages [fig., forever and ever], ¹⁰the twenty-four elders will fall down before the One sitting on the throne and will prostrate themselves in worship before the One living into the ages of the ages [fig., forever and ever], and they will cast their victor's wreaths before the throne, saying, ¹¹"You are worthy, our Lord and God, the Holy [One], to receive the glory and the honor and the power, because <u>You</u> created all [things], and because of Your will they were [fig., existed] and were created!"

5And I saw in the right hand of the One sitting on the throne a scroll having been written inside and outside, having been sealed with seven seals. ²And I saw a strong angel proclaiming with a loud voice, "Who is worthy to open the scroll and to break its seals?" ³And no one in the heaven above nor on the earth nor under the earth was being able to open the scroll, nor to be looking at it. ⁴And I began weeping greatly, because no one was found worthy to open the scroll, nor to be looking at it.

⁵And one of the elders says to me, "Stop weeping! Listen! The Lion overcame, the One from the tribe of Judah, the Root of David, the One opening the scroll and its seven seals." ⁶And I saw in [the] middle of the throne and of the four living creatures, and in [the] middle of the elders, a Lamb having stood as if having been slain, having seven horns and seven eyes, which are the seven spirits [fig., which is the seven-fold Spirit] of God having been sent into all the earth. ⁷And He came and has taken out of the right hand of the One sitting on the throne. ⁸And when He took the scroll, the four living creatures and the twenty-four elders fell down before the Lamb, each one having a harp and golden bowls full of incenses, which are prayers of the holy ones [or, saints, and throughout book].

⁹And they sing a new song, saying, "You are worthy to take the scroll and to open its seals, because You were slain, and You redeemed us to God by Your blood, out of every tribe and tongue [fig., language group, and throughout book] and people and nation, ¹⁰and made them kings and priests to our God, and they will reign on the earth!"

¹¹And I looked, and I heard as [it were the] voice of many angels around the throne and of the living creatures and of the elders; and the number of them was

ten thousand [times] ten thousand, and thousands of thousands, [12]saying with a loud voice, "Worthy is the Lamb, the One having been slain, to receive the power and the wealth and wisdom and strength and honor and glory and blessing!"

[13]And every creature which is in heaven and in the earth and under the earth and on the sea, and the [things] in them, I heard all saying, "To the One sitting on the throne and to the Lamb, [be] the blessing and the honor and the glory and the might [or, dominion] into the ages of the ages [fig., forever and ever]! So be it!" [14]And the four living creatures saying the "So be it" and the elders fell down and prostrated themselves in worship.

6And I saw that the Lamb opened one of the seven seals, and I heard one of the four living creatures saying, like a voice of thunder, "Be coming and see!" [2]And look! A white horse, and the one sitting on it having a bow, and a victor's wreath was given to him, and he went out conquering, and so that he should conquer.

[3]And when He opened the second seal, I heard the second living creature saying, "Be coming!" [4]And another horse, fiery [red], went out. And it was given to the one sitting on it to take peace from the earth, so that [people] should slay one another. And a great sword was given to him.

[5]And when He opened the third seal, I heard the third living creature saying, "Be coming and see!" And look! A black horse, and the one sitting on it having a balance in his hand. [6]And I heard a voice in [the] midst of the four living creatures saying, "A choenix [about one quart or one liter] of wheat for a denarius [i.e., one day's wages], and three choenixes of barley for a denarius, and you shall not damage the olive oil and the wine!"

[7]And when He opened the fourth seal, I heard the voice of the fourth living creature saying, "Be coming and see!" [8]And look! A pale [fig., sickly], green horse, and the one sitting on it, [the] name to him [is] Death, and The Realm of the Dead [Gr., *Hades*] was following him. And authority was given to them over the fourth of the earth to kill with sword and with famine and with death, and by the wild animals of the earth.

[9]And when He opened the fifth seal, I saw under the altar the souls of the ones having been slain because of the word of God and because of the testimony of the Lamb which they were holding. [10]And they cried out with a loud voice, saying, "Until when [fig., How long], O Master [or, Sovereign], the Holy and the True, do You not judge [fig., until You judge] and avenge our blood from the ones dwelling on the earth?" [11]And a long, white robe was given to each of them. And it was said to them that they should rest themselves yet a time [fig., a while longer], until also their fellow-slaves and their brothers [and sisters] and the ones being about to be killed even as they [had been] shall complete [their course; or, their number].

[12]And I saw when He opened the sixth seal, and a great earthquake occurred, and the sun became black as sackcloth [made] of hair, and the whole moon became like blood. [13]And the stars of the sky fell to the earth like a fig tree having cast its unripe figs when shaken by a high wind. [cp. Joel 2:10; 2:31; Matt 24:29] [14]And

the sky was split [fig., receded] like a scroll being rolled up, and every mountain and island were moved out of their places. [cp. Isaiah 34:4] ¹⁵And the kings of the earth and the nobles and the commanding officers [or, Chiliarchs] and the rich and the strong and every slave and free person hid themselves in the caves and in the rocks of the mountains. ¹⁶And they say to the mountains and to the rocks, "Fall on us, and hide us from [the] face of the One sitting on the throne and from the wrath of the Lamb! ¹⁷For the great day of His wrath came, and who is being able to stand?"

7 And after this, I saw four angels having stood at the four corners of the earth holding the four winds of the earth, so that a wind would not blow on the land nor on the sea nor on any tree. ²And I saw another angel ascending from the rising of the sun [fig. from the east] having [the] seal of [the] living God. And he cried out with a loud voice to the four angels, to whom it was given to damage the land and the sea, ³saying, "Do not damage the land nor the sea nor the trees until we seal the slaves of our God on their foreheads."

⁴And I heard the number of the ones having been sealed—one hundred and forty-four thousand having been sealed out of every tribe of [the] sons of Israel: ⁵Out of [the] tribe of Judah twelve thousand having been sealed; out of the tribe of Reuben twelve thousand; out of [the] tribe of Gad twelve thousand; ⁶out of the tribe of Asher twelve thousand; out of [the] tribe of Naphtali twelve thousand; out of the tribe of Manasseh twelve thousand; ⁷out of [the] tribe of Simon twelve thousand; out of the tribe of Levi twelve thousand; out of [the] tribe of Issachar twelve thousand; ⁸out of the tribe of Zebulun twelve thousand; out of [the] tribe of Joseph twelve thousand; out of [the] tribe of Benjamin twelve thousand having been sealed.

⁹After these [things] I saw, and look!, a large crowd, which no one was being able to number, out of every nation and [from] tribes and people and tongues, having stood before the throne and before the Lamb having been clothed in long, white robes and palm branches in their hands. ¹⁰And they cry out with a loud voice, saying, "The salvation [belongs] to our God, the One sitting on the throne, and to the Lamb!"

¹¹And all the angels had stood around the throne, and the elders and the four living creatures, and they fell down on their face[s] before the throne and prostrated themselves in worship before God, ¹²saying, "Amen! The blessing and the glory and the wisdom and the thanksgiving and the honor and the power and the strength [belong] to our God into the ages of the ages [fig., forever and ever]! So be it!"

¹³And one of the elders answered, saying to me, "These, the ones having been clothed with the long, white robes, who are they, and from where did they come?" ¹⁴And I said to him, "My Lord, you know." And he said to me, "These are the ones coming out of the great tribulation, and they washed their long robes and made [them] white in the blood of the Lamb. ¹⁵For this reason they are before the throne of God, and they sacredly serve Him day and night in His Temple. And the One sitting on the throne will spread [His] tabernacle over [fig., will shelter] them.

¹⁶They will not hunger [any] longer, nor by any means will they thirst [any] longer, nor will the sun fall [fig., beat down] on them, nor any heat. ¹⁷Because the Lamb, the [One] in [the] center of the throne, shepherds them. And He leads them to fountains of waters of life, and God will wipe away every tear from their eyes."

8And when He opened the seventh seal, silence occurred in heaven [for] about half an hour. ²And I saw the seven angels who have stood before God, and seven trumpets were given to them. ³And another angel came and stood at the altar holding a golden incense burner. And much incense was given to him, so that he should offer [it] with the prayers of all the holy ones on the golden altar, the [one] before the throne. ⁴And the smoke of the incense with the prayers of the holy ones ascended out of [the] hand of the angel before God. ⁵And the angel has taken the incense burner and filled it from the fire of the altar, and he threw [it] to the earth. And [there] occurred peals of thunder and voices and lightning flashes and an earthquake. ⁶And the seven angels, the ones having the seven trumpets, prepared themselves so that they should sound the trumpets.

⁷And the first [one] sounded [his] trumpet, and there occurred hail and fire having been mixed with blood, and it was thrown to the earth; and the third of the earth was burned up, and the third of the trees was burned up, and all green grass was burned up.

⁸And the second angel sounded [his] trumpet, and [something] like a great burning mountain was thrown into the sea, and the third of the sea became blood. ⁹And the third of the creatures in the sea, the ones having life, died, and the third of the ships were utterly destroyed.

¹⁰And the third angel sounded [his] trumpet, and a great star fell out of the sky, burning like a torch, and it fell on the third of the rivers and on the springs of the waters. ¹¹And the name of the star is called Wormwood ["Bitterness"], and the third of the waters became [fig., turned] into wormwood, and many of the people died from the waters, because they were made bitter.

¹²And the fourth angel sounded [his] trumpet, and the third of the sun was struck and the third of the moon and the third of the stars, so that the third of them would be darkened, and the day should not shine [for] the third of it, and the night likewise.

¹³And I saw, and I heard a single eagle flying in midair, saying with a loud voice, "How horrible! How horrible! How horrible to the ones dwelling on the earth, from the remaining sounds of the trumpet of the three angels, the ones being about to be sounding [their] trumpets!"

9And the fifth angel sounded [his] trumpet, and I saw a star having fallen out of the sky to the earth. And the key of the shaft of the bottomless pit [or, of the abyss, and throughout book] was given to him. ²And he opened the shaft of the bottomless pit, and smoke ascended out of the shaft like [the] smoke of a burning furnace, and the sun was darkened, also the air, from the smoke of the shaft.

³And out of the smoke came forth locusts to the earth. And power [to sting] was given to them, as scorpions of the earth have power. ⁴And it was said to them

that they should not damage the grass of the earth nor any green [plant] nor any tree, except the people who do not have the seal of God on their foreheads. ⁵And it was given to them that they should not be killing them, but that they should be tormented five months. And their torment [was] like [the] torment of a scorpion when it strikes a person. ⁶And in those days people will seek death, and they will by no means find it. And they will desire to die, and death will flee from them.

⁷And the likenesses [fig., appearance] of the locusts [was] like horses having been prepared for battle, and on their heads [was something] like gold victor's wreaths, and their faces [were] like faces of people. ⁸And they had hair like [the] hair of women, and their teeth were like [the teeth] of lions. ⁹And they had breastplates like breastplates of iron, and the sound of their wings [was] like the sound of chariots with many horses running into battle. ¹⁰And they have tails like scorpions, and [with] stingers. And in their tails they have power to harm people [for] five months. ¹¹They have over them a king, [the] angel of the bottomless pit. [The] name to him in Hebrew [or Aramaic] [is] Abbadon ["Destroyer"], but in the Greek he has [the] name Apollyon ["Destroyer"].

¹²The first horror is past. Listen! Two horrors are still coming after these things!

¹³And the sixth angel sounded [his] trumpet, and I heard a voice out of the four horns of the golden altar, the [one] before God, ¹⁴saying to the sixth angel, the one having the trumpet, "Release the four angels, the ones having been bound at the great river Euphrates." ¹⁵And the four angels were released, the ones having been prepared for the hour and for the day and month and year, so that they shall be killing the third of people. ¹⁶And the number of the armies of the horse [fig., of the cavalry] [was] ten thousand [times] ten thousand [i.e. 100 million], and I heard the number of them.

¹⁷And I saw the horses in the vision and the ones sitting on them [looking] like this: having breastplates of fiery [red] and hyacinth [blue] and sulfurous [or, brimstone] [yellow]; and the heads of the horses [were] like [the] heads of lions, and out of their mouths proceed fire and smoke and sulfur [or, brimstone]. ¹⁸The third of the people were killed by these three plagues: from the fire and from the smoke and from the sulfur [or, brimstone] proceeding out of their mouths. ¹⁹For the power of the horses is in their mouth[s] and in their tails, for their tails [are] like serpents having heads, and with them they do harm.

²⁰And the rest of people, the ones not killed by these plagues, did not repent from the works of their hands, so that they should not prostrate themselves in worship before the demons and idols, the [ones] of gold and the [ones] of silver and the [ones] of brass and the [ones] of stone and the [ones] of wood, which are neither able to be seeing nor to be hearing nor to be walking about. [cp. Psalm 115:4-7; 135:15-17] ²¹And they did not repent from their murders nor from their sorceries nor from their sexual sins nor from their thefts.

10 And I saw a mighty angel coming down out of heaven, having been clothed with a cloud, and the rainbow on his head, and his face like the sun, and his feet like pillars of fire, ²and having in his hand a scroll having been opened. And he put his right foot on the sea, but the left on the land, ³and he cried out with a loud voice, just like a lion roars. And when he cried out, the seven peals of thunder spoke their voices. ⁴And when the seven peals of thunder spoke, I was about to be writing, and I heard a voice out of heaven saying, "Seal up what the seven peals of thunder spoke, and do not write these [things]!"

⁵And the angel whom I saw having stood on the sea and on the land, lifted up his right hand to heaven ⁶and took an oath by the One living into the ages of the ages [fig., forever and ever], who created heaven and the [things] in it, and the land and the [things] in it, and the sea and the [things] in it, that [there] will be time [fig., delay] no longer. ⁷But in the days of the voice of the seventh angel, when he is about to be sounding [his] trumpet, then the secret [or, mystery] of God is completed, as He preached the Gospel [or, Good News] to His slaves the prophets.

⁸And the voice which I heard out of heaven [was] again speaking with me, and saying, "Be going; take the little scroll, the one having been opened in the hand of the angel, the one having stood on the sea and on the land." ⁹And I went out to the angel telling him to give the little scroll to me. And he says to me, "Take and devour it, and it will make your stomach bitter, but it will be sweet as honey in your mouth." ¹⁰And I took the scroll out of the hand of the angel and devoured it, and it was sweet as honey in my mouth, and when I ate it my stomach was made bitter. ¹¹And they say to me, "It is necessary [for] you to again prophesy about many peoples and about nations and tongues and kings."

11 And a reed like a rod was given to me, saying, "Get up and measure the temple of God and the altar and the ones prostrating themselves in worship in it. ²And leave out the court, the [one] outside of the temple, and do not measure it, because it was given to the nations [or, Gentiles], and they will trample the holy city forty and two months [i.e. 3½ years]. ³And I will give [power] to My two witnesses, and they will prophesy a thousand, two hundred [and] sixty days [i.e. 3½ years], having been clothed with sackcloth."

⁴These are the two olive trees and the two lampstands, the ones having stood before the Lord of the earth. ⁵And if anyone wants to harm them, fire proceeds out of their mouth and consumes their enemies, and if anyone wants to harm them, it is necessary [for] him to be killed in this manner. ⁶These have power to shut the sky, so that it shall not rain a rain [during] the days of their prophecy; and they have power over the waters to be turning them to blood and to strike the earth as often as they desire with every plague.

⁷And when they complete their testimony, the beast, the one ascending out of the bottomless pit, will make war with them and will overcome them and will kill them. ⁸And their dead body [will lie] on the open street of the great city (which spiritually [or, figuratively] is called Sodom and Egypt, where also their Lord was crucified). ⁹And [those] from the peoples and tribes and tongues and nations look at their dead body three [and] a half days, and they will not allow their dead bodies to be put into a tomb. ¹⁰And the ones dwelling on the earth [will] rejoice

over them, and they will celebrate, and they will give gifts to one another, because these, the two prophets, tormented the ones dwelling on the earth."

¹¹And after the three and a half days, a spirit [or, breath] of life from God entered into them, and they stood on their feet, and great fear fell upon the ones watching them. ¹²And they heard a loud voice out of heaven saying to them, "Come up here!" And they ascended into heaven in the cloud, and their enemies watched them. ¹³And in that day a great earthquake occurred, and the tenth of the city fell, and seven thousand names of people [fig., individuals] were killed in the earthquake; and the rest became terrified, and they gave glory to the God of heaven.

¹⁴The second horror is past. Listen! The third horror is coming quickly!

¹⁵And the seventh angel sounded [his] trumpet, and [there] occurred great voices in heaven, saying, "The kingdom of the world became [the kingdom] of our Lord and of His Christ, and He will reign into the ages of the ages [fig., forever and ever]!"

¹⁶And the twenty-four elders, the ones sitting on their thrones before the throne of God, fell on their faces and prostrated themselves in worship before God, ¹⁷saying, "We give thanks to You, O Lord God, the Almighty, the One being and the One [who] was, because You have taken Your great power and reigned. ¹⁸And the nations were enraged, and Your wrath came, and the time of the dead to be judged [came], and [the time] to give the reward to Your slaves the prophets and to the holy ones and the ones fearing Your name, to the small and to the great, and to destroy the ones utterly destroying the earth."

¹⁹And the temple of God was opened in heaven, and the ark of the covenant of the Lord was seen in His temple, and [there] occurred lightning flashes and voices and peals of thunder and great hail.

*12*And a great sign was seen in heaven: a woman having been clothed with the sun, and [with] the moon underneath her feet, and on her head a victor's wreath of twelve stars. ²And having in [the] womb [fig., being pregnant], she was crying out, suffering birth-pains and being in anguish to give birth. ³And another sign was seen in heaven. And look! A great, fiery [red] dragon, having seven heads and ten horns, and on his head seven royal bands. ⁴And his tail drags away the third of the stars of heaven, and he threw them to the earth; and the dragon had stood before the woman, the one about to give birth, so that when she gives birth, he should devour her child.

⁵And she gave birth to a Son, a Male, who is about to be shepherding [or, ruling] all the nations with an iron staff. And her Child was caught up to God and to His throne. ⁶And the woman fled into the wilderness, where she has there a place having been prepared by God, so that there they shall be nourishing her a thousand two hundred [and] sixty days [i.e. 3½ years].

⁷And war occurred in heaven: Michael and his angels waged war with the dragon, and the dragon and his angels waged war. ⁸And he was not strong [enough], nor was a place found for him [any] longer in heaven. ⁹And the great dragon was thrown down—the ancient serpent [see Gen 3:1], the one being called

[the] Devil ["Slanderer"] and Satan ["Adversary"], the one leading astray [fig., deceiving] the whole inhabited earth—he was thrown down to the earth, and his angels were thrown down with him.

[10]And I heard a loud voice saying in heaven, "Now the salvation and the power and the kingdom of our God and the authority of His Christ [has] occurred, because the accuser of our brothers [and sisters], the one accusing them before our God day and night, was thrown down! [11]And they defeated him because of the blood of the Lamb and because of the word of their testimony, and they did not love their life to the point of death. [12]For this reason, be celebrating, O heavens and the ones tabernacling [or, dwelling] in them! How horrible it will be to the land and to the sea, because the Devil went down to you*, having great rage, knowing that he has little time."

[13]And when the dragon saw that he was thrown down to the earth, he persecuted the woman who gave birth to the Male [Child]. [14]And two wings of the great eagle were given to the woman, so that she should be flying into the wilderness, to her place, in order that she shall be nourished there a time and times and half a time [i.e. 3 ½ years], from [the] face [fig., presence] of the serpent.

[15]And the serpent poured water like a river out of his mouth after the woman, so that he shall cause her [to be] swept away by the river. [16]And the earth helped the woman, and the earth opened its mouth and swallowed up the river which the dragon poured out of his mouth. [17]And the dragon was enraged against the woman, and he went off to make war with the rest of her seed [fig., offspring], the ones keeping the commandments of God and having the testimony of Jesus.

13 And I stood on the sand of the sea. And I saw a beast rising up out of the sea, having ten horns and seven heads, and ten royal bands on its horns, and a blasphemous name on its heads. [2]And the beast which I saw was like a leopard, and its feet like a bear's, and its mouth like a lion's mouth. And the dragon gave to it his power and his throne and great authority. [3]And one of its heads [was] as [if] having been slain to death [fig., mortally wounded], and its wound of death [fig., fatal wound] was healed.

And the whole earth marveled after the beast. [4]And they prostrated themselves in worship before the dragon, the one having given the authority to [the] beast; and they prostrated themselves in worship before the beast, saying, "Who [is] like the beast, and who [is] able to wage war with it?"

[5]And a mouth was given to it speaking great [things] and blasphemy, and authority was given to it to make war forty-two months [i.e. 3½ years]. [6]And it opened its mouth in blasphemy toward God, to blaspheme His name and His tabernacle, [that is], the ones tabernacling [or, dwelling] in heaven. [7]And it was given to it to make war with the holy ones and to overcome them, and authority was given to it over every tribe and people and tongue and nation. [8]And all the ones dwelling on the earth will prostrate themselves in worship before it, the name of whom has not been written in the Scroll of Life of the Lamb having been slain from [the] laying of the foundation of [the] world.

⁹If anyone has an ear, let him hear. ¹⁰If anyone has captivity, he goes away [into captivity]; if anyone kills by a sword, it is necessary [for] him to be killed by a sword. Here is the patient endurance and the faith of the holy ones.

¹¹And I saw another beast rising up out of the earth, and it had two horns like a lamb, and it was speaking like a dragon. ¹²And it exercises all the authority of the first beast before it, and it was making the earth and the ones dwelling in it that they should prostrate themselves in worship before the first beast, whose wound of death [fig., fatal wound] was healed. ¹³And it performs great signs, so that even fire is coming down from heaven on the earth before the people. ¹⁴And it leads astray [fig., deceives] my own [people], the ones dwelling on the earth because of the signs which were given it to do before the beast, telling the ones dwelling on the earth to make an image to the beast which was having the wound from the sword and lived.

¹⁵And it was given to it to give breath [or, a spirit] to the image of the beast, so that the image of the beast should both speak and make [it that] as many as would not prostrate themselves in worship before the image of the beast should be killed. ¹⁶And it makes all [people], the small and the great, and the rich and the poor, and the freemen and the slaves, that they shall give to them marks on their right hand or on their forehead, ¹⁷and that no one is able to buy or to sell, except the one having the mark: the name of the beast or the number of its name.

¹⁸Here is the wisdom—the one having understanding, let him calculate the number of the beast, for it is the number of a person [or, of humanity]. And its number is six hundred sixty-six.

14 And I saw. And look! The Lamb having stood on Mount Zion, and with Him a number, one hundred forty-four thousand, having His name and the name of His Father having been written on their foreheads. ²And I heard a voice out of heaven, like a voice of many waters and like a voice of great thunder, and the voice which I heard [was] like harpists harping with their harps.

³And they sing a new song before the throne and before the four living creatures and the elders, and no one was being able to learn the song except the one hundred forty-four thousand, the ones having been redeemed from the earth. ⁴These are [those] who were not defiled with women, for they are virgins. These are the ones following the Lamb wherever He is going. These were redeemed by Jesus from among people, a first-fruit to God and to the Lamb. ⁵And deceit [or, treachery] was not found in their mouth, for they are blameless.

⁶And I saw an angel flying in midair, having the eternal Gospel [or, Good News] to proclaim to the ones sitting [fig., dwelling] on the earth, and to every nation and tribe and tongue and people, ⁷saying with a loud voice, "Fear the Lord and give glory to Him, because the hour of His judgment came, and prostrate yourselves in worship before Him, the One having made heaven and the earth and the sea and springs of waters."

⁸And another, a second angel, followed, saying, "Fallen [is] Babylon, the great city! From the wine of the rage of her sexual sin she has given to all nations to have drunk."

⁹And another, a third angel, followed them, saying in a loud voice, "If anyone prostrates themselves in worship before the beast and its image and receives a mark on his forehead or on his hand, ¹⁰he also will drink from the wine of the rage of God, the [rage] having been mixed undiluted in the cup of His wrath, and he will be tormented in fire and sulfur [or, brimstone] before the holy angels and before the Lamb. ¹¹And the smoke of their torment ascends to ages of ages [fig., forever and ever]. And they have no relief day and night, the ones prostrating themselves in worship before the beast and its image, also if anyone receives the mark of its name."

¹²Here is [the] patient endurance of the holy ones, the ones keeping the commandments of God and the faith of Jesus. ¹³And I heard a voice out of heaven saying, "Write: 'Happy [or, Blessed, and throughout book] [are] the dead, the ones dying in [the] Lord from now [on]!'" "Yes," says the Spirit, "so that they shall rest from their labors, but their works follow with them."

¹⁴And I saw. And look! A white cloud, and sitting on the cloud [One] like [the] Son of Humanity, having a golden victor's wreath on His head, and a sharp sickle in His hand. ¹⁵And another angel came out from the temple crying out with a loud voice to the One sitting on the cloud, "Send [Fig., Thrust in] Your sickle and reap, because the hour to reap came, because the harvest of the earth was ripened." ¹⁶And the One sitting on the cloud swung His sickle on the earth, and the earth was reaped.

¹⁷And another angel came out from the temple, the [one] in heaven, he also having a sharp sickle.

¹⁸And another angel came forth from the altar, having authority over the fire, and he called with a loud shout to the one having the sharp sickle, saying, "Send [fig., Thrust in] your sharp sickle and gather the clusters of the grapevine of the earth, because her grapes became ripe." ¹⁹And the angel swung his sickle to the earth and gathered the grapevine of the earth, and he threw [it] into the great winepress of the wrath of God. ²⁰And the winepress was trampled outside of the city, and blood came out from the winepress up to the bridles of the horses, for [a distance of] one thousand, six hundred stadia [about 180 miles or 300 kilometers].

*15*And I saw another sign in heaven, great and marvelous: seven angels having the seven last plagues, because in them was completed the wrath of God. ²And I saw [something] like a glassy sea having been mixed with fire and the ones being victorious over the beast and over its image [and] over the number of its name standing on the glassy sea having harps of God.

³And they sing the song of Moses, the slave of God, and the song of the Lamb, saying, "Great and marvelous [are] Your works, O Lord God, the Almighty; righteous and true [are] Your ways, O King of the nations! ⁴Who shall not fear You, O Lord, and glorify Your name? For [You] alone [are] holy; for all the nations will come and will prostrate themselves in worship before You, for Your righteousnesses [or, righteous judgments] were made known."

⁵And after these [things] I saw, and the temple of the tabernacle of the testimony in heaven was opened. ⁶And the seven angels, the ones having the seven plagues, came out from the temple, the ones having been clothed in clean, bright linen, and having been wrapped around the chests with golden belts [or, sashes]. ⁷And one of the four living creatures gave to the seven angels seven golden bowls full of the wrath of God, the One living into the ages of the ages [fig., forever and ever]. ⁸And the temple was filled with smoke from the glory of God and from His power, and no one was being able to enter into the temple until the seven plagues of the seven angels were completed. [cp. 1Kings 8:10,11]

*16*And I heard a loud voice out of the temple saying to the seven angels, "Be going away, and pour out the seven bowls of the wrath of God on the earth."

²And the first went away and poured out his bowl on the earth, and a foul and malignant ulcerated sore occurred on the people, the ones having the mark of the beast and the ones prostrating themselves in worship before its image.

³And the second angel poured out his bowl into the sea, and it became blood as of [one] dead, and every living soul [or, creature] died in the sea.

⁴And the third [angel] poured out his bowl into the rivers and into the fountains of the waters, and it became blood. ⁵And I heard the angel of the waters saying, "You are righteous, the One being and the One [who] was, the Holy [One], because You [have] judged these [things]. ⁶Because they shed [the] blood of holy ones and of prophets, and You gave blood to them to drink. They are worthy [fig., They deserve it]." ⁷And I heard [an angel] of the altar saying, "Yes, Lord God, the Almighty, true and righteous [are] Your judgments."

⁸And the fourth angel poured out his bowl on the sun, and it was given to him to scorch the people with fire. ⁹And the people were scorched with great heat, and the people blasphemed the name of God, the One having authority over these plagues, and they did not repent [so as] to give to Him glory.

¹⁰And the fifth [angel] poured out his bowl on the throne of the beast, and its kingdom has become darkened. And they began gnawing their tongues from the pain. ¹¹And they blasphemed the God of heaven because of their pains and because of their ulcerated sores, and they did not repent from their works.

¹²And the sixth [angel] poured out his bowl on the great river Euphrates, and its water was dried up, so that the way of the kings, the ones from [the] rising of [the] sun [fig., from the east], would be prepared.

¹³And I saw [coming] out of the mouth of the dragon and out of the mouth of the beast and out of the mouth of the false prophet three unclean [or, defiling] spirits like frogs. ¹⁴For they are spirits of demons, performing signs, which go out to the kings of the whole inhabited earth, to gather them together to the battle of that great day of God the Almighty.

¹⁵"Listen! I am coming like a thief! Happy [is] the one keeping watch and keeping his clothes, lest he be walking about naked, and they shall be seeing his shame."

[16]And they gathered them together to the place, the one being called in Hebrew, Armagedon.

[17]And the seventh [angel] poured out his bowl upon the air, and a loud voice came out from the temple of heaven, from the throne, saying, "It has happened!" [18]And [there] occurred lightning flashes and peals of thunder and voices, and a great earthquake, such as did not occur since the people came on the earth, so mighty an earthquake—so great! [19]And the great city became [fig., was split] into three parts, and the cities of the nations fell, and Babylon the great was remembered before God, to give to her the cup of the wine of the rage of His wrath. [20]And every island fled away, and mountains were not found. [21]And huge hail, [each] weighing about a talent [about 95 pounds or 42 kilograms], is coming down out of heaven [or, the sky] on the people, and the people blasphemed God because of the plague of the hail, because its plague is extremely great.

17 And one of the seven angels, [one] of the ones having the seven bowls, came and spoke with me, saying, "Come, I will show to you the judgment of the great prostitute, the one sitting on the many waters, [2]with whom the kings of the earth committed sexual sin, and the ones inhabiting the earth got drunk from the wine of her sexual sin."

[3]And he carried me away in spirit [or, by [the] Spirit] into a wilderness. And I saw a woman sitting on a scarlet beast full [or, covered] with names of blasphemy [or, blasphemous names], having seven heads and ten horns. [4]And the woman had been clothed with purple and scarlet, having been adorned with gold and a precious stone and pearls, having a golden cup in her hand being full of [the] abominations and the uncleanness of her sexual sin. [5]And on her forehead a name had been written: Secret [or, Mystery], Babylon the Great, the Mother of the Prostitutes and of the Abominations of the Earth.

[6]And I saw the woman being drunk from the blood of the holy ones, from the blood of the witnesses [or, martyrs] of Jesus. And having seen her, I was amazed with great amazement.

[7]And the angel said to me, "Why were you [so] amazed? I will tell to you the secret [or, mystery] of the woman and of the beast, the [one] carrying her, the one having the seven heads and the ten horns. [8]The beast which you saw was, and is not, and is about to be ascending out of the bottomless pit and to be going away to destruction. And the ones dwelling on the earth will be amazed, whose names have not been written on the Scroll of Life from [the] laying of the foundation of [the] world, when they see the beast that was, and is not, and will come.

[9]"Here [is] the mind, the one having wisdom: the seven heads are seven mountains, where the woman sits on them. [10]There are also seven kings: the five fell, the one is, the other did not yet come. And when he comes, it is necessary [for] him to remain a short time. [11]And the beast which was, and is not, is himself [or, itself] also an eighth, and is out of the seven, and is going away to destruction.

[12]"And the ten horns which you saw are ten kings, who did not yet receive a kingdom, but they receive authority as kings [for] one hour with the beast. [13]These have one mind [fig., purpose], and they give their power and authority to the

beast. ¹⁴These will wage war with the Lamb, and the Lamb will conquer them, because He is Lord of lords and King of kings, and the [ones] with him [are] called and chosen and faithful."

¹⁵And he says to me, "The waters which you saw, where the prostitute sits, are peoples and crowds and nations and tongues. ¹⁶And the ten horns which you saw, and the beast, these will hate the prostitute and will make her having been laid waste and will make her naked, and they will eat her flesh and will burn her in fire. ¹⁷For God gave into their hearts to do His mind [fig., purpose] and to make [fig., to be of] one mind and to give their kingdom to the beast until the words of God are completed [or, fulfilled]. ¹⁸And the woman which you saw is the great city, the one having kingship over the kings of the earth."

*18*After these [things] I saw another angel coming down out of heaven, having great authority, and the earth was lit up from his glory [or, splendor]. ²And he cried out with a mighty voice, saying, "Fallen [is] Babylon the great! And she became a dwelling place of demons and a prison of every unclean [or, defiling] spirit and a prison of every unclean and having been detested bird. ³For all the nations have drunk of the wine of the wrath of her sexual sin, and the kings of the earth committed sexual sin with her, and the merchants of the earth became rich from the power [fig., wealth] of her luxury."

⁴And I heard another voice out of heaven, saying, "Come out from her, my people, so that you* shall not participate in her sins, and so that you* shall not receive of her plagues. ⁵For her sins [have] piled up to heaven, and God [has] remembered her misdeeds. ⁶Give back to her as she also gave back, and double doubles [fig., give back double] to her according to her works; in the cup which she mixed, mix to her double. ⁷As much as she glorified herself and lived in luxury, [by] so much give to her torment and sorrow; for she says in her heart, 'I sit [as] a queen, and I am not a widow, and I shall by no means see sorrow.' ⁸For this reason, her plagues will come in one day—death and sorrow and famine. And she will be consumed by fire; for mighty [is the] Lord God, the One having judged her.

⁹"And the kings of the earth, the ones having committed sexual sin and having lived luxuriously with her, will weep and will beat their breasts [fig., will mourn] over her when they shall be seeing the smoke of her burning, ¹⁰having stood at a distance because of the fear of her torment, saying, 'How horrible! How horrible! The great city Babylon, the mighty city! For in one hour your judgment came!'

¹¹"And the merchants of the earth will weep and will mourn over her, for no one buys their cargo any more: ¹²cargo of gold and of silver and of precious stone and of pearl and of fine linen and of purple cloth and of silk and of scarlet cloth, and of every citron wood and of every vessel of ivory and of every vessel of most precious wood, and of brass and of iron and of marble, ¹³and cinnamon and incenses and perfume and frankincense, and wine and olive oil and fine flour and wheat, and sheep and cattle, and of horses and of chariots, and of bodies and souls of people.

¹⁴"And the fruit of the desire of your soul [fig., the fruit for which your soul craved] went away from you, and all the elegant and lavish [things] perished from you, and by no means shall you any longer find them. ¹⁵The merchants of these

[things], the ones having become rich from her, will stand at a distance because of the fear of her torment, weeping and sorrowing [16]and saying, 'How horrible! How horrible! The great city, the one having been clothed with fine linen and purple and scarlet, and having been adorned with gold and precious stone and pearls; [17]for in one hour such great wealth was laid waste!'

"And every ship captain and every[one] sailing by [the] place [fig., along the coast] and [the] sailors and as many as work the sea stood at a distance, [18]and were crying out, seeing the smoke of her burning, saying, 'What [city is] like the great city?' [19]And they threw dust on their heads and were crying out, weeping and sorrowing and saying, 'How horrible! How horrible! The great city in which all the ones having the ships in the sea became rich from her abundance of costly things! For in one hour she was laid waste!' [20]Be celebrating over her, O heaven, and the holy ones and the apostles and the prophets, because God judged your* judgment of her [fig., God has pronounced judgment for you* against her]!"

[21]And one mighty angel took up a stone as a great millstone and threw [it] into the sea, saying, "In this way Babylon will be thrown down with violence, the great city, and she shall by no means be found [any]more. [22]And [the] sound of harpists and of musicians and of flutists and of trumpeters shall by no means be heard in you [any]more; and no craftsmen of any craft shall by any means be found in you [any]more; and [the] sound of a millstone shall by no means be heard in you [any]more. [23]And [the] light of a lamp shall by no means shine in you [any]more, and [the] voice of bridegroom and of bride shall by no means be heard in you [any]more; for your merchants were the nobles [or, great ones] of the earth, because by your sorcery all the nations were led astray [fig., were deceived]. [24]And in her was found [the] bloods of prophets and of holy ones and of all the ones having been slain on the earth."

19 After these [things] I heard [something] like a loud voice of a large crowd in heaven, saying, "Praise the Lord [or, Hallelujah]! The salvation and the power and the glory [are] of our God! [2]Because His judgments [are] true and righteous; because He judged the great prostitute who was utterly destroying the earth with her sexual sin, and He avenged the blood of His slaves [shed] by her hand." [3]And a second time they were saying, "Praise the Lord! And her smoke rises up into the ages of the ages [fig., forever and ever]!"

[4]And the twenty-four elders and the four living creatures fell down and prostrated themselves in worship before God, the One sitting on the throne, saying, "So be it! Praise the Lord!"

[5]And a voice came out from the throne, saying, "Praise our God, all His slaves and the ones fearing Him, both the small and the great!" [6]And I heard [something] like [the] voice of a large crowd and like [the] sound of many waters and like [the] sound of mighty peals of thunder, saying, "Praise the Lord! Because our Lord God, the Almighty, reigned [or, has begun to reign]! [7]Let us be rejoicing and be very glad, and let us give the glory to Him, for the marriage of the Lamb came, and His wife made herself ready. [8]And it was given to her that she should clothe herself with fine linen, bright and clean, for the fine linen is the righteousnesses of the holy ones."

⁹And he says to me, "Write: 'Happy [are] the ones having been called to the banquet of the marriage of the Lamb!'" And he says to me, "These are the true words of God." ¹⁰And I fell before his feet to prostrate myself in worship before him, and he says to me, "See [that you do] not! I am your fellow slave and of your brothers [and sisters], the ones having the testimony of Jesus. Worship God! For the testimony of Jesus is the spirit of prophecy."

¹¹And I saw heaven having been opened. And look! A white horse, and the One sitting on it, being called Faithful and True, and He judges and wages war in righteousness. ¹²Now His eyes [are] a flame of fire, and on His head [are] many royal bands [or, diadems] having names having been written [on them], and a name having been written [on them] which no one knows, except Himself, ¹³and having been clothed with a robe having been covered with [or, dipped in] blood, and His name is called, The Word [fig., the Expression of the Logic] of God. ¹⁴And the armies, the [ones] in heaven, were following Him on white horses, having clothed themselves with fine linen, bright and clean.

¹⁵And out of His mouth proceeds a sharp, double-edged sword, so that with it He should strike down the nations. And He will shepherd them with an iron staff. And He Himself treads the winepress of the wine of the rage of the wrath of God, the Almighty. ¹⁶And He has on the robe and on His thigh a name having been written, "King of kings and Lord of lords."

¹⁷And I saw an angel having stood in the sun, and he cried out with a loud voice, saying to all the birds, the ones flying in midair, "Come, be gathered together for the great banquet of God, ¹⁸so that you* shall eat [the] flesh of kings and [the] flesh of commanding officers [or, Chiliarchs] and [the] flesh of mighty [people] and [the] flesh of horses and of the ones sitting on them, and [the] flesh of all [people], both of free persons and of slaves, and both of small and of great!"

¹⁹And I saw the beast and the kings of the earth and their armies having been gathered together to make war with the One sitting on the horse and with His army. ²⁰And the beast was captured, and the false prophet with it, the one having performed the signs before him, by which he led astray [fig., deceived] the ones having received the mark of the beast and the ones prostrating themselves in worship before its image. These two were thrown living into the lake of fire, the one being burned with sulfur [or, brimstone]. ²¹And the rest were killed with the sword of the One sitting on the horse, the [sword] having proceeded out of His mouth, and all the birds were filled from their flesh.

20And I saw an angel coming down out of heaven, having the key of the bottomless pit, and a great chain on his hand. ²And he seized the dragon, the ancient serpent, who is [the] Devil and Satan, the one leading astray [fig., deceiving] the whole inhabited earth, and he bound him [for] a thousand years. ³And he threw him into the bottomless pit, and shut and sealed [it] over him, so that he shall not be leading the nations astray [fig., be deceiving the nations] [any] longer until the thousand years are completed. And after these [things] it is necessary [for] him to be released [for] a short time.

⁴And I saw thrones, and they sat on them, and judgment was given to them, and the souls of the ones having been beheaded because of the testimony of Jesus and because of the word of God, and who did not prostrate themselves in worship [before] the beast nor its image and did not receive the mark on the forehead and on their hand. And they lived and reigned with Christ [for] the thousand years. ⁵And the rest of the dead did not live until the thousand years are completed. This [is] the first resurrection.

⁶Happy and holy [is] the one having a part in the first resurrection! Over these the second death does not have power, but they will be priests of God and of Christ, and they will reign with Him [for] a thousand years.

⁷And when the thousand years are completed, Satan will be released from his prison. ⁸And he will go out to lead the nations astray [fig., to deceive the nations], the [ones] in the four corners of the earth, Gog and Magog, to gather them together for the war, of whom the number [is] like the sand of the sea. ⁹And they went up over the breadth of the earth and surrounded the camp of the holy ones and the beloved city. And fire came down out of heaven from God and consumed them. ¹⁰And the Devil, the one leading them astray [fig., deceiving them], was thrown into the lake of fire and sulfur [or, brimstone], where the beast and the false prophet [are], and they will be tormented day and night into the ages of the ages [fig., forever and ever].

¹¹And I saw a great white throne and the One sitting on it, from whose face the earth and heaven fled away, and a place was not found for them. ¹²And I saw the dead, the great and the small, having stood before the throne, and scrolls were opened, and another scroll was opened, which is [the Scroll] of Life. And the dead were judged by the [things] having been written in the scrolls, according to their works. ¹³And the sea gave up the dead, the [ones] in it, and death and the realm of the dead [Gr. *hades*] gave up the dead, the [ones] in them. And they were judged, each one according to their works.

¹⁴And death and the realm of the dead were thrown into the lake of fire. This is the second death, the lake of fire. ¹⁵And if anyone was not found having been written in the Scroll of Life, he was thrown into the lake of fire.

21 And I saw a new heaven and a new earth, for the first heaven and the first earth went away [fig., had disappeared]. And the sea is not [any]more [fig., the sea no longer exists]. ²And I saw the holy city, New Jerusalem, descending out of heaven from God, having been prepared like a bride having been adorned [for] her husband.

³And I heard a loud voice out of heaven, saying, "Look! The tabernacle of God [is] with the people, and He will tabernacle [or, dwell] with them! And they will be His people, and God Himself will be with them. ⁴And He will wipe away every tear from their eyes, and death will not be [any]more [fig., death will no longer exist], nor sorrow, nor crying, nor will pain be any more [fig., pain will no longer exist], because the first [things] passed away."

⁵And the One sitting on the throne said, "Look! I am making all things new!" And He says to me, "Write, because these words are true and trustworthy." ⁶And He

said to me, "I have become the Alpha and the Omega, the Beginning and the End [or, the Origin and the Fulfillment]. I will give to the one thirsting from the spring of the water of life without cost. ⁷The one overcoming will inherit these [things], and I will be God to him, and he will be a son to Me. ⁸But to the cowardly and unbelieving and sinners and [ones] having been corrupted and murderers and sexual sinners and sorcerers and idolaters and all the liars, their part [will be] in the lake, the one being burned with fire and sulfur [or, brimstone], which is the second death."

⁹And one of the seven angels came, the one having the seven bowls full of the last seven plagues, and he spoke with me, saying, "Come, I will show to you the wife, the bride of the Lamb."

¹⁰And he carried me away in spirit [or, by [the] Spirit] to a great and high mountain and showed to me the great city, the holy Jerusalem, descending out of heaven from God, ¹¹having the glory of God. Its light [is] like a most precious stone, like a crystallizing [or, crystal-clear] jasper stone, ¹²having a great and high wall, having twelve gates and twelve angels at the gates and names having been inscribed, which are [the] names of the twelve tribes of the sons of Israel: ¹³at [the] risings [of the sun] [fig., at the east] three gates, at the north three gates, at the south three gates, at the west three gates, ¹⁴and the wall of the city having twelve foundations, and on them [the] twelve names of the twelve apostles of the Lamb.

¹⁵And the one speaking with me had a measure, a golden reed, so that he could measure the city and its gates and its wall. ¹⁶And the city is laid out in a square, and the length of it [is] as great as the width. And he measured the city with the reed at twelve thousand, twelve stadia [about 1365 miles or 2200 kilometers]; the length and the width and the height of it are equal. ¹⁷And he measured its wall: one hundred forty-four cubits [about 216 feet or 66 meters], [by the] measure of a person, which is of the angel. ¹⁸And the building material of its wall was jasper, and the city [was] pure gold, like pure glass.

¹⁹The foundations of the wall of the city have been adorned with every precious stone: the first foundation [with] jasper, the second [with] sapphire, the third [with] chalcedony, the fourth [with] emerald, ²⁰the fifth [with] sardonyx, the sixth [with] carnelian, the seventh [with] chrysolite, the eighth [with] beryl, the ninth [with] topaz, the tenth [with] chrysoprasus, the eleventh [with] jacinth, the twelfth [with] amethyst. ²¹And the twelve gates [were made from] twelve pearls; each one of the gates was [made] from one pearl. And the open street of the city [was] pure gold, like transparent glass.

²²And I did not see a temple in it, for the Lord God, the Almighty, is its temple, also the Lamb. ²³And the city has no need of the sun, nor of the moon, that they should be giving it light, for the glory of God illuminated it, and its lamp [is] the Lamb. ²⁴And the nations will walk about by its light, and the kings of the earth will bring to it [the] glory and honor of the nations into it. ²⁵And its gates shall never at all be shut [at the end of] day, for night shall not be [fig., exist] there. ²⁶And they will bring the glory and the honor of the nations into it. ²⁷And by no means shall any defiling [thing] and [anyone] doing an abomination and a lie enter into it, but only the ones having been written in the Scroll of Life of the Lamb.

22 And he showed to me a pure river of water of life, bright as crystal, coming out [fig., flowing] from the throne of God and of the Lamb, ²in the middle of its open street. And the river from here and from there [fig., And on each side of the river] [was] a tree of life, producing twelve fruits, according to each month [fig., monthly] yielding its fruits. And the leaves of the tree [are] for [the] healing of the nations.

³And every curse will not be [any] longer [fig., And [there] will be no more curse], and the throne of God and of the Lamb will be in it, and His slaves will sacredly serve Him. ⁴And they will see His face, and His name [will be] on their foreheads. ⁵And night will not be [fig., exist] there, and they have no need of a lamp and of [the] light of [the] sun, because [the] Lord God illuminates them. And they will reign into the ages of the ages [fig., forever and ever].

⁶And he says to me, "These words [are] trustworthy and true, and [the] Lord God of the spirits of the prophets sent His angel to show to His slaves what [things are] necessary to occur with quickness."

⁷"And listen! I am coming quickly! Happy [is] the one keeping the words of the prophecy of this scroll."

⁸And I, John, [am] the one hearing and seeing these [things]. And when I heard and saw, I fell down to prostrate myself in worship before the feet of the angel, the one showing these [things] to me. ⁹And he says to me, "See [that you do] not! I am a fellow-slave of you and of your brothers the prophets and of the ones keeping the words of this scroll. Prostrate yourself in worship before God!"

¹⁰And he says to me, "Do not seal the words of the prophecy of this scroll, for the time is near. ¹¹The one acting unjustly let him act unjustly still, and the filthy [person] let him be made filthy still, and the righteous [person] let him practice righteousness still, and the holy [person] let him be holy still."

¹²"Listen! I am coming quickly, and My reward [is] with me, to render [or, to repay] to each as his work will be [fig., according to his deeds]. ¹³I [am] the Alpha and the Omega, the First and the Last, the Beginning and the End."

¹⁴Happy [are] the ones doing His commandments, so that their right will be to the tree of life, and they shall enter by the gates into the city. ¹⁵Outside [are] the dogs and the sorcerers and the sexual sinners and the murderers and the idolaters and every one affectionately loving and practicing falsehood.

¹⁶"I, Jesus, sent My angel to testify to you* [or, to tell you* about] these [things] concerning the assemblies. I am the Root and the Offspring of David, the Bright, Morning Star!"

¹⁷And the Spirit and the bride say, "Be coming!" And the one hearing, let him say, "Be coming!" And the one thirsting, let him come. The one desiring, let him take [the] water of life without cost.

¹⁸I testify to everyone hearing the words of the prophecy of this scroll, if anyone adds to them, God [is prepared] to add to him the plagues, the ones having been written in this scroll. ¹⁹And if anyone takes away from the words of the scroll of this prophecy, may God take away his part from the tree of life and from the holy city, the [things] having been written in this scroll.

[20]The One testifying to these things says, "Yes, I am coming quickly!" So be it! Yes, be coming, Lord Jesus!

[21]The grace of the Lord Jesus Christ [be] with all the holy ones. So be it!

Appendix #1
Important Textual Variants

This second edition of the *Analytical-Literal Translation of the New Testament of the Holy Bible* is based on the forthcoming second edition of the *Byzantine Majority Text.* The translator believes this Greek text most accurately reflects the original manuscripts. However, there are two other Greek texts which are often used for Bible translation. These are the *Textus Receptus* (which the *King James Version* and the *New King James Version®* are based on) and the Critical Text (which versions like the *New American Standard Bible®*, the *New International Version®*, and the *New Living Translation®* are based on).

For ease in comparing Bible translations, this appendix lists the most important textual variants between these three Greek texts.

The *Textus Receptus* and Critical Text variants are translated as they would appear in the ALT if the ALT was based on these texts. Alternative translations and other bracketed material seen in the ALT are omitted here unless the variant affects such material. However, words added for clarity are included and bracketed as they would be in the ALT. But some versions do not bracket added words. So these words might appear in another translation without any notation.

The following are the primary standards used to decide if a variant was of sufficient importance to be included in this appendix. A variant was included if:

1. The length is significant, such as one Greek text including an entire verse or a significant portion of a verse that another Greek text omits, such as Acts 8:36,37 and Acts 9:5,6.
2. It significantly affects the interpretation of the verse, such as the inclusion or omission of "to repentance" in Matthew 9:13.
3. It bears on a theological issue, such as the inclusion or omission of "the One being in heaven" in John 3:13.
4. It bears on the reliability of the NT, such as the name of a king being listed as Asa or Asaph in Matthew 1:7,8 (the OT has Asa).
5. The differences between texts are rather striking or apparent.

For Further Information

These variants are taken from the more complete lists of textual variants posted on the ALT section of Darkness to Light's Web site (www.dtl.org/alt/). Also posted on the site is a list of alternative readings which are footnoted in the *Byzantine Majority Text* but which are not indicated in the ALT text. These represent places where the Byzantine Greek manuscripts are closely divided.

For an extensive discussion on why the translator believes the *Byzantine Majority Text* is the most accurate of the three Greek texts compared here, see my book *Differences Between Bible Versions*. This book also looks in detail at the different translation principles used in Bible translation. It is available from the publisher AuthorHouse (www.AuthorHouse.com ~ 1-888-280-7715).

Greek Texts

Byzantine Majority Text: The Greek New Testament: Byzantine Textform. Second Edition. Complied, arranged, and thoroughly updated by Maurice A. Robinson and William G. Pierpont. Publication forthcoming.

Textus Receptus: F.H.A Scrivener's 1894 edition.

Critical Text: *The Greek New Testament* edited by Kurt Aland, Matthew Black, Carlo M. Martini, Bruce M. Metzger, and Allen Wikgren, Fourth Edition, Copyright © 1966, 1968, 1975 by the United Bible Societies and 1993, 1994 by Deutsche Bibelgesellsschaft (German Bible Society), Stuggart (which is identical to the Nestle-Aland *27th Edition of the Greek New Testament*).

Abbreviations and Notations

In addition to the abbreviations and notations seen in the ALT itself and which are listed on the page *Abbreviations and Notations*, the following abbreviations and notations are used in this appendix:

CT: – Critical Text
MT: – *Byzantine Majority Text.*
TR: – *Textus Receptus*
MT/ TR: – Both indicated Greek texts have the same reading.
eating ... to God – Words which are identical in all Greek texts have not been written out, or the entire passage enclosed by and including the words around the ellipse are omitted by the other Greek text.
brackets – The Greek text considers the word(s) to be of doubtful authenticity.
double brackets – The Greek text considers the word(s) to be of very doubtful authenticity.
omits – The word(s) do not appear in the indicated Greek text.
{the} – Indicates words for which the Greek text considers the textual evidence to be divided as to whether they are original or not.

The Variants

Matthew

1:7 MT/ TR: Asa – CT: Asaph

1:8 MT/ TR: Asa – CT: Asaph

1:10 MT/ TR: Amon – CT: Amos (twice)

5:22 MT/ TR: without cause – CT: omits

6:13 MT/ TR: Because Yours is the kingdom and the power and the glory into the ages! So be it! – CT: omits

9:13 MT/ TR: to repentance – CT: omits

12:47 MT/ TR: includes verse – CT: brackets verse

15:5 MT: 'and by no means shall he honor his father or his mother.' - TR: moves this statement to the beginning of verse 6 - CT: moves this statement to the beginning of verse 6, and omits *or his mother*

16:2 MT/ TR: includes all of verse 2 and verse 3 – CT: brackets everything after *to them* in verse 2 and all of verse 3.

17:21 MT/ TR: includes verse – CT: omits verse

18:11 MT/ TR: includes verse – CT: omits verse

19:9 MT/ TR: and the one having married the one having been divorced commits adultery – CT: omits

19:17 MT/ TR: "Why do you call Me good? No one [is] good except One—God. – CT: "Why are you asking Me about the good? [There] is [only] One [who] is good.

20:16 MT/ TR: for many are called, but few chosen – CT: omits

20:22 MT: drinking, or … baptized. – TR: drinking, and … baptized. – CT: drinking. (omits *or to be baptized [with] the baptism which I am baptized*)

20:23 MT/ TR: and the baptism which I am baptized [with], you* will be baptized – CT: omits

21:44 MT/ TR: includes verse – CT: brackets verse

23:13 MT: includes verse 13 – TR: includes verse 13 but reverses verses 13 and 14 and moves *But* to the new verse 14 – CT: omits verse 13 and numbers verse 14 as verse 13 and includes *But* in the new verse 13

23:25 MT: unrighteousness. – TR/ CT: lack of self-control.

24:36 MT/ TR: heavens, – CT: heavens, nor the Son,

25:13 MT/ TR: in which the Son of Humanity is coming. – CT: omits

26:28 MT/ TR: new – CT: omits

26:39   MT: having approached [God] a little [distance away] – TR/ CT: having gone a little beyond [them]

26:61   MT: But later two false witnesses having come forward, - TR/ CT: Moves this phrase to the end of verse 60

27:34   MT/ TR: wine vinegar – CT: wine

27:35   MT/ CT: a lot. – TR: a lot, so that the [word] having been spoken by the prophet should be fulfilled, *"They divided My garments among themselves and over My clothing they cast a lot."* [Psalm 22:18]

28:9   MT/ TR: But as they were going to tell to His disciples, – CT: omits

Mark

1:1   MT/ TR: God's Son – CT: {God's Son}

1:2   MT/ TR: in the prophets, – CT: in Isaiah the prophet,

2:17   MT/ TR: to repentance – CT: omits

3:19   MT/ TR: And they come into a house. - CT: moves this sentence to beginning of verse 20

6:11   MT/ TR: Positively, I say to you*, it will be more tolerable for Sodom or Gomorrah in [the] day of judgment than for that city." – CT: omits entire sentence

7:8   MT/ TR: baptisms of pitchers and cups, and many such other similar things you* do. – CT: omits this part of the sentence

7:16   MT/ TR: includes verse – CT: omits verse

9:38   MT/ TR: who does not follow us – CT: omits

9:44   MT/ TR: includes verse – CT: omits verse

9:46   MT/ TR: includes verse – CT: omits verse

9:49   MT/ TR: and every sacrifice will be salted with salt. – CT: omits

10:7   MT/ TR: and will be joined to his wife. – CT: {and will be joined to his wife}

11:26   MT/ TR: includes verse – CT: omits verse

12:15   MT/ TR: "Should we give, or should we not give?" - CT: moves sentence to the end of verse 14

13:14   MT/ TR: the one having been spoken [of] by Daniel the prophet – CT: omits

14:24   MT/ TR: New – CT: omits

14:27   MT/ TR: because of Me on this night – CT: omits

14:70   MT/ TR: and your accent is like [theirs] – CT: omits

15:3   MT/ CT: [things]. – TR: [things], but <u>He</u> answered nothing.

15:28   MT/ TR: includes verse – CT: omits verse

16:9-   MT/ TR: includes passage – CT: double brackets passage. The CT also
20   includes a shorter ending in double brackets. It reads:

Then they promptly reported all these [things] having been instructed to Peter and the [ones] with [him]. Then also Jesus Himself sent out through them from [the] rising [of the sun] [fig., from the east] and as far as [the] west the sacred and imperishable proclamation of the eternal salvation. Amen.

Luke

1:28   MT/ TR: <u>You</u> have been blessed among women. – CT: omits

2:14   MT/ TR: earth, good will among people! – CT: earth among people of good will!

2:33   MT/ TR: Joseph – CT: His father

4:4   MT/ TR: <u>but</u> on every word of God. – CT: omits

4:8   MT/ TR: Get behind Me, Satan! – CT: omits

8:45   MT/ TR: and the [ones] with him – CT: omits

            MT/ TR: and You say, 'Who [is] the one having touched Me?'" – CT: omits

8:48   MT/ TR: Take courage – CT: omits

9:55,56   MT/ TR: [55]and said, "You* do not know of what sort of spirit you* are! [56]For the Son of Humanity did not come to destroy people's lives, <u>but</u> to save!" – CT: omits passage

11:2   MT/ TR: Our Father, the [One] in the heavens, – CT: Father,

            MT/ TR: let Your will be done, as in heaven, [so] also on the earth – CT: omits

11:4   MT/ TR: <u>but</u> deliver us from evil – CT: omits

11:11   MT/ TR: a loaf of bread, he will not give to him a stone, will he? Or also – CT: omits

11:44   MT/ TR: scribes and Pharisees, hypocrites! – CT: omits

12:39   MT/ TR: would have kept watch and – CT: omits

17:9   MT/ TR: I think not. – CT: omits

17:35   MT/ CT: does not include next verse – TR: includes verse 36: "Two [people] will be in the field: the one will be taken, and the other will be left."

20:23   MT/ TR: "Why do you* test Me? – CT: omits

20:30   MT/ TR: took the wife, and this [man] died childless. – CT: omits

22:43,44   MT/ TR: includes verses – CT: double-brackets verses

22:64   MT/ TR: kept striking Him on the face and – CT: omits

23:17	MT/ TR: includes verse – CT: omits verse
23:34	MT/ TR: But Jesus was saying, "Father, forgive them, for they do not know what they are doing." – CT: double-brackets sentence
24:42	MT/ TR: and a honeycomb from a beehive – CT: omits
24:46	MT/ TR: and thus it was necessary – CT: omits

John

1:18	MT/ TR: Son – CT: God
1:27	MT/ TR: who has come to be before me, – CT: omits
3:13	MT/ TR: the One being in heaven – CT: omits
3:15	MT/ TR: shall not perish, <u>but</u> – CT: omits
5:3	MT/ TR: waiting for the moving of the water. – CT: omits
5:4	MT/ TR: includes verse – CT: omits verse
5:16	MT/ TR: and were seeking to kill Him, – CT: omits
6:47	MT/ TR: in Me – CT: omits
6:69	MT/ TR: the Christ, the Son of the living God! – CT: the Holy [One] of God!
7:8	MT/ TR: not yet – CT: not
7:53-8:11	MT/ TR: includes passage – CT: double brackets passage
8:9	MT/ TR: and by the conscience being convicted – CT: omits
8:10	MT/ TR: and having seen no one but the woman, – CT: omits
8:59	MT/ TR: having passed through [the] middle of them, and so He passed by. – CT: omits
11:41	MT/ TR: from where the one having died was lying – CT: omits
16:16	MT/ TR: because I am going away to the Father. – CT: omits
21:15	MT/ TR: of Jonah – CT: of John (and in next two verses)

Acts

2:30	MT/ TR: according to [the] flesh, to raise up the Christ – CT: omits
3:20	MT/ CT: appointed for – TR: previously preached to
4:25	MT/ TR: by [the] mouth of David – CT: by the Holy Spirit, [through] [the] mouth of David
7:16	MT/ TR: the [father] of Shechem – CT: in Shechem

8:36   MT/ CT: does not include next verse – TR: includes verse 37: Then Philip said, "If you believe out of your whole heart, it is permitted." So answering, he said, "I believe Jesus Christ to be the Son of God."

9:5,6   MT/ CT: ⁵Then he said, "Who are You, Lord?" And the Lord said, "I am Jesus whom you are persecuting. ⁶But get up and enter ..." – TR: ⁵Then he said, "Who are You, Lord?" And the Lord said, "I am Jesus whom you are persecuting. [It is] difficult for you to be kicking against [the] goads." ⁶So trembling and astonished, he said, "Lord, what do you want me to do?" And the Lord [said] to him, "Get up and enter ..."

9:28   MT: and speaking boldly in the name of the Lord Jesus, – TR: moves phrase to verse 29 - CT: omits Jesus

10:6   MT/ CT: sea. – TR: sea; this [man] will tell you what it is necessary [for] you to be doing.

10:11   MT/ TR: having been tied at [the] four corners and – CT: omits

10:21   MT/ CT: men, – TR: men, the ones having been sent from Cornelius to him,

10:32   MT/ TR: who having arrived, will speak to you – CT: omits

13:23   MT: brought to Israel salvation – TR: raised up to Israel a Savior, Jesus – CT: brought to Israel a Savior, Jesus

15:18   MT/ TR: "Known from [the] ages to God is all His works. – CT: know from [the] ages.

15:24   MT/ TR: saying [for you*] to continue being circumcised and to be keeping the Law – CT: omits

15:33   MT/ CT: does not include next verse – TR: includes verse 34: But it seemed good to Silas to remain there.

21:15   MT/ CT: having prepared – TR: having packed and carried off [our things]

21:22   MT/ TR: It is certainly necessary [for] the congregation to come together, for they will hear – CT: They will certainly hear

21:25   MT/ TR: judged [that they need] to be observing no such [thing], except to be – CT: judged [for them] to be

23:9   MT/ TR: but if a spirit spoke to him, or an angel, let us not be fighting against God. – CT: but perhaps a spirit spoke to him, or an angel.

24:6-8   MT/ CT: ⁶who also was trying to desecrate the temple, whom also we arrested, ⁸from whom you will be able, ... [Note: There is no verse 7 in MT/ CT.] – TR: ⁶who also was trying to desecrate the temple, whom also we arrested, and we wanted to be judging [him] according to our Law. ⁷But Lysias the commanding officer having come along, with much violence took [him] away out of our hands, ⁸having ordered his accusers to be coming before you, from whom you will be able, ...

28:16   MT/ TR: the centurion handed the prisoners over to the camp commander; but – CT: omits

28:29   MT/ TR: includes verse – CT: omits verse

Romans

1:16   MT/ TR: of Christ – CT: omits

8:1   MT/ TR: [who] do not walk about according to flesh, <u>but</u> according to [the] Spirit. – CT: omits

8:26   MT/ TR: on our behalf – CT: omits

9:11   MT/ TR: not of works, <u>but</u> of the One calling), – CT: moves to beginning of verse 12

9:28   MT/ TR: in righteousness, because [the] matter having been ended abruptly – CT: omits

10:15   MT/ TR: of the ones proclaiming the Gospel of peace – CT: omits

12:2   MT: [you* are] to stop conforming yourselves to this age, <u>but</u> [are] to continue being transformed – TR/ CT: stop conforming yourselves to this age, <u>but</u> continue being transformed

14:6   MT/ TR: and the one not honoring the day, to [the] Lord he does not honor [it]. – CT: omits

14:21   MT/ TR: or is made to fall, or becomes weak – CT: omits

14:24-26   MT: includes in this location – TR/ CT: includes as 16:25-27

16:24   MT/ TR: includes verse – CT: omits verse

1Corinthians

2:4   MT/ TR: human – CT: omits

6:20   MT/ TR: and in your* spirit, which are God's. – CT: omits

10:28   MT/ TR: "for the earth [is] the Lord's, and its fullness." – CT: omits

11:24   MT/ TR: Take, eat – CT: omits

        MT/ TR: being broken – CT: omits

11:29   MT/ TR: unworthily – CT: omits

MT/ TR: of the Lord – CT: omits

15:55   MT/ TR: sting? O realm of the dead, where [is] your victory? – CT: victory? Death, where [is] your sting?

16:24   MT: Jesus. So be it! – TR: Jesus. So be it! To [the] Corinthians first was written from Philippi through Stephanas and Fortunatus and Achaicus and Timothy. – CT: Jesus.

2Corinthians

1:6   MT: and our hope ... you*. If we ... and salvation, – TR: If we ... and salvation; and our hope ... you*. – CT: moves *and our hope ... you** to verse 7.

8:7   MT/ TR: your* love for us – CT: our love for you*

13:12-14   MT/ TR: Numbers verses as given – CT: Moves all of verse 13 to verse 12, and renumbers verse 14 as verse 13

13:14   MT: all! So be it! – TR: all! So be it! To [the] Corinthians second was written from Philippi [a city] of Macedonia through Titus and Luke. – CT: all!

Galatians

3:1   MT/ TR: [so as] not to be obeying the truth – CT: omits

6:18   MT/ CT: So be it! – TR: So be it! To [the] Galatians was written from Rome.

Ephesians

1:6   MT/ TR: by which He bestowed grace – CT: which He graciously bestowed

1:18   MT/ CT: heart – TR: understanding

3:9   MT/ CT: administration – TR: fellowship

MT/ TR: through Jesus Christ – CT: omits

3:14   MT/ TR: our Lord Jesus Christ – CT: omits

5:30   MT/ TR: from His flesh and from His bones – CT: omits

6:24   MT: incorruptibility. So be it! – TR: incorruptibility. To [the] Ephesians was written from Rome through Tychicus. – CT: incorruptibility.

Philippians

1:16,17   MT/ TR: numbers verses as given – CT: reverses order of verses

3:16   MT/ TR: with [the] same standard, to be thinking the same [thing]. – CT: omits

4:23   MT: with you* all. So be it! – TR: with you* all. So be it! To [the] Philippians was written by Paul, through Epaphroditus. – CT: with your* spirit.

Colossians

1:2   MT/ TR: and [the] Lord Jesus Christ – CT: omits

1:14   MT/ CT: redemption, the forgiveness – TR: redemption, through His blood, the forgiveness

2:2   MT/ TR: of both God the Father and of Christ – CT: of God, [which is] Christ

2:18   MT/ TR: has not seen – CT: has seen

4:8   MT/ TR: he shall know the things concerning you* – CT: you* shall know the things concerning us

4:18   MT: So be it! – TR: So be it! To the Colossians was written by Paul through Tychicus and Onesimus. – CT: omits

1Thessalonians

1:1   MT/ TR: from God our Father and [the] Lord Jesus Christ! – CT: omits

2:6   MT/ TR: being able to be burdensome as Christ's apostles. - CT: moves to verse 7

3:2   MT/ TR: a servant of God and our co-worker – CT: a co-worker of God

4:1   MT/ TR: God, – CT: God (just as indeed you* are walking),

5:28   MT: So be it! – TR: So be it! To [the] Thessalonians first was written from Athens. – CT: omits

2Thessalonians

2:3   MT/ TR: sin – CT: lawlessness

2:4   MT/ TR: as God – CT: omits

2:13   MT/ TR: from [the] beginning – CT: as [the] first-fruits

3:18   MT: So be it! – TR: So be it! To [the] Thessalonians second was written from Athens. – CT: omits

1Timothy

1:4   MT/ TR: disputes – CT: speculation

      MT/ CT: administration – TR: building up

3:3   MT/ TR: not greedy for dishonest gain, – CT: omits

3:16   MT/ TR: God – CT: who

4:10   MT/ TR: are insulted – CT: strive

6:5   MT/ TR: Be withdrawing from such people. – CT: omits

6:19   MT/ TR: eternal – CT: real

6:21   MT: So be it! – TR: So be it! To Timothy first was written from Laodicea, which is [the] capital city of Phrygia Pacatiana. – CT: omits

2Timothy

4:22   MT: So be it! – TR: So be it! To Timothy second was written from Rome when Paul was brought [the] second [time] before Nero the emperor. – CT: omits

Titus

3:15   MT: So be it! – TR: So be it! To Titus, chosen as [the] first overseer of [the] assembly of the Cretans, was written from Nicopolis of Macedonia. – CT: omits

Philemon

1:2   MT/ TR: beloved – CT: sister

1:11   MT: whom I sent back - TR/ CT: moves to verse 12, and CT adds *to you*

1:25   MT: So be it! – TR: So be it! To Philemon was written by Paul from Rome through Onesimus, a household servant. – CT: omits

Hebrews

1:1   MT/ CT: in these last days He spoke to us by [His] Son - TR: moves this phrase to the beginning of verse 2

1:3   MT/ TR: by Himself – CT: omits

2:7   MT/ CT: honor, – TR: honor, and set him over the works of Your hands,

3:6   MT/ TR: firm to [the] end – CT: omits

7:21   MT/ TR: according to the order of Melchisedek – CT: omits

10:1   MT: they are never able – TR/ CT: is never able [i.e. referring to the Law]

13:25   MT: all! So be it! – TR: all! So be it! Written to [the] Hebrews from Italy through Timothy – CT: all!

James

4:4   MT/ TR: Adulterers and adulteresses! – CT: Adulteresses!

4:5   MT/ TR: dwelt – CT: He [has] caused to dwell

4:12   MT/ CT: Lawgiver – TR: Lawgiver and Judge

5:12   MT: into hypocrisy. – TR/ CT: under judgment.

1Peter

1:22   MT/ TR: through [the] Spirit – CT: omits

1:23   MT/ TR: [the] word of God [which is] living and remaining into the age. – CT: [the] living and abiding Word of God.

3:13   MT/ TR: imitators of – CT: zealous for

3:15   MT/ TR: the Lord God – CT: Christ [as] Lord

4:14   MT/ TR: On the one hand according to them, He is being blasphemed, on the other hand according to you*, He is glorified. – CT: omits

5:2   MT/ TR: willingly, nor – CT: willingly, according to [the will of] God, nor

5:5   MT/ TR: [continue] being subjected to one another. Clothe yourselves with humility – CT: clothe yourselves with humility towards one another

2Peter

3:10   MT/ TR: will be burned up – CT: will be discovered

1John

2:20   MT/ TR: you* know all [things] – CT: you* all know

2:23   MT: the Father. – TR/ CT: the Father. The one confessing the Son has the Father also.

3:1   MT/ TR: children of God! – CT: children of God, and [so] we are!

4:3   MT/ TR: Christ [as] having come in the flesh – CT: omits

5:7,8   MT/ CT: ⁷Because three are the Ones testifying: ⁸the Spirit and the water and the blood, and the three are into the one. – TR: ⁷Because three are the Ones testifying in heaven–the Father, the Word, and the Holy Spirit–and these three are one. ⁸And three are the Ones testifying on the earth–the Spirit and the water and the blood–and the three are into the one.

5:13   MT/ TR: and so that you* shall be believing in the name of the Son of God. – CT: omits

2John

1:9   MT/ TR: transgressing – CT: going too far

3John

1:14   MT/ TR: Peace to you! Our friends greet you. Be greeting our friends by name. – CT: Brackets passage and gives it as verse 15

Jude

1:1   MT/ TR: having been sanctified – CT: having been loved

1:5   MT/ TR: you* knowing this once for all, that the Lord – CT: {you*} knowing all [things], that {the} Lord once for all

1:22   MT/ TR: making a distinction – CT: [who are] doubting

1:23   MT/ TR: be saving with fear – CT: be saving

       MT/ TR: fire, – CT: fire, but on some be having mercy with fear,

1:25   MT/ TR: To [the] only wise God our Savior, [be] glory and majesty, dominion and authority, both now and to all the ages! So be it! – CT: To [the] only God our Savior, through Jesus Christ our Lord, [be] glory, majesty, dominion, and authority, before all time and now and to all the ages! So be it!

The Revelation

1:8   MT/ CT: Omega, – TR: Omega, [the] Beginning and [the] End,

2:5   MT/ TR: quickly – CT: omits

2:27   MT/ TR: as I also have received [authority] from My Father. - CT: moves this phrase to the beginning of verse 28.

3:2   MT: which you were about to be throwing out – TR/ CT: which are about to die

5:14   MT/ CT: worship – TR: worship before [the One] living into the ages of the ages.

7:5   MT/ CT: Reuben – TR: Reuben twelve thousand having been sealed. And the TR adds *having been sealed* after each tribe through verse eight

8:7   MT/ CT: and the third of the earth was burned up, – TR: omits

8:13   MT/ CT: eagle – TR: angel

9:16   MT: ten thousand [times] ten thousand [i.e. 100 million] – TR: two [times] ten thousand [times] ten thousand [i.e. 200 million] – CT: twenty thousand [times] ten thousand [i.e. 200 million].

15:3   MT/ CT: the nations! – TR: the holy ones!

19:12 MT: names having been written [on them], and – TR/ CT: omit

20:2   MT: the one leading astray the whole inhabited earth, – TR/ CT: omit

20:14 MT/ CT: death, the lake of fire. – TR: death.

21:6   MT: I have become the Alpha – TR: It has taken place! I am the Alpha – CT: They have taken place! I {am} the Alpha

21:24 MT/ CT: nations – TR: nations of the ones being saved

       MT: will bring to it [the] glory and honor of the nations into it. – TR: bring their glory and honor into it. – CT: will bring their glory into it.

22:14 MT/ TR: the ones doing His commandments – CT: the ones washing their robes

22:19 MT/ CT: from the tree of life – TR: from [the] Scroll of the Life

22:21 MT: the Lord Jesus Christ [be] with all the holy ones. So be it! – TR: our Lord Jesus Christ [be] with you* all. So be it! – CT: the Lord Jesus [be] with all.

Appendix #2:
Translation Decisions and
Explanations of Notations

There are many decisions a translator must make when translating the Greek New Testament. And in translating the *Analytical-Literal Translation of the New Testament* (ALT), this translator struggled and prayed over every one.

Translation of Words, Alternative Translations, and Transliterations

First among these decisions is to decide which English word best represents the original Greek word. In most cases this decision is relatively easy. The Greek word has one basic meaning, so the only decision is which of various synonymous English words best expresses the connotation of the Greek word. But in many other cases, the Greek word has more than one basic meaning. But generally, the context indicates which of these meanings best "fits" in the text.

However, in some cases more than one meaning of the Greek word would fit in the particular context. So it is not certain which meaning the author had in mind. It is for this reason that the ALT includes alternative translations within brackets within the text. These are indicated by the notation, "or. "

When alternative translations are used, the reader should realize the alternative translation is just as legitimate of a rendering as the translation in the text. In other words, it could go either way. So the alternative translation in the text cannot be ignored. It must be seriously considered in interpreting the text.

For instance, in John 15:2, Jesus could be saying about His Father, "Every branch in Me not bearing fruit He takes it away." Or the last phrase could be, "He lifts it up." This difference is important as it has a bearing on the theological question of eternal security. But the reader needs to consider the implications of each of these as both are possible translations of the Greek word.

At other times, the alternative translation represents a more traditional translation than the one used in the text. For instance, where the ALT uses "holy ones" most other versions will have "saints" (e.g. Romans 1:7).

The notation "or" is also used when a Greek phrase or sentence can be translated in more than one way. Again, the phrase or sentence in the text and the one in brackets are both legitimate renderings of the Greek text. So when Paul quotes from Habakkuk 2:4, it could be rendered as, *"the [one] righteous by faith will live"* or as *"the righteous will live by faith"* (Romans 1:16).

The notation "or" is also sometimes used when a literal translation of a Greek phrase is particularly awkward. What follows is a slightly less literal rendering of the preceding literal translation. But the deviation from a strictly literal rendering is relatively minor. So this rendering also needs to be seriously considered as it is a legitimate translation.

For instance, in Matthew 5:22, Jesus refers to "the hell of the fire." The alternative translation of "the fiery hell" is given. The former is a strictly literal rendering while the latter is not quite as literal. But it would still be considered a word for word rendering as the grammatical form of the word "fire" can indicate an adjectival sense.

Another notation seen in brackets is "Gr." What follows is the original Greek word, with the Greek letters transliterated (changed) into English letters. These are given when the actual Greek word might be of interest to the reader. For instance, in Titus 1:5, Paul begins to give the qualifications for "elders." Following is, "[Gr. *presbuteros*]." This Greek word is the source of the English word "Presbyterian."

Additional Bracketed Materials

Other than the "or" or "Gr." bracketed materials, all other information seen in brackets is not directly indicative of material seen in the original Greek text. It represents information that has been added as an aid to the reader in understanding the text. So such material can be ignored if the reader so chooses. However, it is this translator's hope and prayer that this bracketed information will prove useful to the reader.

First among such additions are words added for clarity. These are included in the text without any preceding notations. They are included as very often the Greek text omits words that English grammar or normal usage would require. And without these words, the text would be excessively awkward and even "choppy. " If is for this reason that the "Copyright Information" page states that these words cannot be omitted when quoting from the ALT.

For example, the first phrase of Matthew 26:17 without the words added for clarity would read, "Now on the first of the Unleavened Bread." But with the words, it reads, "Now on the first [day] of the [Feast of] Unleavened Bread."

However, in some cases these clarifying words are interpretive, such as the addition of "sexually" to the end of 1Corinthians 7:1. This verse, the possible interpretations thereof, and my reasons for adding the clarifying word are discussed in detail in my book *Differences Between Bible Versions*, so I will not pursue the discussion here. But suffice it to say, cases where the added clarifying words are interpretive are rare in the ALT.

But a couple of instances are of particular note. After the word "brothers" is generally added "[and sisters]," and after the word "sons" is often added "[and daughters]." This is done as the Greek words can indicate a group of only males or a mixed group of males and females. Which is meant can sometimes be difficult to determine but can sometimes have important implications. So the inclusive possibility is given but in brackets so the reader can decide for yourself.

The next type of material seen in brackets is figurative renderings, indicated by the notation "fig." These are used when the preceding literal translation is excessively awkward or hard to understand. So the text has been paraphrased.

For instance, in Matthew 1:16, it is said that Mary, "was found having in [the] womb." Most readers probably could figure out that what this means. But to be sure, following the literal translation is, "[fig., to have become pregnant]."

Also seen in brackets are explanatory notes, indicated by the notation "i.e." These provide the type of information found in commentaries and in the footnotes of study Bibles. I have included such notes when I thought that some kind of explanation was needed to help the reader understand the text.

For instance, at His birth, Jesus was given gifts of "gold and frankincense and myrrh." People know what gold is, but many do not know what the latter two are. So I added, "[i.e., an expensive incense and ointment, respectively]" (Matt 2:11).

Similar to the above, also seen in brackets are modern-day equivalents for measurement and monetary units and time designations. The measurements are introduced by "about" and the monetary units and time designations by "i.e."

For the measurement units I have included both English and metric equivalents. This would seem pretty straightforward, but in many cases it is not exactly certain what an ancient unit referred to. But I have tried my best to research each unit so as to give the most likely equivalent.

Monetary units were even harder to give an equivalent for. Indicating equivalent USA dollar values would be one possibility. But due to inflation and other factors, over time such a value would become out of date. Also, it would not be useful to those from other countries.

So in most cases I decided to indicate the equivalent value in terms of ounces and grams of gold or silver as these precious metals have relatively consistent values over time. But in some cases I have given the equivalent in terms of the typical wage for a day or hour of work. Such values are for field laborers.

For most of the New Testament, equivalents for time designations are based on the Jewish method. With it, the day starts at our 6:00 a.m. and the night starts at our 6:00 p.m. and is broken up into four "watches" each lasting three hours. But in the Gospel of John, Roman time is most likely being used. But there is some debate on this, so both Jewish and Roman time is given. Roman time is the same as ours, with the hour count starting at either 12:00 midnight or 12:00 noon.

Meanings of proper names are sometimes indicated in brackets within quotation marks. This is done only when the meaning has significance to the text. For instance, an angel appeared to Joseph in a dream and told him to call his Son "Jesus." Placed in brackets is, "Yahweh saves." Jesus' mission was to "save His people from their sins," so the meaning of His name is significant (Matt 1:21).

And finally, also seen in brackets are Scripture references. These include the sources for quotations from the Old Testament, along with cross-references. The former are given without any preceding notations while the latter are introduced by "cp." (for "compare") or by "see."

The sources for the OT quotations are generally rather obvious. But in some cases it is difficult to determine exactly which verse the NT writer is referring to as there is no verse in the OT that is identical to how the quote appears. Sometimes this is due to the writer paraphrasing or quoting from memory, and sometimes two or more verses are merged together. In such cases, the various possible sources are indicated.

But more often, the NT writer is quoting from the Septuagint instead of the original Hebrew text. The Septuagint is a Greek translation of the Hebrew OT from the third century B.C. It is abbreviated as "LXX." The name and abbreviation are based on the tradition that 70 or 72 Jewish scholars worked on the translation, six from each of the twelve tribes of Israel.

The "LXX" notation is included in the ALT after the OT verse reference when the wording of the quote in the NT differs from the wording of the source verse in the Hebrew but is similar or even identical to that of the LXX. This will enable the reader to know when the use of the Septuagint is the reason for the difference between the quote as it appears in the NT and the OT source.

The cross-references generally come from my own Bible studies and indicate verses that I have found to be helpful in understanding the particular verse.

Capitalization

The original Greek text was written in all capital letters, with the letters all running together. It was also written without any punctuation marks. This means there was no distinction between small and capital letters in the original text, and the text was not divided into words, sentences, and paragraphs. It should also be noted that the chapter and verses divisions were not added to the text until hundreds of years after the New Testament was completed. So they are not reliable indications of the beginnings of sentences and paragraphs.

The *Byzantine Greek Majority Text* that I used for translating the ALT, as with most published Greek texts, includes spaces between words and includes the chapter and verse divisions. And rather than all capital letters, it prints the entire text in small letters simply because they are easier to read than capital letters. But this still means there is no distinction between small and capital letters. And the Byzantine text does not include any punctuation.

So in every case where a word is capitalized and where a new sentence or paragraph is started, it was this translator's decision without specific backing in the Greek text. But the text must be broken up into sentences and paragraphs for it to be readable by today's standards. And in most cases, this was relatively easy. I simply compared the practice used in other Bible versions and followed them. But in some cases, the versions differed, and so I was "own my own" so speak.

For instance, 1Corinthians 14:33 ends with the phrase "as in all the assemblies of the holy ones." Most versions include this as the last phrase of the paragraph running from verses 29-33. However, some versions make it the first phrase of the next paragraph (verses 34-35). This difference is important as Paul uses the phrase to emphasize the point he is making. But is he emphasizing the point of the former or of the latter paragraph?

In the first edition of the ALT, I included the phrase as the last phrase of the paragraph running from verses 29-33. But after having looked at it carefully, I realized it really could go either way. So for this second edition, I kept the phrase in the same place, but I then added the following note in brackets: "[or, The final phrase could instead be the first phrase of the next paragraph.]." I used the notation "or" since this is the notation used in the text to indicate two equally legitimate possibilities.

Besides the beginning of sentences, English usage also requires the use of capital letters for proper names. In such cases, there usually is not much difficulty in deciding when to capitalize such words. But what was possibly controversial was the decision to capitalize pronouns referring to deity.

I decided to do so for two main reasons. First, I simply believe it is a sign of respect to capitalize such pronouns. Secondly, there are times in the text when it can be difficult to determine who is speaking or being referred to. But the capitalization of such pronouns helps to clear up the confusion.

However, in capitalizing pronouns referring to Jesus, I am making a decision as to the deity of Jesus, and some would disagree with this decision. So I am using this page to indicate that the reader is free to disagree with this decision.

A similar decision was whether or not to use capitals in verses like John 8:58. In this verse, many believe Jesus is making a reference to Exodus 3:14 when He declares, "before Abraham came to be, I Am!"

In the first edition of the ALT, I did not capitalize the "am" as I felt it was too interpretive. But in this second edition I did capitalize the word. The reason for the change is that as I read over the text, it simply seemed inconsistent to capitalize pronouns referring to Jesus but not to capitalize the "am" here. I also included a cross-reference to Exodus 3:14 to indicate the possible connection. But again, the reader is free to disagree with this decision.

Punctuation

As indicated above, neither the original Greek text nor the Byzantine text includes any punctuation. So all punctuation seen in the ALT is added. And this was actually an area that caused me great difficulty. It required a review of proper English punctuation practices and careful proofreading of the text to be sure the correct punctuation was included in the appropriate places.

In most cases, where to use what punctuation was simply a matter of determining the correct English practice. But in some cases, it required a decision that affected the reading of the text.

For instance, probably the most famous verse in the Bible is John 3:16. But who is the source of this verse? Jesus is clearly speaking in the preceding verses. But from verses 16-21, it is unclear if Jesus is continuing His discourse, or if it is narrative by John the Gospel writer.

Similarly, later in the same chapter, John the Baptist is speaking in verses 27-30. But are verses 31-35 continuing discourse from John the Baptist or additional narrative by John the Gospel writer?

In the first edition of the ALT, I punctuated verses 16-21 as Jesus speaking and verses 31-35 as John the Baptist speaking. But after studying the issue for this second edition, I changed the punctuation to indicate both sections are narrative by John the Gospel writer. This change does not affect the interpretation, but it does change what the reader pictures in mind while reading these verses.

Conclusion

I have included this appendix in this second edition of the *Analytical-Literal Translation* to give the reader some idea of the many decisions and difficulties encountered when translating the New Testament. I also hope this appendix helps the reader better understand the reasons for the decisions made and how to best make use of the many helps included within the ALT text.

It is my hope and prayer that God has been guiding me in my decisions and that He uses the ALT to His glory and the spiritual growth of His people.

Appendix #3:
Publication Notes

This *Analytical-Literal Translation* is the ideal Bible version for personal Bible study. However, for more general purposes, there is the possibility of sometime in the future publishing an *Analytical-Literal Translation: Devotional Version* (ALT-DV).

The ALT-DV would be more of a standard formal equivalence version, like the *New King James Version*® or the *New American Standard Bible*®. But the unique feature would be that the ALT-DV would be based on the *Byzantine Majority Text* while these versions are based on somewhat different Greek texts, namely the *Textus Receptus* and the Critical Text, respectively.

The idea behind the ALT-DV is this: the ALT is the ideal version to use for personal Bible study. But due to its literalness and the analytical bracketed materials, the ALT can be rather awkward to use for such purposes as personal devotional reading, reading aloud in church services or Bible studies, or even for evangelism. But the ALT-DV would fill devotional and other such needs with a Majority Text based version.

Other than the ALT, there are currently only a couple of versions available which are based on the Majority Text. Meanwhile, there are dozens if not hundreds of versions available based on the *Textus Receptus* or the Critical Text.

The ALT-DV would still be "literal" in that any significant deviations from a literal translation would be footnoted. It would also be "analytical" in that bracketed analytical materials from the ALT would be footnoted. However, in some cases an alternate, less-literal translation, or a figurative rendering would be used in the text and the more literal reading footnoted.

Whether an ALT-DV is ever produced will depend on the popularity of the ALT itself and on the demand for a devotional version thereof. To express your opinion in this regard, please contact the translator (see Appendix #4).

Also, please note that there are currently no plans to produce an Old Testament to go along with the ALT: New Testament. There would be nothing distinctly unique about an ALT: OT. There are not different texts being used to translate the OT as there is with the NT. Most Old Testaments available are based on the Masoretic Hebrew Text, as an ALT: OT would be. So an ALT: OT would simply a duplication of the effort of others.

For a literal translation of the OT, it is recommended the reader attain a copy of the *Literal Translation of the Bible*, available from: www.chrlitworld.com ~ (800) 447-9142. Recommended formal equivalence translations of the OT can be found in the *New King James Version* or the *New American Standard Bible*.

Appendix #4:
Books and eBooks
by the Translator

In addition to being the translator of the ALT, Gary F. Zeolla is also the author of seven books. All seven books are available in Microsoft Reader® eBook format from the "Books and eBooks by the Director" section of Darkness to Light's Web site (www.dtl.org/books).

Four of the books are also available in paperback and in Acrobat Reader® eBook formats from the publisher via their Web site: www.AuthorHouse.com.

The paperbacks can also be ordered by calling toll-free 1-888-280-7715. They are also available from Amazon.com and other online bookstores.

Companion Volume to the ALT
(eBook)

This eBook contains extensive background information on the *Analytical-Literal Translation*. It will aid the reader in understanding not only why the ALT is translated in the manner it is but also the reasons why other versions are as well.

Included in this volume is an eight-part "Grammatical Renderings" section. It explains the reasons for the somewhat unique translation of Greek tenses seen in the ALT, while comparing the ALT style of translation to that of other versions. It also explains other nuances of Greek grammar which are brought out in the ALT but which are often missed in other versions. This section is detailed enough to be used as a primer on Greek grammar. It also enables the reader to understand why Bible versions differ in their translations of the particulars of Greek grammar.

In addition, the *Companion Volume* includes a glossary explaining the reasons for how important words are translated in the ALT. Also included is a list of reference works which were consulted while working on the ALT. Primary among these was *BibleWorks for Windows®* This program and the many lexicons and other aids on it were indispensable in translating the ALT.

The *Companion Volume* also includes other information helpful in understanding the translations seen in the ALT versus other versions.

Complete Concordance for the ALT
(with Reese Currie; eBook)

This eBook indexes every occurrence of most words in the *Analytical-Literal Translation*. Only minor words are omitted (e.g., a, and, but, the). Sufficient context is provided for the reader to recognize the verse or to get the gist of it.

This concordance will enable the reader to quickly find a verse in the ALT. It will also be invaluable in doing topical studies in the ALT. Looking up every reference to a word like "grace" will enable one to do a study on this important Biblical topic.

The ALT is the ideal version to use for such in-depth Bible study, and having this concordance to use as reference tool will improve these studies.

Differences Between Bible Versions:
Updated and Expanded Edition
(paperback and eBook)

This book answers such questions as: Why do Bible versions differ? Why does the same verse read differently in different versions? Why do some versions contain words, phrases, and even entire verses that other versions omit? Which Bible versions are most reliable? These and many other questions are answered in this book.

This book contains extensive discussions on why the translator of the ALT believes either a literal or a formal equivalence ("word-for-word") translation principle is the best method to use for translating the Bible. These principles of translating are contrasted with the dynamic equivalence ("phrase for phrase") and paraphrase methods seen in many modern Bible versions.

In addition, this book includes detailed discussions on why the translator believes the *Byzantine Majority Text* is the most accurate of the three Greek texts used in Bible translation.

This book also contains an extended section critiquing the claims of "KJV only-ists" (those who claim the *King James Version* is the only "real" Bible).

In addressing these various issues, *Differences Between Bible Versions* compares over thirty different versions of the Bible. ISBN: 0-75962-501-8

The New World Translation:
A Reliable Bible Version?
(eBook)

This eBook evaluates the NWT, the Bible of Jehovah's Witnesses. The NWT is reviewed by looking at select passages from Paul's Epistle to the Ephesians. The standards used are the same standards that are used in the book *Differences Between Bible Versions*. Simply put, does the translation faithfully and accurately render the Greek text into English?

More specifically, are words translated correctly? Are words left untranslated? Are words added without any indication that they have been added? Are the grammatical forms of words altered? Are phrases paraphrased rather than translated? How readable is the text? How reliable is the Greek text being used?

Scripture Workbook:
For Personal Bible Study
and Teaching the Bible
(paperback and eBook):

This book contains twenty-two individual Scripture Studies. Each study focuses on one general area of study. These studies enable individuals to do in-depth, topical studies of the Bible. They are also invaluable to the Bible study teacher preparing lessons for Sunday School or a home Bible study.

The range of topics covered in the different studies is broad: from what the Bible teaches about itself to what the Bible teaches about divorce and remarriage. Contained in each study are hundreds of Scripture references. So there will be no lack of material from which to begin your studies. ISBN: 1-58721-893-3

Creationist Diet:
Nutrition and God-given Foods
According to the Bible
(paperback and eBook)

This book answers such questions as: What did God give to human beings for food? What does the Bible teach about diet and nutrition? How do the Biblical teachings on foods compare to scientific research on nutrition and degenerative disease like heart disease, cancer, and stroke?

In answering these questions, the book starts with God's decrees about foods at Creation, the Fall, and after the Flood, and gleans nutrition information from the rest of the Bible, while correlating this information with scientific research. ISBN: 1-58721-852-6

Overcoming Back Pain
(eBook)

I powerlifted in college, but back pain forced me to stop weightlifting. Eventually, the back pain worsened to the point where I was crippled by it for six years. I tried various traditional and alternative treatments, but all to no avail. But then by utilizing mind-body techniques I was able to completely overcome the back pain, so much so that I was able to start powerlifting again. This eBook discusses all of the treatments I tried and what finally worked.

Appendix #5:
Web Sites and Newsletters
by the Translator

Gary F. Zeolla is the Webmaster for two different Web sites, both of which offer a free email newsletter. Subscription information for the newsletters can be found on the Web sites.

Darkness to Light
www.dtl.org

Darkness to Light ministry is dedicated to explaining and defending the Christian faith. Currently available on the site are over 800 Web pages, eight books and eBooks, and a free email newsletter. In these materials, a wide range of topics are covered, including: theology, apologetics, cults, ethics, Bible versions, and much more. So you are sure to find something of interest.

The name for the ministry is taken from the following verse:
"… to open their eyes [in order] to turn [them] back from darkness [i.e., falsehood and unrighteousness] to light [i.e. truth and righteousness] and [from] the authority of Satan to God, [in order for] them to receive forgiveness of sins and an inheritance among the ones having been sanctified by faith in Me" (Acts 26:18; ALT).

The words "darkness" and "light" have a wide range of meanings when used metaphorically in Scripture, but basically (as the ALT indicates), "darkness" refers to falsehood and unrighteousness while "light" refers to truth and righteousness. People turn from darkness to light when they come to believe the teachings of the Bible and live in accordance with them.

Fitness for One and All
www.FitnessforOneandAll.com

I have a B.S. in Nutrition Science and am a certified personal fitness trainer. I currently hold seven International Powerlifting Association world records. And these records were set after over 20 years of dealing with a variety of serious health problems.

First I was crippled with low back pain. Then I sustained numerous injuries in a near-fatal bicycle accident. Then I was crippled with fibromyalgia pain and fatigue. And finally, I was paralyzed with stiff person syndrome (a very rare auto-immune disorder). I also have suffered with many less serious health problems over the years. But I overcame these problems sufficiently to be able to compete in powerlifting again.

With all I have been through, overcome, and accomplished, it is now my passion to help others achieve their health, fitness, and performance goals. To that end, I set up Fitness for One and All Web site.

Currently available on the site are over 250 Web pages, two books and eBooks, and a free email newsletter. These materials are directed towards a wide range of people, including beginning fitness enthusiasts, athletes, powerlifters, and those dealing with health problems. The name "Fitness for One and All" reflects this diversity of covered topics.

Contacting the Translator

The translator of the ALT can be contacted by using the comments forms on Darkness to Light's Web site and on Fitness for One and All's Web site. Click on the "Contact Information" link near the bottom of any page on either Web site.

About the Author

Gary F. Zeolla is the director of Darkness to Light. This ministry addresses Christian theology, defense of the faith, cults, ethics, and many other issues. Research for these topics and Zeolla's own Bible studies led to his *Scripture Workbook: For Personal Bible Study and Teaching the Bible.*

Also addressed is the subject of Bible versions. This research led to Zeolla's book *Differences Between Bible Versions* and his *Analytical-Literal Translation of the New Testament.*

Zeolla also directs Fitness for One and All, which is dedicated to helping people attain their health, fitness, and performance goals. His efforts in this area and his love of the Bible led to his book *Creationist Diet: Nutrition and God-given Foods According to the Bible.*

CPSIA information can be obtained at www.ICGtesting.com
Printed in the USA
LVOW132033020713

341225LV00011B/867/A